CRIMINAL PROCEDURE AND PUNISHMENT

For Jacob, Erin and Alexander

Always remain inquisitive

CRIMINAL PROCEDURE AND PUNISHMENT

Ed Johnston and Tom Smith

THIRD EDITION

H&S

Hall and Stott Publishing Ltd
27 Witney Close
Saltford
BS31 3DX

British Library Cataloguing in Publication Data

ISBN 978 1 8384824 0 4

Typeset by Style Photosetting Ltd, Mayfield, East Sussex

PREFACE

This book is an introduction to the dual concepts of both criminal procedure and punishment. It is designed to cover the major stages involved in encounters with the police, prosecution and the criminal courts of England and Wales, from a seemingly innocuous stop and search, to how suspects are charged, tried, convicted and sentenced. Along the way, a range of other powers available to the courts and police are also critically examined, with the essential issues highlighted and discussed.

The rationale behind covering these elements of procedure and punishment together is partly because 'punishment' can, in reality, occur at various stages of the criminal process. We would argue that 'punishment' is not limited to a state-sanctioned sentence after conviction; arguably, a person might experience any number of parts of criminal procedure as punitive. For example, being stopped and searched on the street might be viewed as a form of punishment – for many, there is a degree of degradation, humiliation and embarrassment to this encounter. Furthermore, this informal method of punishment may act as a form of social control or discipline.

Suppose a person has never previously experienced this intimidating process. They may be less concerned by its implications, less hostile to police interactions, and therefore less likely to act in a way that arouses police suspicion (or contempt). Conversely, the use (or overuse) of this power may generate a feeling of persecution amongst some populations because the person has been stopped for what could be described, at best, as flimsy reasons (you will see that the requirement of 'reasonable suspicion' does not set a high bar for a police officer to stop someone). This could create resentment towards the police within the local population, regarded as enemies bent on persecution. This can ultimately lead to disengagement, uncooperative behaviour, and sometimes rioting and disorder, as in Brixton (1981) and across London and other major cities (2011), as well as more recent examples concerning Brexit, Kill the Bill and various climate concerns, illustrated by Extinction Rebellion.

Ultimately, we consider criminal procedure and punishment as intertwined and mutually influential. The process shapes the likely punishment, and the nature of the punishment can influence and distort the preceding process (as well as lead some offenders back into the system in the future).

Therefore, we consider it imperative to look at the process of detecting, convicting and punishing offenders holistically and as a continuing cycle. It is of vital importance that the system detects and punishes the 'right' individual, not only to serve the difficult-to-define notion of 'justice' but also to positively impact future crime. That being said, the book will consider the possibility that general deterrence may work no matter which individual is caught, so long as that person (guilty or not) feels the full force of the law, thus impacting crime in society in general. The rights of wrongs of such possibilities – and the implications for individuals drawn into the criminal justice system – will be considered across the various chapters.

This book offers a broadly chronological journey through the criminal process and a theoretical analysis of how things should operate in an ideal world. The book does not suggest that a particular theory is better than the reality, or vice versa, but that theory should underpin and permeate the practical elements of the process, rather than merely being driven by practical considerations like time and cost. This theoretical analysis will allow the book to critique the issues and problems, both longstanding and contemporary, that exist in the practical world of criminal procedure and punishment.

As well as focusing on the fundamental issues in procedure and punishment, we also examine the impact of prison on the families of offenders and the use of the death penalty as a punishment. Additionally, the 3rd edition of the book includes updates to existing chapters, considering topical developments. The book closes with a new chapter examining contemporary issues in criminal procedure. In past editions, we have posited that there has been a push for greater efficiency in the justice system, and we further explore this cultural shift through the lens of Pre-Charge Engagement and the Single Justice Procedure Notice. Both have ramifications for traditional notions of fair trial rights and adversarial norms and values in England and Wales. The chapter also examines the myriad issues surrounding investigating and prosecuting rape and other sexual offences. The chapter argues that despite a raft of initiatives, developments and critical evaluations in recent years, the approach of the police and other agencies continues to be inadequate. The treatment of complainants and levels of prosecution and conviction still need significant improvement.

As always, the aim of our book is to provide students with both detailed knowledge and understanding of how criminal procedure and punishment should work in theory and the ability to evaluate how well this translates into practice. We seek to offer some insight into the day-to-day operation of both criminal procedure and punishment and to enable students to critique these approaches from multiple perspectives. To that end, we have used extensive references to provide broader literature and further avenues for learning, debate and exploration. Finally, we attempt to offer a structured, engaging, coherent and accessible account of criminal procedure and punishment for students and lecturers alike.

We hope you enjoy the book.

Ed Johnston and Tom Smith
1 April 2023

CONTENTS

Preface v
Table of Cases xv
Table of Legislation xxi
Abbreviations xxvii

Chapter 1 Theoretical Approaches to Criminal Procedure 1

1.1 Introduction 1
1.2 An overview of legal traditions 1
1.2.1 Adversarialism 2
1.2.2 Inquisitorialism 3
1.2.3 A brief critique of ideological approaches to criminal justice 5
1.3 The purpose(s) of the criminal trial 7
1.3.1 Truth 7
1.3.2 Argument 8
1.3.3 Catharsis 9
1.3.4 Finality 9
1.4 Adversarial and inquisitorial trials: a different purpose? 10
1.5 The role of the judiciary in different legal traditions 12
1.5.1 The adversarial judiciary 12
1.5.2 The myth of the impartial adversarial umpire? 13
1.5.3 The inquisitorial judiciary 14
1.6 Critical analysis of criminal justice: Packer's models 15
1.7 Conclusion 18

Chapter 2 Policing on the Street (1): Stop and Search 19

2.1 Introduction 19
2.2 Overview of the power to stop and search 19
2.3 Why is stop and search important? 20
2.3.1 Prevalence 21
2.3.2 Impact 23
2.3.3 Stop and search as a crime-fighting tool 24
2.4 The law governing stop and search 25
2.4.1 Section 1(2) of PACE 1984 26
2.4.2 Section 60 of the CJPOA 1994 and s 47A of the TA 2000 27
2.5 Reasonable suspicion 29
2.5.1 Case law and research on stop and search 32
2.6 Racial discrimination 34

2.6.1 Direct racial discrimination 34
2.6.2 Implicit and 'institutional' racial discrimination 35
2.6.3 Poverty and marginalisation 36
2.6.4 Poor relations between the police and minority communities 37
2.7 Reform 38
2.8 Other safeguards 39
2.9 Summary 41

Chapter 3 Policing on the Street (2): The Power of Arrest 43
3.1 Overview of the power of arrest 43
3.2 What constitutes an 'arrest'? 43
3.2.1 Arrest as a factual state of affairs 44
3.2.2 Arrest depends on context and intention 45
3.2.3 Deprivation of liberty 46
3.3 The law governing arrest 48
3.3.1 Code G 49
3.3.2 Reasonable suspicion 49
3.3.3 Necessity 52
3.4 Ancillary powers and duties 55
3.4.1 The caution 56
3.5 Research on the power of arrest 57
3.6 Summary 60

Chapter 4 In Police Custody (1): Detention and Charging 61
4.1 Introduction 61
4.2 History and development 61
4.3 Custody officers 62
4.4 Decisions about detention 63
4.5 Release from police custody on bail 64
4.5.1 Bail without charge 65
4.5.2 Impact of the changes 67
4.6 The 'necessity' of detention prior to charge 70
4.7 The effect of the custody officer 71
4.8 Custody records 73
4.9 Reviews of detention 73
4.10 Detention time limits 74
4.11 Charging a suspect 76
4.11.1 The Full Code Test 76
4.11.2 The Threshold Test 77
4.11.3 Which test is used? 78
4.11.4 Who makes the decision to charge? 78
4.12 Research on charging decisions 79
4.13 Summary 80

Chapter 5 In Police Custody (2): Legal Advice and Interrogation 81
5.1 The right of access to a lawyer 81
5.1.1 The right to a lawyer and human rights 82
5.2 The impact of s 58 on access to a lawyer 83

	5.3	Who provides legal advice at police stations?	86
	5.4	How is legal advice provided?	90
	5.5	The effect of legal advice	93
	5.6	Police interviews	94
		5.6.1 Why do the police interview?	94
		5.6.2 Defining a police 'interview'	96
		5.6.3 When can the police interview?	96
	5.7	Safeguards in police interviews	96
	5.8	Summary	98
Chapter 6	**The Right to Silence**		**99**
	6.1	Introduction	99
	6.2	The origin of the right to silence	100
	6.3	The scope of the right to silence	101
	6.4	Debates about the right to silence	102
		6.4.1 Advantages	103
		6.4.2 Disadvantages	106
		6.4.3 Some counter-arguments	109
	6.5	Using silence against the accused: the Criminal Justice and Public Order Act (CJPOA) 1994	111
	6.6	Section 34	111
		6.6.1 'Facts' and 'reliance' under s 34	112
		6.6.2 'Proper inferences'	113
		6.6.3 Reasonableness	114
		6.6.4 Reasonableness and legal advice	115
	6.7	Section 35	116
	6.8	Sections 36 and 37	117
	6.9	Impact of reform on the use of the right to silence	118
	6.10	Impact of reform on convictions	119
	6.11	Impact of reform on disclosure and legal advice	120
	6.12	The delegitimisation of silence	120
	6.13	Summary	121
Chapter 7	**The Regulation of Confessions**		**123**
	7.1	Introduction	123
	7.2	What is a 'confession' and how is it regulated?	124
		7.2.1 A confession needs to be made by the accused	124
		7.2.2 The confession must be 'adverse' to the accused	124
		7.2.3 A confession can be either partly or wholly adverse	125
		7.2.4 It can be made to a person in authority or not	125
		7.2.5 A confession can be made in words or otherwise	125
	7.3	The regulation of confession evidence	125
	7.4	False confessions	126
		7.4.1 Coerced-internalised confessions	127
		7.4.2 Coerced-compliant confessions	128
		7.4.3 Coerced-passive confessions	128
	7.5	Police-invented confessions	129
	7.6	Prevalence and significance	129

7.7 Regulation of confession evidence in the police station 131
7.7.1 The right to legal advice 131
7.7.2 Oppression and inducements 131
7.7.3 Other safeguards 132
7.8 Regulation of confession evidence at trial: PACE 1984, s 76 133
7.8.1 Oppression 133
7.8.2 Unreliability 135
7.9 Procedure for excluding confession evidence 138
7.10 Summary 138

Chapter 8 'Managing' Criminal Procedure 141

8.1 Introduction 141
8.2 The evolution of disclosure 142
8.3 The birth of the efficient criminal process: CPIA 1996 144
8.4 The Auld Review and evolution of the CPIA 1996 145
8.5 The Criminal Procedure Rules: a 'sea change' in managing criminal justice 147
8.5.1 Paragraph (a): 'acquitting the innocent and convicting the guilty' 147
8.5.2 Paragraph (b): 'dealing with the prosecution and the defence fairly' 148
8.5.3 Paragraph (c): 'recognising the rights of a defendant, particularly those under Article 6 of the European Convention on Human Rights' 148
8.5.4 Paragraph (d): 'respecting the interests of witnesses, victims and jurors and keeping them informed of the progress of the case' 148
8.5.5 Paragraph (e): 'dealing with the case efficiently and expeditiously' 148
8.5.6 Paragraph (f): 'ensuring that appropriate information is available to the court when bail and sentence are considered' 149
8.5.7 Paragraph (g): 'dealing with the case in ways that take into account the gravity of the offence alleged, the complexity of what is in issue, the severity of the consequences for the defendant and others affected, and the needs of other cases' 149
8.6 Case management: the power to control the trial 151
8.7 Truth or proof: the dilution of adversarialism in pursuit of the overriding objective 152
8.8 Conclusion 155

Chapter 9 The Criminal Court (in Theory) 159

9.1 Introduction 159
9.2 Venue of trial and allocation of cases 159
9.2.1 Summary offences 159
9.2.2 Indictable offences 160
9.2.3 Either-way offences 161
9.3 Comparing magistrates' courts and the Crown Court 162
9.4 The 'actors' in the criminal process 163
9.4.1 The judge 164
9.4.2 Lay magistrates 165
9.4.3 The prosecutor 166
9.4.4 The defence lawyer 169
9.4.5 The jury 171
9.5 Conclusion 177

Chapter 10 The Criminal Court (in Practice) 179

10.1 Introduction 179
10.2 Before court: bail and detention 179
10.3 First appearance at court 181
10.3.1 Guilty plea 182
10.3.2 The significance of early guilty pleas 182
10.3.3 Not guilty plea/no plea 186
10.4 Court bail 186
10.4.1 The grounds for withholding bail 187
10.4.2 Unconditional and conditional bail 188
10.4.3 How common is pre-trial detention? 189
10.4.4 Research on the use of pre-trial detention 190
10.5 Pre-trial disclosure 192
10.6 The trial 193
10.7 Sentencing 197
10.8 Summary 198

Chapter 11 Appeals 199

11.1 Introduction 199
11.2 The need for an appeals process 199
11.3 Appeals from a magistrates' court 200
11.3.1 Appeals against conviction or sentence to the Crown Court 200
11.3.2 Appeals 'by way of case stated' 203
11.3.3 Judicial review 204
11.4 Appeals from the Crown Court 204
11.4.1 'Fit for appeal' 205
11.4.2 Prevalence 205
11.4.3 Unsafe convictions 206
11.4.4 Fresh evidence 208
11.4.5 Result of appeals from the Crown Court to the Court of Appeal 209
11.5 Appeals to the Supreme Court 210
11.6 The post-appellate system 210
11.6.1 Introduction 210
11.6.2 The Criminal Cases Review Commission (CCRC) 210
11.7 Summary 216

Chapter 12 Theories of Punishment 219

12.1 Introduction 219
12.2 Why do we punish? 219
12.2.1 Retribution theory 220
12.2.2 Prevention theory 222
12.2.3 Denunciation 226
12.2.4 Reparation theory 228
12.3 Justifications in practice: sentencing 231
12.3.1 Sentencing 232
12.3.2 The death of discretion 233
12.4 Conclusion 234

Chapter 13 Punishment in Practice: Custody and the Alternatives 235

13.1 Introduction 235
13.2 Prison 235
13.2.1 Immediate incarceration: the aims and use of prison 236
13.3 Suspended sentences 241
13.4 Community sentences 243
13.5 Fines 247
13.5.1 How is a fine fixed? 247
13.5.2 Sanctions for non-payment 249
13.5.3 Equal fines: equal impact? 250
13.6 Discharge 251
13.7 Out of court disposals 253
13.7.1 Simple and conditional cautions 253
13.7.2 Penalty notices for disorder 256
13.8 Conclusion 258

Chapter 14 The Ripple Effect of Imprisonment: The Impact on Families 259

14.1 Introduction 259
14.2 Family ties: the impact on marriage 260
14.2.1 Maintaining love in prison 261
14.2.2 Sustaining a relationship in prison 263
14.2.3 The impact on children 266
14.3 The financial impact of imprisonment 270
14.4 Stigma 273
14.5 Reforms for prisoners' families 274

Chapter 15 Capital Punishment: Debates about Death as a Penalty for Crime 277

15.1 Introduction 277
15.2 The abolition of capital punishment in the UK 278
15.3 For or against? Debates about capital punishment 280
15.4 Retribution and denunication 280
15.5 Incapacitation and public protection 282
15.6 Impact on and relationship to individual rights 284
15.6.1 Torture or cruel, inhuman or degrading treatment or punishment (Article 3 ECHR and Article 7 ICCPR) 286
15.6.2 The right to a fair trial (Article 6 ECHR and Article 14 ICCPR) 288
15.6.3 Minimising suffering (ESC Resolution 1984/50, para 9) 288
15.6.4 Individual rights and the relationship with overall use of the death penalty 289
15.7 Deterrence 290
15.8 Practicality 294
15.9 Summary 297

Chapter 16 Miscarriages of Justice 299

16.1 Introduction 299
16.2 What is a miscarriage of justice? 300
16.3 A history of mistakes: how miscarriages have shaped criminal justice 303
16.4 Causes of miscarriages of justice 307

16.4.1 External pressures on the justice process 307
16.4.2 Prosecution misconduct 311
16.4.3 Police misconduct 312
16.4.4 Unreliable witnesses 313
16.4.5 Non-disclosure, faulty forensic evidence and inadequate investigation 315
16.4.6 Ineffective representation 319
16.5 Summary 320

Chapter 17 Contemporary Issues in Criminal Procedure and Punishment 321

17.1 Introduction 321
17.2 New approaches to efficiency in criminal procedure 321
17.2.1 Disclosure and Pre-Charge Engagement 321
17.2.2 The Single Justice Procedure Notice 325
17.2.3 Concluding thoughts: why the push for efficiency? 328
17.3 Criminal justice responses to sex offending 329
17.3.1 Impact on reporting of sexual offences 329
17.3.2 Investigation process 330
17.3.3 Attrition 331
17.3.4 The role of myths and stereotypes 332
17.3.5 Improving investigation 333
17.3.6 Beyond the investigation: prosecution 334
17.3.7 Explanations for prosecution issues 334
17.3.8 Next steps 336
17.4 Conclusion 337

Index 339

TABLE OF CASES

A

A (No 2) [2002] 1 AC 45 208
Adams [2011] UKSC 18 301
Adler v DPP [2013] EWHC 1968 (Admin) 45
AG's References (Nos 14 and 15 of 2006) [2006] EWCA Crim 1335 132
Ahmed [2010] EWCA Crim 2899 208
Alexander [2009] NIQB 20 54
Al-Fayed v Commissioner of Police of the Metropolis (No 3) [2004] EWCA Civ 1579 52, 63
Alladice (1988) 87 Cr App R 380 107
Allan v United Kingdom (2003) 36 EHRR 12 104, 313
Allan v United Kingdom [2002] ECHR 702 96
Argent [1997] 2 Cr App R 27 112
Associated Provincial Picture Houses Ltd v Wednesbury Corporation [1948] 1 KB 223 51
AT & T Istel v Tully [1993] AC 45 99
Atristain v Spain [2022] ECHR 64 82
Attorney General v MGN Ltd and News Group Newspapers Ltd [2011] EWHC 2074 (Admin) 308
Austin v Commissioner of Police of the Metropolis [2009] UKHL 5 47
Austin v UK (2012) 55 EHRR 14 47

B

Baldwin [2002] EWCA Crim 2647 247
Barnes (1970) 55 Cr App R 100 164
Barry (1992) 95 Cr App R 384 136
Beale [2019] EWCA Crim 665 332
Beales [1991] Crim LR 118 133
Beckles [2004] EWCA Crim 2766 115
Beghal v DPP [2015] UKSC 49 101
Bennett (No 1), ex parte [1994] 1 AC 42 313
Bentley (Deceased) [2001] 1 Cr App R 21 279
Betts and Hall [2001] EWCA Crim 224 115
Blake [1991] Crim LR 119 137
Bravender [2018] EWCA Crim 723 317
Bristol [2007] EWCA Crim 3214 40
Brizzalari [2004] EWCA Crim 310 112
Browne v Commissioner of Police of the Metropolis [2014] EWHC 3999 (QB) 41
Bryant and Dickson (1946) 31 Cr App R 146 142
Buckley v Chief Officer of Thames Valley Police [2009] EWCA Civ 356 52

C

Cadder v HM Advocate [2010] UKSC 43 82
Camberwell Green Youth Court, ex parte D [2005] 2 Cr App R 1 195

Carr v The Queen (1988) 165 CLR 314	312
Castorina v Chief Constable of Surrey [1988] NLJR 180	50
Chaaban [2003] EWCA Crim 1012	154, 182
Chalkley and Jeffries [1998] QB 848	207
Chandler [1976] 1 WLR 585	100
Charlton and Ali [2016] EWCA Crim 52	135, 208
Christie [1914] AC 545	100
Chung (1991) 92 Cr App R 314	137
Clarke (1930) 22 Cr App R 58	142
Clewer (1953) 37 Cr App R 37	164
Commission of Metropolis v MR [2019] EWHC 888 (QB)	55
Commissioner of Police of the Metropolis v DSD and another [2018] UKSC 11	19, 302
Compton [2002] EWCA Crim 2835	118
Condron v United Kingdom (2001) 31 EHRR 1	114, 115
Cooper [1969] 1 QB 267	206
Copsey [2008] EWCA Crim 2043	154
Cordingley [2007] All ER (D) 131	154
Cowan, Gayle and Ricciardi [1996] QB 373	114, 117
Crampton (1991) 92 Cr App R 369	136
Cumming v Chief Constable of Northumbria Police [2003] EWCA Civ 1844	51

D

D and Others [2007] EWCA Crim 2485	154
Dallison v Caffery [1965] 1 QB 348, [1964] 2 All ER 610	142, 155
Daniel [1998] 2 Cr App R 373	114
Davison [1988] Crim LR 442	134
Dawes v DPP [1995] 1 Cr App R 65	44
Delaney (1988) 88 Cr App R 338	98, 136
Dhorajiwala [2010] 2 Cr App R 161	138
Director of Serious Fraud Office, ex parte Smith [1993] AC 1	101
Doolan [1988] Crim LR 747	137
Downing (Stephen) [2002] EWCA Crim 263	319
DPP v Blake [1989] 1 WLR 432	137
DPP v Chorley Justices [2006] EWHC 1795 (Admin)	110

E

Embleton [2016] EWCA Crim 1968	215
Emmerson (1991) 92 Cr App R 284	134
Everett [1988] Crim LR 826	137

F

Firth v Epping Magistrates' Court [2011] EWHC 388 (Admin)	153
Fulling [1987] QB 426	133, 313
Furman v Georgia, 408 US 238 (1972)	292

G

George (Barry) [2007] EWCA Crim 2722	310
Gilbert (1977) 66 Cr App R 237	101
Gillan and Quinton v Commissioner of Police for the Metropolis [2006] UKHL 12	20
Gillan and Quinton v United Kingdom (2010) 50 EHRR 45	20
Gleeson [2003] EWCA Crim 3357	110, 153, 154, 155, 165
Goldenberg (1988) 88 Cr App R 285	136
Goonatilleke, ex parte [1986] QB 1	204

Grafton [1992] Crim LR 826 13
Graham v West Mercia Constabulary [2011] EWHC 4 (QB) 54
Gregg v Georgia, and others 428 US 153 (1976) 292
Gunning [1980] Crim LR 592 13

H

Hallam (Sam) [2012] EWCA Crim 1158 318
Haringey Justices, ex parte DPP [1996] 1 All ER 828 13
Hart [2006] EWCA Crim 3239 205
Harvey [1988] Crim LR 241 137
Hasan [2005] UKHL 22 124
Hawthorn, ex parte [1979] 1 All ER 209 204
Hayes [2012] 1 WLR 517 54
Hillard [2004] EWCA Crim 837 118
HM Advocate v Cadder [2010] UKSC 43 106
Hoare and Pierce [2004] EWCA Crim 784, [2005] 1 WLR 1804 109, 116
Hodgson (Robert Graham) [2009] EWCA Crim 490 319
Holgate-Mohammed v Duke [1984] 1 All ER 1054 95
Howarth v Commissioner of Police for the Metropolis [2011] EWHC 2818 (QB) 33
Howell [2005] 1 Cr App R 1 115
Huntingdon Crown Court, ex parte Jordan [1981] QB 857 185, 201
Hussain (Mohammed) [2005] EWCA Crim 1866 223
Hussien v Chong Fook Kam [1970] AC 942 32, 44

I

Ibrahim v R [1914] AC 599 104
Ilijkov v Bulgaria, No 33977/96, 26 July 2001 186
Iqbal [2011] EWCA Crim 273 46

J

Jisl [2004] EWCA Crim 696 150, 182
Johnson and Rowe [2001] 1 Cr App R 8 207
Jones v National Coal Board [1957] 2 QB 55 12

K

Keenan [1990] 2 QB 54 98

L

Lattimore, Salih and Leighton (1976) 62 Cr App R 53 62, 304
Lewis [1990] EWCA Civ 5 300
Lewis [2005] EWCA Crim 859 208
Lewis v Chief Constable of South Wales [1991] 1 All ER 206 44
Li Shu-ling [1989] AC 270 125
Lord Hanningfield v Chief Constable of Essex [2013] EWHC 243 (QB) 55

M

M [2000] 8 Arch News 2 137
Magee v United Kingdom [2000] ECHR 216 128
Maguire and others (1991) 94 Cr App R 133 317
Mahmoud Mattan (Hanged) [1998] EWCA Crim 676 284
Mason [1988] 1 WLR 139 312
McCann, Cullen and Shanahan (1991) 92 Cr App R 239 106
McGovern (1991) 92 Cr App R 228 138

McIlkenny v Chief Constable of the West Midlands Police Force [1980] 2 All ER 227 124, 214
McIlkenny, Hunter, Walker, Callaghan, Hill and Power (1991) 93 Cr App R 287 301
McVeigh (1983) 5 EHRR 71 59
Medcalf v Mardell [2002] UKHL 27 91
Michalko v Slovakia, No 35377/05, 21 December 2010 186
Milford [2001] Crim LR 330 113
Miller [1986] 1 WLR 1191 134
Moss (1990) 91 Cr App R 371 137
Mullen [2000] QB 520 207
Murray v United Kingdom (1996) 22 EHRR 29 105, 113
Mushtaq [2005] 1 WLR 1513 135

N

Newell [2012] EWCA Crim 650 153
Nickolson [1999] Crim LR 61 113

O

O'Hara [1997] AC 286 51
Olden [2007] EWCA Crim 726 51
Oliphant [1992] Crim LR 40 131
Oliva [1965] 1 WLR 1028 13

P

Paris, Abdullahi and Miller (1993) 97 Cr App R 99 90, 106, 125, 282, 313
Parker v Chief Constable of Essex [2018] EWCA Civ 2788 51
Pearson, ex parte [1999] 3 All ER 498 211
Peart [2006] UKPC 5 104
Pendleton [2001] UKHL 66 211
Pinfold [1988] QB 462 209
Polemis, ex parte [1974] 1 WLR 1371 204
Ponting [1985] Crim LR 318 173
Poole and Mills [2003] EWCA Crim 1753 209
Pope [2012] EWCA Crim 2241 207
Pratt and Morgan v Attorney General for Jamaica [1993] UKPC 1 286
Proulx, Re [2001] 1 All ER 57 135

R

R (DPP) v Chorley Justices [2006] EWHC 1795 (Admin) 322
R (DPP) v Leicester Magistrates' Court unreported, 9 February 2016 185
R (Hallam) v Secretary of State for Justice; R (Nealon) v Secretary of State for Justice [2019] UKSC 2 302
R (Kelly) v Warley JJ [2007] EWHC 1836 (Admin); [2008] 1 WLR 2001 152
R (Mullen) v Secretary of State for the Home Department [2004] UKHL 18 301
R (Nunn) v Chief Constable of Suffolk [2014] UKSC 37 214
R (Roberts) v Commissioner of Police of the Metropolis and another [2015] UKSC 79 32
R (Rutherford) v IPCC [2010] EWHC 2881 (Admin) 51
R (TL) v Chief Constable of Surrey Police [2017] 1 WLR 2047 54
R (Westlake) v Criminal Cases Review Commission [2004] EWHC 2779 (Admin) 283
Randall [1998] 6 Arch News 1 114
Randall v R [2002] 2 Cr App R 17 311
Rhodes (1899) 1 QB 77 100
Rice v Connolly [1966] 2 QB 414 101
Richardson [2011] 2 Cr App R 1 53
Roberts [1999] 1 WLR 662 74

Roble [1997] EWCA Crim 118 119
Roderick Ricardo Went v The Queen (Criminal Appeal No 2 of 2014) (2018) Court of Appeal of Barbados 288
Rondel v Worsley [1969] 1 AC 191 169

S

Salduz v Turkey (2009) 49 EHRR 19 319
Salduz v Turkey [2008] ECHR 1542 82
Samuel [1988] QB 615 134
Sander v UK [2000] Crim LR 767 173
Saunders v United Kingdom, A/702 (1997) 23 EHRR 313 101
Sawyer (1980) 71 Cr App R 283 173
Seelig and Spens [1992] 1 WLR 148 134
Senior [2018] EWCA Crim 837 317
Sharp [1993] 3 All ER 225 13
Shields v Chief Constable of Merseyside Police [2010] EWCA Civ 1281 45
Smith (Troy) [2011] EWCA Crim 1098 113
Spicer v Holt [1977] AC 987 44
ST v CC of Nottinghamshire Police [2022] EWHC 1280 (QB) 55

T

Tabbakh [2009] EWCA Crim 464 116
Taylor (Michelle) (1994) 98 Cr App Rep 361 307
Taylor v Chief Constable of Thames Valley Police [2004] 1 WLR 3155 56
The People (at the Suit of the Director of Public Prosecutions) v Phelim McGuinness [1978] IR 189 164
Three Rivers District Council v Governor and Company of the Bank of England (No 6) [2004] UKHL 48 91, 115
Togher [2001] 3 All ER 463 208
Turnbull [1977] QB 224 313
Twomey and Others [2009] EWCA Crim 1035 176

U

Ulcay [2007] EWCA Crim 2379 91

V

Voisin [1918] 1 KB 531 62

W

W [1994] Crim LR 130 138
W [2010] EWCA Crim 2799 137
Walker v Commissioner of Police of the Metropolis [2014] EWCA Civ 897 44
Ward (Judith) (1993) 96 Cr App Rep 1 315
Ward [2018] EWCA Crim 872 318
Webber [2004] UKHL 1 113, 114
Weeks [1995] Crim LR 52 132
Wilson (Jamie Lee) [2019] EWCA Crim 2410 317
Wood v DPP [2008] EWHC 1056 (Admin) 45
Woolmington v DPP [1935] UKHL 1, [1935] AC 462 155, 165, 193

Y

Young, Court of Appeal (Criminal Division), 30 December 1994 174
Yuill v Yuill [1945] 1 All ER 183, 61 TLR 176 12, 164

Z

Zaredar [2016] EWCA Crim 877 320

TABLE OF LEGISLATION

Anti-social Behaviour, Policing and Crime Act 2014
s 175(1) 301
Attachment of Earnings Act 1971 249

Bail Act 1976 65, 186, 191, 192
s 3(1) 188
s 3(4) 188
s 3(6) 65, 188, 189
s 3(6ZAA) 65
s 4 182, 186, 189
s 6 180
s 7(3) 189
Sch 1 180, 186, 187, 188
Bill of Rights 1689 103

Children Act 1908 278
Contempt of Court Act 1981
s 8 174
Coronavirus Act 2020
Sch 21 19
Coroners and Justice Act 2009
s 115(1) 186
Courts Act 1971 163
Courts Act 2003
s 69 147
s 69(4)(a) 147
s 69(4)(b) 147
s 86A 181
Crime and Disorder Act 1998 232
s 51 181
s 80 232
s 81 232
Criminal Appeal Act 1968
s 1 209
s 1(1) 204
s 2(1)(a) 206
s 3 209
s 7 209
s 9(1) 204
s 23 208
s 29 205
Criminal Appeal Act 1968 – *continued*
s 31 205
s 33 209
Criminal Appeal Act 1995 206
Part II 108
s 8(1)–(6) 210
s 13(1)(a) 210
s 13(1)(b), (c) 211
s 13(2) 211
s 17 212
s 18A 212
Criminal Evidence Act 1898 100
s 1 100
s 1(b) 100, 111
Criminal Justice Act 1967 142, 171
s 11 142
Criminal Justice Act 1972 171, 229
Criminal Justice Act 1982
s 37 247
Criminal Justice Act 1987 143
s 2(3) 143
Criminal Justice Act 1988 172
s 133(1ZA) 301
s 139 26
s 139AA 26
Criminal Justice Act 1991 250
Criminal Justice Act 2003 78, 194, 241, 247, 249
s 22(3)(a)–(c) 254
s 23 254
s 24(3) 254
s 28 78
s 34 152
s 44(6)(a)–(c) 176
s 51 327
s 114 194
s 142 232, 234, 236, 282
s 144 183
s 144(1)(a), (b) 183
s 148(1) 244
s 151 244
s 152(2) 241

Criminal Justice Act 2003 – *continued*
s 156 182, 192
s 158 192
s 163 247
s 164 248
s 167 232
s 177 244
s 177(1)(a)–(i) 244
s 177(5) 244
s 190(1) 241
s 300(2) 249
s 301 249
s 321 172
Sch 2 78
Sch 12, para 8 242
Sch 21 197
Sch 33 172
Criminal Justice and Courts Act 2015 172
s 17(2) 253
s 17(4) 253
s 26 300
Criminal Justice and Police Act 2001 256
ss 1–11 256
Criminal Justice and Public Order Act 1994 17, 26, 111, 118, 119, 120, 121, 144
s 25 186
s 34 92, 111, 112, 113, 114, 115, 116, 117, 118, 119, 145
s 34(1) 111
s 34(1)(b) 112
s 34(2) 111
s 35 111, 116, 117, 118, 119, 145, 153
s 35(1)(b) 116
s 35(3) 116
s 35(4) 116
s 36 111, 117, 118, 119, 145
s 37 111, 117, 118, 119, 145
s 38(3) 113, 116
s 60 22, 26, 27, 28, 31
s 60(3) 27
Criminal Procedure and Investigations Act 1996 144, 145, 146, 150, 153, 321
s 1(2) 144
s 3 144, 192, 321
s 5 144, 145, 193, 321
s 6 144, 321
s 6(2) 144
s 6A 144
s 6A(2)(a), (b) 145
s 6B(4) 145
s 6C 152
s 7A 144, 193
s 11 145
Criminal Procedure and Investigations Act 1996 – *continued*
s 11(3)(a), (b) 145
s 11(5) 145
s 11(10) 145
s 12 145
Criminal Procedure Rules 2020 7, 17, 147, 150, 151, 153, 171, 183, 185, 186, 192, 193, 200, 322
r 1.1 147, 322
r 1.1(1) 182
r 1.1(2) 147
r 1.1(2)(a) 147, 185, 302
r 1.1(2)(b)–(e) 148
r 1.1(2)(f), (g) 149
r 1.2(2) 149
r 3.2(1) 149
r 3.2(2)(a) 150
r 3.2(2)(e) 150
r 3.2(2)(f) 186
r 3.5 151
r 3.5(2)(i) 149, 151
r 3.13 151
r 3.13(d) 154
r 3.16(3)(b) 181
r 3.16(5)(a) 181
r 8.2(2) 184
r 8.2(3) 184
r 9.7 181
r 9.8 181
r 14.5(3) 186
r 14.7 187
r 14.8 189
r 14.8(6) 189
r 24.3(3)(d) 194
r 24.7(1)(b) 201
r 34.2(2)(b) 201
Crown Court (Advance Notice of Expert Evidence) Rules 1987 143

Directive 2012/13
Article 7 184
Directive 2013/48 84

Equality Act 2010
s 149 29
European Convention on Human Rights 90, 133, 190, 284, 286
Article 2 285, 286
Article 2(2) 286
Article 3 19, 104, 197, 286, 287
Article 5 19, 20, 104, 304
Article 5(1) 46
Article 5(1)(a), (b) 48

European Convention on Human Rights – *continued*
Article 5(1)(c) 23, 48
Article 5(1)(d)–(f) 48
Article 6 6, 10, 82, 147, 148, 288, 304
Article 6(1) 10, 83, 208
Article 7 197
Article 8 19, 104
Article 8(2) 23
Article 11 290
Protocol 6 285
Protocol 13 285

Fines (Deduction from Income Support) Regulations 1992 249
Firearms Act 1968 26

Habeas Corpus Act 1640 103
Homicide Act 1957 278, 279
Human Rights Act 1998 49

Juries Act 1974 171
Legal Aid, Sentencing and Punishment of Offenders Act 2012 187, 190, 202
s 17 202
s 21 202

Magistrates' Courts Act 1980 182, 200, 325
s 2 181
s 5 182
s 9(3) 182
s 10 182
s 82(4) 249
s 108(1) 200
s 111 203
s 128 182, 189
s 142 185
Sch 1 161
Sch 4 249
Magna Carta (1215) 104
Metropolitan Police Act 1829 101
Misuse of Drugs Act 1971 26
s 23(2) 26
Murder (Abolition of the Death Penalty) Act 1965 279
s 1 197

Official Secrets Act 1911
s 11 174

Police Act 1976
s 1 108
Police and Criminal Evidence Act 1984 17, 25, 26, 27, 43, 44, 48, 49, 62, 63, 67, 69, 70, 71, 72, 73, 74, 76, 78, 81, 82, 83, 90, 96, 97, 105, 107, 108, 125, 126, 131, 133, 139, 304, 319

Police and Criminal Evidence Act 1984 – *continued*
Part II 19
Part IV 65
s 1 21, 22, 26, 27, 29, 39
s 1(1)(b) 26
s 1(2) 26
s 1(3) 26, 29
s 1(7) 26
s 1(8) 26
s 2 40
s 3 40
s 3(1)–(6) 40
s 10 91
s 24 43, 48, 49, 50, 53, 55, 56
s 24(1)(a) 49
s 24(1)(b) 50
s 24(1)(c) 49
s 24(1)(d) 50
s 24(2) 50
s 24(3) 50
s 24(4) 52
s 24(5) 54
s 24(5)(a)–(c) 52
s 24(5)(d)–(f) 53
s 28 56
s 30 62
s 30A 62, 65
s 36(3) 63
s 36(5) 63
s 37 63, 71
s 37(1) 63
s 37(2) 64
s 37(3) 64
s 37(4) 73
s 37(5) 73
s 37(7) 63, 76
s 37A 76
s 38 63
s 38(1) 179
s 38(1)(a) 180
s 38(2A) 180
s 39(1) 63
s 40 73
s 40(1) 74
s 40(1)(a), (b) 74
s 40(2) 74
s 40(3)(a)–(c) 74
s 40(12)
s 41 74
s 41(1) 75
s 41(2) 75
s 42(1) 75
s 43 75

Police and Criminal Evidence Act 1984 – *continued*
s 44 75
s 46(2) 180
s 46A(1) 65
s 46A(1A) 65
s 47(1A) 65, 179
s 47ZB 69
ss 47ZD–47ZG 69
s 50A(1) 64
s 50A(2) 64
s 58 82, 83, 97, 131, 319
s 58(1) 81, 86
s 58(4) 81
s 58(6) 81
s 66 26
s 76 125, 131, 133, 313
s 76(1) 125, 133
s 76(2) 133, 136, 138
s 76(2)(a) 133
s 76(2)(b) 133, 135, 137, 138
s 76(3) 123, 138
s 76(8) 133
s 78 133, 312, 313
s 82(1) 124, 125
s 117 56
PACE Code A 20, 22, 26, 29, 30, 31, 32, 38
para 1.4 20, 25
para 2.2 29, 38
para 2.2B 29, 31
para 2.4 30
para 2.4A 30
para 2.6 31
para 2.6B 39
para 3.3 23, 26
para 3.5 23
para 4 40
para 4.2 40
Note 1 20
Annex A 26
PACE Code C 60, 76, 81, 97, 98, 118, 123, 131, 132, 134
Section 6 97
Section 12 97
para 1.7 131
para 2 73
para 2.1 73
para 2.3 73
para 2.4 73
para 3.1 81
para 6.9 91
para 10.1 96
para 10.4 56
para 10.5 56
para 11.1 96
Pace Code C – *continued*
para 11.1A 96
para 11.5 97, 131
para 11.7 97
para 11.15 131
para 12.2 97
para 12.4 97
para 12.6 97
para 12.8 97
para 15.1 73
para 16.1A 76
Note 6D 92
Note 11C 123
Note E2 123
PACE Code G 49, 50
para 1.2 49
para 1.3 54
para 2.3A 50
paras 2.4–2.9 53
Police, Crime, Sentencing and Courts Act 2022 69, 327
Part 6 25
s 45 69
s 200 327
Sch 4 69
Police Reform Act 2002
s 51 108
Policing and Crime Act 2017 67, 68, 69
s 162 181
Powers of Criminal Courts (Sentencing) Act 2000
s 12(1) 251
s 12(1)(b) 251
Prison and Courts Bill (2016–17) 236
Prosecution of Offences Act 1985 167
s 1 108
s 22 180
s 23 168
Prosecution of Offences (Custody Time Limits) Regulations 1987 180
reg 2(2) 181
Protection of Freedoms Act 2012 26, 28

Senior Courts Act 1981 163
s 28 205
s 28(2) 205
s 48(4) 202
s 81 189
Sentence of Death (Expectant Mothers) Act 1931 278
Sentencing Act 2020
s 342E 29
Serious Organised Crime and Police Act 2005
s 110 49

Terrorism Act 2000 26
s 44 20, 28

Terrorism Act 2000 – *continued*
s 47A 27, 28
Sch 7 101
Tribunals, Courts and Enforcement Act 2007
s 62 249

United Nations Economic and Social Council (ESC)
Resolution 1984/50 285, 286, 288
para 9 287, 288
United Nations International Covenant on Civil and Political Rights 286, 288
Article 6 285
Article 6(2) 285
Article 6(5) 285
Article 7 285, 286, 287
Article 14 288
Article 19 290

Vagrancy Act 1824
s 24 27

Youth Justice and Criminal Evidence Act 1999 195
s 16 195, 197
s 16(2) 195
s 17 195, 196, 197
s 19 148, 195, 196
s 20 148
s 21 148, 196
s 22 148, 195
ss 22A–30 148, 195, 196
s 31 148
s 32 148
s 41 148
s 59 101
Sch 3 101

ABBREVIATIONS

BA 1976	Bail Act 1976
BCM	Better Case Management
CAA 1968	Criminal Appeal Act 1968
CEA	Criminal Evidence Act
CJPOA 1994	Criminal Justice and Public Order Act 1994
CO	custody officer
CPIA 1996	Criminal Procedure and Investigations Act 1996
CPS	Crown Prosecution Service
CrimPR	Criminal Procedure Rules
ECHR	European Convention on Human Rights
ECtHR	European Court of Human Rights
EHRC	Equality and Human Rights Commission
HMCTS	HM Courts and Tribunals Service
HMICFRS	HM Inspectorate of Constabulary and Fire & Rescue Services
JR	judicial review
KBD	King's Bench Division of the High Court
LASPO 2012	Legal Aid, Sentencing and Punishment of Offenders Act 2012
MCA 1980	Magistrates' Courts Act 1980
MPS	Metropolitan Police Service
PACE 1984	Police and Criminal Evidence Act 1984
PCA 2017	Policing and Crime Act 2017
PCSCA 2022	Police, Crime, Sentencing and Courts Act 2022
PND	penalty notice for disorder
PTD	pre-trial detention
RUI	'released under investigation'

chapter 1

Theoretical Approaches to Criminal Procedure

1.1 Introduction

In England and Wales, if a person reports a crime, the police may commence an official investigation into the alleged offence. This represents the formal start of the criminal justice process and may result in a citizen being arrested; detained; interrogated; charged; bailed; tried and convicted. The ramifications of an allegation of and conviction for criminal conduct are significant – they can have a life-changing impact on suspects and defendants, whether they are innocent or guilty. Accordingly, the criminal justice process requires a clear and robust framework of procedural rules that define acceptable practice by the police, the courts and lawyers. Without these rules, the process may be open to abuse and distortion, endangering the individual rights of those drawn into the system, as well as those victims of crime seeking justice for wrongs against them. For example, without the restraint of procedural rules, the police could arrest anyone they wished, and treat them in any way they desired, without the need to justify or moderate their behaviour. This would not only breach the individual rights of the accused person but lead to mistakes, such as miscarriages of justice (see **Chapter 16**). Any society claiming to respect the rule of law[1] would rightly condemn such conduct and recognise the necessity of rules of criminal procedure which restrain and regulate. In turn, this would prevent abuse of power by officials of the state, ensure each suspect and defendant is treated equally, fairly and proportionately, and ultimately achieve a just and accurate outcome.

This chapter considers:

- theoretical approaches to traditional models of criminal procedure;
- the purpose of the criminal trial; and
- the complex role the judiciary plays in adversarial and inquisitorial approaches.

This framework will be applied to later topics as a method of understanding theoretical approaches to criminal procedure.

1.2 An overview of legal traditions

These vital rules of criminal procedure have been developed by centuries of law and practice in the various legal systems of the world, and will have been shaped by the legal 'tradition' within which that jurisdiction falls. A legal 'tradition' is essentially a collective description for the structures, institutions and methods which characterise how a jurisdiction 'does' justice. It is widely accepted that the criminal justice process of a jurisdiction, and the rules governing it, will fall under one of two broad legal traditions: adversarialism or inquisitorialism. These are historic, ideological models

1 In its simplest form, the rule of law states that everyone is equal before and subject to the law. If everyone is treated with equality, the administration of law should be fair, effective and transparent.

that outline the general approach to administering criminal justice in any given jurisdiction. As a general rule, the adversarial tradition can be found in common law jurisdictions, which can be broadly described as systems in which laws are interpreted by judges and created by the legislature. Examples of common law jurisdictions include England and Wales, the United States of America, Australia, and many Commonwealth countries. The inquisitorial tradition is best represented by civil law systems, which generally have a comprehensive, constantly updated legal code. Here, the role of the judge is to establish the facts of the case and apply the appropriate section of the code. It has been said that the decision of the judge is less crucial in shaping the legal landscape. It is those who draft and interpret the code that carry the greater responsibility. Civil law jurisdictions vastly outnumber their common law counterparts, and examples of those who use the civil law approach include much of continental Europe, for example France and Italy. It must be emphasised that these are theoretical or ideal models and do not entirely reflect the reality of criminal procedure. As such, one is unlikely to find a completely adversarial or completely inquisitorial model operating anywhere in the world. This chapter aims to unpick and critique the various components and functions of these different approaches.

1.2.1 Adversarialism

Adversarialism might best be described as a battle: a competition between two sides, with the 'winner' judged by a neutral third party. This is governed by a set of regulations, ensuring that the process is fair and that neither side can 'cheat' each other or those deciding the outcome. Adversarial criminal procedure therefore represents the rules of the game. This is best exemplified in England and Wales; reporting in 1993, the Royal Commission on Criminal Justice described the adversarial legal system of England and Wales in the following terms:

> [A] system which has the judge as an umpire, who leaves the presentation of the case to the parties (prosecution and defence) on each side. They separately prepare their case and call, examine and cross-examine their witnesses.[2]

The adversarial process in England and Wales could therefore be characterised as 'legally regulated debate between [two] parties with the trial as its centrepiece'.[3] The two sides (usually referred to as 'parties') gather and select the evidence before orally presenting their case – their version of the facts – at trial. Traditional adversarial ideology is centred on the notion that 'the truth is best discovered by powerful statements on each side of the argument'.[4] By pitting contrasting arguments against each other and testing the supporting evidence, a more accurate picture of the truth can be obtained. In line with this 'competing truths' theory, the parties are responsible for gathering their evidence and presenting their case in a light that best favours their desired result – a conviction for the prosecution or an acquittal for the defence.[5] This of course raises questions about how likely it is that the truth (in short, an objective,

2 Royal Commission on Criminal Justice, *Report* (London: HMSO, 1993), para 10.

3 Hodgson, J, 'Conceptions of the Trial in Inquisitorial and Adversarial Procedure' in A Duff et al (eds), *The Trial on Trial Volume 1: Truth and Due Process*, 1st edn (Oxford: Hart, 2004), 224.

4 As per Lord Eldon LC in *ex parte Lloyd* (1822) Mont 70 at 72.

5 Although in certain instances, the defence will not seek an acquittal but a conviction on a lesser charge. For example, in the case of homicide, the defence may attempt to seek a conviction of involuntary manslaughter as opposed to murder.

factual account of reality) will be discovered in an adversarial process – and this will be discussed below.

In the adversarial tradition, those who decide on guilt and innocence (hereafter, decision-makers) are only responsible for adjudication and do not possess any investigative function. Professor Michael Zander described the traditional role of the adversarial judge as 'a passive umpire, as in a tennis match …',[6] who considers the evidence offered by both parties, ensures that the rules of the process are adhered to, and decides on the outcome. In order to maintain a passive and neutral stance, decision- makers should not conduct an active role in proceedings. If they were to become overtly active, they would run the risk of compromising the ability to 'neutrally evaluate the adversaries' presentations'.[7] Pre-trial preparation by the parties is at least partially motivated by self-interest rather than public interest, geared towards presenting favourable evidence in the best possible light in order to 'win' the contest. As such, decision-makers must guard against this by ensuring that the desire to win does not outstrip the search for the truth. The rules of the game – the procedural requirements for building and presenting a case – are designed to restrain each party's natural desire to achieve victory (whether by legitimate or illegitimate means). Therefore, decision- makers are charged with both enforcing the rules as well as judging the case.

A key feature of an archetypal adversarial system is the principle of equality of arms – that is, defendants are adequately equipped with tools to defend themselves from the 'oppressive state', an entity with significantly more power and influence than any single citizen, thus levelling the playing field. A primary example would be the right to refuse to testify or to cooperate (referred to as the right to silence).[8] Another would be the right to legal representation – a lawyer who can make sense of the accusations made by the state and help the accused to defend against them. Such tools inevitably hamper the ability of the prosecution to secure convictions – in effect, they present obstacles which must be overcome. In this sense, the adversarial model favours the sacrifice of a swift and efficient criminal process in order to safeguard the individual rights of an accused person. A key justification for this approach is the avoidance of mistakes and miscarriages of justice; if an accused is compelled to give evidence or tried without an advocate to protect them, innocent persons may be convicted. As such, equality of arms operates to enhance the integrity of the deliberations.[9] In summary, the adversarial model hinges on the concept of balance by ensuring that the parties are equally able to make their case, and that decision-makers are able to draw fair, accurate and objective conclusions.

1.2.2 Inquisitorialism

Both the adversarial and inquisitorial models seek to ascertain 'the truth', but employ vastly different mechanisms for deciding upon it. The inquisitorial model does not conceptualise the process in terms of 'sides' or 'competition'; as the name suggests, the central focus of the process is managed inquiry. The responsibility for investigating and adjudicating a criminal case lies not with any partisan prosecution or defence, but with

6 Zander, M, *Cases and Materials on the English Legal System*, 10th edn (Cambridge: Cambridge University Press, 2007).

7 Landsman, S, 'The Decline of the Adversary System: How the Rhetoric of Swift and Certain Justice has Affected Adjudication in American Courts' (1980) *Buffalo Law Review* 487–529 at 491.

8 See **Chapter 6**.

9 Fuller, L, 'The Forms and Limits of Adjudication' (1978) 92 *Harv LR* 353 at 501.

a central judicial authority whose role is to act in the wider public interest in the search for the truth.[10] The rationale behind this is that, in building and presenting a case, its integrity will inevitably be corrupted by the adversarial desire to win. For example, it may be in the best interests of each party to conceal the truth if it does not serve their goals. Bias and subjectivity are unavoidable in an adversarial contest; indeed, the adversarial model actively encourages this with its 'competing truths' paradigm. In contrast, inquisitorialism regards 'the truth' as an objective concept which will only be obscured by allowing parties to control the flow of evidence and information to decision-makers. Inquisitorial tradition does not share the trust placed in adversarial parties to investigate and present a case fairly, instead relying on 'the integrity and capacity of public officials to pursue "the truth", unprompted by party allegiances'.[11] The state, as represented by the judiciary, is therefore best equipped to carry out the investigation into an alleged offence. In theory, the person who conducts the pre-trial investigation is a member of the judiciary, and it is the judiciary that will investigate all evidence and information, both exculpatory and inculpatory, and build a case on this basis. Once completed, the dossier of evidence will be exposed to external scrutiny.

In general, pre-trial investigation of the most serious offences under an inquisitorial model will be the responsibility of an examining magistrate. However, in most other cases, the police, under the supervision of the prosecutor, will conduct the pre-trial investigation. This is therefore not dissimilar to adversarialism. A key point to remember here is that in the inquisitorial approach, the prosecutor and judge are an overlapping class of state official, and the prosecutor will often follow the orders of the judiciary when undertaking the pre-trial investigation. This is in contrast to the adversarial approach where the bodies are independent of one other and neither has any role to play in the pre-trial investigation.

Inquisitorial theory holds that the best person equipped to conduct the investigation is the benevolent state[12] and that judicial supervision is a safeguard from abuse of power by state officials. The pre-trial investigation by the judiciary culminates in the creation of a dossier of evidence; it is this dossier and pre-trial investigation that is the centrepiece of the inquisitorial model.[13] The dossier is passed to a judge in preparation for trial, and it will be for the judge to decide on which witnesses to call and to conduct any examination of the witnesses. The role of adversarial parties is minimal – as such, a converse hierarchy of power exists, in which both parties play a subsidiary role to the proactive judge. There is greater emphasis on the written dossier than on the oral competition of the trial. Writing in 1977, Goldstein and Marcus claimed that uncontested inquisitorial trials merely served as perfunctory proceedings, and often, in the French Correctional Court, not a single corroborating witness was called. The accused made his or her statement, the lawyers made their speeches and sentencing swiftly followed.[14] Essentially, the public trial element of the inquisitorial model is a summary or evaluation of the evidence in the dossier, rather than a forum for oral contest.[15]

---

10 See Ellison, L, 'The Protection of Vulnerable Witnesses in Court: An Anglo-Dutch Comparison' (1999) 3 *International Journal of Evidence and Proof* 29–43.

11 *Ibid.*

12 Simon, WH, 'The Ideology of Advocacy: Procedural Justice and Professional Ethics' (1978) *Wis LR* (29) at 43

13 Moohr, GS, 'Prosecutorial Power in an Adversarial System: Lessons from Current White Collar Cases and the Inquisitorial Model' (2004) *Buffalo Law Review*, Vol 8 at 193.

14 Goldstein, AS and Marcus, M, 'The Myth of Judicial Supervision in Three "Inquisitorial" Systems: France, Italy and Germany', 87 *Yale Law Journal* 240 at 268.

1.2.3 A brief critique of ideological approaches to criminal justice

Duff believes that the models are over-simplified and that no legal system falls purely into the adversarial or inquisitorial bracket.[16] Most adversarial systems now impose limitations on 'ambush defences' (the ability to surprise the prosecution at trial), and most inquisitorial systems allow the defence to confront the prosecution witnesses in person, which traditionally would not occur. Both the adversarial and inquisitorial models reflect the ideology of their respective society's stance on the allocation of power. This is illustrated by the fact that the adversarial process attaches less weight to the goal of fact-finding.[17] This is not because adversarial ideology values fact-finding as unimportant but because it acknowledges the importance of other aims, such as the protection of the citizen from the over-zealous state.[18] Various safeguards are designed to prohibit the state from abusing its powers. The use of lay people (unqualified volunteers) in the criminal justice process and the neutral passivity of decision-makers are examples of the protections afforded to the accused against oppressive or abusive behaviour from state officials. This ethos is also evident in the investigative stage of an adversarial model; for example limitations on the duration of time the suspect can remain in police detention without charge, the right to silence and the right to legal representation. While the adversarial model is grounded in the belief that state power must be checked, the inquisitorial model believes that the state is best equipped to spearhead the investigation of allegations of criminal behaviour, with state officials granted primary responsibility for doing so and adversarial safeguards minimised. For example, legal representation plays a reduced role under the inquisitorial model, characterised as an obstacle to the discovery of truth. It is the duty of the inquisitorial defence lawyer merely to ensure that the state's representatives adhere to the procedural rules of investigation. The defence lawyer can suggest certain avenues of investigation that benefit the case of the accused, but cannot conduct any independent inquiry. In short, legal representation contributes but does not lead; parties to the case have little power in comparison to the judicial authority. The dossier might be described as a safeguard, in that 'it not only forms the basis of the trial, but also a coherent system of supervision and control'.[19] Yet, one might argue that the emphasis placed on this central document – which is not tested and scrutinised in the same manner as adversarial evidence – typifies the trust in the state to investigate fairly and thoroughly. As such, the location of power and control in the criminal justice process is quite different under each model.

As theoretical models, adversarialism and inquisitorialism represent the most common ways of understanding and explaining ways of 'doing' criminal procedure, but these approaches are not universally accepted. Whilst this chapter will not examine alternative frameworks in great detail, it is appropriate here to briefly mention them. Damaska[20] does not reject the models, but believes that their intricate workings can be

15 Jorg, N, Field, S and Brants, C, 'Are Inquisitorial and Adversarial Systems Converging?' in *Criminal Justice in Europe: A Comparative Study* (Oxford: Clarendon Press, 1995), 50.

16 Duff, P, 'Changing Conceptions of the Scottish Criminal Trial: The Duty to Agree Uncontroversial Evidence' in A Duff et al (eds), *The Trial on Trial Volume 1: Truth and Due Process* (Oxford: Hart, 2004), 30.

17 Sanders, A and Young, R, *Criminal Justice*, 3rd edn (Oxford: Oxford University Press, 2007), 14.

18 *Ibid* 48.

19 See further Hodgson (n 3).

20 For more on Damaska's approach to theoretical procedure, see Damaska, MR, *The Faces of Justice and State Authority: A Comparative Approach to the Legal Process* (Yale University Press, 1986).

better understood if they are explanatory rather than normative. The former model is a useful way to explain how a particular procedural method works. A normative approach – whilst useful for understanding the underlying principles and ideals that shape a system – may have less practical value because it is suggestive of how things *should* be done, rather than how they are *actually* done (see figure below).

We stated earlier that using the adversarial and inquisitorial lens to analyse procedure is not universally accepted. Summers challenges and rejects the established opinion that criminal procedure in Europe should be analysed through the dichotomy of adversarialism and inquisitorialism, arguing that, since the 19th century, criminal procedure in Europe can be described as a single tradition.[21] She suggests that one can 'identify a common European concept of criminal procedure',[22] and she details the 'emerging European discourse'[23] amongst jurists in the 19th century which describes the notion of the 'accusatorial trinity' (the defence, prosecution and impartial judge) as the dominant procedural model.[24] Summers argues that the European Court of Human Rights (ECtHR) has neglected this European tradition but that the jurisprudence of the Court has been influenced by developments stemming from the 19th century. She argues that by discarding the traditional adversarial and inquisitorial models and devoting more consideration to the European model, the ECtHR will develop a more coherent and consistent vision of the rights that are outlined in Article 6 of the European Convention on Human Rights (ECHR).[25]

Normative Models	**Explanatory Models**
The model suggests a way things should be done to a particular standard.	The model explains why and how a particular thing works. It is an exploration of a particular phenomenon.

Critique aside,[26] the two traditional models will be used as the primary lens for observing and examining the criminal justice process for the purposes of this book; we believe that the approaches offer the student the greatest clarity when dealing with complex, procedural models. Ultimately, the models represent a useful analytical tool with which to examine the historical development, current state and potential transformation of the criminal justice process in England and Wales. The models are advantageous in that they are easy to understand, and they remain relevant in contextualising any changes in broader patterns of reform; that is, instead of viewing

21 Summers, S, *Fair Trials and Procedural Tradition in Europe* (Oxford: Hart Publishing, 2007), 29.

22 *Ibid* xix.

23 *Ibid* 22.

24 *Ibid* 27.

25 See *ibid* 29, although Field believes that Summers' finding of a single European tradition is stimulating but flawed. He believes that it is difficult to bear a label of 'European' where there is very little mention of developments in legislation or intellectual thought in Southern Europe or Scandinavia. For an in-depth analysis of Field's rejection of Summers' model, see Field, S, 'Fair Trials and Procedural Tradition in Europe' (2009) *Oxford Journal of Legal Studies* 29(2), 365–87.

26 For further reading, see Duff, P, 'Disclosure in Scottish criminal procedure: another step in an inquisitorial direction?' (2007) *International Journal of Evidence and Proof* 11(3), 153–80.

changes as isolated incidents, they can be viewed as expressions of emerging trends. The models can also help identify any potential tension or conflict that changes create within the traditional ideology. Ultimately, the models can be used as a tool to examine the ways other jurisdictions 'do' criminal procedure.

1.3 The purpose(s) of the criminal trial

As the apex of the theoretical criminal process, it is useful to examine why exactly we use this method of examining and judging criminal behaviour. Identifying a single purpose of the criminal trial has proven to be quite troublesome. It is commonly assumed to be the determination of the guilt or innocence of defendants.[27] However, if the nature of the trial is deconstructed, it becomes clear that it aims to attain several goals, including:

- truth;
- argument;
- catharsis; and
- finality

1.3.1 Truth

Adversarial ideology and practice arguably suggest that the adversarial trial is less committed to the discovery of the truth than its inquisitorial counterpart.[28] Each party scrutinises the facets of their counterpart's account, exposing any weaknesses discovered during the public forum of the trial. Advocates endeavour to 'reveal to the tribunal which witnesses can be relied upon and which can be cast aside'.[29] Whilst the search for the truth is central to the adversarial criminal justice process, this is balanced against other considerations, for example maintaining the integrity of the system. In England and Wales, the prosecution will only succeed if it can present a case which convinces decision-makers (normally, magistrates or a jury) that the defendant is guilty of the alleged offence to the requisite standard (in the criminal trial, beyond all reasonable doubt). Procedural safeguards (referred to at the outset of this chapter) not only protect the defendant but also help maintain the integrity of the system. However, these safeguards may also inhibit the search for the truth; for example, if evidence was obtained inappropriately, it should be excluded from trial. This protects the defendant from any abuse of state power and seeks to ensure that evidence is legitimate and reliable. Nonetheless, this may also render a truthful confession inadmissible due to the method by which it was extracted from the defendant. As such, the search for the truth, as a purpose of the trial, is subjugated to another consideration (protection of individual fair trial rights).

Other factors may come into play. The quality of the advocate may indirectly hamper the search for the truth. The prosecution and defence lawyers present their version of an alleged incident, attempting to persuade the jury or the magistrate that their version is the 'truth'. The success of the parties may be as dependent on the skill, knowledge and experience of the advocate presenting the case as it is on the strength of the evidence. The art of advocacy is 'a highly refined one whose very best practitioners may

27 See, for example, the overriding objective of the Criminal Procedure Rules.

28 Because the model insists that both inculpatory and exculpatory evidence are included in the dossier.

29 Solley, S, 'The Role of the Advocate' in M McConville and G Wilson (eds), *The Handbook of the Criminal Justice Process* (Oxford: Oxford University Press, 2002), 312.

manage to persuade in the face of facts',[30] whereas a more inexperienced, less eloquent practitioner may fail to convince that his or her version of events is the truth – even if the facts suggest this is so. Furthermore, the quality and temperament of the witnesses may affect the search for the truth. If the witness is inarticulate or unwilling to answer questions, it may mean that a case founders despite its merits.[31]

At the risk of over-simplifying each model, the relationship with truth-seeking can be broadly defined by the following:

Adversarialism
What truth can you prove?

Inquisitorialism
What truth can be found?

1.3.2 Argument

The adversarial criminal court is, in essence, a civilised combat zone in which only one side can win. If the defence wins, the defendant is exonerated and the prosecution fails. A victory for the prosecution means defeat for the defendant, who will then be subject to the various punishments the court can administer. This description of the trial conveys images of a gladiatorial battle where defeat is fatal to one side. It has been observed that

> trials involve adversaries and adversity, defeats and victories, winners and losers. They pivot around serious allegations presented by their champions as wholly true and their opponents as wholly false. At stake are very grave matters of liberty and confinement, accusation and vindication, reputation and veracity, matters which passionately concern defendants and defence witnesses, victims and prosecution witnesses.[32]

The trial process is emotive, with the most serious issues considered and the most grave consequences possible. In many cases, a fine margin separates winning and losing. These emotions are often most evident during the most confrontational aspect of the trial: the cross-examination. The object of cross-examination is to call into question the moral probity of the other side.[33] Cross-examination seeks to convince the jury or magistrate that a witness cannot be trusted, that their account may be knowingly fabricated or simply unreliable, and by extension that the case of the opposition is therefore not credible. The object and nature of cross-examination therefore means it is not only the facts of the case that are on trial, but the moral character of those involved. This applies to both parties; Zedner comments that the role of the prosecutor is not only to call into the question the veracity of the defendant's claim to innocence but also to debase his very character.[34] This debasement of one's character has led to the trial being termed as a degradation ceremony,[35] one in which both sides must participate. If the defendant is exonerated, he is cleared of all wrongdoing. However, this runs the risk of the witnesses for the prosecution being

30 Zedner, L, *Criminal Justice* (Oxford: Oxford University Press, 2004), 169.

31 Sanders, A, *Victims with Learning Disabilities* (Oxford: Centre for Criminological Research, 1997), 312.

32 Rock, P, 'Witnesses and Space in a Crown Court' (1991) 31 *British Journal of Criminology* 266 at 267.

33 *Ibid.*

34 *Ibid.*

35 Garfinkel, H, 'Conditions of Successful Degradation Ceremonies' (1956) *American Journal of Sociology*, Vol 61, 420.

subjected to humiliation by having their character impugned; under cross-examination they may appear to be spiteful, muddled or greedy, with the implication that their word cannot be relied upon.[36]

The legitimacy of the conflict-airing process is bolstered by the open nature of proceedings. Allowing the public to witness proceedings demonstrates the principle of justice both being done and being visible. It thereby reduces the risk of abuse of power, exemplified by 'show' trials or the pursuit of 'enemies' by the state through the medium of the justice process. Zedner claims that in the Family Court – in which proceedings are not open and are less formalised – authority and legitimacy could, at times, break down.[37] The public nature of the criminal trial therefore ensures that the conduct of the trial complies with the legitimate expectation that the rule of law will be upheld and imposes the social order of the outside world on the court room, as much as it imposes order on the defendant.

1.3.3 Catharsis

As well as the negative connotations of the trial, there are possible positive outcomes. It can provide an opportunity for the accused to publicly air his or her account – the classic idea of 'having your day in court'. For the victim, the trial may provide closure, catharsis or vindication. During the trial of Peter Sutcliffe, the 'Yorkshire Ripper,' the prosecution was willing to accept a plea of guilty to manslaughter by way of diminished responsibility. The prosecution was acutely aware that psychiatrists who had examined Sutcliffe agreed that he suffered from severe mental illness. When this plea was offered to the trial judge, it was rejected; Boreham J insisted that the prosecution ignore its own medical experts and pursue the charge of murder as if Sutcliffe was of sound mind. McEwan doubts that the trial judge disagreed with any of the expert testimony concerning Sutcliffe's mental health, but instead thought that 'a contested criminal trial [was] necessary to provide some kind of healing process following the fear and distress that Sutcliffe's terrible killings had engendered'.[38] McEwan concludes that even those members of society who are used to disposing of criminal cases by way of a guilty plea feel that matters would not be sufficiently brought to a proper close without a fully contested case where all the gruesome evidence is placed before the public.

1.3.4 Finality

The trial is the ultimate arbiter of guilt or innocence. The general assumption is that once a decision has been made about innocence or guilt, this cannot be further challenged and punishment can be allocated accordingly. This guarantees certainty for victims of crime and society, ensures that justice cannot be frustrated by never-ending appeals or prosecution and, of course, prevents a drain on the finances of the state. Most criminal justice systems have an appellate system; this allows parties in criminal proceedings to question the decision made by a court, but this will normally be limited. This ensures finality. The concept of finality had particular importance during the era of capital punishment in England and Wales, primarily because the punishment of death was obviously irreversible. In the second half of the 18th century, there was a growing aversion to capital punishment. Langbein states that it was over-prescribed; in terms of the criminal justice process, he argues that 'too much truth meant too much

36 See Damaska (n 20) at 57–62.

37 Zedner, L, *Criminal Justice* (Oxford: OUP, 2004), Chs 4 and 5.

38 McEwan, JA, *Evidence and the Adversarial Process* (Oxford: Hart, 1998), 171.

death'.[39] As such, the function of the trial became to 'winnow down the number of persons actually executed from the much larger cohort of culprits whom the "Bloody Code" threatened with death'.[40] This objective illustrates not only that the trial could be truth-defeating, but that it was and continues to operate as a dynamic rather than static platform – that is, it flexibly adapts to the needs of the era.

This desire for 'finality' not only applies to victims and witnesses but also to the defendant. Article 6 of the ECHR states that when charged with the commission of a criminal offence, the accused is entitled to a fair and public hearing within a reasonable time by an independent and impartial tribunal.[41] This requirement ensures that the fate of the defendant does not remain uncertain for too long a period and that the alleged incident is fresh in the memory of witnesses, minimising the potential for mistakes.

To some degree, the notion of finality conflicts with the notion of the trial as a search for the truth. If the latter were the primary aim of the trial, the quest for the truth would not be restricted by the concept of finality. Furthermore, to reach the truth, the system should have the capacity to retrospectively correct mistakes by allowing wrongful convictions to be quashed or new prosecutions sought against those acquitted of offences. In England and Wales, the post-appellate system (which will be discussed in **Chapter 11**) exemplifies this idea.

1.4 Adversarial and inquisitorial trials: a different purpose?

According to Duff, the aim of the criminal trial is 'not merely [to] reach an accurate judgement on the defendant's past conduct; it is to communicate and justify that judgement – to demonstrate its justice – to him and others'.[42] In short, it is to deter others from breaking the law. The trial may also be seen as part of the rehabilitation of the convicted person, to influence their future behaviour in a positive way. In this sense, it is not enough to merely punish an offender; he or she must learn what society thinks justice ought to be. In a study of the French inquisitorial criminal process, Field identified an interesting contrast between adversarial and inquisitorial criminal trials. A French judge spent a vast amount of time questioning the accused about his private life, education, history, sexual relationships and hobbies.[43] Field noted that French criminal proceedings were not only designed to discover if the particular individual committed the particular offence; they aimed to ascertain in detail who did what, when, how and why, within the context of a set of general norms about the life of the ordinary French citizen. One might describe this as a form of character mapping, which was considered important because '[t]hese assumptions seemed to be part of a set of reciprocal expectations between the individual on the one hand and the state and community on the other'.[44]

By conducting this examination of the accused's educational and social weaknesses or failings, Field remarked that he had the impression that it was not only the offence in question that was being judged, but also that of the life of the defendant, according to a

39 Langbein, JH, *The Origins of Adversary Criminal Trial* (Oxford: Oxford University Press, 2005), 6.

40 *Ibid.*

41 European Convention on Human Rights, Article 6(1).

42 Duff, R, *Trials and Punishments* (Cambridge, Cambridge University Press, 1986).

43 Field, S, 'State Citizen and Character in French Criminal Process' (2006) *Journal of Law and Society* 33(4) at 523.

44 *Ibid* 523–24.

positive and fairly developed notion of what a French citizen ought to be.[45] Ultimately, the inquisitorial approach could be viewed to take a less retributive stance and a more rehabilitative one as programmes could be provided to match the needs of the defendant. This is a view that is shared by Field; he believes that the criminal trial in France is explicitly part of the process of the accused's rehabilitation and his or her re-entry to society as a reformed citizen of the state. The trial portrays the citizen in a positive manner against which it is deemed appropriate to judge the character and life of the accused.[46] Furthermore, the 'dominance in France of the fact-finding by the professional judiciary changes the attitudes to the social prejudice generated by character evidence'.[47] The adversarial criminal trial presents a far narrower image of the relationship between state and citizens than its inquisitorial counterpart; as such the adversarial criminal law is more distanced from social expectations of the citizen.[48] It should also be borne in mind that much of the fact-finding in inquisitorial procedure has occurred prior to the trial stage, which is in a theoretical sense a formality.

The inquisitorial trial places great emphasis on character evidence. Evidence of both good and bad character is heard prior to pronouncing judgment. In the adversarial trial in England and Wales, the use of character evidence is less significant in determining the culpability of the defendant. It is acceptable for character evidence to be considered at the sentencing stage, but at the trial stage the adversarial process does not permit the use of character evidence to the same extent as its inquisitorial counterpart. This is to ensure that the guilt of the defendant relates to the particular offence in question and its facts, rather than to a broad judgement about the standing of the accused in the community.[49] However, this stance toward character evidence has not always been the norm in England and Wales. Prior to the emergence of the adversarial trial in the last quarter of the 18th century,[50] the trial and sentencing stages were less distinct. The sentencing stage, a clear form of moral judgement about the defendant, would immediately follow the conclusion of the trial, and it was during the sentencing proceedings that juries would sometimes return a partial verdict (where an individual is convicted on a lesser charge that carries a more lenient penalty).[51] This therefore blurs the line between pure consideration of the facts of an allegation and judgement of the accused's character.

Although guilt was rarely contested in early adversarial trials,[52] a defendant was unlikely to plead guilty. A guilty plea would deprive the defendant of the opportunity to give his or her account of events. Furthermore, the accused could call witnesses of his or her own and these witnesses would testify to the good character of the individual. It has been argued that the shift from the pre-adversarial to fully adversarial trial involved a partial shift in the definition of criminal responsibility. Prior to the evolution of the modern adversarial trial, the conviction of the accused was sometimes influenced by his or her character and reputation. Over the last century, great effort has been made to

45 *Ibid* 524.
46 Duff (n 42), 545.
47 *Ibid* 544.
48 *Ibid.*
49 *Ibid.*
50 Beattie, J, *Crime and the Courts in England 1660–1800* (Princeton University Press, 1986), 253.
51 *Ibid* 58.
52 Langbein states that only a small fraction of 18th century criminal trials were genuinely contested inquiries.

ensure that the character of the accused is less influential and that the trial (and any subsequent conviction) are focused on the notion of individual choice and capacity.[53]

It is clear that one single purpose of the criminal trial does not exist, and there is no set definition of the trial in either the adversarial or inquisitorial jurisdictions. What can be said is that the criminal trial is a dynamic mode of justice, which is constantly evolving. This is particularly so in the modern adversarial trial of England and Wales, something that will be discussed later in this book.

1.5 The role of the judiciary in different legal traditions

The classic adversarial judge is both passive and impartial.[54] In the case of *Jones v National Coal Board*,[55] Lord Denning gave what is generally accepted as the classic statement of the modern position of the judge:

> The judge's part ... is to hearken to the evidence, only ... asking questions of witnesses when it is necessary to clear up any point that has been overlooked ... to see that advocates behave themselves seemly and keep to rules laid down by law ... to discourage repetition ... If he goes beyond this, he drops the mantle of a judge and assumes the [role] of an advocate ...[56]

Lord Greene in *Yuill v Yuill*[57] stated that if a judge were to speak 'he ... is liable to have his vision clouded by the dust of conflict'. Both Lord Greene and Lord Denning appear to strike at the distinction between the partisan lawyers who represent each side in an adversarial contest, clarifying that a judge should be an objective figure above the conflict.

1.5.1 The adversarial judiciary

The common law tradition in England and Wales states that it is the duty of the prosecution and defence to conduct the examination of all witnesses. The judge does not engage in this activity, except where supplementary questions may clarify a point. This tradition of passivity dates from the Middle Ages and was once the original method of conducting criminal trials in all European countries. However, this procedure was abandoned in the 12th century in favour of the inquisitorial procedure in many countries.[58] This impartial and passive judicial model was designed to ensure freedom from bias, prevent premature judgement, and provide a balanced view of the case:

> The duty most appropriate ... is to attentively listen to all that is said on both sides. After performing the duty patiently and fully he is in a position to give a jury the full benefit of his thoughts on the subject ...[59]

With that being said, it should be noted that it is well within the right of the adversarial judge to question a witness. Lord Goddard stated, 'if a judge thinks the case has not been thoroughly explored he is entitled to put as many questions as he likes'.[60]

---

53 For a further account of this theory, see Lacey, N, 'In Search of the Responsible Subject' (2001) *MLR* 350.

54 Langbein, J, 'The Criminal Trial Before Lawyers' (1978) 45 *U Ch LR* 263 at314.

55 [1957] 2 QB55.

56 *Ibid* para 64.

57 [1945] 1 All ER 183, 61 TLR 176.

58 Williams, G, *The Proof of Guilt* (London: Stevens and Sons, 1963), 24.

59 Stephen, Sir JF, *History of the Criminal Law* (Kessinger Publishing, 1883) as cited in *ibid* 26.

60 *Per* Lord Goddard CJ in *Williams* (1955) *The Times*, 26 April.

Traditionally, this power was little used, and although Goddard LJ intimated that a judge can put as many questions as he or she likes, that is not entirely the case and there are limits to this power. Where a judge intervenes too frequently, the traditional adversarial role is threatened and the system cannot operate effectively. The Court of Appeal has moved to quash convictions to preserve the notion of judicial impartiality and passivity. In *Gunning*,[61] the defendant's conviction was quashed after counsel asked 172 questions and the judge asked 165 – in essence, usurping the role of the lawyers. The judge also has the authority to call a witness when its purpose is to assist the defence,[62] although this power is rarely used. If the calling of a witness will, in effect, mean that the judge assumes the role of the prosecution then this may lead to a quashed conviction. For example, in *Grafton*,[63] the Court of Appeal emphasised that the judge had to remain impartial and that his or her role was to direct the jury on points of law. By calling the witness, the judge had acted as if he had assumed the mantle of the prosecution. Preventing judges doing so again raises questions about the truth-seeking aspect of the trial. For example, in a 1993 Crown Court Study,[64] nearly 19% of judges questioned were aware of important witnesses who were not called by either side. The Philips Commission recommended that when judges are aware that an important witness has not been called, they should seek counsel to explain the absence of the witness, and, if deemed necessary, the judge should urge counsel to rectify the situation. As a last resort, judges should be prepared to exercise their power to call witnesses.[65] Although, as Zander notes, there is no evidence to suggest that either recommendation has been adopted in practice.[66]

An overly interventional judge risks appearance bias. In *Sharp*,[67] the Court of Appeal held that the judge

> … may be in danger of seeming to enter the arena in the sense that he may appear partial to one side or the other. This may arise from a hostile tone of questioning or implied criticism of counsel who is conducting the examination or cross-examination.

The power to intervene should therefore only be used to satisfy the minimal case management responsibilities of the judge. Proper interventions manage the criminal trial, rather than control it. The traditional adversarial judge should generally do no more than ensure that proceedings are orderly and that the rules of evidence and procedure are followed. When intervening, the judge should ensure that the truth-finding process is not distorted, as in *Sharp*. Above all, interventions should not interfere with the right to a fair trial, the guiding principle behind the judicial role.

1.5.2 The myth of the impartial adversarial umpire?

As alluded to above, the role of the adversarial judge can be likened to an umpire in a cricket match, impartially interpreting information and applying the pre-established standards in the game of law. He or she is simply 'hearkening to the evidence'.[68]

61 [1980] Crim LR592.

62 See *Haringey Justices, ex parte DPP* [1996] 1 All ER 828 and *Oliva* [1965] 1 WLR 1028.

63 [1992] Crim LR826.

64 Zander, M and Henderson, P, 'The Crown Court Study' (Royal Commission on Criminal Justice, Research Study No 19, 1993), section 4.3.12.

65 *Ibid.*

66 Zander (n 6) at 383.

67 [1993] 3 All ER 225, 235.

68 [1957] 2 QB 55.

However, it could be argued that this is an idealistic conception. Judges often become actively involved in proceedings, well illustrated by a *voir dire* ('a trial within a trial') in the Crown Court. During a *voir dire*, the jury will be temporarily discharged and the judge will decide on the admissibility of a piece of evidence. Arguably, the judge enters the realm of the jury: that of the trier of facts. In contrast to the jury in the Crown Court, a magistrate cannot be discharged to alleviate the possibility of prejudice. McEwan believes that when adjudicating on the admissibility of evidence, it is difficult to proceed without the nature of the evidence becoming obvious. If the magistrate feels that, by hearing the disputed evidence, his or her opinion may be prejudiced then there is no remedy – after all, once evidence has been heard it cannot be 'unheard'. Recusal would not be practical for a magistrate, as a later bench would not be bound by the decision, and the new bench would also have to go through the *voir dire*. Ironically, lay magistrates – volunteers with no formal legal training or qualifications – are deemed capable of hearing inadmissible evidence and proceeding to trial with excluded evidence somehow erased from memory. In contrast, professional judges in the 'Diplock Court'[69] are permitted to excuse themselves from a case if they reject evidence that may affect their neutral stance. This example demonstrates the 'myth' of the neutral umpire: the idea that a judge will be unaffected by evidence and will always remain above the fray. In this sense, there is some distance between adversarial theory and the reality of practice.

1.5.3 The inquisitorial judiciary

The traditional concept of judge in the inquisitorial model is vastly different. The inquisitorial judiciary is viewed as the guarantor of individual liberties.[70] This contrasts to adversarialism, which posits that liberties are best defended by equipping each side with the tools to defend themselves. As such, the inquisitorial judiciary is more paternal. To fulfil this function, the judge has a broad range of responsibilities, including the investigation of an offence, adjudication to determine the culpability of the accused, and the authorisation of coercive measures that directly impinge on individual liberty. These measures can include telephone tapping or extending the period for which the suspect is remanded in custody without charge. Historically, the functions of investigation, prosecution and trial were all the responsibility of a single individual,[71] and in theory this remains the case today. As mentioned earlier, this shows a distinctly different approach to the allocation of power within the criminal justice process to that of traditional adversarialism.

This is well exemplified by the French model. In determining the culpability of the accused, the function of the judiciary is not merely to pass judgement on the evidence presented, but to conduct independent enquiries to determine the guilt or innocence of the defendant. This investigation may be conducted via direct questioning of the defendant or by insisting that the police carry out further investigations. The judiciary is also responsible for the discovery of the truth and must therefore seek out evidence that points to the innocence of the defendant (exculpatory) as well as to his or her guilt (inculpatory). The inquisitorial model holds that the truth is best discovered through

69 In a Diplock Court, a professional judge sits without a jury and has to decide on questions of law and fact. For further information on Diplock Courts, see Jackson, J, *Judge Without Jury: Diplock Trials and the Adversary System* (Oxford: Clarendon, 1995).

70 Salas, D, 'The Role of the Judge' in M Delmas-Marty and JR Spencer (eds), *European Criminal Procedures* (Cambridge: Cambridge University Press, 2002), 534.

71 Hodgson (n 3), 230.

unilateral investigation by the judiciary, rather than via the 'check and balance' model of the adversarial partisan contest. Inquisitorialism is therefore defined by

> a concentration of power in the hands of one person, who represents neither the narrow interests of the defence or prosecution but what are claimed to be the wider interests of society.[72]

Therefore, all other interests, including that of the accused, are subordinate to the supremacy of the judge. However, Hodgson found that the judiciary is not as impartial in practice as it is in theory:

> The guilt of the suspect is presumed and denials are rejected. Evidence of violence committed against the suspect by the police was ignored and left for the defence to raise ... the word of the victim or of the police was consistently preferred to that of the suspect; serious cases mean an almost automatic request for a remand in custody, even where evidence is thin.[73]

Despite many jurisdictions utilising an investigating judge, there is a danger that corruption or bias may infiltrate the judiciary – a serious problem when such significant power is vested in one figure. Jackson states that, over time, some officials may come to favour certain kinds of litigants over others. Psychological insight suggests that it is difficult for active investigators to suspend judgement and weigh up evidence dispassionately, creating a risk that a particular hypothesis about a case will be pursued to the exclusion of others – in short, a form of judicial tunnel vision.[74] This is often cited as a problem with police officers in adversarial systems, determined to secure a conviction. One *juge* interviewed by Hodgson was very proud of his record that only two cases sent to him in 10 years had resulted in acquittals.[75] This raises concerns about how genuinely impartial he was – that personal statistics may have been more important to the *juge* than uncovering the truth in each case. Despite the supposed efficiency of the *juge* interviewed by Hodgson, other jurisdictions have ceased to embrace this inquisitorial figurehead. In 1975, Germany abolished the role of examining magistrate over doubts about the role, and Italy abolished the role after a corruption scandal in 1988.[76]

Despite sharing the same title, the theoretical role and the position of the inquisitorial judiciary are quite different to those of their adversarial counterpart. The inquisitorial judiciary is deeply interwoven into the criminal proceedings, possessing more investigative power and greater responsibility for case building. All evidence is given equal weight, and, in theory, no particular result is sought. Of course, this model is somewhat different in reality.

1.6 Critical analysis of criminal justice: Packer's models

Like any academic subject, we should take a critical view when examining criminal procedure and punishment – that is, go beyond merely describing the structure and form of criminal justice, but question what it does, how it does it, and why it does it.

72 *Ibid* 356.

73 Hodgson, J, 'The Police, the Prosecutor and the Juge D'Instruction: Judicial Supervision in France, Theory and Practice' (2001) *British Journal of Criminology*, 41, 342–61 at 357.

74 Jackson, J and Doran, S, *Judge Without Jury* (Oxford: Clarendon Press, 1995), 68.

75 Hodgson (n 73), 347.

76 For an in-depth discussion of the rationale behind the abolition of the examining magistrate in Germany and Italy, see Vogler, R, *A World View of Criminal Justice* (Ashgate Publishing, 2005), 166.

This is important and useful as it allows us to assess the implications the process has for those affected by it and what this might mean for the future direction of criminal justice in England and Wales. Ultimately, it is important to know *how* the criminal justice system works as well as *why* it works in the way it does – and whether it is, in fact, just. One of the most useful ways to analyse criminal procedure in any particular jurisdiction is through the lens of a theoretical model. Theoretical models regarding criminal procedure represent a useful tool for both understanding and explaining how and why criminal justice works in a particular manner. They help us to comment on what has happened or is happening, and why this is relevant. We can, for example, look for patterns in the way criminal procedure has developed; or we can predict what sort of changes may be on the horizon by reference to a consistent philosophy underlying previous reform. Throughout this book, we will refer to Packer's two models of criminal justice. In 1964, Stanford Law Professor, Herbert Packer, created arguably the most influential theoretical models in relation to modern criminal procedure: *Due Process* and *Crime Control.* These models are still taught on law degrees across the world and continue to assist scholars in interpreting the function and development of criminal justice. Each model represents an extreme point of view on a spectrum. The *Due Process* model is concerned with the fairness of the proceedings and prioritises the individual rights of the citizen over that of the state. Unsurprisingly, the *Crime Control* model is the polar opposite – the model holds that the repression of criminal activity is the single most important function played by the criminal justice system and that very little should hinder this. The models identify the competing goals that exist within the system, and each model is a possible way of 'doing' criminal justice.[77]

The *Crime Control* model can be summarised as follows:

- The repression of crime is the most important function of the criminal justice system.[78]
- Failure to adhere to this will lead to the breakdown of public order.
- This is because the criminal justice system is a positive guarantor of social freedom and rules need to be quickly enforced.
- There is full trust in those who investigate and prosecute crime and there is a presumption of guilt. The police can be relied on to identify the correct culprit.
- The model needs a high rate of detection and conviction.
- The process needs to be fast – time is a premium that cannot be wasted.
- There is a focus on speed and efficiency; the process should resemble a 'conveyor belt'.
- The conveyor belt moves an endless stream of cases, never stopping; each stage in a case moves toward the end goal – a finding of guilt. Acquittals should be a rare exception.
- The procedures are based on informality and uniformity; therefore there should be limited exposure to challenge and all decisions are seen as final.
- The model emphasises fact-finding during the pre-trial investigation. Therefore this stage is more valuable than the actual trial when time can be wasted.

Since the models directly contrast, the exact opposite is found in the *Due Process* model:[79]

---

77 Welsh, L, Skinns, L and Sanders, A, *Sanders & Young's Criminal Justice* (OUP, 2021).

78 Packer, HL, *The Limits of the Criminal Sanction* (California: Stanford University Press, 1968), 158–63.

79 *Ibid* 163–70.

- If the *Crime Control* model represents a conveyor belt, the *Due Process* model is an obstacle course.
- Every successive stage should represent a formidable impediment to carrying the suspect any further along the criminal justice process. There is no presumption of guilt.
- The model rejects the importance of the pre-trial investigation as humans are fallible and poor observers; the possibility of error is high.
- Confessions to the police could be induced by physical or psychological coercion and are treated with extreme caution.
- Therefore the model insists on a formal, adjudicative, adversarial fact-finding process.
- This process needs to be heard by an impartial tribunal, and the defendant has the opportunity to refute and discredit the allegations made against him or her.
- Because of the possibility of human error, the demand for finality in the model is low.

The utility of Packer's models

Neither model is designed to be taken entirely literally; in reality, a fusion of both approaches is useful for measuring the changing attitudes and agendas driving criminal justice policy. Arguably, England and Wales has developed a piecemeal crime control agenda over the course of the last three decades. In 1986, the Police and Criminal Evidence Act (PACE) 1984 came into force and represented the high-water mark of a due process revolution. The provisions contained within the Act will be explored in further depth later, but the Act significantly strengthened the rights of the suspect in the police station, with the advent of the custody officer, right to a defence lawyer, time limits on detention. Clearly, if we place this Act on our spectrum, it will be placed more toward the *Due Process* end.[80] However, various pieces of legislation have subsequently been created that dilute the due process spirit of the Act and employ a discreet crime control agenda, for example the curtailment of the right to silence provisions in the Criminal Justice and Public Order Act (CJPOA) 1994. The goal here was to stop the guilty hiding behind the shield of silence and evading justice – a clear attempt at repressing crime. This agenda was accelerated by the Criminal Procedure and Investigations Act (CPIA) 1996, which fundamentally altered the adversarial nature of the procedure and attempted to cultivate an environment of cooperation and early disclosure by the defence (see **Chapter 8**). Questionable motives may exist here – for if you know your opponent's hand, it should be easier to win the game and, ultimately, repress criminal activity. Finally, the Criminal Procedure Rules ensured that the stance of early disclosure cooperation, which was compulsory in the Crown Court but voluntary in the magistrates' court, would now be compulsory in the magistrates' court. Without using Packer's models to analyse these changes, it might be difficult for students to understand the gravity and importance of each successive change. The changes could be viewed in isolation, but by using theoretical models, one can scratch beneath the surface and potentially identify agendas and goals that are not immediately visible. Despite critique of Packer's models, we believe that an understanding of them represents the best way of analysing changes in the criminal process.

80 Although it should be noted that PACE 1984 also expanded police powers significantly.

1.7 Conclusion

This chapter has sought to provide a clear picture of the key differences between adversarialism and inquisitorialism. It is important to reiterate that no single jurisdiction will operate a purely adversarial or inquisitorial system. There is significant crossover between the differing approaches in practice. However, each approach provides a useful and contrasting perspective on how individual jurisdictions tackle the investigation and trial of criminal offences, and what is an appropriate way to allocate power and responsibility within the criminal justice process. Equally, Packer's models provide us with idealised but contrasting versions of 'doing' criminal justice, when the reality is arguably a hybrid of crime control and due process. These concepts will provide an analytical foundation for the rest of this book, enabling you to examine different elements of criminal procedure and punishment through the lens of adversarialism and inquisitorialism. This will hopefully prompt you to question both how and why the systems operate as they do, as well as to explore where the future of the criminal justice process may lie. It is important to remember the key components of each approach, summarised as follows:

Adversarialism

- The unsupervised police investigate an allegation of a crime.
- They pass the evidence to a prosecutor.
- Should the prosecutor decide to charge, the defendant will be taken to court.
- The trial represents the forum where his or her guilt or innocence is decided.
- After two sides present opposing cases, a neutral arbiter will decide on guilt or innocence.

Inquisitorialism

- The key actor in this model is the judge who will identify witnesses and guide the police in investigating.
- The guilt or innocence of the defendant is decided at the pre-trial stage.
- The trial represents a check on the process.
- There is less reliance on oral evidence at trial.
- Lawyers and witnesses play little part in the trial.

chapter 2

Policing on the Street (1): Stop and Search

2.1 Introduction

This and the next chapter are concerned with the powers of the police to investigate crime in the community – on the street, as it were. The subject could feasibly cover a range of matters including powers of entry, search and seizure, and possibly the ability of the police to ask citizens to 'stop and account'.[1] These chapters will focus on two of the most visible and, arguably, significant powers available to the police: stop and search (**Chapter 2**) and arrest (**Chapter 3**). Both involve substantial invasions of privacy and (temporary) restrictions on liberty, therefore affecting the fundamental human rights of citizens.[2] These interferences with civil liberties can be justified if they are done with the aim of investigating and controlling crime, therefore protecting wider society from such behaviour. The right to be protected from crime and to have it investigated by the authorities is an equally important right for all citizens.[3] However, these powers must be used legitimately and proportionately. One must always question the balance between the competing interests of individual citizens and wider society. Stop and search and arrest have significant scope for upsetting this balance. Indeed, all of the above points were particularly well exemplified by the extended scope of police powers – most notably arrest – introduced in response to the Covid-19 pandemic, designed primarily to enforce social distancing and more broadly to protect public health – but which posed a clear challenge to civil liberties.[4] These chapters will explore the scope of these two powers and how they operate in theory and practice, and will examine some of the issues relating to their operation as crime-fighting tools.

2.2 Overview of the power to stop and search

Broadly, stop and search is the power of the police (and other agencies – including port and airport authorities) to stop a person or vehicle, and to search for certain items or articles which they suspect are connected with criminal behaviour. There are several types of stop and search, governed by different statutes, but there is generally no power

1 See Police and Criminal Evidence Act (PACE) 1984, Part II regarding entry, search and seizure; 'stop and account' is arguably not a power since individuals who are stopped and asked to explain their presence in an area are not compelled to do anything.

2 ECHR, Articles 8 and 5 respectively.

3 The failure of the police to properly investigate criminal behaviour may breach Article 3 of the ECHR (prohibition on torture and inhuman or degrading treatment or punishment); see *Commissioner of Police of the Metropolis v DSD and another* [2018] UKSC 11 (this involved the failure to fully investigate the claims of victims of the 'Black Cab Rapist', John Worboys).

4 See, particularly, Schedule 21 to the Coronavirus Act 2020 (now expired).

to stop a person simply to question them, either on suspicion of a criminal offence or not.[5] It is important to note that:

- the police should not use the power because they suspect that a criminal offence has been committed by the person they are searching;
- the power only relates to a search for suspicious items/articles; thus stop and search should only be used when the police suspect that the person has a particular item in their possession (eg drugs).

In this sense, stop and search could be described as relating to acts preparatory to the commission of an offence (such as drug dealing or the use of a weapon to assault someone). When the police believe that an offence has taken place, exercising the power of arrest will be more appropriate (see below). Stop and search is not a form of 'arrest lite' allowing the police to avoid the more stringent safeguards attached to arrest, which is a more intrusive and significant power. In exercising the power to stop and search, the police can compel a person or vehicle not to proceed temporarily; as such, there is still an effect (albeit limited) on a person's right to liberty. If we compare stop and search and arrest, we can notice some similarities:

- Both powers involve forms of compulsion of citizens by police officers.
- Both powers may be used as part of a police investigation strategy and, ultimately, for crime reduction.

And we can see some differences:

- Arrest involves suspicion of a criminal offence; stop and search does not require suspicion of an offence but of possession.
- Stop and search is designed primarily to rule out the need for arrest – PACE Code A states that '[t]he primary purpose … is to enable officers to allay or confirm suspicions about individuals without exercising their power of arrest'.[6] It is therefore, by definition, designed to be a distinct and lower level investigatory power.
- The two separate powers have different requirements and safeguards.

2.3 Why is stop and search important?

Stop and search potentially affects the rights of citizens to freedom and privacy – although not necessarily in a substantial manner.[7] It is both controversial and topical, being the subject of significant criticism and reform in recent years. For example, in mid-2018, a spate of fatal stabbings in London led some media commentators to criticise

5 See Home Office, 'Code A – Revised Code of Practice for the exercise by: police officers of statutory powers of stop and search; police officers and police staff of requirements to record public encounters' (TSO, 2023), Notes for Guidance, [1].

6 *Ibid* [1.4]

7 A series of landmark cases relating to s 44 of the Terrorism Act 2000 considered, among other issues, whether Article 5 (the right to liberty) was engaged during a stop and search by the police. In *Gillan and Quinton v Commissioner of Police for the Metropolis* [2006] UKHL 12, the House of Lords concluded that a person was not deprived of their liberty in such circumstances. In contrast, the ECtHR (hearing an appeal by Gillan and Quinton) considered that the coercive nature of stop and search was 'indicative' of deprivation of liberty (*Gillan and Quinton v United Kingdom* (2010) 50 EHRR 45).

the reduction in stop and search over the last decade.[8] Some commentators (such as then Home Secretary Priti Patel) suggested that England and Wales was in the grip of an 'epidemic' of violent crime,[9] with a number (but not all) calling for the power of stop and search to be deployed more widely by the police.[10] Notwithstanding that this moral panic has somewhat receded in the public consciousness, the previous long-term trend relating to stop and search – that of reduction – was, in effect, turned on its head after 2018 (and was particularly acute during the early stages of the Covid-19 pandemic in 2020). This resulted in annual statistical increases in the use of the power until the most recent statistical year (which saw a 25% decrease in s 1 searches).[11] Clearly, the use of this power, and its relationship to tackling crime, remains a contemporary matter of debate.

2.3.1 Prevalence

Stop and search has seen substantial but varied use over the past two decades. In 2008/09, this peaked at approximately 1.5 million stops conducted by the police.[12] In the decade following this, use of the power declined year on year; in 2017/18, the use of stop and search under PACE 1984, s 1 (accounting for 99% of stops) hit a record low of 282,248 – a reduction of more than 80% in a decade.[13] The obvious question is: why did it reduce so dramatically in such a short period of time? There has been no specific academic research on this, although two things should be noted before suggesting an explanation:

- Individual police officers may choose to exercise the discretionary power to stop someone – they are not compelled to do so; therefore, police decision-making may be more important than external factors in explaining any change.
- Whilst the relevant statutes provide criteria for when an officer is allowed to stop someone, there are a variety of non-statutory factors that may influence their decisions in practice.[14]

---

8 Evans, M, 'Knife crime soars by almost a quarter amid warnings drop in stop and search is fuelling violence' (*Telegraph*, 26 April 2018): www.telegraph.co.uk/news/2018/04/26/latest-crime-statistics-reveal-knife-crime-soaring-stop-search (accessed 5 May 2020). It should be noted that this article mistakenly claims that 'reasonable grounds for suspicion' is a new rule, demonstrating the problems in calling for changes in policy based on misunderstanding of the relevant legislation.

9 Home Office, 'Government lifts emergency stop and search restrictions' (11 August 2019): www.gov.uk/government/news/government-lifts-emergency-stop-and-search-restrictions?utm_source=d1d5a8ad-ed6c-47be-ba62-fe6a245536c2&utm_medium=email&utm_campaign=govuk-notifications&utm_content=daily (accessed 5 May 2020).

10 *Ibid*; for contrasting views, see Padfield, N, 'Offensive weapons and knife crime (Editorial)' (2019) *Crim LR* (6); Hymas, C and Scott, P, 'Knife crime soars in rural areas by as much as 50 per cent as violence epidemic spreads out of cities' (*Telegraph*, 8 August 2019): www.telegraph.co.uk/news/2019/07/18/knife-crime-soars-rural-areas-much-50-per-cent-violence-epidemic/ (accessed 5 May 2020); and Ffrench, K, 'Knife crime is a real problem, but stop and search isn't the solution' (*Guardian*, 13 August 2019): www.theguardian.com/law/2019/aug/13/stop-search-extension-knife-crime-police-home-secretary (accessed 5 May 2020).

11 See **2.3.1**.

12 Home Office, 'Stop and search statistics data tables: police powers and procedures year ending 31 March 2019' (October 2019), Table SS.01: www.gov.uk/government/statistics/police-powers-and-procedures-england-and-wales-year-ending-31-march-2019 (accessed 5 May 2020).

13 *Ibid.*

14 We will discuss some of these; for a fuller account, see Welsh, L, Skinns, L and Sanders, A, *Sanders & Young's Criminal Justice* (OUP, 2021).

A simple theory is that fewer people were carrying suspicious items, with a consequential reduction in the need to stop people. This explanation has two problems. First, it assumes that all police stops accurately and legitimately target persons carrying suspicious items, which is highly doubtful.[15] As Her Majesty's Inspectorate of Constabulary and Fire & Rescue Services (HMICFRS) has stated, '[f]inding the item searched for is one of the best measures of effectiveness and indicates that the grounds for the officer's suspicions are likely to have been strong.'[16] Yet, in 2017, the item searched for was found in only 24% of police searches.[17] Secondly, it is difficult to robustly show that large numbers of people (with varying demography) were being stopped carrying suspicious items (such as knives or drugs).[18]

Another explanation is that changes in policy, at various levels, towards the use of stop and search (primarily at government level, cascading downward into police forces) influenced an overall reduction. In the latter 2000s, there emerged significant pressure on the police to 'rein in' the use of stop and search, most notably from the then Home Secretary, Theresa May.[19] Critical reports suggested that it was being deployed unnecessarily and in a discriminatory manner.[20] Reducing the use of stop and search became a focus of the Home Office, leading to the revision of Code A and the introduction of the 'Best Use of Stop and Search' (BUSS) scheme in 2014.[21] The rapid decline in the use of the power correlates with these changes, providing support for the notion that police powers such as stop and search are not simply a result of objective police encounters with suspicious persons; they can shaped by both police force policy and political influences. This theory is given further credence by the upward turn in the use of stop and search since the emergence of the 'violence epidemic' narrative, and the subsequent ascent to power of the Johnson Government in 2019. 2018/19 saw the first overall increases in the use of stop and search in a decade, with PACE 1984, s 1 searches increasing by 32% and CJPOA 1994, s 60 searches increasing (strikingly) by 426%.[22] It is unlikely to be a coincidence that such figures, indicating a significant change in the use of the power, were recorded in the context of a 'pro' stop and search narrative (mentioned above); the repeal, by the Johnson Government, of restrictions on s 60

---

15 Indeed, one might cite the low numbers of stops leading to arrests as potential evidence that a significant number of persons are stopped unnecessarily. See n 16.

16 HMICFRS, 'PEEL: Police Legitimacy, A national overview' (December 2017), 24.

17 *Ibid* 25.

18 We could cite the drops in numbers of arrest and convictions across the board as evidence of fewer people possessing suspicious items. This does, however, stretch the validity of statistical analysis to extremes.

19 Home Office, 'Stop and search: Theresa May announces reform of police stop and search' (30 April 2014): www.gov.uk/government/news/stop-and-search-theresa-may-announces-reform-of-police-stop-and-search (accessed 5 May 2020).

20 Equality and Human Rights Commission (EHRC), 'Stop and Think: A critical review of the use of stop and search powers in England and Wales' (2010): www.equalityhumanrights.com/sites/default/files/ehrc_stop_and_search_report.pdf (accessed 5 May 2020); EHRC, 'Race disproportionality in stops and searches under Section 60 of the Criminal Justice and Public Order Act 1994' (2012): www.equalityhumanrights.com/sites/default/files/briefing-paper-5-race-disproportionality-in-stops-and-searches-under-s60-of-criminal-justice-and-public-order-act-1994.pdf (accessed 5 May 2020), EHRC, 'Stop and think again: towards race equality in police PACE stop and search' (2013): www.equalityhumanrights.com/sites/default/files/stop_and_think_again.pdf (accessed 5 May 2020); Bowling, B and Phillips, C, 'Disproportionate and Discriminatory: Reviewing the Evidence on Police Stop and Search' (2007) 70 MLR (6).

21 See Home Office, n 19.

22 Home Office, n 12. See **2.4**.

searches, accompanied by open encouragement to use the power more;[23] and new police operations targeting knife crime with stops.[24] As such, accounts of both the 'anti' and 'pro' stop and search narratives of recent years suggest a simple change in policy can be highly influential on prevalence.

Other factors can, of course, be influential. For example, during the most acute stages of the Covid-19 pandemic (in 2020 and 2021), stops under s 1 peaked at their highest levels since 2013.[25] Since the easing and removal of Covid-19 restrictions, the number of searches has reduced (with the most current statistics at the time of writing showing approximately 516,000 s 1 searches in 2021/22) – but remain well above pre-2018 levels.[26] The pandemic undoubtedly accelerated a pre-existing trend of expanded use, and whilst this has reversed (at the time of writing), it remains to be seen whether the general resurgence in the use of stop and search powers will abate or continue.

2.3.2 Impact

Whilst less intrusive than arrest, stop and search can have a significant impact on searched citizens. The actual physical intrusion may be minor (normally limited to a search of an individual's pockets),[27] but there is no specific time limit on the length of a stop, other than it being 'reasonable' and 'kept to a minimum'.[28] Potentially, someone could be detained for a significant period of time. The power can only be exercised in a public place; as such, the potential for a stopped individual to feel shamed, disrespected or embarrassed by the procedure is significant (potentially a form of punishment in itself). It might be argued that such intrusions are minor in the name of public protection; indeed, interference with human rights such as liberty and privacy is explicitly allowed on these grounds.[29] But what is minor for one person may not be for another – particularly if an individual is stopped repeatedly or there is an unspoken subtext to the search. A primary example of this is racial discrimination. The Lammy Review found that black, Asian and minority ethnic communities were three times more likely to be stopped than white people, whilst black people were six times more likely to be stopped than white people.[30] This continues a (sadly) long-running trend of statistical evidence suggesting that minority citizens are subjected to stops much more than the white majority population of England and Wales.

---

23 Home Office, n 9.

24 For example, Operation Sceptre in March 2020 (Metropolitan Police, 'Met contributes to national push to suppress violence' (23 March 2020): http://news.met.police.uk/news/met-contributes-to-national-push-to-suppress-violence-397819?utm_source=rss&utm_medium=rss&utm_campaign= Subscription &utm_content=current_news (accessed 5 May 2020).

25 Home Office, 'Stop and search summary data tables: police powers and procedures, year ending 31 March 2022' (November 2022), Table SS.02: www.gov.uk/government/statistics/police-powers-and-procedures-stop-and-search-and-arrests-england-and-wales-year-ending-31-march-2022 (accessed 23 March 2023).

26 *Ibid.*

27 Code A, [3.5].

28 *Ibid* [3.3].

29 See ECHR, Articles 5(1)(c) and 8(2).

30 Lammy, D, 'The Lammy Review: An independent review into the treatment of, and outcomes for, Black, Asian and Minority Ethnic individuals in the Criminal Justice System' (September 2017), 18: https://assets.publishing.service.gov.uk/government/uploads/system/uploads/attachment_data/file/643001/lammy-review-final-report.pdf (accessed 5 May 2020).

2.3.3 Stop and search as a crime-fighting tool

A common justification for the use of stop and search by the police is its importance in fighting crime – but this might be questioned:

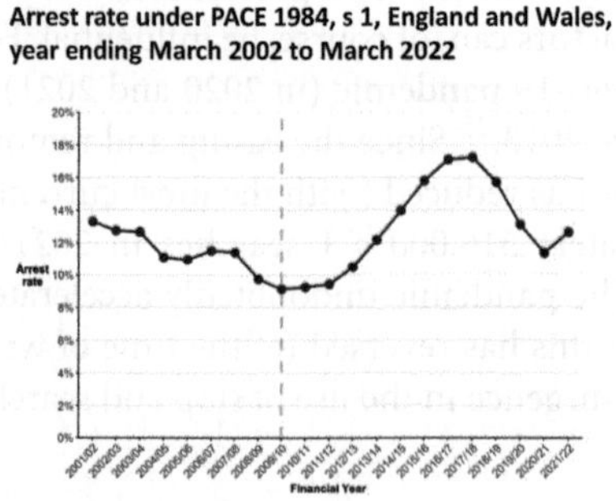

The graph above[31] shows a clear trend until 2018: the 'hit rate' (the proportion of stops which lead to an arrest of an individual) increased – at the same time, the number stops taking place dropped dramatically. This indicates that more stops do not necessarily mean a better rate of detection and prosecution of crime. Indeed, as the number of stops began to rise again after 2018, the arrest rate dropped (to a current rate of 13%).[32] This raises the question: does more stop and search mean less crime? In 2017/18, the number of stops hit a record low, whilst the hit rate reached its highest point in nearly two decades (17%). This suggests that the police were taking a more targeted approach to the use of stop and search, and that, if used sparingly, stop and search may therefore be a more effective crime-fighting tool. This theory is bolstered by the fact that, in 2018/19, two decade-long trends ended: the number of stops increased for the first time and the hit rate declined for the first time (to 15%), again implying that more stops mean fewer conversions to arrest. However, even a 'hit rate' of 17% means that 83% of stops do not lead to an arrest. Broken down, the latest figures seem less impressive:

- In 2021/22, a 13% hit rate equated to approximately 65,000 stops leading to arrest.[33]
- In 2021/22, roughly 663,000 persons were arrested.[34]
- Therefore, we can estimate that only 10% of all arrests were preceded by a stop.

Furthermore, not all those who are arrested will subsequently be prosecuted. Whilst recent data is not available, the 1992 British Crime Survey found that only 3% of pedestrian stops led to prosecution.[35] This suggests that stop and search plays a small role in directly tackling crime.

This does, however, assume that combatting crime only involves the traditional route of arrest, prosecution and conviction. This is misleading. First, other actions or results following a stop can be equally effective (and possibly more proportionate), such as penalty notices for disorder (PNDs); cannabis warnings; or simple confiscation

31 Home Office, 'Police powers and procedures: Stop and search and arrests, England and Wales, year ending 31 March 2022' (November 2022), Figure 2.6: www.gov.uk/government/statistics/police-powers-and-procedures-stop-and-search-and-arrests-england-and-wales-year-ending-31-march-2022 (accessed 23 March 2023).

32 *Ibid.*

33 Home Office (n 25).

34 Home Office (n 31).

35 Skogan, W, 'Contacts Between Police and Public – Findings from the 1992 British Crime Survey' (Home Office, 1994). For a more detailed discussion, see Welsh et al (n 14).

(eg of knives or drugs).[36] Secondly, if the primary purpose of stop and search is to 'enable officers to allay or confirm suspicions about individuals without exercising their power of arrest', it helps officers to avoid unnecessary arrests.[37] HMICFRS found that a person was eliminated from suspicion, and an unnecessary arrest therefore avoided, in 12% of cases it reviewed – arguably an effective use of the power.[38] Thus, hit rate should not be the only measure. Thirdly, another objective of stop and search is deterrence; if criminals are aware that the police are conducting large-scale stops, they may be deterred from carrying prohibited items. As a hypothesis, this is appealing and has often driven the introduction of stop and search 'operations' targeted at reducing criminal behaviour (eg Operation Blunt 2).[39] There may be some truth in the claim that stop and search acts as a deterrent, but this is difficult to measure since, by its nature, deterrence involves people not doing something (in this case, carrying suspicious items due to fear of being stopped). There is generally a lack of robust evidence to support the deterrence argument;[40] moreover, criminals may simply be displaced, resort to underground activity, or be more cautious in areas where police are operating.[41] In 2017, the College of Policing examined the use of stop and search by the Metropolitan Police Service (MPS) between 2004 and 2014.[42] It found that higher overall rates of stop and search were followed by slightly lower than expected rates of crime, but only for some crime types, and concluded that there was generally a very weak link between more stop and search and less crime:

> The inconsistent nature and low strength of these associations … provide only limited evidence of stop and search having had a meaningful deterrent effect.[43]

2.4 The law governing stop and search

Stop and search is governed by various statutes, but the primary ones are:

- the Police and Criminal Evidence Act (PACE) 1984;

---

36 See **Chapter 13** for more on PNDs. Note, however, that significant reform of out of court disposals (including PNDs) is imminent, under Part 6 of the Police, Crime, Sentencing and Courts Act 2022 (not yet in force). The above-mentioned disposals are slated for abolition.

37 Code A, [1.4].

38 HMICFRS (n 16), 24.

39 Operation Blunt 2, May 2008; see McCandless, R, Feist, A, Allan, J and Morgan, N, 'Do initiatives involving substantial increases in stop and search reduce crime? Assessing the impact of Operation BLUNT 2' (Home Office, March 2016): https://assets.publishing.service.gov.uk/government/uploads/system/uploads/attachment_data/file/508661/stop-search-operation-blunt-2.pdf (accessed 5 May 2020).

40 See, for example, Braakmann, N, 'Does stop and search reduce crime? Evidence from street-level data and a surge in operations following a high-profile crime' (2022) *Journal of the Royal Statistical Society* 185 (3).

41 For more on deterrence and displacement, see Miller, J, Bland, N and Quinton, P, 'The Impact of Stops and Searches on Crime and the Community' (Home Office, 2000): www.researchgate.net/publication/265004960_The_Impact_of_Stops_and_Searches_on_Crime_and_the_Community (accessed 5 May 2020); Goldsmith, C, 'Cameras, Cops and Contracts: What Anti-Social Behaviour Management Feels Like to Young People' in P Squires (ed), *ASBO Nation: The Criminalisation of Nuisance* (Policy Press, 2008); Lord Scarman, 'The Brixton Disorders, 10–12 April 1981' (The Scarman Report) (Home Office, November 1981); Hallsworth, S, *Street Crime* (Willan, 2005).

42 Quinton, P, Tiratelli, M and Bradford, B, 'Does stop and search mean less crime? Analysis of Metropolitan Police Service panel data, 2004–14' (College of Policing, 2017): www.college.police.uk/News/College-news/Documents/Stop%20and%20search%20-%20Less%20crime%20-%20Report.pdf (accessed 5 May 2020).

43 *Ibid* 4.

- the Criminal Justice and Public Order Act (CJPOA) 1994;
- the Terrorism Act (TA) 2000 (as amended by the Protection of Freedoms Act 2012).

This chapter will primarily focus on PACE 1984.[44] In addition to legislation, the power is regulated by sub-statutory Codes of Practice (specifically, Code A) and case law.[45] Whilst an important source of regulation and guidance, the Codes of Practice are supplementary to the statute; the power is governed by the statute and its use regulated by the Codes.

2.4.1 Section 1(2) of PACE 1984

The primary power to stop and search, s 1(2) of PACE 1984 allows a police constable to search any person or vehicle for the following:

- stolen or prohibited articles;
- any article in relation to offences under ss 139 and 139AA of the Criminal Justice Act 1988 (that is, having a bladed or pointed article or threatening someone with those items);
- certain prohibited fireworks.

Alongside stolen property, blades and fireworks, officers can search for 'prohibited articles'; but what does this mean? This could potentially cover a broad range of items, and the definition in s 1(7) and (8) suggests that this is by design. The definition includes, unsurprisingly, offensive weapons; but it also covers 'any article made or adapted, or intended for use in the course of or connection with' a variety of offences, including burglary, theft, taking a motor vehicle without consent, fraud and criminal damage. This potentially means that any item (regardless of its normal function) could be considered a prohibited article should it be deemed to be connected to the commission of one of these offences. It might be noted that controlled drugs are not included under s 1 – these are specifically dealt with by s 23(2) of the Misuse of Drugs Act 1971.

An officer can detain any person for the purpose of such a search (hence the semi-formal name 'stop and search') but can only do so in a public place (for example, not in a private dwelling).[46] As mentioned above, the length of time for which a person or vehicle may be detained must be reasonable and kept to a minimum.[47] Without this limitation, the police could theoretically detain someone for a period which might be more akin to arrest, whilst avoiding the various safeguards related to that more serious power.[48]

To conduct a search under s 1(2), a constable must have reasonable grounds for suspecting that they will find one of the items/articles listed above. This requirement is more commonly known as 'reasonable suspicion' (found under s 1(3)). In essence, it means that the police cannot simply exercise the power of stop and search without reason or justification. This places a limitation on police discretion and acts as a

44 Other statutory forms of the power worth noting (but not covered here) are the Misuse of Drugs Act 1971 and the Firearms Act 1968. For a full list, see PACE Code A, Annex A.

45 Code A, as with the other Codes, is issued by the Secretary of State under the authority of PACE 1984, s 66. Code A also regulates the power under s 60 of the CJPOA 1993. The TA 2000 has its own Code of Practice for the exercise of stop and search powers.

46 PACE 1984, s 1(1)(b).

47 Code A, [3.3].

48 Which is not to say that stop and search does not have a variety of safeguards built in.

safeguard against abuse of the power. For example, the police (in theory) cannot simply stop someone because they 'do not like the look of them' (although evidence suggests that this does happen in practice).[49] Reasonable suspicion is foremost amongst a number of safeguards created by PACE 1984. Stop and search as a power existed prior to PACE,[50] but in the wake of the Royal Commission on Criminal Justice (the Philips Commission) in 1981, it was significantly reformed.[51] PACE 1984 created a uniformly regulated power for England and Wales, removing disparate local police powers, with the aim of promoting consistent and fair use of the power. Reasonable suspicion was a key part of this, requiring that police officers provide reasoning for decisions to stop individuals. This will be discussed in more detail below.

2.4.2 Section 60 of the CJPOA 1994 and s 47A of the TA 2000

In contrast to PACE 1984, s 1, individual police officers do not need to have reasonable suspicion in order to exercise their powers under either the CJPOA 1994, s 60 or the TA 2000, s 47A. This is significant as it effectively means that individual officers can exercise their discretion without needing objectively justifiable reasons for doing so. These are therefore substantial powers. Section 60 of the CJPOA 1994 allows police officers to stop individuals without reasonable suspicion, but only in certain circumstances – specifically, when it is authorised by a higher ranking police officer (see further below). Originally, authorisation could only occur if said officer reasonably believed that:

- incidents involving serious violence may take place in any locality in their police area;
- an incident involving serious violence has occurred; a dangerous instrument or offensive weapon used in the incident is being carried by a person in that area; or
- persons are carrying dangerous instruments or offensive weapons in any locality in their police area without good reason.

For all of the above, the officer had to consider it 'expedient' to authorise stop and search without reasonable suspicion.[52] In 2014, the BUSS scheme sought to restrict the use of this power in several respects: stipulating that only a more senior officer (above the rank of Chief Superintendent) could authorise this type of search; that there had to be a reasonable belief that incidents involving serious violence *will* (not *may*) take place in the local area; and that the power was to be used only when it was deemed necessary.[53] All of the above placed a greater burden on authorising officers (of a much higher rank) to demonstrate that s 60 should be invoked – allowing stop and searches for offensive weapons and dangerous instruments by individual officers on the street, without needing to establish reasonable suspicion. Unsurprisingly, this led to a swift decline in the use of the power, from nearly 4,000 stops in 2013/14 to just over 600 in

49 For example, looking 'shifty' ('Viewed with Suspicion: The Human Cost of Stop and Search in England and Wales' (Open Society Justice Initiative and StopWatch, 2013)): www.opensocietyfoundations.org/sites/default/files/viewed-with-suspicion-human-cost-stop-and-search-in-england-and-wales-20130419.pdf (accessed 5 May 2020).

50 Vagrancy Act 1824, s 4.

51 Philips, C, 'Royal Commission on Criminal Procedure' (The Philips Commission) (HMSO, 1981).

52 CJPOA 1994, s 60(3).

53 HM Inspectorate of Constabulary (HMIC), 'Best Use of Stop and Search Scheme' (September 2016), 8–9: www.justiceinspectorates.gov.uk/hmicfrs/wp-content/uploads/best-use-of-stop-and-search-scheme.pdf (accessed 5 May 2020).

2016/17 (less than 1% of all stops that year).[54] However, in the wake of the concerns about knife crime discussed above, the BUSS restrictions were temporarily relaxed (in March 2019) for seven police forces and then for all police forces in August 2019.[55] Specifically, the restrictions outlined above were returned to their original form.[56] Again, the extent of use of s 60 swiftly changed, with a 400% increase in stops in 2017/18 and (following the expansion of the 'relaxed' criteria to cover all police forces in August 2019) a further 426% increase in 2018/19.[57] In short, s 60 stops increased by more than 12,500 in only two years.[58] However, this trend changed significantly during the Covid-19 pandemic, with a 49% decrease in use in 2020/21 and 52% in 2021/22.[59] Arguably, the context of the pandemic – which involved significant restrictions on personal liberty and rapidly changing policing priorities – is a potential explanation for this dramatic decrease.

Section 47A of the TA 2000 also allows police officers to stop individuals without reasonable suspicion in certain circumstances. A senior officer can authorise this if they:

- reasonably suspect that an act of terrorism will take place; and
- consider that stop and search powers are necessary to prevent this.

But this is only allowed within an area that is no larger than necessary and for a period that is no longer than necessary (maximum 14 days). Such an authorisation allows individual officers to stop any person or vehicle to search for evidence that the person is a terrorist or that the vehicle is being used for the purposes of terrorism. This is regardless of whether or not the officer reasonably suspects that such evidence will be present. This power has, in fact, been used rarely since 2010/11 (prior to significant amendments introduced by the Protection of Freedoms Act 2012).[60] Between that year and 2017/18, the power was not used at all; it was used 149 times in the wake of the Parsons Green train bombing in September 2017;[61] and it has not been used since. This suggests that the power is, essentially, dormant, and now reserved for use during emergency situations, rather than as a general policing tool.

The lack of a reasonable suspicion requirement for both s 47A and s 60 potentially creates scope for abuse of the power by police officers – for example, stopping an individual on the basis that they 'look like a terrorist'. Whilst this is of limited concern in regard to s 47A because of its rare use, the risk of police malfeasance in using suspicionless searches is increasing with the wider use of s 60. Both powers were used significantly in the past: s 44 (the forerunner to s 47A) was used to stop individuals on

54 Home Office (n 12), Table SS.01.

55 The initial seven forces – including the Metropolitan Police (the largest force in England and Wales) – 'collectively account for 60% of all knife crime in England and Wales' (Home Office, 'Greater powers for police to use stop and search to tackle violent crime' (31 March 2019): www.gov.uk/government/news/greater-powers-for-police-to-use-stop-and-search-to-tackle-violent-crime (accessed 5 May 2020). The relaxation was made permanent in July 2021 as part of the Government's 'Beating Crime Plan' (Home Office, July 2021): www.gov.uk/government/publications/beating-crime-plan (accessed 23 March 2023).

56 *Ibid.*

57 Home Office, (n 12), Table SS.01.

58 *Ibid.*

59 Home Office (n 25), Table SS.09.

60 In the wake of the decision in *Gillan and Quinton v United Kingdom* (n 7).

61 Home Office, 'Police powers and procedures, England and Wales, year ending 31 March 2018' (25 October 2018), 26: 'https://assets.publishing.service.gov.uk/government/uploads/system/uploads/attachment_data/file/751215/police-powers-procedures-mar18-hosb2418.pdf (accessed 5 May 2020).

210,013 occasions in 2008/09, whilst s 60 was used 150,174 times in the same year.[62] Whilst current figures are dwarfed by these, one can see how dramatically the use of these powers has changed in the past decade: first reducing and then (in the case of s 60) increasing again. We will now return to PACE 1984, s 1 to consider reasonable suspicion in more depth.

2.5 Reasonable suspicion

Reasonable suspicion is another term that is open to interpretation. The requirement under s 1(3) broadly means that an officer must suspect they will find one of the prohibited items (above) if they search someone. They must have grounds (ie reasons or justifications) for this suspicion; and those grounds must be reasonable.

The statute does not expand on this vague definition, but further information is provided by Code A and, to a lesser extent, case law.[63] Paragraph 2.2 of Code A provides a two-part test for 'reasonable suspicion', which officers must satisfy in order to discharge the power lawfully:

> (i) Firstly, the officer must have formed a genuine suspicion in their own mind that they will find the object for which the search power being exercised allows them to search; and
>
> (ii) Secondly, the suspicion that the object will be found must be reasonable. This means that there must be an objective basis for that suspicion based on facts, information and/or intelligence …

The paragraph concludes that '[o]fficers must therefore be able to explain the basis for their suspicion by reference to intelligence or information …'. It should be reiterated that reasonable suspicion relates to an individual's possession of an item, and not to whether they have committed a criminal offence.

Paragraph 2.2B of Code A states that 'personal factors' can never justify a stop (such as dislike for a particular person or group of people). Factors that cannot form reasonable grounds for suspicion include:

- physical appearance (including the 'protected characteristics' under the Equality Act 2010, s 149 – age, race, gender, etc);
- an officer's knowledge of previous convictions;[64] and
- generalisations or stereotypical images that certain groups are 'criminals'.

An exception to this rule is where there is specific intelligence or information describing a suspected individual (for example, a witness description).[65]

---

62 Home Office (n 12), Tables SS.12 and SS.08 respectively.

63 Code A, which was last revised in 2015, is the primary source of guidance for police officers on how to use their stop and search powers.

64 Though see the new stop and search power under s 342E of the Sentencing Act 2020 (as amended), which allows searches based on knowledge of a previous conviction for knife crime.

65 Code A [2.2B].

This is an important restriction which is designed to limit (as far as is possible) the ability for personal prejudice to inform an officer's decision to stop someone. This might derive from an individual officer's personal views (such as racism or homophobia) or from personal experience of policing.[66] For example, if an officer encounters a person with a long list of previous convictions for drug offences, that person might be regarded as being 'likely' to have drugs on their person (even if there is no specific evidence to suggest they do at that particular time).[67] The restriction on generalisations and stereotypical images as grounds for a stop attempts to go beyond individual prejudice or bigotry to tackle conceptualisations of certain groups as being inherently 'criminal'. Typically, ethnic minority groups, the poor, the young, and the mentally ill are most vulnerable to such stereotyping.[68] By attempting to strongly bind stop and search to solid, objective evidence, the intent of Code A is to lessen the influence of irrelevant and unfair factors.

Paragraph 2.4 emphasises this by stating that reasonable suspicion should 'normally be linked to accurate and current intelligence or information', and that such intelligence should relate to 'articles for which there is a power to stop and search, being carried by individuals or being in vehicles in any locality'. Intelligence or information includes reports from members of the public or other officers, and it will normally describe a person who has been seen carrying such an article or a vehicle in which such an article has been seen. It can also relate to descriptions of 'crimes committed in relation to which such an article would constitute relevant evidence, for example, property stolen in a theft or burglary, an offensive weapon … used to assault someone …'. Therefore, the emphasis is on some form of information which has credibility and relevance. Paragraph 2.4A suggests that 'searches based on accurate and current intelligence or information are more likely to be effective', although what is meant by 'effective' is open to interpretation (presumably, a stop that results in finding the item that is specifically being searched for).[69]

Officers may attempt to undertake 'fishing' stops – that is, speculative searches not based on specific evidence – in the hope of finding something prohibited.[70] These often target stereotyped persons or the 'usual suspects' who have a history of criminality in

---

66 Particularly relevant in light of the Casey Review – Casey, L, 'An independent review into the standards of behaviour and internal culture of the Metropolitan Police Service' (March 2023): www.met.police.uk/SysSiteAssets/media/downloads/met/about-us/baroness-casey-review/update-march-2023/baroness-casey-review-march-2023.pdf (accessed 23 March 2023).

67 *Ibid.* Code A is clear on both the need for intelligence or information and on the prohibition on previous convictions forming the grounds for a stop.

68 For more on this, see Bowling and Phillips (n 20); EHRC, 'Stop and Think' (n 20); Hall, S, Lewis, G and McLaughlin, E, 'The Report on Racial Stereotyping' (Milton Keynes: Open University, 1998); Fitzgerald, M and Sibbett, R, 'Ethnic monitoring in police forces: A beginning' (Home Office, 1997); Quinton, P, 'The formation of suspicions: police stop and search practices in England and Wales' (2011) 21(4) *Policing and Society* 357.

69 See the HMICFRS (n 16) report for more on the meaning of 'effective' stops.

70 Cownie, F, Bradney, A and Burton, M, *English Legal System in Context* (OUP, 2013), 243; 'Can an increase in stop-and-search cut knife crime?' (*The Economist*, 18 January 2018): www.economist.com/britain/2018/01/18/can-an-increase-in-stop-and-search-cut-knife-crime (accessed 5 May 2020).

the hope of finding something prohibited.[71] Some commentators have argued that this is inevitable because 'police rarely have all the facts available to them' and they 'inevitably have to begin with surmise'.[72] Equally, it can be argued that it might be justifiable if the 'hit rate' for stops of certain groups were high enough.[73] These arguments are open to question. First, the claim that the police have a paucity of information available to them is open to debate (especially in an age of extensive surveillance); but, even if it is, one has to wonder how effective the strategy of blindly stopping people (based on subjective assumptions) will be. Secondly, the argument regarding the 'hit rate' is problematic – not only because it is fairly low (13%) but because an arrest will not inevitably lead to charge, prosecution or conviction. Clearly, though, Code A – as it is currently drafted – stresses the need for intelligence or information as a 'starting point' and attempts to prevent randomised, stereotype-driven stop and search from happening. Code A also addresses reasonable suspicion in relation to groups of people:

> Where there is reliable information or intelligence that members of a group or gang habitually carry knives unlawfully or weapons or controlled drugs, and wear a distinctive item of clothing or other means of identification in order to identify themselves as members of that group or gang, that distinctive item of clothing or other means of identification may provide reasonable grounds to stop and search any person believed to be a member of that group or gang.[74]

This is a relevant consideration because it allows targeting of gangs (who may be carrying weapons or dealing drugs) and therefore allows, in such circumstances, reasonable suspicion to be based on appearance. This creates a potential conflict with para 2.2B since, normally, basing reasonable suspicion on physical appearance or stereotyping would be prohibited – this is, in effect, a loophole.

One might question whether this seemingly narrow exception leaves stop and search open to abuse and indirect discrimination, primarily affecting young, black males. The Office for National Statistics has asserted that 'by its nature gang membership is a challenging area to collect statistics on'.[75] Research by Disley and Liddle suggested that membership of gangs is defined less by ethnicity and more by factors like 'involvement in drugs markets, violence and geography' and that gangs were diversifying.[76] Yet, stereotypes about involvement in gangs appear to persist. In *Roberts*, the Supreme Court found s 60 of the CJPOA 1994 compatible with the ECHR, stating:

---

71 See Norris, C, Fielding, N, Kemp, C and Fielding, J, 'Black and Blue: An Analysis of the Influence of Race on Being Stopped by the Police' (1992) 43 *Brit J of Crim* (2); Fitzgerald, M, 'Report into Stop and Search' (Metropolitan Police Service, 1999); Medina Ariza, J, 'Police-initiated contacts: young people, ethnicity, and the "usual suspects"' (2014) 24 *Policing and Society* (2); Choongh, C, 'Policing the Dross: A Social Disciplinary Model of Policing' (1998) 38 *Brit J of Crim* (4); and McAra, L and McVie, S, 'The usual suspects? Street-life, young people and the police' (2005) 5 *Criminology & Criminal Justice* (1).

72 McAra (n 71), 8, paraphrasing Smith, D, 'Reform or Moral Outrage — the Choice is Yours' (1998) 38(4) *Brit J of Crim* 616.

73 *Ibid* 8–9.

74 [2.6].

75 The Office for National Statistics (ONS), 'Freedom of Information (FOI): Statistics on gang crime in London and Essex' (24 January 2018): www.ons.gov.uk/aboutus/transparencyandgovernance/freedomofinformationfoi/statisticsongangcrimeinlondonandessex (accessed 5 May 2020).

76 Disley, E and Liddle, M, 'Local perspectives in Ending Gang and Youth Violence areas: perceptions of the nature of urban street gangs' (Home Office, 2016), 17: https://assets.publishing.service.gov.uk/government/uploads/system/uploads/attachment_data/file/491802/horr88.pdf (accessed 5 May 2020); see also Grund, T and Densley, J, 'Ethnic Heterogeneity in the Activity and Structure of a Black Street Gang' (2012) 9 *European Journal of Criminology* (3).

> It must be borne in mind that many of these gangs are largely composed of young people from black and minority ethnic groups. While there is a concern that members of these groups should not be disproportionately targeted, it is members of these groups who will benefit most from the reduction in violence, serious injury and death that may result from the use of such powers. Put bluntly, it is mostly young black lives that will be saved if there is less gang violence in London and some other cities.[77]

This was heavily criticised by campaign group StopWatch as 'appealing to stereotypes of black youth being the predominant members of street gangs hence are the justifiable targets of the stop and search power'.[78] More recently, research was conducted by Amnesty International into the 'Gangs Matrix' (a gang-mapping database used by the MPS, listing nearly 4,000 persons).[79] It found that 78% of those listed were black, despite MPS figures suggesting that only 27% of serious youth violence is committed by black persons.[80] Amnesty also highlighted that the Mayor's Office for Policing and Crime itself had found that

> more than 80% of all knife-crime incidents resulting in injury to a victim aged under 25 in London were deemed not to be gang related.[81]

It concluded that the Matrix was therefore 'part of an unhelpful and racialised focus on the concept of gangs' which led to disproportionate targeting of young black males.[82] As such, despite mixed evidence about gang membership, the aforementioned demographic (young black men) seems more likely to be targeted for stops, creating scope for this exception in Code A to be used in a discriminatory manner. As a result of such criticism, in November 2022 it was announced that the Gangs Matrix would be significantly overhauled.[83]

2.5.1 Case law and research on stop and search

Code A is the primary source of guidance on reasonable suspicion, but there is some case law which helps us to understand its meaning. In *Hussien v Chong Fook Kam*, Lord Devlin described reasonable suspicion as being of

> a lower standard than that which would be required to establish a *prima facie* case. It allows police officers to take into account matters that would not be admissible as evidence.[84]

77 *R (Roberts) v Commissioner of Police of the Metropolis and another* [2015] UKSC 79, [41] per Lady Hale and Lord Reed.

78 Marks, E, 'Unjustified assumptions: The Supreme Court and Section 60' (StopWatch, February 2016): www.stop-watch.org/news-comment/story/unjustified-assumptions-the-supreme-court-and-section-60 (accessed 5 May 2020).

79 Amnesty International, 'Trapped in the Matrix: Secrecy, stigma, and bias in the Met's Gangs Database' (May 2018), 2.

80 *Ibid* 2–3.

81 *Ibid* 31.

82 Amnesty International, 'Press Release: Met Police using "racially discriminatory" Gangs Matrix database' (9 May 2018): www.amnesty.org.uk/press-releases/met-police-using-racially-discriminatory-gangs-matrix-database (accessed 5 May 2020).

83 BBC News, 'Gang Violence Matrix: Met police to overhaul controversial database' (12 November 2022): www.bbc.co.uk/news/uk-england-london-63568880 (accessed 23 March 2023).

84 [1970] AC 942. It should be noted that this case pre-dates PACE 1984, but the principle has continued to be valid for post-PACE stops.

This therefore suggests that any number of factors could satisfy reasonable suspicion; certainly, it implies that the police do not need to have robust or reliable evidence to justify stopping an individual. Indeed, in *Howarth v Commissioner of Police for the Metropolis*, the court stated that '[i]t is well recognised that the threshold for the existence of reasonable grounds for suspicion is low'.[85] These cases are not particularly useful in understanding reasonable suspicion, beyond confirming that the police do not need to have particularly strong grounds to justify stop and search. For example, the cases do not elaborate on the distinction between 'reasonable suspicion' and suspicion falling below this threshold (sometimes referred to as 'mere' suspicion).[86] Reasonable suspicion allows officers significant discretion in satisfying themselves that grounds for a search exist, and it can therefore allow an inconsistent approach to stop and search to develop.[87] This suggests that reasonable suspicion is so flexibly interpreted that it is not a particularly effective safeguard against abuse of the power.

Research seems to support this. In 2000, Miller et al found that reasonable suspicion did not prevent arbitrary stop and search by officers (for example, on the basis of appearance, 'suspicious' behaviour, time and place of the stop).[88] This suggests that reasonable suspicion was not fulfilling its primary function – which is to prevent police discretion being used in an arbitrary manner. This was 18 years ago, but it appears that little has changed. In 2013, HMICFRS (then HMIC) examined records of stops; it found that 27% lacked sufficient grounds to justify the use of the power, thus casting doubt on whether any legal rationale for these searches existed.[89] It concluded that this deficit was partly due to poor understanding of what reasonable suspicion means, implying that the safeguard was either not clear enough in terms of definition and guidance, or that police officers were not adequately trained and supervised in this regard.[90] Despite making a variety of recommendations designed to improve these problems, a follow-up review in 2015 found that slow or insufficient progress had been made in improving officers' training and supervision.[91] Whilst HMICFRS found improvements in recording of reasonable suspicion by 2017, it noted that this progress was inconsistent.[92] More recently again, it inspected several forces with regard to recommendations to improve police use of stop and search powers, noting that '[d]isappointingly, only nine of these forces had sufficiently trained their officers to recognise and overcome unconscious bias to help them treat people fairly'.[93] In 2021, HMICFRS also found that nearly 20% of searches still lacked reasonable suspicion; that

85 [2011] EWHC 2818 (QB). In this case, the suspects were stopped on the basis that they possessed items which would be used to cause criminal damage at a protest – specifically, chalk and molasses.

86 For a discussion of the difference between reasonable suspicion and mere hunches in the USA, see Lerner, C, 'Reasonable suspicion and mere hunches' (2005) 59 *Vanderbilt* LR (2).

87 For an example of this, see the cases of *Francis* and *Slade*, detailed in Welsh et al (n 14).

88 Miller (n 41).

89 HMICFRS, 'Stop and Search Powers: Are the police using them effectively and fairly?' (2013), 30: www.justiceinspectorates.gov.uk/hmicfrs/media/stop-and-search-powers-20130709.pdf (accessed 5 May 2020). There is the possibility that such cases simply represented examples of poor record-keeping, but it should be pointed out that there is a link between a lack of grounds and poor recording practices.

90 *Ibid* 8.

91 HMICFRS, 'Stop and search powers 2: are the police using them effectively and fairly?' (2015): www.justiceinspectorates.gov.uk/hmicfrs/wp-content/uploads/stop-and-search-powers-2.pdf (accessed 5 May 2020).

92 HMICFRS (n 16), 22.

93 HMICFRS, 'PEEL spotlight report: Diverging under pressure' (February 2020), 17: www.justiceinspectorates.gov.uk/hmicfrs/wp-content/uploads/peel-spotlight-report-diverging-under-pressure-2018-19-overview.pdf (accessed 5 May 2020).

the majority (55%) of searches were self-generated by officers (rather than based on external sources); and that only 6% were based on specific intelligence.[94] It is not unreasonable to conclude that the persistent failure to establish reasonable suspicion is likely linked to the apparent under-reliance on robust, objective sources of intelligence and information when deciding to stop.

2.6 Racial discrimination

A long-running problem cited earlier is that of racially disproportionate use of stop and search, which is arguably related to the weakness of reasonable suspicion as a safeguard. Ethnic minority citizens have consistently been more likely to be stopped than their white counterparts for decades, particularly affecting black people. The most recent statistics suggest some improvement but present a picture that remains highly problematic. In 2021/22,[95] there were:

- 6 stops per 1,000 white people (the majority population in England and Wales)
- 28 stops per 1,000 black people (9.5 times more likely than white people)
- 9 stops per 1,000 Asian people (nearly three times more likely than white people)
- 10 stops per 1,000 for people of mixed ethnicity.

Overall, minority citizens were twice as likely to be stopped than white citizens.[96] As HMICFRS has highlighted, '[t]his disproportionate effect is long-standing and may be deteriorating as the use of stop and search powers increases'.[97] Whilst the Casey Review concluded that '[e]nough evidence and analysis exists to confidently label stop and search as a racialised tool.'[98] This is particularly concerning in light of the upward trend described earlier in this chapter. Throughout the decades of its use, a number of reasons have been explored to explain the disproportionate use of stop and search.

2.6.1 Direct racial discrimination

The most obvious explanation is direct racial discrimination – that is, that police officers are racist and target ethnic minorities with unnecessary stops. Bowling and Phillips have argued that, historically, 'racism and racial prejudice in police culture was more widespread and more extreme than in wider society'.[99] Clear examples of overt racism were displayed in the 2003 BBC *Panomara* documentary, the 'Secret Policeman'.[100] Commissioned after the Macpherson Inquiry into the death of Stephen Lawrence,[101] it revealed explicit racist behaviour and views amongst Manchester police trainees and trainers. In the aftermath of the broadcast, the Commission for Racial Equality (now the Equality and Human Rights Commission (EHRC)) launched an

94 HMICFRS, 'Disproportionate use of police powers: A spotlight on stop and search and the use of force' (February 2021): www.justiceinspectorates.gov.uk///hmicfrs/wp-content/uploads/disproportionate-use-of-police-powers-spotlight-on-stop-search-and-use-of-force.pdf (accessed 23 March 2023).

95 Home Office, 'Update to stop and search and arrests statistics using 2021 Census estimates' (March 2023), Table SS.01: www.gov.uk/government/statistics/update-to-stop-and-search-and-arrests-statistics-using-2021-census-estimates (accessed 23 March 2023).

96 HMICFRS (n 93) 17.

97 *Ibid.*

98 Casey Review (n 66).

99 Bowling (n 20), 954.

100 Daly, M, 'Panorama: The Secret Policeman' (BBC, October 2003).

101 Macpherson, W, 'The Stephen Lawrence Inquiry' (Home Office, February 1999).

inquiry and concluded that racism remained a serious problem in the police force.[102] As a result of the documentary, 10 officers resigned and a further 12 were disciplined.[103] More recently, in 2019, eight officers in Hampshire Constabulary were made the subject of gross misconduct proceedings for racist and homophobic language and behaviour (with the investigating force being criticised for providing little transparency or detail about the allegations).[104] Clearly, overt racism remains an undoubted problem for policing; indeed, this reality was openly accepted by the MPS Police Deputy Commission responsible for professional standards.[105] Whilst there is almost certainly truth in this as an explanation for racially disproportionate use of power, it also requires context. Whilst the examples above are demonstrative, they account for a very small number of the roughly 120,000 police officers in England and Wales. As such, there is a lack of evidence to suggest that a large proportion of officers are overtly racist. Indeed, the Macpherson Inquiry did not find evidence of overt (that is, open and conscious) racist attitudes amongst the MPS.[106] Notwithstanding this, recent years have raised concerning evidence of direct racism (and other problematic attitudes) amongst serving officers, with the Institute of Race Relations suggesting there has been an increasing 'culture of extremism' amongst rank-and-file officers.[107] Most recently, the Casey Review highlighted the significant proportion of officers from minority backgrounds who had experienced racism – for example, 46% of black officers (including examples of being stopped and searched).[108]

2.6.2 Implicit and 'institutional' racial discrimination

Racial discrimination can also manifest itself indirectly. For example, this might be through the working assumptions of police officers about 'criminality' – that is, who is likely to be an offender or 'suspicious'.[109] This could include subjective concepts like an 'instinct' or 'hunch' that an individual is carrying a prohibited article. These are of course unmeasurable and not necessarily based on rational and reasonable criteria. Moreover, they could be based on generalised assumptions drawn from an officer's arguably narrow interpretation of their experience and knowledge of policing. High-profile examples of how such assumptions can go wrong include Stephen Lawrence's brother (who lodged a complaint against the MPS after being stopped 25 times over the

102 Commission for Racial Equality, 'Formal Investigation into the Police Service in England and Wales' (March 2005).

103 Dean, N, '12 officers disciplined after "racist police recruits" documentary' (*Independent*, 4 March 2005): www.independent.co.uk/news/uk/this-britain/12-officers-disciplined-after-racist-police-recruits-documentary-7907232.htm(accessed 5 May 2020).

104 Mercer, D, 'Eight Hampshire Police officers to face misconduct hearings after "racism" inquiry' (Sky News, 4 October 2019): https://news.sky.com/story/eight-hampshire-police-officers-to-face-misconduct-hearings-after-racism-inquiry-11827257 (accessed 5 May 2020).

105 Kotecha, S, 'Met Police: Some officers are racist, professional standards chief admits' (BBC News, 15 January 2022): www.bbc.co.uk/news/uk-60379131 (accessed 23 March 2023).

106 An IOPC investigation found evidence of racism (and other behaviour) which was more than 'a few bad apples' (February 2022): www.policeconduct.gov.uk/sites/default/files/Operation%20Hotton%20Learning%20report%20-%20January%202022.pdf.

107 Institute of Race Relations, An increasing 'culture of extremism' amongst rank-and-file police officers (July 2022).

108 Casey Review (n 66).

109 Macpherson (n 101), [6.11].

course of several years) and British athlete, Bianca Williams.[110] In both cases, it appeared that skin colour was the driving factor in establishing suspicion, rather than any evidence of possession of prohibited items. Indirect discrimination might also be driven by context – for example, the time period or place. An example of this would be the period in the mid-to-late 2000s when there was significant public concern about Islamic terrorism; at the same time, stops of Asian individuals were particularly prevalent.[111] Officers relying on working assumptions might not be the type of officers to openly or consciously hold racist beliefs or explicitly target someone because of race – but they may do so 'unwittingly'.[112] This may be the product of implicit or unconscious personal bias or the culture of policing (sometimes described as 'canteen culture'), rather than a product of conscious racial discrimination.[113]

The Macpherson Report concluded that 'institutional racism' existed within the MPS; this refers not to the overt racism of individual officers but to the 'net effect' of police policies, culture and decision-making which target minority groups in particular.[114] Within an institutionally racist organisation (whether it be the police or any other), unconscious bias and working assumptions that are indirectly racist are unlikely to be challenged or changed – and may in fact 'breed'.[115]

2.6.3 Poverty and marginalisation

Whilst a complex issue and not universally the case, ethnic minority groups tend to be disproportionately affected by poverty and marginalisation in society.[116] Research suggests that criminal behaviour has an association with poverty; by extension, this

---

110 Malik, S and Laville, S, 'Stephen Lawrence's brother lodges racism complaint against Met police' (*Guardian*, 9 January 2013): www.theguardian.com/uk/2013/jan/09/stephen-lawrence- brother-racism-police (accessed 5 May 2020); Dodd, V, 'Police who handcuffed Bianca Williams to face gross misconduct charge' (*Guardian*, 26 April 2022): www.theguardian.com/uk-news/2022/apr/26/police-who-handcuffed-bianca-williams-to-face-gross-misconduct-charge (accessed 23 March 2023). See also StopWatch (n 49) for various examples.

111 Home Office statistics show that stops of Asian citizens nearly doubled between 2006/07 and 2010/11 (Home Office, 'Stop and Search: Ethnicity Facts and Figures' (October 2017): www.ethnicity-facts-figures.service.gov.uk/crime-justice-and-the-law/policing/stop-and-search/1.1 (accessed 5 May 2020); Welsh et al (n 14); Casciani, D, 'Muslim anger over stop and search' (*BBC News*, 2 July 2004): http://news.bbc.co.uk/1/hi/uk/3860505.stm (accessed 5 May 2020).

112 See Macpherson (n 101), [6.17].

113 For discussion of canteen culture, see Welsh et al (n 14); Fitzgerald (n 71); Macpherson (n 101), [6.17]. Also see a recent investigation by the IOPC into racist banter ('IOPC recommendations to tackle Met culture after investigation uncovers bullying and harassment in the ranks' (1 February 2022): www.policeconduct.gov.uk/news/iopc-recommendations-tackle-met-culture-after-investigation-uncovers-bullying-and-harassment (accessed 23 March 2023). It is worth mentioning that, since 2014, unconscious bias training for police officers has increased (see Quinton, P and Packham, D, 'College of Policing stop and search training experiment: An overview' (College of Policing, 2016): http://whatworks.college.police.uk/Research/Documents/SS_training OVERVIEW_Final_report.pdf (accessed 5 May 2020).

114 Macpherson (n 101), [6.28].

115 *Ibid* [6.17]. This finding is reinforced by the Casey Review (n 66).

116 See EHRC, 'Is Britain Fairer? The state of equality and human rights 2015' (2015): www.equalityhumanrights.com/sites/default/files/is-britain-fairer-2015.pdf (accessed 5 May 2020); EHRC, 'Healing a divided Britain: the need for a comprehensive race equality strategy' (2016): www.equalityhumanrights.com/en/publication-download/healing-divided-britain-need-comprehensive-race-equality-strategy (accessed 5 May 2020); Garner, S and Bhattacharyya, G, 'Poverty, ethnicity and place' (Joseph Rowntree Foundation, 2011): www.jrf.org.uk/sites/default/files/jrf/migrated/files/poverty-ethnicity-place-full.pdf (accessed 5 May 2020).

may lead police to indirectly target minority groups.[117] For example, the police might choose to target stops at particular geographical areas (referred to as 'stop zones' by Bowling and Phillips) because of a perceived reputation for criminality. These will often be particularly economically deprived areas and have a higher proportion of ethnic minority citizens living there.[118] This in turn means that a disproportionate number of non-white persons are likely to be stopped, simply because they are 'available'.[119] As such, the cycle of reputation, targeting and stopping is self-reinforcing, and, notwithstanding the legal regulation discussed in this chapter, is driven by the use of extensive police discretion. By targeting certain locations, it is inevitable that ethnic minority citizens will be disproportionately stopped – notwithstanding the fact that 'availability' does not 'constitute sufficient grounds for a stop and search'.[120]

2.6.4 Poor relations between the police and minority communities

It has long been argued that the relationship between the police and ethnic minority communities has been damaged by excessive stopping of non-white individuals.[121] The relationship is characterised by a lack of trust, primarily because such communities have felt targeted by the police, and some police officers have characterised these communities as less cooperative or more likely to be 'suspicious'.[122] From the perspective of ethnic minority communities, feelings of persecution, targeting and racism (direct and indirect) have often led to hostility, distrust and frustration. On a smaller scale, this could manifest itself in the form of reactive individual behaviour born of this poor relationship (such as non-white individuals avoiding the police, or being critical or contrary or potentially aggressive towards officers when they feel unfairly targeted).[123] In turn, the police may fail to recognise this as a natural reaction to real or perceived targeting or racism (particularly if they do not recognise any implicit bias on their part). Officers may in fact consider such behaviour to be suspicious, uncooperative or aggressive, providing justification for further targeting. On a larger scale, examples of tensions between the police and minority communities reaching a tipping point include the riots in Brixton, Broadwater Farm, Bristol, and most recently those in London in 2011.[124]

---

117 For a review of the complex relationship between poverty and crime, see Webster, C and Kingston, S, 'Anti-Poverty Strategies for the UK: Poverty and Crime Review' (Joseph Rowntree Foundation, May 2014): http://eprints.lancs.ac.uk/71188/1/JRF_Final_Poverty_and_Crime_Review_May_2014.pdf (accessed 5 May 2020).

118 Bowling (n 20), 947.

119 Waddington, P, Stenson, K and Don, D, 'In Proportion: Race and Police Stop and Search' (2004) 44 *Brit J of Crim*; Fitzgerald (n 68).

120 Delsol, R and Shiner, M, 'Regulating stop and search: a challenge for Police and community relations in England and Wales' (2006) 14 *Critical Criminology*, 249.

121 *Ibid.*

122 Macpherson (n 101), [6.17] and [45.7]; Delsol (n 120), 244–47.

123 Welsh et al (n 14).

124 For more on rioting and the link to racial discrimination (and stop and search), see Riots Communities and Victims Panel, 'After the Riots: The final report of the Riots Communities and Victims Panel' (March 2012), 10; Scarman Report (n 36); Lewis, P, Newburn, T, Taylor, M and Mcgillivray, C, 'Reading the Riots: Investigating England's summer of disorder' (London School of Economics, 2011): http://eprints.lse.ac.uk/46297/1/Reading%20the%20riots%28published%29.pdf (accessed 5 May 2020); and Jefferson, T, 'Policing the riots: from Bristol and Brixton to Tottenham, via Toxteth, Handsworth, etc' (*Criminal Justice Matters*, 2012): www.crimeandjustice.org.uk/sites/crimeandjustice.org.uk/files/09627251.2012.670995.pdf (accessed 5 May 2020).

From a police perspective, the interpretation of reasonable suspicion may be regarded through the lens of this poor relationship – that ethnic minority communities are 'trouble' and therefore are to be treated with greater suspicion.[125] Such reasons can easily drive stop and search because the safeguard has such significant scope for interpretation. The essentially subjective nature of this supposedly 'objective' test allows police officers to impose their own values on decision-making. This is both a good and a bad thing; such discretion is important for flexible, practical and effective policing, but it also creates significant scope for abuse or unconscious misuse. In the context of the poor relationship between the police and minority communities, this flexibility creates a great risk of inappropriate stops (evidenced in the consistent disproportion in statistics). Reasonable suspicion is, in effect, an 'enabling' rule, rather than a restriction, which allows factors like race and ethnicity to influence decision-making.[126]

2.7 Reform

Generally, discussions regarding reform of stop and search have pursued one of two lines: improvement or abolition. Arguments in favour of improvement suggest a reduction in the overall use of the power, coupled with better targeting of stops and better training/understanding of the safeguards by police officers. Arguments in favour of abolition suggest that stop and search is ineffective and counter-productive, and that its continued use cannot be justified.[127] Alternatively, it can be argued that stop and search is simply not used enough and that it should be expanded in scope. The latter two arguments – abolition and expansion – might be regarded as rather extreme. Reform had, until recent years, focused primarily on reduction and improvement of the use of the existing powers.

As discussed above, in 2014, BUSS was introduced by the Home Secretary and the College of Policing, with the aim of increasing public confidence in the use of stop and search, by both reducing and improving its use.[128] Whilst the scheme was voluntary, all 43 police forces signed up to it, suggesting widespread will amongst not only politicians but also the police to address the issues discussed in this chapter. As well as the restrictions imposed on s 60 stops, the scheme required the recording and publication of all stop and search data, with a view to making it more transparent and accessible to scrutiny (and hopefully encouraging better practice as a result).[129] The scheme also required diversity monitoring and local community observations of stop and search.[130] Shortly after the scheme was introduced, the 2015 revision of Code A made significant changes designed to address various criticisms; for example, it introduced the clearer two-part test under para 2.2 (see above). The Code also clarified that '[a] hunch or instinct which cannot be explained or justified to an objective observer can never

125 See n 124; and Bowling (n 20), 954.

126 Welsh et al (n 14).

127 This fits within a wider narrative about 'defunding' the police generally, which has gained momentum since 2020. See Fleetwood, J and Lea, J, 'Defunding the police in the UK: Critical questions and practical suggestions' (2022) *Howard Journal of Criminal Justice*, 61 (2).

128 See Home Office and College of Policing, 'Best Use of Stop and Search Scheme' (Home Office, 2014): https://assets.publishing.service.gov.uk/government/uploads/system/uploads/attachment_data/file/346922/Best_Use_of_Stop_and_Search_Scheme_v3.0_v2.pdf (accessed 5 May 2020).

129 *Ibid* 2.

130 *Ibid* 7 and 2 respectively.

amount to reasonable grounds'.[131] This seemed, in theory, to signal the death of the traditional 'policeman's hunch' as a ground for a stop. There was also extended clarification that personal factors can never be reasonable grounds.

As discussed earlier, there had been a significant drop in the number of stops under all pieces of legislation (although this trend began prior to these changes), and at the same time the arrest rate for stops slowly increased. This trend has now ceased, but even prior to this, closer examination of the use of the power suggested that problems continued to exist notwithstanding attempts at reform. Various inspections by HMICFRS found large-scale failure to comply with BUSS (until 2016),[132] suggesting that the progress of reform was sluggish (possibly due to a lack of resources for training, or resistance from serving officers). Equally, the disproportionate stopping of non-white individuals continued (and continues) to be a serious problem, with the Lammy Review in 2017 finding similar patterns to previous research.[133] HMICFRS also identified a lack of progress regarding consistent application of and training on reasonable suspicion.[134] However, in its 2017 PEEL legitimacy report, HMICFRS found that only 6% of stops lacked reasonable suspicion, commenting that its findings 'indicate that the hard work carried out across the police service has resulted in sustained improvement'.[135] However, as noted earlier in this chapter, more recent findings from HMICFRS suggest these levels have not been sustained, notably as the numbers of stops increased after 2018.[136]

We can argue that reform did achieve its short-term goal (reducing the overall number of stops) but did not comprehensively or effectively address the underlying legal and cultural problems associated with the reasonable suspicion safeguard or the disproportionate stopping of ethnic minority individuals (and arguably the latter is closely linked to the former). Moreover, as discussed earlier, the BUSS scheme has since been relaxed significantly, potentially sapping the motivation of forces to comply fully. Indeed, HMICFRS has argued that, in light of these changes, '[p]roper scrutiny by both forces and the public of the use of these powers is essential and must not be compromised', yet highlighted that '[s]ome forces don't monitor a comprehensive enough set of data on how they use force and stop and search powers'.[137] As such, the best that can be said is that there have been mixed results and that we are still a long way from solving the problems associated with stop and search.

2.8 Other safeguards

Alongside reasonable suspicion, a number of other important safeguards exist in relation to stop and search under s 1 of PACE 1984. The two primary ones are the 'information' and 'recording' requirements, with an additional rule against consensual searches without legal grounds:

131 Code A, [2.6B].

132 See n 91.

133 Lammy (n 30).

134 See n 91.

135 See n 16, 31.

136 HMICFRS (n 94).

137 HMICFRS, 'State of Policing: the Annual Assessment of Policing in England and Wales 2018' (2019), 68: www.justiceinspectorates.gov.uk/hmicfrs/wp-content/uploads/state-of-policing-2018.pdf (accessed 5 May 2020).

- The *'information' requirement*: An officer must tell an individual being stopped their name and station, and the object of and grounds for the proposed search.[138] This was confirmed to be a mandatory requirement in *Bristol*.[139]
- The *'recording' requirement*: An officer must normally make a record of a search, including the object of the search, the grounds for making it, and whether anything was found.[140] Unless impracticable, an officer must tell the person being stopped that a record is being made of the search and must normally give a copy to them.[141]
- *'Consensual searches'*: an officer must not search a person on the basis of consent if legal grounds for conducting it do not exist.[142]

The first two are positive rules, requiring the police to do something. The third is a negative rule, prohibiting the police from doing something. In terms of recording, early research suggested that police recorded less than half of all stops.[143] It was theorised that such low numbers may have been due to the practice of persuading people to consent to stop and search and thus freeing the police from statutory restraints such as recording and information. This is therefore linked to the rule against consensual searches without legal grounds. Whilst recording significantly improved upon historically low levels (75% of stops were recorded in 2000), there continues to be a problem of compliance.[144] In 2013, HMIC expressed significant concerns about a continuing failure to record stop and search.[145] For example, a 2013 inspection by HMICFRS found that only two forces achieved a recording compliance rate of over 95%.[146] More recently, the inspectorate reported that police forces were inconsistently recording the ethnicity of those stopped, with 17% of stops having no ethnicity stated despite being a legal requirement.[147] As a result, this hampered monitoring of disproportionate use.[148] The recording safeguard has also potentially been weakened; since 2009, officers have only had to provide a 'receipt' to individuals who have been stopped (rather than a full record).[149] Individuals must then visit a police station or access the record online. One can speculate on how likely to happen this is, particularly if those searched are vulnerable or juveniles. As such, the purpose of recording – to make the police 'feel' accountable – is undermined since the search record will probably never be viewed.

138 s 2.

139 [2007] EWCA Crim 3214.

140 PACE 1984, s 3(1)–(6).

141 PACE 1984, s 3 and Code A, [4].

142 *Ibid* [1.5].

143 In 1987, approximately 40% of police searches were recorded (based on British Crime Survey estimates as compared with police-recorded searches) (Clancy, A, Hough, M, Aust, R and Kershaw, C, 'Crime, Policing and Justice: The Experience of Ethnic Minorities, Findings from the 2000 British Crime Survey' (Home Office, 2001), 67–68.

144 *Ibid*; and see recent evidence from HMICFRS on recording (n 16).

145 See n 95.

146 *Ibid*, 30.

147 HMICFRS (n 94).

148 HMICFRS (n 16).

149 Code A, [4.2].

2.9 Summary

- Whilst its use has (in general) declined, stop and search remains a widely used power of police investigation; it has begun to increase in use; and it continues to have implications for rights to liberty/privacy, particularly for ethnic minority communities.
- The decline in the mid-2010s appears to be the result of the significant criticism and reform directed at stop and search in previous years – but there has been fairly slow progress in improving the mechanisms of the power, and the trend of decline in use has reversed.
- Stop and search is a high discretion, wide-ranging police power that is subjected to limited external supervision; it may not be susceptible to control through legal rules.[150]
- There are potentially stronger influences on how the power is used, which are hard to tackle:
  - police culture – for example, working practices, core values and beliefs;
  - a lack of training for/supervision of use of stop and search by other police officers or external actors;
  - inconsistent monitoring/recording of how stop and search is used.
- Reasonable suspicion remains a flawed safeguard against abuse/misuse of the power, in that it sets a low standard and is not consistently satisfied in recording.
- Racial discrimination remains a significant problem in the use of stop and search, with a variety of potential explanations.
- There are a lack of consequences for the unlawful use of stop and search. Damages and exclusion of evidence at trial are potential remedies,[151] but such consequences are unlikely.[152]

150 Welsh et al (n 14).

151 Potentially, someone unlawfully searched could sue for damages (see eg *Browne v Commissioner of Police of the Metropolis* [2014] EWHC 3999 (QB)).

152 We should ask whether persons subjected to such searches will have the time, money or even the knowledge to pursue such claims.

chapter 3 Policing on the Street (2): The Power of Arrest

3.1 Overview of the power of arrest

When one thinks of police powers, the archetype is arrest – most typically, a police officer handcuffing a criminal and wrestling them into a police car. Aside from street patrolling and stop and search, arrest is the most visible form of policing, and it is a power that most members of the public hope (and assume) they will never be subjected to. It removes individual liberty (albeit temporarily) and invokes connotations of guilt, unjustified as that may be. It is a significant and widely used power, although its use has declined in recent years. In 2021/22, the police arrested approximately 647,000 people – 2.5% higher than the previous year and the first annual rise in arrests since 2007/08.[1] The Office for National Statistics' (ONS) Crime Survey of England and Wales (CSEW) gives us some context of the scale of crime and its relationship to arrest. In the year ending March 2021, there were an estimated 12 million crimes (including fraud and computer misuse, which have been included since 2017).[2] Of these, 5.4 million were recorded by the police, a 10% decrease on the previous year.[3] This not only indicates the important difference between 'actual' crime (albeit estimated via interviews with the public) and the crime recorded by the police; but also that arrest relates to a small portion of all actual crime in England and Wales. This chapter will be focusing on the primary power of arrest used by the police – that outlined under PACE 1984, s 24. Before examining how this power is regulated, it is important to understand what actions by the police amount to an 'arrest'.

3.2 What constitutes an 'arrest'?

How do we define the concept of an 'arrest'? This is an important question – after all, if a police officer undertakes physical action towards a citizen, we need to know whether they are, in fact, 'arresting' them. If they are not, then the officer will be committing a criminal offence (most likely a form of common assault). If they are arresting someone, then we need to know that an officer is doing so lawfully – that is, they are abiding by the rules laid down in PACE 1984 which tell us what must be done when someone is arrested (for example, being told that you are being arrested). Police officers therefore need to know what actions constitute an arrest so that they can lawfully execute their

1 Home Office, 'Arrest summary tables: police powers and procedures, year ending 31 March 2022' (November 2022), Table A.01a: www.gov.uk/government/statistics/police-powers-and-procedures-stop-and-search-and-arrests-england-and-wales-year-ending-31-march-2022 (accessed 24 March 2023).

2 ONS, 'Crime in England and Wales: year ending March 2021' (July 2021): www.ons.gov.uk/peoplepopulationandcommunity/crimeandjustice/bulletins/crimeinenglandandwales/yearendingmarch2021#overall-estimates-of-crime (accessed 24 March 2023).

3 *Ibid.* The ONS notes that this figure does not include Greater Manchester Police due to data issues. As a large urban police force, this suggests a significant number of recorded crimes are not included in this headline statistic.

duties. Equally, citizens need to know whether they are being arrested or whether the police are using their authority illegitimately. In most cases, it will be obvious that someone is being arrested and there will be no dispute. However, there are situations where a lack of clarity about whether an 'arrest' is taking place can create problems.

The concept of arrest is not defined in PACE 1984. As such, we need to rely on judicial interpretation for its meaning. The courts have, unhelpfully, adopted two distinct and arguably different approaches to the concept, leading to some inconsistency and confusion over when actions taken by the police constitute an arrest. The first approach taken is that an arrest is a factual state of affairs and is dependent on whether a person has been deprived of their liberty. The second approach taken is that an arrest depends on the context and the intention of the police officer conducting the arrest.

3.2.1 Arrest as a factual state of affairs

The first approach outlined by the courts states that whether an 'arrest' has occurred depends on the facts in question – in short, was the person, according to the facts, deprived of their liberty? The main authority for this conceptualisation of arrest is *Spicer v Holt*, in which a police officer arrested a suspect after a breath test, but failed to check the test.[4] The suspect appealed on the basis that the arrest was unlawful as there was no evidence that the breath test was positive (which would indicate he had been drinking and driving). The court said:

> Arrest is an ordinary English word … whether or not a person has been arrested is dependent not on the legality of the arrest but on whether he has been deprived of his liberty to go where he pleases.[5]

The case of *Lewis* confirmed this definition, adding that arrest is a 'situation' which is not dependent on legality but is simply a 'matter of fact'.[6] As such, an arrest seems to require some form of deprivation of the liberty of the suspect.[7] In *Spicer*, this was the officer preventing the suspect from driving away. In *Dawes*, the police set up a car to auto-lock when it was broken into; the suspect did so and was 'arrested' when the car locked.[8] Deprivation of liberty (from these examples) appears to be any restriction of the right to move freely (either at all or from a specific location). Contrast this concept with the case of *Walker*, in which a police officer cornered a suspect in a doorway and prevented him from leaving.[9] The court concluded that the officer did not purport to arrest him, but had falsely imprisoned the suspect. This seems strange when the above cases suggest that deprivation of liberty is the requirement. This does suggest that the term is broad and open to interpretation.

---

4 [1977] AC 987.

5 *Ibid* 1000 *per* Viscount Dilhorne.

6 *Lewis v Chief Constable of South Wales* [1991] 1 All ER 206.

7 For example, in *Hussien v Chong Fook Kam* [1970] AC 942, this amounted to being prevented from leaving (949) – but see *Walker v Commissioner of Police of the Metropolis* [2014] EWCA Civ 897.

8 *Dawes v DPP* [1995] 1 Cr App R 65.

9 *Walker*, n 7.

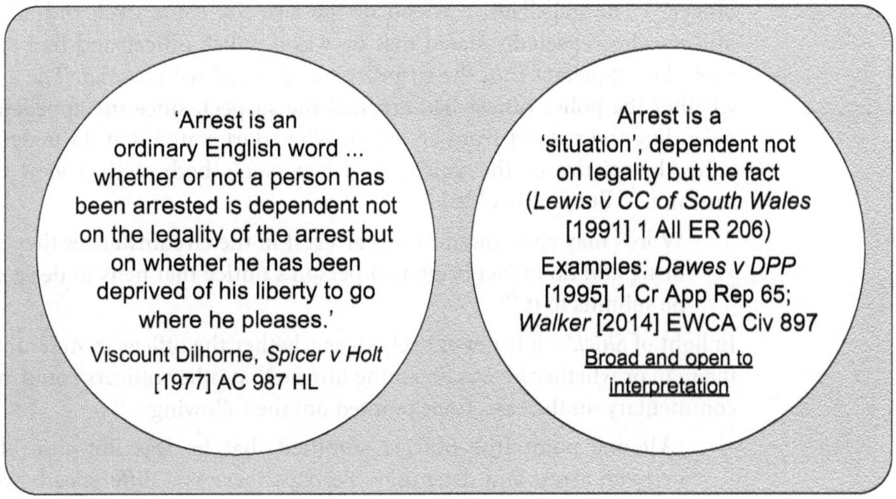

3.2.2 Arrest depends on context and intention

The second approach outlines that whether an action constitutes an 'arrest' depends on the context in which it takes place and the intention of the police officer taking the action. The primary authority is *Shields v Chief Constable of Merseyside Police*, in which a suspect and his father struggled with a police officer, who radioed for support.[10] When other officers arrived, the first officer said that the suspect was under arrest for assault and one of the support officers then seized the suspect physically. The court said:

> The mere act of taking a person into custody does not constitute an arrest unless the person knows, either at the time when he is taken into custody or as soon thereafter as it is reasonably practical to inform him, upon what charge or on suspicion of what crime he is being arrested.[11]

This suggests that simply depriving a suspect of their liberty (as per *Spicer*) is not enough to be an 'arrest' – there must be a clear intention on the part of an officer to arrest the suspect for an offence. In *Wood v DPP*, the court also seemed to draw this conclusion:[12]

> [W]here a police officer restrains a person, but does not at that time intend or purport to arrest him, then he is committing an assault, even if an arrest would have been justified.[13]

These cases seem to blur the line between two separate concepts: the fact that an arrest has *occurred* (ie depriving someone of their liberty, such as handcuffing or physical restraint) and the *lawfulness* of an arrest (for example, telling the suspect that they have been arrested). This confusion is highlighted in case law. In *Adler v DPP*, an off-duty police officer saw a suspect breaking a car window; the suspect tried to get into another car, from which the officer dragged him by the arm, stating that he was a police

10 [2010] EWCA Civ 1281.
11 *Ibid* [15].
12 [2008] EWHC 1056 (Admin).
13 *Ibid* [7].

officer.[14] The appellant, a friend of the suspect, came over and struggled with the officer, who repeatedly stated that he was a police officer and had detained the first man. The appellant (not the suspect) was charged with assault. The appeal hinged on whether the police officer had arrested the suspect, since the appellant claimed to be defending the suspect from an attack. The court stated that '[a]n arrest can be made either by seizure or the touching of a person's body with a view to that person's restraint.'[15] But it also added:

> Words may also amount to an arrest if in the circumstances they are calculated to bring and do in fact bring to a person's notice that he is under a compulsion and he submits to it.[16]

In light of *Shields*, it is not entirely clear whether the officer in *Adler* intended to arrest the man or whether he was detaining him so that other officers could arrest him. In his commentary on the case, Cape pointed out the following:

> [A]t one point [the officer] admitted that he was not sure of the difference between arrest and detention: 'Perhaps there is a difference between restraining somebody's liberty so that they can't get away from you and actually arresting them.'... If a senior police officer is not clear about what constitutes an arrest, how can more junior officers be expected to have a clear understanding of their powers?[17]

This demonstrates some significant confusion as to when exactly an arrest has been effected. In the case of *Iqbal*, similar problems emerged.[18] The suspect was detained and handcuffed by police officers and told he would have to wait to be arrested by other officers; the suspect then fled. The court concluded that because the officer did not intend to arrest the suspect, he had not been arrested. The conviction was quashed. However, one might argue that because the suspect was deprived of his liberty, he was arrested – just not lawfully. One might ask why any of this important. Clearly, interpretation of various actions by officers and suspects at or around the time of an alleged arrest will probably influence whether an arrest is deemed to have taken place. If a police officer grabs someone without intending to arrest them, this is potentially a criminal offence. Equally, it is important to know whether an arrest has occurred as various requirements and safeguards are attached to an arrest. Such confusion therefore creates problems in understanding whether the police have complied with their duties and whether potential defendants have committed criminal offences against officers (which can be punished severely).

3.2.3 Deprivation of liberty

The right to liberty is a fundamental human right, as outlined in Article 5(1) of the ECHR, but lawful arrest is an exception to this. By definition, an arrest must therefore involve some form of deprivation of liberty. In most cases, whether this has occurred will be clear. However, in some cases it may not be – and a broad interpretation of deprivation of liberty may create problems.

14 [2013] EWHC 1968 (Admin).

15 *Ibid* [13].

16 *Ibid.*

17 Cape, E, 'Case Comment: Adler v Crown Prosecution Service' (2014) *Crim LR*, 226.

18 [2011] EWCA Crim273.

An example of a problem area is 'kettling': a police tactic employed to confine or contain a number of people in a specific area (generally at protests and demonstrations or during riots). Those who are 'kettled' are not prevented from moving completely but are severely restricted in terms of how far they can move (sometimes only a few feet). They may also be deprived, for substantial periods of time, of access to food, water and toilet facilities. As such, it has been questioned whether 'kettling' represents a deprivation of liberty and therefore amounts to an arrest. This is important because there is clearly at least some degree of deprivation of liberty involved in 'kettling'; and since an arrest has various safeguards and requirements attached to its use, failing to fulfil or abide by these could potentially constitute an unlawful arrest. For example, if a 'kettle' involved several thousand people, could officers feasibly inform all of them that they were under arrest and why? These kinds of issues were considered in *Austin v Commissioner of Police of the Metropolis*, in which the claimant was 'kettled' along with several thousand other people at a demonstration.[19] The organisers refused to cooperate with the police and some of them were violent and disorderly (though the claimant was not); a 'kettle' was imposed on anyone within a defined police cordon. The claimant argued that she had been deprived of her liberty (and therefore that rights of arrested individuals applied to her). The court stated:

> Whether there is a deprivation of liberty, as opposed to a restriction of movement, is a matter of degree and intensity. Account must be taken of a whole range of factors, including the specific situation of the individual and the context in which the restriction of liberty occurs.[20]

This therefore suggested, based on pre-existing case law, that finding a deprivation of liberty would depend on 'the type, effects, duration and manner of the execution/implementation of the measure in question'.[21] However, based on such factors alone, Oreb argued that it was 'somewhat at odds with the facts to say that there was no deprivation' in *Austin*.[22] Instead, the House of Lords 'effectively added an additional criterion, "purpose", to the existing … factors'[23] – in short, what was the purpose of the police in kettling the protestors and did this enable the court to find that this was not a deprivation of liberty? The House of Lords concluded that the purpose was the protection of the physical safety of the demonstrators and preventing violence against property, and that this was a legitimate restriction of movement rather than a deprivation of liberty.[24] The case proceeded to the ECtHR, which drew the same conclusion – but for different reasons.[25] It found that the purpose of the police was irrelevant in determining whether there had been a deprivation of liberty.[26] Rather, 'the specific context and circumstances' needed to be considered, and where temporary restrictions on movement were 'unavoidable as a result of circumstances beyond the control of the authorities and are necessary to avert a real risk of serious injury or

19 [2009] UKHL 5.

20 *Ibid* [21].

21 Sometimes referred to as the '*Engel/Guzzardi* factors'; Oreb, N, 'The Legality of "Kettling" after Austin' (2013) 76 *Modern LR* (4), 738.

22 *Ibid.*

23 *Ibid.*

24 *Austin* (n 21), [39].

25 *Austin v UK* (2012) 55 EHRR 14.

26 *Ibid* [58].

damage, and are kept to the minimum required for that purpose', no deprivation of liberty could be established.[27] Kettling fell within this classification.[28]

Therefore, it appears that anything that does not constitute a deprivation of liberty is not an arrest (in line with the *Spicer* approach) and will merely be a restriction of movement (for example, in the case of *Walker*). This is an interesting decision; one wonders how much public policy (that is, enabling the police to control large numbers of people) weighed on the minds of the judges in coming to their conclusion. Indeed, Oreb appears to imply a degree of creative interpretation by both the House of Lords and the ECtHR in reaching the same conclusion. If one considers the implication of a 'kettle' being deemed a deprivation of liberty and therefore an arrest, the impracticality of ensuring that this fully complied with the requirements of PACE 1984 would, effectively, have instantly brought the practice to an end.[29] Kettling – and police management of public protest – has remained a live issue, particularly in recent years. Its use during anti-fascist demonstrations in 2013 led to the Metropolitan Police Service (MPS) settling out of court, paying £700,000 to protestors in 2019.[30] Kettling also appeared to have been used (albeit on a very small scale) during the extensive 'Extinction Rebellion' protests of 2018 and 2019,[31] which also involved large-scale arrests.[32] More recently, Black Lives Matter protestors were kettled and compelled to provide personal details to police (including being filmed) in order to leave.[33]

3.3 The law governing arrest

The primary power of arrest available to the police is governed by s 24 of PACE 1984. The power is wide; generally, a police officer may arrest:

- anyone;
- without a warrant;
- for any offence.

Until 2005, the concept of 'arrestable' and 'non-arrestable' offences meant that the police could not arrest a person for a swathe of minor offences. The rationale behind this distinction was 'a basic idea of proportionality … that arrest would not normally be appropriate where the least serious offences were concerned.[34] Thus the police were

27 *Ibid* [59].

28 For more on this generally, see Oreb (n 21).

29 Or at least would require kettling be justified under one of the other exceptions to Article 5 ECHR, which seems almost impossible based on the wording of the exceptions (see Article 5(1)(a)–(f)).

30 Evans, R, 'Met police pay out £700,000 to detained anti-fascist protesters' (*Guardian*, 26 June 2019): www.theguardian.com/uk-news/2019/jun/26/met-police-in-700k-payout-to-detained-anti-fascist-protesters (accessed 6 May 2020).

31 Snaith, E, 'Extinction Rebellion: 92-year-old arrested as climate activists prepare for "Hong Kong-style" occupation of airport' (*Independent*, 9 October 2019): www.independent.co.uk/news/uk/home-news/extinction-rebellion-protests-london-live-updates-police-arrests-trafalgar-square-a9148376.html (accessed 6 May 2020).

32 Approximately 1,600 arrests were made in connection with the protests (Newburn, T, 'The London ban on Extinction Rebellion risks a perilous erosion of public trust' (*Guardian*, 18 October 2019): www.theguardian.com/commentisfree/2019/oct/18/london-ban-extinction-rebellion-erosion-trust-protesting (accessed 6 May 2020).

33 Andersson, J, 'Black Lives Matter protests: London demonstrators were kettled, photographed and had names taken by police' (iNews, 8 June 2020): https://inews.co.uk/news/black-lives-matter-protesters-kettled-photographed-and-names-taken-by-police-440373 (accessed 24 March 2023).

34 Campbell, L, Ashworth, A and Redmayne, M, *The Criminal Process*, 5th edn (OUP, 2019), 123.

legally prevented from excessive use of their power of arrest under PACE for the vast majority of crimes. However, this distinction was abolished by s 110 of the Serious Organised Crime and Police Act 2005, enabling arrest for any offence. As such, this significantly widened the scope of the power. Notwithtanding this extension, these powers can only be exercised when two conditions are satisfied. An officer must:

(a) have reasonable grounds for suspicion that a crime has been, is being, or will be committed;[35] and

(b) reasonably believe that it is necessary to arrest the person (introduced in 2005 to counter-balance the abolition of arrestable/non-arrestable offences).[36]

These act as limiting safeguards against abuse of this discretionary power – they are therefore due process concepts, which align with the idea espoused by Packer's models that police powers must be curbed to ensure that individual rights are respected.[37] It should, however, be recognised that, for necessity, this was accompanied by a substantial expansion of the scope for arrest, demonstrating the ongoing tension (and need for balance) between crime control and due process imperatives.

3.3.1 Code G

Like stop and search, arrest under s 24 is regulated by a Code of Practice (Code G), which provides guidance on the exercise of the power for officers. Paragraph 1.2 states:

> The right to liberty is a key principle of the HRA (Human Rights Act) 1998. The exercise of the power of arrest represents an obvious and significant interference with that right.

This clearly highlights that arrest can impair the ability of citizens to enjoy their fundamental rights. As such, officers should be aware that when they arrest someone, they will be engaging in this 'obvious and significant interference with that right'.

The Code goes on to say:

> The use of the power must be fully justified and officers should consider if the necessary objectives can be met by other less intrusive means ... When the power of arrest is exercised it is essential that it is exercised in a non-discriminatory and proportionate manner.[38]

The message to officers should therefore be clear: use of the power should be carefully considered; it should be justified and necessary; it should be a method of last resort; and it must be used responsibly. All of these requirements derive from the fact that arrest directly impinges upon a fundamental human right, which must be balanced with the police objective of detecting and preventing criminal behaviour.

3.3.2 Reasonable suspicion

Normally, an arrest requires 'reasonable grounds for suspicion' of an offence to be lawful. The police can arrest an individual under s 24 in four circumstances:

(a) When someone is *about to commit* an offence, or when the police have reasonable grounds for suspecting that someone is about to commit an offence.[39]

---

35 PACE 1984, s 24.

36 PACE 1984, s 24.

37 See **Chapter 1**.

38 Home Office, Police and Criminal Evidence Act 1984 (PACE) Code G Revised Code of Practice for the statutory power of arrest by police (TSO, 2012).

39 s 24(1)(a) and (c).

(b) When someone *is committing* an offence or when the police have reasonable grounds for suspecting that someone is committing an offence.[40]

(c) When the police have reasonable grounds for suspecting that an offence *has been committed.* The police can arrest someone who is guilty or whom they have reasonable grounds for suspecting is guilty.[41]

(d) When someone *has committed* an offence. The police can arrest someone who is guilty or whom they have reasonable grounds for suspecting is guilty.[42]

As such, s 24 covers situations where an offence has been committed in the past, is being committed in the present, or will be committed in the future. It also covers situations where an officer *knows* that an offence has been, is being or will be committed and the suspect is guilty, as well as situations where they are *not certain* but have reasonable grounds for suspicion. Moreover, as long as the existence of an offence and the suspect's guilt are proven – for example, by a subsequent conviction for the offence for which they were arrested – the arrest will be lawful, even if the police did not have reasonable suspicion at the time. This is a rather troubling point, as it retrospectively categorises an arrest as lawful, even if it did not stand up to scrutiny at the time because of a lack of reasonable suspicion. This therefore closes the number of potential challenges to unlawful arrests to those people who were arrested but not found guilty and those who challenge their arrest early on (that is, beforeconviction).

As with stop and search, the legislation itself does not provide a definition for what reasonable suspicion means. Code G does provide some information in para 2.3A:

> There must be some reasonable, objective grounds for the suspicion, based on known facts and information which are relevant to the likelihood the offence has been committed and the person liable to arrest committed it.

Whilst this is vague, it does indicate that some form of useful, relevant material (information or facts) should form the basis for reasonable suspicion. The common law provides both guidance on how to assess reasonable suspicion and what information might satisfy the requirement in Code G. The leading case on reasonable suspicion for arrest is *Castorina v Chief Constable of Surrey* – a vital case central to understanding this area of the law.[43] In this case, there was a burglary that appeared to be an 'inside job'; there was only one suspect, whom the police visited and arrested. The claimant argued that she had been wrongfully arrested as the police did not have reasonable grounds for suspecting she had committed the offence. Lord Woolf outlined a three-stage test to determine whether reasonable suspicion existed, which has a subjective and an objective element:

(a) 'Did the arresting officer suspect that the person who was arrested was guilty of the offence? The answer to this question depends entirely on the findings of fact as to the officer's state of mind.' (a subjective test)

(b) 'Assuming the officer had the necessary suspicion, was there reasonable cause for that suspicion? This is a purely objective requirement to be determined by the judge if necessary on facts found by a jury.' (an objective test)

40 s 24(1)(b) and (d).

41 s24(2).

42 s24(3).

43 [1988] NLJR 180.

(c) The decision to arrest must have been '*Wednesbury* reasonable' – that is, a decision that is not 'so unreasonable that no reasonable authority could ever have come to it'.[44]

As such, not only must an officer genuinely believe that they are arresting the right person, but this must be deemed to be a reasonable belief – that is, objectively justifiable. The third limb – *Wednesbury* reasonableness – operates to ensure that a decision to arrest is not so bizarre or irrational that it cannot be allowed to stand (although this test has a very high threshold).[45]

Other cases provide additional information on what might constitute reasonable suspicion for the purposes of arrest. In *Hussien v Chong Fook Kam* (see above), the court said:

> Suspicion arises at or near the starting-point of an investigation … suspicion can take into account matters that could not be put in evidence at all … [and] also matters which, though admissible, could not form part of a prima facie case.[46]

As such, the evidence required to show reasonable suspicion (much like stop and search) is of a much lower standard than that required to prove a case at trial. This sets a fairly low threshold for showing reasonable suspicion – arguably, this is a crime control approach, as it places a very limited restraint on police power.[47]

What kind of information might satisfy this standard? In *R (Rutherford) v IPCC*, the court stated that an arresting officer does not need to identify the precise offence for which a person is being arrested, suggesting that the level of information needed to form reasonable suspicion can be vague.[48] The courts have considered whether orders or information from other police officers will be enough. In *O'Hara*, a police officer arrested the claimant based only on a police briefing in which it had been alleged that the suspect was involved in a murder.[49] Since, according to the principle of original authority, each officer must make an independent decision to arrest, the court concluded:

> Such an order to arrest cannot without some further information being given to the constable be sufficient to afford the constable reasonable grounds for the necessary suspicion.[50]

In *Olden*, the court clarified:[51]

> [T]he arresting officer must himself or herself have the necessary suspicion and reasonable grounds for such suspicion. The mere fact that the arresting officer has been instructed by a superior officer to effect the arrest is not of itself capable of amounting to such reasonable grounds.[52]

The courts have also considered whether the 'opportunity' to commit the offence might constitute grounds for reasonable suspicion. In *Cumming v Chief Constable of*

---

44 In *Parker v Chief Constable of Essex* [2018] EWCA Civ 2788, the Court of Appeal approved an extended version of the *Castorina* test, with additional questions for officers (see [59]).

45 *Associated Provincial Picture Houses Ltd v Wednesbury Corporation* [1948] 1 KB 223.

46 *Chong Fook Kam* (n 7), 948.

47 See **Chapter 1**.

48 [2010] EWHC 2881 (Admin).

49 [1997] AC 286.

50 *Ibid* 294.

51 [2007] EWCA Crim 726.

52 *Ibid* [21].

Northumbria Police, several innocent CCTV operators were arrested on the basis that they had the opportunity to tamper with a CCTV tape.[53] The court said:

> Where a small number of people can be clearly identified as the only ones capable of having committed the offence, I see no reason why that cannot afford reasonable grounds for suspecting each of them of having committed that offence, in the absence of any information which could or should enable the police to reduce the number further.[54]

In *Al-Fayed*, the court expanded on this:[55]

> It is all a matter of degree, in which the strength of the opportunity, whether or not unique to the person or persons arrested, has to be considered in the context of all the other information available to the arresting officer.[56]

As we can see, the definition of reasonable suspicion provided by the courts is therefore quite broad, fairly flexible, and has a low threshold to be satisfied.[57] This therefore raises questions about its effectiveness as a due process safeguard against abuse of the power of arrest.

3.3.3 Necessity

Section 24(4) of PACE 1984 states:

> The power of summary arrest … is exercisable only if the constable has reasonable grounds for believing that for any of the reasons mentioned in subsection (5) it is necessary to arrest the person in question.

First, this provision suggests (although does not state) that the power of arrest should only be used when the officer needs to use it (when it is 'necessary'), implying that it is a last resort that should only be used when there is no other appropriate choice of action. Secondly, the officer must have reasonable grounds for believing it is necessary; that is, they must have some objective basis for believing that they need to arrest someone. Thirdly, the legislation (helpfully) provides an exhaustive list of reasons for believing an arrest to be necessary. Whilst the statute contains six specific reasons for believing that an arrest is necessary, these can be grouped into five basic categories: identity, harm/loss, protection, investigation and disappearance. It should be noted that these are not statutory groupings; they are simply designed to make it easier to remember them:

(i) Arrest is necessary to enable the *identity* of the person to be ascertained. This will be either the suspect's name (s 24(5)(a)) or address (s 24(5)(b)). This reason will arise when an officer does not know or cannot readily ascertain this information, or when an officer has reasonable grounds for doubting whether the information supplied is accurate, for example when an officer believes a false name or address has been given.

(ii) Arrest is necessary to prevent the person in question *causing or suffering physical injury*; *causing loss of or damage to property*; committing an offence against public decency; or causing an unlawful obstruction of the highway (s 24(5)(c)). In short,

53 [2003] EWCA Civ 1844.

54 *Ibid* [41].

55 [2004] EWCA Civ 1579.

56 *Ibid* [56].

57 See the case of *Buckley v Chief Officer of Thames Valley Police* [2009] EWCA Civ 356 for another example case demonstrating the manner in which reasonable suspicion should be established by officers.

it is necessary to prevent a suspect committing these particular offences, which will generally be of an urgent and harmful nature.

(iii) Arrest is necessary to *protect* a child or other vulnerable person from the person in question (s 24(5)(d)).

(iv) Arrest is necessary to allow the prompt and effective investigation of the offence or of the conduct of the person in question (s 24(5)(e)). This is the broadest reason, granting a particularly wide power to the police to interpret an arrest as necessary.

(v) Arrest is necessary to prevent any prosecution for the offence from being hindered by the *disappearance* of the person in question (s 24(5)(f)). That is, it is believed that the individual will flee to evade arrest and prosecution.

In summary, if an officer has objectively based grounds for believing that, for any of these reasons, they need to arrest the suspect, then this condition will be satisfied. It is therefore important to examine how these provisions have been interpreted, particularly the 'prompt and effective investigation' reason.

Code G provides some guidance on the interpretation of the necessity reasons in paras 2.4–2.9. It opens by strongly emphasising that arrest is only exercisable when there are reasonable grounds for believing it is necessary – underlining the importance of this condition.[58] Paragraph 2.6 outlines that in assessing whether it is necessary to arrest a person, an officer must 'examine and justify the reason or reasons why a person needs to be arrested'. This emphasises the importance of the police carefully weighing up whether an arrest is needed – or whether it is simply the most convenient (or possibly desirable) action for the officer to take. Importantly, an officer must be able to justify it – otherwise the arrest may be open to challenge. Paragraph 2.7 underlines that the reasons listed in s 24 are exhaustive (ie they are the only reasons for which an arrest can be considered necessary). However, it also points out that interpreting those reasons is 'a matter of operational discretion of individual officers'.[59] This provides a wide power of interpretation to officers, designed to ensure that they have the flexibility to adapt decision-making to varied situations. Nonetheless, they must go through a process of analysing and justifying the necessity of an arrest. Paragraph 2.8 provides some useful guidance for officers considering which circumstances might make an arrest necessary, suggesting that the following might all be relevant considerations (the last of which is particularly broad):

- the situation of the victim;
- the nature of the offence;
- the circumstances of the suspect; and
- the needs of the investigative process.

Paragraph 2.9 provides guidance on each of the 'reasons' listed in s 24 – this will not be examined in detail here, although it is worth noting that extensive description and detail is dedicated to the 'prompt and effective' investigation reason – the most wide and controversial one.

In interpreting necessity, the courts have attempted to refrain from defining it too restrictively. In *Richardson*, the court said, 'Necessity is an ordinary English word which can be applied without paraphrase.'[60] As with reasonable suspicion, the courts have

58 Code G.

59 *Ibid.*

60 [2011] 2 Cr App R 1, 62.

considered how to assess whether the 'necessity' condition has been satisfied. In *Graham v West Mercia Constabulary*, the court laid down the primary test:[61]

> The test is, did the arresting officer actually believe that it was necessary to arrest the person in question for one of the reasons set out in s. 24(5), and, if so, did he or she have reasonable grounds for that belief?[62]

As such, like reasonable suspicion, this is a mixed subjective/objective test. In satisfying the subjective test – that is, did the officer actually believe it was necessary – the courts have ruled that an officer must assess their options other than arrest. The question is, to what extent? In *Re Alexander*, Lord Justice Kerr said:[63]

> It is necessary that [the officer] make some evaluation of the feasibility of achieving the object of the arrest by some alternative means, such as inviting the suspect to attend for interview.[64]

Again, this suggests that arrest should be a power of last resort, used only when it is needed. An officer should therefore examine whether they have other choices. This analysis is also supported by Code G, which states at para 1.3: 'officers exercising the power should consider if the necessary objectives can be met by other, less intrusive means.' However, the courts have put a limitation on this requirement: an officer does not need to be satisfied that there is no viable alternative to arrest. In *Hayes*, a police officer investigating an assault contacted the suspect by telephone and arranged to meet him; the suspect was then arrested.[65] The assault claim was thereafter withdrawn and the suspect released without charge. The suspect claimed that the officer had not considered alternatives to arrest. The court concluded, relying on *Re Alexander*, that if an officer believed that an arrest was the 'practical and sensible option' then this would be enough to deem it necessary. The court added:

> To require of a policeman that he pass through particular thought processes each time he considers an arrest, and in all circumstances no matter what urgency or danger may attend the decision, and to subject that decision to the test of whether he has considered every material matter and excluded every immaterial matter, is to impose an unrealistic and unattainable burden. Nor is it necessary.[66]

This, therefore, suggests that arrest is not a last resort; an officer needs to make some assessment of alternatives to arrest, but it does not have to be the only option to be deemed 'necessary'. If arrest is the most practical and sensible option, it will satisfy the subjective limb of the necessity test. This appears to be a more crime control-oriented approach, in that it allows for a fairly flexible interpretation of when an arrest will be necessary. It is not particularly restrictive. That being said, recent case law suggests that necessity is not 'envisaged as a synonym for "desirable" or "convenient"'[67] – in short, the fact that it might be easier for an officer to arrest the suspect than to take another course of action will not be enough to make that arrest 'necessary'. Indeed, in the case of *TL*, the court illustrated the unnecessary use of arrest in that case:

---

61 [2011] EWHC 4 (QB).
62 *Ibid* [56].
63 [2009] NIQB 20.
64 *Ibid* [16].
65 [2012] 1 WLR 517.
66 *Ibid* [40].
67 *R (TL) v Chief Constable of Surrey Police* [2017] 1 WLR 2047, [40].

> The claimant was, and is, of good character and there is no evidence that he previously breached any assurance that he had given, or had been imposed on him. Further, there was considerable delay in the investigation of this case … The police log does not give a picture of any particular haste or urgency; or, of any concern that unless appropriate action was taken soon, [the claimant] would be at unacceptable risk.[68]
>
> It is clear from entries in the log that the decision to impose bail conditions was made on general policy grounds rather than the particular circumstances of this claimant.[69]

A particularly poor example of an 'unnecessary but convenient' arrest occurred in the case of *ST v CC of Nottinghamshire Police*.[70] This involved the arrest of a child at 5.30 am for a minor alleged offence; this was done on the basis of an 'arrestogram'– a message from another department asking officers to arrest a suspect. In reviewing the case, the High Court concluded that this had been done 'largely if not solely for … [the requesting] officer's convenience'.[71] Indeed, the Court asserted that:

> The very concept of an 'arrestogram' exposed any arresting officer to the risk that an arrest may be unlawful as the officer simply did not know enough about the offence and/or the offender.[72]

As for the objective limb, the question is whether an officer had reasonable grounds for their belief in arrest being necessary. In this regard, the courts have been fairly robust and favoured a due process approach, interpreting 'reasonable grounds' quite restrictively. In *Lord Hanningfield v Chief Constable of Essex*, the suspect (having been released from prison for false accounting) was arrested at home by police officers.[73] Whilst the police may well have subjectively believed that it was necessary to arrest him, it was argued that there were no reasonable grounds for this belief. The police argued that the suspect might attempt to destroy or conceal evidence relating to ongoing investigations. In response, the court said:

> There were simply no solid grounds to suppose that he would suddenly start to hide or destroy evidence, or that he would make inappropriate contacts. There was only the theoretical possibility that he might do so.[74]

This therefore suggests that reasonable grounds for belief in the necessity of an arrest must be based on 'solid' reasons rather than 'theoretical' possibilities. In deciding whether an arrest is objectively necessary, this places an emphasis on the need for tangible evidence or information, rather than speculation or mere possibility. This arguably represents a due process-oriented interpretation of necessity, prioritising individual liberty over the detection and prevention of crime.

3.4 Ancillary powers and duties

We shall now briefly consider some of the ancillary powers and duties that accompany the power of arrest under s 24 of PACE 1984. 'Ancillary' relates to any power that an

68 *Ibid* [54].

69 *Ibid.* See also *Commission of Metropolis v MR* [2019] EWHC 888 (QB).

70 [2022] EWHC 1280 (QB).

71 *Ibid* [15].

72 *Ibid* [108].

73 [2013] EWHC 243 (QB).

74 *Ibid* [29].

officer may use when effecting an arrest or any duty which an officer must perform when arresting someone. The primary ancillary power relating to the s 24 power of arrest is 'reasonable force', under s 117 of PACE 1984. The main issue raised by this provision is what kind of force (being some form of physical manipulation of a suspect) will be deemed 'reasonable'. There is a variety of case law on this point, which will not be examined in detail here. To summarise, a court must take into account all the circumstances, including:

- the nature and degree of the force used;
- the gravity of the offence;
- the harm that would result from the use of force;
- the possibility of arresting the suspect by other means.

There are also a number of ancillary duties that must be performed by an officer for an arrest to be lawful. Under s 28, an arrest will be unlawful unless the suspect is informed that they are under arrest at the time of the arrest, or as soon as is practicable after the arrest. They must also be informed of the grounds for the arrest (even if they are obvious). Clearly, the key sources of contention here are what 'informed' means and whether communication was 'as soon as practicable after' the arrest. The test for what being 'informed' means was outlined in *Taylor v Chief Constable of Thames Valley Police*, in which the court stated that an officer must use simple, non-technical language that an ordinary person can understand; and tell the suspect the essential legal and factual grounds.[75] The interpretation of 'as soon as is practicable after the arrest' will vary from case to case and will require an assessment of the surrounding circumstances.

3.4.1 The caution

Additionally, a suspect must normally be cautioned by an officer according to para 10.4 of PACE Code C, unless it is impracticable to do so by reason of the suspect's condition or behaviour at the time, or if they have already been cautioned prior to arrest in relation to questioning about an offence or suspected offence. Many people will be familiar with the caution and its terms from TV and film. The official wording used in England and Wales is set out in para 10.5 of Code C:

> You do not have to say anything. But it may harm your defence if you do not mention when questioned something which you later rely on in Court. Anything you do say may be given in evidence.

The caution makes clear that all persons arrested for a suspected offence have a basic right to silence (that is, 'you do not have to say anything'). This therefore emphasises individual rights, such as the presumption of innocence and the prosecution burden of proof – in short, a due process safeguard. However, this is followed by an important caveat; exercising the right to silence may 'harm' a suspect's defence if they later rely on something they did not mention during questioning by the police. If a suspect withholds information from the police and later uses it in court, this may infer guilt (this will be covered in more depth in **Chapter 4**). This element of the caution therefore emphasises a crime control approach – that is, suspects cannot use silence to frustrate an investigation or hide information. This aspect of the caution therefore places the detection and investigation of crime ahead of individual rights.

75 [2004] 1 WLR 3155.

3.5 Research on the power of arrest

Academic commentators argue that police powers of arrest can be used in a 'wide spectrum of circumstances'.[76] Welsh et al assert that 'imprecision' in the legal regulation of the power means that it operates as a set of 'enabling rules' – that is, it allows the police to arrest in a broad range of circumstances and exercise discretion relatively freely.[77] The legal power 'enables' rather than restricts the ability to arrest, which one would consider to be the primary objective of regulation.

Kemp found that the widening of the power of arrest in 2005 (see above) and the continued influence of targets had driven arrests for minor offences.[78] These types of arrest were 'easy hits' (ie straightforward ways of fulfilling targets) and were enabled by wide and flexible powers. Welsh et al draw on wider research to identify a number of factors which they consider to influence the use of arrest.[79] The first is the perceived need of the police to keep order. Reiner argues that maintenance of public order has been the prime concern of the police since it was established in the early 19th century.[80] The ability to do so derives from the moral and legal authority of the police – in short, order is maintained because people believe that the police can and will enforce it. Where this authority is challenged (for example, the London riots of 2011 and the variety of protests and demonstrations in recent years, including those related to the Black Lives Matter movement, the Covid-19 pandemic, Brexit, and the climate crisis), the police seek to control such challenges as quickly as possible so as to protect this perception of authority. For example, in 2022, several journalists were arrested on suspicion of conspiracy whilst covering a controversial 'Just Stop Oil' protest; after being challenged, the arrests were judged to be without justification, disproportionate and unnecessary. Furthermore, arrests were ordered by senior officers as part of a blanket enforcement response to protests – rather than being carefully considered on a case-by-case basis by the arresting officers.[81]

Some research suggests that the police use arrest as a sort of 'parenting' tool – that is, to punish individuals in the same manner as an adult would punish a child, in order to stop others copying or joining in.[82] Another factor is the need to enforce respect for the police. This is linked to the 'order' factor but focuses on the attitude of individual suspects towards the police. Welsh et al argue that arrests for 'contempt of cop' (such as swearing, lack of cooperation, or hostility) are common.[83] They also argue that the attitude of a suspect may justify an arrest in the absence of information such as previous convictions.[84] Brown and Ellis argue that the police will not tolerate disrespect or abuse from suspects because it will encourage such behaviour in the future.[85] A study by Piliavin and Briar suggested that the more uncooperative a suspect was, the more likely

76 Welsh, L, Skinns, L and Sanders, A, *Sanders & Young's Criminal Justice* (OUP, 2021).

77 *Ibid.*

78 Kemp, V, 'PACE, performance targets and legal protections' (2014) *Crim LR*(4).

79 Welsh et al (n 76).

80 Reiner, R, *The Politics of the Police* (OUP, 2010), Ch 5.

81 Gayle, D, 'Senior officers ordered "unlawful" arrests of journalists at Just Stop Oil protests' (*Guardian*, 23 November 2022): www.theguardian.com/media/2022/nov/23/senior-officers-ordered-unlawful-arrests-of-journalists-at-just-stop-oil-protests (accessed 24 March 2023).

82 McConville, M, Sanders, A and Leng, R, *The Case for the Prosecution* (Routledge, 1991),25.

83 Welsh et al (n 76).

84 *Ibid.*

85 Brown, D and Ellis, T, 'Policing Low Level Disorder: Police Use of Section 5 of the Public Order Act 1986' (Home Office, 1994), 42.

they were to be arrested – regardless of the offence.[86] The working rule of targeting those with a poor attitude towards the police therefore leads to a disproportionate focus on groups who dislike or distrust the police (for example, young, socially marginalised males – see **Chapter 2** on racial discrimination in stop and search).

Suspiciousness and previous convictions are two important factors in influencing the use of arrest. Previous convictions can be used as a reference tool by the police at the start of an investigation. Someone with a history of a particular type of offending may, for example, be arrested as a starting point for intelligence gathering rather than with the end-goal of prosecution. Previous convictions can also be used for pre-emptive investigation (such as surveillance) prior to an arrest. As such, those with previous convictions are more likely to be targeted for arrest, whether they have committed an offence or not.[87] Additionally, those who display uncooperative attitudes or who seem suspicious in terms of behaviour or appearance may be more likely to be targeted for arrest – this concept is of course open to very wide interpretation and most certainly does not accord with legislative criteria.

The role of the victim of a crime may also be an important factor in the use of arrest. The law provides no rights for victims in relation to the use of arrest – only that their views may be taken into account. But if the victim desires arrest, and their evidence is vital, this may make arrest more likely. Police officers can, of course, influence the desires of the victim who will often rely on them for advice; as such, if an officer wishes to arrest a suspect, they may be able to convince the victim to support this course of action.[88] The status of a victim may also be important – for example, the rich or powerful who may be able to cause 'trouble' for the police. For those of low status, Kemp et al found that victims' views were ignored, and arrest used if it suited the police.[89]

Organisational factors may also influence how the police exercise the power of arrest. Public policy priorities – often linked to current events – may determine the likelihood of arrests for certain types of offences. For example, if knife crime or drug dealing have generated moral panic, then the police may be more likely to arrest individuals for such offences.[90] For example, as part of Operation Sceptre (aimed at tackling knife crime), police forces across England and Wales arrested 1,733 people in one week during September 2019;[91] similarly, in March 2020, the MPS made 800 arrests in one week.[92] The workload of the police is also important. If the police have too much to do, they are less likely to arrest; conversely, if they have too little to do, they are more likely to arrest. The target-driven culture of the police was cited as a factor by Maguire and Norris (and more recently Kemp) in driving arrest and detection rates.[93]

86 Piliavin, I and Briar, S, 'Police Encounters with Juveniles' (1964) 70 *American Journal of Sociology*; see also Southgate, P, 'Police-Public Encounters' (Home Office, 1986).

87 Welsh et al (n 76).

88 *Ibid* 168.

89 Kemp, C, Norris, C and Fielding, N, 'Legal Manoeuvres in Police Handling of Disputes' in D Farrington and S Walklate (eds), *Offenders and Victims, Theory and Policy* (British Society of Criminology, 1992), 73.

90 See **Chapter 2** for discussion of the knife crime 'epidemic' and the response of the police to this.

91 National Police Chiefs' Council, 'More than 1,700 arrested in targeted knife crime action' (1 November 2019): https://news.npcc.police.uk/releases/more-than-1-700-arrested-in-targeted-knife-crime-action (accessed 6 May 2020).

92 MPS, 'More than 800 arrests during Met's Operation Sceptre week' (31 March 2020): http://news.met.police.uk/news/more-than-800-arrests-during-mets-operation-sceptre-week-398868 (accessed 6 May 2020).

93 Maguire, M and Norris, C, 'The Conduct and Supervision of Criminal Investigations' (HMSO, 1992), 87; Kemp (n 78).

Finally, race and social class appear to influence the use of arrest. It is argued that the police are more likely to arrest for offences committed by disadvantaged sections of society, leading to disproportionate focus on certain minority and class groups. Arrest of ethnic minority individuals is disproportionately high and has been for many years, though the disparity is not as stark as for stop and search.[94] For example, in 2021/22, black people were twice as likely to be arrested than white people, and whilst arrest rates have decreased across all ethnic groups, the reduction has been largest amongst white people.[95] If black people were twice as likely to commit crime, such figures might be defensible. Yet, 'empirical analysis of self-reported offending suggests minority groups are less likely to commit crime',[96] highlighting an incongruity: arrest appears to be disproportionately targeted at those who are, statistically, less likely to commit crime. Thus, this suggests a gap between the theoretical purpose of arrest (investigating likely crime) and its actual day-to-day use (and what drives it). In addition to ethnic minority groups, the unemployed, low paid and working class are also much more likely to be arrested.[97]

Considering all of these factors, Welsh et al conclude that, in practice, arrest has a strong crime control emphasis, focusing on detecting and preventing crime regardless of the rights (or indeed innocence) of large numbers of arrested individuals.[98] They also question the legality of arrests influenced by such factors. In *McVeigh*, the European Commission of Human Rights stated:[99]

> Arrest ... must be for the purpose of securing ... [the] fulfilment [of an obligation prescribed by law] and not, for instance, punitive in character.[100]

In short, this implies that many of the factors outlined above are likely to be in breach of the law, and they certainly do not comply with the requirements of regulations like Code G. It must be questioned whether the conditions of reasonable suspicion and necessity are fulfilled when the aforementioned factors motivate the use of arrest, rather than objective intelligence or information. Indeed, a 2018 study by Pearson et al appears to demonstrate the ineffective nature of the necessity safeguard in practice.[101] They found that officers tended to have an 'all or nothing' approach to arrest – that is, the suspect needed to be arrested or released – with not even 'fleeting' consideration given to alternatives (as suggested by the case law).[102] Despite being more than a decade on from the introduction of the necessity requirement, they argued

94 See **Chapter 2**.

95 Home Office, 'Update to stop and search and arrests statistics using 2021 Census estimates' (2 March 2023): www.gov.uk/government/statistics/update-to-stop-and-search-and-arrests-statistics-using-2021-census-estimates (accessed 23 March 2023).

96 Uhrig, N, 'Black, Asian and Minority Ethnic disproportionality in the Criminal Justice System in England and Wales' (Ministry of Justice, 2016), 12: https://assets.publishing.service.gov.uk/government/uploads/system/uploads/attachment_data/file/639261/bame-disproportionality-in-the-cjs.pdf (accessed 6 May 2020).

97 See Choongh, C, 'Policing the Dross: A Social Disciplinary Model of Policing' (1998) 38 *Brit J of Crim* (4); and McAra, L and McVie, S, 'The usual suspects? Street-life, young people and the police' (2005) 5 *Criminology & Criminal Justice* (1). For an offence-specific example, see Daly, M, 'Britain's Upper Classes are Less Likely to be Busted for Drugs' (*Vice*, 22 June 2014): https://news.vice.com/article/britains-upper-classes-are-less-likely-to-be-busted-for-drugs (accessed 6 May 2020).

98 Welsh et al (n 76).

99 (1983) 5 EHRR 71.

100 *Ibid* [172].

101 Pearson, G, Rowe, M, and Turner, L, 'Policy, Practicalities, and PACE s. 24: The Subsuming of the Necessity Criteria in Arrest Decision Making by Frontline Police Officers' (2018) 45 *J of Law & Soc* (2).

102 *Ibid* 299.

that 'confusion amongst officers as to what establishes a necessary and lawful arrest remains'.[103] Overall, they concluded that 'reasons for arrest and arrest necessity are subsumed by other concerns and pressures which have a far greater influence on whether suspects will find themselves taken into custody'.[104] Ultimately, they questioned (like other commentators) 'the extent to which the law can regulate the police'.[105]

3.6 Summary

- Arrest is widely used but has been in decline for some years; arrest is used for only a portion of all criminal offences (often for violence, theft and sexual offences).
- An arrest involves at least some form of deprivation of a suspect's liberty.
- Whether that deprivation is an arrest may depend on the context/intention of the arresting officer.
- The courts have diverged on how 'arrest' is to be defined, leading to confusion.
- The primary police power of arrest, contained in s 24 of PACE 1984, allows an officer to arrest anyone, for any offence, without a warrant.
- This is restricted by two key safeguards – the requirement of reasonable grounds for suspicion and the requirement that the arrest be necessary.
- The courts appear to have diluted the strength of these safeguards – there is a low threshold to satisfy reasonable suspicion, and arrest can often be justified as necessary.
- An officer can use reasonable force to effect an arrest; they must tell a suspect that they are under arrest and read the caution, prescribed by Code C.
- Research evidence suggests that the legislative power is so wide that other factors – in the form of 'working rules' – can and do influence the use of arrest by the police.

103 *Ibid* 283.
104 *Ibid* 290.
105 *Ibid* 291. Also see, McConville (n 82), 182–84.

chapter 4

In Police Custody (1): Detention and Charging

4.1 Introduction

Once a person is arrested on suspicion of an offence, they will normally be immediately taken to a police station (referred to as 'custody centres' in recent years) so that an investigation into any alleged offences can proceed. This will generally, though not always, involve a suspect being detained and interrogated by the police. Their liberty is, in effect, suspended – perhaps for a lengthy period. The Secret Barrister has previously commented on the 'inestimable … impact of losing your liberty on remand':[1]

> Everything you have built over the course of your lifetime – your relationships, your family, your employment, your income, your home – is suddenly, without notice, snatched away from you and placed on a high shelf beyond your reach … Detention in remand effectively starts the moment you are arrested … From that moment, your freedom is the property of the state. You can be detained at the police station overnight, taken to court from the police cells and then formally remanded until trial. It could be months, if not years, before you are returned to normality.[2]

As such, deprivations of liberty (as discussed in **Chapters 2 and 3**) may be much more than temporary. The police station is key to this, acting as a hub for the filtering, facilitation and progression of cases; here, it will be determined whether unconvicted people should be:

- detained until they appear at a court;
- formally accused of offences;
- released with conditions;
- interviewed about allegations.

This is not to mention being subject to searches; having possessions confiscated; and having access to food, visitors and information controlled by the police (areas which we will not cover in this book). The experience of detention can potentially be extremely distressing, confusing and intimidating for those accused of criminal offences. How this is regulated is of great importance and will be examined in the next two chapters: first (in **Chapter 4**) by considering how detention and charging are regulated, and secondly (in **Chapter 5**) by considering the right of a detained person to access legal advice and the power of the police to interrogate crime suspects.

4.2 History and development

PACE 1984 fundamentally altered the regulation of criminal investigations; prior to this, the framework of regulation in this area was mainly non-statutory and, as such, far

1 The Secret Barrister, *Stories of the Law and How It's Broken* (Macmillan, 2018), 92.

2 *Ibid* 93.

less robust. The primary source of regulation applicable to police investigations were the Judges' Rules, first issued by the senior judiciary in 1912.[3] Prior to this, there was a lack of clarity on the legal boundary between police powers and the individual rights of citizens subject to those powers. Not only did this create a risk of the police abusing those powers, but it led to inconsistent investigation practices by different police forces. The Judges' Rules provided guidance for the police on correct investigative procedures, primarily detention and the questioning of suspects. The aim was to reduce divergent practice, clarify individuals' rights, ensure fair process and reduce the scope for abuse of powers. However, the Rules were greatly undermined by their lack of statutory force.[4]

As such, to call them rules was misleading; they served merely as guides for practice, which due to their limited enforceability were frequently ignored by the police. A major example of this was the Maxwell Confait case.[5] The defendants (all teenagers) were convicted of strangling Confait and setting fire to his house; the convictions were based entirely on confessions, with no other evidence. Fresh evidence emerged which conflicted with the confessions, the case was referred to the Court of Appeal by the Home Secretary, and the convictions were quashed. Whilst the Court did not examine how the confessions were obtained in detail, it did comment that the defendants were 'very suggestible and quite unreliable … [and] of subnormal intelligence'.[6] Clearly, the Rules had not provided adequate protection. In response to such miscarriages of justice (see **Chapter 14**), the Royal Commission on Criminal Procedure (the Philips Commission) was established in 1978. Among its various conclusions regarding defects in the regulation of criminal investigations, it identified the 'voluntary' nature of the Judges' Rules as a serious problem in need of reform.[7] A result of the Commission's findings was PACE 1984, which, for the first time, provided a firm legislative footing for the regulation of detention and questioning of suspects in police custody, rather than the essentially informal and unenforceable Judges' Rules. It introduced major changes, including:

- custody officers: police officers charged with the care and welfare of suspects in custody;
- the regulation of decisions about detention in police custody;
- custody records;
- maximum periods of detention, and reviews of detention; and
- access to legal advice for suspects in police stations.

4.3 Custody officers

Under s 30 of PACE 1984, an arrested person 'must be taken by a constable to a police station as soon as practicable after the arrest'. This is subject to the power of individual officers to grant 'street bail' (s 30A), a discretionary power to release a suspect on bail 'there and then', on the condition that they attend at a police station at a later time. On arrival at a police station, suspects must be brought before a custody officer (CO). A

3 For a summary of the Rules, see St Johnston, T, 'Judges' Rules and Police Interrogation in England Today' (1966) 57 *J of Crim L & Criminol* 1; these were gradually added to by both the judiciary and the executive (Home Office, 'Judges' rules and administrative directions to the police', Home Office Circular No 89/1978 (HMSO, 1978)).

4 See *Voisin* [1918] 1 KB 531.

5 *Lattimore, Salih and Leighton* (1976) 62 Cr App R 53.

6 *Ibid* 62.

7 Philips, C, 'Royal Commission on Criminal Procedure' (The Philips Commission) (HMSO, 1981), [4.70].

CO must be appointed at each 'designated' police station (that is, those that hold suspects in custody) and must be at least of the rank of sergeant (in short, reasonably experienced).[8] The CO, or officers acting in their place should one not be available, cannot be directly involved with the investigation of the suspect or the alleged offence in question.[9] This, importantly, is designed to introduce some independence into custody decision-making, placing the CO as an 'independent filter' in the detention of suspects.[10] This distance between custody and investigation decisions is essential, as it is designed to prevent custody being used as a 'tool' in investigating offences (for example, using the threat of detention to make suspects more compliant). The CO has a duty to ensure that suspects are treated in accordance with PACE 1984 and its attendant Codes of Practice, and must ensure that the custody record is completed.[11] As such, the CO plays a role in ensuring that the law and suspects' rights are respected – a clear due process protection. Crucially, the CO has responsibility for deciding whether to detain a suspect and whether there is sufficient evidence to charge them with an offence.[12] If a suspect is charged, the CO also decides whether to grant bail (that is, whether the suspect is suitable for release from detention).[13] As such, the CO plays a vital role in the early stages of the process.

4.4 Decisions about detention

The decision to detain a suspect in police custody is significant: it is a major suspension of individual liberty prior to any charge or conviction, which the police must justify. Detention gives rise to a number of obligations on the police, and it activates safeguards for suspects. Detention prior to charge primarily allows time for further investigation of an offence by officers – but within limits. It is underpinned by a key principle outlined by the Philips Commission, also applicable to arrest: that detention should only be used when 'necessary':[14]

> [T]he custody officer ... shall determine whether he has before him sufficient evidence to charge that person with the offence for which he was arrested and may detain him at the police station for such period as is necessary to enable him to do so.

There are therefore two key concepts in this process:

(a) There must be 'sufficient evidence' to charge a suspect with an offence.
(b) Detention must only be for as long as is 'necessary' to come to a charging decision.

If the suspect can be charged ...

Should the CO decide that there is sufficient evidence to charge, s 37(7) of PACE 1984 dictates that one of the following must happen:

- The suspect shall be released without charge and on bail or kept in police detention, for the purpose of enabling the Crown Prosecution Service (CPS) to make a charging decision.[15]

---

8 PACE 1984, s36(3).

9 *Ibid* s 36(5).

10 *Al-Fayed v Commissioner of Police of the Metropolis (No 3)* [2004] EWCA Civ 1579, [101].

11 PACE 1984, s 39(1).

12 *Ibid* s 37.

13 *Ibid* s 38.

14 *Ibid* s 37(1).

15 For some offences, a charging decision can only be made by a Crown prosecutor. See **4.11** below.

- The suspect shall be released without charge and without bail unless the pre-conditions for bail are satisfied (see below).
- The suspect shall be released without charge and on bail if the pre-conditions are satisfied but not in order to enable the CPS to make a charging decision (this will be used to allow the police (that is, the CO) to make a charging decision).
- The suspect shall be charged.

Therefore, the first issue to be determined is whether there is sufficient evidence to charge a suspect with an offence.

If the suspect cannot be charged ...

Section 37(2) of PACE states:

> If ... the custody officer ('C') determines that C does not have such evidence before C, and ... the pre-conditions for bail are satisfied ... the person arrested must be released on bail.

The aforementioned pre-conditions are outlined under s 50A(1) – specifically, the CO must be 'satisfied that releasing the person on bail is necessary and proportionate in all the circumstances' having 'considered any representations made by the [suspect] or [the suspect's] legal representative'. The factors the CO should consider when determining whether it is 'necessary and proportionate' include the need to secure the suspect's surrender to custody; the need to prevent offending; and the need to safeguard victims.[16] If these pre-conditions are not met, the suspect must be released without bail. Release either with or without bail is subject to s 37(3): this allows the CO to instead detain a suspect without charge:

> If the custody officer has reasonable grounds for believing that the person's detention without being charged is necessary to secure or preserve evidence relating to an offence for which the person is under arrest or to obtain such evidence by questioning the person, he may authorise the person arrested to be kept in police detention.

In summary:

- When the CO does not believe there is sufficient evidence to charge, there are two basic options: release or detain.
- Unless there are reasonable grounds for believing it necessary to detain a suspect, a suspect will be released: with or without bail.[17]
- When detention is necessary, it is justified either to protect existing evidence or obtain further evidence from the suspect; it is thus oriented towards proceeding with an investigation.

4.5 Release from police custody on bail

The basic concept of bail involves the release of a suspect from police custody, subject to the requirement to attend at the police station or to appear at court at an appointed time in the future. There are three types of police bail, which occur at different stages of the pre-court process and are decided by different people:

16 PACE 1984, s 50A(2).

17 A person released without bail may be 'released under investigation' – see **4.5.2** below.

- Bail following arrest but before arrival at the police station (known as 'street bail'). This will be determined by the arresting officer.[18]
- Bail without charge from the police station. This is decided by the CO. Note that this is called 'without' rather than 'before' charge; 'before' charge would be to assume that a suspect will eventually be charged (which is not necessarily the case).
- Bail following charge. This is also decided by the CO.

4.5.1 Bail without charge

Once a suspect arrives at the police station, the CO adopts responsibility for making decisions about bail (outlined in various sections of Part IV of PACE 1984). The first decision regarding bail will relate to releasing a suspect without charging them – that is, when the police are 'not in a position, or don't want, to charge a person they have arrested'.[19] When the aforementioned pre-conditions for bail are met, if the CO decides to release on bail without charge, this may be without any conditions beyond attending at a police station or court at a later date. However, in some circumstances, further conditions may be attached. The CO has the 'normal powers to impose conditions' on bail without charge, set out in the Bail Act (BA) 1976.[20] Essentially, the CO has the same powers as a court in making bail subject to requirements (see **Chapter 10**). Under s 3(6) of the BA 1976, one or more conditions can be attached to ensure that the person released:

- attends at the police station when required;
- does not commit any offences;
- does not interfere with witnesses/obstruct the investigation.

Conditions could include a curfew; electronic monitoring; being banned from contacting certain people; exclusion from a geographical area; confiscation of a passport; and frequent reporting to a police station.[21] In short, conditions can be used to regulate a person's behaviour when they have been released, whilst the police or CPS decide whether or not to charge them with an offence. A person can be arrested for breach of bail conditions or failing to attend a police station when required;[22] furthermore, a person commits an offence if they fail to attend after release on pre-charge bail.[23] As such, the consequences of breaching bail conditions or failing to attend are signficant; bail therefore has a coercive aspect to it.

Until 2017, bail without charge could be used relatively freely by the police. Of particular concern was the fact that there was no time limit on a person's release on

18 PACE 1984, s 30A; see Cape, E and Edwards, R, 'Police Bail without Charge: The Human Rights Implications' (2010) 69 *Cambridge Law Journal* (3).

19 Cape, E, 'Police bail. A right old mess' (Centre for Criminal Justice Studies, 30 May 2017): www.crimeandjustice.org.uk/resources/police-bail-right-old-mess (accessed 7 May 2020).

20 PACE 1984, s 47(1A).

21 Beyond electronic monitoring (under s 3(6ZAA)), the BA 1976 does not specify what conditions can be imposed, beyond saying that they must be 'necessary' to ensure the aims summarised above. For more on the use of conditions (including examples), see Hucklesby, A, 'Pre-charge bail and release under investigation (RUI): an urgent case for reform' (2021) *Crim LR* 2; and Cape, E and Smith, T, 'The Practice of Pre-trial Detention in England and Wales' (University of the West of England, 2016): www.fairtrials.org/wp- content/uploads/Country-Report-England-and-Wales-MASTER-Final-PRINT.pdf (accessed 7 May 2020).

22 PACE 1984, s 46A(1) and (1A).

23 BA 1976, s 6.

bail. Therefore, persons who had not been charged with any offence could potentially be subjected to coercive conditions for as long the police liked, with the potential for no action ever to be taken. This represented a concerning and possibly excessive interference with the right to liberty under Article 5 of the European Convention on Human Rights (ECHR) and arguably caused significant distress and embarrassment to some persons bailed for lengthy periods, particularly if the original allegations were highly sensitive and if no charge was ever brought.[24]

Statistics and research appeared to demonstrate that significant problems existed in the use of bail without charge by the police.

Time period	Source	Total released on bail without charge	Total released on bail without charge for 6 months or more
12 months from April 2013	College of Policing[25]	Approx. 400,000 (across all police forces)	24,000 (6%)
Snapshot from May 2013	Home Office (via BBC Freedom of Information request)[26]	57,428 (across 34 police forces)	3,172 (6%)
Snapshot from May 2014	MPS[27]	18,898 (MPS area only)	4,630 (25%)

The College of Policing also stated in 2016 that around half of the roughly 80,000 people on pre-charge bail at any one time were never charged.[28] These are very substantial numbers of people who may have been subject to conditions, and essentially placed 'under suspicion', weighed down with the possibility of an investigation and charge, with no guarantee of any conclusion. The Home Office did not (and, at the time of writing, still does not) have data on how conditions were used, what conditions were

24 The broadcaster and journalist, Paul Gambaccini, provides a high-profile example – he was bailed without charge for 11 months in relation to allegations of historical sex abuse and was never prosecuted – see Home Affairs Committee, Oral evidence: Police bail (HC 962, 3 March 2015): http://data.parliament.uk/writtenevidence/committeeevidence.svc/evidencedocument/home-affairs-committee/police-bail/oral/18431.html (accessed 7 May 2020).

25 As part of a Home Office consultation on pre-charge bail, the College of Policing provided data from a sample of 12 police forces which was 'scaled up' to give a national picture (Home Office, 'Pre-Charge Bail: Summary of Consultation Responses and Proposals for Legislation' (March 2015), 25): https://assets.publishing.service.gov.uk/government/uploads/system/uploads/attachment_data/file/418226/150323_Pre-Charge_Bail_-_Responses__Proposals.pdf (accessed 7 May 2020). Also see Cape, E, 'What if police bail was abolished?' (Howard League for Penal Reform, 2015), 10: https://howardleague.org/wp-content/uploads/2016/03/What-if-police-bail-was-abolished-web.pdf (accessed 5 May 2020).

26 Harmes, L, 'Law Society calls for 28-day limit on police bail' (*BBC News*, 28 May 2013): www.bbc.co.uk/news/uk-22624648 (accessed 7 May 2020).

27 Cape (n 19).

28 College of Policing, 'Pre-charge bail: The possible implications of research' (October 2016), 2: www.college.police.uk/News/College-news/Documents/College_of_Policing_Pre-charge_Bail_Briefing.pdf (accessed 7 May 2020).

imposed, and what proportion of those placed on bail were eventually charged. As such, there has been and continues to be a lack of critical information on the use of bail without charge. Between 2011 and 2013, Hucklesby conducted research with two police forces, finding that nearly 50% of those bailed were not prosecuted; that conditions were imposed on two-thirds of people bailed; and that police officers were often able to foresee that there would be no charge when bailing a person – but did so anyway.[29]

As a result of the extensive criticism of bail without charge, the law was changed in 2017.[30] The Policing and Crime Act (PCA) 2017 represented the biggest shake-up of police bail in three decades, amending PACE 1984 extensively. It introduced a presumption of release *without* bail for all suspects (unless the discussed pre-conditions for bail were satisfied); limited a person's initial release on bail without charge to 28 days in standard cases; and required further extensions of bail to be authorised by a senior officer (by up to three months). These changes imposed significant limitations on the use of bail without charge, requiring the police to repeatedly consider whether or not to use it, as well as introducing an element of judicial scrutiny (if seeking an extension beyond three months). Undoubtedly, the purpose of the legislation was to substantially reduce the (ab)use of this police power, particularly in terms of long, unsupervised periods of bail ending with no charge; the police, it was believed, would be incentivised to decide upon charge or, alternatively, seek an extension within the timeframe imposed by legislation. Bail without charge, as predicted, reduced dramatically.[31] Yet, as with many well-intentioned reforms, these changes had unanticipated consequences which have created problems of equal seriousness for suspects, defence lawyers, the police, and complainants of crime[32] – instead of release on bail, a significant number of persons arrested on suspicion of an offence, but not charged, were informed that they were 'released under investigation' (hereafter, RUI).

4.5.2 Impact of the changes

RUI was an operational police term with no formal legal status which, in essence, amounted to the release of a suspect without bail but with an attached status of 'released under investigation', implying that the matter was not simply at an end. This had implications for both suspects and complainants.

Unlike the regime introduced by the PCA 2017, RUI did not impose any time limits, which might be regarded as disadvantageous from the perspective of police seeking to control suspect behaviour. A person released without charge must be told they are 'not to be prosecuted'; but again, this does not mean that they will not be in the future. Otherwise, the supply of further information is not required. Since the police appeared to be informing persons that they were 'released under investigation', this strongly suggested that a police investigation would continue. Yet, as Cape pointed out:

29 Hucklesby, A, 'Pre-charge bail and investigation of its use in two police forces' (University of Leeds, 2015); see also College of Policing, 'Bail report: Pre-charge bail – an exploratory study' (September 2016): www.college.police.uk/News/College-news/Documents/Bail_report_document_439E0816_2.pdf (accessed 7 May 2020).

30 Hughes, D, 'Theresa May proposes 28-day bail limit to stop people being left in legal limbo "for years"' (*Independent*, 18 December 2014): www.independent.co.uk/news/uk/politics/theresa-may-proposes-28-day-bail-limit-to-stop-people-being-left-in-legal-limbo-for-years-9933203.html (accessed 7 May 2020).

31 See College of Policing, 'Pre-charge bail data' (September 2017): www.college.police.uk/News/Collegenews/Documents/Pre-charge%20bail%20data.pdf (accessed 7 May 2020).

32 For an extensive review of the changes under the PCA 2017, see Sosabowski, MH and Johnston, E, 'Released Under Investigation: High Time to Bail Out' (2022) *J of Crim L*: https://doi.org/10.1177/00220183221078935.

> [S]uspects have no idea whether the police are continuing to investigate, how long that is likely to go on for, whether the police will want to interview them again, whether they will be re-arrested, or whether they will eventually be prosecuted.[33]

Since RUI was simply an informal term applied to people released without bail, it had no applicable time limits. Persons so released could not require the police (or any other body for that matter) to review ongoing investigations or provide information. The same applied to complainants. Moreover, the police could not impose conditions on RUI – for example, to protect complainants from domestically violent partners, leaving them, potentially, vulnerable. The Law Society summarised this situation as 'leav[ing] the accused and victims in limbo'.[34] The College of Policing found that, between April and June 2017, bail without charge was used in only 4% of cases (down from 26% in March 2017) whilst 25% of cases involved RUI (which was previously not used at all).[35] A more comprehensive Freedom of Information request (covering 31 police forces, including the MPS) by the Law Society found that the use of pre-charge bail and RUI had changed dramatically between April 2017 and April 2018. Prior to the PCA 2017, just over 200,000 suspects were on pre-charge bail; the year after, this figure had dropped to just over 40,000.[36] In contrast, RUI (virtually unused prior to the PCA 2017) was used for just under 200,000 persons in 2017/18.[37] Strikingly, one force (the MPS) used RUI more times in that year than all 31 forces used pre-charge bail (46,674 compared with 43,923).[38] Furthermore, the average length of time suspects were RUI, before charges were brought or the investigation formally ended, increased significantly. Based on data from 10 forces, the Law Society found that prior to the PCA 2017, the average period spent on bail was 90 days; in contrast, the average period spent RUI in 2017/18 was nearly 140 days.[39]

Such evidence suggests that RUI effectively replaced bail without charge as it 'remove[d] all the pressures associated with a release on bail' and provided the police with a free hand to investigate people.[40] Yet RUI was, in essence, a 'shadow status' assigned to released persons; it was unregulated, had no safeguards or time limits, and it placed no requirements on the police. There was no right to challenge it, there was little data available on its use, and, like bail without charge, the 'whiff' of suspicion remained.

The solution to the problem of pre-charge bail introduced by the PCA 2017 was considered simply unworkable from both a police and defence perspective; as such, it became clear that further reform was inevitably needed. Acknowledging the concerns with the use of RUI, in February 2019, the Home Office launched a public consultation on amending the legislation in various ways, including removal of the presumption against pre-charge bail; extending the length of initial bail to at least two months; and introducing a regulatory framework for the use of RUI.[41] After receiving 844 responses

33 Cape (n 19).

34 The Law Society, 'Released under investigation' (7 November 2019): www.lawsociety.org.uk/policy-campaigns/campaigns/criminal-justice/release-under-investigation/ (accessed 7 May 2020).

35 College of Policing (n 29).

36 The Law Society (n 34).

37 *Ibid.*

38 *Ibid.*

39 *Ibid.*

40 Cape (n 19).

41 See Home Office, 'Police Powers: Pre-charge Bail Government consultation' (February 2020): https://assets.publishing.service.gov.uk/government/uploads/system/uploads/attachment_data/file/879759/20191127_ConDoc_PCB_May.pdf (accessed 7 May 2020).

(64% of which came from police forces),[42] the Government concluded that there was 'generally high agreement' with the proposals, though noted that 'members of the public who had been investigated and lawyers were less supportive of the longest timeframes of bail'.[43] In a particularly damning conclusion, the Government acknowledged that RUI was:

> an unsatisfactory process which does not provide the necessary level of accountability around decision-making, communication with the suspect, victims and witnesses, and timescales for completing the investigation.[44]

The proposed reform package – dubbed 'Kay's Law'[45] – was included in the Police, Crime, Sentencing and Courts Act (PCSCA) 2022, and closely reflected the conclusions of the consultation.[46] Part 1 of Sch 4 amended the provisions of PACE 1984 related to the granting of pre-charge bail by removing the presumption against it, whilst retaining a set of pre-conditions for bail to be granted. Authorisation of bail can now be granted by the CO (as opposed to the more senior level established in the PCA 2017), based on a variety of risk factors (outlined in Part 2). This therefore paves a smoother road for COs inclined to release suspects on bail, reversing the arguably disincentivising position of the PCA 2017.

Several timescale models for release on bail were considered, although all proposed significantly lengthening the initial period of bail from 28 days, with the possibility of further extensions beyond this.[47] In contrast to the PCA 2017, the PCSCA 2022 amended PACE 1984 to allow the police (at increasing levels of seniority) to extend bail without external approval up to nine months; with any further extensions being approved by a magistrates' court.[48] As such, the Act not only substantially increases the potential length of pre-charge bail but grants the police greater independence to utilise bail before the intervention of the courts is necessary. The purported rationale is to strike a balance between the problems identified prior to the PCA 2017 – namely, overuse of long, unjustified, and under-scrutinised periods of pre-charge bail – with the need to regulate the behaviour of released suspects and protect victims, whilst granting enough time for practitioners (particularly the police) to undertake investigative actions.[49]

The legislation is clear in its objective of reviving the use of pre-charge bail. In this sense, the PCSCA 2022 not only reverses virtually the entirety of the scheme created in 2017, but does so with a quite different emphasis of intention. The well-meaning but flawed changes ushered in by the PCA 2017 were primarily driven by long-running concerns about overuse and poorly justified use of bail to the detriment of suspects. In

42 Home Office, 'Police powers: pre-charge bail government response' (September 2021): www.gov.uk/government/consultations/police-powers-pre-charge-bail/outcome/police-powers-pre-charge-bail-government-response-accessible-version#summary-of-responses (accessed 31 August 2022).

43 *Ibid.* It is worth noting these categories of respondent together represented less than a third of the overall responses received.

44 *Ibid.*

45 Named for Kay Richardson, who was killed by her ex-husband whilst he was RUI in 2018. See Cowling, P, Clayton, J and Newman, M, '"Scandal brewing" as thousands of suspects released' (BBC News, 4 December 2019): www.bbc.co.uk/news/uk-50563533 (accessed 31 August 2022).

46 Section 45; and Sch 4, the latter introducing the substantive changes.

47 See PACE 1984, s 47ZB; for an overview, see n 42.

48 PACE 1984, ss 47ZD, 47ZE, 47ZF and 47ZG.

49 See summary at **4.1**.

contrast, the Government's pre-Act factsheet on Kay's Law made clear what it regarded as the primary mischiefs motivating reform, stating that the new legislation would 'encourage the police to impose strict conditions on bail more frequently in high harm cases'; rebalance (in other words, lengthen) the timeframes for bail; and protect victims.[50] Whilst the protection of vulnerable victims (such as Kay Richardson) from violent abusers is undoubtedly necessary and laudable, the language suggests limited interest in, and therefore motivation to address, the disadvantages of RUI (and bail) for suspects. Indeed, the Government declined to create a formal framework (with timeframes) for RUI, on the basis that RUI would likely reduce significantly post-reform.[51]

4.6 The 'necessity' of detention prior to charge

Much like arrest, the requirement for detention to be necessary is designed to be a due process safeguard. How effective this safeguard is may, however, be questioned. The relevant terms are vague and not defined by PACE 1984; it is unclear what exactly constitutes a 'reasonable ground' and what circumstances will render detention 'necessary'. During the passage of PACE 1984 through Parliament, the then Home Secretary, Douglas Hurd, said that detention must be more than 'desirable' or 'convenient' for the police.[52] By this logic, the CO should not approve further detention simply because it would be a helpful or more cost-effective method of furthering an investigation. Ordinary interpretation would suggest that 'necessary' means that there is 'no other way' of proceeding with the investigation (although case law relating to the power of arrest does not accord with this definition). In *Al-Fayed*, Auld LJ stated that even when a CO had 'a genuine and bona fide belief' that detention was necessary, this was not enough.[53] Instead, the court approved the reasoning of Beldam LJ in *Wilding*:[54]

> A court … should ask itself the question … whether the decision of the custody sergeant was unreasonable in the sense that no custody officer, acquainted with the ordinary use of language and applying his common sense to the competing considerations before him, could reasonably have reached that decision.[55]

Importantly, the CO can consider the arresting officer's view of the necessity of detention, although the CO is not bound by it.[56] This arguably dilutes the barrier between the investigation and custody decisions and potentially compromises the independence of the CO. The test outlined in *Wilding* seems to add little clarity to the statutory language. Welsh et al criticised the decision as providing 'convoluted' logic and representing an 'abdication' of judicial responsibility to safeguard suspects.[57]

---

50 Home Office, 'Pre-charge bail: Police, Crime, Sentencing and Courts Act 2022 factsheet' (August 2022): www.gov.uk/government/publications/police-crime-sentencing-and-courts-bill-2021-factsheets/police-crime-sentencing-and-courts-bill-2021-pre-charge-bail-factsheet.

51 *Ibid.*

52 HC Official Report, SC E, 16 February 1984, col 1229.

53 *Al-Fayed* (n 12), [86].

54 Court of Appeal (Civil Division), 22 May 1995.

55 *Al-Fayed* (n 12), [96].

56 *Ibid* [101].

57 Welsh, L, Skinns, L and Sanders, A, *Sanders & Young's Criminal Justice* (OUP, 2021).

4.7 The effect of the custody officer

The intended effect of the CO was to provide a more robust check on detentions and a more independent decision-making process. It was believed that the 'necessity' principle would reduce the proportion of suspects detained without charge. However, research evidence suggests that neither of these predicted outcomes have come to fruition. In 1990, McKenzie undertook an observational study of COs.[58] He argued that if the 'necessity' principle were working effectively then the number of persons being detained without charge should have declined – but at that point there was no evidence suggesting this was the case.[59] The changes brought in by PACE 1984 had seemingly failed to stop 'the almost automatic authorisation of detention'.[60] McKenzie observed only one case where the CO did not authorise detention (in that case, due to the suspect suffering a stroke).[61] The study also reviewed 1,800 post-PACE 1984 custody records and discovered no cases where detention was not authorised by the CO. The study found that COs paraphrased the wording of s 37 (that is, 'detention authorised in order to secure or preserve evidence and to obtain evidence by way of questioning') in order to justify detention, rather than by making specific reference to facts about the case or the suspect. McKenzie concluded that authorisation of detention was a 'rubber-stamping' exercise.[62] This suggested that the introduction of COs had produced none of the effects desired or expected, and the 'necessity' principle appeared to be entirely undermined by the realities of practice. It could therefore be described as a 'presentational' rather than 'working' rule.[63]

McKenzie posited two reasons for the predicted outcomes not occurring:

(a) *The 'always cover yourself' axiom:* authorising detention was the 'safe' decision, with little risk of making a 'wrong' decision (that is, one that would be discovered and challenged by a suspect – which was unlikely).[64] In contrast, releasing a suspect raised the theoretical prospect of further offending or disappearance. The CO might undermine their own authority by refusing to authorise detention, as it essentially 'de-arrested' a suspect. This could cause discontent amongst arresting or investigating officers and lead to complaints against COs.[65] Additionally, there was 'no organisational support' from superior officers to protect COs.[66] It was also suggested that risk avoidance was an attitude inherent in police culture, and that using initiative (by straying from the normal practice of detention) was 'fraught with danger'.[67] As such, this issue of 'covering yourself' appeared to be a cultural problem within policing.[68]

---

58 McKenzie, I, 'Helping the Police with Their Enquiries: the necessity principle and voluntary attendance at the police station' (1990) *Crim LR*.

59 *Ibid* 23.

60 *Ibid* 24.

61 *Ibid.*

62 *Ibid.*

63 That is, rules 'that exist to give an acceptable appearance to the way that police work is carried out' as opposed to rules that are 'internalised by police officers to become guiding principles of their conduct' (Smith, D and Gray, J, *Police and People in London* (Gower, 1983), 171). See also Welsh et al (n 57).

64 McKenzie (n 58), 33.

65 *Ibid* 23; de-arrest is separate concept, covered under PACE 1984, s 30A.

66 *Ibid* (McKenzie).

67 *Ibid* 25.

68 *Ibid* 33.

(b) *Lack of established procedure for release:* Three police forces observed by McKenzie had no instructions on how to deal with cases of non-authorisation by the CO. As such, rejection of detention was avoided because it was unclear what should be done with a suspect – again, detention was the easier choice.[69] This was a procedural problem; a lack of regulatory clarity or preparation for the possibility for release meant that it was avoided.[70]

Research by McConville seemed to make clear the gap between the law, as set out in PACE 1984, and the reality of practice.[71] When asked whether he would ever refuse to authorise detention, one CO responded, 'Probably not in practice, no.' Another described a hypothetical interaction with a suspect:

> Often the bloke's remonstrating saying 'Not me, it wasn't me. I haven't done it, you've got the wrong man', but of course I have to take the policeman's word, so I accept him [into custody] on what the policeman tells me.[72]

These responses show a clear difference between the legal framework (and its predicted effects) in theory, and their application in real-world decision-making. Specifically, the responses highlight three issues:

- The arresting officer can influence the custody decision, despite the intention of the regulatory framework to introduce independence and 'distance' from the investigation.
- A lack of weight is attached to the suspect's perspective.
- There is pressure on the CO (who is after all a police officer) to 'accept' detention.

Such issues partially explain why police culture has undermined the effectiveness of the CO role as a brake on the unnecessary detention of suspects prior to charge.

In 2017, Dehaghani found similar problems with CO practice, reflecting historic research.[73] However, in some ways, the problems encountered are now worse. In an empirical study at two sites, Dehaghani concluded that COs still failed to provide a fully independent check on detention decisions and that they may, in fact, *assist* arresting officers in finding grounds to detain. She found that there was continued routine authorisation of detention. Additionally, some COs confused and conflated the 'necessity' of arrest with the 'necessity' of detention – that is, if it was necessary to arrest, it would also be considered necessary to detain a suspect. These are, of course, two separate safeguards applying to different decisions, and they should be considered separately. Since every arrest *should* in theory be necessary, this logic would imply that *everyone* arrested and brought to a police station would need to be detained (which is clearly not the case, nor the intention of the regulatory framework). The study found a continued lack of institutional support for COs to say no to detention, with COs fearing that their decisions might be overruled.[74] The study also found that, despite formal abolition of targets, internal working targets remained in place and added pressure to make certain decisions (for example, to detain certain numbers of suspects).[75] More

69 *Ibid* 25–26.

70 *Ibid.*

71 McConville, M, Sanders, A and Leng, R, *The Case for the Prosecution* (Routledge, 1991).

72 *Ibid* 44.

73 Dehaghani, R, 'Automatic authorisation: an exploration of the decision to detain in police custody' (2017) *Crim LR* (3).

74 *Ibid* 193.

75 *Ibid* 194–95.

recently, Kemp drew similar conclusions regarding approval of detentions by COs, stating that:

> While the number of people detained by the police in the two areas studied has decreased significantly over recent years, it was acknowledged that custody sergeants rarely refused detention and that suspects could be detained for minor matters. Indeed, a custody officer commented that detention was refused in less than one per cent of cases.[76]

4.8 Custody records

Another safeguard introduced under PACE 1984 was the use of custody records.[77] These must be opened as soon as practicable for each person brought to a police station under arrest or arrested at the police station.[78] If a CO authorises detention prior to charge, the grounds for doing so must be recorded.[79] All major decisions and actions must be included in custody records, such as the time of and grounds for detention; decisions regarding legal advice; decisions on the review of detention and the time they were taken; the times of interviews; and decisions regarding charge and bail. A suspect and their legal representative have a right to see the custody record during detention, and they are entitled to a copy of it after release.[80] The CO is responsible for the 'accuracy and completeness' of the record.[81] Whilst a simple requirement, the custody record is a major due process safeguard, providing transparency and accountability for police actions. It is designed to ensure information is accurate and not open to fabrication at a later point, and it requires the police to provide clear justifications for their decisions regarding issues like detention and access to legal advice.

4.9 Reviews of detention

If a CO authorises detention, another important safeguard becomes relevant: the right to a review of that decision. Once detention is approved, a metaphorical clock starts ticking, limiting not only for how long a suspect can be detained (see **4.10** below) but also for how long they can be detained without considering whether it remains necessary to do so. This also means that there is a limited period in which the police can investigate an offence whilst detaining someone without charging them. Section 40 of PACE 1984 requires that detention be periodically reviewed, although it does not specify what this must entail. Paragraph 15.1 of PACE Code C, however, does provide more guidance:

> The review officer is responsible under PACE, section 40 for periodically determining if a person's detention, before or after charge, continues to be necessary.

76 Kemp, V, 'Digital Legal Rights for Suspects: Users' Perspectives and PACE Safeguards' (University of Nottingham, June 2018), 3: https://nottingham-repository.worktribe.com/output/946048 (accessed 7 May 2020).

77 PACE 1984, ss 37(4) and (5); Home Office, 'Police and Criminal Evidence Act 1984 (PACE) Code C: Revised Code of Practice for the detention, treatment and questioning of persons by police officers' (TSO, July 2018), [2].

78 Code C, [2.1].

79 PACE 1984, s 37(4).

80 Code C, [2.4].

81 *Ibid* [2.3].

Therefore, a specific officer must be responsible for this, and the necessity principle discussed earlier continues to apply (to suspects both prior to and after charge).[82] The desire to keep a distance between detention decisions and the investigation is clear in who must review detention. If charged, the review must be conducted by a CO;[83] if not, the review must be conducted by an officer of the rank of inspector or above who is not directly involved in the investigation.[84] As such, reviews of detention prior to charge must be conducted by a more senior and experienced officer, suggesting a greater level of scrutiny. Whether a CO or senior officer, the person conducting the review is known as 'the review officer'.[85] The review must be undertaken 'periodically', which means:

- six hours after detention was first authorised; and then
- at nine hourly intervals.[86]

The suspect and their lawyer must have the opportunity to make representations, introducing an element of adversarial balance into police station procedure.[87]

As always, this is the theory, and as we have already observed, there is often a gulf between theory and practice. In Roberts, the suspect was arrested on suspicion of conspiracy to burgle, and detention at a police station was authorised.[88] He was then transferred to another police station just over two hours later, when detention was authorised again. Six hours after the second authorisation, detention was reviewed, and it was then reviewed again just under 10 hours later. The suspect was released shortly afterwards, and he initiated proceedings for false imprisonment. The court concluded that his detention was unlawful as there had been a failure to review six hours after the first detention, as required by PACE 1984. The police argued that reasonable grounds for detention did exist, despite the failure to review (in short, had they reviewed it, it would have been reasonable to continue to detain him). However, Clarke LJ stated:

> It is nothing to the point to say that the detention would have been lawful if a review had been carried out or that there were grounds which would have justified continued detention … In the absence of a review he was in principle entitled to his liberty. His further detention was therefore unlawful.

As such, failure to adhere to the letter of the law meant that the police were liable for damages. Whilst this suggests a strict approach to the enforcement of the review process, such challenges are rare. In reality, the review process has not been described favourably by the research. In 1990, Dixon et al interviewed police officers and legal advisers, and reviewed custody records and observed review practices, concluding that reviews were typically 'routinised and insubstantial'.[89]

4.10 Detention time limits

As suggested above, authorisation of detention starts a clock, providing only a limited period for the police to investigate an offence and charge a suspect. Section 41 of PACE

82 PACE 1984, s 40(1).
83 *Ibid* s 40(1)(a).
84 *Ibid* s 40(1)(b).
85 *Ibid* s 40(2).
86 *Ibid* s 40(3)(a), (b) and (c).
87 *Ibid* s 40(12).
88 [1999] 1 WLR 662.
89 Dixon, D, Bottomley, K, Coleman, C, Gill, M and Wall, D, 'Safeguarding the Rights of Suspects in Police Custody' (1990) 1 *Policing and Society* (2), 130.

1984 outlines this crucial safeguard; normally, the maximum period for which a suspect can be detained prior to charge is 24 hours from arrival at the police station.[90] However, under s 42(1), this can be extended up to 36 hours when an officer of the rank of superintendent or above has reasonable grounds for believing that:

- detention is necessary to secure or preserve evidence;
- detention is for an indictable offence; and
- the investigation is being conducted diligently and expeditiously.

This, however, is not the upper limit on detention. Under s 43, a magistrates' court may grant a 'warrant of further detention' beyond the 36-hour limit if a police officer provides information under oath. Importantly, a suspect must be legally represented at such a significant hearing. Section 44 allows an extension of up to 60 hours beyond the 36 hour 'enhanced' limit – for a total of 96 hours of detention. Therefore, suspects can be detained without charge for up to four days. Clearly, this is a very substantial suspension of the right to liberty without, at this stage, sufficient evidence to charge someone with an offence. Critiquing this, Sanders et al described such extensions as 'an unashamedly crime control measure'.[91] In short, these longer periods of detention mean that individual rights are sacrificed to increase the scope of a criminal investigation.

Whilst the merit of this is debatable, detention beyond 24 hours is infrequent when compared with the overall number of arrests (only 4,581 in 2021/22).[92] Warrants for detention beyond 36 hours are almost always granted (but such applications are even rarer than those beyond 24 hours): only 461 persons were held for periods beyond 36 hours in 2021/22, with only 13 requests refused.[93] There is no nationally collected data on detention under 24 hours; however, some sources provide an indication of the scale of its use. In 2018 the MPS created 141,446 custody records in which detention was authorised.[94] Furthermore, a Freedom of Information request shows that the MPS detained an average of approximately 200,000 individuals per year between 2013/14 and 2021/22 (most of whom will have been detained for 24 hours or less).[95] Additionally, research conducted in 2020 suggested that more than 800,000 people were detained for up to 24 hours in the year 2018/19.[96] The average detention time will vary between police forces and by custody suite within each force. In 1998, Phillips and Brown found

---

90 PACE 1984, s 41(1) and (2).

91 Welsh et al (n 57).

92 *Ibid.* Home Office 'Other PACE powers data tables: police powers and procedures year ending 31 March 2022' (November 2022), Table D.03: www.gov.uk/government/statistics/police-powers-and-procedures-england-and-wales-year-ending-31-march-2019 (accessed 7 May 2020).

93 *Ibid* Table D.04. Although over 100 of these suspects were not charged.

94 Custody records are required for every person brought to a police station (Information Rights Unit, 'Custody Records Created in 2017 and 2018' (MPS, 26 May 2019): www.met.police.uk/foi-ai/af/accessing-information/published-items/?q=detention (accessed 7 May 2020). It is also worth noting that authorisation of detention was refused in less than 1% of all custody records created by the MPS in 2018, lending credence to the 'automatic authorisation' arguments presented by McKenzie, Dehaghani and Kemp (see **4.7**).

95 Metropolitan Police, 'Authorised police custody detentions from 2013/14 to 2021/22' (October 2022): www.met.police.uk/foi-ai/metropolitan-police/d/october-2022/authorised-police-custody-detentions-2013-14-2021-22/ (accessed 20 March 2023).

96 Gibbs, P and Ratcliffe, F, '24 hours in police custody — is police detention overused?' (Transform Justice, 2020): www.transformjustice.org.uk/wp-content/uploads/2020/06/TJ_Police_Custody_Report_041.pdf (accessed 20 March 2023).

an average detention period of 6 hours and 40 minutes;[97] and in 2012 Kemp found an average of just under 9 hours.[98] To provide an example, the average detention time prior to a suspect being charged, bailed or RUI for West Midlands Police was 15 hours in February 2020.[99] Most recently, a small-scale study by Kemp found an average of 17 hours.[100] This evidence suggests that whilst full use of the initial 24-hour limit does not appear to be the norm, average detention times are increasing.

4.11 Charging a suspect

'Charging' is the commencement of criminal proceedings against a suspect – when someone is formally accused of a criminal offence. Whether someone is charged is a decision for the CO, who will complete a charge sheet outlining the offence (or offences) with which the suspect is charged, as well as the time and date of their first court appearance. It should be noted that an alternative mechanism for commencing criminal proceedings is the summons (or written charge and requisition), which tends to be used for less serious matters (such as traffic offences). A suspect will normally be charged at one of two points, namely whichever is the earlier of:

- the expiry of a relevant detention limit (eg 24 hours from arrival at a police station); or[101]
- when the conditions set out in s 37(7) of PACE 1984 are satisfied – that is: 'If the custody officer determines that he has before him sufficient evidence to charge the person arrested.'

The phrase 'sufficient evidence to charge' is not defined in PACE 1984, although some guidance is provided in Code C. Paragraph 16.1A states that COs must have regard to the 'Director's Guidance on Charging' when deciding whether to charge a suspect.[102] The Guidance is published under the authority of s 37A of PACE 1984, specifically for the purpose of assisting COs in undertaking this decision. Of particular importance are paras 8 and 11, which require COs and prosecutors to use one of two tests to determine if there is sufficient evidence to charge a suspect: the Full Code Test or the Threshold Test.

4.11.1 The Full Code Test

The Full Code Test is set out in Section 4 of the 'Code for Crown Prosecutors'.[103] This outlines two stages:

---

97 Phillips, C and Brown, D, 'Entry into the criminal justice system: a survey of police arrests and their outcomes' (Home Office, 1998), 109: http://webarchive.nationalarchives.gov.uk/20110221083401/http://rds.homeoffice.gov.uk/rds/pdfs/hors185.pdf (accessed 7 May 2020).

98 Kemp, V, Balmer, N and Pleasance, P, 'Whose time is it anyway? Factors associated with duration in police custody' (2013) *Crim LR* (10), 739.

99 West Midlands Police, 'Custody Stats (252A/20)' (26 June 2020): https://foi.west-midlands.police.uk/custody-stats-252a-20/ (accessed 14 July 2020).

100 Kemp (n 76), 5.

101 At this point, a suspect would normally be charged – but there must still be sufficient evidence to do so. If there is not, the suspect must either be released or extended detention authorised. However, it is still possible for a suspect to be detained for more than 24 (or even 36) hours and still eventually be released without charge.

102 Director of Public Prosecutions, 'Charging (The Director's Guidance')', 5th edn (Crown Prosecution Service, May 2013): www.cps.gov.uk/legal-guidance/charging-directors-guidance-2013-fifth-edition-may-2013-revised-arrangements (accessed 7 May 2020).

103 Director of Public Prosecutions, 'The Code for Crown Prosecutors' (Crown Prosecution Service, January 2013): www.cps.gov.uk/publication/code-crown-prosecutors (accessed 7 May 2020).

(1) *The evidential stage:* is there sufficient evidence to provide a realistic prospect of conviction? A CO or prosecutor (a CPS lawyer) must consider whether:
- an objective, impartial and reasonable jury, magistrates, or judge;
- properly directed; and
- acting in accordance with the law,

would be more likely than not to convict the defendant of the charge alleged. It is therefore a wide test granting significant discretion; but it does have a strong objective element to it (that is, the reasonable person standard).

(2) *The public interest stage:* is the prosecution in the public interest? This will only be considered if the first stage is satisfied. A CO or prosecutor must consider various questions:
   (a) How serious is the offence committed? Note the phrase 'offence committed' rather than 'alleged', raising questions about respect for the presumption of innocence.
   (b) What is the level of culpability (ie blameworthiness) of the suspect?
   (c) What are the circumstances of and the harm caused to the victim?
   (d) Was the suspect under the age of 18 at the time of the offence?
   (e) What is the impact on the community?
   (f) Is prosecution a proportionate response?

This stage does seem to require more rigorous consideration by a CO or prosecutor as to whether it is worthwhile charging the suspect, but it still affords room for interpretation.

4.11.2 The Threshold Test

Section 5 of the 'Code for Crown Prosecutors' also outlines two stages for this test:[104]

(1) *Is there reasonable suspicion?* There needs to be at least a reasonable suspicion that the person to be charged has committed the offence in question. In many (if not most) cases, this test would automatically be satisfied since reasonable suspicion will have already been (in theory) established for arrested suspects. However, a CO will need to establish this for themselves (in accordance with the principle of constabulary independence).

(2) *Can further evidence be gathered to provide a realistic prospect of conviction?* This will be satisfied when there are reasonable grounds for believing that:
- the continuing investigation will provide further evidence;
- within a reasonable period of time;
- so that all the evidence together is capable of establishing a realistic prospect of conviction in accordance with the Full Code Test.

A CO must therefore consider all the available evidence holistically (including any prospective rather than actually gathered evidence). Additionally, 'further evidence' must be identifiable and not merely speculative. This test thus allows a person to be charged even though there is not sufficient evidence to provide a reasonable prospect of conviction, and essentially on the basis of little more than is required to justify an arrest. The Threshold Test provides very significant discretion to COs and prosecutors when they are not sure that a conviction is realistic, but they want to obtain more time to investigate without releasing a suspect.

---

104 *Ibid.*

4.11.3 Which test is used?

Normally, the Full Code Test must be used. However, the Threshold Test may be used in exceptional circumstances. It can be used by a Crown prosecutor (that is, a CPS lawyer) when:

- there is insufficient evidence for the Full Code Test;
- further evidence will be available within a reasonable period of time;
- the seriousness of the case justifies it; and
- the suspect presents a substantial bail risk if released.

It can be used by a CO when:

- an inspector or above authorises it;
- continued detention after charge is justified; and
- the offence normally requires a prosecutor to make a decision on charge, but a prosecutor is not available before the expiry of a relevant detention time limit (ie they need to charge quickly).

As such, there are restrictions on when the much more lenient Threshold Test can be used to charge a suspect, particularly when the decision is being made by a CO. The Threshold Test is likely to be reserved for the most serious and complex cases, where there is some element of urgency involved.

4.11.4 Who makes the decision to charge?

In the past, the charging decision was always made by a CO, but in 2001 the Auld Review recommended that charging decisions should be transferred to the CPS.[105] The Criminal Justice Act 2003 amended PACE 1984 by introducing a practice known as 'statutory charging', which meant that all but the most minor offences would be charged by the CPS rather than a police officer.[106] After 2010, the Coalition Government chose to transfer some charging decisions back to the police. This was trialled between 2010 and 2012 and then fully implemented from 2013 in the 'Director's Guidance'.[107] The current position is therefore as follows:

- A CO makes the charging decision in respect of:
  - any summary-only offence (including criminal damage if the value of loss/damage is less than £5,000), irrespective of plea;
  - any offence of retail theft (shoplifting) or attempted retail theft, irrespective of plea (provided it is suitable for sentence in a magistrates' court);
  - any either-way offence anticipated as raising a guilty plea and suitable for sentence in a magistrates' court, with some exceptions (for example, domestic violence, hate crimes, actual and grievous bodily harm).
- A Crown prosecutor makes the decision in all other cases.

It is interesting to note who makes the decision. The police and CPS may have different priorities and targets; different ways of thinking about charging, influenced by their working practices; and different experiences of the type of case or offence. Therefore, who is responsible for charging may influence the likelihood of a charge and

105 Lord Justice Auld, 'Review of the Criminal Courts of England and Wales' (The Auld Review) (Ministry of Justice, September 2001).

106 Criminal Justice Act 2003, s 28 and Sch 2.

107 The aforementioned trials of police charging is documented in Baksi, C, 'Charging powers passed from CPS to police' (*The Law Gazette*, 9 May 2011): www.lawgazette.co.uk/news/charging-powers-passed-from-cps-to-police/60359.article (accessed 7 May 2020); The Director's Guidance (n 102), [15].

what offence a person is charged with (even if, in theory, such factors should not matter). The CPS was created in order to make decisions about the continuation and conduct of prosecutions more independent and objective, and the expansion of its responsibility for charging offences after the Auld Review sought to do the same.[108] Whether this is or is not the case is open to debate.

4.12 Research on charging decisions

Commentators have been critical of the vagueness of the phrase 'sufficient evidence to charge'.[109] In 2015, a joint report by HM Crown Prosecution Service Inspectorate (HMCPSI) and HM Inspectorate of Constabulary (HMIC, now HM Inspectorate of Constabulary and Fire and Rescue Services (HMICFRS)) contained mixed findings on the quality of charging.[110] In 91.9% of cases, the decision to charge complied with the 'Code for Crown Prosecutors' (that is, under either of the charging tests).[111] In one third of cases, the CO took the decision to charge when it should have been referred to a Crown prosecutor.[112] The record of charging decisions (the MG3 form) was rated less than 'good' in 60% of cases – indicating a lack of clear information about what the charge was and why the decision was made to charge the suspect.[113] Beyond this, there has been little research regarding charging generally in recent years (and none on the impact of statutory charging from 2004 to 2010), but significant attention has been paid to charging suspects with certain offences – most notably rape and sexual assaults. In 2016, HMCPSI raised concerns about how charging decisions were being made in such cases, with specialists in these areas not being used in approximately 40% of cases (despite this being regarded as best practice).[114] It concluded:

> We found that in over 10% of cases the Code for Crown Prosecutors (the Code) was not applied correctly at the charging stage, which is a worse result than our findings in relation to non-specialist cases. It also takes too long for the CPS to provide charging advice, thereby increasing the anxiety for vulnerable victims.[115]

The report found that a greater proportion of rape and sexual assault cases referred to the CPS for a charging decision were in fact charged (59%)[116] – but this figure has slowly declined since 2016, dropping to 52% in 2018/19 (a reduction of 38% in one

108 The Philips Commission (n 7); the Auld Review (n 105); for more on the objectives of the CPS, see Glidewell, I, 'The Review of the Crown Prosecution Service' (The Glidewell Review) (TSO, 1998): https://assets.publishing.service.gov.uk/government/uploads/system/uploads/attachment_data/file/259808/3972.pdf (accessed 7 May 2020).

109 See Cape, E, 'Detention without charge: what does "sufficient evidence to charge" mean?' (1999) *Crim LR*.

110 HMCPSI/HMIC, 'Joint Inspection of the Provision of Charging Decisions' (May 2015): www.justiceinspectorates.gov.uk/hmicfrs/wp-content/uploads/joint-inspection-of-the-provision-of-charging-decisions.pdf (accessed 7 May 2020).

111 *Ibid* [7.2].

112 *Ibid* [7.4].

113 *Ibid* [1.17].

114 HMCPSI, 'Thematic Review of the CPS Rape and Serious Sexual Offences Units' (February 2016), 36: www.justiceinspectorates.gov.uk/hmcpsi/wp-content/uploads/sites/3/2016/02/RASSO_thm_Feb16_rpt.pdf (accessed 7 May 2020).

115 *Ibid* 1.

116 *Ibid* 45.

year).[117] Considering that police-recorded rapes have increased by 350% since 2008/09,[118] this has generated significant concern that incorrect charging decisions are being made, with accusations that the CPS has 'raised the bar' for sufficient evidence to charge (despite there being no change in the relevant law).[119] For more on this issue, see **Chapter 17**.

4.13 Summary

- PACE 1984 and the Codes of Practice regulate police conduct at the investigation stage, and they provide a number of protective provisions for suspects in police detention.
- These provisions have arguably had a variable impact:
  - Some are treated as working rules (that is, they are consistently adhered to and implemented in practice).[120] Examples include maximum limits on the length of detention and the tape-recording of interviews.
  - Some are treated as inhibitory rules.[121] That is, they act as obstacles for the police and reduce the scope for unfair or abusive behaviour (eg the right to legal advice and the requirement for interviews to take place at police stations).
  - Some are treated in practice as presentational rules; they are for 'show' and are not properly implemented.[122] Examples include the 'necessity' principle for detention decisions or the requirement of senior officers to oversee reviews of detention.
  - Breach of these protective provisions does not automatically lead to exclusion of evidence; we should question whether they deter police malpractice.

---

117 HMCPSI, 'Rape inspection 2019: All rape figures 2016-2019': www.justiceinspectorates.gov.uk/hmcpsi/inspections/rape-inspection-on-report-december-2019/ (accessed 7 May 2020).

118 Office for National Statistics, 'Crime in England and Wales: year ending June 2019' (17 October 2019), Table 3: www.ons.gov.uk/peoplepopulationandcommunity/crimeandjustice/bulletins/crimeinengland andwales/yearendingjune2019 (accessed 7 May 2020).

119 Dearden, L, 'Police accuse prosecutors of "raising bar" for rape cases after scandal over collapsed trials' (*Independent*, 2 November 2018): www.independent.co.uk/news/uk/crime/rape-case-police-evidence-phones-messages-prosecutions-cps-victims-a8615406.html (accessed 7 May 2020).

120 See n 63.

121 Smith and Gray (n 63), defined as rules 'which are not internalised, but which police officers take into account when deciding how to act and which tend to discourage them from behaving in certain ways in case they should be caught and the rule invoked against them' (at 171).

122 See n 63.

chapter 5

In Police Custody (2): Legal Advice and Interrogation

5.1 The right of access to a lawyer

The right to detain suspects is an important power of the police, tempered by various safeguards and rights. One of the most important is the right of access to a lawyer in police custody. Pre-PACE 1984, this was governed by the less robust Judges' Rules. Suspects were supposed to be informed of this right and allowed access to representation, as long as it did not unreasonably 'hinder' the police.[1] This ill-defined concept allowed the police to frequently deny access to legal advice for suspects. Indeed, the Fisher Inquiry (which examined the Maxwell Confait case) found that suspects were often not told about this right.[2] In contrast, individual citizens are now generally much more aware of this right (it may be one of the few rights that people are aware they have in a police station). Importantly, the CO is required by Code C to inform suspects of this right, ensuring that the police cannot restrict access by relying on the ignorance of suspects.[3] The importance of legal advice in the police station is difficult to overstate. It provides an adversarial counter-balance to police power and a check on abuse. It allows suspects – who may be unable to fully understand their situation – to comprehend their rights and obligations (particularly suspects who are vulnerable). The right to a lawyer combats potential intimidation of suspects by the police and promotes legitimate processes in obtaining evidence. The presence of a lawyer can also be helpful to the police; for example, an unnecessarily difficult or uncooperative suspect may damage their own interests as well as frustrate the police – a legal adviser can often help in this situation as a mediator between the two parties, engaging suspects in more cooperative dialogue with the police.

Section 58(1) of PACE 1984 enshrined this right in legislation for the first time:

> A person arrested and held in custody in a police station or other premises shall be entitled, if he so requests, to consult a solicitor privately at any time.

Generally, this must be allowed 'as soon as is practicable';[4] however, access can be delayed (in contrast to the Judges' Rules, which allowed the police to refuse access). Delay can only be authorised by an officer of the rank of superintendent or above; for a maximum of 36 hours; and only for an indictable offence.[5] Furthermore, a delay can only be justified if the authorising officer has reasonable grounds for believing that

1 Principle (c), in the Introduction to the revised Judges' Rules of 1964. See St Johnston, T, 'Judges' Rules and Police Interrogation in England Today' (1966) 57 *J of Crim L & Criminol* 1, 88.

2 Fisher, H, 'Report of an inquiry into the death of Maxwell Confait and the fire at 27 Doggett Road, London SE6' (The Fisher Inquiry) (HMSO, 1977), [17.6]: https://assets.publishing.service.gov.uk/government/uploads/system/uploads/attachment_data/file/228759/0090.pdf (access 7 May 2020).

3 PACE Code C, [3.1].

4 PACE 1984, s 58(4).

5 *Ibid* s 58(6).

exercising the right to legal advice will lead to some negative impact on the investigation and any prosecution, including:

- interference with or harm to evidence;
- alerting persons connected to an offence but not yet arrested;
- hindering the recovery of property; and
- allowing the suspect to benefit from the criminal conduct in question.

More practically, access to legal advice may be delayed purely on practical grounds – for example, when a lawyer needs to travel some distance to the police station. This, of course, falls within the 'as soon as is practicable' caveat. As such, we can summarise the right to a lawyer under s 58 as a fundamental due process safeguard which is tempered by crime control values, as it can be delayed in certain circumstances where an investigation may be hampered.

5.1.1 The right to a lawyer and human rights

The importance of the defence lawyer in police custody was clearly explained in a case before the European Court of Human Rights in 2022:

> Prompt access to a lawyer constitutes an important counterweight to the vulnerability of suspects in police custody. Such access is also preventive, as it provides a fundamental safeguard against coercion and ill-treatment of suspects by the police.[6]

Access to a lawyer at the earliest stage of the criminal justice process (that is, in the police station) is considered essential to the Article 6 right to a fair trial. This was made clear in the landmark case of *Salduz v Turkey*, heard by the European Court of Human Rights (ECtHR).[7] A Turkish citizen participated in a demonstration and was arrested and detained by the Turkish police. The suspect was interrogated without a lawyer and made certain admissions, allegedly under duress. The suspect was then convicted and his appeal was dismissed. A further appeal was made to the ECtHR, arguing that the Article 6 right to a fair trial had been breached because the suspect had not had access to a lawyer in police custody. The court agreed:

> In most cases, [the] particular vulnerability [of a suspect] can only be properly compensated for by the assistance of a lawyer whose task it is, among other things, to help to ensure respect of the right of an accused not to incriminate himself.[8]
>
> The rights of the defence will in principle be irretrievably prejudiced when incriminating statements made during police interrogation without access to a lawyer are used for a conviction.[9]

As such, access must be provided from the very first stage of the investigation, and only compelling reasons will justify denial. PACE 1984, of course, goes further than this, prohibiting the police from denying access (although allowing delay).

In another significant case, the Supreme Court in *Cadder v HM Advocate* highlighted the importance of the right to a lawyer and the principle of early access.[10] Applying *Salduz*, the Court rejected the argument that other safeguards in the Scottish legal system compensated for lack of access to legal advice, with Lord Rodger stating:

6 *Atristain v Spain* [2022] ECHR 64.

7 [2008] ECHR 1542.

8 *Ibid* [54].

9 *Ibid* [55].

10 [2010] UKSC 43.

> [T]here is not the remotest chance that the European Court would find that, because of the other protections that Scots law provides for accused persons, it is compatible with article 6(1) and (3)(c) for the Scottish system to omit this safeguard … and for suspects to be routinely questioned without having the right to consult a lawyer first.[11]
>
> On this matter Strasbourg has spoken: the courts in this country have no real option but to apply the law which it has laid down.[12]

This decision overturned an unbroken chain of Scottish case law, in favour of *Salduz*, demonstrating the importance of human rights law in reinforcing legal protections for suspects and the value attributed to legal advice in the police station. Indeed, it is arguably more important than ever for defence lawyers to be involved from the very start of the process. There has been a general shift away from courts as the focus of the criminal justice system, towards early resolution in police stations.[13] This has been accompanied by a general encouragement of the use of out of court disposals (OOCDs) and diversion, incentivised by the large court backlog in England and Wales.[14] Such factors therefore invest more importance in effective defence work at the police station than ever before.[15] This was made very clear in the Independent Review of Criminal Legal Aid (the Bellamy Review):

> This is not only stressful and challenging work; the first interview with the police will often be critical in determining the whole later course of the case.[16]

5.2 The impact of s 58 on access to a lawyer

The recommendations of the Philips Commission and the passage of PACE 1984 were intended to have a positive impact on the uptake of legal advice at the police station, with the belief that this would reduce miscarriages of justice, such as in the Maxwell Confait case. Before PACE 1984, the rate at which suspects requested advice was

11 *Ibid* [93].

12 *Ibid.*

13 See, for example, the work of John Jackson on this shift (Jackson, J, 'Silence and proof: extending the boundaries of criminal proceedings in the United Kingdom' (2001) *Int J of E & P* 5(3); Jackson, J, 'Responses to Salduz: Procedural Tradition, Change and the Need for Effective Defence' (2016) *Modern LR* 79(6)).

14 Castro, B, 'Nightingale courts will remain open to tackle backlog' (*The Law Gazette*, 17 February 2023): www.lawgazette.co.uk/news/nightingale-courts-will-remain-open-to-tackle-backlog/5115182.article (accessed 8 March 2023).

15 Johnston, E and Cape, E, 'Legal Assistance at the Police Station: Shifts and contradictions in the context of COVID-19', in Johnston, E (ed), *Challenges in Criminal Justice* (Routledge, 2022), 8–10.

16 Sir Christopher Bellamy, 'Independent Review of Criminal Legal Aid' (November 2021), 70: www.gov.uk/government/groups/independent-review-of-criminal-legal-aid (accessed 13 March 2023).

around 10%, of which a third were refused by the police.[17] Statistical evidence[18] suggests that it has achieved, to some degree, its goals.

Year	Source	Requested	Received
1988	Sanders et al	25%	19%
1991	Brown et al	32%	25%
1995/96	Bucke & Brown	40%	34%
2007	Skinns	60%	48%
2008	Kemp & Balmer	54%	Approx 40%
2013	Kemp	47%	35%
2014	Blackstock et al	Approx 30%	Not recorded
2018	Kemp	48%	Not recorded

Clearly, s 58 has had a significant impact on both requests for legal advice and actual receipts over time. We might conclude that the introduction of a legislative right (and therefore a more stringent approach to both enforcing access to the right and informing suspects about it) has made suspects more aware of their entitlement to legal advice, with a consequent increase in the numbers exercising this right. However, there is (and always has been) a substantial gap between the numbers of suspects who request advice and those who actually receive it (that is, meet with a lawyer and receive legal advice). The latter is, after all, the most important figure. This is interesting in light of the fact that, in 2013, the EU issued a directive requiring Member States to ensure access to a lawyer at police stations, which the UK chose not to opt into.[19] Whilst this jurisdiction has a long established right under s 58, the decision not to opt in might

17 Philips, C, 'Royal Commission on Criminal Procedure' (The Philips Commission) (HMSO, 1981), [87]. See also Softley, P, 'Police Interrogation: An Observational Study in Four Police Stations' (HMSO, 1980), which found a request rate of 9% and a receipt rate of 7%.

18 1988 statistics from Sanders, A, Bridges, L, Mulvaney, A and Crozier, G, 'Advice and Assistance in Police Stations and the 24-Hour Duty Solicitor Scheme' (Lord Chancellor's Department, 1989); 1991 statistics from Brown, D, Ellis, T and Larcombe, K, 'Changing the Code: Police Detention under the Revised PACE Codes of Practice' (HMSO, 1992); 1995–96 statistics from Bucke, T and Brown, D, 'In Police Custody: Police Powers and Suspects' Rights under the Revised Codes of Practice' (HMSO, 1997); 2007 statistics from Skinns, L, '"I'm a Detainee: Get Me Out of Here"'(2009) 49 *Brit J of Criminol* (3); 2008 statistics from Kemp, V and Balmer, N, 'Criminal Defence Services: Users' Perspectives (Interim Report)' (Legal Services Research Centre, 2008); 2013 statistics from Kemp, V, '"No time for a solicitor": implications for delays on the take-up of legal advice' (2013) *Crim LR* (3); 2014 statistics from Blackstock, J, Cape, E, Hodgson, J, Ogorodova, A and Spronken, T, *Inside Police Custody: An Empirical Account of Suspects Rights in Four Jurisdictions* (Intersentia, 2014); 2018 statistics from Kemp, V, 'Digital Legal Rights for Suspects: Users' Perspectives and PACE Safeguards' (University of Nottingham, June 2018), 7: https://nottingham-repository.worktribe.com/output/946048 (accessed 7 May 2020).

19 Directive 2013/48/EU of the European Parliament and of the Council of 22 October 2013 on the right of access to a lawyer in criminal proceedings and in European arrest warrant proceedings, and on the right to have a third party informed upon deprivation of liberty and to communicate with third persons and with consular authorities while deprived of liberty [2013] OJ L 294.

suggest a misplaced belief in the effectiveness of the arrangements for accessing legal advice for suspects.[20]

It is therefore important to examine why suspects do not exercise their right to legal advice. In 2011, Skinns outlined a range of reasons:[21]

- *Characteristics:* for example, age or ethnicity. Black suspects are more likely to request advice and less likely to receive it.
- *Haste:* that is, the desire of a suspect to leave the police station quickly – in essence, an attitude of 'let's get it over with'. This could be a key contributor to the gap between requests and receipts of legal advice.[22 23]
- *Seriousness:* where the offence was not perceived as being very serious by a suspect, they were 'less likely to view consulting with a legal adviser as a necessity'.[24]
- *Innocence:* suspects might conclude that they did not need advice because they were innocent, asking 'What do I need a solicitor for?'. Equally, they might decline a solicitor because they are guilty.[25]
- *Experience:* where suspects had previous experience of police stations – and therefore 'knew the ropes' – they were less likely to request a solicitor.
- *Distrust:* some suspects had a negative attitude towards lawyers, particularly those they did not know, regarding them as part of the system. An example from a recent study is illustrative:

  > Fifty per cent of the time I've always felt that [lawyers have] taken … the police officer's side and they're basically with them, they're a team with the police … So, I'd say fifty per cent of the time I've felt not to have full trust in them.[26]

- *Discouragement:* the police might also discourage suspects from making requests for legal advice – for example, by providing incomplete or incomprehensible summaries of rights, or suggesting that legal advice would prolong detention.

Whilst the right to a lawyer is essential, its utility is dependent on the quality of the lawyer provided. Important as assessing quality is, doing so raises several problems. It requires agreement on a number of issues which are not clear-cut, such as what the purpose of police station legal advice is; what criteria are to be treated as significant (that is, what factors make good legal advice); and the relevant standards for measuring the quality of legal advice. Research has tended to focus on factors that are easier to measure, such as:

- who provides legal advice – for example, solicitors or non-solicitors;
- how it is provided – for example, in person or by telephone; and

20 Although the extent to which legal rules, particularly cross-continental ones, can ensure access is perhaps questionable; see generally, Cape, E and Hodgson, J, 'The right of access to a lawyer at police stations: Making the European Union directive work in practice' (2014) 5 *NJECL* (4).

21 'The Right to Legal Advice in the Police Station: Past, Present and Future' (2011) *Crim LR*.

22 For a concise summary of the key reasons for haste and the link with discouragement from seeking legal advice, see the comments of one solicitor in Kemp, V, 'Effective Police Station Legal Advice Country Report 2: England And Wales' (April 2018), 6: http://eprints.nottingham.ac.uk/51145/1/Country%20Report%20England%20and%20Wales%20Final%20.pdf. (accessed 7 May 2020).

23 In her 2018 study (n 18), 7, Kemp found that 30% 'declined legal advice because they were concerned that having a solicitor would lead to delays (as it would take time for the solicitor to get to the station)'.

24 Skinns (n 21).

25 Also see Kemp (n 18), 7.

26 Legal Services Board, 'Vulnerability in legal services Research report' (March 2022), 21: https://legalservicesboard.org.uk/wp-content/uploads/2022/06/Vulnerability-in-legal-services-research-FINAL-REPORT.pdf (accessed 13 March 2023).

- the behaviour of lawyers in police interviews – for example, interventionist or passive.

These metrics, whilst potentially useful, make assumptions that may not be accurate (an obvious one being that solicitors provide better quality advice than non-solicitors).

5.3 Who provides legal advice at police stations?

The question of who provides legal advice requires consideration of the status of those providing advice (particularly their training and experience) as well as the relationship they have with the suspect (their client). According to s 58(1), legal advice in custody is to be provided by solicitors. However, since the passage of the legislation, there has been an increase in the number of legal advisers, who are not qualified solicitors, representing suspects in police stations.[27] These have included solicitors' clerks, trainee solicitors and accredited police station representatives (hereafter accredited representatives). None have the same training and qualifications as solicitors, and they may not have the same amount of practical experience either (although this is not always the case). Whilst this different status does not automatically mean that advice is of a lower quality, it does raise reasonable questions about whether a different standard is provided. Research has offered varying estimates of the levels of non-solicitors providing advice. In 1989, Sanders et al suggested that a large minority received advice from non-solicitors (30%).[28] In 1992, Brown et al suggested a much lower number (only 9% of cases).[29] In 1993, McConville suggested that a very high proportion did so (76% of cases).[30] In the late 1990s, Phillips and Brown provided a similar figure to Sanders (26% of cases).[31] Whilst there is significant divergence in these figures, all imply that at least a sizeable minority received advice from a non-solicitor. It is therefore an issue of significance in considering the quality of police station advice.[32]

Another important aspect is the relationship between the lawyer and their client. Police station representation will often be provided by a 'duty' solicitor – that is, a solicitor automatically assigned to deal with a case and who may have no prior relationship with the suspect (although this may not be the case). This lack of a relationship may create difficulties of communication and trust, which may of course hamper the provision of advice to a suspect. Many suspects will have 'own' solicitors – that is, lawyers they essentially retain and deal with on a regular basis, whom they know and trust. For a client, the major difference between a 'duty' and 'own' solicitor is

27 See Welsh, L, Skinns, L and Sanders, A, *Sanders & Young's Criminal Justice* (OUP, 2021); Pearse, J and Gudjonsson, G, 'A review of the role of the legal adviser in police stations' (1996) 6 *Criminal Behaviour and Mental Health*; Bridges, L and Choongh, S, 'Improving Police Station Legal Advice: The Impact of the Accreditation Scheme for Police Station Legal Advisers' (Law Society's Research and Policy Planning Unit, 1998); and more recently Kemp (n 18), which details the use of external 'agents' by firms of solicitors to provide police station legal advice.

28 Sanders et al (n 18).

29 Brown 1992 (n 18).

30 McConville, M and Hodgson, J, 'Custodial Legal Advice and the Right to Silence. Royal Commission on Criminal Justice Research Study No 16' (HMSO, 1993).

31 Phillips, C and Brown, D, 'Entry into the criminal justice system: a survey of police arrests and their outcomes' (Home Office, 1998).

32 For an account of this issue, see Bridges, L and Cape, E, 'CDS Direct: Flying in the face of the evidence' (Centre for Crime and Justice Studies, 2008), Ch 1: http://eprints.uwe.ac.uk/10488/1/CDSDirect.pdf (accessed 7 May 2020).

therefore choice, which in turn influences the level of trust in their lawyer (an important factor in the effectiveness of the relationship).[33]

It is important to re-emphasise that non-solicitor advice is not necessarily of a lesser quality. Well-trained and supervised non-solicitors will be equally able to provide good representation. However, in 1993, McConville and Hodgson identified several problems with advice provided by non-solicitors, including a lack of legal expertise and confidence, and over-identification with the police.[34] Since the mid-1990s, the situation has improved with the introduction of more stringent training for non-solicitors. In 1995, an accreditation scheme was established, testing non-solicitor advisers for knowledge, skills and practical application of knowledge and skills. In 1998, research by Bridges and Choongh found that the accreditation scheme had resulted in significant improvements, with advice of better quality, more time spent with clients, and more adversarial behaviour in police interviews.[35] Moreover, Bucke et al suggested that the scheme had led to a reduction in the number of non-solicitors providing advice (only 6% in their study).[36] In 2000, the accreditation scheme was extended to all police station duty solicitors, and finally to all solicitors by 2006. The police station accreditation scheme is a mandatory qualification for all lawyers providing legal advice to suspects in custody. The logic is therefore that, with comprehensive and tailored training, there will be improved quality of legal representation from both solicitors and non-solicitors.

An issue influencing who provides legal advice in police stations (and how they do so) is the fee paid for such work. Since 2008, police station advisers have received a fixed fee. The financial crisis in the late 2000s – and a subsequent reduction of 8.75% in fees for such work in 2015 – has placed significant pressure on those firms providing such services. The influence of money on lawyer behaviour has been examined on numerous occasions. Confirming and building on the earlier work of Samuel, Duff and others,[37] a 2007 study by Tata suggested that when choosing courses of action, defence lawyers lend greater weight to choices which promote both client and lawyer interests, particularly those which benefit the financial viability of the latter.[38] This demonstrates, perhaps unsurprisingly, that money can affect lawyer decision-making (even if it does not necessarily damage the client's interests). It also suggests that the breadth of professional discretion afforded lawyers in making decisions about action or inaction in representing a suspect means that money may act as an unintentional or unconscious influence on their assessment of what is or is not required in serving the client. In relation to police stations, Kemp suggested that fixed fees – incorporating travel, waiting and actual representation within one payment – caused legal advisers to spend less time in the police station, as well as encouraging firms to send less qualified staff, in

33 See Smith, T, 'Trust, Choice and Money: Why the legal aid "u-turn" is essential for effective criminal defence' (2013) *Crim LR*; and Skinns (n 21).

34 McConville and Hodgson (n 30); Choongh, S, *Policing as Social Discipline* (OUP, 1997).

35 Bridges and Choongh (n 27).

36 Bucke, T, Street, R and Brown, D, 'The right of silence: the impact of the Criminal Justice and Public Order Act 1994' (Home Office, 2000): http://library.college.police.uk/docs/hors/hors199.pdf (accessed 7 May 2020), 22.

37 Samuel, E, 'Criminal Legal Aid Expenditure: Supplier or System Driven? The Case of Scotland' (1996) in Young, R and Wall, D (eds), *Access to Criminal Justice: Legal Aid, Lawyers and the Defence of Liberty* (Blackstone Press, 2001); Duff, P et al, 'The Public Defence Solicitors Office: An Independent Evaluation' (Scottish Executive Central Research Unit, 2001).

38 Tata, C, 'In the interests of clients or commerce? Legal Aid, Supply, Demand, and "Ethical Indeterminacy" in Criminal Defence Work' (2007) 34 *J of Law & Soc* (4), 492.

order to lower costs.[39] She has also argued that because the fixed fee is insufficient to cover the whole range of work in the police station, this has led to 'some lawyers focusing on the police interview only, and not contacting clients until they attend at the station'.[40] In short, such a funding structure incentivises the provision of minimal service, as quickly as possible, and using the least expensive adviser available. The issue of funding as a factor influencing both availability and quality has been in the spotlight in recent years. In 2021, the Bellamy Review provided a generally grim picture of the financial situation in the sector.[41] One example was illustrative:

> [The lawyer was paid] a total of £249.11 for 13 hours which represents an hourly rate of £19.16 per hour. This does not seem to me a sensible way of remunerating serious work.[42]

As a result, the Review recommended a bare minimum 15% increase in fees for police station representation in December 2021. This was superficially implemented in September 2022, but with serious limitations (for example, no account was taken of soaring inflation during that year); the reality amounted to a 9% increase, far short of Bellamy's bare minimum.[43]

In this challenging context, there is an increasing body of evidence of an impact on who provides legal advice. In a 2018 study by Kemp, one solicitor commented that 'the low fee means that his firm often uses accredited representatives to provide advice rather than a qualified solicitor'.[44] In contrast, another stated, 'We haven't got the reps anymore because we've had to make them redundant.'[45] However, this did not mean that solicitors were filling this vacuum; in contrast, other respondents suggested that unregulated 'agencies' of non-solicitors had been set up to provide such work as cheaply as possible.[46]

These agencies operate outside of the normal framework applicable to traditional solicitors' firms, which requires a direct contract with the Legal Aid Agency (LAA) to provide police station advice. Instead, individual agents employed by the agencies are 'hired' on a temporary basis by firms, who do have a contract to provide police station advice. Agents have no specific internal supervising solicitor (required for accredited representatives employed by firms), though firms are contractually responsible for 'properly' supervising agents.[47] Instead, the firm – by virtue of hiring the agent – provides a form of 'surrogate' supervision. In essence, agents act in a similar manner to temporary or casual employees in other sectors, brought in for support on an ad hoc

39 See Kemp, V, 'Transforming Legal Aid: access to criminal defence services' (Legal Services Research Centre, 2010); see also Welsh, L, 'The Effects of Changes to Legal Aid Provision in Summary Criminal Cases: A Case Study' (2017) 44 *Journal of Law and Society* (4).

40 Kemp, V, 'Digital legal rights: exploring detainees' understanding of the right to a lawyer and potential barriers to accessing legal advice' (2020) *Crim LR* 2, 145.

41 Bellamy (n 16).

42 *Ibid* 69.

43 The Law Society, 'British justice in crisis: the end of criminal legal aid?' (28 March 2022): www.lawsociety.org.uk/topics/legal-aid/british-justice-in-crisis-the-end-of-criminal-legal-aid (accessed 13 March 2023).

44 Kemp, V (n 22), 20.

45 *Ibid* 4.

46 *Ibid* 25.

47 Legal Aid Agency, '2017 Standard Crime Contract standard terms' (2018), [3.3]: https://assets.publishing.service.gov.uk/government/uploads/system/uploads/attachment_data/file/819173/Standard_terms_-_version_2__current_version__effective_from_25_May_2018_.pdf (accessed 7 May 2020).

basis. One might question how robust this arrangement is as a check on quality. Agents are unlikely to have the same working relationship with a supervising solicitor as a firm's salaried employees. Moreover, they are not subject to the LAA tendering process to acquire work (although the LAA can require that agents appointed by a firm 'possess such experience, qualifications, or membership of such panel, or hold such accreditation as we may specify').[48]

Why do separate agencies exist and why do firms rely on them? From the perspective of the firm, provision of police station advice is both contractually required and valuable. It not only provides a reliable form of income (albeit an increasingly unprofitable one), it also enables firms to acquire new 'own' client work by converting 'duty' clients into long-term customers. Losing them would affect not only a firm's short-term income stream but its long-term client base, meaning that firms with a contract will strive to retain such work. Such work could be lost, depending on the firm's ability to provide representation when it is requested, and it will therefore do everything it can to avoid losing this to a competitor. In the increasingly challenging climate of modern legal aid funding, firms may lack employed solicitors or accredited representatives to service demand when it arises, or they may receive multiple requests whilst their lawyers are already engaged with other clients. This has led to another modern phenomenon known as 'stacking', where firms accept cases regardless of their immediate ability to deliver legal advice, adding clients to a 'queue'.

For the firm, this retains work (in theory), but this arrangement arguably threatens the best interests of police station suspects, due to delays in actually receiving advice – and the potential for them to change their mind and decline it entirely.[49] One method of relieving the 'stacking' conundrum is for firms to obtain external assistance – hence, the use of agencies who provide temporary cover when firms cannot adequately service the cases they have accepted. However, there are legitimate concerns about this model, with solicitors suggesting that agents are primarily interested in providing a swift service rather than a good quality one, which could leave clients feeling 'rushed'.[50] Additionally, it has been suggested that agencies are not underpinned by the same ethos of criminal defence practice as firms of solicitors, which cultivate a client- oriented culture.[51] Ultimately, the implication is that the use of agencies is primarily about maximising profit (for both the firm and the agency) rather than providing quality legal advice. This is clearly regarded as a problem by both those regulating lawyers, and lawyers themselves. In 2021, the Legal Aid Agency stated that 'the inappropriate use of inexperienced caseworkers on serious cases at the Police Station is frequently noted as a concern'.[52] For lawyers, the suggestion from research is that they are in a no-win situation:

---

48 *Ibid* [3.5].

49 See **5.2** above.

50 Kemp (n 22), 25.

51 Although for a more critical view of this claim regarding the ethos of criminal defence lawyers, see Newman, D, *Legal Aid Lawyers and the Quest for Justice* (Hart, 2013).

52 Legal Aid Agency, 'Improving your quality in Crime: A guide to common issues identified through Peer Review' (February 2021), 2: https://assets.publishing.service.gov.uk/government/uploads/system/uploads/attachment_data/file/966765/Crime_Guide_Quality_February_2021__2_.pdf (accessed 13 March 2023).

> If you're stuck you use an agent. I would rather not … but I've got no choice because sometimes I can't find any [solicitor] who will go out in the middle of the night for very poor pay.[53]

5.4 How is legal advice provided?

Alongside questions about who provides advice are questions about how such advice is provided. Previous research has suggested that in about 20% of cases, police station advice is provided by telephone only (but this has declined to around 10% according to recent statistics).[54] Generally, there is considerable variation in terms of provision between:

- duty solicitor and own solicitor cases, as referred to earlier; and
- different areas of the country, for example, rural and urban areas.

The Criminal Defence Service (CDS) Direct Scheme provides for telephone-only advice in less serious cases. This was criticised by Bridges and Cape, who argued that it had been rushed into service without proper evaluation and was of questionable legality in light of PACE 1984 and the ECHR.[55] They believed that the service created bureaucratic obstacles and delays to access to advice for suspects (for example, neither the police nor suspect could have direct contact with a requested lawyer) and criticised the fact that paralegals (rather than solicitors) were used to provide advice.[56] They concluded that it was aimed at reducing costs and deterring the take-up of legal advice.[57] More recent research by Kemp also highlights concerns about the privacy of telephone legal advice.[58] All legal advice is meant to be confidential, and s 58 of PACE 1984 entitles suspects to consult with their lawyer in private. Yet, in Kemp's study, 'solicitors said they would warn [clients] that the conversation can be overheard', concluding that '[t]his lack of privacy limits what solicitors can discuss with their clients over the phone, thereby undermining access to legal advice'.[59]

For those lawyers who do attend (which Kemp's 2018 study suggested would be most lawyers), an important aspect of police station representation is behaviour in police interviews.[60] Police coercion and intimidation can lead to false confessions and miscarriages of justice. As such, interventions by advisers in interviews are an important measure of how well protected suspects are. This was demonstrated in the 'Cardiff Three' case, in which one of the defendant's solicitors sat passively and failed to intervene whilst the police bullied and pressured the suspect to confess.[61] In 1992, research by Baldwin et al found that in 66% of interviews, solicitors said nothing (that

---

53 Gibbs, P and Ratcliffe, F, 'Criminal defence in an age of austerity: Zealous advocate or cog in a machine?' (Transform Justice, July 2019), 18: https://barrowcadbury.org.uk/wp-content/uploads/2022/01/TJ_JULY2019_The-Good-Lawyer.pdf (accessed 13 March 2023).

54 Phillips and Brown (n 31), 65; Ministry of Justice and Legal Aid Agency, 'Legal Aid Statistics England and Wales bulletin Jul to Sep 2022' (Ministry of Justice, 2022).

55 Bridges and Cape (n 32), Chs 2 and 3.

56 *Ibid* 3.

57 *Ibid* Chs 3 and 4.

58 Kemp (n 22). See also Pattenden, R and Skinns, L, 'Choice, Privacy and Publicly Funded Legal Advice at Police Stations' (2010) 73 *MLR* (3).

59 *Ibid* (Kemp) 5.

60 *Ibid.*

61 *Paris, Abdullahi and Miller* (1993) 97 Cr App R 99.

is, they did not challenge the police).[62] In 8% of interviews, solicitors 'pushed client's interests' – in short, they acted as an advocate for their client.[63] In 12% of interviews, solicitors sought to clarify matters – they were not aggressively adversarial but attempted to obtain more information for the client.[64] Troublingly, in 9% of interviews, solicitors adopted the role of a third (police) interviewer – they supported the police rather than their client.[65] Commentators have speculated that such passivity may have been due to a Code C emphasis on the lawyer's role as an adviser who should not obstruct the police interview.[66] After all, the police had, and still have, powers to eject solicitors who are disrupting or obstructing an interview.[67] Roberts rejected criticism of the contemporary Law Society guidance for police station advisers (which he authored) as facilitating this; yet he also stressed the need for cooperation and 'mutual respect'.[68] Baldwin argued that solicitors saw their role as ensuring 'fair play' and facilitating the process, rather than protecting or advancing the rights of a suspect. Dixon suggested that solicitors needed to maintain harmonious relations with work colleagues (the police).[69] These provide some explanations for why legal advisers adopted, in the past, a more passive role in police stations.

From a theoretical standpoint, this is somewhat problematic. In line with professional codes of conduct – and long-standing ethical principles – criminal defence lawyers arguably owe several important duties to accused persons, which require specialised skills, experience and an appropriate attitude towards such service. They should be loyal, non-judgmental partisans for clients' interests;[70] they must preserve confidences;[71] and they must be diligent in performing their role.[72] To effectively discharge these duties, they need a healthy working relationship with clients, based on trust. If clients do not trust that their lawyer will act loyally in their interests, guard their confidences or act diligently, they will disengage from any meaningful relationship; effective criminal defence becomes virtually impossible, rendering representation a merely symbolic gesture. Because of the circumstances in which they find themselves (that is, arrested and detained in police custody, with the possibility of criminal prosecution), suspects are often stressed, anxious, angry or scared. Ensuring that a client is communicative and cooperative may be challenging for a defence lawyer, but it

62 Baldwin, J, 'The Role of Legal Representatives at Police Stations' (HMSO, 1992); this study is summarised in 'Editorial: The conduct of police investigations' (1993) *Crim LR* (1) and Roberts, D, 'Questioning the suspect: the solicitor's role' (1993) *Crim LR* (1).

63 *Ibid.*

64 *Ibid.*

65 *Ibid.*

66 *Ibid*; Welsh et al (n 27).

67 PACE Code C, [6.9] and the notes for guidance which limit when the police can do so – but in broad terms.

68 Roberts (n 62) – a defence which Welsh et al (n 27) have questioned.

69 Dixon, D, 'Common sense, legal advice and the right of silence' (1991) *Public Law*, 236.

70 Examples include the classic 'zealous advocate' statement of Lord Brougham during the trial of Queen Caroline (1821); *Medcalf v Mardell* [2002] UKHL 27; *Ulcay* [2007] EWCA Crim 2379; and r C15 of the Bar Code of Conduct (Bar Standards Board, 'The BSB Handbook' (February 2020), Part 2: The Conduct Rules).

71 See PACE 1984, s 10; the relevant professional codes of conduct for solicitors and accredited representatives; and case law such as *Three Rivers District Council v Governor and Company of the Bank of England (No 6)* [2004] UKHL 48.

72 See Solicitors Regulation Authority, 'SRA Code of Conduct for Solicitors, RELs and RFLs' (November 2019), Part 3: Service and Competence: www.sra.org.uk/solicitors/standards-regulations/code-conduct-solicitors/ (accessed 7 May 2020).

is essential. They need to hear the client's account of a case, including relevant facts and details. The suspect may know of alibis or witnesses who should be contacted; alternatively, they may be vulnerable and have specific needs that have to be met. Whilst COs are also expected to identify such vulnerabilities, this can be missed. Once a defence representative has established this relationship (often in a short space of time), the provision of loyal, robust, discreet and accurate advice and representation becomes achievable. If the defence lawyer can effectively perform their role and satisfy these professional obligations, the client will generally be well served, their fundamental rights protected, and the risk of miscarriages of justice lowered. In contrast, passivity and disengagement are unlikely to fulfil the above requirements and leave the suspect without the legal (and moral) support they need in a hostile environment.

Since the early 1990s, the role of the lawyer in the police station has arguably developed beyond mere adviser to active defender. A more positive, adversarial, description of the defence lawyer's role was incorporated into Code C in 1995 under Note for Guidance 6D:

> The solicitor's only role in the police station is to protect and advance the legal rights of his client.

This appears to implicitly rule out any role other than a client-oriented one and couch it more adversarial terms than the past. Nonetheless, Jackson argues that the current conception of the police station legal adviser 'falls short of giving lawyers any full-blooded adversarial role that is reserved for the trial process'.[73] This is unfortunate considering the enormous influence the police investigation has on all future stages of a case. The nature of the charge and the extent of the evidence available to all parties are generally determined at the investigative stage, and they will shape the direction of the case – from first hearing, to trial, to sentencing. Indeed, the provisions in s 34 of the Criminal Justice and Public Order Act (CJPOA) 1994, enabling inferences to be drawn from silence (see **Chapter 6**), invest even greater importance in the police station stage. The role of the lawyer in advising a suspect on whether to remain silent must be carefully considered. This provision has, however, arguably made adversarial behaviour on the part of the defence lawyer more difficult, possibly discouraging it. All of the above is worth considering in the context of the well-established gaps that emerge between legal rules and the reality of practice.

Even if regulation conceptualises lawyers as adversarial defenders of suspects' rights, their actual behaviour may not reflect this:

> I think a lot of people can forget what their role is in the interview. They don't want to upset anybody. Unless you're an assertive person, someone who can speak up and be confident about it, then you're going to struggle. Your client doesn't want you to upset the police a lot of the time, but this is ridiculous because we're there to protect them.[74]

Newman suggested that defence lawyers may consider themselves to be champions of the accused in a theoretical sense, but in fact they fall short of this in reality (sometimes

73 Jackson, J, 'Responses to Salduz: Procedural Tradition, Change and the Need for Effective Defence' (2016) 79(6) *MLR* 1011.

74 Gibbs and Ratcliffe (n 53), 18.

showing active disdain for clients).[75] Some of the behaviour observed by Newman can perhaps be explained in terms of economics. A theme throughout his study was the lack of respect afforded to clients by their lawyers, arguing that lawyers had 'moved away from client-centeredness and towards managerial, profit centred concerns', and that 'the values that informed these lawyers should take centre stage over and above how they coped financially'.[76] Indeed, a repeated complaint by the defence lawyers interviewed was the underfunding of the legal aid system and inadequate personal remuneration. However, Thornton has more recently argued that, in the context of police station representation, poor pay for challenging work 'reward[s] and encourage[s] perceived poor practices and values to thrive at the expense of other concerns … such as the conviction of the guilty, acquittal of the innocent, fair treatment of both victims and defendants, and value for the taxpayer'.[77] In short, he argued that 'criminal legal aid lawyers are set up to fail by the current financial conditions within which they must work',[78] with an example quote from a practitioner: 'You either do the job properly and lose money or you don't do the job properly'.[79]

As such, it is arguable that the financial devaluation of the criminal defence profession, and the concomitant lack of respect conferred, has led to a collective collapse in self-esteem. Indeed, Thornton suggests that this has severely affected the autonomy, integrity and morale of police custody lawyers, which impacts on both retention and recruitment.[80] In turn, this demoralised and under-appreciated profession projects this disrespect onto its clients. Such an attitude may make it less likely that lawyers will provide adversarial protection.

5.5 The effect of legal advice

It is important to examine what, if any, effect legal advice has on suspect behaviour in police stations. In assessing this, there is a need to distinguish between the effect on outcomes (for example, whether suspects remain silent, are charged or are convicted) and the effect on process (for example, a suspect's experience of being detained and interrogated by the police). In 1998, Phillips and Brown conducted research on the outcomes of advice, and found that suspects who received it were much less likely to make admissions and much more likely to remain silent in police interviews than suspects who did not receive advice.[81] They offered the following explanation for these findings:

> [I]t is highly likely that those who plan to fight the case and who are not inclined to assist the police by answering questions are more likely to seek legal advice.[82]

---

75 Newman (n 51). An overview is provided in Newman, D, 'Why do some defence lawyers regard their clients as "a problem"?' (*The Justice Gap*, 1 November 2017): www.thejusticegap.com/defence-lawyers-regard-clients-problem/ (accessed 14 July 2020). Newman argues that there may be complex reasons to explain this discrepancy, including 'neurosis' relating to the positive attitude lawyers have towards the 'welfarist' aspects of their work, and the reality of low pay and limited respect.

76 Newman (n 51), 158–9.

77 Thornton, J, 'The Way in Which Fee Reductions Influence Legal Aid Criminal Defence Lawyer Work: Insights from a Qualitative Study' (2019) *J of Law and Soc* 46(4), 581.

78 *Ibid.*

79 *Ibid*, 581.

80 Thornton, J, 'Is publicly funded criminal defence sustainable? Legal aid cuts, morale, retention and recruitment in the English criminal law professions' (2019) *Legal Studies* 40(2).

81 Phillips and Brown (n 31), Ch 5. For more on this see **Chapter 6.**

82 *Ibid* 77.

This suggests that legal advice does not tend to encourage suspects to fight and obstruct, but it is in fact sought out by those inclined to such an approach. In short, legal advice does not cause people to remain silent or fight a case; rather suspects who are pre-disposed to challenge the police seek legal advice. Research has also been conducted into the impact of legal advice on the process. In 2010, research by Kemp suggested that the ability of a suspect to choose their lawyer improved the relationship and led to a better experience.[83] She stated that:

> Where the client has 'trust and confidence' in their solicitor … it is likely to encourage them to experience the process as being fair and thus to be more accepting … of [its] legitimacy.[84]

However, in their 2014 study 'Inside Police Custody', Blackstock et al came to less favourable conclusions.[85] They suggested that lawyers in the police station tended to be 'interrogation focused' and were less likely to value other aspects of their role, such as:

- identifying vulnerable suspects, for example those with mental health or addiction issues;
- advising on other investigative actions;
- checking the legality of police action; and
- negotiating release of their client.

Failure to address these aspects can potentially have a substantial impact on the suspect's 'experience' of the process.

5.6 Police interviews

The police have a significant degree of freedom as to when and how they interview suspects. Moreover, the prosecution can use the product of interviews as evidence against the accused, and the exclusion of such evidence is limited. However, a variety of due process safeguards exist in relation to police interrogations; for example, there are limits on the police power to require a suspect to submit to interviewing; the police have no power to pressurise or coerce suspects into admissions of guilt during interviews; and they are not allowed to use confessions as evidence unless they are made voluntarily.

5.6.1 Why do the police interview?

In 1993, John Baldwin published the results of research into police interview techniques.[86] Among various conclusions, he argued:

> Instead of a search for truth, it is much more realistic to see interviews as mechanisms directed towards the 'construction of proof'.[87]

This has long been a working theory regarding the objective of police interviews – that is, to prove an allegation as true, as opposed to a more open inquiry into a suspect's perspective on events. Securing admissions of guilt (a primary form of proof) has

83 Kemp (n 39).

84 *Ibid* 92.

85 Blackstock (n 18).

86 Baldwin, J, 'Police Interview Techniques: Establishing Truth or Proof?' (1993) 33 *Brit J of Criminol* (3).

87 *Ibid* 327.

therefore been considered to be the main goal of an interview.[88] In 2009, the now defunct National Policing Improvement Agency (NPIA) published its 'National Investigative Interviewing Strategy'.[89] It stated:

> An effective interview of a suspect will commit them to an account of events that may include an admission. In the admission, the suspect may detail how the offence was committed and thus the investigation can be more focused … a properly obtained admission can prove the *mens rea* of the offence, beyond doubt.[90]

This lends support to the theory that confessions are valuable to the police because they help to prove an offence. More recent guidance is less explicit regarding the goal of obtaining confessions. Principle Five of the College of Policing's 'Investigative Interviewing' practice guidance highlights the 'positive impact of an early admission'.[91] It outlines the various 'benefits' of an early admission to various parties (including victims and the court). Most relevant are the benefits to the police, who

> gain valuable intelligence, increase detected offences rates, record a fuller picture of offending for possible use in future cases or to support applications for anti-social behaviour orders, or other restrictive orders.[92]

Whilst less emphatic about the 'proof' element, this still demonstrates that an admission of guilt is important to police interviewers.

A confession or admission by a suspect is the easiest way of securing a conviction. Unless there are serious questions about abuse of process or intimidation of a suspect, a confession in interview will be taken to be the 'truth'. Confessions largely eliminate the need to secure other evidence, as a case can usually be firmly based on this one foundation (and there is no requirement for corroboration in England and Wales).[93] They provide a very clear explanation of the internal thought process of a suspect at the time of an offence, thus supplying the mental element of an offence (*mens rea*). Confessions enable more cases to be 'cleared up' or resolved quickly; in short, they are more efficient and cost-effective for the police. Indeed, as Principle Five of 'Investigative Interviewing' asserts, confessions create 'the potential for savings … as offences can be dealt with promptly without additional court hearings' and 'resources … are used efficiently'.[94] Sanders et al have also argued that an unspoken, and perhaps controversial, reason for interviewing is to exercise power over the suspect population – a form of social and political control over, or 'ownership' of, certain portions of the citizenry.[95]

88 Welsh et al (n 27). According to the courts, this appears to be a legitimate reason for detaining and interviewing a suspect (see *Holgate-Mohammed v Duke* [1984] 1 All ER 1054 and **Chapter 7**).

89 NPIA, 'National Investigative Interviewing Strategy' (2009): http://library.college.police.uk/docs/npia/BP-Nat-Investigative-Interviewing-Strategy-2009.pdf (accessed 7 May 2020).

90 *Ibid* 6.

91 College of Policing, 'Investigative Interviewing' (11 January 2016): www.app.college.police.uk/app-content/investigations/investigative-interviewing/ (accessed 7 May 2020).

92 *Ibid.*

93 This can be contrasted with criminal procedure in Japan, where Article 38 of the Constitution states that 'No person shall be convicted or punished in cases where the only proof against him is his own confession'. See **Chapter 7**.

94 College of Policing (n 91).

95 Welsh et al (n 27).

5.6.2 Defining a police 'interview'

It is important to specify how an interview is formally defined. Certain safeguards will apply to all police interviews, designed to protect the rights of suspects and the legitimacy of the process. If an exchange between the police and a suspect is not classified as an interview, the safeguards do not apply. Equally, if something falls within the definition and the safeguards are not upheld, there may be a breach of PACE 1984 and its Codes. The police may attempt to circumvent such safeguards by using interrogation techniques that amount to an interview but are disguised as something else. A good example is *Allan v United Kingdom*, in which a coached police 'stooge' was used to interrogate a suspect who had been remanded in custody.[96] According to para 11.1A of Code C:

> An interview is the questioning of a person regarding their involvement or suspected involvement in a criminal offence or offences which ... must be carried out under caution.

Paragraph 10.1 of Code C emphasises that the administering of the caution before interview is essential 'if [a suspect's] answers or silence may be given in evidence to a court in a prosecution'. In short, making the suspect aware of their rights (and the potential impact of silence) is a due process protection applicable to those interviews which are geared towards prosecution.

5.6.3 When can the police interview?

Generally, an interview must take place at a police station. There are limitations on the ability of the police to interview a suspect outside of the police station (for example, at a suspect's home). Paragraph 11.1 of Code C states:

> Following a decision to arrest a suspect, [the suspect] must not be interviewed about the relevant offence except at a police station or other authorised place of detention, unless the consequent delay would be likely to:
> (a) lead to ... interference with, or harm to, evidence connected with an offence ... interference with, or physical harm to, other people; or ... serious loss of, or damage to, property;
> (b) lead to alerting other people suspected of committing an offence but not yet arrested for it; or
> (c) hinder the recovery of property obtained in consequence of the commission of an offence.

As such, interviews should only take place away from the police station in circumstances where the investigation would be substantially impaired – in short, when it is urgent. A prime motivation for requiring interviews to take place at the police station is to ensure that a CO can properly assess whether a suspect should be released, charged or detained, and whether they are vulnerable. It also ensures that suspects can exercise their rights (eg to legal advice) as swiftly and effectively as possible. This is therefore a due process-oriented safeguard.

5.7 Safeguards in police interviews

A variety of safeguards exist to protect suspects in police interviews, recognising the potential for abuse and unfairness. We have already covered the right to legal advice in

96 *Allan v United Kingdom* [2002] ECHR 702.

interviews (PACE 1984, s 58 and Code C, Section 6). Additionally, para 11.15 of Code C requires that an appropriate adult be present in a police interview of a juvenile or vulnerable suspect, with limited exceptions. This will usually be a parent or someone otherwise charged with the care of the suspect. It could also be a social worker or other relevant adult connected to the juvenile, as long as it not a police officer or police employee. The exceptional circumstances when an interview can take place without an appropriate adult are the same as those applicable to interviews away from police stations (see above). Interestingly, Code C makes it clear that an appropriate adult is 'not expected to act simply as an observer' but to 'advise the person being interviewed' and to check that 'the interview is being conducted properly and fairly'.[97] This therefore suggests a quasi-lawyer role, designed to ensure that an appropriate adult is not simply another warm body in the room – that is, it is more than a 'presentational' safeguard. Importantly, the police also have an obligation to record interviews.[98] It ensures that a record of what was said in interview is contemporaneous, has not been doctored or fabricated, and it deters pressure or coercion of suspects by the police (since it would be captured).

Paragraph 11.5 of Code C prohibits the use of oppression in order to obtain answers or statements from a suspect. This might be in the form of overly aggressive interviewing, offering of inducements or the use of subtle threats (for example, an officer suggesting negative consequences should the suspect not comply, such as prosecution, searching of personal property, etc). This provision is clearly designed to uphold due process principles of legitimacy, reliability, fairness and the supremacy of individual rights. The creation of this provision recognised the problems identified by the Philips Commission in the late 1970s, namely that oppressive and coercive police interrogation techniques were leading to unsafe convictions and miscarriages of justice. Section 12 of Code C places limits on the length of interviews, when interviews can take place (for example, not normally at night), and it sets minimum environmental conditions for interview locations. As such, the provision recognises that long interviews, inappropriately timed interviews and poor conditions can effectively amount to oppression and substantially raise the risk of a suspect offering a false confession. It therefore seeks to minimise their use as a 'passive' interrogation tactic. The length of the interviews conducted in the 'Cardiff Three' case was strongly criticised by the Court of Appeal; indeed, one of the defendants was interviewed for a total of 13 hours over the course of five days, denying his involvement in any offence over 300 times.[99] Code C does not set a maximum length for an interview, but it specifies that in a 24-hour period, a suspect must have eight continuous hours of rest and that there should be breaks approximately every two hours.[100] Interview rooms must be adequately heated, lit and ventilated, and suspects must not be made to stand during interviews.[101]

There are some limitations to the due process-oriented safeguards applicable to police interrogations, outlined under PACE 1984 and Code C. For example, as stated above, para 11.1 does permit interviews away from a police station in some circumstances. These circumstances are open to interpretation; for example, how will

97 Code C, [11.17].

98 According to Code C, [11.7] and Codes E (Audio recording interviews with suspects) and F (Visual recording with sound of interviews with suspects).

99 *Paris* (n 61).

100 Code C, [12.2] and [12.8].

101 *Ibid* [12.4] and [12.6].

the police show that evidence may be interfered with? What is the standard of proof for this? In terms of the definition of an interview, some conversations or unprovoked admissions are not classed as such. Therefore, the safeguards attached to interviews (such as cautioning, the right to legal advice and the length of interviews) will not be applicable. Yet such exchanges could form part of the case against a suspect or assist the police in their investigation. Moreover, breaches of Code C (or any other Code of Practice) will not necessarily result in exclusion of evidence.[102] Such breaches need to be significant and substantial, and they need to lead to unfairness.[103] As such, whether some of the safeguards mentioned above represent, in reality, a protection for suspects can be questioned, as breaching them may have little negative consequence for the police.

5.8 Summary

- All suspects in a police station have the right to a lawyer. The effectiveness of this right depends on factors such as trust, quality, funding and method of delivery.
- Police interviews are the primary method of investigation. They are arguably more than an information-gathering exercise; they are a statement of power and control and a key tool for securing convictions – in particular by securing admissions of guilt.
- The definition of an interview is essential to ensuring that the process is not abused and that suspects' rights are protected.
- Interview safeguards may be undermined if suspects can be interrogated through casual conversations or other techniques, or if breaches have limited consequences.

102 Cape, E, 'Transposing the EU Directive on the right to information: a firecracker or a damp squib?' (2015) *Crim LR* (1), 61.

103 See *Keenan* [1990] 2 QB 54 and *Delaney* (1988) 88 Cr App R 338.

chapter 6

The Right to Silence

6.1 Introduction

Nemo tenetur seipsum accusare ('no man is bound to accuse himself')

Having examined the processes of detaining and interrogating suspects of crime, one can conclude that there is much significance in what the suspect says at the police station and that the police have substantial power to influence this. We have discussed a variety of safeguards designed to protect suspects from abuses of power and promote legitimate evidence gathering. Many of these are relatively new innovations; they are also (to some extent) dependent on other figures (eg the police or lawyers) undertaking their roles in a fair manner. It therefore seems imperative to examine a principle that underlies all stages of the criminal justice process and has particular importance in the police station. In contrast to other safeguards, this right is (comparatively) ancient and dependent only on a suspect's or defendant's willingness to exercise it. It is the right to silence.

> **definition**
>
> The **right to silence** allows suspects and defendants in criminal proceedings to refuse to answer questions put to them; to refuse to provide information to authority figures; or to refuse to address allegations made against them.

Those accused of crimes can essentially decline to communicate anything to the police, the prosecution or the court – most specifically, information that would harm their own interests. As such, a suspect does not have to answer the questions of the police about criminal accusations, and a defendant is not compelled to give evidence at their own trial. This right is key to upholding every accused person's privilege against self-incrimination: that is, protection from being compelled to provide information or evidence which damages their legal interests or implicates them in criminal behaviour. This is, in itself, an essential due process safeguard because it 'discourages ill-treatment of a suspect and secondly … it discourages the production of dubious confessions'.[1]

The privilege thus facilitates the accuracy and legitimacy of criminal proceedings; reinforces the burden of proof borne by the prosecution; and underlines the presumption that all are legally innocent until proven guilty, and therefore should not be forced to undermine their own interests. The right to silence is an essential part of the privilege against self-incrimination; if we see the privilege as the 'goal', then silence is a 'means' by which that goal is achieved. The right to silence is a thread running through and binding together all the key tenets of fair and legitimate criminal justice. This is the theory; in this chapter we will explore how this right is expressed in practice,

1 *AT & T Istel v Tully* [1993] AC 45, *per* Templeman LJ at 53.

and why this theory seems somewhat idealistic in the modern age of criminal procedure.

6.2 The origin of the right to silence

Langbein argues that the right to silence was essentially the creation of defence lawyers, originating alongside the rise of adversarial criminal procedure in the 18th century.[2] Prior to this, the defendant's right to speak was considered the key safeguard in the criminal justice process (generally referred to as the 'accused speaks' form of trial – see **8.7**).[3] After a series of miscarriages of justice in the late 1600s, the expectation that the defendant would speak was gradually supplanted by a desire that they would say nothing and that a lawyer would be their voice.[4] Indeed, until the late 1800s, there existed a common law prohibition on criminal defendants providing testimony at their own trial on the grounds of 'interest' – that is, a defendant's evidence might be partial and perjured. With lawyers and (eventually) witnesses to speak in their defence, defendants were sidelined. This changed with the passage of s 1 of the Criminal Evidence Act (CEA) 1898, which allowed defendants to appear as witnesses at their own trials if they chose to.[5] Furthermore, a failure to give evidence would 'not be made the subject of any comment by the prosecutor'.[6] Therefore, the CEA 1898 not only allowed a defendant to give evidence, but it enshrined two mutually dependent concepts:

- giving evidence should be *voluntary*; and
- declining to do so should not allow the prosecution to undermine the defence.

The CEA 1898 represented the first legislative foundation for the right to silence at trial, later built on and adapted by 20th century case law.[7] However, it was clear from an early point that the right was not absolute. Shortly after the passage of the CEA 1898, the courts clarified that judges could comment on silence, even if prosecutors could not.[8] Thus, if a defendant chose not to testify, there could be 'evidentiary consequences stemming from such a decision'.[9]

---

2 Langbein, J, 'The Historical Origins of the Privilege Against Self-incrimination at Common Law' (1993-1994) 92 *Mich LR* 1084.

3 Langbein notes that, prior to the emergence of defence lawyers, a defendant's silence was tantamount to 'suicide' (*ibid*).

4 The primary example is the 'Popish Plot' in the late 1670s – a fabricated treason conspiracy, which led to several trials and executions of innocent persons. After the Glorious Revolution of 1689, legislation was passed (the Treason Trials Act 1696) allowing defence counsel for defendants in treason trials. This reversed a ban on defence lawyers for serious crimes, which had stood since the 13th century. This arguably kickstarted a gradual change in the culture of criminal justice in England and Wales. For more on this, see Langbein, J, *The Origins of Adversary Criminal Trial* (OUP, 2005) and Smith, T, 'Zealous Advocates: The historical foundations of the adversarial criminal defence lawyer' (2012) 2 *Law, Crime & History* (1).

5 Section 1 states that 'Every person charged with an offence ... shall be a competent witness for the defence at every stage of the proceedings', and that a defendant could not be called as a witness unless 'upon his own application'.

6 *Ibid* s 1(b).

7 Maloney, R, 'The Criminal Evidence (NI) Order 1988: A Radical Departure from the Common Law Right to Silence in the UK?' (1993) 16 *Boston College Int & Comp LR* (2), 426.

8 *Rhodes* (1899) 1 QB 77.

9 *Chandler* [1976] 1 WLR 585, 589. For the classic articulation of this judicial discretion to comment prior to legislative reform in the 1990s, see *Christie* [1914] AC 545, 554.

The establishment and development of the police as the primary agency for detecting and preventing crime raised issues about the right to silence during criminal investigations.[10] The key principle that evolved was that suspects should not be compelled to answers questions, on pain of punishment. This was clearly recognised in *Rice v Connolly*, when Lord Parker stated:

> It seems to me quite clear that though every citizen has a moral duty or, if you like, a social duty to assist the police, there is no legal duty to that effect, and indeed the whole basis of the common law is that right of the individual to refuse to answer questions put to him by persons in authority.[11]

Occasionally, the police and other investigative agencies have effectively been granted the power to compel suspects to speak, in that a failure to do so results in a criminal sanction.[12] This subversion of the right to silence – and by extension the privilege against self-incrimination – was recognised by the ECtHR in *Saunders v United Kingdom*, declaring such evidence inadmissible at trial.[13]

6.3 The scope of the right to silence

Michael and Emmerson argue:

> [The right to silence] is not a single, discernible, right ... but rather, consists of a cluster, composed of crumbs from different procedural rules ... each related, in one way or another, to the protection against self-incrimination.[14]

This is evident in its lengthy, piecemeal evolution through (at times conflicting) case law.[15] The characterisation of the right as a 'cluster' was well articulated in *Director of Serious Fraud Office, ex parte Smith*, which summarised the basic entitlement as 'immunity from being compelled to answer questions or give evidence, on pain of punishment'.[16] The court divided the right into two general immunities (possessed by everyone) and four specific immunities (possessed by certain people in certain situations).

The 'general' immunities

The court in *Smith* stated that all persons and bodies possess a general immunity from being compelled:

- to answer questions posed by other persons or bodies; or
- to provide answers which may incriminate them.

10 The modern, centralised, professional police force we are familiar with arguably originated with the Metropolitan Police Act 1829, which replaced disparate local constables with the MPS.

11 [1966] 2 QB 414, 419.

12 For an example, see the Terrorism Act 2000, Sch 7, particularly [5] and [18] which make it an offence to 'wilfully' fail to give an examining officer information when questioned at a port or border area.

13 (1997) 23 EHRR 313. Section 59 and Sch 3 of the Youth Justice and Criminal Evidence Act (YJCEA) 1999 amended various statutes to give effect to this. There are arguably some gaps in protection, however; see *Beghal v DPP* [2015] UKSC 49, in which the Supreme Court judged Sch 7 to be compatible with the ECHR because evidence gathered would not be used in subsequent criminal proceedings against suspects.

14 Michael, J and Emmerson, B, 'Current Topic: The Right to Silence' (1996) 1 *European Human Rights Law Review*, 6.

15 *Gilbert* (1977) 66 Cr App R 237, 244.

16 [1993] AC 1. 'On pain of punishment' is a relic from the era of torture, but still relevant even today – see below.

These immunities therefore form the most basic and broad description of the right to silence.

The 'specific' immunities

The court also identified four specific immunities existing in a narrow category of circumstances:

(a) immunity possessed by all persons suspected of a criminal offence from being compelled to answer questions during a police interview (reflecting the dicta of *Rice v Connolly*);

(b) immunity possessed by a defendant at trial from being compelled to give evidence or to answer questions put to them;

(c) immunity possessed by persons charged with an offence from having questions material to that offence addressed to them by police officers. Once a suspect is charged, they can no longer be interrogated about the offence by the police because the court becomes the primary investigative body;

(d) immunity possessed (in certain circumstances) by a defendant at trial from having adverse comment made on any failure to answer questions before trial or to give evidence at trial. This was, for a long time, a key part of right to silence and seen as essential to the effective functioning of the right. It protected suspects and defendants from being openly labelled as 'suspicious' or 'guilty' for refusing to answer questions, and it implicitly recognised the idea that silence does not always indicate guilt. Whilst this had been gradually restricted via case law, this fourth specific immunity has been severely eroded by modern legislation.

6.4 Debates about the right to silence

The right to silence has evolved over several centuries, accompanied by passionate debate regarding its place in the criminal justice system. We will now briefly review some of its theoretical advantages and disadvantages. They can be summarised as follows:

Advantages

- It protects suspects and defendants against mistreatment and unfairness.
- It respects individual rights such as liberty, privacy and fair trial.
- It is necessary due to the limitations of other protections.

Disadvantages

- It is exploited by the guilty to frustrate legitimate criminal justice processes.
- It is an unnecessary and excessive safeguard in the modern era.
- It is counter-productive, increasing the possibility of mistreatment and unfairness.

The debate illustrates the basic conflict between civil libertarian and utilitarian arguments. Civil libertarians emphasise the protection of individual rights for all and therefore 'tend towards favouring protection of the minority'. [17] In contrast, 'utility tends towards favouring control by the majority' and ensuring that the interests of the greater good are advanced.[18] Civil libertarians would argue that, in an adversarial system, the prosecution must prove guilt and the defendant should not be coerced or

17 MacPartholan, C, 'Evolution of an Erosion: The Historico-legal Development of Sections 34–38 of the Criminal Justice and Public Order Act 1994' (2017) 81 *JCL* (2), 105.

18 *Ibid.*

compelled to help (particularly by having their own silence used against them). In contrast, utilitarians would argue that the public interest should not allow criminals to hide behind rights designed to protect the innocent, and that courts should be able to interpret the meaning of a suspect's silence for themselves (specifically that it indicates guilt).[19]

6.4.1 Advantages

The right to silence protects against mistreatment and unfairness

To some extent, the right to silence is justified by the imperfect history of criminal procedure in England and Wales and a desire to avoid repeating it. The use of torture to extract evidence from criminal suspects is an example of this. Whilst this was primarily an issue in European inquisitorial systems for many centuries, it was undeniably a problem in England and Wales in the late Middle Ages (particularly during England's so-called 'century of torture').[20] Lawfully sanctioned torture was abolished in 1640;[21] and the Bill of Rights later prohibited 'cruel and unusual punishment'.[22]

Some courts also had the scope to treat defendants unfairly, with particularly bad examples being the Courts of Star Chamber and High Commission. These institutions – controlled by the Monarch and the Church – operated arbitrarily and without scrutiny. They involved no juries or witnesses; hearings were held in secret; and procedures were flexible, lacking basic safeguards for defendants.[23] At times, they were used by sitting Monarchs to punish political enemies, not achievable through conventional channels. Moreover, they used *ex officio* procedure, in which the accused was told to swear an oath that they would answer the courts' questions – on pain of punishment.[24] In the face of significant opposition from reformers (particularly John Lilburne), these courts were dissolved in 1641.[25] Despite these changes, it would clearly be naïve to assume that these new laws immediately translated into practice.[26] It might be more accurate to argue that the courts gradually developed the privilege against self-incrimination and the right to silence as part of a shifting culture rather than as a direct reaction, forming a bulwark against such practices re-emerging.[27]

In the 19th century, Parliament and the courts further strengthened the right to silence as a counter-balance to other disadvantages suffered by defendants in the

---

19 Clearly, this also represents a tension between crime control and due process perspectives (see **Chapter 1**).

20 Between the years 1540 and 1640 (Langbein, J, *Torture and the Law of Proof* (University of Chicago Press, 1977), 140). For more on the history of torture in criminal procedure in England and Wales, see Langbein (above); Hope, D, 'Torture' (2004) *ICLQ* 53; Friedman, D, 'Torture and the Common Law' (2006) *EHRLR* (2) 180; and Heath, J, *Torture and English Law: An Administrative and Legal History from the Plantagenets to the Stuarts* (Greenwood Press, 1982).

21 Habeas Corpus Act 1640 (16 Charles I, c 10). Torture had been conducted under warrants from the Privy Council. The statute transferred jurisdiction over the estates and liberties of citizens to the ordinary courts, and the Privy Council lost this ability. Thereafter, torture 'played no part in the legal system of England after the Restoration' (Hope (n 20), 812).

22 1689 c 2, 1 Will and Mar Sess 2.

23 See Quirk, H, *The Rise and Fall of the Right of Silence* (Routledge, 2016), Ch 1: 'The origins of the right of silence'.

24 Langbein (n 20), 1073.

25 MacNair, M, 'The Early Development of the Privilege against Self-Incrimination' (1990) 10 *OJLS* (1), 66–67.

26 For example, torture played a part in the Popish Plot conspiracy – see n 4.

27 See MacNair (n 25). For more on the conflicting accounts of the origins of the right to silence/privilege against self-incrimination, see Quirk, H, 'The Right of Silence in England and Wales: Sacred Cow, Sacrificial Lamb or Trojan Horse?' in J Jackson and S Summers (eds), *Obstacles to Fairness in Criminal Proceedings: Individual Rights and Institutional Forms* (Hart, 2018).

criminal justice system, for example the poor quality of juries, magistrates and lawyers; the excessive speed of trials; and the lack of any mechanism of appeal for defendants.[28] The use of torture and secret courts might appear to be old problems; but the original ideas behind the right to silence – ensuring freedom from threats, violence or punishment, and ensuring the legitimacy of evidence – remain important justifications for the right today, for both practical and principled reasons.[29]

The influence of this flawed history is evident in the now well-established principle that evidence is inadmissible if obtained from suspects who are compelled to speak on 'pain of punishment'. This clearly includes evidence resulting from the use of violence and threats (which may or may not amount to torture). In *Peart*, the Privy Council highlighted the moral objection to such evidence, asserting that 'reliance on statements so obtained shocks the conscience, abuses or degrades judicial proceedings and involves the state in moral defilement'.[30] Moreover, such evidence may have little practical value, in that innocent suspects may admit guilt simply to escape severe mistreatment. There is also the 'positive rule' that statements which have been 'obtained from [the accused] either by fear of prejudice or hope of advantage exercised or held out by a person in authority' are not admissible.[31] The right to silence helps to enforce these rules by providing the accused with legal (if not literal) protection from compulsion when faced with coercion. Other safeguards (such as recording of interviews or the provision of a lawyer) help with this, but they are inevitably dependent on others (particularly police officers) respecting such safeguards. In contrast, the right to silence is truly 'controlled' by the suspect and may be their only form of power in the police station.[32] Its importance is underlined by the argument that the police search for 'proof' rather then 'truth' when dealing with suspects.[33] Rather than searching for objective truth, the police may focus on demonstrating a suspect's guilt, in the belief that they have 'the right person'. Again, the right to silence mitigates this by allowing suspects to refuse to give the police an account which may be used to confirm their prejudices.

The right to silence protects individual rights

In *Allan v United Kingdom*, the court stated that 'the right to silence ... serves in principle to protect the freedom of a suspected person to choose whether to speak or to remain silent under police questioning'.[34] Arguably, the key word in this quote is 'freedom'. Citizens in England and Wales have long-established rights to liberty, privacy and dignity, confirmed most recently and authoritatively by the ECHR and its related jurisprudence.[35] All are facets of the concept of individual freedom in a liberal democracy, and the right to silence is an expression of this. The right to privacy is well justified when one considers that suspects in criminal proceedings may have non-suspicious reasons for maintaining silence: for example, the desire to protect another person; embarrassment; fear; confusion; or the possibility that (as a non-lawyer) a

28 MacPartholan (n 17), 103.

29 One might also point to a modern example of a 'secret' court in England and Wales – the Special Immigration Appeals Commission (SIAC).

30 [2006] UKPC 5, [23].

31 *Ibrahim v R* [1914] AC 599, 609.

32 Quirk (n 23), Ch 3: 'Police custody, cop culture and the caution'.

33 Baldwin, J, 'Police Interview Techniques: Establishing Truth or Proof?' (1993) 33 *Brit J of Criminol* (3).

34 (2003) 36 EHRR 12, [50].

35 See particularly Articles 3, 5 and 8. Historical examples include *Magna Carta* (1215) and the Bill of Rights (1689).

suspect recognises that they may inadvertently damage their own interests, even if they are innocent. In *Murray v United Kingdom*, the ECtHR described the right to silence and the privilege against self-incrimination as 'generally recognised international standards which lie at the heart of the notion of a fair procedure'.[36] As a key part of the broad individual right to a fair trial, the right to silence reinforces the right to be presumed innocent until proven guilty, and the prosecution's burden of proof. Indeed, Ashworth commented:

> If there is to be a presumption that a person is innocent until proved guilty by the prosecution, there appears to be some inconsistency in holding that the defendant can through his or her silence supply an element of that case.[37]

This is logical; if accused persons are *in law* innocent, their silence should (by extension) be treated as innocent. Furthermore, since it is solely the responsibility of the prosecution to demonstrate guilt, the defendant should not be compelled to help it – including through their silence. These thus form an interconnected and mutually supportive web of individual rights and protections, of which the right to silence is a crucial thread. The importance of the right in upholding fair trials was underscored in *Murray*:

> By providing the accused with protection against improper compulsion by the authorities these immunities contribute to avoiding miscarriages of justice and to securing the aims of Article 6.[38]

The right to silence provides particular protection for vulnerable suspects and defendants (and many are vulnerable).[39] This might include persons with mental health issues, drug and alcohol addictions, learning difficulties, or physical injuries or disabilities. Vulnerable suspects are more likely to succumb to pressure, making the police station a perilous environment. Additionally, rules of criminal procedure and evidence are complex and may be difficult for vulnerable suspects and defendants to comprehend. Attempting to engage with the police based on a misunderstanding of law and procedure could be highly damaging for a suspect or defendant. Therefore, the ability to remain silent provides a safe haven for vulnerable suspects, ensuring that their legal rights are protected.

The right to silence is necessary due to the limitations of other protections

As discussed in **Chapter 4**, the regulatory framework of PACE 1984 does have weaknesses, including the varying effectiveness of and access to legal advice; the weakness of the 'necessity' principle regarding detention; the lack of robust reviews of detention; and problems with the role of the CO. In the 'Cardiff Three' case, the Court of Appeal said:

36 (1996) 22 EHRR 29, [45].

37 Ashworth, A, *The Criminal Process: An Evaluative Study* (Clarendon, 1998), 96.

38 *Murray v United Kingdom* (1996) 22 EHRR 29, [45].

39 For example, Loucks estimated that between 20–30% of offenders 'have learning difficulties or learning disabilities that interfere with their ability to cope within the criminal justice system', which is of course only one type of vulnerability (Loucks, N, 'The prevalence and associated needs of offenders with learning difficulties and learning disabilities' (Prison Reform Trust, 2007), 1. See also HM Inspectorate of Constabulary (HMIC), 'The welfare of vulnerable people in police custody' (2015): www.justiceinspectorates.gov.uk/hmicfrs/wp-content/uploads/the-welfare-of-vulnerable-people-in-police-custody.pdf (accessed 11 May 2020).

> [W]e should comment on the apparent failure of the provisions in PACE … In our judgment, the circumstances of this case do not indicate flaws in those provisions. They do indicate a combination of human errors.[40]

This suggests that whilst other protections for suspects and defendants are (in theory) good, they can be, and are, circumvented in practice. Research suggests that most suspects in the police station do not receive legal advice (see **Chapter 3**). Therefore, this key safeguard does not actually protect the majority of suspects from pressure or mistreatment in police stations. Indeed, in *Cadder*, the Supreme Court made it clear that the mere existence of other protections alongside legal advice did not compensate for a failure to provide a lawyer.[41] The same logic might be applied to the right to silence; denying the benefit of such a fundamental right cannot arguably be compensated for simply by providing other safeguards, especially when they have significant limitations and flaws. In contrast, the right to silence, when conceptualised as an inviolable right which can be autonomously engaged by a suspect or defendant at any time (unlike the other safeguards), is vital when these other protections fail.

6.4.2 Disadvantages

The right to silence is exploited by the guilty and frustrates justice

As far back as the early 1700s, William Hawkins argued that the honest account of an innocent suspect offered better protection against a miscarriage of justice than the use of lawyers or the cloak of silence.[42] Jeremy Bentham argued that '[i]nnocence never takes advantage of [silence] … Innocence claims the right of speaking, as guilt invokes the privilege of silence.' In short, the 'accused speaks' form of criminal justice worked in the interests of the truly – that is, *factually* – innocent, whereas silence did not. The logical concomitant of these arguments is that the guilty exploit the right to silence. Bentham suggested that it naturally attracted those wishing to evade justice, arguing:

> If all the criminals of every class assembled, and framed a system after their own wishes, is not this rule the very first which they would have established for their security?[43]

Similarly, Lord Denning asserted that 'only the guilty' would exercise the right, since 'the innocent man would want to give his explanation and be cleared'.[44] Indeed, Glanville Williams argued that 'immunity from being questioned is a rule which from its nature can protect the guilty only … It is not a rule that may operate to acquit some guilty for fear of convicting some innocent.'[45] Rupert Cross provided an illustration of this:

> Innocent men do not normally keep out of the witness box, so the risk that one such man will occasionally court conviction by doing so is one which may legitimately be taken.[46]

40 *Paris, Abdullahi and Miller* (1993) 97 Cr App R 99, 109.

41 *HM Advocate v Cadder* [2010] UKSC 43, [93].

42 Hawkins, W, *A Treatise of the Pleas of the Crown, Vol 2* (J Walthoe, 1716), 400.

43 Bentham, J, *A Treatise of Judicial Evidence* (Baldwin, Craddock and Joy, 1825), 241.

44 *McCann, Cullen and Shanahan* (1991) 92 Cr App R 239, 249–50.

45 Williams, G, *The Proof of Guilt* (Stevens & Sons, 1955), 51.

46 Cross, ARN, 'The right to silence and the presumption of innocence: Sacred cows or safeguards of liberty?' (1970–71) *J Society Pub Tchrs L* 11, 70.

By this logic, silence should be treated as suspicious and indicative of guilt, such is the rarity of an innocent defendant refusing to testify. In its arguments for reform of the right to silence, the Criminal Law Revision Committee placed great emphasis on the scope for 'hardened criminals' to abuse the right in order to 'hamper the police and even bring their investigation to a halt'.[47] Others have raised similar concerns in relation to suspects of serious offences: those engaged in 'professional' criminal activity such as organised crime and people trafficking; and terrorists.[48] Undoubtedly, some factually guilty persons must benefit from the protection of silence. For commentators such as Denning and Bentham, the central objection is that it does so disproportionately, whilst offering little advantage to innocent persons. For such critics, a utilitarian, crime control approach that restricts the right to silence is fairer.

Related to this is the argument that the right to silence allows unscrupulous individuals to unfairly undermine a prosecution by 'ambush'.[49] This involves a suspect in a police station refusing to talk, waiting until the prosecution case has been presented at court, and then offering a defence. This therefore provides a tactical advantage for the defendant; the prosecution will have had no opportunity to prepare for such a defence and its case will consequently be weakened. Critics suggest that this thwarts justice through technicality; frustrates the truth-seeking purpose of criminal justice; and disproportionately favours defendants. Critics argue that justifying such behaviour on the pretext that it is a legitimate adversarial tactic is unsustainable. As Lord Justice Auld stated:

> A criminal trial is not a game under which the guilty defendant should be provided with a sporting chance. It is a search for the truth. The right to silence is to protect the innocent from wrongly incriminating themselves, not to enable the guilty, by fouling up the criminal process to make it as procedurally difficult as possible for the prosecution to prove their guilt regardless of the cost and disruption to others involved.[50]

The right to silence is an unnecessary and excessive safeguard

In 1987, Home Secretary Douglas Hurd argued for reform of the right to silence on the basis that PACE 1984 had greatly improved the safety of procedures for suspects and defendants.[51] This was echoed by both the police[52] and the judiciary.[53] In *Alladice*, Lord Chief Justice Lane asserted:[54]

> [I]t seems to us that the effect of section 58 (the right to legal advice) is such that the balance of fairness between prosecution and defence cannot be maintained unless proper comment is permitted on the defendant's silence in such circumstances. It is high time that such comment should be permitted together with the necessary alteration to the words of the caution.

47 Criminal Law Revision Committee, 'Eleventh Report, Evidence: General' (HMSO, 1972), [17].

48 Association of Chief Police Officers (ACPO), 'ACPO Right of Silence Survey' (unpublished); Bucke, T, Street, R and Brown, D, 'The right of silence: the impact of the Criminal Justice and Public Order Act 1994' (Home Office, 2000), 2 and 36–37.

49 Criminal Law Revision Committee (n 47).

50 Lord Justice Auld, 'Review of the Criminal Courts of England and Wales' (The Auld Review) (Ministry of Justice, September 2001), [154].

51 Hurd's various statements are summarised in Greer, S, 'The Right to Silence: A Review of the Current Debate' (1990) 53 *MLR* (6).

52 *Ibid* 716.

53 *Ibid.*

54 (1988) 87 Cr App R 380, 385.

The argument behind these statements was fairly simple: this swathe of new protections for suspects and defendants rendered the right to silence obsolete. It was once necessary – but could now be sacrificed in exchange for the new set of safeguards granted by PACE 1984 (hence, the name given to this argument – 'exchange abolitionism').[55] But more than this, maintenance of the right to silence was, in fact, damaging the fairness of criminal justice because it gave *too much* power to suspects and defendants. As discussed in **Chapter 5**, PACE 1984 transformed criminal procedure by introducing (amongst other provisions):

- the right to legal advice and, for some, an appropriate adult;
- limits on detention periods, and periodic reviews of decisions;
- recording and regulation of police interviews; and
- the right to inform someone of detention.

Moreover, since then, a variety of other developments have both reduced the scope for police abuses of power and increased the levels of scrutiny directed at police behaviour towards suspects, for example:

- the creation of an independent prosecution service;[56]
- the creation of an independent body for examining miscarriages of justice;[57]
- the creation of an independent body for handling complaints against the police;[58] and
- the advent of independent custody visiting schemes.[59]

As argued above, there are undoubtedly limitations to these protections, and cases such as the 'Cardiff Three' demonstrate this. However, whilst such cases are troubling, there is little evidence to suggest they are the norm; one might argue that using exceptional 'outliers' as evidence of the need for a right to silence for all suspects is disproportionate and misleading.

Additionally, it is argued that arguments in favour of the right to silence are over-reliant on historical experiences that are no longer applicable in the modern era. Williams said of the right to silence:

> [T]he rule cannot … be supported by an argument referring to torture. No one supposes that in present-day England a permission to question an accused person … would result in any ill treatment of him.[60]

Many of the systemic problems that were common in 16th and 17th century criminal justice are certainly no longer problematic (at least on the same scale). This argument therefore concludes that since time has passed and criminal justice is now fundamentally different, the right to silence is a relic of a bygone era and should not be

55 Greer (n 51), 718.

56 The CPS – created under the Prosecution of Offences Act 1985, s 1.

57 Criminal Cases Review Commission (CCRC), created by Criminal Appeal Act 1995, Part II – see **Chapter 11**.

58 Currently the Independent Office for Police Conduct; formerly the Independent Police Complaints Commission, and originally the Police Complaints Board (first created in 1977 under the Police Act 1976, s 1).

59 Under these schemes, lay persons can visit and inspect police custody suites to ensure they are safe and that the welfare of suspects is respected. After the Scarman Report (Lord Scarman, 'The Brixton Disorders, 10–12 April 1981' (The Scarman Report) (Home Office, November 1981), police forces allowed this on a voluntary basis; this was given a statutory, compulsory basis under the Police Reform Act 2002, s 51.

60 Williams (n 45), 48.

retained on the basis that threats such as torture and oppressive procedure remain a risk or might re-emerge.

The right to silence is counter-productive and may encourage mistreatment
Glanville Williams argued:

> The risk, if there is one, is ... that if dangerous criminals cannot be questioned before a magistrate or judge, the frustrated police may resort to illegal questioning and brutal 'third degree' methods in order to obtain convictions.[61]

The basic logic of this argument is as follows:

- There will always be pressure on the police to obtain confessions from suspects, since this is the most effective way of obtaining convictions (see **Chapter 5**).
- If suspects use their right to silence to frustrate police inquiries, this cannot be used as evidence against the suspect.
- As such, the police may calculate that using force or threats to extract answers from a suspect is worth the risk, since the alternative may well be a failure to convict.
- The likelihood of this scenario happening would reduce if silence could be used as evidence.

This perhaps represents a concession to the reality of criminal investigations. The right to silence aims to deter mistreatment of suspects, but it only does so if the police fully respect that right and look elsewhere for evidence. This may be somewhat idealistic if we consider that:

- a suspect is often the best source of information about their involvement in an alleged offence; and
- there may be great pressure on the police to identify and convict offenders (particularly when dealing with high-profile or sensitive cases).

A 'no comment' response from someone that the police suspect is a dangerous terrorist or serial rapist is unlikely to elicit an accepting shrug of the shoulders from investigating officers. This is not to say that most police officers will, at this point, resort to violence to get answers; but the risk exists that silence may counter-productively encourage mistreatment rather than combat it. As such, this argument asks us to consider: would it not be more desirable to allow a suspect's silence to be used as a form of evidence than to indirectly encourage unfair and illegal practices by the police?

6.4.3 Some counter-arguments

It is worth raising a few further points regarding the criticisms of the right to silence outlined above.

Curtailing the right to silence (particularly by allowing it to be used against suspects) is aimed at 'flushing out innocence at an early stage' and ensuring that it does not 'shelter ... the guilty'.[62] However, it might be suggested that these arguments, whilst superficially appealing, lack weight.

---

61 *Ibid.*

62 *Hoare and Pierce* [2004] EWCA Crim 784, [54]; quoting Judge Henry Friendly, in Leshem, S, 'The benefits of a right to silence for the innocent' (2010) 41 *RAND Journal of Economics* (2),399.

First, most suspects do not appear to exercise the right to silence. Records are not kept by authorities, and research has 'produced widely varying figures'.[63] Estimates have traditionally tended to range from 5–20% of suspects exercising the right in some form.[64] More recently, Sukumar et al found that as many as 65% of suspects exercised silence;[65] whilst analysis by Garbutt identified just under a third of suspects remaining silent in some form.[66] It does not appear, however, that most suspects rely on silence as a shield or tactic in police interviews (even when they should arguably be entitled to do so – for example, when faced with limited police disclosure or denied a lawyer). Thus, the argument that silence is commonly used to frustrate justice is perhaps exaggerated.[67]

Secondly, the so-called 'ambush defence' is not common in practice. In *DPP v Chorley Justices*, the court stated:[68]

> Most people approach a case on the basis that they want justice done as they wish to be acquitted if they are innocent; it is our experience that the case where a defendant refuses to identify the issue is rare indeed.

Furthermore, the courts (via the Criminal Procedure Rules) have effectively outlawed ambushes. In *Gleeson*, Lord Justice Auld asserted:[69]

> For defence advocates to seek to take advantage ... by deliberately delaying identification of an issue of fact or law in the case until the last possible moment is, in our view, no longer acceptable.

Even if one accepts that ambushes are a common phenomenon, to criticise the defence for failing to help the prosecution arguably conflicts with the presumption of innocence, the burden of proof, and the privilege against self-incrimination. In practice, there is a lack of robust evidence to suggest that it is a substantial problem. Indeed, Leng found no evidence of a link between exercising the right to silence and ambushes.[70]

Thirdly, the idea that silence can only be of assistance to the guilty is arguably misplaced and certainly an over-simplification. Academics have argued that the mere existence of the right is beneficial to the innocent. A game theoretic analysis by Seidmann and Stein asserted that the right to silence indirectly benefits the innocent because rational guilty suspects will utilise silence to avoid justice. This 'helps

63 Bucke (n 48), 30. A number of problems exist in identifying a reliable figure; for example, the varying definitions of 'silence' used in research; gaining access to interviews in order measure the use of silence; and varying sample sizes.

64 *Ibid.* The Runciman Commission found that silence was exercised only in a minority of cases, but was used more often in serious cases and as a result of legal advice (Viscount Runciman, 'Report of the Royal Commission on Criminal Justice' (The Runciman Commission) (HMSO, 1993), 53.

65 Sukumar, D, Hodgson, J and Wade, K, 'Behind closed doors: live observations of current police station disclosure practices and lawyer-client consultations' (2016) *Crim LR*, 911–12. This included 'total' and 'selective' silence.

66 Garbutt, J, 'The Use of No Comment by Suspects in Police Interviews', in M Schroter and C Taylor (eds), *Exploring Silence and Absence in Discourse* (Palgrave Macmillan, 2018).

67 The Runciman Commission found no evidence that it was used disproportionately by 'professional' criminals, and it did not believe that any change would be likely to alter the behaviour of this class of suspects and defendants. The Commission believed that less experienced and more vulnerable suspects would likely be most affected by any reform of the right to silence (n 64, 53–54).

68 [2006] EWHC 1795 (Admin), [26].

69 [2003] EWCA Crim 3357, [35].

70 Leng, R, 'The Right to Silence in Police Interrogation: a study of some of the issues underlying the debate' (HMSO, 1993)

distinguish the guilty from the innocent by inducing an anti-pooling effect that enhances the credibility of innocent suspects'.[71] In short, the very existence of the right to silence makes those who speak seem (by comparison) less 'guilty' to a jury. Bibas criticised this characterisation of silence as merely a pre-trial ploy, highlighting its assumption that most rational guilty suspects remain silent (which is not the reality) and the fact that most cases never reach trial.[72] Leshem developed on this to argue that the existence of the right more directly benefits innocent suspects, recognising the assistance it provides for those who may legitimately wish to remain silent because they fear police distortion or false prosecution witness testimony.[73] Whichever theory one accepts, the binary argument that silence can only assist the guilty is simplistic.

6.5 Using silence against the accused: the Criminal Justice and Public Order Act (CJPOA) 1994

After several high-profile miscarriages of justice in the 1980s and early 1990s, a Royal Commission on Criminal Justice (the Runciman Commission) was established. The Commission recommended that no changes should be made to the right to silence due to the risk that 'extra pressure on suspects to talk in the police station and the adverse inferences invited if they do not may result in more convictions of the innocent'.[74] Nonetheless, the Government proceeded to pass the Criminal Justice and Public Order Act (CJPOA) 1994.[75] The legislation created four main provisions relating to the right to silence:

- s 34: silence at the police station, about facts which are relied on at trial;
- s 35: silence at trial;
- s 36: silence at the police station, about an object, substance or mark; and
- s 37: silence at the police station, about presence at a particular place.

The effect of these provisions is to allow the prosecution, at trial, to comment on the silence of the accused (either in the police station or at trial); and to allow magistrates and juries to draw adverse inferences about the defendant from their silence.[76]

6.6 Section 34

Section 34 of the CJPOA 1994 allows adverse inferences to be drawn from the unreasonable failure of a suspect to tell the police about any fact, which is later relied on at trial.

Section 34 is the broadest provision and probably the most significant of those affecting the right to silence. Section 34(1) and (2) allows the court to 'draw such inferences ... as appear proper' when a defendant relies on facts at trial which they unreasonably failed to mention during police questioning or when charged with an

71 Seidmann, D and Stein, A, 'The Right to Silence Helps the Innocent: A Game Theoretic Analysis of the Fifth Amendment Privilege' (2000) 114 *Harvard LR* (2), 433.

72 Bibas, S, 'The right to remain silent only helps the guilty' (2003) 88 *Iowa LR* 421.

73 Leshem (n 62).

74 The Runciman Commission (n 64), 54.

75 For a full account of the period leading up to reform, see Welsh, L, Skinns, L and Sanders, A, *Sanders & Young's Criminal Justice* (OUP, 2021).

76 Therefore, the CJPOA 1994 repealed s 1(b) of the CEA 1898 ('The failure of any person charged with an offence ... to give evidence shall not be made the subject of any comment by the prosecution.')

offence. In *Argent*, Lord Bingham outlined six conditions that must be fulfilled before this can occur:[77]

(a) Criminal proceedings must have been brought against the accused.
(b) An alleged failure to mention a fact must have occurred before the accused was charged, although it should be noted that s 34(1)(b) states that alleged failure can take place 'on being charged … or informed [they] might be prosecuted'.
(c) The alleged failure must have taken place whilst the accused was undergoing police questioning about the alleged offence, under caution. Again, s 34(1)(b) explicitly includes at the point of charge, which will occur after questioning by the police
(d) The questioning 'must be directed to trying to discover whether or by whom the alleged offence had been committed'.[78] The police do not necessarily need to be asking questions which specifically relate to the facts that the accused has failed to mention: so long as the accused could reasonably have been expected to mention them during questioning, inferences can be drawn.[79] Sanders et al argue that inferences can only be drawn 'if the police through their questioning made it reasonable to expect suspects to volunteer the facts which they later relied on at trial'.[80] As such, the simple fact of being in a police interview and being questioned does not in and of itself allow inferences to be drawn.
(e) The accused must have failed to mention 'any fact' which they later relied on at trial. If 'any fact' not mentioned in the police station is *not* relied on at trial, proper inferences cannot be drawn. Both 'reliance' and 'failure' are questions for the jury to determine.
(f) The accused could have reasonably been expected to have mentioned the fact later relied on at trial, in the circumstances existing at the time. The accused means 'the actual accused with such qualities, apprehensions, knowledge and advice as he is shown to have had at the time' (ie during questioning in the police station).[81] This could include factors such as 'time of day, the defendant's age, experience, mental capacity, state of health, sobriety, tiredness, knowledge, personality and legal advice'.[82]

The provision raises a number of questions, including:

- What is a 'fact' for the purposes of the legislation?
- When will a defendant be considered to have 'relied' on a fact?
- What is the meaning of 'proper inferences'?
- In what circumstances will it be 'reasonable' to expect a suspect to mention such facts?

6.6.1 'Facts' and 'reliance' under s 34

The meaning of a 'fact' has been construed fairly widely by the courts. In *Milford*, the court stated that 'the words "any fact" do not fall to be read only in the narrow sense of an actual deed or thing done' and should be interpreted as

77 [1997] 2 Cr App R 27.
78 *Ibid* 33.
79 See, for example, *Brizzalari* [2004] EWCA Crim 310.
80 Welsh et al (n 75).
81 *Argent* [1996] EWCA Crim 1728, 33.
82 *Ibid.*

> something that … is actually the case … hence, a particular truth known by actual observation or authentic testimony, as opposed to what is merely inferred, or to a conjecture or to fiction.[83]

The court reasoned this by arguing:

> The facts relevant to establishing whether or not the defendant is guilty of the crime in respect of which he is being interrogated go far wider than the simple matter of what might have been observed to happen on a particular occasion and frequently involve what reasons or explanations the defendant gives for his involvement in the particular event observed which, if true, would absolve him from the suspicion of criminal intent or involvement which might otherwise arise.[84]

However, a 'fact' does not appear to include a basic denial of part of the prosecution's case by the defendant at trial, after having remained silent at the police station.[85] This means that a 'fact' must involve the defendant advancing some positive case of innocence, rather than simply putting the prosecution 'to proof'.

A defendant's 'reliance' on a fact at trial for the purposes of s 34 has also been interpreted widely. In *Webber*, the court concluded as follows:

> We consider that a defendant relies on a fact or matter in his defence not only when he gives or adduces evidence of it but also when counsel, acting on his instructions, puts a specific and positive case to prosecution witnesses, as opposed to asking questions intended to probe or test the prosecution case. This is so whether or not the prosecution witness accepts the suggestion put.[86]

6.6.2 'Proper inferences'

'Proper inferences' can be broadly summarised as negative or adverse conclusions about an aspect of the defendant's case (such as its accuracy or truthfulness), which may consequently impact on the verdict in their case. As such, when a defendant does not mention a 'fact' pertaining to their defence at the police station but relies on it at court, this might suggest that the 'fact' has, for example, been invented in the intervening period. This logically infers that the defendant is lying about this defence; this may, by extension, raise doubts about their innocence, although this is not inevitably the conclusion and is not the specific inference that a jury should necessarily draw (but possibly will). This provision transforms the right to silence into a disadvantage as it undermines the defendant and contributes to the prosecution case. 'Proper inferences' can be used together with any other evidence to determine a defendant's guilt. However, s 38(3) makes it clear that a conviction cannot be 'solely or mainly' based on adverse inferences, as confirmed in *Murray*.[87] As such, the prosecution cannot simply use the defendant's pre-charge silence as its only evidence of

---

83 *Milford* [2001] Crim LR 330, [32].

84 *Ibid.* A good example of a 'non-fact' is provided in *Nickolson* [1999] Crim LR 61, where the defendant was asked how semen might have gotten onto a complainant's nightdress. The explanation he put forward (which had not been mentioned before) was not considered to be a 'fact' because it was 'a theory, a possibility … a speculation only', presented in response to an invitation to speculate. Therefore, adverse inferences could not be drawn.

85 *Smith (Troy)* [2011] EWCA Crim 1098.

86 *Webber* [2004] UKHL 1, [34].

87 (1996) 22 EHRR 29.

guilt – it must have a *prima facie* case to present to the court.[88] A failure to mention a fact to the police should therefore only be a contributing factor to a finding of guilt, although how significant a contribution this makes is a matter for magistrates or the jury. There is, however, limited scope for controlling how much weight is given to silence, beyond judicial directions.

One might ask what specific negative conclusions magistrates or a jury might draw about a defendant. In *Condron*, the ECtHR asserted that a jury should be directed that they can only draw proper inferences if they are satisfied that silence could only 'sensibly be attributed to their having no answer or none that would stand up to cross-examination' and that such a direction was 'more than merely "desirable"'.[89] The standard inference is, therefore, that the defendant has fabricated or invented the facts relied upon at trial, after the police interview.[90] It might also be inferred that a false account was prepared in advance of an interview, but was not revealed as it would not withstand police scrutiny.[91] Magistrates or a jury might also conclude that the accused had no innocent explanation and therefore chose to remain silent rather than lie to the police or further incriminate themselves.[92] The specific meaning notwithstanding, all adverse inferences essentially amount to the same finding: that the defendant is either lying or hiding something relating to their defence. Even if their explanations at court are compelling, this can fatally undermine a defendant's case as it raises serious doubt in the minds of the fact-finders about their trustworthiness. Ultimately, we cannot be sure what inferences juries will draw from silence as juries do not need to explain their reasoning (see **Chapter** 7).

6.6.3 Reasonableness

Inferences cannot be drawn unless it was reasonable (in the circumstances existing at the time) to expect the suspect to have mentioned any facts later relied upon at trial. This essentially asks fact-finders to step into the shoes of the suspect in the police station and ask: would a reasonable person expect me to tell the police the relevant fact? As such, it is an objective test, with subjective elements. In *Murray*, the ECtHR stated that it will be reasonable to expect the accused to mention such facts 'in situations which clearly call for an explanation'.[93] In determining this, magistrates and juries should apply 'common sense' – a phrase used frequently by the courts in interpreting s 34. This was explained in *Webber* in the following terms:

> Common sense would suggest that the jury should be free … to ask themselves whether, if the appellant's version were true, he would not have mentioned it earlier when he was questioned by the police.[94]

As such, 'common sense' suggests that innocent suspects are likely to answer police questions.[95] The question of reasonableness is to be determined objectively (using 'common sense'), although the surrounding context must be considered (*per Argent*, above). However, the phrase 'common sense' does raise questions. Easton argues that

88 *Cowan, Gayle and Ricciardi* [1996] QB 373, 379.
89 *Condron v United Kingdom* (2001) 31 EHRR 1, 22–23.
90 Emson, R, *Evidence* (Palgrave Macmillan, 2010), 224.
91 *Randall* [1998] 6 *Arch News* 1; *Milford* (n 83).
92 *Daniel* [1998] 2 Cr App R 373, 378.
93 *Murray* (n 38), [47].
94 [2004] UKHL 1, [34].
95 This simplistic assumption might be questioned for reasons discussed earlier.

common sense is generally 'unreliable, impressionistic and unsystematic' in that it has no form or structure and is potentially subjective.[96] We might question if this is a good model for understanding what is 'reasonable'.

6.6.4 Reasonableness and legal advice

Will it be reasonable for a suspect to remain silent about facts later relied on at trial on the basis of legal advice? A court cannot demand an explanation for why the suspect relied on the advice because such interactions are subject to legal professional privilege; they are confidential and cannot be revealed without consent.[97] In theory, this enables the accused to use their lawyer as a shield against adverse inferences by claiming that they remained silent because they were advised to do so – even if the reality is that they did so because they had no robust answer to the allegations against them. By exploiting this legitimate due process protection, the accused can 'driv[e] … a coach and horses through section 34'.[98] Confidential legal advice is essential; Lord Chief Justice Woolf highlighted in *Beckles*:

> It is of the greatest importance that defendants should be able to be advised by their lawyer without their having to reveal the terms of that advice if they act in accordance with that advice.[99]

Nonetheless, the courts have determined that it can still be reasonable to expect suspects to mention facts even if they were advised otherwise. Various cases have determined that the fact that silence is a result of legal advice is not, in itself, a barrier to inferences, and that the reasons for the advice will be key.[100] In *Condron*, the suspects argued that they remained silent because of their solicitor's 'grave doubts about their fitness to cope with police questioning'.[101] The jury needed to consider whether this was a plausible explanation; but if they concluded, notwithstanding this explanation, that 'silence could sensibly be attributed to the accused having no answer or none that would stand up to questioning' then they could draw adverse inferences.[102] A suspect's reliance on legal advice to remain silent must still be reasonable and needed 'soundly based objective reasons' to justify it – in short, blindly following legal advice without question is not an adequate explanation.[103] In *Beckles*, the court set out two elements magistrates or a jury must consider when deciding if reliance on legal advice could justify silence and therefore prevent inferences:[104]

(a) there was genuine reliance on legal advice to remain silent (a subjective question); and
(b) it was reasonable to rely on that advice (an objective question)

In *Hoare and Pierce*, the court clarified:

96 Easton, S, 'Legal Advice, Common Sense and the Right to Silence' (1998) *Int J of Ev & Proof* 2, 114.
97 See *Three Rivers District Council and others v Governor and Company of the Bank of England* [2004] UKHL 48.
98 *Beckles* [2004] EWCA Crim 2766, [43].
99 *Ibid.*
100 Including *Condron* (n 89), *Beckles* (n 98) and *Betts and Hall* [2001] EWCA Crim 224.
101 (2001) 31 EHRR 1, [61].
102 *Ibid.*
103 *Howell* [2005] 1 Cr App R 1, 14.
104 [2004] EWCA Crim 2766.

> Genuine reliance by a defendant on his solicitor's advice to remain silent is not in itself enough to preclude adverse comment.[105]
>
> It is not the purpose of section 34 ... to exclude a jury from drawing an adverse inference against a defendant because he genuinely or reasonably believes that, regardless of his guilt or innocence, he is entitled to take advantage of that advice to impede the prosecution case against him. In such a case the advice is not truly the reason for not mentioning the facts.[106]

Therefore, even when a suspect *genuinely* relies on advice to remain silent, and subjectively believes it is reasonable to do so, this will not prevent inferences being drawn if magistrates or a jury conclude it was not objectively reasonable to rely on that advice.

6.7 Section 35

Section 35 of the CJPOA 1994 allows inferences to be drawn from the failure of a defendant to give evidence at trial.

Section 35(2) states that a court or jury may draw such inferences as appear proper from either:

- the failure of a defendant to testify in their own defence; or
- a defendant's refusal to answer any questions, without good cause.

In contrast to s 34, s 35 does not require the defendant to rely on any facts not previously mentioned. They must simply exercise their right to silence at trial (either in whole or in part). Section 35(3) states that 'in determining whether the accused is guilty of the offence charged, [the court or jury] may draw such inferences as appear proper'. Thus, as Owusu-Bempah highlights, inferences under this section 'may go straight to the issue of guilt rather than the likelihood of any specific facts'.[107] However, as with s 34, any verdict of guilt cannot be solely based on inferences according to s 38(3). Section 35(4) clarifies that the provision does not 'render the accused compellable to give evidence on his own behalf'. In short, a defendant cannot be made to give evidence or testify at trial, maintaining their right to silence in principle. Moreover, s 35(1)(b) states that inferences cannot be drawn from silence when the physical or mental condition of the defendant makes it undesirable for them to give evidence.[108]

If a defendant is capable of testifying but does not, any adverse inferences drawn may strengthen the case against them. As discussed above, the right to silence is a logical concomitant of the prosecution burden of proof, the presumption of innocence, and the privilege against self-incrimination. By essentially making a defendant's silence part of the prosecution case, these principles appear to be eroded. Section 35 presents a stark choice between:

- remaining silent, and therefore risking the consequences of adverse inferences; or
- testifying, leading to possible self-incrimination or at least assisting the prosecution case.

---

105 *Hoare and Pierce* [2005] 1 WLR 1804, [51].

106 *Ibid* [54].

107 Owusu-Bempah, A, 'Judging the desirability of a defendant's evidence: an unfortunate approach to s 35(1)(b) of the Criminal Justice and Public Order Act 1994' (2011) *Crim LR*, 691.

108 The courts have left this caveat open to broad interpretation, with simple difficulty in giving evidence not sufficient. See *Tabbakh* [2009] EWCA Crim 464.

We should question whether this presents a real choice for such defendants and whether this fully respects the rights mentioned above. In Cowan, the court dismissed such criticism, asserting that the argument that s 35 'alters the burden of proof or "waters it down"' was 'misconceived'.[109] As with s 34, the prosecution must establish a *prima facie* case before the section can be raised. There must be a case for the defendant to answer, and if the prosecution's case is weak and the defendant opts not to testify, no inferences can be drawn.[110] If the defendant refuses to give evidence or answer questions when there is a case to answer, inferences can only be drawn if the jury conclude that 'the only sensible explanation for that silence was that [the defendant] had no answer to the case against him or none that could have stood up to cross-examination'.[111] As such, inferences are not automatic – but again, whether magistrates and juries truly respect these limitations is hard to know.

6.8 Sections 36 and 37

Section 36 of the CJPOA 1994 allows inferences to be drawn from the failure of a suspect to account for an object, substance or mark on their person or in their possession. Section 37 allows inferences to be drawn from the failure of a suspect to account for their presence at a particular place.

These provisions therefore allow inferences to be drawn from silence, in specific circumstances. Section 36 permits magistrates or a jury to draw inferences when:

- a suspect is arrested with an object, substance or mark on their person, in their clothing, in their possession, or in any place in which they were at the time of their arrest;
- the police reasonably believe this may be attributable to the suspect's participation in or commission of an offence;
- the police inform the suspect of this belief and request an account for the presence of the object, substance or mark;
- the suspect fails or refuses to do so.

Classic examples of an 'object, substance or mark' include weapons, drugs or injuries (but there are many potential things that could be included, hence the broad language). Additionally, finding the above is not limited to the suspect's physical person – it can include the surrounding area (such as the house or street where they were arrested).

Section 37 permits a court or jury to draw inferences when:

- a person is arrested in a place at the time of an offence;
- the police reasonably believe that their presence there is attributable to participation in or commission of an offence;
- the police inform the suspect of this belief and request an account for the suspect's presence in that place at that time; and
- the suspect fails or refuses to do so.

'Presence' can relate to any range of situations, but it might include being in a stolen vehicle shortly after it was so reported, or being at or in the vicinity of a crime scene.

109 [1996] QB 373, 379.

110 It is in fact likely that the defence will make a submission of no case to answer (see **Chapter 10**).

111 *Cowan, Gayle and Ricciardi* [1996] QB 373, 381.

To draw inferences under ss 36 and 37, a suspect must simply fail to give an account. Unlike s 34, there are no pre-requisites for such a failure to be unreasonable or for any facts to be relied on at trial. According to PACE 1984 Code C, inferences can only be drawn if the accused has been told:[112]

- what offence is being investigated;
- what fact they are being asked to account for;
- that the police believe the object/substance/mark or presence at a certain place may be due to their involvement in the offence; and
- that adverse inferences may be drawn from a failure to account.

Therefore, it must be made very clear to suspects that they are specifically being questioned about the relevant 'fact' and why. This can be contrasted with s 34, where questioning does not necessarily have to focus specifically on any fact later relied on at trial.[113] Similarly to ss 34 and 35, inferences can only be drawn if the jury 'are sure that [the defendant] had no acceptable explanation to offer'.[114]

6.9 Impact of reform on the use of the right to silence

Whilst the CJPOA 1994 has had some impact on the use of the right to silence by suspects in police stations and at trial, it has perhaps been less significant than was envisaged by its architects. This may be because of the apparent disparity between beliefs about the right to silence (that it was exercised widely) and the reality (that it was never exercised that often). Prior to the legislation, a study by Phillips and Brown found that 10% of suspects exercised 'total' silence in the police station (for example, a 'no comment' interview); and 13% exercised 'selective' silence (answering some questions, but not others).[115] After the legislation, a study by Bucke et al found that these numbers had dropped to 6% and 10% respectively.[116] These are estimates, and, as mentioned above, calculating the number of suspects exercising silence is very difficult. This evidence does, however, suggest that any reduction in the use of silence was relatively small. Interestingly, more recent research (albeit involving a small sample) by Sukumar et al found that 53% of suspects exercised 'total' silence; 12% exercised 'selective' silence; and 35% answered all questions.[117] This would suggest that, in the long term, 'total' silence has not been impacted at all (and has in fact increased in use). The biggest impact occurred amongst those groups of suspects who had previously been most likely to remain silent. This included suspects arrested for serious offences; suspects who received legal advice; and black suspects.[118] In these categories, there was a more significant reduction in the exercise of silence; thus, we can observe that:

- silence primarily affected minority suspect groups, rather than most suspects; and

112 Home Office, 'Police and Criminal Evidence Act 1984 (PACE) Code C: Revised Code of Practice for the detention, treatment and questioning of persons by police officers' (TSO, July 2018), [10.11].

113 Although if the nature of the police questioning made it reasonable to expect the suspect to volunteer such facts, that would allow inferences. For an example, see *Hillard* [2004] EWCA Crim 837.

114 *Compton* [2002] EWCA Crim 2835, [37]. For more on ss 36 and 37, see Owusu-Bempah, A, 'Silence in suspicious circumstances' (2014) *Crim LR*.

115 Phillips, C and Brown, D, 'Entry into the Criminal Justice System: a survey of police arrests and their outcomes' (Home Office, 1998).

116 Bucke (n 48), 31.

117 Sukumar (n 65), 911.

118 Bucke (n 48), 31–32.

- the target groups (such as 'professional' criminals) did not appear to be affected as much.

There also appears to be consensus that fewer defendants were refusing to testifying at court – suggesting that s 35 may have had a more substantial impact.[119]

6.10 Impact of reform on convictions

There is also little evidence to suggest that reform has been of benefit to the pursuit of convictions. For example, confessions of guilt (which will significantly increase the likelihood of conviction – see **Chapter** 7) have not increased. The proportion of suspects who confessed in interview remained the same before and after the legislation (55%).[120] More recent research suggests that this has, if anything, decreased. Soukara et al found a confession rate of 39% in police interviews;[121] and in the aforementioned study by Sukumar et al, 12% of suspects fully admitted guilt.[122] For suspects accused of serious crimes, the confession rate is also low – only 23% fully or partially admitted guilt in a study by Leahy-Harland and Bull.[123] Court conviction rates have remained relatively stable – and they certainly do not appear to have increased as a result of the provisions of the CJPOA 1994.[124] Before and after the legislation, convictions rates in magistrates' courts remained the same (98%); and remained steady in the Crown Court (91%; 89%).[125] In the 2000s, conviction rates actually *declined* quite significantly. By 2017, the conviction rates in magistrates' courts and the Crown Court were 87% and 83% respectively.[126] Additionally, research by Bucke et al found little change in charging or caution rates for suspects who remained silent, before and after the CJPOA 1994.[127] As such, the changes to the right to silence do not appear to have positively impacted on the success of prosecutions in either the short or long term.[128] These findings are worth bearing in mind when one considers the purpose behind the changes. Citing Roble, Munday argues that s 34 intended to 'discourage an accused from fabricating a defence late in the day' and 'encourage the accused to make speedy disclosure of any genuine defence or any fact that may go towards establishing a genuine defence'.[129] Similar arguments can be applied to ss 36 and 37. We might therefore question whether these objectives have been achieved.

---

119 *Ibid* 52; Quirk (n 23), Ch 5.

120 Bucke (n 48), 34.

121 Soukara, S, Bull, R, Vrij, A, Turner, M and Cherryman, J, 'What really happens in police interviews of suspects? Tactics and confessions' (2009) 15 *Psych, Crime & Law* (6), 502.

122 Sukumar (n 65), 911.

123 Leahy-Harland, S and Bull, R, 'Police Strategies and Suspect Responses in Real-life Serious Crime Interviews' (2016) 32 *J of Police and Crim Psych* (2).

124 From the perspective of those who advocated curtailing the right to silence, 'improved' might be used in place of 'increased' – after all, one of the justifications for reform was to more successfully prosecute professional criminals and other nefarious characters.

125 Bucke (n 48), 65.

126 Ministry of Justice, 'Criminal Justice Statistics Quarterly: December 2017, Overview Tables' (17 May 2018), Table Q3.3: www.gov.uk/government/statistics/criminal-justice-system-statistics-quarterly-december-2017 (accessed 11 May 2020).

127 There were in fact some decreases. Bucke (n 48), 41.

128 Although it should be remembered that a wide range of factors can influence conviction rates.

129 *Roble* [1997] EWCA Crim 118; Munday, R, *Evidence* (OUP, 2017), 486.

6.11 Impact of reform on disclosure and legal advice

Research suggests that police attitudes to disclosure to suspects and their lawyers can impact on the exercise of silence, and this is particularly the case in the post-CJPOA 1994 era.[130] Police may use disclosure tactically, luring suspects into silence so that inferences may be drawn at court.[131] Police may aim to 'surprise or pressure' silent suspects by revealing key information during interview, rather than before.[132] In a recent study, Sukumar et al concluded that

> lawyers who are given pre-interview disclosure are generally more cooperative, in that they are less likely to advise their clients to make no comment than lawyers who are given no disclosure before the interview.[133]

Generally, research has suggested that defence lawyers have become less likely to advise clients to remain silent when questioned by the police, primarily because of the potential risks later in the criminal process.[134] That being said, Sukumar et al found that lawyers advised 59% of suspects to remain silent (although some suspects disregarded this advice).[135]

6.12 The delegitimisation of silence

In the aftermath of the CJPOA 1994, O'Reilly argued that the legislation had 'shifted the criminal justice system from its accusatorial focus … to an inquisitorial focus'.[136] Quoting this argument, in 2001, Jackson suggested that the potential for adverse inferences at the earliest stages of the criminal investigation meant that, in effect, proceedings against suspects commenced once the caution was administered rather than at court, as was traditional.[137] As such, there had been a shift in power and authority towards the police and prosecution, particularly in regard to obtaining information in the police station.[138] This suggests a significant change in the nature of criminal justice in England and Wales: away from the adversarial, trial-based system of the last 300 years (with its focus on witnesses and extrinsic evidence), towards a continental, inquisitorial model (with the focus on interrogation of the suspect). Leng added that this has led to the 'normative' expectation that suspects will answer police

---

130 See generally Sukumar, S, Hodgson, J and Wade, K, 'How the timing of police evidence disclosure impacts custodial legal advice' (2016) 20 *Int J of Ev & Proof* (3); and Blackstock, J, Cape, E, Hodgson, J, Ogorodova, A and Spronken, T, *Inside Police Custody: An Empirical Account of Suspects' Rights in Four Jurisdictions* (Intersentia, 2014).

131 Cape, E, 'Transposing the EU Directive on the right to information: a firecracker or a damp squib?' (2015) *Crim LR* (1), 57.

132 Sukumar (n 65), 911. For recent evidence on this, see Kemp, V, 'Effective Police Station Legal Advice Country Report 2: England And Wales' (University of Nottingham, April 2018): http://eprints.nottingham.ac.uk/51145/1/Country%20Report%20England%20and%20Wales%20Final%20.pdf (accessed 11 May 2020).

133 *Ibid* 902.

134 Bucke (n 48), 21; Quirk (n 23), Ch 4.

135 Sukumar (n 65), 912.

136 O'Reilly, G, 'England Limits the Right to Silence and Moves towards an Inquisitorial System of Justice' (1994) 85 *J of Crim L & Criminol* (2), 405.

137 Jackson, J, 'Silence and proof: extending the boundaries of criminal proceedings in the United Kingdom' (2001) 5 *Int J of Ev & Proof* (3), 167.

138 *Ibid* 165.

questions.[139] Equally, one might argue that adverse inferences may distract courts (and particularly juries) from their primary function, which is arguably to scrutinise the prosecution case. The prosecution bears the burden of proof, and the defendant has a right to silence and a presumption of innocence. Logically then, the focus should primarily be on the strength of the case brought by the prosecution. However, these complex provisions – which have the statutory seal of approval – create the danger that 'emphasis can fall on whether and how the accused co-operated during police questioning, rather than the prosecution case'.[140]

In 2016, Quirk suggested that the CJPOA 1994 marked a significant change for England and Wales, a jurisdiction that had 'led the world in establishing the right to silence … then became a leader in its retrenchment'.[141] She described the legislation as a 'legal tremor … that led to a shift in the tectonic plates of the criminal justice system in England and Wales',[142] creating 'a culture of expectation that suspects should cooperate'.[143] From a broader perspective, it is interesting to note that during the 1990s, many European jurisdictions moved to prevent adverse inferences being drawn;[144] in contrast, England and Wales has moved in the opposite direction. Moisidis therefore argued that this represents a return to the pre-16th century 'accused speaks' form of criminal justice.[145] All of the above suggest that the right to silence has been gradually delegitimised, facilitated by the provisions above. It was once viewed as a fair and necessary safeguard in the criminal justice process; since the CJPOA 1994, it has acquired a noxious meaning within the culture of criminal justice. Whether intentional or not, the legislation formally 'branded' the right as something negative: as a refuge for the guilty and an obstruction to legitimate inquiry by the police and prosecution.

6.13 Summary

- The right to silence is an expression of the privilege against self-incrimination, which arguably evolved alongside the rise of adversarialism and in reaction to abusive practices in criminal justice in England and Wales.
- It consists of various 'immunities' from being compelled to answer questions, on pain of punishment.
- There are a variety of arguments that both support and oppose giving suspects and defendants a right to silence.
- The CJPOA 1994 fundamentally altered the right to silence by allowing adverse inferences to be drawn from a failure to answer questions, provide information or testify at trial.
- The changes have had a fairly modest impact on the exercise of the right to silence, with limited benefit in successful convictions; but they have created a 'normative' expectation that suspects and defendants will not remain silent.

---

139 Leng, R, 'Silence pre-trial, reasonable expectations and the normative distortion of fact finding' (2001) 5 *Int J of Ev & Proof* (4).

140 Owusu-Bempah (n 114), 128.

141 Quirk (n 23), Ch 6.

142 *Ibid* Ch 5.

143 *Ibid* Ch 6.

144 Van Kessel, G, 'European perspectives on the accused as a source of testimonial evidence' (1998) *West Virginia LR* 100, 821.

145 Moisidis, C, *Criminal Discovery. From Truth to Proof and Back Again* (Institute of Criminology Press, 1998), 3.

chapter 7 The Regulation of Confessions

7.1 Introduction

Confessions of guilt by suspects are very useful for the police and prosecution in an adversarial system. Whilst there is oversight to regulate the integrity of the evidence, the two parties are largely allowed to build their case without interference from the judiciary.[1] For the police and prosecution, a suspect's confession saves time, money and effort. The need to investigate further is eliminated or at least minimised, and the job of discharging the burden of proof in court is either eradicated (should there be a guilty plea) or easier to satisfy. As such, a confession is often a 'golden ticket' to a swift, low-cost conviction. In this sense, confessions are *too* useful, providing an incentive for the police to pursue admissions from suspects, with the potential for neutral, objective investigation to be sidelined. This can lead to over-zealous police officers pressuring, bullying or manipulating suspects into confessing or (in extreme circumstances) fabricating confessions.

The default assumption is that a confession is accurate; whilst this is logical and often true, it is not always the case. Suspects in police stations do confess to crimes they have not committed for a variety of reasons, which will be explored below. A confession is normally taken at face value; there is no requirement for corroboration once someone pleads guilty; and a court will not normally independently question the veracity of a confession.[2] Whilst PACE 1984 Code C provides notes for guidance which emphasise the need to corroborate admissions by vulnerable suspects, this is far short of a general duty on the police to check that a confession is accurate.[3] With this in mind, it should be remembered that the police have substantial power and authority, particularly in the police station – where most confessions take place.[4] They are trusted to exercise this power responsibly and use their significant discretion fairly. Largely, this is the case, but when it is not, the results can be catastrophic for innocent individuals, revealing the disturbing reality that *some* police officers may not be trustworthy and can abuse their

---

1 For example, the common law 'abuse of process' power allows judges to exclude evidence where the police have overstepped the boundaries of their authority in obtaining evidence (see Wells, C, *Abuse of Process* (OUP, 2017)).

2 For example, see Article 38 of the Constitution of Japan, which states that 'No person shall be convicted or punished in cases where the only proof against him is his own confession'. Yet, there is a general consensus that Japanese criminal justice relies heavily on confessions and has a very high conviction rate, so it might be questioned how much of a benefit this protection is in practice. Corroboration of confessions was recommended by Hirst (Hirst, J, 'Royal Commission Research Papers: A Policing Perspective' (Police Research Group, 1993)). It should also be noted that judges can question the veracity of a confession under s 76(3) of PACE 1984 (see below at **7.9**).

3 Home Office, 'Police and Criminal Evidence Act 1984 (PACE) Code C: Revised Code of Practice for the detention, treatment and questioning of persons by Police Officers' (TSO, July 2018), Notes for Guidance 11C and E2.

4 Quirk, H, *The Rise and Fall of the Right of Silence* (Routledge, 2016), Ch 3.

power. This can be a difficult truth to face.[5] Thus, whilst confessions are beneficial in the criminal justice system, they have attendant dangers which make regulating such evidence essential.

7.2 What is a 'confession' and how is it regulated?

In common parlance, a confession might be described as an admission or acknowledgment of culpability or blame. In the context of criminal justice, the stereotypical confession is an admission or acceptance of guilt for a criminal offence, normally in a police interview. However, for the purposes of criminal procedure in England and Wales, a 'confession' is broader than either of these definitions. This is specifically dealt with under s 82(1) of PACE 1984, which states:

> 'confession' includes any statement wholly or partly adverse to the person who made it, whether made to a person in authority or not and whether made in words or otherwise.

This definition will be used to decide whether such evidence should be excluded at trial and therefore not used against a defendant. There appear to be five elements required to constitute a 'confession' according to this provision.

7.2.1 A confession needs to be made by the accused

A confession must actually be made by the accused. Whilst this seems obvious, it is relevant in relation to police-invented confessions (see below). If it is claimed that a suspect confessed, but the suspect argues that they did not, the said 'confession' will not fall within the definition of s 82(1) since it will not (according to the suspect) have been 'made'. A suspect must at the very least have made some form of statement or indication (in whatever form this might take) for it to be considered a 'confession'. This also implies that a 'confession' cannot be made on someone's behalf.

7.2.2 The confession must be 'adverse' to the accused

That is, the confession needs to have some form of inculpatory element, which demonstrates guilt or involvement in the criminal offence being investigated. In short, it will be contrary to a suspect's or defendant's interests. This could include:

- an explicit admission of guilt;
- providing information or evidence that indicates guilt of an offence; and
- making admissions that might undermine or damage any defence.

Aside from obviously 'adverse' statements, the courts have considered the difficult issue of statements which 'become' adverse. This is when a statement made by the accused, which is neutral or even exculpatory (and therefore not a confession), is subsequently used against them at trial. The question is whether this subsequent use of the statement, which has transformed it into something 'adverse' to the accused, can be classed as a confession and therefore be excluded. In *Hasan*, the accused was charged with burglary, and during the trial an 'off the record' interview with the police was used by the prosecution against him.[6] The interview was concerned with a separate police investigation and was entirely neutral regarding the burglary, and it did not therefore

5 For an example of judicial 'denial', see the speech of Lord Denning in *McIlkenny v Chief Constable of the West Midlands Police* [1980] 2 All ER 227.

6 [2005] UKHL 22.

contain a confession at the time it was made. However, the accused later gave evidence at trial which showed some inconsistencies with the interview; the prosecution argued that this demonstrated the unreliability of the accused as a witness. As such, the interview had become 'adverse' at a later point; the accused argued that this was therefore a confession within the definition of s 82(1) and should be excluded. The court concluded that a statement should be interpreted 'at the time' it was made; if it was neutral or exculpatory, it could not be considered a confession even if it became adverse to the accused's interests at a later stage. Lord Steyn suggested that the argument that s 82(1) included statements which were neutral or exculpatory was 'wholly implausible' and that 'the plain meaning of the statute is against such a strange interpretation'.[7] As such, the accused's argument was rejected, and the interview was accepted as evidence against him.

7.2.3 A confession can be either partly or wholly adverse

A confession does not need to entirely damage the case of the accused, and it could include exculpatory material (that is, material supportive of innocence). For example, a suspect accused of starting a bar fight might admit to being in the bar at the relevant time (which is inculpatory), but state that he was with a friend in another room and so could not have committed the offence (which is exculpatory). This is known as a 'mixed statement', as only part of it is adverse to the accused.

7.2.4 It can be made to a person in authority or not

Most confessions will be made to persons in authority (normally, a police officer), but confessions can also be made to friends, colleagues, relatives and so on. A good example is the 'Cardiff Three' case, in which all three defendants allegedly made confessions to non-police figures (Miller to two women who visited him in prison; Paris to a prison informer; and Abdullahi to his common law wife).[8]

7.2.5 A confession can be made in words or otherwise

The word 'statement' is not defined by PACE 1984, but logically it includes spoken and written words. The word 'otherwise' suggests non-verbal indications, such as a nod of the head or a thumbs-up. For example, in *Li Shu-ling*, a re-enactment of the alleged offence by the accused with the police was considered to be a confession.[9]

7.3 The regulation of confession evidence

The admissibility of evidence falling within the above meaning of a 'confession' is governed by s 76 of PACE 1984. Section 76(1) broadly summarises the circumstances in which a confession can be admitted as evidence:

> In any proceedings a confession made by an accused person may be given in evidence against him insofar as it is relevant to any matter in issue in the proceedings and is not excluded by the court ...

In short, a confession by a suspect or defendant can be used against them at trial. However, the confession must be 'relevant to any matter in issue' and must be

---

7 *Ibid* [56].

8 *Paris, Abdullahi and Miller* (1993) 97 Cr App R99.

9 [1989] AC 270.

admissible; that is, it must not have been excluded by the court. We will explore the basis on which confessions can be excluded below; but before doing so, it is worth examining why it is important to regulate confessions in this manner. A primary reason for doing so is to guard against the risk of non-genuine confessions – that is, confessions which are either false or fabricated. A 'false' confession is when a suspect makes an adverse admission which is not in fact true. The most obvious example of this would be explicitly admitting guilt for an offence which the accused has not in fact committed. It could also include the admission of other facts related to an offence which indicate guilt – such as admitting to being present at the scene of a crime, when the suspect was in fact elsewhere. An 'invented' or 'fabricated' confession occurs when the police claim that the suspect has made an admission of guilt which the suspect has not, in fact, made. The confession will have been fabricated by the police (either entirely or through distortion of a suspect's words) and then attributed to the suspect.

7.4 False confessions

A key rationale for reform of criminal procedure in the 1970s and 1980s was the phenomenon of false confessions by those accused of criminal offences. Whilst PACE 1984 has done much to tackle them, the problem has persisted. Broadly, there are two kinds of false confession: voluntary and coerced. Voluntary false confessions occur when – without pressure or threat from the police or others – a person chooses to make a false confession. Research suggests that those accused of criminal offences make voluntary false confessions for a variety of reasons, including:[10]

- to relieve feelings of guilt (either real or imagined);
- to pre-empt or avoid investigation of a more serious offence;
- to protect someone else, for example a loved one;
- to gain notoriety or attention (particularly an issue in high-profile cases);
- due to mental illness, which may prevent a person from distinguishing between fact and fantasy;
- to hide non-criminal facts (for example, an extra-marital affair or embarrassing personal habits).

Coerced false confessions are non-voluntary, in that the accused confesses as a result of coercion or pressure. We will concentrate on this type of confession, as it is the primary focus of the safeguards under PACE 1984. There are three forms of coerced false confession that have been identified:[11]

- coerced-internalised false confessions;
- coerced-compliant false confessions (described in research by Gudjonsson and MacKeith);[12]

---

10 Generally, see Gudjonsson, G, *The Psychology of Interrogations and Confessions: A Handbook* (Wiley, 2003); Huff, C, Rattner, A and Sagarin, E, 'Guilty Until Proved Innocent: Wrongful Conviction and Public Policy' (1986) 32 *Crime & Delinquency* (4); Sigurdsson, J and Gudjonsson, G, 'Psychological characteristics of "false confessors": A study among Icelandic prison inmates and juvenile offenders' (1996) *Personality and Individual Differences* 20; Kassin, S and Wrightsman, L, 'Confession evidence', in S Kassin and L Wrightsman (eds), *The psychology of evidence and trial procedure* (Sage, 1985); Kassin, S, 'False Confessions: Causes, Consequences, and Implications for Reform' (2014) 1 *Policy Insights from the Behavioral and Brain Sciences* (1).

11 Originally by Kassin and Wrightsman (*ibid*).

12 Gudjonsson, G and MacKeith, J, 'Retracted confessions: legal, psychological and psychiatric aspects' (1988) *Medicine, Science and the Law* 28.

- coerced-passive false confessions (described by McConville et al).[13]

7.4.1 Coerced-internalised confessions

Coerced-internalised (or 'false belief') confessions occur when the accused believes (at least temporarily) that they have committed the offence in question, when they are in fact innocent. In short, the suspect 'internalises' the evidence or account of guilt presented to them by the police or others. The accused trusts the version of events presented to them rather than their own memory (or lack thereof). This demonstrates the problem of human memory and its fallibility – generally, people are prone to create false memories in order 'gap-fill' (known as confabulation).[14] This can be particularly problematic for suspects due to the high level of stress associated with both criminal activity and police investigations, as stress causes issues in terms of memory recall. Furthermore, memories can be distorted or fabricated with relative ease in the right circumstances, generating false confessions which suspects believe are true. In a study by Shaw and Porter, 70% of participants provided 'rich' false confessions to crimes in adolescence, underlining the unreliability of memory in the right circumstances.[15] Vulnerable suspects – like children or those with mental health issues – are particularly susceptible to providing false confessions when pressured or manipulated. Coerced-internalised confessions tend to be associated with some of the following conditions or states:

- *The influence of drugs or alcohol:* the accused may be unable to recall events due to intoxication; or may believe they did not have control over their own behaviour. They may therefore believe that they have committed the offence in question.
- *Poor memory*: this may be related to intoxication but can exist independently. A person may be unable to remember committing an offence, due to a general inability to recall facts and events.[16]
- *Low self-esteem:* this may or may not be due to a mental health issue such as depression or anxiety. A suspect may hold an unjustified negative opinion of their own integrity or trustworthiness, and may therefore be inclined to trust the police rather than themselves.
- *Immaturity or suggestibility:* juveniles or those with mental health issues may be easily manipulated, allowing the police to convince them of their own guilt through suggestion or persuasion. They may be unable or unwilling to challenge the police account, perhaps because of undue respect for figures of authority and a belief that they would not lie.

---

13 McConville, M, Sanders, A and Leng, R, *Case for the Prosecution: Police Suspects and the Construction of Criminality* (Routledge, 1991).

14 Shaw, J and Porter, S, 'Constructing Rich False Memories of Committing Crime' (2015) 26 *Psychological Science* (3).

15 *Ibid.* Similarly, a study by Nash and Wade placed students in a controlled environment and played fake video evidence of them cheating in a gambling exercise (Nash, R and Wade, K, 'Innocent but proven guilty: Eliciting internalized false confessions using doctored-video evidence' (2009) 23 *Applied Cognitive Psychology* (5). Using specific interview techniques, they found that 70% of the students falsely confessed to cheating.

16 However, even someone with a good memory may, if subjected to pressure over time, come to doubt their ability to recall their involvement in an offence and therefore conclude that they are guilty. A good example is the 'Kerry Babies' case (see O'Mahony, P, 'The Kerry Babies case: Towards a Social Psychological Analysis' (1992) *Irish Psychology* 13).

- *Guilt:* some accused persons may possess feelings of guilt unrelated to the offence in question, confusing or associating those feelings with the suggestion that they have committed an offence.[17]

7.4.2 Coerced-compliant confessions

This occurs when a suspect agrees with the suggestion of guilt presented to them by an interrogator, without internalising it; in short, they confess to their guilt externally, but maintain belief in their innocence internally. They 'comply' or cooperate with the police by confessing their guilt and can do so for different reasons. A suspect might confess in order to please the interrogator (an authority figure, and normally the dominant party in the interview). They might also confess in order to gain a short-term advantage or relief from stress or pressure, for example to secure release on bail, or to end a particularly unpleasant or oppressive interview. A suspect might also be 'induced' to confess (see below). Coerced-compliant confessions are often associated with aggressive questioning of a suspect by the police, but they can also be related to the period of detention, the stress of the environment, fear of or submission to authority figures, lack of sleep, and physical violence (all present in *Magee v United Kingdom*).[18] Vulnerable suspects are particularly at risk of providing coerced-compliant confessions. Moreover, some innocent suspects falsely confess in the belief that this would later be corrected by the justice system and that they would not be punished unjustly.[19]

7.4.3 Coerced-passive confessions

Coerced-passive confessions occur where questioning 'leads suspects to "admit" to committing an offence without necessarily adopting or even understanding the substance of this admission'.[20] As such, an interrogator guides or directs the suspect towards a police objective – securing a confession. This will normally be subtle, to the extent that the suspect does not realise or appreciate the weight of their statement.

Such confessions therefore involve some form of manipulation, exploitation or deception on the part of the police; and a lack of understanding on the part of the accused about what is happening to them. Confusion as to the law or facts is a particular problem in relation to coerced-passive confessions, as an accused may either:

- think that they are guilty of an offence when they are not; or
- agree with facts or assertions which confirm their guilt, without realising this.[21]

This is a particular problem with vulnerable suspects, who may struggle to understand the nature and significance of the interaction between themselves and a police officer, the words used, or their meaning. Furthermore, such problems will be exacerbated – and such confessions made more likely – where there is no legal representative to protect the interests of the suspect by both asserting their rights and interpreting the law.[22]

---

17 This is particularly problematic where the feelings of guilt are non-specific. This could also relate to mental health issues, such as depression or anxiety.

18 [2000] ECHR 216.

19 Leo, R, 'False Confessions: Causes, Consequences, and Implications' (2009) 37 *J of the American Academy of Psych & the Law* (3); Kassin, S, 'On the Psychology of Confessions: Does Innocence Put Innocents at Risk?' (2005) 60 *American Psychologist* (3).

20 Welsh, L, Skinns, L and Sanders, A, *Sanders & Young's Criminal Justice* (OUP, 2021).

21 For an example of this in practice, see McConville (n 13), 70.

22 Clearly, this is heightened by the uptake of legal advice in the police station – see **Chapter 5**.

7.5 Police-invented confessions

Police-invented confessions occur when the police say that the accused has confessed when, in fact, they have not. Police-invented confessions can be sub-divided into two categories:

- *Embellishment:* distortion of what the accused has actually said by the addition of incriminating detail or information to existing statements.
- *Fabrication:* the creation of totally new material, which is then attributed (falsely) to the suspect.

Clearly, there is a grey area between legitimate but robust interrogation, and unfair and coercive behaviour. In contrast, police-invented confessions clearly involve outright deception and abuse of trust. The main issue is one of evidence: proving that the police have invented the confession and that the accused did not make the confession is challenging. This will usually be a question of whom the jury finds more credible: the police or the accused. This leaves the accused at an obvious disadvantage; the police are, generally, trusted authority figures, whereas jurors may take a dim view of an unknown defendant in the dock.

7.6 Prevalence and significance

The question of prevalence (how commonly something occurs) is important in determining the extent to which we should regulate confession evidence. If confessions are rare, then false confessions (which are even less common) arguably pose a minor threat to the integrity of the criminal justice system. Gudjonsson suggested that confession rates ranged from 40–76% of cases;[23] these findings were subsequently confirmed by other studies.[24] This suggests that they are relatively common. It is much harder to calculate the prevalence of false confessions, as many will go undiscovered. Data from the Innocence Project suggests that between 15–30% of DNA exoneration cases in the USA (that is, where those convicted of a crime are later proven innocent due to DNA evidence) involve defendants incriminating themselves, confessing or pleading guilty.[25] Research in this area is hampered by a lack data on false confessions from authorities such as the police or central government.[26] Researchers would need to

23 Russano, M, Meissner, C, Narchet, F and Kassin, S, 'Investigating True and False Confessions Within a Novel Experimental Paradigm' (2005) 16 *Psychological Science* (6), 481; also see Gudjonsson (n 10).

24 According to Baldwin, suspects made confessions or self-incriminating statements in more than half of cases where there was an interrogation (Baldwin, J, 'Police interview techniques: establishing truth or proof?' (1993) *Brit. J of Criminol* 3; Moston et al found a confession rate of 55% (Moston, S, Stephenson, G and Williamson, T, 'The incidence, antecedents and consequences of the use of the right to silence during police questioning' (1993) *Criminal Behaviour and Mental Health* 3; Bucke and Brown found that 58% of suspects confessed in police interview (Bucke, T and Brown, D, 'In police custody: police powers and suspects' rights under the revised PACE codes of practice' (Home Office, 1997); more recently, Sukumar et al found that only 12% made full admissions – but this was a small sample (Sukumar, D, Hodgson, J and Wade, K, 'Behind closed doors: Live Observations of Current Police Station Disclosure Practices and Lawyer-Client Consultations' (2016) *Crim LR*).

25 Quoted in Kassin (n 19); see Innocence Project, 'DNA exonerations in the United States': www.innocenceproject.org/dna-exonerations-in-the-united-states/ (accessed 11 May 2020).

26 The police do not routinely record numbers on confessions, let alone those which are later proven to be inaccurate. Demonstrable false confessions would result from the appeal process in the courts, meaning that the police would not have any reason to record such data. The government does not publish any data highlighting successful appeals involving alleged or proven false confessions; a systematic analysis of available information on successful appeals and cases involving false confessions is possible, but outside of the scope of this book.

identify cases where suspects and defendants have confessed their guilt, and then positively establish their 'innocence'. This is extremely challenging, for a variety of reasons.[27] There are, however, plenty of high-profile examples of false confessions.[28] A due process perspective would argue that even one wrongful conviction based on a false confession is unacceptable, and that protections for suspects should be strengthened to avoid this. In contrast, a crime control perspective would argue that the relatively small risk of false confessions resulting from police interrogation is a price worth paying for a greater chance of convicting the guilty.

Confessions are not only prevalent, but also significant in the criminal justice process. Decades of research suggests that confessions are regarded as 'particularly weighty in the courtroom, such that when a confession is present, juries are much more likely to convict'.[29] In 1993, McConville found that 94% of suspects who confessed in police interview pleaded guilty, whilst a further 4% were convicted after trial.[30] In 1998, Philips and Brown studied defendants in magistrates' courts and found that 92% of those who had made self-incriminating statements or confessions went on to plead guilty, compared with only 76% who had made no admissions.[31] More recently, a US study in 2018 by Redlich et al found that 100% of suspects who made partial confessions and 97% of suspects who made full confessions pleaded guilty.[32] As such, confessions in police interviews appear to make a guilty plea more likely and an acquittal more difficult. It has also been argued that confessions have a broader influence on the nature of the proceedings that follow it. Leo argued:

> Suspects who provide incriminating information to detectives are significantly more likely to be treated differently at every subsequent stage of the criminal justice process than those suspects who did not provide incriminating information during interrogation.[33]

As such, confessions not only 'funnel' suspects towards an eventual conviction, but they appear to lead to less favourable treatment in the proceedings that follow – including charging and sentencing.[34] Confessions are therefore highly impactful on the nature and outcome of cases. Both the prevalence and significance of confessions therefore seem to justify a robust system of safeguards to protect the accused and ensure that admissions of guilt are in fact valid.

---

27 Lack of access to case files and relevant evidence, as well as the ability to clearly demonstrate innocence to the requisite standard. For an account of this sort of work see Field, S and Eady, D, 'Truth-finding and the adversarial tradition: the experience of the Cardiff Law School Innocence Project' (2017) *CrimLR*.

28 Such as the Cardiff Three, the Guildford Four (1989), the Tottenham Three (1991), the Darvell Brothers (1992) and the 2009 case of Sean Hodgson – who wrongly spent 27 years in jail as a result of a false confession.

29 Redlich, A, Yan, S, Norris, R and Bushway, S, 'The Influence of Confessions on Guilty Pleas and Plea Discounts' (2018) 24 *Psychology, Public Policy, and Law* (2), 147.

30 McConville, M, 'Corroboration and Confessions: The impact of a rule requiring that no conviction can be sustained on the basis of confession evidence alone' (HMSO, 1993), 33.

31 Phillips, C and Brown, D, 'Entry into the criminal justice system: a survey of police arrests and their outcomes' (Home Office, 1998), 159.

32 Redlich (n 29), 152. Interestingly, nearly 95% of suspects who made no statement (ie remained silent) pleaded guilty. This therefore has implications for the issues discussed in **Chapter 4**.

33 Leo, R, 'Inside the Interrogation Room' (1996) 86 *J of Crim L & Criminol* (2), 298.

34 *Ibid.*

7.7 Regulation of confession evidence in the police station

7.7.1 The right to legal advice

Section 58 of PACE 1984 grants all suspects the right to a lawyer, and this represents an important form of regulating confession evidence at the police station. A suspect can obtain legal advice on whether to answer police questions and, if so, in what form. The presence of a lawyer in the police interview and the police station generally can protect the accused from verbal or physical intimidation, as well as ensure that police questioning is appropriate and that evidence has not been fabricated. A legal representative is also charged with negotiating the release of the accused; as such, a suspect will feel less inclined to take matters into their own hands to secure their release by confessing. In the 'Cardiff Three' case, the court emphasised:

> It is of the first importance that a solicitor fulfilling the exacting duty of assisting a suspect during interviews should ... discharge his function responsibly and courageously.

The provision of an appropriate adult is a safeguard designed to protect an accused person who is a juvenile or otherwise vulnerable.[35] Whilst they do not provide legal advice in the same manner as a lawyer, they do provide advice and assistance, vital moral support, and reassurance to the accused.

7.7.2 Oppression and inducements

According to para 11.5 of Code C, the police cannot use 'oppressive' methods when interviewing the accused. This is a crucial safeguard; the use of oppression, overt or not, can force the accused to falsely confess due to fear of the consequences of non-compliance; due to immediate fear of violence; or due to the influence of a dominant, authority figure. Oppressive interview techniques may lead to a resultant confession being deemed non-admissible at trial under s 76 of PACE 1984 (see below). It is worth noting, however, that police interrogation which actively seeks a confession is not necessarily prohibited. In *Oliphant*, the police suggested that it was 'in [the suspect's] interest to tell the truth' and that he would 'feel better ... if he got it off of his chest'.[36] The suspect proceeded to make full and extensive admissions to the offence without a solicitor present. Whilst the Court of Appeal found several breaches of Code C and a failure to provide legal advice, it also concluded that this made no difference; the accused confessed because he wanted to and 'it was permissible to seek admissions'.[37]

Whilst the police can pursue confessions, the way in which they do so is limited by the protections under PACE 1984 and its Codes of Practice. Alongside 'oppression', para 11.5 of Code C prohibits 'inducements', which is when the police attempt to obtain a confession by outlining 'what action will be taken by the police if the person being questioned answers questions, makes a statement or refuses to do either'. As such, the police cannot tempt a suspect to confess by offering positive or negative incentives – for example, the promise of release or the threat of prosecution. However, Sanders et al argue that this rule is arguably presentational and ineffective.[38] This is

35 Code C (n 3), various paras – particularly [11.15] which states that juveniles, mentally disordered or otherwise vulnerable suspects 'must not' be interviewed without an appropriate adult (unless it is urgent). Appropriate adult is defined at [1.7].

36 [1992] Crim LR 40.

37 *Ibid.* They also added that it was not the court's job to 'control or discipline the police'.

38 Welsh et al (n 20).

partly because the courts have insisted on a clear causal link between the inducement and confession;[39] and there is extensive evidence that informal negotiations and bargaining between police and suspects are, regardless of this rule, an important part of the dynamic of police interrogation.[40] Moreover, it is not necessarily clear when police are merely offering information to a suspect and when they are inducing them.[41]

7.7.3 Other safeguards

Other protections in Code C set clearer boundaries (see **Chapters 4** and **5**). Some are designed to ensure that the circumstances and environment in which interviews and detention occur (such as heating, lighting, access to food, and sleep) are not so poor that a suspect 'breaks', confessing simply to escape the situation.[42] Another practical but equally important safeguard is the regulation of the period of detention and of police interviews. Placing limits on the detention of suspects without charge helps to prevent the police using custody as a tool for extracting admissions. Equally, long interviews clearly pose a risk; hours or even days of continuous questioning can break a suspect's psychological resistance and lead them to confess – perhaps in order to obtain relief or because they have come to believe the account suggested by the police.

Interviews should also normally take place at police stations, since they provide ready access to the facilities (such as appropriate interview rooms), equipment (such as recording equipment) and personnel (such as the custody officer, a duty lawyer or an appropriate adult) required to protect the accused and hold police officers to account. Other locations will not have these protections in place and may therefore facilitate the production of non-genuine confessions. Police interviews must be recorded (and will often be filmed) to ensure that there is a contemporaneous, objective record of exchanges between the police and the accused. The effectiveness of such limitations is easier to measure than, for example, oppression or inducements, since one can plainly observe the state of an interview room or time the length of detention.

When it comes to the conduct of the police, the rules are open to interpretation. Whilst this has the potential to embrace a range of behaviours, it also makes it difficult for lawyers, judges and (perhaps most importantly) police officers to determine when an interview has gone too far in the pursuit of an admission. A fundamental challenge in designing a regulatory structure for confession evidence is striking a balance between:

- encouraging guilty suspects to confess (a crime control imperative);
- not causing innocent suspects to confess falsely (a due process imperative); and
- protecting all suspects from police-invented confessions, regardless of guilt or innocence.

---

39 That is, the inducement clearly led to the suspect providing a confession (*ibid*). For example, see *Weeks* [1995] Crim LR 52.

40 Often, the suspect will want something (for example, bail, a lesser charge, disclosure, or discharge) which the police can provide. Equally, the police may also want something (for example, *any* form of conviction or intelligence). For more, see Welsh et al (n 20).

41 A good example would be the possibility of a sentence discount for an early admission. For example, see *AG's References (Nos 14 and 15 of 2006)* [2006] EWCA Crim 1335. For discussion of this, see Ashworth, A, *The Criminal Process* (OUP, 2010), 98–99.

42 A classic example of an environment designed to break a suspect would be Castlereagh Holding Centre in Belfast, Northern Ireland. See Fitzpatrick, B and Walker, C, 'Holding centres in Northern Ireland, the Independent Commissioner and the rights of detainees' (1999) *European Human Rights LR* 1.

7.8 Regulation of confession evidence at trial: PACE 1984, s 76

As stated earlier, s 76(1) allows a confession to be used against the accused if it is 'relevant' and has not been excluded by the court. The court's power to exclude confession evidence is a key safeguard, allowing the accused to argue that a confession should be inadmissible on two basic grounds – that is, 'the confession was or may have been obtained':

- 'by oppression of the person who made it' (s 76(2)(a));
- 'in consequence of anything said or done which was likely, in the circumstances existing at the time, to render unreliable any confession which might be made by [the accused] in consequence thereof' (s 76(2)(b)).

When the accused raises one of these two grounds for exclusion, a judge must (not may) exclude it unless 'the prosecution proves to the court beyond reasonable doubt that the confession (notwithstanding that it may be true) was not obtained as aforesaid'.[43] If the accused claims that a confession has been invented by the police, s 76 will not be applicable as it applies only to 'a confession made by an accused person'. It therefore cannot cover the situation where an accused claims never to have made a confession. This is a factual question for the jury to decide.[44]

7.8.1 Oppression

Section 76(8) provides some definition of this term:

> 'oppression' includes torture, inhuman or degrading treatment, and the use or threat of violence (whether or not amounting to torture).

Generally, these might be considered the most obvious types of oppression that involve undisputed breaches of PACE 1984, its Codes of Practice and the ECHR. Beyond this, the courts have provided guidance on what this means. The leading case is *Fulling*, in which Lord Chief Justice Lane stated that '"oppression" ... should be given its ordinary dictionary meaning', specified as follows:

> [The] exercise of authority or power in a burdensome, harsh, or wrongful manner; unjust or cruel treatment of subjects, inferiors, etc.; the imposition of unreasonable or unjust burdens.[45]

In addition, Lord Lane commented:

> We find it hard to envisage any circumstances in which such oppression would not entail some impropriety on the part of the interrogator.[46]

In short, oppression will nearly always involve some form of improper behaviour by the police (although this is not absolutely necessary).

Other cases have explored what kind of behaviour might fall within the *Fulling* definition. In *Beales*, the accused was arrested on suspicion of assaulting the 2-year-old son of his girlfriend.[47] He was arrested and interviewed for just over half an hour, with

43 PACE 1984, s 76(2).

44 It is worth noting that s 78 of PACE 1984 may be relevant for police-invented confessions, particularly if there has been a breach of PACE or a Code of Practice. Section 78 gives the court a discretion to exclude any evidence – including confession evidence – if it believes it may have 'an adverse effect on the fairness of the proceedings'.

45 [1987] QB 426, 432.

46 *Ibid.*

47 [1991] Crim LR 118.

only one officer present. The officer used a variety of false and exaggerated statements to convince the accused he had swung the child around by his ankles, even though the accused claimed to have no recollection of doing so. Hyam J concluded that the accused had been 'hectored and bullied from first to last' and that the officer had deliberately misstated the evidence in order to pressure the accused.[48] This 'stepped into the realm' of oppression.[49] A more extreme version of such behaviour was displayed in the 'Cardiff Three' case, which involved the 'relentless refusal to entertain the possibility that a suspect's answers may be truthful', combined with repeated assertions that he was guilty.[50] In contrast, in *Emmerson*, the suspect admitted to taking money from 'one-armed bandit' machines after two interviews in which he protested his innocence.[51] During the third interview, the interviewing officer spoke in a raised voice and swore at the accused. The accused argued that he had confessed out of concern for his family and due to intimidation by the police officer. Whilst Lord Justice Lloyd conceded that the officer's behaviour was 'rude and discourteous', this 'was not in any sense oppressive', and to exclude it would 'give oppression a completely false meaning'.[52] In *Davison*, the defendant made admissions after being interviewed without a lawyer (despite requesting one); being unlawfully detained by the police after the first interview; and being confronted with an informer.[53] The court concluded that the failure to provide a solicitor was a breach of Code C but not, in itself, oppressive;[54] however, the unlawful detention after the first interview was a wrongful exercise of power within the *Fulling* definition. Therefore, everything after the first interview was excluded.

The character and attributes of the suspect may also be relevant to whether a confession has been obtained by oppression. In *Seelig and Spens*, a suspect was described as 'an experienced merchant banker' and therefore it was concluded that no oppression occurred.[55] In *Miller*, the accused was a diagnosed paranoid schizophrenic who was questioned about the murder of his girlfriend.[56] The police were aware of his condition; in interview, he made a confession but shortly afterwards tried to retract it. Miller argued that the interview was oppressive, claiming it had caused hallucinations and delusions which an ordinary person would not have experienced. Concluding that the interview was not oppressive, the court stated:

> It may well be ... that in all probability some of the questions triggered off hallucinations and flights of fancy, but that by itself is not, in our view, indicative of oppression. Whether questions skilfully and deliberately asked so as to produce that kind of disordered mind could amount to oppression is an altogether different matter. The judge did not find that such obviously wicked conduct had taken place.[57]

In short, the police had acted in good faith; had they sought to obtain a confession by inducing delusions, the court may well have found otherwise.

48 *Ibid* 119.
49 *Ibid.*
50 Welsh et al (n 20); *Paris* (n 8).
51 (1991) 92 Cr App R 284.
52 *Ibid* 287.
53 [1988] Crim LR 442.
54 *Ibid* 444. Although not explicitly confirmed, this was also implied in *obiter* in *Samuel* [1988] QB 615.
55 [1992] 1 WLR 148, 159.
56 [1986] 1 WLR 1191.
57 *Ibid* 1201.

More recently, the Court of Appeal in Charlton considered whether it could 'infer' that there had been oppressive behaviour by police officers who had been connected to other previous misconduct cases (specifically the 'Cardiff Three' case).[58] However, the court rejected a general 'culture of police misconduct' amongst a particular police force as being sufficient to establish oppression, since there was nothing specific to suggest that this had happened in the instant case.[59] To summarise, *Blackstone's Criminal Practice* suggests that exclusion for oppression is

> likely to be reserved for those rare cases where an accused has been subjected to misconduct of a deliberate and serious nature, and where the court is anxious to mark its disquiet at the methods employed.[60]

Whilst case law does provide guidance, this tends to be on a case-by-case basis; as the court in *Charlton* noted, 'each case has to be considered on its merits'.[61] Beyond the *Fulling* definition, it is uncertain what sort of behaviour will be considered oppressive, limiting its value as a deterrent for police malpractice. That being said, even if a confession is not excluded by a judge under s 76(2)(b), the jury retains the discretion to disregard one which they consider has been obtained through oppression – and in fact should do so, even if they consider it to be true confession.[62]

7.8.2 Unreliability

It is worth reminding ourselves of s 76(2)(b), which is a rather convoluted provision:

> [T]he confession was or may have been obtained … in consequence of anything said or done which was likely, in the circumstances existing at the time, to render unreliable any confession which might be made by [the accused] in consequence thereof.

There are four elements needed to allow exclusion under s 76(2)(b):

- something 'said or done' (this can be 'anything');
- the confession was obtained 'in consequence' of whatever was 'said or done';
- whatever was 'said or done' was 'likely to render' *any* confession 'unreliable';
- the likelihood of unreliability must be considered in the 'circumstances existing at the time'.

As highlighted above, the question for a court is not whether *the* confession was unreliable (that is, the confession made by the suspect in the case before it) but whether *any* confession which a suspect might make was likely to be rendered unreliable. This was confirmed in *Re Proulx*:[63]

> The word 'any' must … be understood as indicating 'any such' or 'such a' confession as the applicant made … the test is not whether the actual confession was untruthful or inaccurate. It is whether whatever was said or done was, in the circumstances existing as at the time of the confession, *likely* to have rendered such a confession unreliable.

58 [2016] EWCA Crim 52.

59 *Ibid* [116].

60 Ormerod, D and Perry, D (eds), *Blackstone's Criminal Practice 2023* (OUP, 2022), F18.14.

61 [2016] EWCA Crim 52, [116].

62 *Mushtaq* [2005] 1 WLR 1513.

63 [2001] 1 All ER 57.

This also confirms (as is stated in s 76(2)) that it is irrelevant whether the confession is actually true. In *Crampton*, the court clarified the meaning of the section:[64]

> The word 'unreliable' ... means 'cannot be relied upon as being the truth.' What the provision ... is concerned with is the nature and quality of the words spoken or the things done by the police which are likely to, in the circumstances existing at the time, render the confession unreliable ... It is quite plain that if those acts and words are of such a quality, whether or not the confession is in fact true, it is inadmissible.

One could argue that this represents a strong due process approach. If the police employ questionable tactics that are likely to lead to unreliable confessions, this will not be excused simply because a confession is genuine and a suspect, in fact, guilty. The means cannot justify the end. This places individual rights and a fair process above securing convictions.

'Anything said or done'

'Anything said or done' clearly allows the court to consider a wide range of behaviours or circumstances that may have caused unreliability. As demonstrated in Barry, this should not be confined to 'a narrow analysis' of verbal exchanges between the police and the accused, 'analogous to offer and acceptance in the law of contract'.[65] Whilst the relevant behaviour or words will usually, but not inevitably, be that of the police, *Goldenberg* confirmed that 'anything said or done' must be 'external' to the accused (that is, it cannot be the words or actions of the accused).[66] In *Delaney*, the suspect – a juvenile with a low IQ – was accused of indecently assaulting a 3-year-old girl and was questioned at his home by the police, 12 days after the event.[67] He initially denied the accusations, but admitted the offence after 90 minutes of questioning, which was not recorded or written up until the next day. The confessions were the only inculpatory evidence. The court pointed out that the 'mere fact that there has been a breach of the Codes ... does not of itself mean that evidence has to be rejected', and it did not believe that the lack of recording had directly caused the defendant to confess.[68] However, the court did believe that the breaches had had an indirect effect, stating:

> By failing to make a contemporaneous note ... the officers deprived the court of what was ... the most cogent evidence as to what did indeed happen during these interviews and what did induce the appellant to confess ... The judge of course is entitled to ask himself why the officers broke the rules. Was it mere laziness or was it something more devious? Was it perhaps a desire to conceal from the court the full truth of the suggestions they had held out to the defendant? These are matters which may well tip the scales in favour of the defendant in these circumstances and make it impossible for the judge to say that he is satisfied beyond reasonable doubt, and so require him to reject the evidence.[69]

Since the court could not be sure how the confession had been obtained, the prosecution could not dispel a reasonable doubt that the confession had not been so

64 (1991) 92 Cr App R 369.

65 *Barry* (1992) 95 Cr App R 384, as described in Ormerod (n 60), F18.19.

66 (1988) 88 Cr App R 285. This is logical, as the suspect could otherwise 'spoil' their confession by some other action or words.

67 (1988) 88 Cr App R 338.

68 *Ibid* 341.

69 *Ibid* 342.

obtained (that is, as a consequence or things said or done in the circumstances, which were likely to make a confession unreliable). This case also confirms that an omission – the failure to do something – can be something 'said or done'.

In *Blake*, the accused was arrested after a witness in a major fraud investigation identified two taped voices as possibly (but not definitely) being that of the offender.[70] Whilst one of the voices was in fact the accused, the police wrongly told him that his voice had been recognised, leading to a confession. The court held that misleading the suspect as to the existence of evidence against him fell within s 76(2)(b). In *Harvey*, a psychopathically disordered woman of low intelligence heard her lover confess to a murder, leading her to confess her own guilt due to a 'child-like desire' to protect her lover.[71] The court found that hearing her lover confess was considered something 'said or done', demonstrating that this is not limited to the police or authority figures. Equally, the court drew a similar conclusion in *M*, when the suspect's own solicitor intervened during an interview in an attempt to secure a confession.[72] Several cases involve clear breaches of the PACE 1984 Codes of Practice; these may constitute something 'said or done' which causes a confession to be unreliable – but there is no guarantee. Examples of breaches leading to exclusions for unreliability include:

- *Doolan*: in which the police failed to caution the accused and did not maintain a proper interview record or show it to the accused, leading to exclusion of a confession.[73]
- *Chung*: in which the police questioned the accused before allowing access to a solicitor; this was considered something 'done'.[74]
- *DPP v Blake*: in which the police insisted on the use of the accused's estranged father as the appropriate adult in interview.[75]
- *Moss*: which involved a combination of breaches and circumstances; the accused was of low intelligence, was interviewed nine times during a lengthy period of detention, had access to legal advice denied, and had no independent person in interview.[76]
- *W*: a confession made by a vulnerable person without an appropriate adult would be unreliable when there was a realistic likelihood that no admissions would have been made had an appropriate adult been present.[77]

Nonetheless, it is important to note that 'the mere fact that there has been a breach of the Codes of Practice does not of itself mean that evidence has to be rejected'.[78]

'Circumstances existing at the time'

The courts have also considered the meaning of 'the circumstances existing at the time'. In *Everett*, the court concluded that this should 'obviously include' the mental condition of the suspect (in this case, a 42-year-old with a mental age of 8, who was in the bottom 2% of the population for intelligence) and that this should be based on

70 [1991] Crim LR119.
71 [1988] Crim LR241.
72 [2000] 8 Arch News 2.
73 [1988] Crim LR 747.
74 (1991) 92 Cr App R 314.
75 [1989] 1 WLR 432.
76 (1990) 91 Cr App R 371.
77 [2010] EWCA Crim 2799.
78 *Delaney* (n 67), 341.

objective medical evidence (not the subjective beliefs of the police officers).[79] In *McGovern*, the physical and mental state of the accused – who was 6 months pregnant and of limited intelligence – formed 'part of the background' and should be included in the definition of 'circumstances existing at the time'.[80] However, it is unclear whether this extends beyond the accused for the purposes of s 76(2)(b). In *W*, the confession of a 13-year-old was considered reliable even though the appropriate adult (her mother) was psychotic at the time and unable to support her daughter.[81]

7.9 Procedure for excluding confession evidence

Generally, the prosecution does not have to prove the admissibility of a confession unless:

- the defence 'represents' that it is inadmissible under s 76(2); or
- the court, of its own motion, requires proof of admissibility under s 76(3).

The defence must make a representation, which is 'a statement by responsible counsel, upon the basis of documents or proofs of evidence in his possession at the time of speaking', that a confession was or may have been obtained in breach of s 76(2).[82] This must take place prior to the prosecution's use of the evidence at trial. If the judge accepts that there is a reasonable argument to be made about admissibility, the jury will retire and the matter will be considered by the judge alone in a *voir dire* (a 'trial within a trial'). This ensures that the jury are not aware of any disputed evidence until it is deemed admissible. A *voir dire* can involve the submission of evidence and the production of witnesses to aid the judge in deciding on admissibility. If the prosecution does not prove beyond reasonable doubt that a confession was not obtained in a manner prohibited by s 76(2), the confession *must* be excluded – the judge has no discretion.

7.10 Summary

- A confession is a statement that is wholly or partly adverse to the person who made it (the accused); and it can be made to a person in authority or not, in words or otherwise.
- Confessions are useful to the police and prosecution as they make convictions easier and quicker; confessions are both common and significant.
- Confessions are regulated in order to reduce the incidence of false confessions, police-invented confessions and the use of illegitimate methods to obtain confessions.
- Safeguards exist at the police station to protect suspects from pressure and coercion, and thus to reduce the likelihood that suspects will confess falsely or in unfair circumstances.
- Section 76 of PACE 1984 requires the exclusion of confession evidence if it has been obtained by oppression or as a result of anything said or done which might render it unreliable.

79 [1988] Crim LR 826.
80 (1991) 92 Cr App R 228.
81 [1994] Crim LR 130.
82 *Dhorajiwala* [2010] 2 Cr App R 161.

- Breaches of PACE 1984 do not automatically amount to oppression or unreliability.
- If raised by the defence, the prosecution must prove (beyond reasonable doubt) that a confession was not obtained in the manner above.

chapter 8

'Managing' Criminal Procedure

8.1 Introduction

In **Chapter 1**, we explained that there are different theoretical approaches to the delivery of criminal justice. Whilst the chapter analysed these approaches in a theoretical context, it was accepted that England and Wales has traditionally adopted an adversarial approach to criminal procedure. One significant distinction between adversarialism and inquisitorialism is the contrast in the approach to 'truth', as illustrated below:

Adversarialism	**Inquisitorialism**
What truth can you prove?	What truth can be found?

The difference between proof and truth can be exemplified by illustrating how the procedure in each approach is carried out. Adversarialism is centred on a partisan battle between the prosecution and defence. Each side battles to convince the neutral adjudicator that their side's case represents the most credible, evidential and provable version of the truth and, as such, that their side should win. This approach accepts that an objective 'truth' is very difficult to obtain in reality; therefore, the most well supported account of the facts should be victorious. Inquisitorialism does not involve this partisan battle between the prosecution and defence. Instead, the process is conducted by a neutral state official who will supervise an investigation, which will be condensed into a *dossier* of evidence. This *dossier* will present the 'truth' of the matter, and as a result it will acquit or convict the suspect. An adversarial trial process is regarded by inquisitorial theory as a waste of resources, with 'the truth' unlikely to be discovered. The criminal process, and any trial as a part of that, should focus on truth and not proof.

This conflict of 'truth vs proof' has permeated traditional adversarial justice since the dawn of the new millennium. In his 'Review of the Criminal Courts of England and Wales' (the 'Auld Review'), Auld LJ suggested that

> A criminal trial is not a game in which a guilty defendant should be provided with a sporting chance. It is a search for the truth in accordance with the twin principles that the prosecution must prove its case and a defendant is not obliged to inculpate himself, the object being to convict the guilty and acquit the innocent. Requiring a defendant to indicate in advance what he disputes about the prosecution case offends neither of those principles.

This statement marked the symbolic birth of a more 'managerial' approach to criminal procedure. This chapter will return to the Auld Review's comments to ascertain whether the modern process offends traditional adversarial principles, including the burden of proof and the privilege against self-incrimination.

8.2 The evolution of disclosure

definition

Disclosure is the provision of material by each party to the court and each other, with the aim of ensuring that all relevant information is shared between the relevant stakeholders in the criminal justice process.

The regime requiring disclosure by parties is a relatively recent creation and represents the beginnings of the 'managerial' approach to criminal justice. As **Chapter 1** established, the adversarial criminal trial emerged in the mid-18th century. However, obligations to disclose information to the opposing party were absent for some 200 years. The Devlin Report, published in 1976, noted that until the mid-1940s, there was no duty to disclose any information prior to trial by either party.[1] The judgment in *Bryant and Dickson*[2] is commonly regarded as the beginning of the process in which the courts began to impose a duty on the prosecution to disclose material that may lead to the acquittal of the accused.[3] The case established an obligation upon the prosecution to make available to the defence details of any witnesses whom the prosecution knew could give material evidence. The rule in *Bryant and Dickson* was extended further by *Dallison v Caffery*.[4] Lord Denning sought to broaden the disclosure obligations of the prosecution:

> [I]f [the prosecutor] knows of a credible witness who can speak [of] material facts which tends to show the prisoner to be innocent, he must either call that witness himself or make his statement available ... it would be highly reprehensible to conceal ... the evidence which such a witness can give.[5]

For Denning, disclosure was concerned with ensuring that justice was done and not simply ensuring that a particular rule was followed; it was the spirit of the rule that should prevail, not its letter. Until the 1960s, obligations to disclose information were placed exclusively upon the prosecution. The Criminal Justice Act 1967 was the first exception to this general rule; s 11 (now repealed) stated that in trials on indictment:

> (1) ... the defendant shall not without the leave of the court adduce evidence in support of an alibi unless, before the end of the prescribed period, he gives notice of particulars of the alibi.

---

1 Devlin Committee Report, *Report of the Committee on Evidence of Identification in Criminal Cases* (CMND 338, 1976, 134/135, 42 para 5.

2 (1946) 31 Cr App R 146. Prior to *Bryant and Dickson*, in *Clarke* (1930) 22 Cr App R 58, the court held that where there is a discrepancy between a witness's evidence at trial and his or her statements made previously to the police, the prosecution should consider if an actual copy of the witness's statement should be disclosed rather than just information given about it.

3 Corker, D and Parkinson, S, *Disclosure in Criminal Proceedings* (Oxford: Oxford University Press, 2010), 3.

4 [1965] 1 QB 348.

5 *Ibid* per Lord Denning MR at para 369.

Alibi disclosure remained the only form of defence disclosure until the mid-1980s. In 1986, the Fraud Trials Committee, chaired by Lord Roskill, published a report leading to the second major development in the area of defence disclosure. The Committee found that the public was correct; the legal system was too archaic, cumbersome and unreliable. Every stage of the legal process was an 'open invitation to blatant delay and abuse'.[6] The Committee concluded that radical reform was necessary. Although the terms of reference for the report related to fraud trials, the Committee argued that the changes could 'be of benefit to a wider range of criminal cases'.[7] The Committee believed that forcing the defence to outline its case in advance of trial would make the trial both 'shorter and more efficient'. Furthermore, this would make the trial clearer for the jury, if they were told at the outset what part of the prosecution's case the defence was intending to challenge (although the Committee accepted that it had been unable to empirically test this assertion). Requiring the defence to disclose a case outline would, it argued, reduce the risk of fabricated defences, and the prosecution would be able to investigate in advance any defence claims that required closer scrutiny.[8]

The Committee considered a number of objections to the proposal. First, it accepted that the main objection was that the proposal was an infringement of the prosecution burden of proof. A further objection to the proposal was the lack of an effective sanction against a defendant who failed to comply with the provisions. To alleviate any fear that a defence disclosure regime would weaken the burden of the proof, the Commission stated:

> [T]he prosecution will be required to prepare their case thoroughly ... and this will include making early disclosure of their evidence ... We recognise that the burden of proof would be affected if the prosecution were allowed to alter the nature of their case once the defence had been disclosed. To avoid this possibility, any proposal would therefore have to involve the prosecution's case being 'fixed' before the defence could be required to show their hand. If the prosecution sought to change their ground ... to overwhelm the case put forward by the defence, the judge might well be justified in interfering to stop the case ... or, if it were not too late, to ensure that the prosecution adhered to their original case.[9]

Following the Committee's report, the Government enacted the Criminal Justice Act 1987. The Act provided that in serious fraud cases, persons could be required to give information about and produce documents concerning the investigation. Section 2(3) allowed the Director of the Serious Fraud Office '... to require the person under investigation or any other person to produce ... any specified documents which appear to the Director to relate to any matter relevant to the investigation ...'.[10] The Crown Court (Advance Notice of Expert Evidence) Rules[11] provided that any statement in writing of any finding or opinion of an expert upon which a party intended to rely had to be disclosed as soon as practicable after committal.[12] These obligations in the mid-

6 The Fraud Trials Committee, Chairman: The Right Honourable Lord Roskill, PC (HMSO, 1986).

7 *Ibid* p 2 at para 4. The Committee did stop short of recommending proposals for anything other than fraud cases; it would leave that discussion for those with wider concerns than its own.

8 The Fraud Trials Committee, Chairman: The Right Honorable Lord Roskill PC (HMSO, 1986), para 6.75.

9 *Ibid* p 104 at para 6.75.

10 Criminal Justice Act 1987, s 2(3).

11 SI 1987/716.

12 'Committal' means to transfer a defendant from a magistrates' court to the Crown Court. Formerly, committal hearings were held to achieve this; these were abolished in 2013 as part of a drive for swifter and more efficient proceedings. It is now correct to refer to cases being 'sent' to the Crown Court.

1980s were the first formal deviations from the traditional notion that the accused does not have to outline any aspect of their defence prior to trial, save for any alibi notifications.

Until 1996, the regime of defence disclosure could be summarised as follows:

- the defence had to disclose two parts of its defence: (a) alibi evidence; and (b) expert evidence;
- the prosecution was not entitled to receive anything else in advance of trial.

However, this stance was changed dramatically with the advent of the defence statement.

8.3 The birth of the efficient criminal process: CPIA 1996

The Criminal Procedure and Investigations Act (CPIA) 1996 could be described as a politically influenced piece of legislation.[13] The Conservative Government at the time was trying to take a 'tough on crime' approach; when introducing the Bill at the second reading, Michael Howard said that the Act was 'designed to restore balance in our criminal justice system – to make life tougher for the criminal and to improve the protection of the public'.[14] Arguably, the end result of the CPIA 1996 disclosure regime was to tip the balance more in favour of the prosecution rather than the defence.[15]

To summarise the key aspects of the current disclosure process:

- The prosecutor has an initial duty to disclose information to the defence (CPIA 1996, s 3).
- The accused has to provide a defence statement for trials on indictment (CPIA 1996, s 5).
- For summary trials, any defence disclosure is voluntary (CPIA 1996, s 6).
- The prosecutor is under a continuing duty to disclose information that may undermine the prosecution's case or assist the accused (CPIA 1996, s 7A).

Section 5 of the CPIA 1996 deals with compulsory disclosure by the accused. The provisions apply when a person is charged with an indictable offence and sent to trial.[16] They do not apply to summary trials, although s 6(2) does allow the accused to voluntarily provide a defence statement to the prosecution in such cases.[17] The content of the defence statement is laid down in s 6A and includes:

(a) setting out in general terms the nature of the accused's defence, including any particular defences on which he intends to rely;
(b) indicating the matters on which the accused takes issue with the prosecution;
(c) setting out, in the case of each such matter, the reason why the accused takes issue with the prosecution.

If the accused is relying on alibi evidence, the accused must include the particulars of that evidence in the statement. This must include the name and address of any witness

13 As could the preceding piece of major criminal justice legislation – the Criminal Justice and Public Order Act 1994 (see below and **Chapter 6** on the right to silence).

14 Leng, R and Taylor, R, *Blackstone's Guide to the Criminal Procedure and Investigations Act 1996* (Blackstone Press, 1996), 1.

15 *Ibid* 2.

16 CPIA 1996, s 1(2).

17 Card and Ward believe the section is unnecessary as it is always open to the accused to disclose facts about their defence. For further discussion, see Card, R and Ward, R, *The Criminal Procedure and Investigations Act 1996* (Bristol: Jordan Publishing, 1996), 37.

that the accused believes can give evidence to support the alibi.[18] Further, the accused must provide any information that may be of material assistance in finding any such witness, if the name and address are not known.[19]

Bearing in mind that, in theory, the defence should not have to assist the prosecution, it is now very difficult in practice for the defence to withhold information about its case until trial. Section 12 states that the defence statement must be served within the period prescribed by the CPIA 1996.[20]. Additionally, ss 34 to 37 of the Criminal Justice and Public Order Act 1994 effectively curtailed the accused's right to withhold his defence until trial (see **Chapter 6**). Under s 34, the court or jury can draw such inferences as appear proper from the accused's failure to mention, in the police interview, any fact he later relies on in court.

Sanctions for non-compliance with the defence disclosure regime are governed by s 11 of the CPIA 1996 and apply where s 5 applies and the accused:

(a) fails to give a defence statement;
(b) gives a defence statement but does so after the end of the period which, by virtue of s 12, is the relevant period for s 5;
(c) is required to give an updated defence statement or a statement of the kind[21] but fails to do so;
(d) gives an updated defence statement or statement of the kind but does so after the end of time period;
(d) sets out inconsistent defences in his defence statement; or
(f) at his trial:
   (i) puts forward a defence which was not mentioned in his defence statement or is different from any defence in that statement;
   (ii) relies on a matter which was not mentioned in his defence statement;
   (ii) adduces evidence in support of an alibi without having given the particulars of the alibi in the defence statement; or
   (iv) calls a witness to give evidence in support of an alibi without having complied with s 6A(2)(a) or (b) as regards the witness in his defence statement.

Should the accused fail to comply with the defence statement provisions, two sanctions are available: the court or the prosecution, with leave of the court, may make such comment as appears appropriate;[22] and/or the court or the jury may draw inferences as appear proper in deciding whether the accused is guilty of the offence concerned.[23] Despite the fact that the court may draw inferences from non-compliance with the disclosure obligations, the defendant cannot be convicted by mere inferences alone.[24]

8.4 The Auld Review and evolution of the CPIA 1996

Lord Justice Auld was tasked with examining the workings of both the criminal justice system and the criminal courts in England and Wales with a view to reform. More specifically, the review aimed to improve the management of the process and enhance

18 CPIA 1996, s 6A(2)(a).
19 *Ibid*, s 6A(2)(b).
20 *Ibid*, s 12.
21 CPIA 1996, s 6B(4) defines a statement of the kind as 'a written statement stating that he has no changes to make to the defence statement'.
22 CPIA 1996, s 11(3)(a).
23 *Ibid*, s 11(3)(b).
24 *Ibid*, s 11(5) and (10). For more on adverse inferences, see **Chapter 6**.

the quality, effectiveness and efficiency of justice delivered.[25] The Auld Review stated that '... fairness, efficiency and effectiveness of the criminal justice system demand that its procedure should be simple, accessible and, so far as is practicable the same for every type of criminal jurisdiction'.[26] Lord Justice Auld commented that the 1996 Act 'was not working as Parliament intended and its operation did not command the confidence of criminal practitioners'.[27] He also argued that there was a high level of non-compliance by the defence in its duty of completing an adequate defence statement, and that this was a major deficiency in the disclosure provisions.

The Review suggested that any test for disclosure should be anchored to the issues in the case, as the police and prosecutor know or believe them to be, and proposed the following construction as a test for disclosure: 'material that, in the prosecutor's opinion, might reasonably affect the determination of any issue in the case of which he knows or should reasonably expect'.[28] The Review clarified this with a definition:

> [M]aterial which in the prosecutor's opinion might reasonably weaken the prosecution case or assist that of the defence.[29]

With regards to the defence statement, Lord Justice Auld believed that the requirements were adequate as they stood. He did not believe that a general obligation to identify defence witnesses and the content of their expected evidence, save for alibi or expert evidence, should be introduced.[30]

The legal reform charity JUSTICE published its response to the Auld Review in January 2002, commenting that the disclosure regime contained in the CPIA 1996 provisions had taken England and Wales closer to an inquisitorial approach to criminal procedure. The response stated that 'there can be no connection between proper disclosure by the prosecution and participation by the defence',[31] and it argued that the Auld Review had not adequately recognised this central challenge to the burden of proof, despite widespread and long-standing criticism of the CPIA 1996 regime on this basis. Furthermore, the Auld Review failed to recognise the logical extension of the burden of proof and privilege against self-incrimination, which should entitle the defence to refuse to cooperate, no matter how much it was cajoled or pressurised. In short, the defence lawyer should not have to do the prosecution's work since it is for the prosecution in an adversarial system to prove the case against the accused. As such, the defence statement provided the prosecution with the opportunity to investigate further and use any mistakes or admissions against the defendant, therefore obligating (by law) a form of self-incrimination. The JUSTICE response was also critical of the three-stage process that the CPIA 1996 had created, endorsed by the Auld Review. It argued that the current regime was wrong in principle, as it legitimised the withholding of relevant information by the prosecution, as secondary disclosure was dependent on the submission of a defence statement. JUSTICE believed this to be incorrect because it delayed the disclosure of all relevant material to the defence, which is at a distinct disadvantage in the criminal justice process. Ultimately, this could unfairly impede the defendant's chance of running a legitimate defence.[32]

---

25 Auld, R, 'A Review of the Criminal Courts of England and Wales' (HMSO, 2001), Ch 1, para 1.

26 *Ibid* Ch 10, para 271.

27 *Ibid* Ch 10, para 163.

28 *Ibid.*

29 *Ibid.*

30 *Ibid* Ch 10, para 180.

31 JUSTICE (2002) 'A Response to the Auld Review', para 75.

32 *Ibid* para 78.

8.5 The Criminal Procedure Rules: a 'sea change' in managing criminal justice

In keeping with the recommendation of the Auld Review, the Criminal Procedure Rules Committee was established 'to create a single and simply expressed instrument'[33] that codified criminal procedure. The Rules produced by the Committee would govern the practice and procedure to be followed in the Criminal Division of the Court of Appeal, the Crown Court and for criminal proceedings in magistrates' courts. Furthermore, the Committee was responsible for the development of the necessary procedures to bring about the closer alignment of the criminal courts. The Rules were created under the authority of s 69 of the Courts Act 2003, and the Act explicitly states that they should secure that 'the criminal justice system is accessible, fair and efficient and the rules are simple and simply expressed'.[34]

Rule 1.1 of the Criminal Procedure Rules (CrimPR) 2020 explicitly states that the overriding objective of this 'procedural code' is that criminal cases should be dealt with 'justly'. Rule 1.1(2) provides a non-exhaustive list of what this means:

(2) Dealing with a criminal case justly includes–
- (a) acquitting the innocent and convicting the guilty;
- (b) dealing with the prosecution and the defence fairly;
- (c) recognising the rights of a defendant, particularly those under Article 6 of the European Convention on Human Rights;
- (d) respecting the interests of witnesses, victims and jurors and keeping them informed of the progress of the case;
- (e) dealing with the case efficiently and expeditiously;
- (f) ensuring that appropriate information is available to the court when bail and sentence are considered; and
- (g) dealing with the case in ways that take into account–
  - (i) the gravity of the offence alleged,
  - (ii) the complexity of what is in issue,
  - (iii) the severity of the consequences for the defendant and others affected, and
  - (iv) the needs of other cases.

A number of these propositions have the potential to impact on the notion of adversarial justice in England and Wales.

8.5.1 Paragraph (a): 'acquitting the innocent and convicting the guilty'

Paragraph (a) appears, on face value at least, to give equal weight to acquitting the innocent and convicting the guilty. Whilst this is initially appealing and logical, it is difficult to reconcile with the adversarial criminal process of England and Wales that has traditionally embraced Blackstone's formulation that it is better for the guilty to be acquitted than for the innocent to be convicted. This conception may have theoretical implications for the presumption of innocence and by extension the adversarial defence lawyer's role. For example, are defence lawyers expected to assist in 'convicting the guilty'? If there is equal weighting between these goals, does it dilute the effectiveness of defence representation? Will the accused see their shield in the police

33 Auld (n 25), para 184.

34 Courts Act 2003, s 69(4)(a) and (b).

station tempered and effectively scaled back, if convicting the guilty is viewed as being just as important as acquitting the innocent?

8.5.2 Paragraph (b): 'dealing with the prosecution and the defence fairly'

Proposition (b) is also concerning. Again, it appears to provide equal weight to the prosecution and defence, by requiring that they be treated fairly. Again, whilst this initially seems reasonable (reflecting, in theory, the equality of arms – see **Chapter 1**), it fails to recognise the reality: that the state has significantly greater resources than the accused, as well as the legitimacy of authority. In contrast, in the accused's corner stands only the defence lawyer, normally funded by legal aid; it is he or she who is tasked with defending the accused against the allegations of the state. Perhaps the Rules would be enhanced if they more explicitly recognised the equality of arms principle.

8.5.3 Paragraph (c): 'recognising the rights of a defendant, particularly those under Article 6 of the European Convention on Human Rights'

Proposition (c) is a welcome addition, especially when one considers that the CrimPR do not explicitly acknowledge the presumption of innocence (although this is considered a key feature of the Article 6 ECHR right to a fair trial). This paragraph appears to provide some recognition that the defence is, by default, at a disadvantage and needs special protection within the criminal justice process. Providing a broad definition, this paragraph leaves room for interpretation, which is arguably both a benefit and a hazard. However, as one of a number of overarching objectives as opposed to prescriptive, detailed rules, para (c) is an important and symbolic nod to the adversarial nature of criminal justice in this jurisdiction.

8.5.4 Paragraph (d): 'respecting the interests of witnesses, victims and jurors and keeping them informed of the progress of the case'

Regarding paragraph (d), one wonders if it means that the defence lawyer will be prohibited from carrying out certain functions because such action may not respect the rights of witnesses and jurors, for example zealously questioning a prosecution witness. We have already established (see **Chapter 6**) that managerial desires have blunted the adversarial arsenal by seeking to eradicate the ambush defence. This explicit obligation could theoretically mean that the defence lawyer cannot pursue certain lines of questioning.[35] The Rules lend procedural credibility to any negative judgements the jury may make regarding defence behavior. At the same time, this provision is welcome in the sense that respect for all parties is desirable, but the proposition offers no guidance on the limits of this potential restriction and what the impact may be.

8.5.5 Paragraph (e): 'dealing with the case efficiently and expeditiously'

Proposition (e) is directly linked into the case management provisions that will be considered below. This is an explicit obligation that aims to improve the efficiency of the criminal justice process. The impact of this drive for efficiency in the defence lawyer's traditional role will be considered at **8.6**.

---

35 Youth Justice and Criminal Evidence Act 1999, ss 19–32 already make provision to tailor questioning to witnesses with different needs, and s 41 restricts the use of evidence of a person's sexual history.

8.5.6 Paragraph (f): 'ensuring that appropriate information is available to the court when bail and sentence are considered'

Proposition (f) also feeds into the managerial culture of efficiency. By ensuring that all information is presented to the court when sentencing and bail are being considered, there can, in theory, be no reason for delays or unjust decisions. This would include any reports that the court would need to make a decision. Plowden argues that this is a welcome requirement for all agencies but could catch 'defence lawyers who intended to make available expert or other reports at the sentencing stage'.[36]

8.5.7 Paragraph (g): 'dealing with the case in ways that take into account the gravity of the offence alleged, the complexity of what is in issue, the severity of the consequences for the defendant and others affected, and the needs of other cases'

At face value, this paragraph appears to be introducing some notion of proportionality into criminal proceedings. However, does the closing line of the 'needs of other cases' impose a notion of 'justice on the cheap'? If so, what does this mean for the defendant? It certainly gives no thought to what the stigma of a criminal conviction can mean for a person, for example the loss of employment or a negative perception attached to them in their local community.

The overriding objective applies to all participants in a criminal case, defined as 'anyone involved in any way with a criminal case'.[37] Clearly, this includes the defence lawyer. Further to complying with the overriding objective, any party must inform the court of any 'significant failure' to take any step required by the Rules. Atkinson and Moloney explain that a significant failure is defined as 'one which might hinder the court in furthering the overriding objective'.[38] Should one lawyer make a significant failure, the onus would be another lawyer to report this to the court; indeed, failure to do so may lead to the lawyer that fails to report being sanctioned by the court. The raises two potential problems: first, it might require one side (within the adversarial model) to effectively highlight the flaws in the other side's case; and secondly, it may strain the professional relationships of opposing lawyers (goodwill being an undervalued cog in the machinery of criminal justice). Under r 3.5(2)(i) of the CrimPR, the case management provisions of the court allow the court to 'specify the consequences of failing to comply with a direction'.

It is the responsibility of the court to further the overriding objective by 'actively managing'[39] the case. Active case management is defined as including:

(a) the early identification of the real issues;
(b) the early identification of the needs of witnesses;
(c) achieving certainty as to what must be done, by whom, and when, in particular by the early setting of a timetable for the progress of the case;
(d) monitoring the progress of the case and compliance with directions;
(e) ensuring that evidence, whether disputed or not, is presented in the shortest and clearest way;

---

36 Plowden, P, 'Make Do and Mend, or a Cultural Evolution?', *New Law Journal*, March 2005 at p 331.

37 CrimPR, r 1.2(2).

38 Atkinson, D and Moloney, T, *Blackstone's Guide to the Criminal Procedure Rules 2005* (Oxford: Oxford University Press, 2005), 13, para 2.13.

39 CrimPR, r 3.2(1).

(f) discouraging delay, dealing with as many aspects of the case as possible on the same occasion, and avoiding unnecessary hearings;
(g) encouraging participants to cooperate in the progression of the case; and
(h) making use of technology.

Arguably, the case management provisions are nothing new to the court. The Auld Review had already stressed the importance of case management prior to the implementation of the CrimPR. It is worth reiterating here the importance ascribed to active case management. In the case of *Jisl*,[40] Judge LJ described the starting point for any criminal case as follows:

> The starting point is simple. Justice must be done. The defendant is entitled to a fair trial: and, which is sometimes overlooked, the prosecution is equally entitled to a reasonable opportunity to present the evidence against the defendant. It is not however a concomitant of the entitlement to a fair trial that either or both sides are further entitled to take as much time as they like, or for that matter, as long as counsel and solicitors or the defendants themselves think appropriate. Resources are limited ... time itself is a resource. Every day unnecessarily used, while the trial meanders sluggishly to its eventual conclusion, represents another day's stressful waiting for the remaining witnesses and the jurors in that particular trial, and no less important, continuing and increasing tension and worry for another defendant or defendants, some of whom are remanded in custody, and the witnesses in trials who are waiting their turn to be listed. It follows that the sensible use of time requires judicial management and control.[41]

This judgment occurred prior to the creation of the CrimPR, but the influence this statement had on the rules is clear. It implies that time is a resource that is required to be managed effectively; it also gives consideration to the stress levels of the jurors, and waiting witnesses, as well as the accused in engaging with the system, which should be minimised as much as is possible without compromising justice.

In the post-CrimPR era, judges are focused on cases being actively managed, so what impact does that have on the defence lawyer? Rule 3.2(2)(a) of the CrimPR requires the early identification of the real issues. This potentially, and presumably intentionally, widens the disclosure requirements for the defence as well as the prosecution. The accused is already required to provide the prosecution with a defence statement under the CPIA 1996; one must question whether this rule creates an expectation of disclosure beyond the legislative requirements.

Another provision that gives rise to the 'managerial' approach is r 3.2(2)(e) ('ensuring that evidence, whether disputed or not, is presented in the shortest and clearest way'). The issues are twofold: first, when will brevity go too far and compromise the ability of the parties to make their case; and secondly, what does 'clear' mean and who decides? Adversarial theory would suggest that the defence lawyer selects the evidence to present in the way that best benefits his or her client. Under this rule, this approach could arguably be altered on the basis that the level of content and method of presentation are not considered efficient. One might speculate whether this could potentially lead to a gradual reduction in the presentation of oral evidence, with more focus on written submissions (akin to inquisitorial theory). As the Auld Review stated, the starting point is simple: 'justice must be done'. Whether justice can be

40 [2004] EWCA Crim 696.
41 *Ibid* per Judge LJ at [114].

sufficiently 'done' if either side is hampered by onerous obligations, which contradict their natural inclinations, is questionable. The defendant already has to indicate the matters on which they take issue with the prosecution and any potential defences they intend to rely upon. As this chapter has argued, this potentially conflicts with the adversarial theory of the English and Welsh criminal justice process; arguably, the defendant should not be required to assist the prosecution in building a case, which ultimately will be used as a basis upon which to convict them.

8.6 Case management: the power to control the trial

The case management powers of the court can be found in r 3.5 of the CrimPR. They are largely unsurprising in their nature, although r 3.5(2)(i) allows the court to 'specify the consequences of failing to comply with a direction'. The rule does not specify what the sanction might be. The threat of sanctions could raise further conflict with the classic concept of the defence lawyer; theoretically, the defence lawyer is the shield for the defendant and will do anything to protect them, whilst furthering their best interests (to not be convicted!). However, in reality, the sanctions are designed to keep lawyers in order. The rules permit the court to require each party to identify:

(a) which witnesses they intend to give oral evidence;
(b) the order in which they intend those witnesses to give their evidence;
(c) whether they require an order compelling the attendance of a witness;
(d) what arrangements, if any, they propose to facilitate the giving of evidence by a witness;
(e) what arrangements, if any, they propose to facilitate the participation of any other person, including the defendant;
(f) what written evidence they intend to introduce;
(g) what other material, if any, they intend to make available to the court in the presentation of the case;
(h) whether they intend to raise any point of law that could affect the conduct of the trial or appeal; and
(i) what timetable they propose and expect to follow.

This may arguably have the effect of transforming the traditional adversarial trial, where the defence battles the prosecution, into something more akin to a strictly timetabled meeting. Rule 3.13 does not, for example, leave much scope for the defence lawyer to act as an accused's 'zealous advocate' or 'white knight' in the traditional sense. The CrimPR do not appear to embrace this classic conception of the defence lawyer's role. One might argue that such developments move the defence lawyer away from the traditional partisan role into a more managerial one, creating almost 'organisational' pressure to conform with timetables and disclosure requirements. How this complies with the duty to further the best interests of his or her client is moot. One wonders whether the lawyer can realistically satisfy both requirements without impinging either his or her duty to the client or his or her duty to the court and the administration of justice.

The CrimPR consolidated over 50 different sets of rules into a single document, drawing together each step of the criminal process and dividing them into 10 sections. The rationale behind this was to enable '… those who are not legally qualified to find all relevant provisions in one place …'.[42] If the CrimPR were created merely to consolidate

42 Plowden (n 36), 329.

existing law, one would expect the impact to be modest.[43] Yet, it is clear that the Rules have become more than mere consolidation, expanding the scope and power of judges to manage cases via the 'overriding objective' and imposing various new requirements for case management. Both have the potential to impact on all actors in the criminal justice process, including the defence lawyer and the accused.

In May 2010, an expansion of the defence disclosure regime was introduced. Not only did the defence have to complete the defence case statement and/or comply with the case management forms, now, when the defendant intends to call witnesses, those witnesses also have to be disclosed. The new rule requires the defendant to give notice to both the prosecution and the court regarding the name, address and date of birth of any proposed witness and any other information that may assist in identifying and finding the witness.[44] Failure to disclose the information about a witness may lead to that witness being subjected to cross-examination as to why the information was withheld, which may call into question their credibility. This sets aside the decision in *R (Kelly) v Warley JJ*,[45] where the court ruled that the general powers of case management did not extend to the defence having to identify its witnesses. Does this pose a problem in that it allows the prosecution and the police to build a stronger case against the defendant by using the advance notification of witnesses, for example to attack their credibility based on opposition research. Another concern is the fact that the defence witnesses may be less willing to offer evidence if they fear being interviewed by the police and/or prosecution.

8.7 Truth or proof: the dilution of adversarialism in pursuit of the overriding objective

Undoubtedly, the criminal process has evolved over time. In the early period of its development, adversarialism had to essentially compete with the established 'accused speaks' form of trial (discussed in **Chapter 6**), which most courts were still trying to preserve. This form of trial had traditionally allowed the court to treat the defendant as an 'informational resource'[46] through open testimony at trial under the control of the judiciary.[47] In contrast, adversarial theory regards the trial as, essentially, a dispute between the parties, in a position of equality, which is conducted before a passive and neutral adjudicator. The evidence is predominately oral, and it is the responsibility of the adjudicator to ensure that the parties stay within the rules.[48] Each side is responsible for the presentation of their individual case, the trial being the forum in which the guilt or innocence of the defendant is resolved.[49]

The 'accused speaks' trial reflected the notion that the trial was not a competition but an investigation designed to establish the truth of a particular accusation. The implementation of the CrimPR, alongside the judiciary assuming a more interventionist

43 *Ibid.*

44 Criminal Justice Act 2003, s 34, inserting s 6C into the CPIA 1996.

45 [2007] EWHC 1836 (Admin); [2008] 1 WLR2001.

46 Langbein, J, *The Origins of Adversary Criminal Trial* (Oxford: Oxford University Press, 2003), 48.

47 Although it should also be noted that for nearly two centuries, defendants were prohibited from speaking at their own trial – see **Chapter 6**.

48 For a critical evaluation of adversarial theory, see Damaška, MR, *Evidence Law Adrift* (New Haven: Yale University Press, 1997).

49 McEwan, J, 'From Adversarialism to Managerialism: Criminal Justice in Transition', *Legal Studies*, Vol 31, No 4 at 520.

role, might suggest a return to this approach after several hundred years of predominantly adversarial criminal justice. The truth-seeking nature of the trial is exemplified by the case management provisions of the CrimPR and its extension, the policy of the Courts and Tribunals Judiciary's 'Better Case Management', which is designed to ensure that the case management provisions are strictly adhered to. Never before has the judiciary or magistracy had such explicit directions as to what constitutes its role of active case management. Furthermore, the traditionally voluntary nature of the defendant's participation in the trial (at least since the late 1800s) has been diluted by compulsion to make disclosures in 'pursuit of efficient fact-finding' and provisions such as those contained under s 35 of the CJPOA 1994.[50]

Much of this arguably threatens the notion of adversarialism in England and Wales. It is reasonable to suggest that the case management forms required of the defence are akin to completing a defence case statement under the CPIA 1996.[51] Furthermore, there is a potential danger that the forms could be used as part of the prosecution's evidence. In *Firth v Epping Magistrates' Court*,[52] the prosecution introduced the forms as evidence to prove that the defendant was present at the scene. When completing the forms, the defendant stated that she was acting in self-defence, thereby proving she was at the scene, something which the prosecutor struggled with. The court allowed the forms to be admitted and the defendant was convicted. The courts quickly moved to halt this practice. In *Newell*,[53] the court stated that the prosecution could not rely on the forms as evidence if the defendant keeps to the spirit of the CrimPR. Whilst this is somewhat opaque, the court effectively protects the defendant if the Rules are adhered to and the defendant does not play tactical games. Effectively, the case management forms erode the voluntary nature of the statutory legislation. Whilst defence disclosure is not an entirely novel proposition, the defendant had never before had to disclose so much information in advance.[54] It might be argued that active case management, driven by the desire for more expeditious and efficient trials, has had the effect of partially resurrecting the 'accused speaks' trial.

However, the modern day version has a notable difference; the accused is now primarily speaking through written case management disclosures, as opposed to orally disclosing information. It has been claimed that defence disclosure does weaken a fundamental adversarial foundation, namely that the burden of proof rests solely on the prosecution. However, the Roskill Committee suggested that the prosecution would not be permitted to amend its case once defence disclosure is made.[55]

The approach offered by the Roskill Committee was admirable, acknowledging as it did the serious impact of defence disclosure on the burden of proof. Yet, the 'sea change' signalled by the Auld Review almost ignores the due process safeguard highlighted by the Committee. As *Gleeson* demonstrates, the prosecution may alter

50 Owusu-Bempah, A, *Defendant Participation in the Criminal Process* (London: Routledge, 2017), 163.

51 Keogh argues that the case management form is analogous to the defence statement in the Crown Court. See Keogh, A, 'Criminal Case Management – Is the Game Over? (Eldon Lecture Series, Northumbria University School of Law, 2001).

52 [2011] EWHC 388 (Admin).

53 [2012] EWCA Crim 650.

54 Previously, defence alibi witnesses had to be disclosed by virtue of s 11 of the Criminal Justice Act 1967, and in fraud trials the defendant had to outline their defence in general terms. However, if the defence to the fraud charge was based on alibi or expert evidence then fuller disclosure was required.

55 See **8.2** and Roskill (n 8) at para 6.75.

an indictment to ensure that cases are not frustrated by its own error.[56] This completely contradicts the principle expressed by the Committee, and whilst this decision satisfies the goals of an efficient and expeditious criminal process, it is certainly non-adversarial. This is not to deny the reality of criminal practice; the court in *Chaaban*[57] was entirely correct when it stated that the time available to a court is not unlimited, but the dual goals of efficiency and case management should not be fulfilled at the expense of unfairness to the defendant. The evolution of the judicial role of active case manager has caused further confusion. It appears there is some difficulty in ascertaining the boundaries between the judge as 'neutral umpire' and the judge as 'active manager'. In *Cordingley*[58] the judge was discourteous and rude to the defence lawyer, and in *Copsey*[59] the Court of Appeal deemed the judge's interventions all too frequent and, as such, the defendant's conviction was rendered unsafe. So, whilst the court has fully adopted the era of case management, the Court of Appeal has not been afraid to temper the notion of judicial intervention.

Arguably, active case management stands at odds with many of the due process protections built into traditional adversarial criminal procedure. Adversarial systems are focused on the interests of the state and the defendant.[60] The goal of active case management is to increase the efficiency of the criminal trial process. In Herbert Packer's *Due Process* model, a central component of the adversarial process is the accused's opportunity to have 'his day in court', should he or she elect to do so.[61] The model looks much like an obstacle course, with each successive stage designed to present formidable impediments to carrying the accused any further through the process.[62] Packer's opposing model, the *Crime Control* model is almost managerial in nature. The metaphor used by Packer was a conveyor belt, moving an endless stream of cases smoothly through the system, never stopping. Traditional trial elements such as cross-examination have no real value in this model; facts are more easily established at the police station, and the procedures followed need to be uniform.[63] Arguably, the CrimPR reflect this uniform approach, and the active case management powers allow the judiciary to supervise the conveyor belt of criminal cases, ensuring that the process does not slow down or stop. The judiciary can pursue the goal of efficiency and expedited trials by adopting a role that intervenes in proceedings where a delay may occur. This could, for example, potentially lead to the curtailment of oral evidence by not allowing advocates to take an unlimited amount of time to present their case.[64] The judiciary can also substitute written evidence for oral evidence (the latter being the traditional format) in order to expedite proceedings.[65]

The requirement of cooperation between the parties is a distinctly non-adversarial feature of the modern criminal justice process. Dempster[66] suggests that cooperation is

---

56 See *Gleeson* [2003] EWCA Crim 3357.

57 [2003] EWCA Crim 1012.

58 [2007] All ER (D) 131.

59 [2008] EWCA Crim 2043.

60 McEwan (n 49), 520.

61 Packer, HL, *The Limits of the Criminal Sanction* (California: Stanford University Press, 1968), 157. See the summaries of Packer's models in **Chapter 1**.

62 *Ibid* 163.

63 *Ibid.*

64 CrimPR, r 3.13(d).

65 *D and Others* [2007] EWCA Crim 2485.

66 Dempster, J, 'Show your Hand or Have it Cut Off', *Criminal Bar Association Newsletter*, 1 March 2005.

both unnecessary and unwelcome, arguing that the post-*Gleeson*[67] approach is incorrect. He states that 'it is the Crown's job to draft an appropriate indictment, not the job of the defence to proof read it'.[68] The central idea that trials should be efficient and that resources should be used appropriately is commendable and one that should, in theory, be embraced. Unnecessary delay and waste serves the interest of no one involved in criminal process (including lawyers, subjected as they are to limited fees). The key question is how far these goals should be pursued and at what point they encroach on valuable aspects of adversarial justice, designed to protect defendants and guarantee fair trials. Clearly, the overriding objective of the CrimPR and the tools it makes available to the judiciary are designed to improve efficiency. However, in meeting this goal, the judiciary may act in a manner that appears incongruent with the classic principles of an adversarial system. The presence of non-adversarial traits in a nominally adversarial system certainly appears, at face value, to sit rather awkwardly. The desire of an interventionist judiciary to meet the overriding objective through active case management is distinctly non-adversarial. McEwan suggests that a new ethical code is needed if the criminal justice system is no longer adversarial.[69] There has een no official recognition that adversarialism has been, or should be, abandoned, and it would perhaps be somewhat excessive to make such a claim. However, the desire to move away from adversarialism towards something altogether different is implicit in the piecemeal changes to the criminal justice process and the increasing significance of judicial intervention. Since the turn of the century, it would be reasonable to argue that a new form of process has been created.[70]

8.8 Conclusion

A long-established and fundamental principle of English and Welsh criminal justice requires the prosecution to prove its case. Viscount Sankey LC famously stated that 'throughout the web of English Criminal Law one golden thread is always to be seen, that it is the duty of the prosecution to prove the prisoner's guilt …'.[71] Originally, the majority of the disclosure provisions, save for two exceptions,[72] placed the onus on the prosecution to disclose information to the defence, a recognition of the significant disadvantage burdening ordinary people faced with criminal prosecution. If we follow Lord Denning's view from *Dallison v Caffery*,[73] the disclosure regime was created to ensure that the defendant was not subjected to an injustice and that following the 'spirit' of this was of more importance than the letter of the law. The modern disclosure regime is completely different from the one that was designed to even the scales between prosecution and defence. In the modern criminal process, the defence now has to disclose witness details; defence statements that outline the nature of the accused's defence; and alibi and expert evidence. Further to this, if the defence lawyer spots a flaw

67 [2003] EWCA Crim 3357.

68 Dempster (n 66).

69 Garland, F and McEwan, J, 'Embracing the Overriding Objective: Difficulties and Dilemmas in the New Criminal Climate' (2012) *International Journal of Evidence and Proof*, 16, 233–62 at 262.

70 Inter alia, the dilution of the right to silence, the growing importance of the pre-trial investigation in deciding criminal matters. See Jackson, J, 'Police and Prosecutors after PACE: The road from case construction to case disposal' in E Cape and R Young, *Regulating Policing: The Police and Criminal Evidence Act 1984: Past, Present and Future* (Hart, 2008) 255–77.

71 *Woolmington v DPP* [1935] AC 462 at 481.

72 Alibi and expert notifications.

73 [1964] 2 All ER 610, CA.

in the prosecution's case, he or she has to notify the court, and the court can then permit the prosecution to alter its indictment. All of these elements are distinctly non-adversarial in nature, and the quest for a more efficient criminal justice process appears to have created an expectation that the accused and his or her defence lawyer will participate in aiding the prosecution. This is achieved under the guise of managing the case, but it is arguably a much greater change than mere bureaucracy. The adversarial fabric of the criminal justice system in England and Wales is torn. Ashworth and Redmayne believe that, post-*Gleeson*, the courts are close to placing the accused under a duty of cooperation with the prosecution.[74]

Furthermore, there is evidence to suggest that the duty to cooperate is no longer limited to the trial preparation and trial stage of the process. **Chapter 17** examines a new efficiency driver called Pre-Charge Engagement (PCE) and suggests that the police and the defence engage to possibly divert the case from going to court. This is a further example of how the adversarial fabric is torn and how the pre-trial process in the 21st century is centred around the quest for greater efficiency.

The evolution of the disclosure regime can be viewed as follows:

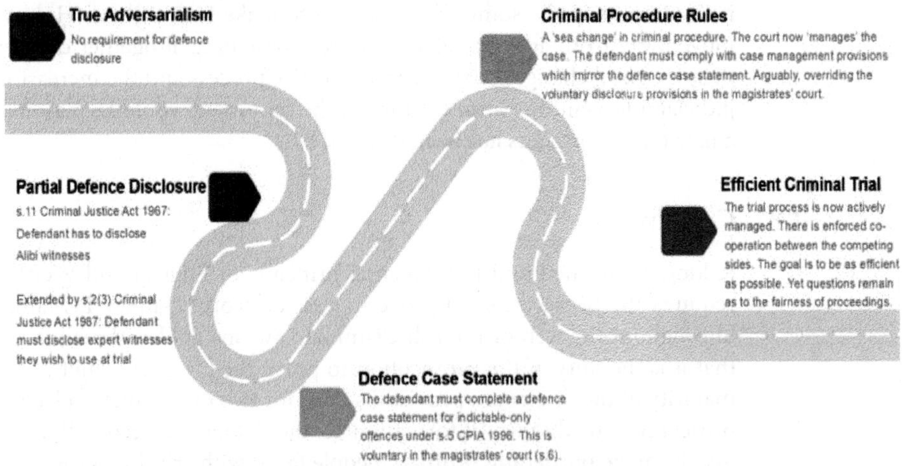

As highlighted by the above 'roadmap', there has been a clear departure from the entrenched, traditional notion of adversarialism. The goal of the criminal trial is to reconstruct historical events in respect of which neither party is in possession of all the facts.[75] Moisidis believes that it is the problem of insufficient fact possession that reveals the tension between truth and proof in a criminal trial. He states that the essence of a criminal trial is a search for the truth, rather than a sporting contest between the prosecution and defence (reflecting the words of the Auld Review).[76] It is this sporting contest that the CrimPR have assisted in eradicating. The criminal trial in

74 Ashworth, A and Redmayne, M, *The Criminal Process*, 3rd edn (Oxford: Oxford University Press, 2003), 245.

75 Moisidis, C, *Criminal Discovery: From Truth to Proof and Back Again* (Sydney: Institute of Criminology, 2008), 250.

76 *Ibid.*

England and Wales now reflects aspects of the old 'accused speaks' trial, where the defendant is an informational resource of the court – but with a different approach.[77]

Whereas the ancient 'mining' of the defendant for information focused on extracting oral admissions of guilt, modern procedure would regard the defendant as a conduit through which the court can establish the 'real issues' of the case. Should the defendant delay or refuse identification of such information, the court can exert pressure (for example, through sanctions for non-compliance) in order to extract details or even a plea (even if the defence lawyer does not hold all the facts). Furthermore, the defendant may ultimately be compelled to compromise their privilege against self-incrimination in order to satisfy the overriding objective. As such, it is very difficult to argue that criminal procedure in England and Wales reflects one that fully shares adversarial values, as it once did. This new form of process, what might be termed the rise of managerialism, has arguably tipped the equality of arms so far in favour of the prosecution that the defendant is placed at a distinct disadvantage. As Lord Bingham argued, 'no one has rights [more important than] those of the defendant because it is he alone who is at risk of being punished by the state.'[78] Considering that the defendant arguably has the most to lose, the erosion of such rights by managerialism (focused on economy and efficiency) is, at best, questionable.

77 Hawkins, W, *A Treatise of the Pleas of the Crown*, Vol II (London, 1721) cited in Langbein, J, *The Origins of Adversary Criminal Trial* (Oxford: Oxford University Press, 2003), 171.

78 HL Deb, col 1270, 15 December 1998.

chapter 9

The Criminal Court (in Theory)

9.1 Introduction

Chapter 1 explained that different legal jurisdictions adopt differing approaches in the way they 'do' criminal procedure. An adversarial system holds the trial as its centrepiece, whereas its inquisitorial counterpart places great weight on the pre-trial investigation; the trial represents a forum in which the dossier of evidence is reviewed, rather than a battle between competing versions of the 'truth'. This chapter will build upon this, focusing on the court stage of the criminal justice process in England and Wales. We shall examine how it works in theory, by exploring the conceptual ideas that underpin proceedings and the figures (or 'actors') who comprise the court. In England and Wales, formal criminal proceedings against defendants are heard in a magistrates' court or the Crown Court. There are roughly 330 magistrates' courts, although more than 120 have been closed since 2010.[1] There are currently approximately 16,000 magistrates sitting in such courts (a 36% reduction since 2012).[2] All adult cases begin in magistrates' courts; they will dispose of the vast majority of cases, but the actual trial may be heard in the Crown Court, depending on the type of offence with which the accused is charged.

This chapter will consider:

- the differing types of criminal trial in England and Wales;
- the actors and roles involved;
- recent developments within the criminal trial which are distinctly non-adversarial.

9.2 Venue of trial and allocation of cases

All cases begin in magistrates' courts, but those that remain for trial are heard 'summarily'; this means that the case is not suitable to be held in the Crown Court as it is not sufficiently serious or complex. Which venue a case will ultimately be resolved in will depend on the classification of the offence (which is set by primary legislation).

9.2.1 Summary offences

Magistrates' courts will primarily deal with *summary* offences – minor offences that must be heard in the lower court (see below). These will include cases such as motoring offences, common assault, minor criminal damage, and drunk and disorderly conduct. Indictable offences (the most serious) will always by dealt with by the Crown Court. Both courts can deal with offences classed as 'either-way'; whether the lower court will

1 www.judiciary.gov.uk/you-and-the-judiciary/going-to-court/magistrates-court/; www.parliament.uk/business/publications/written-questions-answers-statements/written-question/Commons/2018-02-08/127599/ (accessed 11 May 2020).

2 www.judiciary.gov.uk/about-the-judiciary/who-are-the-judiciary/diversity/judicial-diversity-statistics-2017/ (accessed 11 May 2020).

retain jurisdiction over an either-way case will depend on the nature of the particular case (see also below). Magistrates' courts have maximum sentencing powers: six months in custody (or 12 months if there are two or more either-way offences) or a financial penalty (up to the specified level):

- Level 1 offence: £200
- Level 2 offence: £500
- Level 3 offence: £1,000
- Level 4 offence: £2,500
- Level 5 offence: unlimited

The unlimited fine is a relatively new creation; until March 2015 the maximum fine in a magistrates' court was £5,000. However, should the appropriate sentence fall outside the scope of the court's powers, the court is permitted to send the defendant to the Crown Court for sentencing (which is not subject to such stringent limitations, particularly in relation to custody).

In May 2022, an extension was granted to the sentencing powers in the magistrates' courts. In an attempt to tackle the backlog of criminal cases, the sentencing powers increased to allow magistrates to impose a prison sentence of 12 months' imprisonment for a single offence. According to the then Lord Chancellor, Dominic Raab, this doubling of powers illustrated that 'we are doing everything in our power to bring down the court backlog, and doubling the sentencing powers … will create more capacity in the Crown Court to hear the most serious cases'.[3] However, this change lasted less than a year as, in March 2023, the powers were reduced to six months' imprisonment for a single offence. This move was welcomed by the Criminal Bar Association which claimed that the original rationale to increase the powers 'was a bad idea for reasons of increasing short-term prison sentences; increasing defendants electing to go to Crown Court, and increasing appeals [to the] Crown Court'.[4] However, the reversal was met with disappointment from the Magistrates' Association, which claimed to be 'incredibly disappointed' by the reduction as the extension to powers was 'something we have long campaigned for as a vital means of ensuring speedier justice for all'.[5] As you will see in **Chapter 13**, there is a quest for a more efficient system, but perhaps the rise in the prison population means that whilst the state will not stop sending people to prison, it ought to be less inclined to do so.

9.2.2 Indictable offences

Offences that are *indictable* include murder, rape, GBH with intent, and such cases can only be heard in the Crown Court. Generally, the Crown Court is reserved for the most serious of offences. Whilst the case will begin in the magistrates' court, that court will only deal with the issue of initial plea and bail (see **Chapter 10**). Should the defendant enter a plea of 'not guilty', the case will be sent to the Crown Court for trial. The maximum levels of sentence and any fines will be set by statute and generally far exceed that of the lower court.

---

3 Ministry of Justice, 'Magistrates to help tackle backlog as sentencing powers doubled', 2 May 2022: https://www.gov.uk/government/news/magistrates-to-help-tackle-backlog-as-sentencing-powers-doubled (accessed March 2023).

4 Fouzder, M, 'Magistrates' sentencing powers scaled back', *Law Society Gazette*, 10 March 2023: www.lawgazette.co.uk/news/magistrates-sentencing-powers-scaled-back/5115396.article (accessed March 2023).

5 *Ibid.*

9.2.3 Either-way offences

There are number of offences that are classified as *either-way* offences. Schedule 1 to the Magistrates' Courts Act 1980 contains a list of either-way offences, including theft, burglary, ABH, and possession of or possession with intent to supply drugs. If the defendant is charged with an either-way offence and enters a plea of 'not guilty', a magistrates' court must decide if it can hear the case and has the appropriate sentencing powers – this is known as allocation. The traditional rule has been that if the court believes that any sentence, if the defendant is convicted, will exceed its sentencing powers, it will 'decline jurisdiction'. The case will then be sent to the Crown Court for trial. However, if its sentencing powers are considered sufficient, the defendant can choose if they wish to have their case heard in the magistrates' court or the Crown Court. Allocation will not be an issue for summary or indictable offences, but does raise broader questions in relation to either-way offences. The Sentencing Council guideline on allocation of cases states that:

> In general, either way offences should be tried summarily unless:
>
> - the outcome would clearly be a sentence in excess of the court's powers for the offence(s) concerned after taking into account personal mitigation and any potential reduction for a guilty plea; or
> - for reasons of unusual legal, procedural or factual complexity, the case should be tried in the Crown Court.[6]

Sending a case to the Crown Court for the latter reason (complexity) will be 'rare and case specific';[7] as such, there is an emphasis on keeping as many either-way cases in magistrates' courts as possible.

One might argue that this is at least partially motivated by a desire to reduce the overall cost of hearings and drive the agenda of efficiency (see, generally, **Chapter 8**). As the National Audit Office (NAO) highlighted in 2016, hearings in the Crown Court are more costly (an average of £1,900 per day, compared to £1,150 per day in a magistrates' court).[8] It identified the increase in the sending of either-way cases to the Crown Court as an example of inefficiency; between 2013/14 and 2014/15, 2% more cases of this nature were sent to the higher criminal court at a cost of £5.5 million.[9] This led the NAO to speculate that £45 million could be saved if all either-way cases heard in 2014/15 were dealt with by the magistrates' court.[10] This highlights a key justification for retaining either-way cases in the lower court; the more expensive trial stage can be heard in the less expensive court, and if the appropriate sentence exceeds the powers of a bench of magistrates, the case can be sent to the higher court for a judge to deal with. Such arguments led Sir Brian Leveson to recommend as follows:

> Magistrates' Courts must be encouraged to be far more robust in their application of the allocation guideline which mandates that either way offences should be

---

6 Sentencing Guidelines, 'Allocation guideline: Determining whether cases should be dealt with by a magistrates' court or the Crown Court' (March 2016): www.sentencingcouncil.org.uk/wp-content/uploads/Allocation-definitive-guideline-web.pdf (accessed 11 May 2020).

7 *Ibid.*

8 National Audit Office, 'Efficiency in the criminal justice system' (HC 852, Session 2015–16, 1 March 2016), 10: www.nao.org.uk/wp-content/uploads/2016/03/Efficiency-in-the-criminal-justice-system.pdf (accessed 11 May 2020).

9 *Ibid* 23.

10 *Ibid.*

tried summarily unless it is likely that the court's sentencing powers will be insufficient.[11]

To summarise:

- Summary and indictable offences pose no issue in terms of venue – they will always be heard in the same court.
- Either-way offences are, in theory, heard in either; but, in practice, there is now a presumption that they will be heard in magistrates' courts, except in unusual circumstances.

Case type	Venue	Sentencing powers
Summary only	Magistrates' court	6 months (or 12 months for two or more either-way offences). Unlimited fine.
Indictable only	Crown Court	Dependent on offence – set by statute.
Either-way	Either magistrates' court or Crown Court	Dependent on offence – set by statute.

It is debatable whether the modern policy of allocating most cases to magistrates' courts is based on the need/desire to save money or the reasonable expectation that criminal justice should be proportionate, swift and efficient. Again, this represents a battle between crime control and due process, with the current policy favouring the comparative 'conveyor belt' of summary justice in the magistrates' court.

9.3 Comparing magistrates' courts and the Crown Court

Magistrates' courts have been described as 'the workhorse of the system'.[12] Ministry of Justice Criminal Statistics show that, in 2007, the number of defendants prosecuted through the magistrates' court peaked at around 2 million.[13] However, more recent figures suggest that this has reduced and stabilised at a little over 1 million cases a year:[14]

Year	Number of cases prosecuted in magistrates' courts
2013	1.53m
2014	1.60m
2015	1.59m
2016	1.52m
2017	1.51m
2018	1.45m
2019	1.44m
2020	1.12m
2021	1.44m

11 Leveson LJ, 'Review of efficiency in criminal proceedings' (Judiciary of England and Wales, 2015), 25: www.judiciary.gov.uk/wp-content/uploads/2015/01/review-of-efficiency-in-criminal-proceedings-20151.pdf (accessed 11 May 2020).

12 Welsh, L, Skinns, L and Sanders, A, *Sanders & Young's Criminal Justice* (OUP, 2021).

13 Ministry of Justice, Criminal Statistics 2007 (London: MoJ, 2008), Table 2.1.

14 Ministry of Justice, Criminal Statistics Quarterly, England and Wales, April to June 2022 (London: MoJ, 29 September 2022), Table M1: www.gov.uk/government/statistics/criminal-court-statistics-quarterly-april-to-june-2022 (accessed March 2023).

The decline since the high water mark of 2007 could be attributed to a number of differing factors, including the rise in the use of out-of-court disposals issued by the police (including cautions and penalty notices – see **Chapter 13**) and the rise of the Single Justice Procedure Notice (see **Chapter 17**). Regardless, magistrates' courts are the stalwart of the English and Welsh criminal justice system; they deal with all low-level crimes of which there is a high volume. In contrast, the Crown Court could be referred to as the 'specialist' court. The higher criminal court, with its jury-based trial and bewigged advocates, is the quintessential image when thinking of criminal justice in this jurisdiction. The Courts Act 1971 created the Crown Court, replacing the courts of assize and quarter sessions which had previously dealt with indictable-only offences, with much of the regulation later superseded by the Senior Courts Act 1981. The Crown Court has three main responsibilities:

- It has exclusive jurisdiction over trials on indictment.
- It deals with offenders who have been sent (previously 'committed') by the magistrates' court for sentencing (because the magistrates' sentencing powers were not sufficient) or for trial in the case of either-way offences.
- It hears appeals from magistrates' courts against conviction and/or sentence (see **Chapter 11**).

Courtroom dramas have populated British television for decades, from *Rumpole of the Bailey*, *Kavanagh QC*, *The Brief* and *Silk* to the recently-aired *The Verdict*, to name but a few. All depict a romanticised, thrilling notion of the traditional adversarial trial. However, in reality, trials in the Crown Court are rare when compared to magistrates' courts:[15]

Year	Number of cases prosecuted in the Crown Court
2013	37,710
2014	36,780
2015	34,722
2016	32,392
2017	32,199
2018	26,884
2019	27,388
2020	29,092
2021	23,837

The table above clearly shows two key points: first, the receipt of cases by the Crown Court has not exceeded 38,000 cases in the last decade; secondly, there has been a steady decline in the number of cases heard in the Crown Court since 2013. However, despite the fact that the Crown Court is comparatively underused, it still presents the image that most of us picture when thinking about criminal trials.

9.4 The 'actors' in the criminal process

Having examined the conceptual role of the courts in the criminal process, we will now examine the people who make this process come alive – the 'actors'.

15 *Ibid.*

9.4.1 The judge

As was outlined in **Chapter 1**, traditionally, the adversarial judge was viewed as someone who was extremely passive and did little to intervene in proceedings. In 1944, Lord Greene, who was Master of the Rolls, stated that if a judge conducts cross-examination, '[he] descends into the arena and is liable to have his vision clouded by the dust of conflict'.[16] By reverting to his former role as an engaged participant, it was thought that the judge would lose his position as an observer because, as a result of his clouded vision, 'he unconsciously deprives himself of the advantage of calm and dispassionate observation'.[17] The trial judge should refrain from entering the arena of the adversarial battle, save for clearing up a point.

In *Clewer*[18] the defendant appealed on the basis of undue interruption by the judge. The judge was of the opinion that the defence advanced was improbable. Lord Chief Justice Goddard stated that if 'counsel was interrupted ... his task becomes impossible'.[19] The judge went as far as to suggest to the jury that the defence was raising 'false issues'.[20] The Court of Criminal Appeal quashed the conviction, taking a very dim view of the illegitimate conduct of the judge. In *Barnes*[21] the judge informed the defence that he took 'a serious view of hopeless cases ... contested at public expense'. The Court of Appeal quashed the conviction because of the 'wholly improper' conduct of the judge in exerting pressure to enter a guilty plea.[22] Lord Chief Justice Parker outlined the adverse impact of the conduct of the judge as follows:[23]

(a) There was extreme pressure to plead guilty.
(b) The defendant would undoubtedly think that the view of the judge would not result in a fair trial.
(c) The judge interfered with the independence of counsel by giving his advice.
(d) The lawyer–client relationship was destroyed.
(e) The lack of adjournment forced the defendant to continue with counsel he had no confidence in. This was wholly unreasonable.

If the judiciary resumes the role of an active participant in proceedings, it clearly runs the risk of jeopardising the right to a fair trial of the accused. In the Irish case of *Phelim McGuinness*,[24] the accused was granted leave to appeal, as the interventions of the trial judge rendered the trial unsatisfactory and the verdict potentially unsafe. The Appeal Court held that the active participation by a judge in examination-in-chief is undesirable as it may purport to the accused that the judiciary lacks impartiality.[25] During the examination of a defence witness, the judge interjected with 20 consecutive questions. As a result, the Appeal Court ordered a retrial.

However, as discussed in **Chapter 8**, the landscape of the adversarial criminal trial has changed, with the advent of the disclosure regime and the managerialist elements of the CrimPR leading to the resurrection of the interventionist judge. This might suggest that the pendulum has swung towards a more inquisitorial search for some 'objective

16 *Per* Green MR in *Yuill v Yuill* [1945] 1 All ER 183 at 189.
17 *Ibid.*
18 (1953) 37 Cr App R 37.
19 *Ibid per* Goddard LCJ at 40.
20 *Ibid* at 41.
21 *Barnes* (1970) 55 Cr App R 100.
22 *Ibid* per Parker LCJ at 106.
23 *Ibid* at 106–7.
24 *The People (at the Suit of the Director of Public Prosecutions) v Phelim McGuinness* [1978] IR 189.
25 *Ibid* per Kenny J at 193.

truth', as opposed to the adversarial approach of 'proof'. This can be illustrated in several post-Auld Review criminal trials. *Gleeson*[26] is a clear example of the court emphasising the discovery of the truth over proving the allegation. As discussed in **Chapter 6**, this stands in contrast to the purist 'penalty shoot-out theory' of criminal procedure. Additionally, this new landscape arguably contradicts a vital tenet of English and Welsh criminal procedure – that the burden of proof is the prosecution's to discharge. This notion comes from Viscount Sankey's famous judgment in *Woolmington v DPP*:

> Throughout the web of the English Criminal Law one golden thread is always to be seen that it is the duty of the prosecution to prove the prisoner's guilt subject to ... the defence of insanity and subject also to any statutory exception. If, at the end of and on the whole of the case, there is a reasonable doubt, created by the evidence given by either the prosecution or the prisoner ... the prosecution has not made out the case and the prisoner is entitled to an acquittal. No matter what the charge or where the trial, the principle that the prosecution must prove the guilt of the prisoner is part of the common law of England and no attempt to whittle it down can be entertained.[27]

The prosecution still has to prove the guilt of the defendant, but the defendant is now compelled to assist the prosecution by providing information in advance of trial (and the judge will reprimand an advocate who has not complied with the pre-trial obligations). As such, the judge's role of case manager, which has been actively embraced, reflects the change in the adversarial landscape.

9.4.2 Lay magistrates

Magistrates, sometimes referred to as Justices of the Peace, are lay (unqualified) volunteers who reside in the locality of the court they sit in. The Justices of the Peace Act 1361 provided for the appointment in each county of 'one lord and three or four of the most worthy in the county' whose duty would be to 'pursue, arrest ... and chastise' those who 'were not of good fame' (ie those who had breached the King's Law). By the 18th century, their judicial and administrative powers had grown significantly. They tried minor crimes summarily and had the administrative powers to grant licences to ale houses, appoint surveyors of highways and levy rates in their counties. By the 19th century, their administrative functions were greatly diluted and handed to elected local authorities. However, their judicial powers remained. Like their 14th century counterparts, a magistrate today does not require any formal legal qualifications, although a training programme will be completed prior to adjudicating cases. The training will provide new magistrates with a grounding in law and evidence, illustrate the types of cases they are likely to encounter and help them understand the role of others who work in the courts. This training is conducted through formal lectures, court observations and group discussion on the common issues faced by magistrates. Their formative training programme should look something like this:

(a) *Initial training*: this is introductory training on the basics of the role. Following this, the new magistrate will sit in court with two other experienced magistrates.
(b) *Mentoring*: each new magistrate has a specially trained magistrate mentor to guide him or her through the first months. There are six formal mentored sittings in the

26 [2003] EWCA Crim 3357.
27 *Woolmington v DPP* [1935] AC 462, HL.

first 12–18 months, where the new magistrate will review his or her learning progress and talk over any training needs.

(c) *Core training:* During the first year, further training, visits to penal institutions and/or observations take place to equip magistrates with the key knowledge they need. Every magistrate is given a core workbook for further optional self-study.

(d) *Consolidation training:* at the end of the first year, consolidation training builds on the learning from sittings and core training. This is designed to help magistrates plan for their ongoing development and prepare for their first appraisal.

(e) *First appraisal:* About 12–18 months after appointment, when both mentor and magistrate agree that he or she is ready, the new justice is appraised. Another specially trained magistrate appraiser will sit as part of the bench, observing whether the new magistrate is demonstrating that he or she is competent in the role, against established competences. When successful, the magistrate is deemed fully competent.

However, training does not stop at the 18-month appraisal, as the Magistrates' Association (the representative body of magistrates) has a commitment to provide ongoing training and development. Throughout their career, magistrates will have:

- *appraisals*, which take place every three years to ensure that magistrates maintain their competency in whichever court they sit;
- *continuation training*, which takes place once every three years, usually before appraisals;
- *update training* on new legislation and procedure, which is delivered to magistrates as required;
- *threshold training*, which accompanies each development in a magistrate's role, for which there is a matching training process. For instance, magistrates may go through comprehensive training to become a chairman or presiding justice. Alternatively, they may choose to undergo training in the specialist skills needed for family or youth courts.

Magistrates can be appointed from the age of 18 and they retire at 70. Anybody can apply to be a magistrate but, to be appointed, they need to demonstrate six 'key qualities':

- good character;
- commitment and reliability;
- social awareness;
- sound judgement;
- understanding and communication;
- maturity and sound temperament.

9.4.3 The prosecutor

Historically, the duty of prosecution in England was a private responsibility. The creation and development of the modern police force in the early 1800s shifted the responsibility of conducting prosecutions from the private individual to professional crime-fighters, albeit in a non-explicit capacity. Eventually, the Crown Prosecution Service (CPS) was established by the Prosecution of Offences Act 1985, finally creating an independent national agency of lawyers who were responsible for conducting the court stage of criminal prosecutions. This section will examine the role of the prosecutor, the rationale for the creation of this role and the prosecutor's relationship with the police through the course of the criminal justice process.

A Royal Commission established in 1962[28] recommended that a new body should be created to separate the investigative and prosecution stage. This added a layer of independence which would ensure that tension between the two stages would not arise. However, this recommendation was not implemented, and many police forces continued to prosecute their own cases in magistrates' courts. For cases that would be heard in the Crown Court, the police instructed solicitors and barristers to prosecute cases on their behalf.[29] As this situation evolved, the police gradually started to employ their own in-house prosecuting solicitors who would act on the instructions of the police.[30] The prosecutor would have little recourse if the police wanted to go ahead and prosecute a weak case or 'overcharge' a suspect.

This arrangement between the police and the prosecution came under attack in the report of the Fisher Inquiry on the 'Confait Affair'.[31] This case raised questions about the procedures followed by the police in the interrogation of three youths, which led the youths to falsely confess to the murder of Maxwell Confait. In 1977, an inquiry was opened into the investigation. This revealed that the officer in charge of the investigation was willing to breach the Judges' Rules and put severe pressure on the suspects when questioning them. The prosecutor was deemed unable or unwilling to act independently of the police, and the youths were wrongly convicted of murder.[32] The report was chaired by Sir Henry Fisher, who proposed a number of recommendations: the Judges' Rules should be overhauled, and the safeguards provided to suspects, such as having a right to have a solicitor present during interrogation and the right of young people to have an appropriate adult present, should be made more clear.[33]

Following this case, the Royal Commission on Criminal Procedure (the Philips Commission) proposed that an independent body be created to take over cases that the police decided to prosecute. If the prosecutor did not believe that the case should be taken to court then he or she would have the authority to discontinue the case, have the charges changed or have the police investigate further in order to obtain more evidence.[34] The Government accepted the majority of the recommendations made by the Philips Commission. This acceptance resulted in the Prosecution of Offences Act 1985 and established the CPS. The head of the CPS would be the Director of Public Prosecutions (DPP). The Director's position was not a new creation; it was initially created in the late 19th century to advise the police on criminal matters and handle serious cases. Despite the CPS having a national identity, prosecutors are based in 14 regional teams and prosecute cases locally. Each of the 14 teams are headed by a Chief Prosecutor and they work closely with the police force of that area.[35]

28 Royal Commission on the Police (Cmnd 1728, 1962).

29 For a further discussion on the police's use of solicitors and barristers in the 1970s, see Sigler, J, 'Public Prosecutions in England and Wales' [1974] Crim LR 642.

30 Royal Commission on Criminal Procedure, *Investigation and Prosecution of Criminal Offences in England and Wales: Law and Procedure* (Cmnd 8092-1, 1981), 49–52.

31 See 'Inquiry into the Circumstances leading to the Trial of Three Persons on Charges arising from the Death of Maxwell Confait' (HCP 90, 1977).

32 *Ibid.*

33 For a further in-depth account of the Confait Affair and the recommendations made by Sir Henry Fisher, see *ibid.*

34 *Ibid* at Ch 7.

35 The 14 CPS areas can be found here: www.cps.gov.uk/cps-areas-and-cps-direct (accessed 11 May 2020).

The creation of the CPS

The CPS was established in 1986. This was a radical overhaul of the prosecution process in England and Wales, and, as result, a national service of prosecuting lawyers was created instead of the fragmented local authority-based structure.[36] It was envisaged that the service would be independent from both government and the police. The idea was to create a layer of distance between the investigation and the prosecution of a crime. The prosecutors would provide a due process safeguard for the suspect. Such independence was needed because it was thought that suspects required an extra layer of protection from the arrangements between lawyers and police. This was particularly apparent in the wake of the Confait Affair.

As well as having the power to prosecute cases, the DPP also has the power to discontinue a case she believes should not progress to court.[37] However, the DPP has to provide the police with reasons why a case is discontinued.[38] The Philips Commission believed the creation of a National Prosecution Service would 'promote more consistent prosecution and cautioning policies [and] reduce the number of weak cases currently prosecuted …'.[39] The Commission went on to state that these aims would only be achieved if the service were independent, a view which was endorsed by the Government's White Paper[40] and discussions in Parliament.[41] The Code for Crown Prosecutors[42] sets out a dual test which prosecutors use to determine whether to prosecute or discontinue a case. In order to prosecute a case, the prosecutor has to be satisfied that the sufficiency of evidence test will be met; this means that there has to be a realistic prospect of conviction. Furthermore, the case has to pass the public interest test, namely, prosecuting the case has to be in the public interest.[43]

Independent or police dependent?

The establishment of the CPS was envisaged to introduce an external review of the decisions made by the police. Despite this explicit goal, the prosecutor is still heavily dependent on the police. It is the police who make the initial decision to charge or release a suspect. If the police release a suspect without charge, the prosecution has no power to reverse this decision. Once the initial charge decision has been made, the police file will be passed to the prosecutor for review. Therefore, the prosecutor is reliant on the police file to make his or her decision. Sanders argues that this has been created with a particular goal in mind – the successful prosecution of the suspect. Because of this goal, any exculpatory evidence will not be present in the file. He goes on to state that 'cases being prosecuted are shaped to appear prosecutable …'.[44] Therefore,

36 O'Doherty, S (2004) 'The Changing of the Guard: CPS Charging', *Justice of the Peace.*

37 Prosecution of Offences Act 1985, s 23.

38 *Ibid* s 23(5). See McConville, M, Sanders, A and Leng, R, *The Case for the Prosecution: Police Suspects and Construction of Criminality* (Routledge, 1991), 5.

39 Royal Commission (n 30), Ch 6, para 7.

40 Home Office, *An Independent Prosecution Service for England and Wales*, Law Officers Department, (Cmnd 9074, 1983).

41 Lord Elton introducing the Second Reading of the Prosecution of Offences Bill in the House of Lords on 29 November 1984.

42 Crown Prosecution Service, *The Code for Crown Prosecutors* (London: CPS, 2000).

43 However, former Home Secretary Theresa May indicated her desire to hand the decision to charge back to the police: www.guardian.co.uk/uk/2010/may/19/police-power-to-charge-restored (accessed 1 July 2018).

44 Sanders, A, 'Prosecution Systems' in McConville and Wilson (eds), *The Handbook of the Criminal Justice Process* (Oxford: Oxford University Press, 2002), 158.

the prosecutor may only become aware of the exculpatory facts at trial, as they have no idea of any gaps in the evidence.

The prosecution service has historically been under-resourced, and this merely exacerbates the position of structural dependence on more experienced police officers whose decision to prosecute is rarely opposed.[45] The fact that the police have already decided that there is sufficient evidence to prosecute proves to be a structural obstacle for a prosecutor in deciding to discontinue the case. By being over-reliant on the findings of the police, the prosecutor is left in a role that endorses the findings of police, rather than challenging the decisions that have been made. The success of both the prosecutor and the police is judged by various performance indicators. The Full Code Test indicates that there 'must be a realistic prospect of conviction'.[46] Therefore, the prosecutor will be mindful to avoid weak cases that will not result in a successful prosecution.

9.4.4 The defence lawyer

Originally, the defence lawyer in the 17th century was seen as an unnecessary addition to the criminal process; the court was deemed to be better suited to protecting the accused than any lawyer. To emphasise the point that the lawyer was deemed superfluous, Sir Edward Coke observed that 'it is far better for a prisoner to have a judge's opinion for him, than many counsellors at the Bar. The judges … have special care of the indictment and see that … justice be done to the party.'[47] In this statement, Coke is effectively reinforcing the notion that the defence lawyer is an unnecessary addition to the trial; the judge can carry out the role that a prisoner would want a lawyer to carry out. In the early 18th century, there was growing unease about the reliability of the evidence generated by both the prosecution and defence counsel.[48] There are examples of the defence lawyer being cast in a shady or murky light. Langbein cites an example of a lawyer who, with three other people, concocted a false highway robbery in order to claim the reward of £40. One witness claimed that the lawyer told him that it was his business to 'set people together by the Ears and foment Law-Suits …'.[49] These examples illustrate that the defence lawyer in the 17th and 18th centuries was seen as someone who may not be trustworthy and certainly did not have the interests of justice in the forefront of their mind; they would rather further their own selfish goals of self-gain instead of dealing with their clients justly.

The role of the defence lawyer can be seen to operate on three interwoven levels: first, he or she is the mouthpiece of his or her client; secondly he or she is an officer of the court; and finally he or she acts as a zealous protector of the rights of his or her client.[50] Despite being charged with advancing his or her client's case, the defence lawyer's obligation to his or her client is, at times, tempered by obligations owed to other parties in the criminal justice process; this notion was expressed by Lord Reid in the case of *Rondel v Worsley*:[51]

45 Zedner, L, *Criminal Justice* (Oxford: Oxford University Press, 2004), 149.

46 The Code for Crown Prosecutors, para 4.5: www.cps.gov.uk/publications/code_for_crown_prosecutors/codetest.html (accessed 11 May 2020).

47 *Walter Thomas*, 2 Bulstrode 147, 80 Eng Rep 1022 (KB 1613) as cited in Langbein, J, *The Origins of Adversary Criminal Trial* (Oxford: OUP, 2005).

48 *Ibid* 136.

49 These events were reported in 2 *Gentleman's Magazine* 975 (Sept 1732), entry for 11 September as cited in *ibid* at 138.

50 Blake, M and Ashworth, A, 'Ethics and the Criminal Defence Lawyer' (2004) *Legal Ethics*, Vol 7, 167–90.

51 [1969] 1 AC 191.

> Counsel has a duty to fearlessly raise every issue, advance every argument and ask every question, however distasteful, which he thinks will help his client's case. But as an officer of the court concerned with the administration of justice, he has an overriding duty to the court, to the standards of his profession and to the public, which may and often lead to a conflict with his client's wishes ....[52]

It is clear from this statement that the role of the defence lawyer is not as clear-cut as merely advancing the case of his or her client and acting in their best interests. At times, he or she will be charged with actively engaging in ethical decision-making. It has been claimed that the defence lawyer operates on the horns of a trilemma: he or she needs to accumulate as much knowledge about the case as possible; to hold it in confidence; and yet never to mislead the courts.[53]

The adversarial criminal process in England and Wales is rooted in the image of the defence lawyer acting as the accused's shield from the powerful state; this notion has in turn cultivated the ideal of neutral partisanship as a central tenet of the role of the defence lawyer.[54] This duty of neutral partisanship reflects a dual part of the adversarial ethos; the accused is to be adequately protected from the 'oppressive' state, and the truth is best discovered by arguments on both sides of the question.[55] A key element of being a fearless partisan advocate is assertiveness; this is clear when the lawyer is faced with a prosecution witness. In these circumstances, the priority of the defence is clear; at times it may have to 'go after the [witness] aggressively – to destroy [their] credibility or even reputation – when the alternative is that the client will be hurt'.[56] Another aggressive tactic the partisan defence lawyer has at his or her disposal is the weapon of an ambush defence. This occurs when a defence lawyer introduces evidence at trial at the last possible moment; it does not allow the prosecution a chance to rebut, so this evidence may result in an acquittal. For example, if a defence lawyer spots a flaw in the prosecution's case, he or she should point it out to the judge or jury. However, not pointing the flaw out, whilst possibly being beneficial to the client, is frowned upon by the court: '... to look the other way and not point it out ... is to violate your commitment as a lawyer'.[57] These tactics can be used as effective weapons for the partisan criminal defence lawyer in the fight to protect his or her client and further their interests. It is clear, though, that these weapons may conflict with the other obligations the lawyer owes to both the court and to the public.

The notion of partisanship is permitted in an adversarial environment; a long-standing ethic of adversarial justice is that it is better to allow a number of criminals to go free rather than to subject one innocent individual to wrongful conviction.[58] This cornerstone principle of the adversarial justice system gives rise to the notion of partisan representation because 'the criminal justice system is less a device for discovering the truth than it is a series of "screens" designed to make it exceedingly difficult for the innocent to be convicted'.[59] Therefore, by permitting a rigorous,

52 *Ibid* at 227–28.

53 *Ibid* 153.

54 *Ibid* 169.

55 *ex parte Lloyd* (1822) Montagu's Reports 70n, 72 per Lord Eldon.

56 Curtis, C, *The Ethics of Advocacy* (1951–1952) *Stan L Rev* 12 at 529.

57 Van Susteren, G, 'Responsibility' (1996–1997) 30 *Loy LAL Rev* 128.

58 For further discussion, see Luban, D, 'The Adversary System Excuse' in R Abel (ed), *Lawyers: A Critical Reader* (The New Press, 1997), 5.

59 Hodes, W, 'Lord Broughman, the Dream Team and Jury Nullification of the Third Kind' (1996) 67 *U Colo LR* 1086.

aggressive, partisan defence, wrongful convictions should be more rare in their occurrence as the prosecution's case has to pass through the many 'screens'. The process becomes more expansive and transparent, and in theory it protects the innocent and only allows convictions to be based on comprehensively examined evidence. Without the partisan participation of the defence lawyer, the adversarial justice system would mirror its inquisitorial counterpart, which has far fewer 'screens' for a conviction to pass through. As we have seen, ultimately, the defence lawyer can be seen to have three core and conflicting duties:

- the duty to zealously advance the best interests of his or her client;
- the duty to not mislead the court; and
- the duty to the public and the administration of justice.

The difficulty the lawyer faces is in trying to prioritise the duties when they so clearly conflict.[60] The duty to the administration of justice may mean that the lawyer *has* to comply with the case management forms under the CrimPR. However, these forms may directly impact the best interests of the client, who may wish to remain silent and put the prosecution to proof. Whilst this is a fundamental and fair adversarial tactic, **Chapter 6** on the CrimPR illustrated just how difficult this is becoming to achieve.

9.4.5 The jury

Trial by jury is designed to allow the defendant to be judged by their peers, which in theory means that the decision-makers are people from the local community and of a similar social status to the defendant. How accurate a description this is in reality is a different question. As mentioned above, jury trials are used in the Crown Court, when the defendant enters a plea of 'not guilty;' if the plea is guilty, then the process advances directly to the sentencing stage where there is no role for the jury. The jury are 'triers of fact'; therefore, they hear the evidence advanced by the prosecution and the defence at trial, and they objectively weigh its value before determining the guilt or innocence of the defendant. Until 1967, the decision had to be unanimous – all 12 members had to agree on the decision. However, the Criminal Justice Act 1967 allowed the outcome to be determined by a majority of 10:2. In essence, the judge will prefer a unanimous verdict and will only allow a majority verdict when it is abundantly clear that the jury will not reach the aforementioned, unanimous verdict.

The composition, selection and work of juries are primarily governed by the Juries Act 1974, which both consolidated previous legislation and has been subject to numerous amendments since. Jury selection has been reformed a number of times over the last 40 years. Until 1972, it was paramount that a juror was a home owner; however, the Criminal Justice Act 1972 abolished this requirement and stated that if you were on the electoral roll and aged between 18 and 65 years old, you would be eligible for jury service. This reform was designed to increase the number of people who would be eligible for service. There were a number of potential jurors who were ineligible or excused from service:

- *The ineligible:* you would not be eligible for jury service if you were a member of the judiciary, the legal profession, the police, the prison service or the clergy, or had a recognised mental health disorder.

60 For a detailed exploration of the conflict faced by defence lawyers, see Johnston, E, 'The adversarial defence lawyer: Myths, disclosure and efficiency – A Contemporary Analysis of the role in the era of the Criminal Procedure Rules' (2019) *International Journal of Evidence and Proof,* 24(1), 35–58.

- *Excusals:* if you were a Member of Parliament or in the armed forces, you could decline to serve.
- *The disqualified:* if you had served (or were serving) a prison sentence or a community punishment, you would automatically be disqualified from serving.

Increasing the maximum age of jurors is something we have seen governments do periodically over the last 20 years. The Criminal Justice Act 1988 increased the upper age limit to 70 years old, and this was extended to 75 years old more recently by the Criminal Justice and Courts Act 2015. The Auld Review proposed a number of new reforms to jury service, and s 321 and Sch 33 of the Criminal Justice Act 2003 eliminated excusals as a right (except for serving military personnel), therefore widening the pool from which jurors can be drawn. This means that lawyers, police officers and prison officers are now eligible to serve on a jury. Despite these changes, we have seen a decline in the number of Crown Court cases and therefore the decline of the jury trial; approximately 1.6% of all cases prosecuted are heard by a jury.[61]

The role of the jury is as follows:

- The judge decides the law and the jury decide the facts.
- After hearing the evidence, the jury will look to convict or acquit the defendant.
- They will need to reach a unanimous verdict.
- If they cannot reach a unanimous verdict, they will look for a majority (10:2) verdict.

There is no need to provide reasons for their decision.

Equity and secrecy: the advantages of jury trials?

Despite its dwindling use, jury trials offer the adversarial process a number of distinct advantages.

definition

Jury equity – the jury can refuse to convict a defendant even if the prosecution proves their guilt beyond a reasonable doubt.

The jury can look beyond the law and can examine the motives behind the offending behaviour. Even in the face of the most damning evidence, the jury can return a 'not guilty' verdict and acquit the defendant, if they *think* it is the *right* thing to do. However, research by Baldwin and McConville suggests that this romantic notion of fairness is not played out in practice. What they found was in fact the opposite: juror performance did not acquit itself in accordance with the fundamental adversarial idea that it is 'better to acquit those who are probably guilty than to convict those who are possibly innocent'. In fact, they found that the jury appeared to be insufficiently prepared to protect the 'possibly innocent'.[62]

The deliberations in the jury room are secret. Beyond the 12 jurors, nobody is privy to what is said, how the case is discussed or how any particular juror voted. It is argued that this secrecy allows for a better decision-making process as nobody will be singled

61 Of the 1.5 million cases processed in the criminal justice system, around 113,000 were heard in the Crown Court, of which 25% contained a not guilty plea. This means that the percentage of cases heard by a jury was approximately 1.6%.

62 See Baldwin, J and McConville, M, *Jury Trials* (Oxford: Oxford University Press, 1979).

out for what they have decided. However, this secrecy can give rise to problems. Whilst there are 12 members of the jury, if we do not know what occurs in the deliberation room, it is impossible to know if all 12 jurors have an equal voice. It is not beyond the realms of possibility to believe that the room can be dominated by a small number of jurors. By having two or three jurors guide and drive the deliberations in a particular direction, it could be argued that this dilutes the due process safeguard of having 12 jurors, which was designed to offset any potential bias individual jurors may hold. However, by allowing a small number to be the 'voices of the room', this impartiality and unbiased approach may be lost.

Furthermore, the verdict returned may be influenced by factors that are not related to the evidence heard at trial. This is a dangerous proposition – if extraneous evidence is being considered, the fairness of the trial process may be jeopardised. Such extraneous evidence might include one's own biases or preconceptions concerning the defendant, complainant or witness. For example, a juror may dislike a person on the basis of their race, gender, religion, disability, dress, accent, levels of communication, occupation or any other bias that permeates the human mind. Although the jurors will be directed on how to deal with their own biases and preconceptions, it is impossible to say that each and every juror can discharge his or her mind of such thoughts. If the jurors think that there is bias during their deliberations, they can raise it with the court. The ECtHR in *Sander v UK*[63] stated that any allegation of bias must be examined from an objective and subjective point of view, ie a finding that the jury were not biased would not necessarily be the end of the mater. A further question would be asked: are there 'sufficient guarantees to exclude any legitimate doubts as to the impartiality of the jury'? In *Sawyer*[64] the judge observed three jurors speaking to prosecution witnesses. The judge asked the jurors the nature of the conversation, and they informed him that the conversation concerned matters that were unrelated to the trial. In this instance, the judge stated that there was no bias and no danger of prejudice occurring, so he elected not to discharge the jury.

Further to these internal issues, such as bias, there are a number of external issues that could cloud the mind of a jury, and, because of the secrecy surrounding the deliberation room, we cannot ascertain if these worries exist in reality. However, it is not unrealistic to think that some jurors may struggle with the process of being on a jury. They may not be able to grasp the law, understand all of the legal arguments or comprehend the final summing up of the judge. Tied into this concern is the idea of losing track of evidence. Can the untrained jury have the ability to listen to complex and persuasive legal arguments for hours on end, if the trial is lengthy? Do they have the comprehension to remember evidence they heard days ago? Whilst these concerns are theoretical, they present an interesting dilemma for the jury – should deliberations remain secret or should the rest of society be able to understand how a complex, important decision has been reached?

Jury cases: a twist in the tale?

As well as the issue of secrecy, there have been a number of controversial cases surrounding the use of juries in England and Wales. The case of *Ponting*[65] is an excellent example of a 'perverse verdict' – a verdict 'that is entirely against the weight of

63 [2000] Crim LR 767.

64 (1980) 71 Cr App R 283.

65 [1985] Crim LR 318.

the evidence or contrary to the judge's direction'.[66] Ultimately, this means that the jury can pass any sentence they wish, even if it is contrary to the evidence they have heard. In *Ponting*, the jury acquitted a civil servant for breaching s 2 of the Official Secrets Act 1911. Ponting had been charged with leaking an internal Ministry of Defence memo concerning the sinking of the cruise liner, the General Belgrano, during the Falklands War. The Conservative Government at the time stated that the Belgrano was threatening British lives when it was sunk by a British submarine. However, the leaked memo indicated that the liner was sailing out of an exclusion zone. At trial, Ponting claimed that the disclosure of the memo to an MP was in the public interest. The presiding judge, Sir Anthony McCowen, indicated that the jury should convict Ponting as it was his official duty not to disclose the memo and that the public interest 'is what the government of the day says it is'. This case arguably showed that, despite his breaking the law, the jury believed that the defendant was correct in his actions and therefore should not suffer any repercussions for his breach. This controversial example illustrates the aforementioned 'jury equity'; despite all the evidence pointing to a conviction, the jury still returned a 'not guilty' verdict and acquitted Ponting.

There are examples where juror behaviour is so deplorable that it needs to be questioned whether ordinary people should be charged with this important civic duty. In *Young*[67] the defendant was convicted of a double murder of a newlywed couple in East Sussex. However, it later transpired that, during the jurors' overnight stay at a hotel, some jurors had a few alcoholic drinks and then four of them had consulted a ouija board in order to 'speak' with the deceased victims. Having believed that they had made contact with the dead, it was reported that the deceased had named the defendant as the murderer. The next day, the jury returned a 'guilty' verdict and the defendant was convicted of the double murder. Shortly after this, a juror disclosed these facts to the court, leading the defendant to appeal against his conviction. It was held that there had been a material irregularity and the court needed to investigate what had occurred. It was found that the period in the hotel was not part of the official 'deliberations' and, as such, any investigation would not contravene s 8 of the Contempt of Court Act 1981. Accordingly, affidavits[68] were taken from the 12 jurors and the two bailiffs who were looking after them at the hotel. Lord Taylor of Gosforth CJ stated that 'having considered all the circumstances, we conclude that there was a real danger that what occurred during this misguided ouija session may have influenced some jurors and may thereby have prejudiced the appellant.' As such, the court allowed Young's appeal but ordered a retrial. In the subsequent retrial, he was again convicted – albeit through ordinary deliberations, rather than by summoning the dead!

More recently, the issue of trial by jury was thrust into the spotlight in the 'Colston Four' case, referring to the trial of four people charged with criminal damage for their involvement in the toppling of a statue of Edward Colston in Bristol, United Kingdom, during a Black Lives Matter protest on 7 June 2020. Edward Colston was a prominent 17th century slave trader who made his fortune through the transatlantic slave trade. His statue had long been a source of controversy, with many people arguing that it was inappropriate to celebrate someone who profited from the enslavement and exploitation of human beings. During the protest, the statue was pulled down and thrown into Bristol Harbour. The four defendants were subsequently arrested and charged with

66 *Oxford Dictionary of Law*, 8th edn (Oxford: Oxford University Press), 458.

67 Court of Appeal (Criminal Division), 30 December 1994.

68 An affidavit is a written statement confirmed by oath.

criminal damage. The case went to trial in December 2020, and in February 2021 all four were acquitted of the charges.

However, the case caused great consternation that people can wilfully cause criminal damage without suffering any legal sanction. There were arguments for and against the decision, which once again points to the importance of the jury trial – it is the jury alone that hears all the evidence and can draw on the full factual basis in order to come to a conclusion. Whether you think justice was delivered or not is a matter of opinion; it is a matter of fact that the jurors, in this case, chose to be on the 'right side of history'.[69]

Should jury trials be reformed?

Jury trials are designed to ensure that the defendant's case is heard by a representative cross-section of society. However, is this actually the case? This problem has plagued jury trials for decades, and in 1956 Lord Devlin[70] found that jurors were predominantly 'male, middle-aged and middle-class'. In the late 1970s it was found that both women and members of minority ethnic communities were under-represented.[71] In the early 1990s, the Commission for Racial Equality found that outside of urban areas, a black defendant was likely to face an all-white jury.[72] It is thought that this under-representation of certain demographics is because juror selection is tied to the electoral register and, historically, non-registration for voting is lower for both young people and ethnic minority groups. However, since the turn of the century, this problem has arguably improved. Cheryl Thomas suggests:

- There is no under-representation of ethnic minority groups among those summoned for jury trials at virtually all Crown Courts in England and Wales.
- There was no significant difference between the proportion of ethnic minority jurors serving and the ethnic minority population levels in the local catchment area for each court.
- However, racially mixed juries were only likely to exist in courts where ethnic minority groups made up 10% of the catchment area.[73]

Despite this, there appears that little can be done to broaden the social representation of differing demographic groups that sit on a jury. However, there are a number of other reforms that may be employed to reform jury trials.

One is reducing the number of offences eligible for jury trial. Doing so would not only improve the speed and efficiency of cases, but save money. Casey[74] estimated that by removing the defendant's right to choose where their case is heard, the criminal justice system would save around £30 million per year. This is because around 70,000 cases per year that are currently heard in the Crown Court could now be heard in the magistrates' court. Not only would there be an economic and efficiency saving, victims and defendants would also have the matter settled far quicker. This reform has been advanced by a number of review bodies[75] and would allow our legal process to replicate

69 Liam Walker KC represented one of the defendants in this case. Ed Johnston interviewed him on his YouTube Channel, *Criminal Justice Natters*, and you can view the interview here: www.youtube.com/watch?v=DobAOM2mRaw (accessed March 2023).

70 See Lord Devlin, *Trial by Jury* (London: Stevens and Sons, 1956).

71 See Baldwin, J and McConville, M, *Jury Trials* (Oxford: Oxford University Press, 1979).

72 See Commission for Racial Equality (1991) 'Evidence to the Royal Commission on Criminal Justice'.

73 Thomas, C and Barmer, N (2007) 'Diversity and Fairness in the Jury System', Research Series 2/07 (London: Ministry of Justice).

74 www.bbc.co.uk/news/uk-11680382 (accessed 11 May 2020).

75 See Royal Commission on Criminal Justice, *Report* (London: HMSO, 1993).

the system seen in Scotland. Michael Howard's 'crime control' agenda of the 1990s was a huge proponent of modifying the right to choose trial by jury.[76] He believed that jury trials allowed defendants to manipulate the legal system by looking to delay their trial in the hope that witnesses would fail to turn up. These proposals were not acted upon, but the New Labour Government gleefully took up Howard's baton. Proposals of the then Home Secretary, David Blunkett, included a provision that a judge could hear a case alone if there was a 'real and present danger that jury tampering would take place', which was diluted by the House of Lords in 2003.[77] Whilst this power exists, it has rarely been used in practice. The case of *Twomey and Others*,[78] also known as the 'Heathrow Heist,' where four men stole £1.75 million, is an example of this power. Three previous trials collapsed, which led to the first jury-less trial for a serious crime in more than 350 years. In the jury-less trial, the men were all convicted and appealed on the basis that the rationale for a jury-less trial was not disclosed to them. The appeal was dismissed and Lord Judge suggested that the four men 'received a fair trial before a court vested with the appropriate jurisdiction … [and] if criminals choose to subvert the process of trial by jury, they have no justified complaint if they are deprived of it … [T]hat is the consequence they face.'

The Coalition Government and Louise Carey continued to attempt to reform jury trials in the early part of this decade. Carey was keen to point out that the magistrates' court is not 'second-class justice' but 'there is no question that the trial in the magistrates' court is cheaper, at around half the cost of a jury trial'.[79] The notion of things being cheaper is something that permeated **Chapter 8**; it appears that governments want justice to be done but to be done as cheaply as possible. There have been a number of reforms designed to speed up justice in the magistrates' court:

- the enhanced use of technology at trial (ie video link) since 2009;
- Stop Delaying Justice Initiatives in 2012;
- the Early Guilty Plea Scheme which was established in 2013;
- the changes to the sentence discount for an early guilty plea in 2017.

Undoubtedly, these will not be the last initiatives designed to speed up the process and save money. However, if jury trials were eradicated or reduced, what would our process look like?

76 www.thelawyer.com/issues/24-february-1997/howards-political-posturing-over-justice/ (accessed 1 July 2018).

77 Criminal Justice Act 2003, s 44(6)(a)–(c).

78 [2009] EWCA Crim 1035.

79 www.bbc.co.uk/news/uk-11680382 (accessed 1 July 2018).

9.4.5.1 A comparison: lay vs professional justice?

Jury trials	Judge or magistrate trials
Juries often apply common sense to their decisions. They are better placed than professionals to weigh up evidence and reach the 'right' decision.	Justice is best left to highly qualified or highly trained professionals (although we might raise questions about whether this fully applies to magistrates).
Jurors are similar to the people who appear in court – they can understand their circumstances better.	Some trials are lengthy; they need to be tried by professional or well-trained individuals who can concentrate for long periods of time on complex arguments.
Juries bring a fresh approach to justice. They are not case hardened by the fact that they see the same crime, committed by the same type of person, day in, day out.	As they are professionally trained, such individuals should not succumb to being case hardened. They can try each case on its individual merits, regardless of how frequently they try defendants from similar socio-economic backgrounds.
Jury trials show that ordinary people can understand complex legal rules and procedures.	The professional or well-trained will not be influenced by constant media accounts of the alleged crime. This is especially true for horrific crimes, such as child sexual assault or murder.
There is public confidence in juries.	There should be public confidence in the professional or well-trained.
Jury trials show that the justice system is open, accountable and transparent.	The system is accountable and transparent; there are avenues for appeal should mistakes be made.
Jury trials keep the power of the state in check and help protect citizens from any abuse of authority by the state.	The professional or well-trained will take their obligations seriously; they would not turn to an ouija board for assistance!

As you can see, there are many arguments for abolishing jury trials or reducing their availability. However, the majority of such arguments are centred on efficiency. This is something we might be wary of, as any change should come from an evidenced-based standpoint that the quality of justice would be improved, rather than on the basis of saving money. Whilst the saving of resources is important, the democratic symbolism offered by the jury points to its retention. The jury trial is an indispensable feature of legal system, albeit a little used one. It allows the local community, who are often the most affected by crime, to pass judgement on those who have broken the law. It offers a degree of flexibility in the often rigid world of criminal procedure, and its flexibility and common-sense approach should be retained and not further diluted.

9.5 Conclusion

As this chapter and **Chapter 8** have illustrated, the adversarial theory advanced in **Chapter 1** does not necessarily exist in practice. The judge is not a passive participant; he or she is active and wants to reach a conclusion as quickly as possible. Whilst the prosecutor and defence lawyer are adversaries, there is a great deal of cooperation between the two, which raises the question: what is the role of the defence lawyer? It is difficult to suggest that the defence lawyer is purely a zealous advocate for the defendant, whereby advancing the client's best interests is his or her primary goal. The notion of defence disclosure means that information relevant to the defendant's case will be known prior to trial. The trial process itself is evolving, and there is a great desire to make it quicker and cheaper, with consistent calls to reduce the availability of trial by jury in order to streamline the process. We have seen that the jury can make flawed, surprising and sometimes outright foolhardy decisions. Nevertheless, they represent a fundamental part of the criminal justice process, and any calls to impinge further into the domain of the jury should be greatly resisted.

chapter 10 The Criminal Court (in Practice)

10.1 Introduction

Having explored the conceptual form and function of the court stage and its 'actors', we will now examine how the criminal court operates in practice. Up to this point, we have broadly followed the criminal process in chronological order, from arrest through to the police station. We now arrive at the most recognisable stage of the criminal process: court hearings, most particularly the criminal trial. This chapter will explain and critique the process by examining the arrival of the suspect at court; the matters to be resolved at their first appearance; decisions in relation to release or detention pending trial; the structure of the trial itself; and finally sentencing of those convicted of offences. The court stage is the most visible part of the criminal justice process. Any member of the public can normally attend criminal proceedings. This is a key part of upholding the principle of open justice – that is, that justice is both done and seen to be done. Crucial issues will inherently be determined by the procedure used by the court, including whether defendants accept or reject accusations against them, whether they are granted their liberty prior to trial and conviction, and how convicted offenders are to be dealt with. It is no exaggeration to say that lives are made and broken in the criminal courts of England and Wales. It is thus essential to understand how the criminal court works in practice.

10.2 Before court: bail and detention

Once a suspect is charged with an offence by the police, they will appear in court. Before they do so, they will either be:

- released by the police with at least the condition to appear at court on a set date; or
- detained by the police until their first appearance at court (also known as a 'remand in custody').

This decision must be made by a CO, and it will be the CO's first key decision post-charge.[1] There is a presumption that a suspect will be released (either with or without bail).[2] If released without bail, the only condition is that they surrender to the custody of the court on a specified date (normally, their first appearance – see **10.3** below). If a charged suspect is released on bail, a variety of conditions can be attached.[3] For example, a suspect can be released on 'money bail' (known as a surety or security) – but this is very rare in England and Wales.[4] More common conditions include curfews, a requirement to report to a police station at certain intervals (eg once a day), or a condition to stay away from a location or person (normally, the complainant). If a

1 PACE 1984, s 38(1).

2 *Ibid.*

3 *Ibid* s 47(1A).

4 See **10.4** below.

suspect fails to go to court when required (known as failing to surrender) or breaches the conditions of bail, they will normally be arrested, detained and brought to court.[5]

The presumption of release can be overturned and a suspect detained for a number of reasons, including the following:

- The suspect's name and address cannot be ascertained.
- The CO has reasonable grounds for believing that the suspect will fail to appear in court or answer to bail.
- Where the suspect is charged with an imprisonable offence, detention is necessary to prevent the suspect committing an offence.
- Detention is necessary to prevent the suspect interfering with the administration of justice or with the investigation.[6]

When deciding whether to overturn the presumption of release, the CO must have regard to the same considerations a court would have in deciding whether to detain a defendant.[7] Should the CO decide to detain, a suspect will be kept in custody until their first appearance at a magistrates' court, which must take place 'in any event not later than the first sitting after the suspect is charged with the offence' (normally, the same or next working day).[8]

In deciding whether to release or detain a suspect after charge, a conflict emerges between private and public interests. Before a trial or a guilty plea, a suspect or defendant is legally innocent. Denying or restricting their liberty before they have been tried or convicted *prima facie* contradicts the presumption of innocence, as to do so operates on the assumption that the suspect is in some form guilty (or at least suspicious or untrustworthy) and thus needs to be detained or controlled. A person should not be punished unless and until they are found guilty of a criminal offence; if a person is kept in custody pending their trial, they are arguably being subjected to a form of punishment despite their legal innocence (and of course they may be factually innocent too). However, important public interests must be balanced. Once a person is charged with an offence, there is at least (in principle) sufficient evidence against them to give a realistic prospect of conviction.[9] There may be justified concern that they will present a danger to others (perhaps in the form of further offences) or that they may interfere with the course of justice (for example, by intimidating witnesses). As such, detention or control through bail is a practical acknowledgement that the public interest must be protected even before someone is formally convicted of an offence.

This conflict is faced by all criminal justice systems; the major distinction is the way in which private and public interests are balanced in different jurisdictions – for example, by placing limits on the length of pre-trial detention or establishing a presumption of release. Both of these protections exist in England and Wales: the presumption of release has already been mentioned, and custody time limits exist which impose maximum periods for the detention of suspects before trial.[10] For summary offences, the maximum is 56 days; for indictable offences, the maximum is 182 days.[11] These run from the day after a defendant is detained at their first

5 Failure to surrender is an offence under s 6 of the Bail Act (BA) 1976; although breaching bail conditions is not.

6 PACE 1984, s 38(1)(a).

7 *Ibid* s 38(2A). These considerations are outlined in Sch 1 to the BA 1976 – see below at **10.4.1**.

8 PACE 1984, s 46(2).

9 See **Chapter 4** on charging.

10 Prosecution of Offences Act 1985, s 22.

11 Prosecution of Offences (Custody Time Limits) Regulations 1987.

appearance in court, and therefore do not apply to police detention.[12] Statistics relating to the remand population (that is, persons detained at some point before conviction) can be divided into three categories:

(1) those detained (by the police) after charge but before appearing at court;
(2) those detained (by courts) prior to any trial; and
(3) those detained (by courts) after conviction but before sentence.

The latter two will be dealt with below (at 10.4). In terms of the first, it is reasonable to state that the use of detention by the police after charge but before a court appearance is significant, though not the norm. In 2022 the police held 109,955 persons in custody who had been 'directed to appear at magistrates' courts' (in short, having been charged with an offence).[13] This figure accounts for less than 9% of persons so directed, and fits a pattern of decline in police detentions after charge.[14] The majority of those detained were charged with either indictable or either-way offences (though just under a third were charged with summary offences).[15] For those detained prior to charge, statistics are routinely published in relation to suspects detained for more than 24 hours before charge (see **Chapter 4**). However, there is little information available on the number of suspects detained prior to charge for less than a day, leaving this population of unconvicted detainees, effectively, invisible.

10.3 First appearance at court

As mentioned in **Chapter 9**, there are three categories of criminal offence in England and Wales. Regardless of the offence the suspect is charged with, all cases will start in a magistrates' court; as such, all suspects charged with criminal offences will make their first appearance in this court.[16] This will normally be the next working day (including Saturdays) for detained suspects; for those released by the police after charge, the wait may be longer, primarily because those who have been detained have been deprived of their liberty and are thus given priority. Once a suspect reaches the court stage of the criminal process, they are referred to as a defendant (until they are either convicted or acquitted). The first appearance at court will normally involve fairly simple procedures focused on information gathering and the management of future hearings. The court will confirm basic information about the defendant (eg name, date of birth, address and nationality).[17] The defendant will be told what offence or offences they are charged with, and they will be asked to enter a plea (a formal answer to the charges).[18] Defendants have three basic choices at this stage. They can:

- *plead guilty* – the defendant accepts that they committed the offence(s);
- *plead not guilty* – the defendant rejects (or at least refuses to confirm) that they committed the offence(s); or

12 *Ibid* reg 2(2). As mentioned above, if a suspect is detained by the police after charge, they will normally be brought to court within a day.

13 Ministry of Justice, 'Criminal Justice System statistics quarterly: September 2022, Overview Tables' (February 2023), Table Q4.1: www.gov.uk/government/statistics/criminal-justice-statistics-quarterly-september-2022 (accessed 7 March 2023).

14 *Ibid.*

15 *Ibid.*

16 See Magistrates' Courts Act (MCA) 1980, s 2 and Crime and Disorder Act 1998, s 51.

17 Courts Act 2003, s 86A (as amended by the Policing and Crime Act 2017, s 162); Criminal Procedure Rules (CrimPR) 2020, r 3.16(5)(a).

18 CrimPR, rr 9.7, 9.8 and 3.16(3)(b).

- *enter no plea* – a defendant can also choose not to enter a plea; if this happens, the court will decide whether it can deal with the case and proceed to trial or send it to the Crown Court if it cannot.

Depending on what plea the defendant enters, the first appearance may also involve:

- the court making decisions about a trial, if necessary;
- sentencing a defendant for an offence, if necessary.

Unless the first appearance ends with the defendant pleading guilty and being sentenced (and therefore the case formally ending), the court must always decide whether to release or detain the defendant until the next hearing.[19]

10.3.1 Guilty plea

Courts generally accept guilty pleas without questioning them or hearing any evidence (although a prosecutor normally provides a summary of the case).[20] The court must determine whether it can sentence the defendant, as magistrates' courts have limited powers (see **Chapter 9**). If the court cannot sentence the defendant because the likely sentence exceeds its powers, the case will be sent to the Crown Court. If the court can sentence, it may do so at the same hearing or adjourn, normally so that reports can be prepared which may help it decide on an appropriate sentence for the defendant.[21]

10.3.2 The significance of early guilty pleas

Modern development of the criminal trial has been characterised by an agenda of 'non-adversarial' transformation. In the wake of the Auld Review, the courts of England and Wales acted quickly in prioritising both 'efficiency and economy'.[22] The primary example of this was implementation and expansion of the Criminal Procedure Rules (CrimPR); its implicit goals of cost effectiveness and increased efficiency in the conduct of criminal trials is most evident in the overriding objective of 'dealing with cases justly'.[23] Despite this focus, the managerialist approach did not appear to be as effective as anticipated. In 2015, Sir Brian Leveson concluded that all parties still needed to do more to 'identify the issues so as to ensure that court time is deployed to maximum effectiveness and efficiency'.[24] Following this, the goals of efficiency and economy were further consolidated in the genesis of the Better Case Management (BCM) initiative.[25] The initiative endeavoured to link several different concepts designed to improve the way in which cases were processed through the criminal justice system. The overarching aims of BCM are as follows:

- robust case management;
- reduced number of hearings;
- maximum participation and engagement of every participant within the system; and

19 See BA 1976, s 4 and various sections of the MCA 1980, including ss 5, 10 and 128.

20 MCA 1980, s 9(3); Part D, Criminal Practice Directions 2015, Division VII: Sentencing.

21 See Criminal Justice Act 2003, s 156.

22 See *Chaaban* [2003] EWCA Crim 1012 and *Jisl* [2004] EWCA Crim 696.

23 CrimPR, r 1.1(1).

24 Sir Brian Leveson, 'Review of Efficiency in Criminal Proceedings' (Judiciary of England and Wales, 2015), [38].

25 Senior Presiding Judge for England and Wales, 'Better Case Management: Information Pack' (2015): www.judiciary.gov.uk/wp-content/uploads/2015/09/better-case-management-information-pack-3.pdf (accessed 4 May 2020).

- efficient compliance with the CrimPR, Practice and Court Directions.[26]

To assist in fulfilling these goals, BCM introduced a new case management initiative: the Early Guilty Plea scheme.

There has long been a policy of offering credit to defendants who plead guilty at an early stage – namely, a reduction in the sentence handed down by the court.[27] This can be up to a maximum of one third; thus, a sentence of nine years in custody would be reduced by three years. However, the longer a defendant waits to enter a guilty plea, the smaller the discount (with no discount if a defendant is convicted after trial). From 1 June 2017, a new scheme dealing with early guilty pleas came into force, which arguably reflects the managerialist mantra which has existed since the Auld Review in 2001.[28] The Definitive Guideline on dealing with early guilty pleas explicitly states that in order to be entitled to the maximum discount, a defendant must indicate a guilty plea at the first court hearing. Those who enter a guilty plea after the first hearing can be given a maximum reduction of one quarter, reducing to one tenth on the day of the trial. Previously, the court would broadly consider the stage in proceedings when the offender indicated his intention to plead guilty[29] and the circumstances in which this was given.[30] By insisting on a plea at the first appearance, the new scheme significantly reduces judicial discretion concerning the application of a reduction.

The key principles underpinning the scheme are that acceptance of guilt reduces the impact of crime upon victims, saves victims and witnesses from having to testify, and is in the public interest as it saves both time and money.[31] The scheme can be regarded as an incentive for those who are guilty to indicate a guilty plea as soon as possible. However, it is this incentive that arguably threatens the adversarial nature of the criminal justice process in England and Wales. The guidelines stress that 'the purpose … is to encourage those who are going to plead guilty to do so as early in the court process as possible' and that 'nothing in the guideline should be used to put pressure on a defendant to plead guilty'.[32] Yet, it is arguably naïve and idealistic to think that this translates simply into practice, especially considering that the discount may be the difference between a custodial and non-custodial sentence. The temptation to avoid custody at any cost may well be overwhelming. It is also worth considering that defendants, innocent or not, may not have confidence in the criminal justice process to either acquit them or provide them with what they perceive to be a fair trial. For example, the Lammy Review identified a serious deficit of trust in the institutions of the criminal justice system amongst ethnic minority defendants.[33] If defendants have little faith that they will be exonerated by a system they regard as 'stacked against them', they may well take a pragmatic approach and accept an early guilty plea as the most

26 *Ibid.*

27 This discretionary court practice was given a statutory footing under the Criminal Justice Act (CJA) 2003, s 144 (although it remains a discretion – it is not mandatory).

28 Sentencing Council, 'Reduction in Sentence for a Guilty Plea Definitive Guideline' (1 June 2017): www.sentencingcouncil.org.uk/publications/item/reduction-in-sentence-for-a-guilty-plea-definitive-guideline-2/ (accessed 4 May 2020).

29 CJA 2003, s 144(1)(a).

30 *Ibid* s 144(1)(b).

31 See, for example, the Explanatory Notes to the CJA 2003, s 144.

32 Sentencing Council (n 28), 4.

33 Lammy, D, 'The Lammy Review: An independent review into the treatment of, and outcomes for, Black, Asian and Minority Ethnic individuals in the Criminal Justice System' (September 2017): https://assets.publishing.service.gov.uk/government/uploads/system/uploads/attachment_data/file/643001/lammy-review-final-report.pdf (accessed 4 May 2020).

acceptable outcome – regardless of their innocence or guilt.[34] Such issues, which may also include the ability to comprehend the consequences of decisions about plea, are even more acute if defendants are unrepresented (which emerging evidence suggests is a growing problem).[35]

When considering the impact of the Early Guilty Plea regime, we should remember the long established issues which the defence experiences in obtaining information from the prosecution prior to the first appearance. As this is the only time the maximum discount is available, this presents an obvious dilemma. There is clear evidence that pre-trial disclosure by the CPS is often inadequate.[36] The CrimPR obligate the prosecution to disclose 'Initial Details of the Prosecution Case' if the defence requests it or, if it does not, to 'make them available to the defendant at, or before, the beginning of the day of the first hearing'.[37] In practice, this rule is inconsistently adhered to.[38] The scope of this disclosure is narrow; it is merely a brief summary of the case against the defendant, which has normally been prepared by a police officer and passed on to the CPS.[39] Furthermore, the ability of the CPS to fulfil its disclosure obligations is very much dependent on disclosure of exculpatory material by the police – which has been heavily criticised in reports by the House of Commons Justice Committee[40] and the Attorney General.[41] Despite the above, the defendant is still expected to enter a plea at the first stage of proceedings. The failure to plead guilty

---

34 *Ibid* 18.

35 See Transform Justice, 'Justice denied? The experience of unrepresented defendants in the criminal courts' (April 2016): www.transformjustice.org.uk/wp-content/uploads/2016/04/TJ-APRIL_Singles.pdf (accessed 4 May 2020); in May 2018, it emerged that the Ministry of Justice had commissioned, and then withheld, research into the extent of problems with unrepresented defendants in the Crown Court (Dugan, E, 'The Ministry Of Justice Has Just Released A Report It Denied Even Existed' (*Buzzfeed*, 1 June 2018): www.buzzfeed.com/emilydugan/ministry-of-justice-legal-aid-report-released?utm_term=.mxrNdQ3MN#.plNjD4QLj (accessed 4 May 2020). The report is now available in full (through the link above). Furthermore, the Ministry is under criminal investigation by the Information Commissioner's Office for its failure to disclose the report under a Freedom of Information request.

36 See Plotnikoff, J and Woolfson, R, 'A Fair Balance? Evaluation of the Operation of Disclosure Law' (Home Office, 2001): http://library.college.police.uk/docs/homisc/occ76-disclosures.pdf (accessed 4 May 2020); HM Crown Prosecution Inspectorate (HMICPS) and HM Inspectorate of Constabulary (HMIC), 'Making It Fair: A Joint Inspection of the Disclosure of Unused Material in Volume Crown Court Cases' (July 2017): https://www.justiceinspectorates.gov.uk/cjji/wp-content/uploads/sites/2/2017/07/CJJI_DSC_thm_July17_rpt.pdf (accessed 4 May 2020); Cape, E and Smith, T, 'The Practice of Pre-trial Detention in England and Wales' (University of the West of England, 2016): http://eprints.uwe.ac.uk/28291/1/Country-Report-England-and-Wales-MASTER-Final-PRINT1.pdf (accessed 4 May 2020).

37 CrimPR, r 8.2(2) and (3).

38 See Cape and Smith (n 36); and, more recently, Transform Justice, 'Presumed innocent but behind bars – is remand overused in England and Wales?' (March 2018): www.transformjustice.org.uk/wp-content/uploads/2018/03/TJ_March_13.03-1.pdf (accessed 4 May 2020).

39 Referred to as the 'police package' (see Cape and Smith (n 36)). The limited scope of 'Initial Details of the Prosecution Case' may arguably breach EU law. Article 7 of Directive 2012/13 on the right to information in criminal proceedings requires that 'access is granted at least to all material evidence in the possession of the competent authorities, whether for or against suspects or accused persons, to those persons or their lawyers in order to safeguard the fairness of the proceedings and to prepare the defence' and must be done so 'at the latest upon submission of the merits of the accusation to the judgment of a court'.

40 Justice Committee, 'Disclosure of Evidence in Criminal Cases: Eleventh Report of Session 2017–19' (20 July 2018): https://publications.parliament.uk/pa/cm201719/cmselect/cmjust/859/859.pdf (accessed 4 May 2020).

41 Attorney General's Office, 'Review of the efficiency and effectiveness of disclosure in the criminal justice system' (Cm 9735, 15 November 2018). See further **Chapter 17**.

at this stage is tantamount to an automatic increase in sentence in the event of a guilty verdict. Furthermore, the defence lawyer has to consider his or her professional obligations to the client, not least because the Law Society has suggested that lawyers could potentially be liable in negligence if the advice they give regarding plea is inadequate.[42] This poses a very serious question: how are defence lawyers expected to give sound legal advice as to plea when they are only advising on a partial representation of the evidence?

There is undoubtedly an agenda, for better or worse, to encourage defendants to enter early guilty pleas. Moreover, it seems that, should a defendant regret doing so, a remedy will rarely be offered by the courts. In *R (DPP) v Leicester Magistrates' Court*, the claimant sought to re-open his conviction for common assault.[43] The offence had allegedly been committed against a 14-year-old boy, who was in the care of the defendant as an agency worker in a care home at the time of the alleged offence. At his first appearance in court, the defendant intended to enter a plea of not guilty on the basis of self-defence. However, he changed this on the first day of his trial. He asserted that his solicitor had pressured him into entering an early guilty plea; he was convicted, and, as a result, was no longer able to find work in the social care sector. Whilst a magistrates' court can make an order to re-open a conviction when it is in the interests of justice to do so, it can only be exercised where there has been a mistake or a situation akin to a mistake.[44] A subsequent change of heart or regret at entering a guilty plea will not suffice as a mistake, and as such the defendant's conviction stood. One might argue that this was a result of the systemic pressure to obtain a plea early, filtering down from the court to the figure charged with protecting the defendant – the defence lawyer.

In such cases, there is a risk that the overriding objective of the CrimPR is undermined – that is, to deal with cases justly, which includes acquitting the innocent and convicting the guilty.[45] Whilst it is important to consider the effects of lengthy criminal proceedings on victims and witnesses, it is often the defendant who is forgotten in the process of reform. The emergence of the CrimPR has placed an emphasis on cooperation between all parties and their compliance with a new set of goals that focus on efficiency. Piecemeal changes over the last 15 years (including, but not limited to, the Early Guilty Plea scheme) arguably represent a departure from the traditional adversarial foundations of English and Welsh criminal justice, moving towards a more managerial process. The ramifications for fair trial rights have been largely ignored. Considering its impact, it is imperative that any decision to enter a guilty plea is based on full and accurate evidence from the police and prosecution. If cooperation is to be encouraged, it should be done so on an equal basis, and the defence should be in receipt of a greater amount of prosecution disclosure prior to entering a plea. This would ensure that the defence lawyer can adequately advise the client as to plea. Moreover, it would arguably re-assert basic adversarial tenets of criminal justice in England and Wales, for example improving compliance with the prosecution burden of proof by requiring revelation of the totality of its case from the beginning.

42 The Law Society, 'Response of the Law Society of England and Wales to the Sentencing Council consultation on the Reduction in Sentence for an Early Guilty Plea' (May 2016), 5.

43 Unreported, 9 February 2016.

44 MCA 1980, s 142. The defendant can also appeal against their conviction if they entered an 'equivocal plea' (that is, the defendant was not definitive about accepting guilt). An example of this would be when a defendant pleads guilty under duress (eg threats), as occurred in *Huntingdon Crown Court, ex parte Jordan* [1981] QB 857. See **Chapter 11** for more on appeals against conviction.

45 CrimPR, r 1.1(2)(a).

10.3.3 Not guilty plea/no plea

When a defendant either pleads not guilty or enters no plea, the prosecutor will summarise the case against the defendant, and the defence lawyer will provide basic information about the defendant's case. The court must then determine whether it can try the defendant. For an indictable offence, or an either-way offence where the defendant chooses jury trial, the case will be sent to the Crown Court. If the case involves a summary offence, the trial will always take place in a magistrates' court and a date will be set for this. The court will normally engage in some form of case management before ending the hearing; this might include setting timetables, requesting or making court directions and the completion of case management forms. The court may have further separate hearings, but this will be exceptional as there is a general expectation that courts should deal with 'as many aspects of the case as possible on the same occasion, and [avoid] unnecessary hearings'.[46] Finally, as mentioned above, the first appearance must end with the court deciding whether the defendant should be released on bail or detained in custody until trial.

10.4 Court bail

Decisions regarding court bail are governed by the Bail Act (BA) 1976. At the court stage, even an unconditional release is regarded as a form of bail; in contrast to the pre-charge stage, a defendant is no longer simply considered as 'released' since they have now been formally charged with an offence and must return to court at some point. All defendants (with limited exceptions)[47] have a *prima facie* right to release on bail.[48] However, the court can choose to overturn this and withhold bail, remanding a defendant in custody until their next appearance at court.[49] The statute does not formally place the burden of proof on the prosecution (the court must be 'satisfied' that bail should be refused); however, it is in effect the job of the prosecution to show why the defendant should be detained, aligning with key due process principles like the presumption of innocence and ECtHR jurisprudence.[50] The CrimPR do, however, make it clear that the prosecution must make 'representations' to the court if it opposes the release of a defendant on bail, justifying why it should be refused.[51]

For the defence, the situation is slightly different. Defence lawyers commonly refer to the conduct of 'bail applications' in courts; that is, making representations as to why the defendant should be released on bail (and, occasionally, why they should be detained).[52] In a purely technical sense, a 'bail application' should not be necessary, since the defendant has the benefit of a presumption of release. They should thus not need to ask the court to be freed from custody. However, from a practical perspective, a diligent defence lawyer will normally make representations on his or her client's behalf,

46 CrimPR, r 3.2(2)(f).

47 The exceptions include murder (bail can only be granted by the Crown Court – Coroners and Justice Act 2009, s 115(1)) and defendants charged with certain serious offences who already have a conviction for such an offence (CJPOA 1994, s 25).

48 BA 1976, s 4.

49 *Ibid.*

50 See the various Parts of Sch 1 to the BA 1976; key cases from the ECtHR include: *Michalko v Slovakia*, No 35377/05, 21 December 2010; and *Ilijkov v Bulgaria*, No 33977/96, 26 July 2001.

51 CrimPR, r 14.5(3).

52 In some cases, the defence may wish to see the defendant remanded in custody (for example, for their own protection).

explaining why custody will be inappropriate (if the prosecution is requesting it or the court is considering it). A 'bail application' is therefore a term of art rather than a legal concept.[53] Generally, rebutting the presumption of release is easier for the prosecution if the defendant is charged with an imprisonable offence (normally, indictable or either-way offences). The law is much more restrictive in allowing detention of defendants charged with non-imprisonable offences (normally, summary offences).[54] Again, this might be considered a due process protection, in that it makes it more difficult for the court to deprive a defendant of their liberty before conviction when the offence involved is relatively minor and will not end with a custodial sentence. This is arguably fair because imprisoning someone before conviction when they will not end up in prison afterwards would be disproportionate.

10.4.1 The grounds for withholding bail

Schedule 1 to the BA 1976 outlines the reasons a court can overturn the presumption of bail. As mentioned above, when the defendant is accused of at least one offence which is imprisonable, they need not be granted bail if the court is satisfied that there are substantial grounds for believing that, if released, the defendant would:

- fail to surrender to custody;
- commit an offence on bail; or
- interfere with witnesses or otherwise obstruct the course of justice.

However, since the passage of the Legal Aid, Sentencing and Punishment of Offenders Act (LASPO) 2012, there must be a 'real prospect' of a custodial sentence should the defendant be convicted.[55] Again, this attempts to ensure that the seriousness of the allegation alone does not lead to unnecessary detention; if it is unlikely that the defendant will be imprisoned, then a remand in custody will be disproportionate. When the defendant is charged with a non-imprisonable offence, it is much harder for a prosecutor (or the court of its volition) to rebut the presumption of bail. Generally, detention on the grounds above will be applicable only if there is previous similar behaviour by the defendant (for example, they failed to surrender to the court in previous criminal proceedings).[56] These are the primary grounds for withholding bail, but there are others detailed under Sch 1:

- If the defendant was already on bail when they were brought before the court (in short, they are suspected of committing an offence whilst already on bail), the court must not grant bail unless satisfied that there is no significant risk of the defendant committing another offence.
- Bail can also be denied if the court is satisfied that the defendant should be detained for their own protection.
- Bail will be denied if the defendant is already serving a custodial sentence (as such, this will apply to prisoners accused of offences).
- The court is also unlikely to grant bail when a defendant has been bailed at a previous point in the case and subsequently arrested as an absconder.[57]

53 Although CrimPR, r 14.7 clarifies that the defence does need to apply in writing and explain why the defendant should be released when they want a magistrates' court to 'reconsider' bail that has previously been refused, or wishes to appeal to the Crown Court after a previous refusal by the lower court.

54 See BA 1976, Sch 1, Pt II.

55 BA 1976, Sch 1, Pt I, para 1A.

56 See BA 1976, Sch 1, Pt II.

57 See BA 1976, Sch 1, Pts I and II.

In making its decision, the court must take into account statutory factors – that is, features of the case that justify detaining the defendant. These factors might suggest that one or more of the grounds for withholding bail listed in Sch 1 are satisfied. For example, evidence of a poor record of answering bail in the past may be a *factor* which helps establish a *ground* for denying bail (eg the defendant may fail to surrender to custody). There are a number of factors that the court must consider, including:

- the nature and seriousness of offence;
- the probable method of dealing with the offence – that is, what is the likely sentence, if the defendant is convicted;
- character and antecedents (previous convictions);
- the defendant's record regarding previous grants of bail; and
- the strength of the prosecution case.[58]

These factors therefore provide *evidence* for finding one of the grounds for detention and denying bail – they do not, in themselves, allow denial of bail. For example, the fact that the offence is a serious one (eg rape) does not in itself justify remanding a defendant in custody.

10.4.2 Unconditional and conditional bail

If the presumption is not overturned, the court will release the defendant on bail. They have two options – unconditional or conditional bail:

- *Unconditional bail*: the defendant is released without any requirements other than to return to court at the next scheduled appearance.[59]
- *Conditional bail* (BA 1976, s 3(4) and (6)): the defendant will be released and requirements may be imposed on them for several reasons:
  - to ensure they surrender to custody; do not commit offences on bail; do not interfere with witnesses or obstruct the administration of justice;
  - for their own protection or to protect a child or young person;
  - to ensure that the defendant is available for any enquiries or reports necessary for dealing with the offence;
  - to ensure, before the next appearance, that the defendant meets a defence lawyer.

In short, conditions are a way of controlling the defendant's behaviour without detaining them. Detention is in theory the least desirable outcome, due not only to concerns about interference with the presumption of innocence and the right to liberty, but also due to the cost (financial and otherwise) of remanding someone. A prison space will be required and this is expensive (for more on this, see **Chapter 13**).

Like the police, the court can impose a wide range of conditions on release, falling under three basic categories:

- *A security*: this involves depositing something valuable to the defendant with the court (for example, a passport).
- *A surety:* this is a promise by a third party to pay money if the defendant fails to appear at court (sometimes known as 'money bail'). This is very rare in England and Wales.

58 See BA 1976, Sch 1, Pt I, para 9.

59 BA 1976, s 3(1).

- *Other conditions*: 'such requirements as appear to the court to be necessary'.[60] In short, this can theoretically mean anything.

The court thus has wide discretion to impose restrictions on 'at liberty' defendants; there is no exhaustive list of conditions a court can and does impose, but common conditions include:

- requiring the defendant to stay away from a person (eg a complainant) or a location (eg where the offence allegedly took place);
- electronic monitoring (ie tagging);
- curfew;
- reporting to a police station;
- residence (that is, a requirement to live at a particular address – this could be their own address, that of another person, or a bail hostel).[61]

As always, the interpretation of what will be 'necessary' is rather loose; the court only has to perceive 'a real, rather than a fanciful, risk' in releasing a defendant to justify the attachment of conditions.[62] This arguably sets a fairly low threshold for allowing the court to impose conditions on defendants, with no particular evidential requirements attached. Breach of a condition is not an offence – but the defendant may be arrested, brought to court, and remanded in custody.[63] Once a defendant has been released on bail or detained, the court adjourns until the next scheduled hearing, when the decision will be reviewed.[64] For those charged with indictable offences, the next bail decision will be made by the Crown Court – therefore, decisions regarding pre-trial detention made in the Crown Court will always be a review of a previous decision by a magistrates' court. For defendants detained after the first appearance, a review hearing must take place within eight days.[65] If they are denied bail again, they can appeal to the Crown Court (regardless of the type of offence).[66] As such, these represent fairly robust due process protections to ensure that defendants are not detained for unnecessarily long periods and that decisions are scrutinised (in the case of appeals, by professional judges within a day).[67]

10.4.3 How common is pre-trial detention?

Considering that remanding defendants in custody (which we will hereafter refer to as pre-trial detention (PTD)) deprives them of their liberty without a conviction, it is important to know how extensively it is used. A common measure is the proportion of the prison population that has not yet been tried or, if tried and convicted, not yet sentenced. England and Wales had, until recent years, consistently maintained one of

60 BA 1976, s 3(6).

61 Bail hostels – formally known as 'approved premises' under s 13 of the Offender Management Act 2007 – provide temporary housing for defendants released on bail who do not have other suitable accommodation. They are run by the National Probation Service or independent organisations.

62 *ex parte Sharkey* [1985] QB 613.

63 BA 1976, s 7(3).

64 The presumption of release under s 4 applies at each hearing. If a defendant is refused bail, the court considers whether to grant bail at each subsequent hearing (BA 1976, Sch 1, Pt IIA, para 1). The court does not have to hear arguments of fact or law that it has already heard (BA 1976, Sch 1, Pt IIA, para 3).

65 MCA 1980, s 128.

66 Senior Courts Act 1981, s 81; CrimPR, r 14.8.

67 CrimPR, r 14.8(6).

the lower PTD populations in Europe and globally,[68] at approximately 12% of the overall prison population.[69] However, the jurisdiction also has one of the highest per capita prison population rates in Europe (139 prisoners per 100,000 people).[70] Therefore, the actual number of people in PTD at any one time is comparatively high, and has grown significantly since 2020. As of 31 December 2022, there were 81,806 persons in prison; 14,143 of them were on remand – a 40% increase since 2020 and the last edition of this book.[71] The majority of those on remand are untried (66% of the remand population, and roughly 11% of the overall prison population).[72] These figures represent the highest number of individuals remanded in custody in half a century.[73]

10.4.4 Research on the use of pre-trial detention

Research literature examining PTD has identified a number of issues, suggesting problems in the use of and decision-making about pre-trial remands in custody and court bail.[74] Until recently, these areas had received fairly limited attention from legislators and academics. Exceptions included the reforms introduced under LASPO 2012, an HMIP report on remand prisoners in the same year, and some research conducted by the Howard League for Penal Reform in 2014.[75] In 2016, Cape and Smith published the findings of fieldwork examining the practice of PTD, focusing on four issues:[76]

(a) *Process – how decisions were made:* The process was found to be broadly compliant with ECHR standards. However, decisions were often uncontested; were very short (a matter of minutes in length); and were reliant on police information/summaries and limited evidence, with witnesses rarely called. This is particularly important since one of the 'factors' to be considered is 'the strength of the prosecution case'. One wonders how sure courts can be about the 'strength' of a case on such a restricted basis, and therefore whether grounds for detention are

68 Office for National Statistics, 'Reporting on the Sustainable Development Goals: People on remand in custody in England and Wales' (3 August 2018), 2: www.ons.gov.uk/releases/reportingonthesustainabledevelopmentgoalspeopleonremandincustodyinenglandandwales (accessed 14 July 2020).

69 Ministry of Justice, 'Offender management statistics quarterly: October to December 2019 and annual 2019' (30 April 2020): www.gov.uk/government/publications/offender-management-statistics-quarterly-october-to-december-2019/offender-management-statistics-quarterly-october-to-december-2019-and-annual-2019 (accessed 4 May 2020).

70 World Prison Brief, 'United Kingdom: England and Wales' (as of March 2020): www.prisonstudies.org/country/united-kingdom-england-wales (accessed 4 May 2020).

71 Ministry of Justice (n 69).

72 Ministry of Justice, 'Prison Population: 31 December 2022' (23 January 2023), Table 1.1: www.gov.uk/government/statistics/offender-management-statistics-quarterly-july-to-september-2022 (accessed 7 March 2023).

73 Fair Trials, 'Highest number of people on remand in England and Wales for over 50 years' (22 November 2022): www.fairtrials.org/articles/news/highest-number-of-people-on-remand-in-england-and-wales-for-over-50-years (accessed 7 March 2023).

74 For an overview, see Smith, T, '"Rushing Remand"? Pretrial Detention and Bail Decision Making in England and Wales' (2021) *Howard J of Crime & Justice*, 60(1).

75 HM Inspectorate of Prisons (HMIP), 'Remand Prisoners: A thematic review' (August 2012): www.justiceinspectorates.gov.uk/hmiprisons/wp-content/uploads/sites/4/2012/08/remand-thematic.pdf (accessed 4 May 2020); Howard League for Penal Reform, 'Revealed: The wasted millions spent on needless remand' (18 August 2014): https://howardleague.org/news/needlessremand/ (accessed 4 May 2020).

76 See n 36.

satisfied.[77] Defence lawyers felt courts favoured prosecution submissions. Disclosure to the defence before hearings was largely unregulated and inconsistent, arguably in breach of the EU Directive on the right to information in criminal proceedings.[78]

(b) *Substance – the content and nature of the decisions made:* The most common ground for detention was 'fear of further offences'; the most important factor influencing such decisions was the defendant's history of offending (a logical finding). Occasionally, characteristics of defendants influenced decisions to detain (eg drug addiction, homelessness and mental illness). This was generally to protect the defendant or due to a lack of viable alternatives (ie conditional bail would not be effective or where bail hostels were not available). Decisions tended to be formalistic (that is, reflecting the wording of the BA 1976 rather than engaging with the facts of the case – probably in breach of ECtHR jurisprudence). Magistrates tended to confuse *grounds* for detention with *factors* to be taken into account (eg detaining someone due to the seriousness of the offence). Again, if a factor like 'strength' of the case is given too much weight and treated as a reason to detain a defendant, this will be particularly problematic without a full picture of the case.[79]

(c) *Review – the process for reviewing bail/detention decisions:* Reviews of initial decisions to detain defendants were generally swift. Defendants were generally not present at Crown Court PTD hearings (which are always reviews of magistrates' court decisions); this appeared to be a working rule with no clear justification. Reviews generally had the same issues as at initial hearings (brief reasoning, limited evidence offered, short length). There was also some evidence to suggest an informal 'reversal' of the burden on the prosecution to show why the defendant should be detained (ie the defendant was expected to show why they should be released from detention). This was contrary to the legislation as the presumption of release is applicable at all stages of proceedings

(d) *Outcomes – the outcomes from PTD hearings for defendants (ie detention, bail and final outcome in cases overall):* Nearly 25% of defendants who were detained at some stage were later acquitted or had the case against them dropped (which might suggest legally and factually innocent defendants were detained unnecessarily). Nearly half of defendants detained at some stage prior to trial did not receive a custodial sentence; that is, they did not go to prison despite being remanded in custody earlier in the process. Of those who did receive a custodial sentence, nearly all received a sentence longer than the time spent in PTD,

---

77 In Cape and Smith's study, magistrates and prosecutors highlighted that the strength of the case was an important factor which they considered in their decision-making (see Ch V).

78 See n 36.

79 This is particularly concerning where there has not been complete disclosure prior to the hearing. For example, see the cases of Isaac Itiary and Samson Makele. Both cases collapsed after non-disclosure of key evidence was revealed; Itiary spent four months in custody prior to this, whilst Makele spent 18 months on restrictive bail (including a curfew and seizure of his passport). See Evans, M, 'Scotland Yard reviews all ongoing rape cases after second trial involving same officer collapses as "evidence withheld"' (*Telegraph*, 20 December 2017): www.telegraph.co.uk/news/2017/12/19/met-orders-review-rape-cases-second-trial-collapses/ (accessed 4 May 2020); and Dearden, L, 'Rape case against Eritrean man collapses after photos showing woman "snuggling" with him uncovered' (*Independent*, 15 January 2018): www.independent.co.uk/news/uk/crime/rape-case-collapses-disclosure-eritrean-man-makele-photos-cuddling-snuggling-woman-metropolitan-a8160816.html (accessed 4 May 2020).

suggesting that when PTD is used appropriately it is not generally excessive in length.

In the wake of this report, changes to the Criminal Procedure Rules were introduced to remedy some of these issues; yet these were found to have been relatively ineffective.[80] Most recently, the issue of the fast-rising PTD population has drawn the attention of legislators, with the House of Commons Justice Committee publishing a report on remand in early 2023.[81] It drew largely critical conclusions about current law and practice, recommending (among other things) 'an independent review into whether the Bail Act 1976 is still operating as intended'.[82]

10.5 Pre-trial disclosure

Once a decision regarding bail or detention has been made, the first appearance ends; the manner in which the case will proceed from here will depend on the plea. If the defendant pleaded guilty, the next hearing will normally be to sentence them. In some cases, this can take place later in the same day but may be delayed by a number of weeks (for example, if a complex pre-sentence report is required).[83] If the defendant pleaded not guilty or did not enter a plea, the case will progress towards trial. The next hearing will not necessarily be the trial; for example, there may be some further pre-trial case management hearings. There are various important procedures that must be considered prior to trial, among them the issue of disclosure of evidence and unused material (discussed in **Chapter 8**). Described by HMCPSI and HMIC as 'one of the cornerstones of the criminal justice system', disclosure is designed to ensure that all relevant material goes before the court.[84] In an adversarial system where each party istrying to 'win', the scope for either side to hide unfavourable evidence is apparent – particularly, for the police and prosecution, who have a distinct advantage in terms of resources and power. The potential for miscarriages of justice is significant, exemplified by a series of collapsed trials in late 2017 in which the police (and, as a result, prosecution) failed to disclose vital evidence.[85] Generally, s 3 of the Criminal Procedure and Investigations Act (CPIA) 1996 states that the prosecution must

> [d]isclose to the accused any prosecution material which has not previously been disclosed to the accused and which might reasonably be considered capable of

---

80 Smith, T, 'The Practice of Pre-trial Detention in England & Wales – Changing Law and Changing Culture' (2022) *European J of Crim Policy & Research*, 28.

81 House of Commons Justice Committee, 'The role of adult custodial remand in the criminal justice system: Seventh Report of Session 2022–23' (January 2023, HC 264): https://committees.parliament.uk/publications/33530/documents/182421/default/ (accessed 14 March 2023).

82 *Ibid* 3.

83 CJA 2003, s 158: a pre-sentence report is a report which, 'with a view to assisting the court in determining the most suitable method of dealing with an offender, is made or submitted by an appropriate officer' (this being a probation officer for adult offenders). A pre-sentence report must be prepared when a court seeks to impose a custodial or community sentence (CJA 2003, s 156).

84 HMCPSI and HMIC, 'Making it Fair: The Disclosure of Unused Material in Volume Crown Court Cases: Summary' (18 July 2017): www.justiceinspectorates.gov.uk/cjji/inspections/making-it-fair-the-disclosure-of-unused-material-in-volume-crown-court-cases/ (accessed 4 May 2020).

85 The most high profile was that of Liam Allan – see Metropolitan Police Service (MPS) and Crown Prosecution Service (CPS), 'A joint review of the disclosure process in *R v Allan*' (January 2018): www.cps.gov.uk/sites/default/files/documents/publications/joint-review-disclosure-Allan.pdf (accessed 4 May 2020). See further **Chapter 17**.

undermining the case for the prosecution against the accused or of assisting the case for the accused.

The prosecution has a 'continuing duty' to review disclosure in this manner.[86] In turn, defendants charged with indictable offences (which will be heard in the Crown Court) must give a 'defence statement' to the court and prosecution.[87] The CrimPR also place extensive requirements on the defence to provide information about its case to the court in cases conducted in the magistrates' courts.

10.6 The trial

definition

A **trial** is a court hearing in which the arguments supporting and disputing (with evidence) a defendant's guilt are presented in full by lawyers.

A verdict on the evidence presented is delivered by a neutral adjudicator, determining whether the offence(s) has been proven beyond all reasonable doubt. If it has, the defendant is guilty and is convicted; if not, the defendant is not guilty and is acquitted.[88]

In England and Wales, the trial courts (the courts of first instance) for criminal cases are magistrates' courts and the Crown Court. Trials in both venues have common features:

- *Adversarialism* – trials in both courts involve two opposing sides (prosecution and defence) 'battling' each other to convince the adjudicator that their version of events is the truth (see **Chapter 1** for more on this).
- *The burden and standard of proof* – the prosecution must prove the case against the defendant, and it must do so beyond all reasonable doubt.
- *The presumption of innocence* – all defendants are presumed innocent until proven guilty (ie once the adjudicator delivers such a verdict, after a full and fair trial).[89]
- A *neutral adjudicator* determines whether a defendant is guilty or not.
- *Lawyers appear for both sides* (though this is not guaranteed for the defence),[90] and there is a focus on orality (that is, verbal presentation of evidence in court).
- There will be *cross-examination* of witnesses and the defendant (unless the defendant declines to give evidence, as is their right – see **Chapter 6**).
- The final delivery of a *verdict* by the adjudicator takes place in open court.

Proceedings (that is, the way in which a trial runs) in both courts have a similar structure and order:

---

86 CPIA 1996, s 7A.

87 *Ibid* s 5.

88 Note: an acquittal is not the same as 'innocence'. It merely means that the offence has not been proven to the requisite standard, and therefore the defendant is legally innocent (although they could, in reality, be factually guilty). Contrast this to Scotland's three verdict system: guilty, not proven, and not guilty.

89 In *Woolmington v DPP* [1935] AC 462, this was described as the 'golden thread' running through all criminal cases.

90 There is evidence of an emerging problem of unrepresented clients in magistrates' courts and the Crown Court. See n 35.

- The prosecution makes an opening speech, summarising the case; this is generally briefer in magistrates' courts than in the Crown Court, as magistrates are normally more experienced than jurors in trying cases and do not require an extensive summary.
- The prosecution case is then presented, which is normally focused on the calling of witnesses. In both courts, the order of questioning for each witness is:
  - evidence in chief (prosecution questioning its own witness);
  - cross-examination (defence questioning the prosecution witness);
  - re-examination (further questioning by the prosecution);
  - questions from the bench (ie the magistrates or a judge in the Crown Court).
- At this stage (in certain circumstances), the defence can make a submission of no case to answer; that is, that the prosecution should be dismissed as the case against the defendant is too weak or unreliable to prove guilt.[91]
- Otherwise, the defence can (but does not have to) set out its case, normally by presenting the defendant and others as witnesses. The same order of questioning applies as above but with the roles of defence and prosecution reversed (ie evidence in chief is conducted by the defence, etc).
- Both the prosecution and the defence will normally make a closing speech or representation; this will then be followed by a period of deliberation by the adjudicator and delivery of a verdict.[92]

There are, however, some significant differences between trials in magistrates' courts and the Crown Court. Generally, magistrates' court trials are shorter and less complex. They are normally adjudicated by lay magistrates, supported by a legal adviser (or 'clerk'); however, District Judges (who are legally trained) can also hear trials alone. Juries only sit in Crown Court trials. Advocacy (that is, oral presentation of the case in court) is normally conducted by solicitors in magistrates' courts and barristers in the Crown Court.[93] Crown Court trials are often lengthy and complex. The role of the judge is quite different in the Crown Court, tasked primarily with presiding over the running of proceedings and the explanation of the relevant law to the jury.

It should be noted that the summary above provides a very basic overview of the trial process in both courts. There are many potential variations and aspects of the process that are beyond the scope of this book. It is worth noting that whilst the general principle in English and Welsh criminal procedure is that hearings should be oral and open, there are notable divergences from this. For example, since the Criminal Justice Act 2003, there has been a relaxing of the rule against hearsay – that is, 'that a statement made out of court is inadmissible as evidence of any fact stated'.[94] This therefore means that statements not presented during the trial can be admitted as evidence against a defendant (but also in support of the defence case).

Adapting trials: special measures

It is also worth mentioning another significant example of an alteration to standard trial procedures – special measures. These are adjustments to the normal conduct of a trial in order to 'facilitate the gathering and giving of evidence by vulnerable and intimidated

91 CrimPR, r 24.3(3)(d).

92 Generally, for more detail on the various stages of the trial process, see Sprack, J, *A Practical Approach to Criminal Procedure* (OUP, 2020).

93 Solicitors with Higher Rights of Audience may also conduct trials in the Crown Court.

94 Welsh, L, Skinns, L and Sanders, A, *Sanders & Young's Criminal Justice* (OUP, 2021); see CJA 2003, s 114.

witnesses'.[95] Primarily regulated by the Youth Justice and Criminal Evidence (YJCEA) Act 1999, these are available to prosecution and defence witnesses (but not defendants) who may be particularly affected or inhibited by the trial process. The process of going to court is crucial for securing convictions, but it can be a distressing and traumatic experience for complainants, witnesses and defendants in general. This is especially true for individuals considered to be vulnerable, and as such there is a consensus that the trial process can and should be modified to some extent for certain individuals. This is justified on the basis that special measures can help them give their best evidence during a trial and relieve some of the stress associated with giving evidence. As explained in *R v Camberwell Green Youth Court, ex parte D* [2005] 2 Cr App R 1:

> [T]he theory underlying these provisions is that the use of special measures will maximise the quality of … evidence in terms of its completeness, coherence and accuracy … the measures will enable [witnesses] to give the best evidence of which they are capable.

However, it is essential to ensure fair trials for defendants, and therefore special measures (SMs) are considered exceptional and not the norm.

The YJCEA 1999, the primary legislation for SMs, enshrined several such measures in statute for the first time, although some required additional legislation before they could be implemented. Certain SMs are not currently in force, and their use still generally requires judicial discretion on a case-by-case basis.[96] The available SMs under the YJCEA 1999 include the use of screens in court, giving evidence by live link, giving evidence in private, removal of wigs and gowns, use of video recordings for evidence in chief, recording of cross-examination or re-examination, use of an interpreter or intermediary, and aids to communication.[97]

To be eligible for SMs, two hurdles must be overcome: the relevant individual must be eligible, and the trial judge must exercise discretion to implement SMs (though there are some situations where granting of SMs is mandatory). Two groups are eligible under the legislation: the first covers individuals who are vulnerable due to their age and/or issues of capacity; the second covers individuals who are vulnerable due to fear or distress about testifying. Section 16 defines eligibility for the first group, which includes witnesses under 18 at the time of the hearing, or with mental or physical impairments affecting evidence.[98] Judges must decide whether the quality of evidence given by the witness is likely to be diminished, and factors affecting completeness, coherence and accuracy of evidence are taken into account. Section 17 concerns witnesses who are vulnerable due to fear or distress about testifying in court. The court must be satisfied that the quality of evidence is likely to be diminished as a result of the fear or distress experienced by the witness in connection with the proceedings. The source of the fear or distress which can be considered include the nature and circumstances of the offence, the age of the witness, and the witness's social, cultural and ethnic background, as well as any behaviour towards the witness by the accused, their family, associates or anyone else who is likely to be involved in the case. The legislation defines fear or distress broadly, encompassing anything that might be deemed to cause these emotions in a witness.

95 Ministry of Justice, 'Achieving Best Evidence in Criminal Proceedings' (March 2011), [1.14]: https://www.cps.gov.uk/sites/default/files/documents/legal_guidance/best_evidence_in_criminal_proceedings.pdf (accessed 4 May 2020).

96 Section 19.

97 See ss 22–30.

98 More detail on what this means can be found in s 16(2).

Eligible witnesses are not automatically entitled to all available SMs. If the witness is eligible under s 16, SMs under ss 23–30 may be implemented, whilst witnesses eligible under s 17 may be granted SMs under ss 23–28; as such, ss 29 and 30 (intermediaries and aids to communication) are reserved for Group 1. Moreover, these are granted at the discretion of the court, though there are two situations in which SMs must be granted: these are for child witnesses and complainants in sexual offences cases in the Crown Court.[99] For children, the primary rule is that the court must grant SMs under s 27 (recorded evidence in chief) or, if this is not possible, under s 24 (evidence by live link). However, there are exceptions to this rule. If the witness does not want SMs, and the court does not believe that SMs would diminish the quality of the evidence, then they may not be granted. The court will consider various factors, such as the age and maturity of the witness, their understanding of consequences, the relationship between the witness and the accused, and the social/cultural background and ethnic origins of the witness, as well as the nature/circumstances of the alleged offence. In cases of sexual offences in the Crown Court, SMs are mandatory for complainants under s 22A. This requires the admission of the complainant's video-recorded evidence in chief (under s 27), unless it is believed that this would not maximise the quality of the complainant's evidence. SMs can be raised by either party in relation to any witness other than the accused, or by the court itself. Prior to the trial, the court usually hears submissions from advocates and then decides whether to exercise its discretion to order special measures under s 19.

The effectiveness of SMs is a significant subject of research and debate.[100] Evidence generally suggests that while there is significant praise and high demand for SMs, there are difficulties with availability. SMs have been found to be a crucial factor in some witnesses' decision to give evidence, yet a continuing issue has been late or confusing information about SMs. Indeed, there has been criticism suggesting that witness needs are not always fully assessed, leading to SMs being wrongfully denied or not considered. Witness choice has been found to be problematic, with some describing the process as disempowering. Additionally, SMs have been hampered by logistical challenges in different courts. Despite being considered a 'success story', the effective use of SMs in practice is far from perfect.[101] SMs also raise a range of issues relating to both fair trials and the administration of justice. They are rationalised on the basis that justice should not be denied simply because a victim of crime is unable to provide evidence to the best of their ability (or at all in many cases). This is particularly problematic in sexual offences cases where a successful prosecution may be heavily dependent on the complainant's testimony, which may be undermined simply by the stress of the trial process. At the same time, shielding witnesses or removing them from court altogether may impact on the right of a defendant to a fair trial. It may impede the ability of the defence to properly question a witness, or it may imply that the defendant is guilty because the witness needs 'protection'. Moreover, defendants are not entitled to access SMs under the legislative framework, raising questions about fairness for vulnerable

---

99 Sections 21 and 22A.

100 For a good summary of literature in the area, see Fairclough, S, 'Special Measures: Literature Review (Victims Commissioner, July 2020): https://victimscommissioner.org.uk/document/special-measures-literature-review/ (accessed 8 March 2023).

101 Victims Commissioner, 'Next steps for special measures: A review of the provision of special measures to vulnerable and intimidated witnesses' (May 2021), 7: https://s3-eu-west-2.amazonaws.com/jotwpublic-prod-storage-1cxo1dnrmkg14/uploads/sites/6/2021/12/2021-05-18_Special-measures_FINAL.pdf (accessed 8 March 2023).

defendants.[102] These issues are the subject of significant debate in the courts and amongst researchers.[103] However, what should be remembered is that the *way* in which a trial takes place can influence the outcome. Adjustments to its nature may or may not promote justice or fair trials, and (as with most other aspects of the criminal justice system) they often represent a tug of war between crime control and due process principles.

10.7 Sentencing

Whilst the consensus suggests that a sentence is generally defined as 'the imposition by a court of a criminal sanction', Ashworth points out that 'some criminal sanctions are not imposed by courts, and … some non-judicial agencies are able to alter significantly the length and impact of sentence'.[104] We will examine examples of sanctions falling both within and outside the jurisdiction of the courts more fully in **Chapter 13**. For now, we will briefly examine the role of the court in sentencing.

Once a guilty verdict is returned by either a bench of magistrates or a jury, the court will proceed to sentence the defendant. As mentioned above, this may happen within the same hearing as the trial or may take place after an adjournment. A major (and important) difference between sentencing in a magistrates' court and the Crown Court is *who* delivers sentence. In the lower court, magistrates (or a District Judge) are responsible; in the Crown Court, the judge hands down the sentence. As such, magistrates and District Judges decide on both guilt and determine the punishment (ie verdict and sentence), whilst these functions are separated in the Crown Court. Arguably, this is because sentences delivered in the Crown Court are likely to be both more serious and more complex; the weight of this decision (which may be to imprison a defendant, and in the past to execute them) is therefore borne by a professionally trained and experienced judge. Importantly, magistrates and judges generally have a degree of discretion in determining what sentence is appropriate.

Legislation sets upper and lower limits for sentences, which vary depending on the offence. The rationale behind this is to ensure that magistrates and judges do not exercise their discretion to impose either unduly lenient or unduly harsh sentences, and to ensure consistency. By placing clear 'ranges' on the likely sentence for an offence, the law upholds various fundamental principles, such as certainty[105] and proportionality.[106] In some cases, an offence will attract a mandatory sentence (for example, murder results in an automatic custodial life sentence).[107] A judge or magistrate will therefore have no choice about the sentence passed, although he or she will have discretion over the 'tariff' (that is, the minimum term that must be served before an offender is eligible to apply for parole).[108] To assist in exercising their discretion, guidelines are issued by the Sentencing

102 This is made clear in ss 16 and 17, explicitly restricting eligibility to witnesses 'other than the accused'. For a discussion of this issue and attempts to address this gap in relation to intermediary services, see Taggart, T, 'Vulnerable defendants and the HMCTS court appointed intermediary services' (2022) *Crim LR* 6.

103 See, for example, Henderson, E, '"A very valuable tool": Judges, advocates and intermediaries discuss the intermediary system in England and Wales' (2015) 19 *Int J of Ev & P* (3).

104 Ashworth, A, *Sentencing and Criminal Justice* (CUP, 2015), 13.

105 See ECHR, Article 7 and related ECtHR jurisprudence.

106 See ECHR, Article 3 and related ECtHR jurisprudence – a grossly disproportionate punishment may breach Article 3.

107 Murder (Abolition of the Death Penalty) Act 1965, s 1.

108 For example, see CJA 2003, Sch 21 for the guidelines for determining a tariff for a mandatory life sentence.

Council so that magistrates and judges can decide upon the appropriate sentence within the statutory limits. There are a variety of sentence types which will be covered in depth in **Chapter 11**. The primary ones used by the courts are:

- financial penalties (fines);
- community sentences;
- prison (custody) – immediate or suspended.

In 2022, just over 1 million offenders were sentenced in England and Wales (approximately 93% of which sentences were handed down in magistrates' courts).[109] Of these, approximately 790,000 were fined and 64,000 were sentenced to immediate custody, with 65% of Crown Court convictions resulting in custody.[110] It should be noted that all of these figures, to varying degrees, represent decreases on figures from previous years (though the significant larger drop during the height of the Covid-19 pandemic should be taken into account). In subsequent chapters, we consider the argument that over the last three decades, criminal justice and sentencing has taken a 'punitive turn';[111] that is, it has become harsher. Whilst one might argue that a decrease in the above figures contradicts this theory, it is worth remembering that the throughput of criminal justice has decreased across the board. There are, therefore, less people to sentence. It might also be added that statistics are nuanced and must be treated with caution. For example, even if a smaller proportion of people were imprisoned in 2022, these decreases are modest and the average length of custodial sentences has increased.[112]

10.8 Summary

- Before arriving at court, the police will decide whether a charged suspect can be released or detained; if the latter, they will normally appear in court the next day.
- The first appearance at court is one of the most important stages of the criminal process – a defendant will enter a plea and decisions will be made about trial and, possibly, sentence.
- At the end of the first appearance, all defendants (with some exceptions) have a presumption of release on bail; but the court can overturn this and remand in custody.
- Trials are an adversarial battle between the prosecution and defence; magistrates or a jury will deliver a verdict based on the evidence presented.
- Magistrates' court trials are generally short and simple; trials in the Crown Court are longer, more complex and heard by a jury; trials can be modified by the use of special measures.
- Sentencing is the formal announcement of a convicted defendant's punishment, delivered by magistrates and judges.
- Sentences are subject to upper and lower limits, and guidance is issued to assist in determining an appropriate sentence.

109 Ministry of Justice (n 13), Table Q5.1a.

110 *Ibid.*

111 Matthews, R, 'Rethinking penal policy: towards a systems approach' in R Matthews and J Young (eds), *The New Politics of Crime and Punishment* (Willan, 2003), 224.

112 Ministry of Justice (n 13), Table Q5.2c.

chapter 11

Appeals

11.1 Introduction

Appeals are the process by which decisions of courts regarding convictions and sentences can be challenged, either by those convicted of offences or the prosecution. If an appeal is accepted, this implies that an unfair or incorrect verdict was returned by a magistrates' court or jury (perhaps because of a misdirection in relation to the law) or that the sentence imposed was overly lenient or harsh. Broadly, an appeal can relate to the integrity or accuracy of the factual evidence in the case; the fairness of the process involved; the application of the law by the court; or the proportionality of the sentence. Criminal appeals are primarily dealt with through the court-based appellate system, but a limited post-appellate appeal (that is, after the court process has been exhausted) is also available as a form of last resort. The latter is comparatively rare but has led to many significant reversals of convictions over the years.[1] This chapter will examine the forms of appeal available through the criminal court system, as well as the post-appellate system.

11.2 The need for an appeals process

The existence of an appellate system is premised on the notion that the criminal justice system sometimes makes mistakes. Until the early 20th century, there was significant resistance to the idea that such a process was needed for criminal justice; it was felt that the system of jury trial, coupled with some judicial oversight from either the trial court or the High Court, was, in itself, an adequate safeguard.[2] As a 'fail-safe', outside of the court system, there was also the rarely used prerogative of mercy (exercisable by the Home Secretary).[3] After 50 years of debate and attempted legislation, the high-profile miscarriages relating to Edalji and Beck led to the creation of the Court of Criminal Appeal in 1907.[4] This represented formal acceptance of the idea that criminal trials (and their underpinning investigations) could make serious errors, which needed to be open to reconsideration at a senior judicial level. This reform presented a major adjustment to the concept of finality within the criminal justice process. Finality is an important principle in criminal procedure for several reasons. First, finality means certainty, which is important (for moral and practical reasons) to victims, the offender, the public and the court system. Secondly, finality prevents those who wish to avoid justice from manipulating the system by challenging their conviction or sentence

1 Specific examples will be discussed in **Chapter 16**.

2 See Pattenden, R, *English Criminal Appeals: 1844–1994* (Clarendon, 1996), Ch 1.

3 For a concise summary, see Malone, D and Snell, C, 'The Royal Prerogative of Mercy' (*The Law Gazette*, 6 November 2015): www.lawgazette.co.uk/practice-points/the-royal-prerogative-of-mercy/5052062.article (accessed 4 May 2020).

4 See **Chapter 15**.

continuously. Finality therefore means that the number of appeals allowed should be limited, as should the circumstances in which one can appeal against a decision – for example, when there is a question relating to a plain error as to factual guilt, or when there may be such gross procedural impropriety that the reliability of the guilt-determining process is called into question.

Clearly though, limitations on the opportunity to appeal can only be justified if the police and prosecution are effective in screening out innocence at an early stage. Ensuring that people can appeal decisions acknowledges the importance of rectifying errors and thus upholds the moral integrity of the criminal process. The court system is meant to be a model of legitimacy, fairness and reliability – the embodiment of the rule of law. It is therefore arguable that appeals should go beyond simply correcting verdicts which are demonstrably incorrect – they should enforce adherence to the rules of the system. As Packer noted:

> When an appellate court finds it necessary to castigate the conduct of the police, the prosecutor, or the trial court, but fails to reverse a conviction, it simply breeds disrespect for the very standards it is trying to affirm.[5]

In this sense, the principle of finality should not mean that the appeals process is overly restrictive in terms of both opportunities to challenge decisions and the scope of the issues that can be examined. We can therefore observe a tension between crime control and due process imperatives – the former favouring restricted appeals which ensure finality; the latter emphasising extensive individual rights to challenge unfairness.

An appeal effectively questions the validity of an existing decision by a court. It is therefore necessary for any subsequent inquiry into that decision to be considered at a more senior level – not unlike progression of a complaint to 'management' level within a business. An appeal moves consideration of the case up the court hierarchy. In England and Wales, a criminal appeal is possible at all levels of the court structure, up to the Supreme Court. It should be noted that whilst an appeal is possible against both a conviction and a sentence, this chapter will mainly focus on appeals against convictions – but similar rules exist for appeals against sentence.

11.3 Appeals from a magistrates' court

Magistrates' courts are the lowest tier of the criminal court system (see **Chapter 9**). Since they deal primarily with summary offences, magistrates' courts hear the vast majority of criminal trials in this jurisdiction. Three forms of appeal are available:

- against conviction or sentence to the Crown Court;
- by way of case stated to the Divisional Court of the King's Bench Division of the High Court (KBD);
- judicial review.

11.3.1 Appeals against conviction or sentence to the Crown Court

Appeals from a magistrates' court to the Crown Court are governed by the Magistrates' Courts Act (MCA) 1980 and the Criminal Procedure Rules 2020. Section 108(1) of the MCA 1980 states:

5 Packer, H, *The Limits of the Criminal Sanction* (Stanford University Press, 1968), 232.

> A person convicted by a magistrates' court may appeal to the Crown Court … if he pleaded guilty, against his sentence [or] … if he did not [plead guilty], against the conviction or sentence.

On its face, this indicates that defendants who plead guilty in a magistrates' court *cannot* appeal to the Crown Court against their conviction, therefore barring the vast majority of those convicted in the lowest court.[6] However, this is not entirely accurate: a very limited exception to this rule does exist in relation to equivocal guilty pleas. Generally, a guilty plea will be 'unequivocal', that is, 'a clear acknowledgement of guilt'.[7] However, the defendant may enter an equivocal guilty plea, described as a plea which 'does not answer directly or qualifies what purports to be a guilty plea with words suggesting that [the defendant] is really putting forward a defence'.[8] Such situations are generally limited,[9] though they do include guilty pleas entered under duress (for example, due to threats or pressure).[10] To appeal an equivocal guilty plea, the defendant must make a complaint to the Crown Court. If it finds that there is substance to the complaint, the Court must return the case to a magistrates' court for a full trial.[11] This is arguably a concession to due process logic – that when significant uncertainty threatens the integrity of a conviction (particularly in cases of duress when guilt has formally been admitted by the defendant), there should be the possibility of an appeal. In reality, very few of the 276,351 guilty pleas in magistrates courts in 2021/22 would have been 'equivocal', and the courts should resolve any ambiguity before a plea is accepted.[12] Generally, as discussed in **Chapter 5**, an admission of guilt is taken at face value.

An appeal from a magistrates' court to the Crown Court by the defendant is as of right; there is no leave requirement (that is, the defendant does not need permission to lodge an appeal). In contrast, the prosecution does not have a right of appeal under the MCA 1980. A notice of appeal must be lodged by the defendant within 15 days of the conclusion of magistrates' court proceedings; this therefore emphasises swift resolution of the case notwithstanding the automatic right to challenge a conviction or sentence.[13] The actual appeal takes the form of a complete re-hearing of the case in the Crown Court, heard by a professional judge and two magistrates. It is interesting to note that despite it being a *de novo* (fresh) hearing, appeals heard in the Crown Court have been found to be significantly shorter than Crown Court trials. In 2011, the average length of an appeal hearing in the Crown Court was one hour, compared to an indictable-only trial in the Court lasting an average of 19 hours.[14] This might suggest a cursory approach to appeals; however, trials in the Crown Court involving indictable offences are likely to be complex and time-consuming (particularly considering the involvement

6 In 2021/22, the guilty plea rate in magistrates' courts was 76.1% (Crown Prosecution Service (CPS), 'Annual Report and Accounts 2021-22 (HC 487, July 2022), 43: www.cps.gov.uk/sites/default/files/documents/publications/CPS%20Annual%20Report%20and%20Accounts%202021-22_2.pdf (accessed 13 February 2023).

7 Criminal Procedure Rules (CrimPR) 2020, r 24.7(1)(b).

8 Ormerod, D and Perry, D, *Blackstone's Criminal Practice 2023* (OUP, 2022), D22.4.

9 See Taylor, P, *Taylor on Criminal Appeals* (OUP, 2012), [2.65].

10 *Huntingdon Crown Court, ex parte Jordan* [1981] QB 857.

11 *Ibid.*

12 CPS (n 6).

13 CrimPR, r 34.2(2)(b).

14 Ministry of Justice, 'Judicial and court statistics (annual) 2011: Chapter 4, Crown Court' (June 2012), Table 4.18: www.gov.uk/government/statistics/judicial-and-court-statistics-annual (accessed 4 May 2020).

of juries). Legal aid is not automatically granted for an appeal to the Crown Court; it is subject to an interests of justice (merits) test and (since the passage of LASPO 2012) may be subject to a means test depending on the disposable income of the defendant.[15]

11.3.1.1 Limitations

In general, it might be argued that this form of appeal is reasonably generous in terms of its nature and scope. For example, it is an appeal as of right; a full re-hearing takes place rather than a limited review; and funding is available (albeit limited). However, pleading guilty will almost certainly kill the right to appeal against conviction. This rule does not take into account factors which influence guilty pleas, such as being unrepresented in court or at the police station, or receiving poor legal advice.[16] The fact that funding is subject to a merits test (which includes consideration of the seriousness of the offence) and a means test (in some circumstances) places restrictions on the practical ability of all defendants to exercise this right. Indeed, just under 2,000 people were granted legal aid for appeals heard in the Crown Court in 2021/22 – roughly a third of the total number of people who appealed from magistrates' courts in 2021.[17]

The appeal hearing does not involve a jury (which may be seen as a disadvantage) or a legal clerk, who would take the role of assisting unrepresented defendants in magistrates' court trials (important if legal aid is not available).[18] Moreover, should funding be denied, there is no duty solicitor scheme for appeals to the Crown Court; in short, the state will not provide a lawyer to an unrepresented defendant. In terms of decision-making, the Crown Court has a wide power to vary the decision of a magistrates' court or make additional orders (including costs). If a defendant is unsuccessful, the Crown Court can actually increase the sentence. This must fall within magistrates' court sentencing limits, rather than Crown Court sentencing limits (which are much greater), and it does not, in practice, happen often.[19] It might also be noted, from a practical perspective, that a defendant who received a custodial sentence at the original trial may have served it by the time the appeal is actually heard by the Crown Court, thus rendering an appeal merely symbolic.

11.3.1.2 Prevalence

In general, appeals are rare. In 2021, there were approximately 1.1 million summary cases disposed of in magistrates' courts,[20] although it should be borne in mind that the majority will have pleaded guilty, thus excluding them from the appeal process (see n 6). There were 6,018 appeals to the Crown Court; approximately half were against

15 LASPO 2012, ss 17 and 21.

16 See **Chapter 10.**

17 See **11.3.3** and Ministry of Justice, 'Legal aid statistics quarterly: July to September 2022, Legal aid statistics England and Wales tables Jul to Sep 2022 (December 2022), Table 3.2: www.gov.uk/government/statistics/legal-aid-statistics-july-to-september-2022 (accessed 13 February 2023). These figures should be treated with caution; not only do the time periods not directly overlap, but there is no account taken of those defendants who were represented/assisted on an appeal by their trial solicitor. In such cases, legal aid may have been granted for the original trial and therefore, in practice, extended to assisting at the appeal stage.

18 Though, in the Crown Court, the professional judge would adopt the role of protecting/assisting unrepresented defendants; as such, the absence of a clerk is not particularly problematic.

19 Senior Courts Act (SCA) 1981, s 48(4).

20 Including convictions and acquittals. Ministry of Justice, 'Criminal court statistics quarterly: July to September 2022 (tables)' (January 2023), Table M1: www.gov.uk/government/statistics/criminal-court-statistics-quarterly-july-to-september-2022 (accessed 13 February 2023).

conviction and half against sentence, the number of appeals against verdict falling, year on year, at a faster rate.[21] Therefore, less than 1% of summary cases disposed of were appealed – a very small number of challenges to the decision-making of the lower court (especially considering that many will be able to appeal automatically). This might indicate that magistrates' courts deliver reliable justice; alternatively, it might be an indication that there are too many restrictions on the right to appeal (particularly funding). In terms of success, between 2008 and 2012, 41–45% of appeals were allowed by the Crown Court;[22] this peaked in 2019 at 48%, but then stabilised at 45% in 2021.[23] Again, these figures are open to interpretation; they might suggest that most of those who appeal are doing so without merit or that the (formally) unrestricted right to appeal allows a greater number of cases of poor decision-making by magistrates' courts to be uncovered and remedied.

11.3.2 Appeals 'by way of case stated'

The next form of appeal from magistrates' courts is 'by way of case stated' to the KBD, under s 111 of the MCA 1980:

> Any person who was a party to any proceeding before a magistrates' court or is aggrieved by the conviction, order, determination or other proceeding of the court may question the proceeding on the ground that it is wrong in law or is in excess of jurisdiction by applying to the justices composing the court to state a case for the opinion of the High Court on the question of law or jurisdiction involved.

This form of appeal proceeds directly to the KBD and therefore skips the Crown Court entirely. The legislation specifies two grounds:

- a magistrates' court has acted in excess of its jurisdiction (beyond its powers); or
- a magistrates' court was wrong in law

An appeal by way of case stated requires that the magistrates (or District Judge) who convicted or sentenced the defendant provide a statement of their findings of fact and law, and set out questions for the KBD to consider. Such an appeal is limited to legal argument; the KBD does not hear evidence. It is therefore unlike an appeal to the Crown Court, which is a full, fresh hearing. After considering the case, the KBD may reverse, confirm or amend the decision made by a magistrates' court and can also remit it (ie send it back) to a magistrates' court for reconsideration. Unlike appeals to the Crown Court, this form of appeal is available to both the prosecution and defence. Leave is not required as such, but the appellant must apply to a magistrates' court to state its case within 21 days of the decision to convict or sentence. A magistrates' court can refuse to state its case if it considers the appeal to be 'frivolous', although the KBD can overrule this and compel it to do so.[24] Appeals by way of case stated are extremely rare. In 2021, the KBD heard only 24 such appeals from magistrates' courts and allowed 11 (roughly the same success rate as a standard appeal to the Crown Court).[25] This thus provides another method of challenging the conclusions of magistrates' courts, engaging a more senior court and requiring rationalisation of the decisions made by the

---

21 *Ibid* Table C11.

22 *Ibid.*

23 *Ibid.*

24 Magistrates' Courts Act (MCA) 1980, s 111.

25 Ministry of Justice, 'Civil justice statistics quarterly: January to March 2022, Royal Courts of Justice Annual Tables - 2021' (June 2022), Table 5.6: www.gov.uk/government/statistics/civil-justice-statistics-quarterly-january-to-march-2022 (accessed 13 February 2023).

lower court, although its rarity in practice means that it makes a limited contribution to the appellate system.

11.3.3 Judicial review

The final form of appeal available from magistrates' courts is judicial review (JR). Although this is not strictly an appeal, it does fulfil a similar 'checking' function. JR empowers the KBD to review the decision-making process of public bodies (which can include magistrates' courts). There are three grounds available:

- an error of law on the face of the record (which essentially means that a magistrates' court is mistaken in law);
- bias or irrationality in the decision-making process (that is, *Wednesbury* unreasonableness); or
- a breach of natural justice (sometimes known as fundamental unfairness).

Again, JR is available to both the prosecution and defence. Whereas appeal by way of case stated is only available in respect of a 'conviction, order or determination', JR is available in respect of any aspect of magistrates' court proceedings. As such, it provides a more wide-ranging opportunity to challenge its decisions. There are various examples of JR being used to challenge magistrates' court decisions. In *ex parte Polemis,*[26] the unreasonable refusal of a magistrates' court to grant an adjournment to enable the defendant to prepare his case was deemed to be a breach of natural justice because it did not give him a reasonable chance to present his case. In *ex parte Goonatilleke,*[27] the prosecution failed to notify the defendant that a key prosecution witness had a previous conviction for wasting police time, arising out of a false allegation of theft – and in this case the defendant was accused of theft by shoplifting. This was deemed a breach of natural justice because the information was vital and the defendant was entitled to it. In *ex parte Hawthorn,*[28] the police failed to tell the defendant about two witnesses whose statements would help him; this denied the defendant a fair trial and was, again, a breach of natural justice. It should be noted though that remedies via JR are discretionary; the KBD may therefore agree with the applicant's argument but decline to remedy the issue. Since the court is not bound to correct errors or unfairness, this suggests a rather restrictive approach to appeal; for example, the court may decide that the broader public interest overrides the need to remedy the breach of an individual's rights.

11.4 Appeals from the Crown Court

We now move on to consider appeals from the Crown Court – therefore dealing with more serious offences. Section 1(1) of the Criminal Appeal Act (CAA) 1968 states:

> A person convicted of an offence on indictment may appeal to the Court of Appeal against his conviction.

Section 9(1) states:

> A person who has been convicted of an offence on indictment may appeal to the Court of Appeal against any sentence (not being a sentence fixed by law) passed

26 [1974] 1 WLR 1371.

27 [1986] QB 1.

28 [1979] 1 All ER 209.

on him for the offence, whether passed on his conviction or in subsequent proceedings.

Importantly, appeal against conviction or sentence is available regardless of plea. Unlike in magistrates' courts, leave to appeal must be granted: either by the Court of Appeal or by the trial judge deeming the case fit for appeal. If leave is granted, the case proceeds directly to the senior court, bypassing the KBD. According to s 28 of the Senior Courts Act (SCA) 1981, appeal by way of case stated is available in respect of decisions of the Crown Court;[29] but this is not applicable to trial on indictment.[30] This therefore rules out the majority of cases in the Crown Court; in practice, appeal by way of case stated from the Crown Court is very rare.

11.4.1 'Fit for appeal'

The generally accepted test to determine whether a case is 'fit for appeal' is that an appeal must be 'reasonably arguable' for leave to be granted.[31] An application can be on a question of law, a question of fact, or a mixed question of law and fact. Generally, an application is heard by one High Court judge (exercising the powers of the Court of Appeal) rather than the full Court of Appeal. A theoretical criticism of this arrangement would suggest that a single judge may not make as thorough a decision as the full court, being only one (less senior) judge with one perspective. Malleson found that High Court judges normally considered applications to appeal from the Crown Court in their spare time, taking only a matter of minutes to decide.[32] Should the application to appeal be refused and the applicant want more robust consideration, they can request that the hearing be renewed to the full Court of Appeal; however, a disincentive to do so exists in the form of the 'loss of time' rule. This means:

> If leave to appeal is refused by the full court, any time spent in custody between the commencement of the application and the refusal will not count as 'time served' towards the appellant's sentence.[33]

This therefore has the effect of lengthening the applicant's sentence if their application to appeal fails. According to *Hart*,[34] the rule applies even if it is based on legal advice; this places the onus on lawyers to carefully consider whether to renew an application to the full court.

11.4.2 Prevalence

The Crown Court deals with a much lower volume of cases than magistrates' courts, and appeals from the Crown Court are comparatively rare. They are, however, more serious due to the nature of the offences being dealt with. Below are figures demonstrating the rarity of appeals from the higher trial court:[35]

- In 2021, approximately 96,000 cases were disposed of by the Crown Court.[36]

29 That is, the Crown Court must provide a statement of its findings to the QBD to review.

30 SCA 1981, s 28(2).

31 As outlined by Lord Justice Auld in his review of the criminal courts in 2001 (Lord Justice Auld, 'Review of the Criminal Courts of England and Wales' (The Auld Review) (Ministry of Justice, September 2001).

32 Malleson, K, 'Decision-making in the Court of Appeal: the burden of proof in an inquisitorial process' (1997) 1 *Int J of E & P* (4).

33 CAA 1968, ss 29 and 31.

34 [2006] EWCA Crim 3239.

35 Again, caution should be exercised, partly because the timeframes for these figures do not directly overlap. These figures are, however, illustrative of how rare appeals are.

36 Ministry of Justice (n 20), Table C1.

- 3,940 applications for leave to appeal were received by the Court of Appeal (22% against conviction; 78% against sentence): a reduction of 14% on 2019.[37]
- 2,671 of these were considered by a single judge, with 21% granted leave to appeal;[38] 592 were renewed to the full Court of Appeal, with 32% of these granted leave.[39]
- In 2021, the Court of Appeal heard 906 appeals – a significant decrease in the wake of the Covid-19 pandemic and its impact on the criminal court – with roughly 60% being successful.[40]

As such, a defendant convicted or sentenced in the Crown Court has less than a 1% chance of a successful appeal in the Court of Appeal; although those who make it through this extensive filtering process are more likely than not to be successful. It is thus open to debate as to whether these figures suggest that Crown Court justice is of a very high quality or whether the means and mechanisms are simply not in place to expose poor decisions.

11.4.3 Unsafe convictions

For appeals against conviction in the Crown Court, there is only one ground of appeal available: that the conviction was 'unsafe', as specified by s 2(1)(a) of CAA 1968 (as amended by the Criminal Appeal Act 1995). We might ask what this means; there are two basic potential interpretations:

- A conviction should only be considered 'unsafe' if it is factually unreliable. Procedural errors or malpractice associated with the investigation, prosecution or trial that do not affect the *reliability* of the result should not render the verdict unsafe.
- A conviction should be considered 'unsafe' if it results from unfairness, for example being secured through unfair or unlawful means. This should be the case regardless of the factual accuracy of conviction.

The reality is somewhere between these two interpretations. The meaning of unsafe – and what it covers – has been the subject of significant debate in the courts over the last half century. Prior to the amendments of the 1995 Act, the wording of s 2(1)(a) stated that a conviction had to be 'unsafe or unsatisfactory' for an appeal to be successful.[41] Clearly, this implied a significantly wider meaning than simply 'unsafe'. Case law on appeals suggested that problems with the process (regardless of the accuracy of the result) might therefore allow a conviction to be quashed on appeal. In the leading case of *Cooper*,[42] Lord Widgery described 'unsafe and unsatisfactory' as meaning the following:

> [T]he court must in the end ask itself a subjective question, whether we are content to let the matter stand as it is, or whether there is not some lurking doubt in our minds which makes us wonder whether an injustice has been done. This is a reaction which may not be based strictly on the evidence as such; it is a reaction which can be produced by the general feel of the case as the court experiences it.[43]

37 Ministry of Justice (n 25), Table 2.1. Note, there was a reduction of more than a quarter in 2020, which can partly be explained by the Covid-19 pandemic.
38 *Ibid.*
39 *Ibid.*
40 *Ibid* Table 3.8.
41 CAA 1968.
42 [1969] 1 QB 267.
43 *Ibid* 271 *per* Widgery LJ.

Whilst the law has since been amended (and 'unsatisfactory' removed), the 'lurking doubt' rule continues to be referenced by the courts, suggesting that it still has relevance when the court decides whether a conviction is unsafe. However, subsequent case law has significantly complicated matters.

The Court of Appeal has taken a fairly narrow view of when a conviction will be 'unsafe'. In *Chalkley and Jeffries,*[44] the defendant pleaded guilty after an incorrect ruling on the admissibility of evidence by the trial judge. The Court of Appeal concluded that a reliable verdict of guilty could not be overturned, however unfair the trial process might have been:

> The fact that an erroneous ruling of law as to admissibility of certain prosecution evidence drives a defendant to plead guilty because it makes the case against him factually overwhelming will not do [for an appeal].
>
> Neither the misconduct of the prosecution, nor the fact that there had been a failure to observe some general notion of 'fair play', are in themselves reasons for quashing a conviction ... '[U]nsafe' ... is clearly intended to refer to the correctness of the conviction.[45]

In *Pope,*[46] the court appeared to dismiss the continuing applicability of the much wider 'lurking doubt' rule from *Cooper*:

> If ... there is a case to answer and, after proper directions, the jury has convicted, it is not open to the court [of appeal] to set aside the verdict on the basis of some collective, subjective judicial hunch that the conviction is or may be unsafe.[47]

This also suggests a disinclination to overturn jury verdicts, a frequent theme in (and source of criticism of) the Court of Appeal's approach to appeals.[48] In contrast, in *Mullen,*[49] the Court of Appeal took a wider view. The defendant had been forcibly and unlawfully extradited to England and Wales. The court felt that *Chalkley* 'cannot ... properly be regarded as having concluded the matter', asserting:[50]

> [F]or a conviction to be safe, it must be lawful; and if it results from a trial which should never have taken place, it can hardly be regarded as safe.[51]

This therefore embraced a broader definition of unsafe – not simply where verdicts are unreliable, but where the process has been unfair.

The Court of Appeal has continued to provide contradictory messages on the meaning of unsafe, particularly in the post-Human Rights Act 1998 era. In *Davis, Johnson and Rowe,*[52] the court explicitly rejected the *Chalkley* approach in favour of the *Mullen* approach, saying:

> [A] conviction may be unsafe even where there is no doubt about guilt but the trial process has been 'vitiated by serious unfairness or significant legal misdirection'.[53]

---

44 [1998] QB 848.

45 *Ibid* 861 and 869.

46 [2012] EWCA Crim 2241.

47 *Ibid* [14].

48 See Viscount Runciman, 'Report of the Royal Commission on Criminal Justice' (The Runciman Commission) (HMSO, 1993); Malleson, K, 'Appeals Against Conviction and the Principle of Finality' (1994) 21 *J of Law and Society*.

49 [2000] QB 520.

50 *Ibid* 539.

51 *Ibid* 540.

52 [2001] 1 Cr App R 8.

53 *Ibid* 132.

But it added:

> We reject … [the] contention that a finding of a breach of Article 6(1) … leads inexorably to the quashing of the conviction.[54]

Thus, this implies that a breach of the right to a fair trial does not, in itself, mean that a conviction is unsafe. Yet, in *Togher*, the court stated:

> If a defendant has been denied a fair trial it will almost be inevitable that the conviction will be regarded as unsafe.[55]

Furthermore, in *A (No 2)*,[56] the court said that 'it is well established that the guarantee of a fair trial under Article 6 is absolute: a conviction obtained in breach of it cannot stand'.[57] However, since then the Court of Appeal has reiterated the implication in cases like *Rowe and Pope* that a breach of Article 6 does not necessarily lead to a conviction being quashed; in short, a breach does not equal 'unsafe'.[58]

Therefore, these themes of contradiction and tension between the narrow definition of unsafe and commitment to modern human rights law may or may not be resolved. To summarise:

- The Court of Appeal has taken an inconsistent and contradictory approach to the meaning of 'unsafe', although procedural issues can still lead to a conviction being quashed.
- 'Lurking doubt' appears to still be relevant, but in exceptional cases with a high threshold to show it.
- Breach of Article 6 may mean that the conviction was unsafe, but not inevitably. This raises questions as to whether the right to a fair trial is indeed absolute.

In defining 'unsafe', the Court of Appeal has at times swung between crime control and due process approaches. However, it appears to generally favour a more restrictive, narrow interpretation of 'unsafe', underpinned by a disinclination to overturn jury verdicts. This approach impacts on the work of the Criminal Cases Review Commission (see **11.6** below). A recent example is the case of *Charlton and Ali*,[59] where the court concluded that general police misconduct in an investigation did not necessarily render all resulting convictions unsafe.

11.4.4 Fresh evidence

Generally, evidence is not adduced in appeals against Crown Court decisions, as there is no re-hearing (as is the case for appeals from magistrates' courts). However, under s 23 of the CAA 1968 (as amended), 'fresh evidence' – that is, evidence not adduced at the original trial – may be heard if:

- it is capable of belief;
- it may afford any ground for allowing the appeal;
- it would have been admissible at the trial; and
- there is a reasonable explanation why it was not adduced at trial.

In circumstances where fresh evidence can be introduced on appeal, the Court of Appeal must decide whether a conviction is therefore unsafe. The case of *Ahmed*

54 *Ibid* 135.
55 [2001] 3 All ER 463.
56 [2002] 1 AC 45.
57 *Ibid* 65.
58 *Lewis* [2005] EWCA Crim 859.
59 [2016] EWCA Crim52.

provides guidance on this.[60] The Court of Appeal must ask whether the fresh evidence causes it to doubt the safety of the verdict; the primary question is for the Court of Appeal itself, rather than the effect the fresh evidence would have had on a jury. So, the Court of Appeal is not stepping into the jury's shoes – it is deciding for itself whether the fresh evidence leads to an unsafe conviction.

11.4.5 Result of appeals from the Crown Court to the Court of Appeal

If an appeal is upheld, the Court of Appeal can either:

- quash the conviction (under s 1 of the CAA 1968);
- order a retrial if it is in the interests of justice (under s 7); or
- substitute a conviction for an alternative offence (under s 3).

If the appeal is unsuccessful, the appellant (which can be either the defence or prosecution) can appeal to the Supreme Court (with the leave of either the Court of Appeal or the Supreme Court), which is, in practice, very rare. The Court of Appeal must certify that the case raises a point of law of general public importance, and either the Court of Appeal or Supreme Court believes that it should be considered by the higher court.[61] If leave to appeal to the Supreme Court is refused, there is no further right of appeal. In *Pinfold*,[62] the Court of Appeal confirmed that it would only permit a person to appeal once. In justifying its view, the court said:

> [T]here is nothing on the face of the Criminal Appeal Act 1968 which says in terms that one appeal is all that an appellant is allowed. But in the view of this court, one must read these provisions against the background of the fact that it is in the interests of the public in general that there should be a limit or a finality to legal proceedings.[63]

Lord Justice Auld confirmed the importance of this principle in *Poole and Mills*,[64] stating that the court must keep in mind

> alongside safety of convictions, the public and private interests in an orderly, as well as just, system that secures finality of decisions.[65]

These cases uphold the principle of finality discussed earlier. This view was endorsed by the Runciman Commission in 1993:

> We consider that with the need for finality and the existence of the alternative route to reopening a case via a reference to the Home Secretary, the present position is correct and should be retained.[66]

Thus a second appeal is not permitted even if the matter to be raised at a second appeal would be different to that raised at the first appeal, and even if fresh evidence has come to light. The only way of returning a case to the Court of Appeal for reconsideration is for it to be considered at the post-appellate stage: the 'alternative route' described by the Runciman Commission (see **11.6** below).

---

60 [2010] EWCA Crim 2899.

61 CAA 1968, s 33.

62 [1988] QB 462.

63 *Ibid* 464.

64 [2003] EWCA Crim 1753.

65 *Ibid* [61].

66 Runciman (n 48); see also Malleson (n 48) for more on finality.

11.5 Appeals to the Supreme Court

As mentioned above, the prosecution or defendant can appeal to the Supreme Court from a decision of the Court of Appeal, subject to leave being granted by either court for the reasons above. In addition, there is a similar right of appeal from the KBD – known as a 'leapfrog' appeal.[67] Both forms of appeal are very rare. In practice, the Supreme Court plays a very limited role in criminal cases; for example, in 2021/2022, the Supreme Court heard only four criminal appeals.[68] If the Supreme Court rejects permission to appeal or the appeal itself, the appellate system is exhausted, leaving only the post-appellate system available as a means of correcting a miscarriage of justice.

11.6 The post-appellate system

11.6.1 Introduction

The post-appellate system refers to appeals considered by a non-judicial body after a person has exhausted the internal appeal process of the courts. At the time of the Runciman Commission report, a reference to the Home Secretary was the only post-appellate method of appealing a decision. Whilst the Commission felt that one appeal to the Court of Appeal alongside the post-appellate structure was enough, it did recommended a change in the nature of the post-appellate system. Since 1995, this has been undertaken by the Criminal Cases Review Commission (CCRC). The post-appellate process might be described as the 'fail-safe element in the system'.[69]

11.6.2 The Criminal Cases Review Commission (CCRC)

The Government acted on the Runciman Commission's recommendation by establishing the Criminal Cases Review Commission (CCRC) under s 8(1) of the CAA 1995, with the body operating from March 1997. The statute specified several requirements for the CCRC. It must consist of not fewer than 11 members, to be appointed by the King on the recommendation of the Prime Minister.[70] At least one-third must be legally qualified, and two-thirds must have knowledge or experience of the criminal justice system.[71] To emphasise independence, the CCRC is not to be 'regarded as the servant or agent of the Crown'.[72]

The CCRC may refer a case to the Court of Appeal in respect of a conviction in the Crown Court, or a conviction or sentence in a magistrates' court. The CCRC cannot make a reference unless it 'considers that there is a real possibility that the conviction, verdict, finding or sentence would not be upheld if a reference were to be made'.[73] For a

67 Supreme Court of the United Kingdom, 'Practice Direction 1' (2015), 1.2.17: www. supremecourt.uk/procedures/practice-direction-01.html (accessed 4 May 2020); and The Supreme Court of the United Kingdom, 'Practice Direction 3' (2016), 3.6.1: www.supremecourt.uk/procedures/ practice-direction-03.html#06 (accessed 4 May 2020).

68 Supreme Court of the United Kingdom, 'The Supreme Court and Judicial Committee of the Privy Council Annual Report and Accounts 2021-2022' (HC 499, July 2022), 101: https://assets.publishing.service.gov.uk/government/uploads/system/uploads/attachment_data/file/1089485/supreme-court-jcpc-annual-report-accounts-2021-22.pdf (accessed 23 February 2023).

69 Zander, M, 'The Criminal Cases Review Commission, the Court of Appeal and Jury Decisions — A Better Way Forward' (2015) 179 *Criminal Law and Justice Weekly*, 75.

70 CAA 1995, s 8(3) and (4).

71 *Ibid* s 8(5) and (6).

72 *Ibid* s 8(2).

73 *Ibid* s 13(1)(a).

conviction, verdict or finding, this must be 'because of an argument, or evidence, not raised in the proceedings which led to it or on any appeal or application for leave to appeal against it'.[74] For a sentence, this must be 'because of an argument on a point of law, or information, not so raised'.[75] In addition to the above criteria, an appeal must have already been determined (that is, gone as far as it can through the appellate system) or leave to appeal must have been refused,[76] unless 'exceptional circumstances' apply (known as 'no appeal' cases).[77] Thus, normally, the CCRC provides a mechanism for further appeals only when there is something new and legally relevant to say, and the appeals process has been exhausted. Without fresh evidence or new legal argument, an applicant is almost doomed to fail. Applications which simply assert that the jury 'got it wrong' make little headway, particularly in light of the general unwillingness of the appellate courts to 'usurp' juries by overturning their decisions.[78] Since its creation,approximately 40% of applications to the CCRC have been 'no appeal' cases (in short, claiming to involve 'exceptional circumstances'), most of which, the CCRC asserts, should have pursued a standard appeal.[79]

In 2018, Hodgson et al found that 70% of such cases had no 'exceptional circumstances' and were not reviewed (beyond initial screening) by the CCRC.[80] In 2018/19, the CCRC received 493 'no appeal' applications, and pursued a review of only 22% of them.[81] The CCRC has invoked the 'exceptional circumstances' power to refer a 'no appeal' case rarely, again due to a desire to avoid supplanting established processes (in this case, normal routes of appeal via the courts).[82] If the CCRC did otherwise, it would likely encourage unmeritorious challenges to convictions and sentences without pursuing an appeal in the normal way described in this chapter, therefore bypassing proper scrutiny by the courts. The referral rate for such cases was 2.2% in 2010, dropping to 1.2% by 2016; between 2014 and 2018, the CCRC referred only eight 'no appeal' cases.[83] As such, Hodgson et al argue that the CCRC has, in the absence of a legislative definition, taken an increasingly narrow approach to defining and accepting 'exceptional circumstances'.[84]

11.6.2.1 'A real possibility'

In *ex parte Pearson*,[85] the court considered what the role of the CCRC was in examining whether there was a 'real possibility' that a conviction would be quashed. It concluded that the Commission's task is to predict what decision the Court of Appeal

74 *Ibid* s 13(1)(b)(i).

75 *Ibid* s 13(1)(b)(ii).

76 *Ibid* s 13(1)(c).

77 *Ibid* s 13(2); and see Criminal Cases Review Commission, 'Exceptional Circumstances in "No Appeal" cases: Casework Policy' (April 2020), 2: https://s3-eu-west-2.amazonaws.com/ccrc-prod-storage-1jdn5d1f6iq1l/uploads/2020/04/EXCEPTIONAL-CIRCUMSTANCES.pdf (accessed 4 May 2020).

78 See *Pendleton* [2001] UKHL 66, [12]; and Malleson (n 48).

79 Criminal Cases Review Commission, 'Annual Report and Accounts 2018/19' (HMSO, HC2438, July 2019), 10: https://s3-eu-west-2.amazonaws.com/ccrc-prod-storage-1jdn5d1f6iq1l/uploads/2019/07/CCRC-Annual-Report-and-Accounts-2018-19_Web-Accessible.pdf (accessed 4 May 2020).

80 Hodgson, J, Horne, J and Soubise, L, 'The Criminal Cases Review Commission: Last resort or first appeal?' (Warwick Law School, October 2018), 4: https://warwick.ac.uk/fac/soc/law/research/centres/cjc/news/65867_law_a4_report_1.pdf (accessed 4 May 2020).

81 CCRC (n 79), 11.

82 CCRC (n 77), 2.

83 Hodgson et al (n 80), 21.

84 *Ibid* 5.

85 [1999] 3 All ER 498.

would make as to whether a conviction was unsafe. As such, the CCRC must 'step into the shoes' of the Court of Appeal in determining the prospect of success. The Commission is therefore obliged to consider the Court of Appeal's generally narrow interpretation of its own power to overturn jury decisions (as suggested by Zander). That being said, the Lord Chief Justice commented that a 'real possibility' must be

> more than an outside chance or a bare possibility, but which may be less than a probability or a likelihood or a racing certainty.

This suggests that the CCRC should not take too restrictive an approach and should, instead, tolerate a higher proportion of failed cases, which would ultimately mean that many more miscarriages are remedied. More radically, the Justice Committee recommended that the Law Commission review the 'real possibility' test, by examining 'the benefits and dangers of a statutory change'.[86] Whilst no action has been taken on this yet, it does highlight the underlying and long-running concern that the current test is not fit for purpose (implying that the Court of Appeal's approach to referrals is not satisfactory).

11.6.2.2 CCRC casework, applications and referrals

The CCRC assembles primary materials, obtains fresh evidence and expert advice, and interviews witnesses. It can compel public bodies (and since 2016, private bodies and individuals) to provide documents and materials to the Commission to help in its investigations.[87] In practice, the CCRC normally carries out its own investigations using its own staff. When investigations are conducted on behalf of the CCRC, they are generally carried out by the police. The CCRC can direct a chief officer of a police force to appoint a person from their own force or another force to carry out the investigation.

After being established, the CCRC saw an initial surge in applications: 1,105 in 1997/98; 1,035 in 1998/99; and 774 in 1999/2000.[88] By 2022, the CCRC had received 29,569 applications (including 279 inherited from the Home Office in 1997).[89] Of these, 28,679 had been completed, with 809 referred to the Court of Appeal.[90] This equates to a referral rate of 2.8%; therefore, the chances of an applicant to the CCRC having their case referred back to the Court of Appeal is about 1 in 37. Between 1999-2015/16, the CCRC had a referral rate of 3.43%, suggesting that the chances of success are becoming increasingly slim.[91] However, the CCRC has shown itself to be more ready to refer cases than the previous system run by the Home Office. Of the 809 cases referred by 2022, 782 cases had been heard by the Court of Appeal; of these, 548 appeals had been

86 Justice Committee, *Justice – Twelfth Report: Criminal Cases Review Commission* (HC 850, 25 March 2015), Conclusions and Recommendations, [5]: https://publications.parliament.uk/pa/cm201415/cmselect/cmjust/850/85006.htm (accessed 4 May 2020).

87 CAA 1995, ss 17 and 18A (the latter added by the Criminal Cases Review Commission (Information) Act 2016).

88 Criminal Cases Review Commission (CCRC), 'Annual Report 1999/2000' (August 2000), 17: http://webarchive.nationalarchives.gov.uk/20070705132612/http://www.ccrc.gov.uk/CCRC_Uploads/report1999_2000.pdf (accessed 4 May 2020).

89 Criminal Cases Review Commission, 'Facts and Figures': https://ccrc.gov.uk/facts-figures/ (accessed 23 February 2023).

90 *Ibid.*

91 Westminster Commission on Miscarriages of Justice, 'In the interests of justice: an inquiry into the Criminal Cases Review Commission' (March 2021), 12: https://appgmiscarriagesofjustice.files.wordpress.com/2021/03/westminster-commission-on-miscarriages-of-justice-in-the-interests-of-justice.pdf (accessed 23 February 2023).

allowed – a success rate of roughly 70%, which has remained consistent for a number of years.[92]

11.6.2.3 Issues with the CCRC

Since its creation, concerns have been expressed about the CCRC, reflecting some of the issues that existed within the old system of post-appellate challenge.[93]

Independence

- Commissioners on the CCRC generally represent the 'establishment' – that is, people drawn from disciplines of authority, power or wealth.[94]
- The selection procedure for appointments to the CCRC is run by the Home Office, raising questions about the independence of those chosen to serve.
- All external investigating officers between the years 1997 and 2006 were police officers, with a tendency to draw them from the original prosecuting police force related to the appeal in question.[95]

Referral rates

- Whilst the success rate of references has been consistently high, this might suggest that the CCRC refers mostly cases with a high likelihood of success.
- This arguably sets a prohibitive threshold which excludes cases that may be more likely than not to succeed – but which are not 'safe bets'.
- Sanders et al argue that the success rate should be allowed to fall, which would allow more miscarriages of justice to be discovered and remedied. To illustrate, currently, approximately seven out of 10 referrals are successful (a 70% success rate). If the number of referrals rose from 10 to 30, it is almost certain that a greater *number* (as opposed to proportion) would be successful. For example, if 15 out of 30 referrals were successful, the success rate would drop to 50%, but the overall number of miscarriages remedied would more than double.

Resources

- As of 2022, the CCRC has 99 staff, including Commissioners (which has reduced from an initial 16 to 12).[96] Funding is a critical issue for the CCRC. In 2015, CCRC Chair Richard Foster told the Justice Committee that, 'for every £10 that my predecessor had to spend on a case a decade ago, I have £4 today', which amounted to 'the biggest cut that has taken place anywhere in the criminal justice system'.[97]

---

92 CCRC (n 89).

93 For extensive review of these, see Welsh, L, Skinns, L and Sanders, A, *Sanders & Young's Criminal Justice* (OUP, 2021).Welsh, L, Skinns, L and Sanders, A, *Sanders & Young's Criminal Justice* (OUP, 2021); and Naughton, M (ed), *The Criminal Cases Review Commission: Hope for the Innocent?* (Palgrave Macmillan, 2012).

94 The 13 current Commissioners include lawyers (only two of whom work in criminal defence), civil servants, a professional judge, and a member of the Sentencing Council.

95 Welsh et al (n 93).

96 As of October 2022. The statutory minimum number of 'members' of the Commission is 11, though neither the statute nor the CCRC itself make it clear whether the 'Commission' consists only of the 'Commissioners' or whether members of the Commission's board (such as the Chief Executive, directors and non-executive directors) are counted for this purpose. As such, it is unclear whether (at present) the CCRC actually has the statutory minimum number of members or not.

97 Justice Committee (n 86), Ch 3, [31].

- Under-resourcing had led to a chronic problem of lengthy delays for applicants, though this has improved in recent years. In 2009, it was reported that 90% of applicants had to wait 18 months for a decision.[98] Whilst caseload appears to have increased substantially in recent years (up 74% between 2010 and 2013),[99] the CCRC appears to have improved its throughput. For example, as of December 2022, roughly 80% of applications progressed through to completion (either rejection or referral back to the Court of Appeal) within 12 months.[100] However, the number of long-running cases (over two years) has been a persistent problem for the CCRC. Its target in this regard is for only 5% of cases to be long-running cases; this peaked at nearly 12% in 2020, reducing to 5.4% by December 2022.[101]

Relationship with the Court of Appeal

- The courts have traditionally resisted acceptance of police malpractice, often central to CCRC referrals. In *McIlkenny v Chief Constable of the West Midlands Police Force*,[102] the Birmingham Six brought a civil action for assault against the police. Lord Denning struck out the action since it would mean accepting that 'the police were guilty of perjury, that they were guilty of violence and threats, and the confessions were involuntary', which was an 'appalling vista'.
- Such striking levels of denial about miscarriages of justice gradually changed; by the time the CCRC was created, the Court of Appeal regarded such extra-judicial scrutiny as 'necessary and welcome' and an important 'safety net'.[103] However, Nobles and Schiff argue that the threat posed by the CCRC as a competing review body leads to inevitable tension, which 'can be expected on occasions to result in criticism, and even public rebuke, from the Court of Appeal'.[104]
- In determining what to refer, the CCRC is, in some ways, in an impossible position; in addition to managing this delicate relationship, it must attempt to predict and follow the inconsistent decision-making of the Court of Appeal.[105]

Legal representation and funding

- Extremely limited legal aid is available for applications to the CCRC; this potentially limits the proportion of represented applicants and therefore the number of well-drafted, persuasive applications.
- In the first year, only 10% of applicants were helped by lawyers, usually acting *pro bono*.[106]
- Lawyers are largely unwilling to take on applications to the CCRC because 'miscarriage work is regarded by many as at the bottom of the pile, purely because of finances'.[107]

---

98 Welsh et al (n 93).

99 Justice Committee (n 86), Ch 3, [31].

100 CCRC (n 89).

101 *Ibid.*

102 [1980] 2 All ER 227.

103 *Mattan* (1998) *The Times*, 5 March; *R (Nunn) v Chief Constable of Suffolk* [2014] UKSC 37, [39].

104 Nobles, R and Schiff, D, 'The Criminal Cases Review Commission: establishing a workable relationship with the Court of Appeal' (2005) *Crim LR*, 189. See also Elks, L, *Righting Miscarriages of Justice? Ten Years of the Criminal Cases Review Commission* (Justice, 2008) which describes how the Court of Appeal had already 'wearied' of CCRC referrals after a decade of its operation.

105 Heaton, S, 'The CCRC – is it fit for purpose?' (2015) *Arch Rev* (5), 9.

106 CCRC, 'Annual Report 1997–1998' (TSO, 2005), 18.

107 Former CCRC Commissioner Ewen Smith in Arkinstall, J, 'Unappealing Work: The Practical Difficulties Facing Solicitors Engaged in Criminal Appeal Cases' (2004) 1 *Justice Journal* (2), 101.

- The CCRC asserted that 62% of applicants were legally represented between 2003 and 2005.[108]
- The CCRC estimated that this had dropped to between 40–50% by 2006, but independent research by Hodgson and Horne suggested an even lower figure of 33% for the period 2001-07.[109]
- Vogler et al found that representation 'declined to an average of 23% in the period 2012–2014, and to as low as 10% towards the end of that period'.[110]

11.6.2.4 The CCRC: some conclusions

The CCRC represents an important mechanism for uncovering miscarriages of justice. Prosecution cases that might appear to be watertight at trial and on appeal may, in fact, be very leaky. An example is the case of Jonathan Embleton. After discovering a serious failure to disclose evidence to the defence, the CCRC referred his case back to the Court of Appeal. The Court concluded that the new information discredited a witness whose evidence was 'pivotal ... in shoring up the otherwise weak case against him' and quashed his conviction for murder.[111]

A problem is that courts are not dealing with moral certainties and absolute truth; rather they are dealing with degrees of proof. As Sanders et al say:

> [T]he realities of case construction by police and prosecution agencies strengthens the argument for always leaving open the possibility of a further challenge to the factual basis for a conviction.[112]

Overall, there are some mixed opinions on the success of the CCRC as a replacement for the Home Secretary's reference. In evidence to the Justice Committee, the Court of Appeal commented that 'the current functions and form of the CCRC work well and have led to a valuable working relationship'.[113] Zander argued that the CCRC is an 'efficient, competent and responsible body', whilst the Justice Committee concluded that it was 'performing its functions reasonably well' and 'remains as necessary a body now as when it was set up'.[114] The CCRC has argued that it has brought more miscarriages to light and provides a crucial confidence-boost for the criminal justice system. Statistics indicate that many more cases have been referred back to the courts since the Commission was established (an average of 30 per year).[115]

However, many commentators are critical of the CCRC. Sanders et al argue that the CCRC primarily focuses on high-profile, long sentence cases rather than 'less

---

108 CCRC, 'Annual Report and Accounts 2004–2005' (TSO, 2005), 38.

109 Hodgson, J and Horne, J, 'The extent and impact of legal representation on applications to the Criminal Cases Review Commission (CCRC)' (University of Warwick, 2009), 11. This research is now several years out of date; however, academics at the University of Sussex are currently undertaking research into the effect of the recent legal aid reforms on representation for applicants to the CCRC (as yet to be published).

110 Vogler, R, Welsh, L, Clarke, A, Wiedlitzka, S and McDonell, L, 'The Criminal Cases Review Commission: Legal Aid and Legal Representatives' (March 2021), 4: https://legalaidandrepresentatives.files.wordpress.com/2021/05/210420_ccrc_finalreport-2.pdf (accessed 23 February 2023).

111 *Embleton* [2016] EWCA Crim 1968, [53].

112 Welsh et al (n 93).

113 Justice Committee, 'Inquiry: Criminal Cases Review Commission, Written evidence from the Court of Appeal Criminal Division (CCR 22)' (December 2014): http://data.parliament.uk/writtenevidence/committeeevidence.svc/evidencedocument/justice-committee/criminal-cases-review-commission/written/16091.html (accessed 4 May 2020).

114 Zander (n 69); Justice Committee (n 86), Conclusions and Recommendations.

115 CCRC (n 89) – 692 references in 23 years.

glamorous' miscarriages (eg summary convictions).[116] Indeed, it has been highlighted that the power to refer summary cases is little used, with '[a]n applicant convicted in the Crown Court ... nearly twice as likely to succeed in achieving referral as an applicant convicted by magistrates'.[117] Nobles and Schiff have suggested that reform of the post-appellate system had been designed to 'mollify public opinion' rather than to solve underlying problems.[118] In 2015, investigative journalist Bob Woffinden described the CCRC as 'an almost complete failure', as cases 'disappeared into a black hole and were not heard about for years'.[119] He suggested that this had 'disengaged' the press from the issue of wrongful convictions, in contrast to the late 1980s and early 1990s:

> The media have become uninterested in publishing reports about miscarriages of justice, primarily because they ... would be followed not by administrative action but, seemingly, by inertia. Cases now spend years hidden from public scrutiny while they are examined by the CCRC.[120]

His damning conclusion was that the current existence of the CCRC 'institutionalises miscarriages of justice' by giving 'the impression that we are content to continue with a fallible criminal trial system because we have the semblance of a process offering ex post facto rectification'.[121] The Justice Committee appeared to echo this, stating that '[t]he existence of the CCRC is not enough in and of itself'.[122] Marking its 20th anniversary, campaigner Paul May concluded that the CCRC was 'partly excellent and partly abysmal', held back primarily by underfunding and the attitude of the Court of Appeal.[123] It can perhaps be concluded that the CCRC is 'far from perfect but it represents a major improvement over its lamentable predecessor'.[124]

11.7 Summary

- Courts make mistakes – hence the need for a system of appeals.
- There are three forms of appeal from magistrates' courts: as of right against conviction or sentence; by way of case stated; and judicial review.
- Appeal from the Crown Court is only available if leave is granted; an appeal against conviction will only be allowed if the conviction is considered 'unsafe'.
- Appeals are rare and the success rate is moderate.
- The courts have significant flexibility in both granting appeals and remedying miscarriages.
- The meaning of 'unsafe' has been subject to inconsistent interpretation by the Court of Appeal.

---

116 Welsh et al (n 93).

117 Kerrigan, K, 'Miscarriage of justice in the magistrates' court: the forgotten power of the Criminal Cases Review Commission' (2006) *Crim LR*, 127.

118 Welsh et al (n 93), 660.

119 Quoted in Robins, J, 'CCRC suffers deepest cut of entire criminal justice system' (The Justice Gap, March 2015): www.thejusticegap.com/ccrc-suffers-deepest-cut-entire-criminal-justice-system/ (accessed 14 July 2020).

120 Justice Committee, 'Inquiry: Criminal Cases Review Commission, Written evidence from Bob Woffinden (CCR 33)' (December 2014), [33].

121 *Ibid* [36].

122 Justice Committee (n 86), Conclusions and Recommendations, [55].

123 May, P, '"Partly excellent, partly abysmal": 20 years of the CCRC' (*The Justice Gap*, March 2017).

124 Justice Committee, 'Inquiry: Criminal Cases Review Commission, Written evidence from Paul May (CCR 03)' (December 2014), [27].

- The post-appellate system allows people to challenge decisions after the court process of appeals has been exhausted.
- The Criminal Cases Review Commission (CCRC) receives applications to examine such cases; it has the power to refer cases back to the Court of Appeal.
- The CCRC has a reasonably high success rate in terms of referrals – although there are a number of issues relating to its operation.

chapter 12 Theories of Punishment

12.1 Introduction

The previous chapters have explained how criminal procedure works in England and Wales. When the defendant is convicted at trial, they will then be given an appropriate punishment. However, a number of interesting questions arise at this stage: how should we punish people, why should they be punished and, most interestingly, 'how much' punishment should we give them. By the end of this chapter, you should be able to give an answer to all of these questions.

The *Oxford English Dictionary* defines punishment as: 'The infliction or imposition of a penalty as retribution for an offence.' It is clear that the idea of punishment has two key aspects:

(a) somebody needs to do something wrong; and
(b) the sanction for that wrongdoing needs to hurt the wrongdoer.

What is clear is the desire that a punishment should harm. If you ask the person on the street, it is likely that they would suggest that the offender needs to 'pay' for what they have done. There are a number of differing themes that tie into this idea of 'paying' for wrongdoing. The first type of payment could be to inflict pain on the person; that could be physical pain but it is more than likely to be the pain of imprisonment. The second type of payment could be payment of an offender's time, ie in doing community service in their free time in order to repay society. The third type of payment could actually be a financial transaction – the offender has committed a wrong and will pay a certain amount of money in order to go some way to rectifying that wrong. Whilst we will discuss forms of punishment in the next chapter, it is important to keep in mind the idea of 'paying' something when we look at the different theoretical approaches to punishment.

12.2 Why do we punish?

If we are punishing an offender, we almost certainly need to justify why we have taken this particular course of action. As discussed above, sending someone to prison has connotations that reach far and wide. First, there is the impact on the prisoner – prisons are generally uncomfortable, cramped and overcrowded, often dangerous and may exacerbate or create mental health problems. Furthermore, the pain of imprisonment could stretch further than merely the prisoner. For example, it may have an impact on the prisoner's family: they may have lost their primary source of income, the children may be bullied or teased at school, and all of this could lead to a distrust of the criminal justice process.

As such, the infliction of punishment on an offender needs a strong justification, and any punishment will generally sit in one of four categories of justification:

(a) *Retributive theory*: 'the essence of judicial punishment … is the deliberate imposition of pain'.[1] This approach looks backward to punish wrongs that have already occurred. Arguably, this is rather primitive in nature and is steeped in the desire for revenge. However, to mitigate the desire for revenge, it is important to ensure that the punishment is proportionate and deserving of the wrong that has been committed.

(b) *Prevention theory*: '[preventing] repetition of the offence by the same individual, whether by his reform or removal, is clearly of incalculably less importance (desirable as it is in itself) than … the prevention of crime generally, by the terror of example or of threat'.[2] This is a forward-looking approach. We are looking to prevent future crimes being committed. This can be done by a number of different approaches that are geared toward preventing crime. For example, we can try to deter individuals from committing crime, we can take away the opportunity to commit crime by incarcerating them or we can attempt to make the individual better by using reform or rehabilitation.

(c) *Denunciation theory:* 'the ultimate justification of punishment is not that it is a deterrent but that it is the emphatic denunciation by the community for the crime'.[3] Here we are sending a message to wider society that the criminal conduct of the individual is unacceptable. Society's abhorrence at the crime can be seen from the reaction the punishment receives from the media and general public. This is a mixed approach that contains elements of retribution, ie the expressive denunciation being made, and elements of prevention theory, ie sending a message that this conduct will not be tolerated and therefore we will attempt to reduce criminal conduct by punishing these acts. The central feature of denunciation theory is shaming the individual.

(d) *Reparation theory:* '[Reparation] could have significance and impact in terms of rehabilitating offenders and restoring them to useful lives in society.'[4] We are looking to make things better, to repair the wrongs that have been done and to try to reintegrate the offender back into society. Ultimately, this theory seeks to put things right, to make amends for what has gone on. Arguably, this is less of a punishment or a sanction and more a resolution to wrongdoing.

What this chapter will highlight is that a fusion of all these approaches could be used. This is called 'integrative theory', and it uses elements of retribution, deterrence and rehabilitation throughout the punishment. The differing elements are equally legitimate and none seemingly takes priority; the approach allows a balancing of aims, which will vary according to the particular offender and the crime that has been committed.

12.2.1 Retribution theory

Generally speaking, the public want the courts to sentence offenders harshly. People equate the idea of a harsh punishment with the notion of 'justice'. A 2013 Home Office

1 Morgan, R, 'Public criminology?' (2011) *British Journal of Criminology*, Vol 51, No 4, 716–19 at 717.

2 Nihill, D, *Prison Discipline in its Relations to Society and Individuals: As Deterring from Crime and as Conducive to Personal Reformation* (1839).

3 Lord Denning, 'The Royal Commission on Capital Punishment' (1953), para 53.

4 Jacob, BR, 'Reparation or Restitution by the Criminal Offender to His Victim: Applicability of an Ancient Concept in the Modern Correctional Process' (1970) *Journal of Criminal Law and Criminology* 61(2) at 167.

study found that most people thought the courts too lenient.[5] However, the authors of the study found that knowledge about crime and sentencing largely remained poor, eg a large majority of the population wrongly believed that crime was rising when in fact it had been decreasing.[6] However, it is clear that the criminal justice system 'is harsher, more punitive and more dehumanising than ever'[7] as the length of the average custodial sentence has increased by 4.5 months in the period 2007–17.[8] So whilst the general public may view the criminal justice process as 'soft' or 'too lenient', the evidence suggests that this opinion is misinformed and not reflective of the reality of the process. So what drives this desire for a harsh, punitive, retributive sanction?

Retribution and just deserts

In the mid 1970s, Andrew Von Hirsch wrote his seminal work *Doing Justice*,[9] advancing the idea that the punishment should fit the offence that has been committed. This is the idea of proportionality and giving the offender exactly what their actions 'deserve'. The court will look back in time to the commission of the offence and look to give the offender their 'deserts'. When using the retributive approach, the court does not consider the future ramifications of the punishment. It is not attempting to prevent future crime or reform the offender. Any positive benefits that occur as a result of the punishment are incidental and should not be seen as the purpose of punishment; the court is merely seeking to hand out a punishment it deems proportionate. Kant argued that 'punishment can never be administered merely as a means for promoting another good' and should be 'pronounced over all criminals proportionate to their internal wickedness'.[10] Cavadino and Dignan suggest that the notion of retributivism 'claims that it is somehow morally right to return evil for evil, that two wrongs can make a right'.[11]

The more serious the offender's crime, the more severe the response will be from the court. The court will be guided by various tariffs that will assist it in the sentencing process, and, using the just deserts model, the court should arrive at the correct sanction. The notion of retribution and just deserts is often equated to the Old Testament idea of *lex talionis*,[12] which means that any punishment should resemble the offence that has been committed in both kind and degree, ie an eye for an eye. This barbaric approach provided the rationale for the brutal punishment regime that occupied the criminal justice process until the end of the 18th century; the regime of corporal punishments, including flogging, branding and the pillory, were all underscored by a desire for brutal retribution. With the advent of the prison being used to house and punish offenders, there was a departure from the traditional use of these primitive, brutal punishments.

5 Hough, M, Bradford, B, Jackson, J and Roberts, J, 'Attitudes to Sentencing and Trust in Justice: Exploring Trends from the Crime Survey for England and Wales' (Ministry of Justice, 2013), 1.

6 *Ibid* 52.

7 Garside, R, 'Criminal justice harsher and more punitive than ever' (2014): www.crimeandjustice.org.uk/resources/criminal-justice-harsher-and-more-punitive-ever (accessed 14 May 2020).

8 Criminal Justice Statistics, England and Wales 2017, Ministry of Justice: https://assets.publishing.service.gov.uk/government/uploads/system/uploads/attachment_data/file/707621/criminal-justice-statistics-infographic.pdf (accessed 14 May 2020).

9 Von Hirsch, A, *Doing Justice: The Choice of Punishment* (New York: Hill and Wang, 1976) (Report of the Committee for the Study of Incarceration).

10 Kant, I (1952) 'The science of right' (Hastie, W (trans) in R Hutchins (ed), *Great books of the Western world*, Vol 42, Kant (pp 397–446) (Chicago: Encyclopedia Brittanica), 397.

11 Cavadino, M and Dignan, J, *The Penal System: An Introduction*, 4th edn (London: Sage Publishing), 44.

12 Book of Exodus 21:23–21:27.

Is just deserts fair?

If the desire to harm offenders is paramount, this raises a number of interesting questions. If we are to follow Kant's idea that punishment should be used to punish and any other positive gains are merely incidental, what should we do with those who are convicted of murder? Surely, the only 'deserving' response would be to kill those who kill? Yet, the vast majority of western countries do not use capital punishment, even if it remains available in law. This represents the difficulty in employing retributive theory. The only 'deserving' response to murder would be to kill, but that response would be disproportionate and, as such, offenders are sentenced to a determinate period of incarceration because it is difficult to reconcile that two wrongs (ie the offence of murder and the state-sanctioned execution of the murderer) make a right. If we want a healthy and functioning society, is it correct that we inflict pain and/or suffering on those we value as 'undesirable' or 'bad'? Henry Powell suggested that if we took an eye for an eye, or a tooth for a tooth, we would be left with a world populated with the blind and the toothless.[13] A retributive approach leaves us with the question of whether or not the offender, victim and society heal when we are effectively inflicting more pain because of an offence.

Perhaps retribution is too harsh. By examining further justifications for punishment, we may be able to find an appropriate punishment regime.

12.2.2 Prevention theory

Prevention theory, also referred to as reductivisim, looks to stem the levels of offending in order to reduce the occurrence of future crimes. Cavadino and Dignan suggest that the idea of punishing someone in order to try to stop future offending is a form of 'moral reasoning'[14] that justifies the use of punishment, as this is the mechanism that reduces crime. Prevention theory is centred around three key elements:

- deterrence;
- reform and rehabilitation; and
- incapacitation and protection.

Deterrence

The *Oxford English Dictionary* defines deterrence as: 'The action of discouraging an action or event through instilling doubt or fear of the consequences.' Effectively, a person is scared of committing a criminal act because they are fearful of the consequences they face, should they be apprehended. The problem with focusing on deterrence is that you are reliant of people fearing the available sanctions in the criminal justice process. There are two forms of deterrence that require consideration: specific deterrence[15] and general deterrence.

When examining road safety, the European Commission defined the different types of deterrence as follows:[16]

13 Powell, HS, *What is Truth* (University of Wisconsin, 1944), 10.

14 Cavadino (n 11), 37.

15 Note that some scholars, such as Phillip Bean, use the phrase 'individual deterrence' (the phrases are interchangeable).

16 https://ec.europa.eu/transport/road_safety/specialist/knowledge/speed_enforcement/general_introduction_to_traffic_law_enforcement/general_deterrence_vs_specific_deterrence_en (accessed 14 May 2020).

- Specific deterrence involves the punishment being inflicted on the individual who has committed the offence.
- General deterrence can be defined as the impact of the threat of legal punishment on the public at large.

Writing in the early 1980s, Phillip Bean[17] stated that specific deterrence rests on three core elements. First, it is linked to limiting the physical freedom of the offender. He stated that the roots of specific deterrence lie in the fact that the criminal justice process can remove the offender from the public and place strict limitations on their physical freedom by incarcerating them, thereby removing the threat of that person committing crime. Secondly, we need to condition the offender. This means that any punishment should also contain an element of bringing psychological change in the offender. By making this change, the offender will acknowledge that their offending behaviour is unacceptable and look to rejoin society as a law-abiding citizen. The final element is the individual fear calculus. Scott neatly defines this to mean that the offender's desire to commit offences is balanced by the fear of the consequences of being caught. The 'reward' of committing the offence is vastly outweighed by the consequences of what will happen should the person be caught.[18]

Scott suggests that general deterrence is centred on a 'social fear calculus'.[19] This works in a similar vein to the individual fear calculus, but the key difference is that society is fearful of the consequences of the action, not the individual. Scott suggests that society sees the pain of others and that individuals are deterred from wrongdoing. A good example of general deterrence in action is the change in penalty for use of a mobile phone whilst driving. In March 2017, the Government announced that if drivers were caught using their mobile phone whilst driving, they could receive a fine of up to £200 and six penalty points on their licence. This was widely covered in the media,[20] and some outlets reported the fact that being caught could lead to higher rates of insurance premiums.[21] It is clear that the use of the general deterrence was being used at the rollout of this offence – the pain and suffering of being caught is clear; hopefully the message deters people from using their phones whilst driving. In *Brooke (Simon)*,[22] the defendant was convicted of attempted robbery. He had intentionally targeted a vulnerable adult who suffered with cerebral palsy, and the crime had a severe psychological impact on the victim. The court sentenced the defendant to 63 months in prison, and the defendant appealed on the basis that it was an unduly harsh sentence. The Court of Appeal indicated that the judge was permitted to give a 'deterrent sentence'. Another example of a deterrent sentence is *Hussain (Mohammed)*,[23] in which the defendant stole postal votes. A sentence of three years was handed down as the court was aiming to deter electoral fraud.

17 For further information, see Bean, P, *Punishment: A Philosophical and Criminological Inquiry* (Oxford: Martin Robertston, 1981).

18 Scott, D, *Penology* (Sage: London, 2008), 22.

19 *Ibid.*

20 All major news agencies covered this story; see, for example: www.bbc.co.uk/news/uk-northern-ireland-43307954; www.nidirect.gov.uk/articles/using-your-mobile-phone-while-driving; www.express.co.uk/life-style/cars/930925/McDonalds-drive-thru-mobile-phone-driving-law-fine-Apple-Pay (accessed 14 May 2020).

21 www.telegraph.co.uk/money/consumer-affairs/true-cost-using-phone-driving-200-fine-40pc-higher-car-insurance/ (accessed 14 May 2020).

22 Court of Appeal (Criminal Division), 26 August 2015.

23 [2005] EWCA Crim 1866.

However, there are notable critiques to this justification. How do we know what actually deters people successfully? What deters one person may not deter others. Take, for example, the mobile phone offence above. Despite the clear warnings that the law was changing and the sanctions for breaking this law were harsh, more than 200 people a day were caught using a mobile phone at the wheel in the four weeks after the law changed.[24] So, clearly, general deterrence does not work for all. Furthermore, how do you deter crimes that are impulsive or opportunistic. Say, for example, an individual comes home from work and finds their partner cheating on them. All manner of impulses may rush through their mind, the red mist may descend and they may even end up attacking one of the parties. Will that person be deterred in that instance or even stop and think of the consequences? In opportunistic crimes, consider, for example, a person who sees a lorry parked with its doors open whilst the driver is in a store delivering a parcel. If they think, 'I'll just nip in the back and help myself to the latest console, TV or BluRay player', is there an effective deterrent for that?

Further, if the goal is to focus on general deterrence and thereby deter the greater number of people, does it matter if the courts convict the wrong people? If the goal is to show the severity of crime, it should not matter if the defendant has been wrongfully convicted. However, as **Chapter 16** on miscarriages of justice shows, not only does the system convict the wrong people, often resulting in lengthy sentences, it does so frequently.

Reform and rehabilitation

> **definition**
>
> **Reform:** 'make changes to something in order to improve it.'
>
> **Rehabilitation:** 'the action of restoring someone to former privileges or reputation after a period of disfavour.'

Reform and rehabilitation are often connected, but each concept means a rather different thing. Reform means that we are looking to alter the behaviour of the offender in order to help them recognise the fact that their offending is unacceptable. The punishment handed down will educate, train or create a new moral fabric in the offender; that way we should reduce the chances of them reoffending in the future. Rehabilitation is somewhat different; the offender will not be retrained or re-educated but instead they will be 'fixed' and they will be returned to the point in time when they were deemed to be a good citizen, ie before the commission of the criminal offence. Rehabilitation will assume that the offender was a good person but that committing crime has led them to change. Arguably, this rehabilitation is looking to give the offender a course of treatment in order for them to return to their previous 'good' state. Despite the fact that the terms should be defined separately, Scott suggests that they are generally applied together.[25] This view asserts that a person's delinquent behaviour can be treated, much like an illness, and in effect be cured. But is that the correct way to view criminal offending?

---

24 www.bbc.co.uk/news/business-40079382 (accessed 14 May 2020).

25 Scott (n 18), 22.

This treatment model was the predominant approach in the 1970s until its demise at the end of that decade.[26] Bean's work in the early 1980s highlighted the core strengths of the treatment model, and even though the work is almost 40 years old, it represents a solid foundation for any reformative or rehabilitative sentence. Bean stated[27] that it allows the court to treat the offender as an individual; as such, any sentence can be tailored to their individual needs. It deals with the individual in the context of their offending, ie why does Person X continually burgle people's homes. This could be the desire to feed an addiction or support their family. Accordingly, the treatment model would allow the individual to serve their sentence and receive treatment at the same time. Not only would this improve the life of the individual, but it would promote an idea of self-worth and self-governance in the offender as well. The ultimate benefit is a fluid and flexible sentence. However, it is not without its drawbacks. We illustrated earlier that the general public (incorrectly) believe that punishment in England and Wales is already too lenient, with a focus on improving the offender at the expense of a retributive goal. Thus a reform and rehabilitation model is unlikely to prove popular with the electorate and indeed the popular press. Arguably, offenders have their own autonomy and we should not try to train or condition them like obedient dogs. It may not be possible to use reform or rehabilitation as a stand-alone punishment, but its fluid and flexible nature should mean that it garners serious consideration to be implemented alongside other punishments. **Chapter 13** will highlight the problems with sending people to prison, and perhaps now is the time to start thinking about what punishments will work best for both society and the offender.

Incapacitation and protection

By using incapacitation, we are looking to (a) protect society by removing the physical freedom of the offender, and (b) reduce reoffending by physically limiting the potential for crimes being committed. **Chapter 13** will provide an in-depth analysis of the use of prison as a form of punishment. However, here we introduce theoretical ideas about sending offenders to prison. O'Donnell states that 200 years ago, there was a fourfold rationale for the use of prison:[28]

(a) to contain debtors until what was owed was paid;
(b) to detain the accused pending a trial;
(c) to hold convicted persons pending the execution of the sentence, ie corporal punishment, capital punishment or transportation;
(d) to profit gaolers.[29]

Obviously, some of these goals are somewhat outdated. We no longer have debtors' prisons, use corporal and capital punishment or transport people as a form of punishment. So what are the aims of prison today? In England and Wales, the goal of prison is to 'keep those sentenced to prison in custody, helping them lead law-abiding and useful lives, both while they are in prison and after they are released', thus attempting to include an element of reform and rehabilitation.[30] Interestingly, there is

26 See Bottoms, E, *The Coming Penal Crisis: A Criminological and Theological Exploration* (Scottish Academic Press, 1980).

27 For further information, see Bean (n 17).

28 O'Donnell, I, 'The aims of imprisonment' in Y Jewkes, J Bennett and B Crewe (eds), *Handbook on Prisons*, 2nd edn (London: Routledge, 2016), 40–41.

29 A gaoler was a person who was in charge of the prison.

30 www.gov.uk/government/organisations/hm-prison-service (accessed 14 May 2020).

no mention of those held on pre-trial detention,[31] despite the high levels of those remanded in custody pending a trial.

The use of prison can be justified on the following grounds:

(a) It is a legitimate punishment to deprive a person of their physical freedom. Depending on the crime, the response of imprisonment could be justified on the basis that it is deserving.
(b) Prison is the most severe sanction the court can impose in England and Wales; this *should* act as a deterrent both at the specific and general level. Ultimately, this should result in lower rates of offending in the future.
(c) We need to remove dangerous offenders from society in order to protect the public.
(d) Prison is a place where rehabilitative programmes can be provided. The offender will then be presented with an option to change their offending behaviour.
(e) For habitual offenders, we are left with no other course of action, especially if previous attempts at rehabilitation have failed.

As you can see, this justification of prison incorporates ideas concerning retributive, preventative and rehabilitative theory. When we look at prison in practice, we shall examine how successfully these aims are met.

12.2.3 Denunciation

This is a forward-looking punishment that seeks to reduce crime by allowing society to expressly denunciate the conduct of the offender. The idea is that punishment can be justified on the basis that society is appalled by the objectionable conduct of the individual. In theory, this rejection by society fulfils both specific and general deterrence. The individual is shamed by their community and therefore they are deterred from committing crime. The general public see and feel the level of shame and do not want to be in that position, and, as such, they are deterred from committing similar actions. A degree of proportionality is required; the shame the individual feels needs to be proportionate to the crime that has been committed. However, in cases that involve high levels of emotion, sometimes the level of revulsion far outweighs the crime that has been committed.

During the Soham murders investigation, it transpired that Maxine Carr had provided a false alibi for her boyfriend, Ian Huntley, to the police. As such, the police did not investigate Huntley for a number of days. Carr was subsequently convicted of perverting the course of justice and sentenced to 21 months in prison. She was not directly involved in the murder of the two young victims, Holly Wells and Jessica Chapman. However, Carr was demonised by the public, so much so that she had to be given a new identity upon her release from prison. She received the kind of treatment from the press and public that was 'usually saved for murderers like child killer Mary Bell [or] killers' wives or partners like Rosemary West, Primrose Shipman or the notorious Moors murderer, Myra Hindley'.[32] Carr has anonymity for life, which means her own child cannot know of her past (although her husband does know). The Guardian described Carr as an unwitting accomplice; she knew nothing of the crime and was not near Soham when Huntley murdered the two children.[33] Despite her

31 As discussed in **Chapter 10**.

32 http://news.bbc.co.uk/1/hi/uk/3714579.stm (accessed 1 July 2018).

33 www.theguardian.com/commentisfree/2011/nov/02/maxine-carr-no-ghoul-we-are (accessed 14 May 2020).

anonymity, Carr has been re-homed, at least once, because people recognised her. In 1993, Jon Venables and Robert Thompson murdered 2-year-old, Jamie Bulger. Both defendants were 10 years old at the time of the killing and both were given lifetime anonymity order in order to protect them. The order was granted because the court concluded that the revelation of Venables' and Thompson's new identities would be likely to have 'disastrous consequences', up to 'the real possibility of serious physical harm and possible death from vengeful members of the public or the Bulger family'. Whilst these two cases are obviously very different, they are conjoined by the notion that the defendants are all subject to lifetime anonymity orders to protect them from the vengeful public, who are seeking to further denunciate their past actions with retribution.

However, one has to wonder how healthy this is. All three defendants have served their prison sentences and have been released. Should they still be punished for their crimes? This relates back to the question regarding proportionality: how much public shaming is the correct amount? Is it right for society to administer its own form of justice – what if society gets it wrong? That is what happened when the *News of the World* ran its 'name and shame' campaign against people it believed were guilty of child sex offences. In June 2000 and in the wake of the Sarah Payne murder trial, the paper published the pictures and names of 100 offenders. A mob mentality broke out and vindictive attacks took place all over the country. In South Wales, a paediatrician was mistakenly attacked as people believed her to be a paedophile. There was a clear climate of both fear and panic, and a named paedophile, James White, committed suicide for fear that he would be subjected to reprisals. It is arguable that this level of public shaming goes too far and, ultimately, does not assist with the reintegration of offenders back into the community. If we think back to the aforementioned use of prison, its goal is to 'keep those sentenced to prison in custody, helping them lead law-abiding and useful lives, both while they are in prison and *after they are released*'.[34] Does the shaming of offenders run counter to the goal of having people live law-abiding lives upon release?

John Braithwaite suggests that there are two types of shaming: reintegrative and disintegrative shaming. He argues that shaming is a form of social control.[35] Reintegrative shaming works on the idea that whilst the offender is punished for their crime, they are ultimately welcomed back into society upon completion of their sentence. This form of shaming allows an offender to become a valued member of society once again. The mirror of this is disintegrative shaming, which occurs when an offender is both stigmatised and rejected from society, even after completion of their initial punishment.[36]

Arguably, Thompson, Venables and Carr have all been subjected to disintegrative shaming. According to Braithwaite, this treatment may create individuals who become habitual in a criminal lifestyle, and this therefore reinforces their deviant 'label'.[37] Furthermore, disintegrative shaming is considered to be detrimental to an offender's self-esteem.[38] A study in New Jersey examined the correlation between depression and hopelessness in sex offenders who were subject to community notification. The study

34 www.gov.uk/government/organisations/hm-prison-service (accessed 14 May 2020).

35 Braithwaite, J, *Crime, Shame and Reintegration* (Cambridge University Press, 1989).

36 *Ibid.*

37 *Ibid* at 103.

38 Katz, R, 'Re-examining the integrative social capital theory of crime' (2002) *Western Criminology Review* at 32.

found that offenders who experienced higher levels of notification demonstrated more elevated levels of depression and hopelessness.[39] This suggests that the core goal of rehabilitation of offenders is aligned with appropriate reintegration, and that, without this, such offenders are at greater risk of reoffending.[40] Ultimately, the public shaming of sex offenders via dissemination of information through community notification is a secondary punishment as it leads to a great deal of stigmatisation, often resulting in offenders being unable to find accommodation or employment.[41] Furthermore, it can cause members of the community to inflict their own sanctions, such as vigilantism, which could lead to the harming or suicide of the offender. The US Supreme Court has acknowledged that shaming can have a detrimental effect on offenders but concluded that the purpose was to improve public safety and not to further punish sex offenders.[42] However, it appears that the public clamour to find out the identification of offenders, who have court-mandated anonymity orders, means that the secondary punishment of societal revulsion is impossible to dismiss.

12.2.4 Reparation theory

The final justification of punishment is reparation theory. This basically means that the offender should make amends for their wrongdoing. However, it is argued that it involves more than merely 'making good the damage done to property, body or psyche. It must also entail recognition of the harm done to the social relationship between the victim and offender ...'[43] There are many different forms of reparation theory; it can take the form of:

- redress;
- reparation and restitution; and
- restorative justice.

One of the major problems with reparation theory is that there is no settled definition of what the theory should be. Many scholars who talk about the theory draw upon a variety of different sources that fit their analysis, rather than painting a picture as a whole.[44] Van Ness and Strong suggest that the development of the field in a 'piecemeal fashion' means that different countries are at vastly different stages in their use of reparation theory.[45] Redress has been used to settle disagreements and conflicts for centuries,[46] and De Haan defines it as meaning 'to put right or in good order again, to remedy ... to repair, rectify something suffered'.[47] In practical terms, this approach could be used as a response to minor offending, such as low-level criminal damage. Should an offender spray graffiti on walls or buildings, they could be made to repaint

39 Jeglic, E, Mercado, C and Levenson, J, (2002) 'The Prevalence and Correlates of Depression and Hopelessness among Sex Offenders Subject to Community Notification and Residence Restriction Legislation' at 54.

40 *Ibid.*

41 La Fond, J, *Preventing Sexual Violence: How Society Should Cope with Sex Offenders* (American Psychological Association, 2005), 88.

42 *Smith v Doe*, 538 US 84 (2003).

43 Zedner, L, 'Reparation and Retribution: Are They Reconcilable?' (1994) *MLR* 57(2), 228–50 at 234.

44 See Zher, H and Toews, B, *Critical Issues in Restorative Justice* (Monsey: NY Criminal Justice Press, 2004), Chs 1–3; van Ness, D and Strong, KH, *Restoring Justice: An Introduction to Restorative Justice*, 3rd edn (Cincinnati: Anderson Publishing, 2006), 22–23.

45 van Ness (n 44), 33–35.

46 Scott (n 18).

47 De Haan, W, *The Politics of Redress* (London: Sage, 1990), 158.

the damaged areas and thereby rectify their wrongdoing. By forcing the person to fix the problem, they also witness the damage their action has caused and the impact it has had on the local community.

Reparation and restitution basically means that a monetary payment is made by the offender to the victim, in the form of compensation. Since the Criminal Justice Act 1972, the courts have been able to attach a compensation order to a conviction where any loss, injury or damage had resulted. However, there is a danger with this approach being seen as the predominant form of punishment as 'orders are set with reference to the ability of the offender to pay and, given that the majority of offenders are of limited means, they rarely result in complete restoration'.[48] As such, questions remain whether a monetary sanction carries enough punitive weight to be a valid punishment. When the Dunpark Committee examined the use of compensation in Scotland, it concluded that the only justification for a monetary payment was so that the justice system could be seen to be doing something for the victim and it carried no penal function. In effect, it was a way of settling a dispute in a manner akin to that of the civil court.[49] Zedner further suggests that it 'is questionable whether a compensation order can be properly seen as no more than a civil instrument riding on the back of a criminal trial'.[50] It is hard to justify the use of compensation as a criminal sanction if, as Zedner suggests, we are shoehorning a civil approach into the criminal sphere.

According to the Restorative Justice Council,[51] the act of restorative justice brings those harmed by crime or conflict and those responsible for the harm into communication, enabling everyone affected by a particular incident to play a part in repairing the harm and finding a positive way forward. Johnstone believes that once a crime has been committed, the priority should not be to punish the offender but to (a) meet the needs of the victim, and (b) ensure that the offender is aware of the damage their actions have caused and the need to repair that damage.[52] Johnstone believes that traditional trial and sentencing do not allow for these aims to succeed. Instead, there should be a face-to-face meeting between the victim and the offender, in a neutral and safe venue. Any professionals involved will act merely as facilitators rather than acting in any adjudicative function, amounting to a form of mediation. The practice allows the victim to articulate their feelings, levels of hurt and anger towards the offender, who will, in theory, show accountability for their actions. The Restorative Justice Council suggests that there is a 85% satisfaction rate with the practice and a 14% reduction in the frequency of reoffending.[53] In 2001, the government funded a seven-year research study into the use of restorative justice.[54] The study found the use of restorative justice to have positive results:

- The offenders who participated in the programme committed significantly fewer offences that led to reconvictions over the next two years than the offenders in the control group.

48 Zedner (n 43) at 235.

49 Lord Dunpark, *Reparation by the Offender to the Victim in Scotland* (Cmnd 6802, 1977).

50 Zedner (n 43) at 239.

51 https://restorativejustice.org.uk/what-restorative-justice (accessed 14 May 2020).

52 Johnstone, G, *Restorative Justice: Ideas, Values and Debates*, 2nd edn (Routledge, 2011), 1.

53 https://restorativejustice.org.uk/criminal-justice (accessed 14 May 2020).

54 Shapland, J et al, 'Does Restorative Justice Affect Reconviction: The Fourth Report from the Evaluation of three schemes', Ministry of Justice Research Series 10/08, June 2008: https://restorativejustice.org.uk/sites/default/files/resources/files/Does%20restorative%20justice%20affect%20reconviction.pdf (accessed 14 May 2020).

- The extent to which the offenders felt that the conference had made them realise the harm done; whether the offender wanted to meet the victim; the extent to which the offender was observed to be actively involved in the conference; and how useful offenders felt the conference had been, were all significantly and positively related to decreased subsequent reconviction.
- There were no statistically significant results pointing towards any criminogenic effects of restorative justice (making people worse) in any scheme.
- Offenders who said that they particularly wanted to meet their victim at a conference were less likely to be reconvicted and had lower frequency and cost of reconvictions.
- Restorative justice can produce costs savings up to £9 per £1 spent on it depending on the setting.

However, the approach is not without its critics. It has been argued that it is not a magic solution and is not suitable for all offences. Wood and Suzuki believe that restorative justice has been hybridised and used in an variety of different settings, such as schools, prisons and workplaces. Therefore the definition of restorative justice continues to expand. They argue that what people call restorative justice has far exceeded the purist position of representing meetings between victims and offenders, and ultimately this hybrid definition of restorative justice is essentially meaningless.[55] Furthermore, they point to the rebranding of community service as restorative, ie repairing the harm and restoring order. However, they see little change in the substance of the community service: it involves offenders in degrading and menial work in often stigmatising conditions or settings.[56] The authors believe that restorative justice is in danger of becoming outdated unless it develops new ways to address problems of race, gender and social class within its own practices.[57] Morris addresses a number of criticisms concerning the use of the programme. She states that a common criticism is that restorative justice erodes the legal rights of the defendant. But Morris suggests that legal rights will not be eroded. Practitioners have to follow certain guidelines or practice manuals, and in certain US states a lawyer is present at proceedings and can interrupt at any time if he or she thinks that the offender's rights are being breached.[58] She also defends the claim that it widens the net of social control as it draws in offenders who would otherwise be disposed of by way of police warnings. However, she advances its use in New Zealand, which does not focus on lower level crime but instead is being used for the most serious and persistent offenders in the youth justice system.[59] There is a potential danger that restorative justice trivialises crime and, in the context of domestic abuse, returns it to the sphere of being a private or in-house matter. This is rejected by Morris, who suggests that it 'arguably takes crime more seriously than conventional criminal justice systems because it focuses on the consequences of the offence for victims and attempts to address these and to find meaningful ways of holding offenders accountable'.[60]

---

55 Wood, WR and Suzuki, M, 'Four Challenges in the Future of Restorative Justice' (2016) *Victims and Offenders: An International Journal of Evidence-based Research, Policy and Practice* 11(1), 149–72 at 150–51.

56 *Ibid* 152.

57 *Ibid* 163.

58 Morris, A, 'Critiquing the Critics: A Brief Response to Critics of Restorative Justice' (2002) *Brit J Criminol* 42, 596–615 at 601.

59 *Ibid* 602.

60 *Ibid* 603.

Whilst it is clear that restorative justice is not perfect, it does hold a useful place in the criminal justice process, and in an era that is looking to become more efficient, we could expect restorative justice to be rolled out more widely as it has the potential to be very cost effective.

12.3 Justifications in practice: sentencing

This chapter has sought to address the many different approaches to and justifications for punishment, but a question remains concerning how valid any of these approaches are. Writing in 1954,[61] Flew proposed five rules to which any punishment must conform. It must:

(a) create human suffering;
(b) arise as a direct consequence of the offence;
(c) be directed at the person who committed the offence;
(d) be an intentional creation; and
(e) be inflicted by an authorised body.

In essence, Flew suggested that the punishment must hurt or harm the offender. There needs to be an element of pain in the punishment. The punishment needs to occur because someone has committed a wrong; we cannot punish those who have committed no wrongdoing. It is of paramount importance that we punish the correct person. Whereas general deterrence could work on the basis that society sees 'someone' being punished, Flew suggested that we need to punish the correct offender in order for the punishment to be valid. The punishment needs to be an intentional creation. Say, for example, that an offender was breaking into a high-rise flat by climbing on the balcony and, during the subsequent police chase, he slipped from the balcony, fell to the ground and was paralysed. It would not be valid for the court to turn around and say 'well, son, you have suffered enough because you have lost the use of your legs.' According to Flew, that would invalidate the punishment. Finally, only those with the correct power should be allowed to give out punishments. If a mob mentality broke out, much like the aforementioned *News of the World* 'name and shame' campaign, any punishments handed out would be invalid; by having an authorised body give punishments, the rule of law is respected and any desire for vigilante behaviour should be quashed.

When looking for a justification of punishment, it is impossible to single out one theory and claim that it is the most useful. What any just society ideally needs is a fusion of a number of different theories. Society believes that punishment is too lenient, so it would be difficult to completely rid the justice system of the retributive goals, for fear of public backlash. However, the wider public could be better educated to the fact that sentencing has become tougher over the course of the last 10 years. Prevention theory would also be needed as offenders and the public at large need to be deterred from crime. However, it is important to punish the correct offender, rather than fulfilling the goals of general deterrence to show society how bad the punishment can be. It would be important to include the duel goals of attempting to reform and rehabilitate the offender in order to reduce future delinquent behaviour. Furthermore, an element of shaming could be incorporated, but it is very important to focus on reintegrative rather than disintegrative shaming, as the latter further punishes the

61 Flew, A, 'The Justification of Punishment' in HB Acton, *The Philosophy of Punishment* (London: Macmillan, 1954).

offender through society demonising their previous bad character. Finally, the idea of redress needs to be considered: is restorative justice, restitution or redress appropriate for this offender? Ultimately, aspects of all of these approaches should be mixed together in order to generate a tailored punishment. This integrated theory is based on the idea that balance is the key to punishment and that a fluid approach is more likely to result in a punishment that is successful in its goals.

So how does this fluid model work in practice? Section 142 of Criminal Justice Act 2003 codifies the purpose of sentencing in one neat place. The section states:

> (1) Any court dealing with an offender in respect of his offence must have regard to the following purposes of sentencing—
> (a) the punishment of offenders,
> (b) the reduction of crime (including its reduction by deterrence),
> (c) the reform and rehabilitation of offenders,
> (d) the protection of the public, and
> (e) the making of reparation by offenders to persons affected by their offences.

It is interesting to note that, despite no individual weighting being attached to the aims, purpose (a) is purely retributive in nature. The notion of reparation is represented with purpose (e), and purposes (b), (c) and (d) focus on prevention theory. Despite the inclusion of other theories of sentencing, Dingwall argues that retribution and just deserts still take precedence in sentencing policy.[62]

12.3.1 Sentencing

When determining a sentence, it is important that judges and magistrates are fair. If the sentence is either too harsh or too lenient, this will need to be addressed, and as such the criminal justice process will slow down. It is therefore vital that those passing sentence get the decision correct in the first instance. In order to assist the judiciary and magistracy, the Crime and Disorder Act 1998[63] created the Sentencing Advisory Panel. This panel would draft sentencing proposals and feed their suggestions to the Court of Appeal, which was under no obligation to accept the recommendations of the panel. Both judges and magistrates were in opposition to the formation of the panel but, nevertheless, the panel was established.[64] In 2001, the Halliday Report recommended that England and Wales needed to move toward a comprehensive set of sentencing guidelines, and the Criminal Justice Act 2003[65] created the Sentencing Guidelines Council. The panel continued to draft guidelines, but it was the Council, not the Court of Appeal, which had the authority to create and publish sentencing guidelines. This marked the first time that anyone other than a judge or magistrate had been involved in setting sentencing guidelines.[66] In 2010, the Sentencing Council replaced both the panel and the Guidelines Council; the 'struggle for supremacy in sentencing'[67] was over. The discretion of judges and magistrates to set individual sentences has now been

62 Dingwall, G, 'Deserting Desert? Locating the Present Role of Retributivism in the Sentencing of Adult Offenders' (2008) *Howard Journal*, Vol 47(4), 400–10.

63 Crime and Disorder Act 1998, ss 80–81.

64 Easton, S and Piper, C, *Sentencing and Punishment: The Quest for Justice*, 4th edn (Oxford: OUP, 2014), 37.

65 Criminal Justice Act 2003, s 167.

66 https://www.sentencingcouncil.org.uk/about-us/history/ (accessed 14 May 2020).

67 Ashworth, A, *Sentencing and Criminal Justice*, 4th edn (Cambridge: Cambridge University Press, 2005).

extremely fettered, and the creation of the Council should mean that sentences are more consistent throughout England and Wales.

12.3.2 The death of discretion

The idea of fettering the discretionary powers of the judiciary and magistracy was to make sentencing consistent. At the turn of the millennium, the use of incarceration in the magistrates' court was wildly inconsistent. Easton and Piper offer a comparison of Elbes in Lincolnshire, which had a rate of 0.8%, whereas Luton and South Bedfordshire had a rate of 23.4%. A Ministry of Justice study in 2007[68] found the following:

- Custody rates and the average custodial sentence lengths varied significantly over the 42 Criminal Justice Areas in England and Wales.
- This variation in rate and length was not explained by the case and defendant make-up coming before the court.
- Variations in sentencing practice may be the result of 'local justice', which is the need to establish and maintain consistent policy in an individual court, which takes priority over being consistent on a national level.
- The relationship between those sentencing offenders and the police and probation service presented another factor which could influence the sentencing decision.

Easton and Piper argue that 'sanctions cannot give a clear deterrent message to past or future offenders' if it is difficult to predict the sentencing outcome.[69] However, they argue that some level of discretion in the sentencing process is a positive element, and they provide a fivefold rationale for its use:[70]

(1) Justice cannot be tailored to an individual if there is little discretion, as this may lead to an injustice.
(2) The aims of prevention theory may not be met with the use of mandatory sentences.
(3) Judges and lawyers may look to 'negotiate justice' by way of a plea bargain where the defendant will enter a guilty plea for a lesser sentence to avoid a more severe mandatory penalty.
(4) The lack of discretion may increase the likelihood of more 'not guilty' pleas if the accused thinks that the mandatory penalty is severe, so they 'take their chances at court'. This defeats the efficiency drivers that the criminal justice process is trying to establish.
(5) The lack of discretion may lead to human rights violations.

With the advent of the Sentencing Council, the level of discretion of the judiciary and magistracy has been extremely diluted. They are now governed by maximum and minimum penalties, which have been created to achieve consistency and efficiency throughout the courts. If two people commit the same crime in Elbes and in Luton, the sentence should be broadly the same. This lack of variation means that the notion of 'local justice' will dissipate, and a clear and consistent message regarding sentencing will be sent. This message can in turn enforce the retributive, prevention and reparative

---

68 Mason, T et al, 'Local Variation in Sentencing in England and Wales' (London: Ministry of Justice, 2007): https://assets.publishing.service.gov.uk/government/uploads/system/uploads/attachment_data/file/217971/local-variation-sentencing-1207.pdf (accessed 14 May 2020).

69 Easton and Piper (n 64) at 40.

70 *Ibid.* See p 41 for further detail.

aims of the multi-faceted purpose of sentencing as set out in s 142 of the Criminal Justice Act 2003.

12.4 Conclusion

This chapter has illustrated that both the justifications for punishment and the art of sentencing are complex fields. There are many reasons why we punish, each with a unique driving force behind them, from the desire to harm, to deter, to reform/rehabilitate, to finally making good. Each punishment has a varied philosophical stance which underpins a particular goal, and despite their age, these theories of punishment remain at the heart of dealing with offenders in the 21st century. We have seen that the practical application of these justifications is no longer left to the discretion of the courts; the creation of the Sentencing Advisory Panel, the Sentencing Guidelines Council and ultimately the Sentencing Council has worked to dilute judicial discretion. This move should make sentencing decisions more consistent throughout England and Wales and ensure that offenders are punished in a similar way, for the same offence, irrespective of where the offence took place.

chapter 13

Punishment in Practice: Custody and the Alternatives

13.1 Introduction

Chapter 12 examined a range of justifications for punishment. This chapter will illustrate how such theories are used in practice. A criminal sanction can be imposed in one of two settings. For low-level offending, a penalty can be imposed by the police or another authorised body; this is called an out of court disposal. It is a popular method of disposing of low-level offending without clogging up the already overworked criminal justice process. The types of offences that would warrant this response could include being drunk and disorderly, trespassing on the railway or littering, amongst other offences. Other types of sanctions are handed down by the court. There are a number of different punishments available in the following hierarchy (ranging from most to least serious).

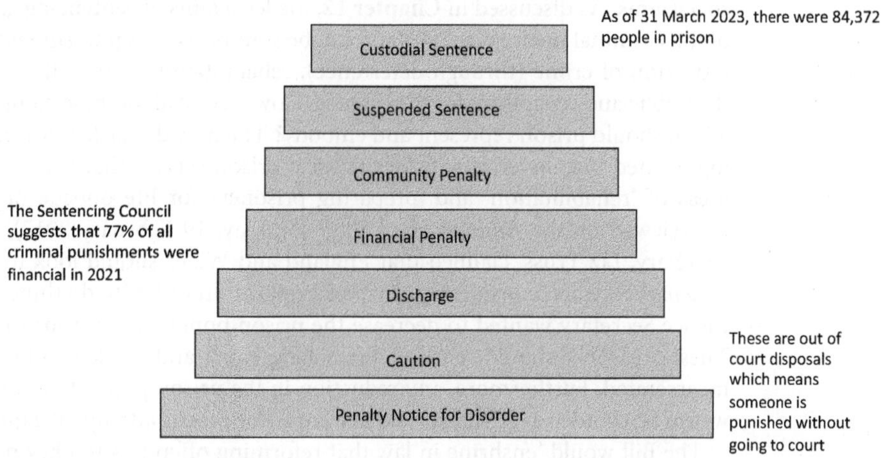

This chapter will analyse the use and implications of each of these penalties.

13.2 Prison

In 2018/19, there were 117 operational prisons in England and Wales,[1] most of which are publicly owned, but a small percentage are privately owned. The goal of prison is to keep the offender incapacitated; it represents the ultimate loss of liberty and should be reserved for the most serious and persistent offenders. Sentences can range from a single day in prison to a whole life tariff, meaning that the prisoner will spend their entire life in prison and never be eligible for parole, although this is extremely rare. Of

1 Prison figures taken from: www.instituteforgovernment.org.uk/publication/performance-tracker-2019/prisons (accessed 14 May 2020).

the prison population of 84,372[2] as of 31 March 2023, only 64 were in prison for a whole life tariff.[3]

There are four different categories of prison in England and Wales:

- Category A: These prisoners are those that would pose the biggest threat to the general public, police or national security should they escape from prison. The security conditions in a Category A prison are designed to ensure that escape is impossible.
- Category B: The prisoners are not required to have the highest level of security but they still represent a potential danger to the public. Whilst this is not a high-security prison, the potential for escape should be made very difficult.
- Category C: These prisoners cannot be trusted in open conditions but areunlikely to attempt an escape.
- Category D: The prisoners can be trusted in open conditions. These prisons have minimum restrictions on the movements and activities of prisoners. There is minimal perimeter security and the prisoners are not locked in their cells. It may be possible for some prisoners to gain employment in the local community whilst completing their sentence.

13.2.1 Immediate incarceration: the aims and use of prison

In order to analyse how effective the use of prison is, we need to examine its legal and social aims. As discussed in **Chapter 12**, the legal aims of sentencing are found in s 142 of the Criminal Justice Act 2003 and can be summarised as punishment of the offender, reduction of crime (through deterrence), rehabilitation of the offender, protection of the public and reparation for the offence. However, of all of these competing objectives, which should prison represent and embody? The now discarded Prison and Courts Bill highlighted the Government's desire for a prison service that heavily emphasised the ideas of 'rehabilitation' and 'preparing prisoners for life outside of prison'.[4] When interviewed on the *Andrew Marr Show* (Sunday, 19 February 2017), the then Justice Secretary, Liz Truss, claimed that England and Wales should look to *The Shawshank Redemption* when considering any penal reform. In order 'to do things differently', the Justice Secretary wanted to decrease the prison population but for the 'right reasons'. These reasons should ensure that dangerous and violent offenders remained incarcerated. Furthermore, any reduction in the prison population, by a cap or quota, was to be avoided as such provisions were a 'dangerous attempt at a quick fix'.

The Bill would 'enshrine in law that reforming offenders is a key purpose of prison and the Secretary of State has a responsibility to deliver this', but in the run-up to the 2017 General Election, the Bill was shelved indefinitely.[5]

---

2 The weekly prison population statistics are published by the Ministry of Justice, HM Prison Service and HM Prison and Probation Service; most recent figures are taken from: www.gov.uk/government/publications/prison-population-figures-2023 (accessed April 2023).

3 Prison Reform Trust, 'Prison: the facts', Summer 2022: https://prisonreformtrust.org.uk/wp-content/uploads/2022/07/Prison-the-facts-2022.pdf (accessed March 2023).

4 Prison and Courts Bill (2016–2017) [170] Pt 1, cl 1.

5 Hyde, J, 'Prisons and Courts Bill Scrapped', *Law Gazette*, 20 April 2017: www.lawgazette.co.uk/news/prisons-and-courts-bill-scrapped/5060715.article (accessed 1 July 2018).

The prison population and its impact

Over the course of the last decade, the prison population has remained relatively stable, at around 83,000–85,000 people, but there is a concerning trend of an increase over the course of the last 2–3 years:

Year	Males	Females	Total
2014	81,402	3,905	85,307
2015	81,741	3,885	85,626
2016	81,493	3,854	85,347
2017	80,613	4,035	84,648
2018	78,603	3,781	82,384
2019	79,311	3,712	83,023
2020	75,421	3,197	78,618
2021	75,881	3,211	79,092
2022	79,036	3,140	82,176
2023	81,057	3,315	84,372

In the early part of this century, there was a lot of talk about the ever-increasing prison population. 2014 saw the start of a largely gradual decrease in the prison population. However, since 2021, there has been a steady increase in the number of people serving prison sentences. This represents a problem for the criminal justice system as the prison estate is overcrowded, with diminishing room to house its prisoners.

Since 1990 there has been a 158% increase in the prison population.[6] In 2006, the population exceeded 80,000 people and by 2012 reached its peak with 86,635 people in prison. To put the table above into context, the prison population equals approximately the capacity of Wembley Stadium, with a rate of imprisonment of 159 per 100,000 of the population.[7]

The overcrowding in prison is just as problematic as the high population. As of 31 March 2023, there were 84,372 people in prison.[8] The International Centre for Prison Studies indicates that prisons are at a 109.8% occupancy level. This is because the official capacity of prisons is actually regarded as 76,808 – the level at which a prison can be viewed as 'certified for normal accommodation use'.[9] However, the issue of overcrowding does not impact all prisons. Piper states that overcrowding is not evenly distributed,[10] so some prisons are overcrowded and others are not. Additionally, overcrowding is not a new problem as 'the prison system as a whole has been

6 UK Prison Population Statistics, House of Commons Library (April 2017) at p 5: http://researchbriefings.files.parliament.uk/documents/SN04334/SN04334.pdf (accessed 14 May 2020).

7 House of Commons Library, UK Prison Population Statistics: https://commonslibrary.parliament.uk/research-briefings/sn04334/ (accessed March 2023).

8 World Prison Brief data: www.prisonstudies.org/country/united-kingdom-england-wales (accessed April 2023).

9 *Ibid.*

10 Piper, C, '"What's Sentencing Got to Do With it?" Understanding the Prison Crisis' (2008) 8(4) *Contemporary Issues in Law*, p 368.

overcrowded since 1994' and this has an impact which 'affects access to resources to assist prisoners in rehabilitation'.[11]

The dire state of the prison estate was highlighted in December 2022 when the Justice Minister announced that hundreds of police cells would be used to house prisoners, because there was no room in the prison estate for them.[12] This may go some way to explaining why magistrates have had their sentencing powers reduced – there is simply not space to house all the people the state would like to send to prison.

Previous convictions and the rate of reoffending

To measure how effective prison is at rehabilitating offenders, reoffending rates will point us in the direction of whether or not prison is fulfilling that goal.

	Apr 2017–Mar 2018	Apr 2018–Mar 2019	Apr 2019–Mar 2020	Apr 2020–Mar 2021
No previous custodial sentences				
Proportion of offenders who reoffend %	16.1	15.4	14.1	14.0
1 previous custodial sentence				
Proportion of offenders who reoffend %	31.6	29.8	27.9	26.2
2 previous custodial sentences				
Proportion of offenders who reoffend %	38.9	37.1	33.7	31.1
3 previous custodial sentences				
Proportion of offenders who reoffend %	43.8	42.4	39.0	35.6
4 previous custodial sentences				
Proportion of offenders who reoffend %	47.7	45.5	41.6	37.7
5 previous custodial sentences				
Proportion of offenders who reoffend %	49.7	47.7	44.5	41.5
6 to 10 previous custodial sentences				
Proportion of offenders who reoffend %	57.0	54.9	50.5	46.7

11 Prison Reform Trust, 'Bromley Briefings Prison Factfile: Autumn 2017', p 18: http://criminaljusticealliance.org/wp-content/uploads/2017/07/Autumn-2017-factfile.pdf (accessed 17 July 2020).

12 Dearden, L, 'UK Prisons near capacity triggering emergency plan to use 400 police cells', *The Independent*, 1 December 2022: www.independent.co.uk/news/uk/home-news/prisons-full-police-cells-safeguard-b2236133.html (accessed March 2023).

	Apr 2017–Mar 2018	Apr 2018–Mar 2019	Apr 2019–Mar 2020	Apr 2020–Mar 2021
11 or more previous custodial sentences				
Proportion of offenders who reoffend %	72.7	70.0	65.2	61.0
All adult offenders				
Proportion of offenders who reoffend %	**28.5**	**27.4**	**25.1**	**24.0**

The 'Proven Reoffending Statistics'[13] suggest a rather bleak picture concerning success rates in preventing the reoffending of those who have previously been given a custodial sentence. Adult offenders had a proven reoffending rate of 24%. This is a decrease of 0.2 percentage points since the same quarter in 2020 but an increase of 1.2 percentage points over the last quarter. Adults released from custodial sentences of less than 12 months had a proven reoffending rate of 53.9%. This is a decrease of 3.6 percentage points from the same quarter in the previous year. Those released from sentences of less than or equal to six months had a proven reoffending rate of 57.0%, which is a decrease of 2.2 percentage points since the same quarter in the previous year. Ultimately, it appears that sending someone to prison is not an absolute deterrent to committing further offences once released.

The crisis in the prison system and how to tackle it

Arguably, the high rates of reoffending can be linked to the prison 'crisis'. The term 'crisis' has been widely accepted by academics since the early 1980s but this represents something of a misnomer. The *Oxford English Dictionary* defines a 'crisis' as 'a period of time when a difficult or important decision must be made'. It is difficult to imagine that such a critical decision could wait for over 30 years. Despite the lack of a clear label, the prison 'crisis' consists of eight component parts culminating in grave problems for the prison system:

(1) the high prison population leads to both:
(2) overcrowding, and
(3) bad conditions (for both staff and inmates).

In turn, this leads to:

(4) understaffing,
(5) staff unrest, and
(6) poor security.

Cavadino and Dignan suggest that these factors symbolise the end product of the crisis:

(7) the toxic mix of prisoners which ultimately leads to:
(8) riots and disorder.

To combat these factors, the government published a White Paper ('Prison Safety and Reform') detailing a £1.3 billion investment in new prisons over the next five years, and it subsequently plans to employ an additional 2,100 prison officers. Despite the influx

13 Data drawn from Ministry of Justice, 'Proven Re-offending Statistics', January to March 2021, published 26 January 2023: www.gov.uk/government/statistics/proven-reoffending-statistics-january-to-march-2021 (accessed March 2023).

of new officers, this would still leave a deficit of almost 4,500 officers when compared to staffing levels in 2010.

What is clear is that both the White Paper and the Justice Minister's plans were seeking both to improve the prison service and subsequently lower reoffending rates of those released from prison. However, perhaps a complete culture change is called for, in order to see the success of Truss's reformation ideas. If England and Wales were willing to depart from the custodial model of punishment and adopt the Nordic approach to criminal justice, we may see such a cultural shift. In Scandinavia, imprisonment is used only for the more serious offences, with a greater utilisation of community sanctions, such as community payback and suspended sentences, for low- and middle-tiered offences. If England and Wales were to follow the Nordic lead, perhaps we could work to lower the prison population, resulting in better staff morale, and improve prison security, especially when considering the extra 2,500 staff due to be hired over the next few years. This could tackle and resolve two of the key components of the prison crisis.

By departing from the current model and prioritising alternatives to custody, England and Wales could offer a more punitive community sentence for those who do not commit violent or dangerous offences. A House of Commons Briefing Paper (published in July 2016) on prison population statistics stated that 10% of all those incarcerated had a sentence of 12 months or less. Potentially, this 'short-term' custody sentence could be replaced with one that is served in the community. A Ministry of Justice study ('The Impact of Short Custodial Sentences, Community Orders and Suspended Sentences Orders on Re-Offending') suggested that these sentences were frequently associated with higher rates of proven reoffending when compared to both community orders and suspended sentences. Furthermore, the short-term custody option was associated with up to one more new offence per person than both community orders and suspended sentences. In essence, a tangible benefit can be derived from using an alternative to short-term custody.

In 2015, a study by the Centre for Crime and Justice Studies suggested that there had been a shift toward the greater use of community sanctions, which have been 'repackaged' in order to ensure that the punitive element of the sanction is visible. The study suggested that there had been four trends in the development of alternatives to custody:

(1) Community sanctions had become more onerous, eg curfews were extended from 12 to 16 hours a day.
(2) The punishment was visible, eg the use of high visibility jackets with the words 'Community Payback' on the back.
(3) The private sector was playing a far greater role with financial incentives to cut reconviction rates.
(4) A greater use of electronic monitoring had been made.

These provisions amplify the punitive element of a community sanction and represent a viable alternative to custody. If the success of any punishment regime is measured by its rate of recidivism, perhaps it is best to support the method with the lower rate of reoffending. By replacing short-term custody with a community sentence for non-dangerous offenders, there would be a tangible reduction in the high prison population, and in turn this could stem the need for new prisons. Furthermore, a reduction in population would improve the conditions for both staff and inmates alike, as prison overcrowding and staff unrest should reduce. Finally, this would dilute the 'toxic mix' of prisoners, which, arguably, is the catalyst for disorder inside the prison walls.

By continuing with a commitment to the greater use of community penalties, the prison crisis may subside and there would be no need for flamboyant calls to focus on reform and rehabilitation. Especially when you consider that the opportunity to focus on rehabilitation has existed since the inception of the Criminal Justice Act 2003. Furthermore, by showing a continued commitment to consider alternatives to custody, the Justice Minister would not have to look to Hollywood for the answers to the prison crisis.

justification: retribution

With the high rate of reoffending, it is difficult to suggest that prison has any justification other than punishment. Whilst it can hold reform and rehabilitative goals, the levels of reoffending are so high that one simply cannot suggest that prison meets these goals.

13.3 Suspended sentences

A suspended sentence is a prison sentence handed down by the courts, but the actual incarceration is 'suspended' or put on hold for a determinate period of time. The rationale for this delay in sending the offender to prison is to allow them one final attempt at reform or rehabilitation. As such, the court will allow the offender to undertake a treatment programme or put them on a period of probation, although there are many different requirements that can be attached to a suspended sentence. The requirements can be found in s 190(1) of the Criminal Justice Act 2003 and they include:

(a) an unpaid work requirement (as defined by s 199),
(b) an unpaid activity (as defined by s 201),
(c) a programme requirement (as defined by s 202),
(d) a prohibited activity requirement (as defined by s 203),
(e) a curfew requirement (as defined by s 204),
(f) an exclusion requirement (as defined by s 205),
(g) a residence requirement (as defined by s 206),
(ga) a foreign travel prohibition (as defined by s 206A)
(h) a mental health treatment requirement (as defined by s 207),
(i) a drug rehabilitation treatment requirement (as defined by s 209),
(j) an alcohol treatment requirement (as defined by s 212),
(k) a supervision requirement (as defined by s 213),
(l) in a case where the offender is aged under 25, an attendance centre requirement (as defined by s 214).

It is important to remember that the custody threshold test needs to be met when the courts are handing down this punishment. This means that the court should not pass a custodial sentence (suspended or otherwise) unless it views the offence, or combination of offences, as 'so serious that neither a fine alone nor community sentence can be justified'.[14] However, a suspended sentence must not be imposed as a more severe form

14 Criminal Justice Act 2003, s 152(2).

of community order. A suspended sentence is a custodial sentence, and the courts have to remember that, if the power to suspend a sentence was not available, they would still sentence the offender to imprisonment. If they cannot be clear on this fact, the court should use a non-custodial sanction.

If the court passes an imprisonment term of at least 14 days but no more than two years then the court is allowed to suspend the sentence.[15] This means that the prison sentence will be deferred and the offender will not serve a prison sentence unless:

(a) during a period specified in the order, the offender commits another offence in the UK (whether or not punishable with imprisonment); and
(b) a court having the power to do so subsequently orders under para 8 of Sch 12 to the Criminal Justice Act 2003 that the original sentence is to take effect.

So, if an offender commits another offence whilst serving a suspended sentence, they will be sentenced for the new crime *and* have to serve the period in prison that was original suspended.

A recent example of suspended sentences working in practice is the high-profile case of Tommy Robinson, the founder of the far-right group, the English Defence League.[16] In May 2017 Robinson claimed that he was looking to 'expose Muslim paedophiles' and recorded himself at Canterbury Crown Court, both on the court steps and inside the court building. There was an obvious risk of his actions prejudicing the trial, and so the judge sentenced him to three months in prison which would be suspended for 18 months. Now, if Robinson did not offend and complied with any additional requirements, he would not be incarcerated. However, 12 months later, Robinson was arrested after broadcasting an hour-long video from outside Leeds Crown Court. He was attempting to video the defendants entering the court building. In his video, he referred to the defendants 'as Muslim child rapists' and 'Muslim paedophiles'. As he was filming on the court steps, he risked identifying a juvenile defendant entering court. When in court, he admitted his guilt, resulting in a sentence of 10 months in prison. This offence also trigged the suspended sentence and the three months from the original offence would run consecutively, meaning that Robinson would serve a total of 13 months in prison. Had this offence occurred outside of the suspended period, he would only have been convicted of the second offence, and thus only been liable to serve the 10-month prison sentence.

The suspended sentence is one the sanctions used least frequently by the court.[17]

Sentencing outcomes	2022
Immediate custody	64,090
Suspended sentence	41,724
Community sentence	69,493
Fine	789,896
Discharge	26,874

15 *Ibid*, s 189(1).

16 Perraudin, F, 'EDL Founder Tommy Robinson jailed for contempt of court', *Guardian*, 29 May 2018: www.theguardian.com/uk-news/2018/may/29/edl-founder-tommy-robinson-jailed-13-months (accessed 14 May 2020).

17 Ministry of Justice, 'Criminal Justice System statistics quarterly: September 2022, Overview Tables' (February 2023), Table Q4.1: www.gov.uk/government/statistics/criminal-justice-statistics-quarterly-september-2022 (accessed 23 May 2023).

Sentencing outcomes	2022
Caution	49,336
Penalty notice for disorder	11,156

In 2022, there were a total of 42,805 suspended sentences handed down by the courts. This figure represents a decline in use since 2018.

	2018	2019	2020	2021	2022
Suspended sentence	45,224	39,350	35,243	44,631	41,724

Justification: deterrence and reform/rehabilitation

Owing to the fact that offenders are not immediately incarcerated, it is clear that retribution is not the primary goal of suspended sentences. There is a high level of prevention theory contained within a suspended sentence; there is an element of specific deterrence, where the courts are attempting to deter the offender, but there are also elements of general deterrence, whereby the courts are highlighting the impact of the offence should other members of the general public undertake similar offences. Furthermore, there are elements of reform and rehabilitation present within the use of suspended sentences, as certain offenders can be enlisted in various treatment programmes in order to tackle their addiction or behavioural problems, where applicable.

13.4 Community sentences

Community sentences are non-custodial sentences that are handed down by the courts. These sentences may be suitable because the offence does not satisfy the custody threshold (for a custodial or suspended sentence) or because the court believes that a community sentence would be more appropriate and productive than a prison sentence. A community sentence is sometimes referred to as a 'community order', 'community service' or 'community payback'.

Whilst community sentences are a viable alternative to custody, they should be not viewed as a soft option. In 2012, the desire to make community sentences hold more retributive value was clear. The then Prime Minister, David Cameron, wanted to toughen up community sentences by allowing the courts to confiscate the credit cards, passports and driving licences of offenders.[18] Cameron wanted to stiffen the penalties to ensure they had added bite and that offenders were not perceived to be 'getting away' with their crimes. He was not alone in thinking that the penalties did not represent much of a deterrent. In a 2012 study, it was found that victims had doubts about how seriously offenders took community penalties and what consequences existed should they not complete their sentence. Furthermore, the study raised doubts about the credibility of certain elements of community sentences, including the aspects of unpaid work, restorative justice and electronic tagging.[19] It concluded that further action was needed to ensure that community sentences effectively delivered the type of justice

18 See Batty, D, 'Community sentences to get tougher under David Cameron plan', *Guardian*, 24 February 2012: www.guardian.co.uk/society/2012/feb/24/community-sentences-tougher-david-cameron (accessed 14 May 2020).

19 Victim Support, 'Out in the open: What victims really think about community sentencing' (September 2012): www.victimsupport.org.uk/sites/default/files/Out%20in%20the%20open%20-%20what%20victims%20really%20think%20about%20community%20sentencing.pdf (accessed 14 May 2020).

victims wanted. Improvements were needed to ensure that victims were aware of and understood community sentences. Finally, the study found that the victims' voice should be heard and engagement with community sentences met.

Section 177 of the Criminal Justice Act 2003 allows the court to make a community order and permits the attachment of any of the following requirements: [20]

(a) an unpaid work requirement (as defined by s 199),
(b) an unpaid activity (as defined by s 201),
(c) a programme requirement (as defined by s 202),
(d) a prohibited activity requirement (as defined by s 203),
(e) a curfew requirement (as defined by s 204),
(f) an exclusion requirement (as defined by s 205),
(g) a residence requirement (as defined by s 206),
(ga) a foreign travel prohibition (as defined by s 206A),
(h) a mental health treatment requirement (as defined by s 207),
(i) a drug rehabilitation treatment requirement (as defined by s 209),
(j) an alcohol treatment requirement (as defined by s 212),
(k) a supervision requirement (as defined by s 213),
(l) in a case where the offender is aged under 25, an attendance centre requirement (as defined by s 214).

If the offender fails to comply with any element of their community sentence, they can be recalled to court and resentenced. Section 177(5) of the Criminal Justice Act 2003 states that the order must not exceed three years in duration. The 'threshold test' for a community sentence can be found in s 148(1),[21] which states:

> A court must not pass a community sentence on an offender unless it is of the opinion that the offence, or combination of the offence and one or more offences associated with it, was serious enough to warrant such a sentence.

However, even if this threshold is not met, s 151[22] provides that 'in relation to an offender aged 16 or over on whom, on 3 or more previous occasions, sentences had been passed consisting only of a fine, a community sentence may be imposed (if it is in the interests of justice)'. So, even if the current offence does not meet the sentencing threshold, an offender can still receive a community penalty if they have previously received three financial penalties. The sentencing guidelines are very fluid regarding community sentences, and sentencers need to: [23]

(a) assess the seriousness of the individual offence;
(b) consult the sentencing guidelines for that offence;
(c) examine the factors that would indicate that custody is likely; and
(d) if not, consider what other disposal is most appropriate.

The Sentencing Council suggests that there are three types of offences that may warrant a community order: [24]

(a) *Low:* These are offences that only just reach the community order threshold. But the seriousness of the offence or the offender's previous record means that

20 Criminal Justice Act 2003, s 177(1)(a)–(i).
21 Criminal Justice Act 2003.
22 *Ibid.*
23 See Sentencing Guidelines Council, 'Overarching Principles: Seriousness' (2004), para 1.35: www.sentencingcouncil.org.uk/wp-content/uploads/Seriousness-guideline.pdf (accessed 14 May 2020).
24 The Community Orders Table is available here: www.sentencingcouncil.org.uk/droppable/item/community-orders-table/ (accessed 14 May 2020).

discharge or a fine would be inappropriate. The Council suggests that only one requirement would be appropriate from the following list:

(i) any appropriate rehabilitative requirement(s),
(ii) 40–80 hours of unpaid work,
(iii) a minor curfew requirement, eg up to 16 hours per day for a few weeks,
(iv) an exclusion requirement for a short period of time,
(v) a prohibited activity requirement.

(b) *Medium:* These offences are such that it is clear that they fall within the community penalty banding. The following sanctions are deemed appropriate for these offences:

(i) any appropriate rehabilitative requirement(s),
(ii) 80–150 hours unpaid work,
(iii) a curfew requirement, eg 16 hours for 2–3 months,
(iv) an exclusion requirement lasting in the region of 6 months,
(v) a prohibited activity requirement.

(c) *High:* These offences are so serious that they only just fall below the custody threshold, or they pass the custody threshold but the community penalty is deemed to be more appropriate in the circumstances. This order is designed to be intensive and may combine two or more appropriate requirements, which include:

(i) any rehabilitative requirement(s),
(ii) 150–300 hours of unpaid work,
(iii) a curfew requirement up to 16 hours per day for 4–12 months,
(iv) an exclusion requirement lasting in the region of 12 months.

Despite the raft of available requirements, the use of the penalty has dwindled significantly over the course of the last decade.[25]

	2018	2019	2020	2021	2022
Community sentence	90,629	89,853	62,385	72,733	69,493

As you can see, there has been a decrease of almost 22,000 offences being sentenced via a community sentence since 2018. The CREST Report, 'Where did it all go wrong? A study in the use of community sentences in England and Wales'[26] found the following:[27]

- Offenders were not properly held to account for not complying with their sentence and one-third of offenders breached their order. Furthermore, 33% of offenders serving a community sentence were reconvicted within a year of being originally sentenced.
- The orders represented little more than a stepping-stone to custody and had little reformative or rehabilitative impact. 35% of those sentenced to custody had received *at least* five community sentences.
- Magistrates had lost confidence in the validity of the orders. A survey commissioned by the CREST Report found that 37% of magistrates were not

25 Criminal Justice Statistics Quarterly (n 17).

26 CREST, 'Where did it all go wrong? A study into the use of community sentences in England and Wales' (2017): www.crestadvisory.com/post/community-sentences-where-did-it-all-go-wrong (accessed 14 May 2020).

27 *Ibid* 6.

confident that community sentences were an effective alternative to custody and 65% were not confident that community sentences reduced crime.

The Report recommended 11 policy changes that aim to increase the validity of punishment in the community:[28]

(1) Creation of Project Hope for England and Wales – this will focus on the most prolific drug and theft offenders. Specific judges would be designated for the programme and conduct hearings within 24 hours of a breach.
(2) Greater flexibility for magistrates – this will allow magistrates to tailor community sentences to match the offender's needs.
(3) Amending sentencing guidelines – this will introduce a presumption of intensive community orders for young adults who would ordinarily be imprisoned for 12 months or less.
(4) Remove the assumption that suspended sentence orders are less onerous than a community order – sentencing guidelines should make it clear that the numerous community order requirements can be as onerous. In time, the Ministry of Justice should abolish the requirement orders issued under a suspended sentence.
(5) Give magistrates the power to review prolific offenders serving short custodial sentences – furthermore, Police and Crime Commissioners should be given powers to monitor the outcome of court sentences.
(6) Train magistrates further – magistrates need additional training to understand the range of requirements available to them.
(7) Improve the quality of pre-sentencing advice – the Report indicates a decline in the quality of pre-sentencing reports over the last decade. By re-establishing the importance of the report, the sentence can be further tailored to the individual offender.
(8) Provide feedback about the outcome of sentences to magistrates – magistrates lack basic information about evidence-based sentencing decisions.
(9) Support greater transparency of community sentences, especially the nature of unpaid work – this could show the local community that the sanction is onerous or tough. It could lead to a change in culture and mean that people no longer 'get away with it' if they are sentenced to a community sentence.
(10) Ensure that sentences start more promptly – if an offender is incarcerated, they are sent to prison immediately. However, it can be several weeks before the community order starts.
(11) Enable Police and Crime Commissioners to co-commission offender management services locally – this would enable local areas to invest in more intensive/innovative alternatives to custody.

Whilst these goals are both ambitious and expensive, they do have a clear theme running through them. Simply put, more needs to be done to enhance the quality and validity of any community punishment. The public, magistrates and offender need to feel that there is a deterrent offered by these punishments. The CREST Report asserts that, rather than being a pathway to prison, the community punishment can divert offenders from future offending and, ultimately, stem the tide of incarceration. Not only will this lower the prison population and help abate the prison crisis, but it will also have a dual impact. It will save the taxpayer millions of pounds each year, and it will also increase the confidence of both sentencers and the public that community sentences are an effective alternative to prison.

28 *Ibid* 56.

justification: prevention

Community sentences look not only to reform or rehabilitate the offender; they attempt to offer a deterrent to crime. Currently, such sentences lack the confidence of both the sentencers and the public that they offer an alternative to prison. However, with some investment and tweaks, that outlook could be reversed and the community sanction could represent an effective and viable alternative to prison but also offer a deterrent to others, whilst addressing the individual needs of the offender.

13.5 Fines

A fine is a financial penalty that can be imposed for any offence, save for one which has a mandatory life sentence, ie murder. Whilst a fine may not be suitable for every offence, at times the courts have attempted to use the penalty to a greater degree. In *Baldwin*,[29] Lord Woolf CJ suggested that with the prison system suffering from a severe degree of overcrowding, the fine could be a useful sanction 'if there are good prospects that an offender is not going to prey upon the public again …'.[30]

The Criminal Justice Act 2003 allows the court to impose a fine on an offender in lieu of, or in addition to, dealing with him in another way.[31] However, in reality, the use of a fine is generally reserved for low-level offenders and will often be an inadequate response in indictable-only cases, where use of the fine is extremely low.

The fine is the most popular form of criminal sanction in the magistrates' court. In 2022, some 789,896 people were handed a fine in all courts. The next most frequently used punishment was community service, with 69,493 sentences handed down. Custodial and suspended sentences made up 105,814 decisions, whereas 26,874 cases resulted in a discharge. So, it is clear that the fine is by far the most commonly used sanction. Furthermore, the use of the fine has remained relatively stable over the last three years.

	2018	2019	2020	2021	2022
Fine	915,675	923,383	675,860	722,973	789,896

13.5.1 How is a fine fixed?

Section 37 of the Criminal Justice Act 1982 created the standard scale of fines for summary offences. There are five levels of fine:

Level	Current Maximum Fine (£)
1	200
2	500
3	1,000
4	2,500
5	Unlimited

29 [2002] EWCA Crim 2647; (2002) *The Times*, 22 November.
30 *Ibid* [9].
31 Criminal Justice Act 2003, s 163.

Until March 2015, the maximum fine the magistrates' court was permitted to hand down was £5,000, but it is now unlimited. This adds further retributive bite to the penalty, as well as enhancing the general deterrent effect. To assess how much a particular individual or company should be fined, the court turns to s 164 of the Criminal Justice Act 2003, which states:

(1) Before fixing the amount of any fine to be imposed on an offender … a court must inquire into his financial circumstances.
(2) The amount of any fine fixed by a court must be such as, in the opinion of the court, reflects the seriousness of the offence.
(3) In fixing the amount of any fine to be imposed on an offender …, a court must take into account the circumstances of the case including, among other things, the financial circumstances of the offender so far as they are known, or appear, to the court.
(4) Subsection (3) applies whether taking into account the financial circumstances of the offender has the effect of increasing or reducing the amount of the fine.

There are six different bands that an offender's fine could fall into, and each of the bands has a different starting point and range:

Band	Starting point	Range
Fine Band A	50% of relevant weekly income	25–75% of relevant weekly income
Fine Band B	100% of relevant weekly income	75–125% of relevant weekly income
Fine Band C	150% of relevant weekly income	125–175% of relevant weekly income
Fine Band D	250% of relevant weekly income	200–300% of relevant weekly income
Fine Band E	400% of relevant weekly income	300–500% of relevant weekly income
Fine Band F	600% of relevant weekly income	500–700% of relevant weekly income

The relevant weekly income is calculated using the following formula: Where an offender is in receipt of income from employment and that income is more than £120 per week after deduction of tax and national insurance, that remaining amount is the relevant weekly income. If the offender's only source of income is state benefits, the relevant weekly income is deemed to be £120.[32] If an offender provides no information regarding their financial situation or the court believes it has not been furnished with reliable information, the court will proceed on the basis that the assumed relevant weekly income is £440. This figure is derived from the national median pre-tax figure.

The fine is payable on the day that it is imposed and the court should seek payment immediately. However, with potentially large sanctions being handed down, this will not always be possible. The court will accept a fine being paid in instalments but it is

32 Details on the definition of relevant weekly income can be found here: www.sentencingcouncil.org.uk/explanatory-material/item/fines-and-financial-orders/approach-to-the-assessment-of-fines-2/3-definition-of-relevant-weekly-income/ (accessed 14 May 2020).

expected that it will be paid within a 12-month period. For Band E and F fines, this period can be extended to 18 or 24 months.

Any instalment plan should be realistic and reflect the disposable income of the offender. The Sentencing Council suggests the following approach:

Net weekly income	Suggested start point for weekly payments
£60	£5
£120	£10
£200	£25
£300	£50
£400	£80

13.5.2 Sanctions for non-payment

If a fine is not paid, there are a number of different outcomes that could occur:

- A warrant of control[33] could be issued against the offender. This means that bailiffs will be authorised to both seize and sell goods belonging to the offender. The proceeds of the sale will be deducted from the outstanding fine amount.
- If the offender is employed, an attachment of earnings order[34] could be made. This means that the employer will deduct a regular sum of the offender's salary and pay the court directly.
- If the offender is on state benefits, a similar order could be made to deduct a regular sum from the benefit and pay the court directly.[35]
- If the fine was issued for an offence that could warrant a custodial sentence, the offender could be sent to prison. The court needs to believe that the offender has the means to pay but will not comply with payments, or that the failure is due to 'wilful refusal or culpable neglect'.[36]

The period of imprisonment will depend on the amount the offender was fined. [37]

Fine amount	Prison term
An amount not exceeding £200	7 days
An amount exceeding £200 but not exceeding £500	14 days
An amount exceeding £500 but not exceeding £1,000	28 days
An amount exceeding £1,000 but not exceeding £2,500	45 days
An amount exceeding £2,500 but not exceeding £5,000	3 months
An amount exceeding £5,000 but not exceeding £10,000	6 months
An amount exceeding £10,000 but not exceeding £20,000	12 months

However, the Criminal Justice Act 2003 allows the court to substitute unpaid work or curfew requirements for prison.[38] Or the offender could be disqualified from driving for a period of up to 12 months.[39]

33 Tribunal, Courts and Enforcement Act 2007, s 62.
34 Attachment of Earnings Act 1971.
35 Fines (Deduction from Income Support) Regulations 1992 (SI 1992/2182).
36 Magistrates' Courts Act 1980, s 82(4).
37 *Ibid*, Sch 4.
38 Criminal Justice Act 2003, s 300(2).
39 *Ibid*, s 301.

13.5.3 Equal fines: equal impact?

One disadvantage with the fixed fine is the fact that it will impact people differently. If a wealthy person and someone in receipt of benefits are both fined £200 for their separate offences, the actual effect of the fine will be very different. Hypothetically, the wealthy person would not be deterred from their offending behaviour as the money might mean very little to them, whereas the less well-off offender would feel a greater impact of the same punishment.

In order to combat this disparity between different offenders, England and Wales could revert to the unit fine system of the early 1990s. A brief flirtation with this system was quickly abandoned some seven months after its inception.[40] The Criminal Justice Act 1991 created a system that financially punished offenders based on their means and not the seriousness of their offence.[41] However, Warner suggested[42] that the system had two key flaws. First, the system was very complex in terms of what was classed as disposable income, and, secondly, the media suggested that the high amount of fines levied meant that the system was attacking the middle class, without giving any explanation that the level of fines was based on disposable income. One example focused on a defendant being fined £1,200 for littering, albeit that the fine was imposed because he had neglected to provide evidence of his disposable income. On appeal, the fine was reduced to £48.

In 2006, the Labour Government suggested a similar approach known as 'day fines', which would look at the daily income of the offender. However, this proposition lapsed when the parliamentary session ended. Whilst, in theory, the notion of unit fines or day fines would represent a system that could ensure that the retributive and deterrent effects of a penalty were felt by everyone, regardless of wealth, the system could not shake off the shackles of disproportionate penalties for very low-level and minor offending. The importance of a punishment being proportionate and deserving is an equally legitimate goal as ensuring that there is retribution or deterrence attached to a penalty. The danger of disproportionate penalties was one of the reasons why the Scottish Commission rejected the use of such systems.[43] Whilst, in theory, the idea of equal impact is attractive, the notion that the better-off could be punished more severely for committing the same crime as a less well-off offender smacks of disproportionality. If penalties are disproportionate and offer a sanction that an offender does not deserve, there is a danger that the criminal justice process is undermined by illegitimate sentences. The public might lose faith in the justice system if offenders were given more than their 'just deserts'.

---

40 Roberts, J, Zedner, L and Ashworth, A, *Principles and Values in Criminal Law and Justice: Essays in Honour of Andrew Ashworth* (Oxford: Oxford University Press, 2012), 231.

41 Home Office, *Crime, Justice and Protecting the Public* (Cm 965, 1990), 7, 26.

42 'Equality Before the Law and Equal Impact of Sanctions: Doing Justice to Differences in Wealth and Employment Status' in Roberts (n 40), 231.

43 Sentencing Commission for Scotland, 'Basis on which Fines are Determined' (Report, 2006) at p 11: www.cjscotland.co.uk/wp-content/uploads/2011/03/basis-fines1.pdf (accessed 14 May 2020).

justification: retribution and prevention

The fine is designed to create financial hardship for the offender – that is the pain that the retributivist seeks. It satisfies prevention theory by offering both specific and general deterrence. However, there is a problem with this; it only offers a deterrent to the very poor. The wealthy might be able to easily afford the financial sanction, and therefore the penalty offers little deterrence. An argument exists that any financial penalty should be tailored to an individual's income, so that the offender feels the impact of the sanction. Otherwise we are left with a disproportionate penalty that penalises the very poor but has little impact on the wealthy. However, if penalties are too disproportionate, it could challenge the legitimacy of the justice system, and the public might lose faith in the ability of the system to deal with offenders justly.

13.6 Discharge

When sentencing, the courts can decide that 'it is inexpedient to inflict punishment'[44] on the offender. They can:

- discharge the offender absolutely; or
- discharge the offender subject to a condition that he does not commit a further offence during the period specified[45] in the order.

If a defendant receives an absolute discharge, it is effectively a final chance to stop offending or they will feel the feel the full force of the law and be sanctioned accordingly. Arguably, some may view this response to offending as a 'let off'. These 'let-offs' occur where an offender is technically guilty of the crime but the court finds it difficult to attach any culpability to them. Whilst these cases are rare, they are not limited to trivial offences. In 2017, in Scotland, a 19-year-old man was given an absolute discharge for raping a 12-year-old girl. The man got into a taxi with the drunk girl who she suggested that she was 17 years old. The taxi driver estimated that her age was around 20. The judge held that there were a number of exceptional circumstances in this case:

- The defendant was a first-time offender and the judge did not believe that the defendant would reoffend.
- When he first learned of the victim's age, he became visibly distressed.
- He had to change his college course and suspend his university plans.
- He would need professional help to deal with this situation in the future.
- There was no evidence of predatory conduct, grooming, manipulation or deception.

As a result of these factors, the judge elected to discharge the defendant absolutely. This is a rare example of an absolute discharge for a serious offence. It is important to remember that this happened outside the jurisdiction of England and Wales, but it nevertheless illustrates the judicial discretion of the judge in passing any sentence he or she deems appropriate, regardless of the severity of crime.

44 Powers of Criminal Courts (Sentencing) Act 2000, s 12(1).

45 *Ibid*, s 12(1)(b) states that the period of condition cannot exceed three years.

A conditional discharge is similar to a suspended sentence. If the offender does not commit any further offences during the period of the 'conditions', then no punishment will be inflicted on them. Should the offender breach the conditions, the court can sentence the offender for the original offence anew, and therefore the whole range of sentencing options are open to the court. This differs from the suspended sentence where, should the offender breach the suspension, the court will quash the suspended nature of the sentence and incarcerate the offender. Like absolute discharges, the conditional discharge can be used for both serious and trivial offences. In 2016, a former aide to the Prime Minister received a conditional discharge for making indecent images of children. Patrick Rock entered a plea of guilty; however, the trial judge indicated that a custodial sentence was not appropriate. Because Rock had previously attempted to address his behaviour at a clinic, the judge also concluded that a community sentence would be inappropriate. In deciding upon a conditional discharge, the judge believed that this would serve both as a warning and as an incentive to not reoffend.[46] Furthermore, as part of the conditions, the judge made a sexual harm prevention order that disbarred Rock from possessing any device that could connect to the internet but not retain the search history. He would also be compelled to turn the device over to the police upon request.

Despite the sanction's deployment in these serious cases, it is clear that its use is on the decline.

	2018	2019	2020	2021	2022
Absolute discharge	5,251	4,228	3,055	2,300	2,430
Conditional discharge	44,290	38,246	28,417	29,646	24,444
Total	49,541	42, 474	31,472	31,946	26,874

As you can see, over the course of the last five years there has been a substantial drop-off in the use of both the absolute and conditional discharge. The use of the discharge has dropped by nearly half over the course of the last five years, which indicates that any leniency offered by the court is dwindling.

justification: prevention

The idea of both the conditional and absolute discharge is to deter the offender from future reoffending. The absolute discharge allows the offender to walk free from court and have a final chance to stop their offending behaviour. Any further offences will generate a harsher response from the court. Whilst the conditional discharge is looking to deter crime and stop the offending behaviour, the conditions attached could lead to the offender being reformed or rehabilitated. There is little retributive bite to either discharge. The punishment uses other elements to ensure that it meets the purpose of sentencing.

46 For the full sentencing comments, see www.judiciary.uk/wp-content/uploads/2016/06/r-v-rock-sentencing.pdf (accessed 14 May 2020).

13.7 Out of court disposals

As well as punishments that can be handed down by the court, an offender can also be sanctioned without going through the entire criminal justice process. These are called out of court disposals and, essentially, they are punishments which are administered by the police. Whilst there are a number of safeguards to the formal criminal justice sanctions, these out of court disposals have very few safeguards attached to them. They are mainly used for low-level offending but, nevertheless, they can hold stark ramifications should the offender accept the punishment. There are two main out of court disposals that this chapter will consider:

- simple and conditional cautions; and
- penalty notices for disorder.

13.7.1 Simple and conditional cautions

There are two types of caution with which an offender can be punished: a simple caution and a conditional caution. An analysis of the use of both cautions is set out below.

The simple caution

Effectively, a caution is a disposal used by the police in relation to low-level offending. The caution is not a criminal conviction. A caution requires an offender to admit their guilt; it should not be offered to someone who wishes to contest their guilt. The caution is a speedy response to low-level offending, such as minor criminal damage or theft. In order for the police to give the offender a caution, they need to be satisfied that there is a realistic prospect of conviction; that is, if the case went to trial, the 'Full Code Test' would be satisfied.[47] Generally, it would not be appropriate for a person to be cautioned where they have already been cautioned or convicted for the same offence (within the last two years). As such, an offender who has been caught spraying graffiti, who admits their guilt, should not be given a caution if they have already received a caution for the same offence in the previous two years.

In order to administer a caution, the police officer must consider a number of factors. The police can offer a caution for any summary or triable either-way offence. For indictable-only offences, s 17(2) of the Criminal Justice and Courts Act 2015 prohibits the police from offering a caution unless the CPS agrees that a caution is acceptable in these circumstances.

The decision to caution will consider the following factors:

(a) Whether there is an admission of guilt from the offender. The caution cannot be offered as an inducement for the offender to admit their guilt.

(b) The seriousness of the offence – the more serious the offence, the less likely it is that a caution will be appropriate. Whilst cautions are available for all offences, s 17(4) of the Criminal Justice and Courts Act 2015 sets out restrictions on the use of cautions. Furthermore, there needs to be consideration of the likely penalty should the person be convicted at trial.

(c) The age, mental well-being and previous criminal history of the offender. As stated above, repeat offenders are unlikely to receive a second caution.

(d) What is the impact on the victim? Will the victim be satisfied if the offender receives a caution?

---

47 See **Chapter 4**.

When the above criteria have been fulfilled, the police can now offer the offender a caution. If the offender accepts a caution, *it is not a criminal conviction*. However, there are number of implications in accepting a caution:

(a) It will be recorded on the offender's criminal record. Should the offender commit further offences, it could influence how the police deal with that person – a repeat offender is more likely to be charged with an offence than a first-time offender.

(b) There is the potential that the caution might be disclosed on a person's DBS (disclosure and barring service) check, and it may hamper their ability to gain employment.

(c) If the caution relates to a sexual offence, the offender will be placed on the Sex Offenders Register.

(d) If the person needs to go through the civil justice system, such as the family courts, the caution may be submitted as evidence against the offender.

(e) There are potential implications surrounding travel and immigration. The caution may bar the offender from entering certain countries.

The above illustrate the potential dangers of accepting a police caution, but it is important to note that the accused does not have to accept the caution. Should the accused decline the caution, it is likely that they will be charged with the criminal offence and the case will proceed to trial. (Remember that the caution criteria state that there must be a realistic prospect of conviction, should the case go to trial. Otherwise, it is inappropriate to administer a caution.) Furthermore, there is no right to appeal once the caution has been administered and accepted. If the caution was administered incorrectly (in terms of procedure), it can be quashed in the High Court via judicial review, but this would be a very lengthy and expensive endeavour.

The conditional caution

A conditional caution is designed to halt criminal proceedings before the offence is prosecuted at trial. Generally, a police officer will be the person who administers the caution, and it can have one or more conditions attached to it. According to the Code of Practice for Adult Conditional Cautions, the conditional caution acts:

- as a proportionate response to low-level offending;
- as an opportunity to make reparation to the victims/local community;
- as an opportunity to engage with rehabilitative services, which should reduce the likelihood of reoffending;
- in order to punish an offender by way of a financial penalty.

The cautioning criteria for a conditional caution are the same as for a simple caution. However, the caution will not result in a prosecution so long as the offender complies with the 'conditions' of the caution. The conditions can serve a number of differing purposes, including the rehabilitation of the offender,[48] to make reparation for the offence,[49] or to punish the offender.[50] Should the offender not comply with the conditions attached to the caution or within the prescribed timescale then the caution will cease to have effect and criminal proceedings can commence.[51]

Section 23 of the Criminal Justice Act 2003 sets out a five-stage process that must be followed before a conditional caution is administered:

---

48 Criminal Justice Act 2003, s 22(3)(a).

49 *Ibid* s 22(3)(b).

50 *Ibid* s 22(3)(c).

51 *Ibid* s 24(3).

(1) The authorised person[52] must have evidence that the offender has committed the offence.
(2) There must be sufficient evidence to charge the offender with the offence.
(3) There must be an admission of guilt from the offender.
(4) The authorised person must explain the effect of the conditional caution and the consequences should the offender not comply with the conditions.
(5) The offender needs to sign a document which contains details of the offence, an admission of guilt, consent to being given the conditional caution and the conditions attached to the caution.

The overall use of cautions

The use of cautions has dramatically decreased over the last decade. The table below illustrates this:[53]

	2018	2019	2020	2021	2022	Percentage change 12 months ending September 2021 to September 2022
OOCD: cautions	72,286	65,731	58,034	50,701	49,336	−2.7%

Whilst the number of cautions has dwindled over the course of the last five years, cautions are still being handed out for a number of very serious offences heard in the Crown Court.[54]

Offence type	Offence group	Year	
Indictable	Indictable offences total	2022	25,488
Indictable	Violence against the person	2022	6,790
Indictable	Sexual offences	2022	490
Indictable	Robbery	2022	57
Indictable	Theft offences	2022	3,392
Indictable	Criminal damage and arson	2022	369
Indictable	Drug offences	2022	9,761
Indictable	Possession of weapons	2022	2,136
Indictable	Public order offences	2022	1,985
Indictable	Miscellaneous crimes against society	2022	1,052
Indictable	Fraud offences	2022	464

As this table makes clear, there were over 7,000 offences involving either violence against the person or sexual offences that were sanctioned by a caution in 2022. Considering the mantra of being tough on crime and sending more people to prison, this makes for surprising reading.

52 This will generally be the police officer.
53 Criminal Justice Statistics Quarterly (n 17).
54 *Ibid.*

13.7.2 Penalty notices for disorder

A penalty notice for disorder (PND) is effectively a police-administered fine, introduced by the Criminal Justice and Police Act 2001.[55] The level of fine is fixed between two tiers. Whilst the fines are given for low-level offending, there is a distinction between the two types of offending. The lower tier offences, such as trespassing on a railway, throwing stones at a train and littering, attract a fixed penalty of £60. The upper tier offences, including shoplifting (under the value of £100), throwing fireworks, causing harassment, alarm or distress and wasting police time, attract a penalty of £90. The offender has 21 days from the date the PND is issued to pay the penalty. Unlike the caution, no admission of guilt is required to administer or accept the penalty; once the penalty has been paid, the offender discharges any liability to be convicted of the penalty offence. Should the offender not pay the penalty within the required timeframe, a fine of one and a half times the penalty will be registered in the offender's local magistrates' court as enforcement of the fine.[56]

In total, there are 16 upper tier offences that will attract the £90 fine:

- wasting police time/giving a false report;
- sending electronic communications in order to cause annoyance, inconvenience or anxiety;
- knowingly raising a false fire alarm;
- using words or behaviour that are likely to cause harassment, alarm or distress;
- throwing fireworks;
- being drunk and disorderly in a public place;
- criminal damage under £300 in value;
- retail theft (under £100);
- breach of a firework curfew (between 11pm–7am);
- possession of a category 4 firework;
- selling or attempting to sell alcohol to person who is drunk;
- supplying alcohol by or on behalf of a club to a person aged under 18;
- selling alcohol anywhere to a person under 18;
- buying or attempting to buy alcohol for consumption on relevant premises by a person under 18;
- delivering alcohol to a person under 18;
- possessing a Class B drug, eg cannabis.

As you can see, there is a heavy element of trying to curb the ability of those under age to drink alcohol. However, there are some quirky offences that attract the £90 fine – how many times have bar staff served people who are drunk, and how many people have set off fireworks past the curfew on New Year's Eve?

As you would expect, the lower tier offences are more trivial in nature. The offences that attract the £60 fine are:

- trespassing on a railway;
- throwing stones at a train or railway;
- being drunk in a highway, public place or licensed premises;

55 Criminal Justice and Police Act 2001, ss 1–11.

56 See Ministry of Justice, *Penalty Notices for Disorder (PNDs)*, June 2014, para 1.8: https://assets.publishing.service.gov.uk/government/uploads/system/uploads/attachment_data/file/403812/penalty-notice-disorder-police-guidance.pdf (accessed 14 May 2020).

- consuming alcohol in a designated public place, contrary to a requirement not to do so;
- littering;
- allowing consumption of alcohol by a person under 18;
- littering in a Royal Park or other open space;
- using pedal cycle/skates/blade/board or foot-propelled device in a Royal Park or other open space;
- failure to remove animal faeces from a Royal Park or other space (unless the person is registered blind);
- possessing a Class C drug, eg khat.

Despite their relatively trivial nature, the PND evidently covers a vast array of offences. However, there is almost no oversight or supervision from the authorities in relation to the penalty; in practice, the use of the sanction is left entirely to the police. Sanders, Young and Burton suggest that the use of PNDs is 'not about prosecutions but about controlling suspect populations and should be viewed as part of a wider goal to increase surveillance and curb anti-social behaviour'.[57]

An example of curbing anti-social behaviour is something one of the authors witnessed first hand. In December 2008, Millwall played Bristol Rovers at the New Den. Bristol Rovers equalised late in the game to level the game at 2–2, and, unsurprisingly, the goal sparked joyous scenes amongst the travelling fans. One of the author's group witnessed a police officer push over a fan, which caused him to topple back into the seats. Incensed with that he had witnessed, the member of the group told the police officer that he would be filing an official complaint. Within minutes, three officers marched up the stand to arrest the group member for being drunk and disorderly in a public place and subsequently issued a PND. Whilst this is one anecdotal example, it does point to the idea that 'attack is the best form of defence'. As such, the officer felt under threat from the group member and elected to quash that threat by using the power of arrest. Ultimately, the use of this power allows the police to 'get a result'[58] but does not allow any further scrutiny from those in authority and very little due process protection for the offender.

However, the use of the PND has been declining over the course of the last decade:

	2018	2019	2020	2021	2022	Percentage change 12 months ending September 2021 to September 2022
OOCD: penalty notices for disorder	21,934	20,728	17,427	13,555	11,156	−17.7%

As previously stated, the offences for which one can receive a PND are relatively trivial. What this disposal permits is potentially more people being drawn into the criminal justice process, where previously they would have been told to 'knock off that behaviour and go home'. This notion is called 'net widening' – effectively, the fisherman (the police) have a wide net on their trawler and therefore they should be able to catch more fish (offenders). The aforementioned lack of scrutiny means that

57 Welsh, L, Skinns, L and Sanders, A, *Sanders & Young's Criminal Justice* (OUP, 2021).

58 *Ibid.*

this may be a very attractive disposal for a target-driven police officer and bring more offenders under the umbrella of social control. The lack of due process protections to this sanction means that the police have a rather unfettered amount of discretion in their use of PNDs.[59]

> **justification**
>
> There are a number of different justifications for using an out of court disposal as a response to crime. At one level, the sanction contains elements of retributive theory: the sanction contains an element of punitive harm in terms of financial penalty. The notion of preventative theory also runs through out of court disposals. They attempt to offer a deterrent and allow the offender to reform and rehabilitate their criminal behaviour to divert them from any future offending.

13.8 Conclusion

As this chapter has highlighted, there are a number of different sanctions that are available to both the courts and police as a response to criminal acts. They differ in what crimes they are appropriate for, but we have seen examples of sanctions that are generally seen to be at the lower end of the scale, such as the caution, being used for crimes that are very serious. In the main, out of court disposals are reserved for low-level crime, and they also give rise to less scrutiny. This allows the police to use their discretion with very little worry of complaint or validation.

Whilst prison is deemed the most severe punishment available in England and Wales, it has very high rates of reoffending, suggesting that prison does not, in reality, work as a deterrent from future crime. With the general public incorrectly believing that the criminal justice system is 'soft', it is arguable that the community sanction could provide a punishment that works, if there could be more retributive bite attached to it. Whilst the authors do not believe that sanctions have to get harsher, if the general public do not believe that sanctions are harsh, they are unlikely ever to be debated by MPs. It is clear that the punishment process in England and Wales is not fit for purpose and needs a radical overhaul to focus on elements that reduce levels of reoffending whilst simultaneously offering a deterrent to stop others from offending.

59 For more on social control and net widening, see Brown, AP, 'Anti-social Behaviour, Crime Control and Social Control' (2004) *Howard Journal of Criminal Justice*, 43(2), 203–11.

chapter 14 The Ripple Effect of Imprisonment: The Impact on Families

14.1 Introduction

This chapter will examine the impact that imprisonment has on the family remaining on the outside and in their community. We suggest that this effect is viewed through an analogy of throwing a rock into a lake. The rock hitting the water is the loved one being sent to prison. It is easy to observe the immediate splash. However, what is sometimes ignored is the ripple effect caused by the splash. For the purposes of this chapter, the ripple effect makes up the differing impacts suffered by families on the outside.

As this book has highlighted, there are almost 85,000 people currently in prison. What is often ignored is the effect that such sentences have on the offender's families who remain living their everyday lives outside of prison. This chapter will examine the impact that imprisonment has on relationship stability, children and the household finances of those with an incarcerated family member. Whilst this is a non-exhaustive list of the wider impacts of prison, they are the most important. This is an under-researched area and, for the purposes of this chapter, the data is drawn from England and Wales, Scotland and the United States. Reporting in 2002, the Social Exclusion Unit suggested that 55% of male prisoners described themselves as living with a partner prior to a custodial sentence being handed down by the court.[1] Crest, an independent consultancy body specialising in criminal justice and policing, estimates that there are 312,000 children in England and Wales who have a parent in prison.[2] This figure is based on its data simulation as no concrete data concerning children is collected during the criminal justice process. The Social Exclusion Unit also explained that 43% of sentenced prisoners and 48% of remand prisoners (that is people who are incarcerated as they await trial) lost contact with their families after entering the prison estate.[3] Finally, almost a quarter of prisoners (22%) who were married when entering prison were believed to have divorced or separated whilst serving their sentence.[4] However, information regarding the family of prisoners is collected 'inconsistently, for different purposes and not used in a systematic way … [making it difficult] to understand the wider family picture'.[5] As such, this chapter will take research from differing jurisdictions in order to build a picture of how prison can impact families, which can be pieced together like a jigsaw to demonstrate its overall effect. Ultimately, the chapter will highlight that the effect of imprisonment on the family can be viewed as a 'shadow

---

1 Social Exclusion Unit, *Reducing Re-offending by ex-prisoners* (2002), p 112: www.bristol.ac.uk/poverty/downloads/keyofficialdocuments/Reducing%20Reoffending.pdf (accessed 15 May 2020).

2 Crest, *Children of Prisoners: Fixing a Broken System* (2019), p 7: www.crestadvisory.com/post/children-of-prisoners-fixing-a-broken-system (accessed 15 May 2020).

3 Social Exclusion Unit (n 1) at p 112.

4 See the Illustrated Empathy Gap: http://empathygap.uk/?p=1717 (accessed 15 May 2020).

5 Crest (n 2) at p 7.

punishment'[6] – generally invisible or ignored by the criminal justice system and the general public. This chapter will make clear that it is not only the prisoner who is 'punished' by their period of incarceration but often their families; and this 'punishment' can come in a number of different and unwarranted guises. Further, the impact of imprisonment represents an element of social injustice, which Lacey suggests needs tackling as we 'cannot deliver effective criminal justice without offering a remedy for social injustice'.[7]

14.2 Family ties: the impact on marriage

The importance of maintaining family ties throughout a prison sentence cannot be overstated. Strong family ties can help reduce future reoffending upon release as well as improving the life chances of children whose parents have been imprisoned.[8] The Farmer Review, published in 2017, suggested that these ties provide the prisoner with 'hope',[9] with one prisoner commenting that 'if I don't see my family, I will lose them, if I lose them, what do I have left?'[10] This paints a picture of despair for the prisoner. They need their family and if they receive regular visits from their family, their chances of reoffending are 39% lower than for those who do not receive regular visits.[11] As such, maintaining ties is clearly important and that stability will be an underlying factor in whether or not the relationship can survive the period of imprisonment.

When a defendant is going through the criminal justice process, they will be able to communicate with family members throughout the process. However, when a person is convicted and subsequently sent to prison, this could come as shock to family members and leave no time for discussion of how those on the outside will continue living their lives. It will be left to the partner on the outside to determine issues such as housing, child care and finances, and almost immediately the family will be placed under considerable stress. The result of this stress could put potentially already strained marriages under a greater deal of further pressure, which could culminate in the collapse of the marriage. In 2005, a US study highlighted that declining marriage among such couples increased the likelihood of a child being disadvantaged, with a heightened risk of offending behaviour.[12] Siennick, Stewart and Staff suggest that a spouse can provide a wall of support for a partner in prison as they offer a bridge to 'kinship'. [13] They suggest that these relationships are beneficial and that society ought

6 See generally, Codd, H, *In the Shadow of Prison: Families, Imprisonment and Criminal Justice* (Willan, 2008).

7 Taken from Nicola Lacey's podcast for the Howard League: Lacey, N, ' Rethinking justice: penal policy beyond punishment' *Howard League for Penal Reform* (2013): https://howardleague.org/what-is-justice-conference-podcasts/ (accessed 15 May 2020).

8 See Laub, J, Nagin, D and Sampson, R, 'Trajectories of Change in Criminal Offending: Good Marriages and the Desistance Process', (1998) *American Sociological Review* (63) 225–38.

9 Ministry of Justice, *The Importance of Strengthening Prisoners' Family Ties to Prevent Reoffending and Reduce Intergenerational Crime* (2017), para 157: https://assets.publishing.service.gov.uk/government/uploads/system/uploads/attachment_data/file/642244/farmer-review-report.pdf (accessed 15 May 2020).

10 *Ibid.*

11 *Ibid* p 4.

12 See Uggen, C and Wakefield, S, 'Young Adults Re-Entering the Community from the Criminal Justice System: The Challenge of Becoming an Adult', in Osgood, W et al (eds), *On Your Own Without a Safety Net: The Transition to Adulthood for Vulnerable Populations* (University Press of Chicago, 2005).

13 Siennick, S, Stewart, E and Staff, J, 'Explaining the Association between Incarceration and Divorce' (2014) *Criminology* (52(3)) 371–98 at p 371.

to work to counteract the corrosive impact of imprisonment on the wellbeing of the family. They indicate that imprisonment poses a great threat to the stability of the marriage, not only when the prisoner is incarcerated but also after their release, and that the chances of divorce 'are almost double' that of marriage without incarceration.[14] The risk of divorce is increased for those serving long-term prison sentences, with each additional year in prison increasing the odds of divorce by 32%.[15] In summary, a stable and loving relationship can help the offender to be diverted from a life of crime and ultimately reduce the likelihood that their child will offend in the future. However, imprisonment poses a great threat to this relationship, and the collapse of a marriage or relationship may result in further reoffending, thus defeating the sentencing objective of reducing crime. Therefore, more needs to be done to help protect such relationships upon entry into the prison estate and to maintain this relationship throughout the duration of the prison sentence.

14.2.1 Maintaining love in prison

If stability provides a key to maintaining a pre-existing relationship in prison, how can this be done during the forced separation of a prison sentence? Helen Codd suggests that imprisonment does not have to be the death knell for a relationship, but it obviously provides challenges in maintaining that relationship. Codd suggests that imprisonment can bring couples closer together emotionally: one man (whose wife was in prison) commented that 'you've never had a love letter until you have had one from a prisoner'.[16] Codd suggests that this period can allow joint day-dreaming of a better future and allow space for each other's hopes and dreams to be shared and grown. Furthermore, the space afforded by the period of imprisonment might allow for some of the relationship wounds to heal and offer a break from the day-to-day stresses and strains from which the relationship was suffering and allow a new loving foundation to be cultivated.[17] However, with any prison sentence, there comes a loss of autonomy for those on the outside. Anna Kotova[18] constructed 33 semi-structured interviews with married and unmarried partners of men serving 10 years' imprisonment or longer. The study found that imprisonment had an impact of the trajectory of the women's life. For example, some may have had plans to get married and start a family prior to the male's imprisonment, but those plans went up in smoke when he was sentenced to prison.[19] When asked 'Do you have any children?', a participant named Susan responded: 'No, I don't. Umm … you know it's a bit of a sore subject really … we were thinking about it [trying for a baby] and then this [imprisonment] comes along and its effectively ruled out our chances.'[20] Another participate named Elly went through the menopause during her husband's prison sentence and therefore would never have the opportunity to have a family. However, the impact of the enforced separation has the ability to cause relationship strain even if the couple were not looking to start a family.

Kotova interviewed a woman named Susan, who was in her early twenties. The strain of imprisonment impacted her through the loss of a regular sex life. She commented

14 *Ibid.*
15 *Ibid.*
16 Codd (n 6), p 49.
17 *Ibid* Ch 3.
18 Kotova, A, 'Time … Lost Time: Exploring how partners of long-term prisoners experience the temporal pains of imprisonment' (2018) *Time and Society* (28(2)) 478–98 at p 484.
19 *Ibid* at 486.
20 *Ibid.*

that her 'best sexual years' were passing her by, as England and Wales do not permit conjugal visits.[21] Casey was of a similar age and felt that the opportunity to get married was slipping by. She alluded to her physical appearance declining with age. Whilst admitting that this might be construed as vain, she said 'you don't want to get married when you are older. You want nice wedding pictures.' Casey's view might be somewhat dated, as statistics released in April 2020 identify that the average age for a heterosexual marriage is 38 years old.[22] But as Kotova notes, the cultural change in terms of age marriage is 'not always applied to their own individual life courses … [and] their landscapes are altered by long term imprisonment'. It is not just young couples who have their lives altered by imprisonment. Those who are older face a change in their retirement plans. They would have expected to spend their golden years with their partners, offering care and various forms of other support as they grow older together. Another interviewee, Iris, was concerned that her partner would die alone in prison, identifying this as an additional strain.[23]

Foster's 2019 study found that women believed their life was 'on hold' whilst their partner was in prison.[24] However, the women interviewed by Kotova countered this point, and it was identified that whilst their lives were lacking some elements of normality, you would be hard pressed to suggest that their lives were on hold. Kotova found that the women she interviewed did not pause their lives whilst their partners served their sentence. Whilst their lives were somewhat dictated by phone calls and visiting times, 'they worked, engaged in parenting, hobbies and housework'.[25] So whilst they missed their partners in terms of future planning, companionship and regular sexual intercourse, they were still able to maintain a somewhat ordinary life. One participant, Elsa, likened it to a long-distance running event (for which she started training prior to the imprisonment of her partner). She alluded to the difficulty of facing a 40-mile run. Looked at as a whole, this might appear to be an impossible task, but when the course is broken down into 5-mile chunks, it becomes so much more manageable. She equated this to looking at her partner's long-term sentence and the fact that her life simply cannot be put on hold; she needed to move forward as pausing her life for the duration of a lengthy sentence would be impractical.

However, we should conclude with a note of caution. The impact of imprisonment is very much a subjective experience, and Kotova's findings, whilst detailed, are taken from a small sample of 33 women. It would be unwise to draw absolute conclusions from such a small sample. Nevertheless, this excellent research opens a window onto the myriad of relationship problems that stem from a partner's imprisonment. Further, the differing impacts should carry an equal weighting despite the fact that some problems differ vastly in their severity. Just because person A suggests that life can go on and that they are looking forward to their future does not automatically mean that person B will feel the same. Impacts can also be measured entirely differently and yet the manifestation of imprisonment pains should not be diluted. If one person is losing

---

21 A conjugal visit is where a prisoner is allowed an allotted amount of time, usually a few hours, to spend with a visitor. It is permitted to engage in sexual intercourse during this period. See *ibid* at 487.

22 ONS, Marriages in England and Wales 2017, p 4: www.ons.gov.uk/peoplepopulationandcommunity/birthsdeathsandmarriages/marriagecohabitationandcivilpartnerships/bulletins/marriagesinenglandandwalesprovisional/2017#age-at-marriage (accessed 15 May 2020).

23 Kotova (n 18) at p 488.

24 Foster, R, '"Doing the Wait": An exploration into the waiting experiences of prisoners' families' (2016) *Time and Society* (28(2)) 459–77 at p 471.

25 Kotova (n 18) at p 493.

the opportunity to have a family and the other is missing regular sex, each impact is as valid as the other.

> **impact**
>
> There are a myriad of potential problems for relationships where a family member is imprisoned. One person might be losing the opportunity to start a family; another might be missing her sexual peak. Others might be concerned about looking older in their wedding pictures, whilst there may be some who are worried about retirement or their partner dying in prison. Finally, those on the outside of the prison estate might worry about dying alone.

14.2.2 Sustaining a relationship in prison

We have seen above that there is a high rate of divorce where one partner is imprisoned, and whilst statistics do not exist to identify the number of relationships that collapse beyond repair during a prison sentence, we can assume that the impact is high. However, a question remains as to how a relationship can survive the enforced period of separation when one half of the couple is sent to prison. Research suggests that there a number of avenues that couples can use to maintain contact, and ultimately it is imperative that this contact occurs. As highlighted above, if family ties are maintained, there is a much greater chance that the prisoner will not reoffend in the future. As such, couples can engage in letter writing, phone calls and regular visits to help heal the wounds of enforced separation.

Letters home

The most common and cost-effective method of communication is letter writing, with prisoners needing only paper, pens, envelopes and postage stamps. In her 2008 book, Doing Time Together, Helen Comfort suggested that 98% of her sample of prisoners and their families communicated via letter writing.[26] Comfort added that this method of communication was 'highly satisfying and central to their experiences of courtship and relationship development'.[27] Furthermore, this activity can be done in the prisoner's own time, whilst in their cell, so it can be done at almost any time during their day. In England and Wales, a prisoner can send one free letter a week, but any additional letters have to be paid for.[28] However, it is important to note that any letter can be opened and read by prison staff as long as it is not from the prisoner's lawyer or the courts. Letters can pertain to almost anything, but letters (both sending and receiving) will be stopped if they:[29]

- contain anything that relates to escape plans or compromises the security of the prison;
- are connected to criminal activity or anything that breaches prison rules;
- contain threats to national security or the letter is written in code;
- contain threats of blackmail;

26 Comfort, M, *Doing Time Together: Love and Family in the Shadow of Prison* (Chicago University Press, 2008) at p 68.

27 *Ibid.*

28 For details on how to communicate with those in prison, see https://www.prisonersfamilies.org/contact/ (accessed 15 May 2020).

29 *Ibid.*

- are racially offensive or obscene.

Comfort's study indicates that letter writing is a very popular method of communication. She found that 20% of her sample wrote to each other almost every day, and 22% sent multiple letters per week. Owing to the time and separation faced by the prisoner, Comfort noted that 36% of women said that their partner wrote more prolifically than they did outside of prison. This can have both a positive and negative effect in terms of overwhelming the recipient outside of prison.[30] One woman, who received a 21-page letter from her incarcerated husband, told Comfort that she hated writing and struggled to return letters to her husband. This is unsurprising as 16% of Comfort's sample did not graduate from secondary education and unsurprisingly found writing a chore.[31]

However, some liked to romantise their letters, for example spraying perfume on the paper so that their husband or partner could experience their scent.[32] Bernice, a participant from Comfort's study, suggested that she could no longer afford to actually wear the perfume because she sprayed so much of it on her letters.[33] Further to this type of romantic gesture, women of imprisoned males will sometimes write 'steamy' or sexually graphic letters to their partners in prison and even include 'risqué' pictures of themselves. However, these letters could of course be viewed by prison staff and this could become difficult to maintain. Another interview participant, Laura, told Comfort that she sent her partner a sexual photograph, but the more he thought about the picture, the more he realised that prison staff might have seen her in such a pose. She said '... he couldn't stand it, it was really bothering him ... he didn't want other people looking at me in such a way.'[34] Her partner eventually tore up the pictures and disposed of them.

Kotova's study found that women sometimes became bored of writing and receiving letters. Elly told her 'there's not really a lot he can tell me'.[35] Her letters to her partner were more detailed than the responses she received, but she was determined to continue to share the everyday detail of her life outside of prison.

It is clear that letters can offer not only a means of contact but also symbolise a loving relationship. The prisoner who poured his soul into a 21-page letter to his partner must have believed that this would show her just how much she meant to him, with little knowledge that his partner actually disliked replying to his letters. By spraying perfume or wearing lipstick to kiss a piece of paper or perhaps even taking risqué pictures, the bonds of a relationship can be fortified in this enforced period of separation. Whilst this might appear to strengthen the relationship during the period of imprisonment, some partners were not convinced that anything would change once the prisoner was released. Keisha believed that '[he will] say anything whilst he is in jail. They'll tell you I won't get in trouble again ... they are cool for three months [after release] and then they are in trouble again because they have hit you.'[36] Comfort suggested that Keisha was not representative of the women in her sample, who would generally suppress any cynicism and instead chose to use letters as a vehicle of optimism and hope to rebuild their futures upon release.

---

30 Comfort (n 26) at p 69.
31 *Ibid* at p 70.
32 *Ibid* at p 73.
33 *Ibid* at p 74.
34 *Ibid*.
35 Kotova (n 18) at p 490.
36 Comfort (n 26) at p 79.

Phone calls

All prisoners in England and Wales have access to a telephone whilst in prison; usually they have a PIN which, once punched into a phone, will bring up their account with their stored numbers and then they can make a call. According to Insidetime.org, prisoners can only make calls during prescribed periods, which is usually in the evenings.[37] Some prisons will limit the duration of a call to ensure that the waiting period for other prisoners is not too long. The calls are not free and cost up to 20p per minute depending on the time the call is made.[38] Calls to a landline are cheaper than those made from outside of prison. However, it is important to remember that prisoners have very little income whilst serving their sentence, so money for calls might have to come from family on the outside, further raising the burden of supporting a loved one in prison (see below). If prisoners were to fund these costs themselves, regular phone calls would eat up a vast amount of the money they earn. A report by HM Inspectorate of Prisons[39] in 2016 found that:

- if prisoners are in employment, they earn a minimum of £4.00 per week;
- if a prisoner is over retirement age, or cannot work for health reasons, the mandatory rate of pay is £3.25;
- those who wish to work but cannot due to a lack of employment places are paid £2.50 per week.

This means that if a person made a 10-minute mobile phone call every day, during the peak-cost period, this would cost them £2.00 a day or £14.00 a week, outstripping their wage and clearly requiring funds from elsewhere. Furthermore, whilst a prisoner does not have to 'pay' for their cell, if they wish to rent a TV, they will have to cover that themselves as well as anything they purchase from the prison shop.[40] Such purchases can include tobacco, which is unsurprisingly popular. A 25g pouch of Amber Leaf tobacco would cost the prisoner £8.57, comparable to prices charged by three supermarkets surveyed by HM Inspectorate of Prisons in 2016.[41]

As described above, phone calls can be made on a regular basis and are far more readily available than prison visits. All phone calls, save for calls made to lawyers, can be recorded and listened to. However, much like the letter writing, it is very difficult for the prisoner to share the experiences of their family on the outside. In Kotova's study, Elsa suggested that phone calls heightened, rather than mitigated, the proximate distance between her and her partner. She commented '… it's the hard fact of leading separate lives … some of the things I have in my life, he wouldn't understand, wouldn't relate to … [my experiences] wouldn't have any significance to him.'[42] Both Fishman and Comfort have made startling claims relating to the use of phone calls. Some male prisoners would use the time allocated to exert their control or dominance over their partner on the outside. This could be termed an element of coercive control and, rather than be a positive trait, could have a negative impact on the health of the relationship. Fishman suggested that men would deliberately call at irregular times to restrict the

37 See Inside Time for further information: https://insidetime.org/prisoner-communications/ (accessed 15 May 2020).

38 *Ibid.*

39 HMIP, 'Life in Prison (Spending and Earning Money)', January 2016: www.justiceinspectorates.gov.uk/hmiprisons/wp-content/uploads/sites/4/2016/01/Earning-and-spending-money-findings-paper-final-draft.pdf (accessed March 2023).

40 *Ibid.*

41 *Ibid* at para 1.40.

42 Kotova (n 18) at p 490.

movements or activities of their partners.[43] Comfort found that men would 'often use telephone conversations to exert their authority and dominance by making demands or checking up on their wives ... [and] demanding that their wives stay more or less confined to their homes ...'.[44] Comfort found that 50% of the women in her sample 'felt imprisoned in their own homes'.[45]

Whilst telephone calls represent an opportunity to maintain relationship bonds, at times they weaken them. The cost of the calls requires funding, either through prison work or, more likely, funding from loved ones. Furthermore, calls can be made at inopportune times which could leave the partner on the outside effectively tethered to the phone, not allowing them the opportunity to fully continue with their lives. In essence, this could be construed as both partners effectively serving the prison sentence, although only one of them has committed a criminal offence and been sanctioned by the courts.

impact

Whilst letters and phone calls provide a mechanism for those in prison to stay in contact with loved ones and the outside world, varying problems arise. Letters might lack engagement from the prisoner because there is little to say, or the distance between partners might become wider as those inside are unable to comprehend what is going on in their partners' lives. Phone calls represent an immediate sense of togetherness as they occur in real time, but there are related costs to making the calls. Furthermore, those in toxic relationships might continue to feel the coercive control of their imprisoned partner by virtue of calls at inopportune times. This may give rise to the partner at home actually feeling a degree of imprisonment themselves.

14.2.3 The impact on children

Much like other loved ones with a family member in prison, there is a dearth of data surrounding the impact on children. Children of incarcerated parents are often described as the victims of a hidden sentence,[46] and this section will examine how far that claim is correct. This is another example of the 'ripple effect' of prison sentences; and the effects can stretch out for a period of time.

Children are a distinctly vulnerable group and often are affected most when a parent is sentenced to prison. Crest suggests that 54% of offenders are parents at the time of their imprisonment and that 7% of school-aged children will experience the imprisonment of a parent during their schooling period.[47] At face value, the disadvantages of having a parent in prison are obvious. These children will often have poorer outcomes in terms of both education and health. They have a higher probability of growing up in poverty and are at an increased risk of both anti-social behaviour and delinquency in later life.[48] It has been stated that two-thirds of boys who have a parent

43 Fishman, L, 'Prisoners and Their Wives: Marital and Domestic Effects of Telephone Contacts and Home Visits' (1988) *International Journal of Offender Therapy and Comparative Criminology* (32(1)) 55–66 at p 60.

44 Comfort (n 26) at p 91.

45 *Ibid* at p 92.

46 Crest (n 2) at p 11.

47 *Ibid.*

48 *Ibid.*

in prison will go on to be involved with the criminal justice system at some point in their lives.[49] Finally, such children will have a myriad of emotional and behavioural needs that might be overlooked if they have difficulty in expressing their anger, grief and assumed rejection.[50] Therefore, this section will explore why it is imperative that children are not impacted by the ripple effect of imprisonment and no longer remain the victims of a hidden sentence.

Both Parke and Codd[51] suggest that imprisonment is a dynamic process which unfolds over time, with the impacts being felt long before the start of the actual prison sentence. The stresses and strains felt by children can actually start when the parent is arrested, which is especially true if the child witnesses their parent being arrested. Van Nijnatten suggests that

> impressions of arrest are burned into the child's mind and are likely to return at night: the violence of the police, the yelling and crying mother, the faces of curious neighbours and above all the father removed in handcuffs or with a bag over his head, are sensations that a child will never forget.[52]

This paints a very brutal picture of arrest, which could have ramifications on the psyche of a child who has witnessed this event. Of course, not all arrests occur in this manner, but should a child witness their parent being arrested, it is safe to say that the image will be ingrained in their mind. These worries and strains have been likened to a child experiencing the divorce of their parents or perhaps the death of one parent.[53] The feelings generated by a death allow the child to grieve 'legitimately', as they have lost their parent. When a parent is imprisoned, the child assumes the status of a 'disenfranchised griever',[54] where they are assuming the mantle of someone who is suffering grief but 'do not have a socially recognised right, role or capacity to actually grieve'.[55] This means that the child will likely feel a raft of emotional and behavioural consequences. The loss of the imprisoned parent is the cause, but children might struggle for an avenue to receive sympathy or even to recognise why they feel the way they do. Boswell and Wedge suggest that it '[is] apparent that [no children are] untouched by the loss of their [parent's] imprisonment [and] all would prefer to not be in the situation in which they find themselves'.[56] However, it must be noted that the absence of one parent will not always have a negative impact on the child. There could be some positives to removing one parent from the family home. Eddy and Reid suggest that if the imprisoned parent is a substance abuser or brings other substance abusers into the home, the temporary removal of this parent could have a positive

---

49 See further Murray, J et al, 'Effects of Parental Imprisonment on Child Antisocial Behaviour and Mental Health' (2009) *Campbell Systematic Reviews* (4), 1–105.

50 *Ibid.*

51 See Parke, R and Clarke-Stewart, K, 'The Effects of Parental Incarceration on Children: Perspectives, Promises and Policies' in Tarvis, J and Waul, M (eds), *Prisoners Once Removed: The Impact on Incarceration and Re-Entry on Children, Families and Communities* (Urban Institute Press, 2003). See also Codd (n 6).

52 Van Nijnatten, C, *Detention and Development: Perspectives of Children of Prisoners*, Forum Verlag Godesberg: Monchengladbach, at p 82.

53 Codd (n 6) at p 67.

54 *Ibid.*

55 See generally Hames, C and Pedreira, D, 'Children with Parents in Prison: Disenfranchised Grievers Who Benefit from Bibliotheraphy' (2003) *Illness, Crisis and Loss*, 11(4) 377–86.

56 Boswell, G and Wedge, P, *Imprisoned Fathers and Their Children* (Jessica Kingsley, 2001) at p 79.

impact on the child's life.[57] Furthermore, if the parent has already left the home and become estranged, then the likely impact of imprisonment will be somewhat diluted. However, much like the problem of maintaining a relationship, discussed earlier, there are many issues and concerns should the imprisoned parent play an active role in the family home. What follows assumes that the imprisoned parent is active and provides a positive influence on the child's life.

If the arrest and subsequent imprisonment of a parent can impact a child's life, it is clear that there are a multitude of differing impacts on the child. The behavioural and emotional impression left by imprisonment can manifest in a number of different ways, which are highlighted below:[58]

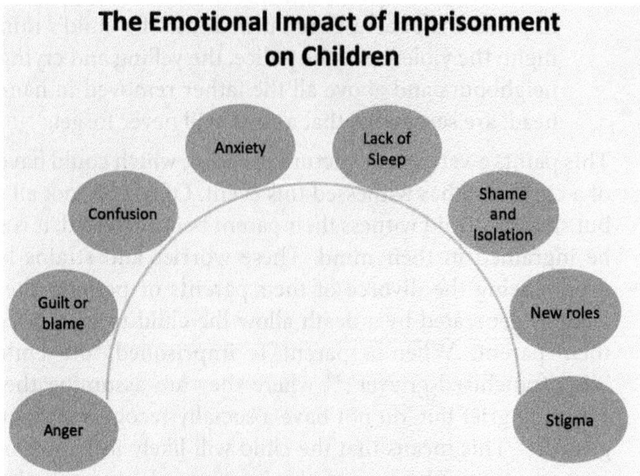

In light of a parent's imprisonment, the child could become angry that their parent has been taken away. This anger could be directed at the remaining parent, the police or at the whole system. Being a child, they might not be aware of the offending behaviour of the parent and, as such, blame the criminal justice system for removing the parent from the house. This blame could also manifest itself as guilt; they might start to believe that they, the child, were at fault for the parent's imprisonment. This would be especially true if the child was the victim in the offending behaviour of the parent. For example, if the parent had sexually or physically abused them, their feelings could manifest in guilt, for example 'if I did not report this, my parent would not be in prison'.

Young children might suffer a great deal of confusion if they witnessed the arrest of the parent, which could be confounded by 'white lies' offered by the remaining parent to justify the absence. For example, Crest reported one example where the parents told their children that 'Daddy is working away' and that is why he cannot be at home.[59] The parents commented that they were comfortable with the lie because they did not believe the children needed to know the true reason for the absence as it 'would be more upsetting for them to see [the father in prison]'. At face value, this approach makes sense, but confusion might overwhelm the child if they are teased at school. This

57 Eddy, J and Reid, J, 'The Adolescent Children of Incarcerated Parents' in Tarvis and Waul (eds) (n 51) at p 240.

58 Crest (n 2) at p 14.

59 *Ibid* at p 15.

would be especially true of small, close-knit communities, where secrets are harder to keep. In the same Crest report, there are examples of children being bullied at school. One parent commented that 'the kids were bullied quite a bit for their dad being in prison. I think that was their downfall at school … it made my children's lives hell … [I] put them in another school to still be harassed again.'[60] So, whilst a white lie may spare the child's feelings about the imprisonment, there is a danger that other people in the community will know about the criminal offence (especially true of a high-profile crime), resulting in bullying. The effect of this bullying and confusion could lead to the child suffering from anxiety, impacting on their home and school life. Some of the symptoms of anxiety include feeling restless/being unable to sit still, feeling nauseous, needing to the use toilet more, headaches and/or feeling light-headed.[61] All of these symptoms would impact the sleep pattern of the child and cause further difficulties when trying to study at school. These symptoms could well exacerbate the internal shame they feel and result in the child becoming more withdrawn and isolated from their friends and family.

The parentification of the child: new household roles

When a parent is imprisoned, the children of that parent can sometimes be given or assume new roles in the household. For the purpose of this section, we will assume that it is the father who has been imprisoned and therefore the mother remains on the outside effectively as a single parent. We will later discuss the financial impact of imprisonment, but it is likely that all households will suffer a reduction in their finances when one parent is imprisoned. This may result in the mother taking on additional work in order to make ends meet. This knock-on effect means that a child (most probably the eldest in the family) assumes the responsibility for caring for their younger siblings and, as such, becomes a 'helper' to the mother.[62] Further to looking after the younger siblings, the child might have to do more of the household chores, go to the shop and cook for other children, as well as bearing some of the emotional burden of listening to their mother. This process is called the 'parentification of the child'[63] and ultimately promotes the child to 'quasi-adulthood'[64], which propels the child into premature adulthood, resulting in a loss of childhood itself. In reality, this transformation means that the child is ill-equipped to deal with the challenges of their new role. Children should be attending school, learning new skills, playing with their friends and developing at their own pace. By removing the childhood experience from the child, they will be left with a sense of deprivation; that they once had something, did not fully experience it and now it is gone. As well as the raft of emotional responses to imprisonment listed above, parentification could result in further negative consequences from the imprisonment of the parent. It is within this process that the ripple effect of imprisonment is most hidden. Most people will not understand how household dynamics change and the resultant impact of this change.

60 *Ibid.*

61 For further information on the impact of anxiety, please refer to the specialist guidance from Mind: www.mind.org.uk/information-support/types-of-mental-health-problems/anxiety-and-panic-attacks/anxiety-symptoms/ (accessed 15 May 2020).

62 Codd (n 6) at p 69.

63 *Ibid* at p 70.

64 *Ibid.*

impact

It is clear that there are a raft of emotional and behavioural issues concerning children with an imprisoned parent. They may become socially isolated, confused and develop anxiety. Furthermore, they might be transplanted to new roles in the family, meaning they lose elements of their childhood through parentification, as the non-imprisoned parent has to seek additional employment.

14.3 The financial impact of imprisonment

As alluded to above, the household finances are likely to be diminished when one parent is imprisoned. As such, it is likely that this hole in the finances will need plugging. The financial consequences have been well documented over the last 20 years,[65] and much like the parentification of the child, the financial ripple effect of imprisonment is 'largely invisible to the public gaze'.[66] If the family are attempting to maintain family ties with an imprisoned parent, this could cause stark ramifications for the family on the outside. As described earlier, prison wages are meagre and prisoners have to pay for their own luxury items like tobacco, TV rental and branded soap products. This could see the family taking on further debt in order to provide the prisoner with gifts and money, as well as trying to maintain the family home in some semblance of the status quo.

These financial implications are many layered. The first layer is the immediate loss of income into the household. Whilst the imprisoned family member may not have held a law-abiding job, they may have been raising money via other means, such as drug dealing, burglary or handling stolen goods, to name but a few. As such, the financial situation in the household could best be described as fragile and certainly something that needs fortifying. To replenish the household situation, the parent on the outside of prison may have to take on additional work (leading to the parentification of older children as mentioned above). Furthermore, if both parents were in receipt of benefits prior to one going to prison, this change is likely to need a recalculation of the household benefits and could lead to delays of up to 12 weeks as government departments reassess the means of the household.[67] In 2003, Action for Prisoners' Families commented that 'going to prison in the UK is considered a change that can immediately remove the right to the majority of state support. If the prisoner is the named benefit receiver, their imprisonment will alter the entitlement of the family … Income Support [now Universal Credit] can fall dramatically or stop all together … [and the family will] fall below the poverty line.'[68] The financial picture for these families is startling. In 2010, the Prison Reform Trust and UNLOCK painted a picture of the stark financial difficulties faced by families. They found as follows:[69]

65 See generally Codd (n 6); Davies, A, 'Men's Imprisonment: The Financial Cost to Women and Children' in Shaw, R (ed), *Prisoner's Children: What are the Issues?* (Routledge, 1992); and Smith, R et al, *Poverty and Disadvantage Among Prisoners' Families* (Joseph Rowntree, 2007).

66 Codd (n 6) at p 50.

67 Dickie, D, 'The Financial Impact of Prison, Families Outside' (2013), p 3: www.familiesoutside.org.uk/content/uploads/2017/12/The-Financial-Impact-of-Imprisonment-on-Families.pdf.

68 *Ibid* at p 4.

69 See Bath, C and Edgar, K, 'Time is Money' (Prison Reform Trust, 2010): www.prisonreformtrust.org.uk/Portals/0/Documents/Time%20is%20Money_8a_Layout%201.pdf (accessed 15 May 2020).

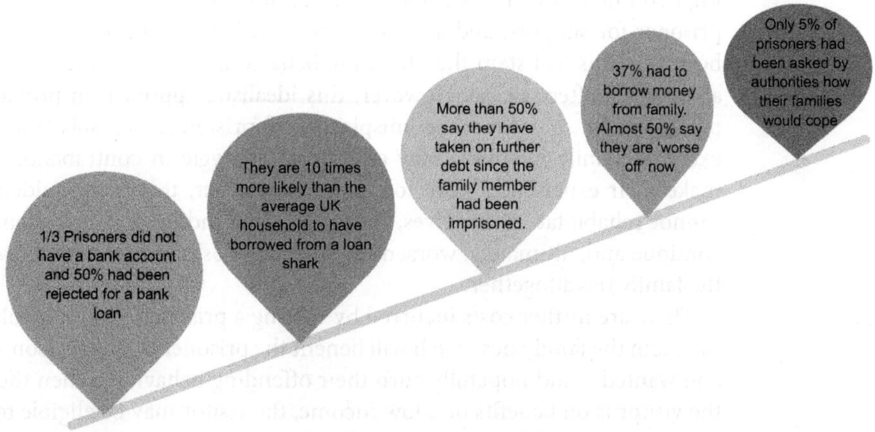

As the figure above indicates, the financial outlook for prisoners' families is bleak. In order to keep their heads above the poverty line, some families may need to take out loans to cover the immediate gap in income. This loan could come from family members or friends, or the family might have to look toward more unscrupulous avenues. Codd suggests that families may look to plug their financial hole through credit cards or high-interest debt consolidation loans.[70] However, these families are disproportionately poor, and such avenues might not be open to them due to a non-existent or poor credit rating. There is a danger that they will turn to loan sharks to allow them to live. Furthermore, Codd indicates that it would be unusual for a prisoner to be debt-free upon entry into prison. [71]This poses another problem for the family: how do they pay the existing debts, to these marginal lenders, once the breadwinner is in prison. Not only do the family have to find a way to eat, pay rent and bills, they may also have to pay loans they might not know existed. Store cards and loans from private, second-tier companies, are being deliberately marketed to the poor and socially excluded at exorbitantly high rates of interest with punitive charges for late payments.[72] It appears that to live day-to-day and replenish the missing financial contribution is very hard, with a number of knock-on effects.

Other financial burdens

It is not only day-to-day living that causes a great deal of financial hardship. The family on the outside might want to improve the experience of the prisoner when serving their sentence. We have already seen above that the family might have to supplement the prisoner's wages in order to fund telephone calls to help maintain family ties, but further costs will arise if the family want to furnish the prisoner with magazines, clothes, books, educational or hobby materials in order to pass their time in prison as productively as possible.[73] However, Codd suggests that the 'provision of food and other items is not simply of practical significance. Food and gifts signify expressions of love and caring.'[74] This is another example of maintaining ties whilst a family member is in prison and illustrates how relationship stability and the financial impact of

70 Codd (n 6) at p 54.

71 *Ibid.*

72 See Smith (n 65).

73 Codd (n 6) at p 56.

74 *Ibid.*

imprisonment are interwoven. If the family can show that they are there for the prisoner for support, and as a reminder of what they have on the outside, there is a hope that this will stem the offending behaviour and allow the prisoner to live a law-abiding life after release. However, this idealistic approach in providing gifts for the prisoner can sometimes be misplaced. If prisoners are substance dependent, for example, family members may attempt to smuggle in contraband, such as drugs, to make their experience more tolerable.[75] However, this is misguided. If the prisoner cannot rehabilitate themselves, the cycle of offending and imprisonment is likely to continue and, ultimately, worsen the financial position of the family and perhaps snap the family ties altogether.

There are further costs incurred by visiting a prisoner. Again, regular visits will help maintain the family ties which will benefit the prisoner both in prison – by feeling loved and wanted – and hopefully curb their offending behaviour when they are released. If the visitor is on benefits or a low income, the visitor may be eligible to claim help with expenses incurred for the prison visit. The Assisted Prison Visits Unit (APVU)[76] will allow one claim every 14 days to provide some financial relief. Helpfully, the Unit can claim for payment prior to travel, in which case it will send the visitor a code to exchange for train tickets, thereby mitigating the need for up-front expenditure. However, taxis are not covered by this scheme, a problem identified by Davis in the early 1990s. Davis found that families found travelling long distances to be tedious and expensive, and if trains were delayed or missed, a taxi was the only alternative to ensure that the family did not miss their visiting slot.[77] Furthermore, submitting a claim to the APVU requires the completion of forms which could be off-putting to some, owing to a lack of a basic education or time to complete the forms.[78] The forms also require the applicant to reveal various details regarding their finances, which some may be reluctant to provide. *The Financial Impact of Imprisonment on Families* report published in 2013 found the following concerns about visiting family members in prison:

- One partner lived a long distance from the prison and was not eligible to receive financial assistance from the APVU.
- A mother was keen to travel to the prison but was worried about the costs involved.
- Another parent found the cost of going to prison with two children a drain on their resources.
- A mother was anxious for information about what help would be available to see her son.[79]

It is clear that the costs associated with prison visits are of great concern to families. And, of course, travel expenses will not be the only cost incurred in visiting a loved one in prison. A long journey will require the purchase of food and drink, especially when travelling with young children.[80] Furthermore, families will want to eat and drink with the prisoner (Dickie's report from Scotland suggests that this is the 'norm'),[81] often

75 *Ibid.*

76 See further government advice on obtaining assistance to visit prison: www.gov.uk/help-with-prison-visits (accessed 15 May 2020).

77 Davies (n 65) at p 81.

78 Dickie (n 67) at p 14.

79 *Ibid* at p 15.

80 *Ibid.*

81 *Ibid.*

having to buy snacks from expensive vending machines inside prison. In a vacuum, this might appear to be an inconsequential detail, but we have already recognised the struggle to stay above the poverty line, and such purchases will only exacerbate the dire financial situation of some families.

impact

The financial consequences of imprisonment are stark. There will be a reduction in household income, even if this income was illicitly earned. Benefits will be recalculated which could result in delays. There might be additional debts that were incurred prior to imprisonment and without the family's knowledge that now need repayment. To plug this gap, the family might seek to obtain high-interest loans, store or credit cards. Finally, there are unforeseen expenses concerning visiting someone in prison. We have previously discussed the tangible benefits to maintaining family ties, but the expense of a prison visit can also be punitive.

14.4 Stigma

We have seen above that children suffer from bullying due to the fact that their parent is in prison. However, negative connotations of a family member's imprisonment are not only aimed at children. Partners of prisoners have been stigmatised by both prison officers and fellow visitors when on prison visits.[82] One participant told Condry, Kotova and Minson that they were 'treated appalling'[83] during prison visits. This appears to worsen for the families of those convicted of the most heinous crimes, for example sexual offences. They approach visits with worry and apprehension: 'how am I going to be treated [by the prison staff] this week and what sort of rubbish am I going to have to put up with from these people.'[84] We have to remember that those outside of prison have not committed any criminal offence; it is the prisoner who has committed the offence and they have been punished by the state. Yet throughout this chapter we have seen how prisoners' families are marginalised and subjected to the ripple effect of their loved ones' imprisonment. This stigmatisation does not reside exclusively with prison visits; some partners have suffered stigmatisation in their local communities as well. Participants in Condry, Kotova and Minson's study described how people would cross the road to avoid them in the street and that dog mess had been put through their letterboxes.[85] One participant recorded: 'I've got quite a few friends that do not speak to me anymore.' Earlier, we stated that children with a parent in prison have been described as 'disenfranchised grievers' in so far as they are grieving the loss of a parent but there is no societal box to put this grief in. If you are grieving the loss of somebody because they have died, can you imagine your local community and friends shunning and abandoning you? Yet, that happens to innocent families all over the world when they are stigmatised for having a loved one in prison. This stigmatisation is not only limited to friends. One participant highlighted that '[my husband and I] have been disowned by the family … my husband's son is getting married this year and obviously

82 Condry, R, Kotova, A and Minson, S, 'Social Injustice and Collateral Damage: The Families and Children of Prisoners' in Jewkes, Y et al, *Handbook on Prisons*, 2nd edn (Routledge, 2016) at p 634.

83 *Ibid* at p 635.

84 *Ibid.*

85 *Ibid.*

my husband is not going but I've not been invited either … so I'm clubbed along with my husband … it is so hurtful.'[86] This indicates that there is little to no distinction between how society treats both those inside prison and their families on the outside. Both the prisoner and their family can be ostracised, an example of the social injustice that Lacey observed (see the introduction to this chapter). Both prisoners and their families can be 'clubbed together' and treated as if they have all committed the criminal act.

impact

Stigmatisation that the family has to face comes in many guises. Children may be bullied and need to change schools. The local community might shun and judge the family. Further, their own wider family might ostracise them, leaving the prisoner's family to feel isolated and alone.

14.5 Reforms for prisoners' families

It is clear that prisoners' families suffer a great deal of informal punishment for having a loved one in prison. We opened the chapter with the analogy of throwing a rock into a lake. The rock hitting the water is the offender being sent to prison, and the ripples caused by the rock are the varying different impacts suffered by family. These might not be of great concern to the vast majority of us, as the impact is often hidden or invisible to the public. Nevertheless, more needs to be done to mitigate the impact of imprisonment on families. *The Financial Impact of Imprisonment on Families* report proposed a number of ways to improve the lives of those on the outside of prison. One suggestion was that families should receive information on the financial implications of prison prior to their loved one being sent to prison. This would allow them to mitigate the change in their financial circumstances and reduce any payment delays. Families also need to be made aware about the support for travel costs through the Assisted Prison Visits Unit and be given assistance in the completion of the forms. Visitor centres in every prison should be created to provide for low-cost snacks and drinks, thereby reducing the financial pressure on families.[87]

However, the biggest change that can be made is one made by society as a whole. Prisoners' families need to be viewed as victims as well. Not necessarily in the sense that they are the victims of crime, rather victims of the offending behaviour. With this in mind, prisoners' families should not be subjected to vilification and stigmatisation; they have not committed any crime and as such need to be treated as ordinary people and not ostracised from their wider family and friends. However, as this chapter has illustrated, this stigmatisation comes in many guises and can impact the family in a myriad of ways. It sadly appears that society is not ready to view these families as forgotten or hidden victims and are happy to 'club them in with' the prisoner. In 2013, the Coronation Street actress, Catherine Tyldesley, won £10,000 on a celebrity gameshow called *All Star Family Fortunes*. Her nominated charity to receive the prize money was a Manchester charity called 'Out There', which provides emotional and practical support to the families of those in prison. However, some viewers were

86 *Ibid.*

87 For a full list of the recommendations, see Dickie (n 67) at p 21.

appalled by this decision, and the *Daily Mail* reported a number of comments berating Ms Tyldesley for her choice. One wrote, 'What about a victim's charity? You are a disgrace.' The family of the murdered toddler, James Bulger,[88] also commented that victims' charities were more deserving. Neither Ms Tyldesley nor ITV made any comment on whether the prize was returned, but this goes some way to illustrate the guilt by association that the families suffer. Society needs to realise that these families need assistance, charitable support and acknowledgment that they are not generally implicated in the offence. Until we accept that fact and remove the stigmatisation of being associated with a prisoner, life for the innocent members of the family will continue to be mired in confusion and shame. If this cannot be fixed, we will be unable to attend to the larger problems concerning the finances of the family and the impact imprisonment holds for the children. Ultimately, this means that the ripple effect of imprisonment will continue.

88 For more on the James Bulger case, see **Chapter 12** and the various news stories and reports from the *BBC* at: www.bbc.co.uk/news/topics/cxwkxyvg4pet/murder-of-james-bulger (accessed 15 May 2020).

chapter 15

Capital Punishment: Debates about Death as a Penalty for Crime

15.1 Introduction

Debates around the death penalty have existed since time immemorial and are inevitably emotive and polarising. The arguments for and against have, to a degree, remained similar in their nature for centuries; yet they have also evolved in light of new knowledge and changing societies. Concerns about stopping and appropriately punishing the most serious types of criminal behaviour have driven arguments in favour of capital punishment. Emphasis on the protection of individual rights and questions about the efficacy of the death penalty as a deterrent have underpinned criticism. This chapter will examine these various debates, including their logic and evidence. Before doing so, it will provide an overview of the history of the death penalty in the UK, examining the evolution – and eventual abolition – of the ultimate punishment, which nonetheless remains a live issue in the 21st century. The chapter will proceed to summarise and then examine in detail the arguments for and against the death penalty, taking into account subjects including retribution, deterrence, miscarriages of justice, methods of execution, individual rights, and costs. These issues have been and continue to be debated, with discussions broadly falling into two broad categories: moral and practical. Moral debate focuses on the values and norms underpinning the use of the death penalty. They tend to be highly subjective, depending on the perspective of the person. They rely on appeals to individual or collective conceptions of good and bad behaviour (for example, ethical frameworks, religious or philosophical ideals, or legal rules). As such, moral debate is concerned with what might be termed the 'right and wrong' of the death penalty. Practical debate, whilst still subjective to an extent (and informed by moral debate), focuses on the efficacy of the death penalty. It examines factors like effectiveness, logistics and cost in the context of the real world, setting aside moral concerns.

It has been a little over 50 years since the initial abolition of the death penalty for murder was given a permanent footing in the UK, and just over two decades since it was finally abolished for all offences. Yet, capital punishment continues to be used across the globe, with new sentences being passed and executions conducted every year. At the end of 2021, nearly 30,000 people were awaiting execution having been sentenced to death,[1] with just over 2,000 new death sentences passed in that year.[2] However, the overall trend is one of decline. At the end of 2021, the majority of the world's countries (108) had abolished the death penalty for all crimes, with two-thirds (144) having abolished it in law or practice (for example, through moratoriums – a temporary suspension of executions).[3] In 2021, figures produced by Amnesty

1 Amnesty International, 'Death Sentences and Executions 2021' (May 2022), 13: https://www.amnesty.org/en/documents/act50/5418/2022/en/ (accessed 10 February 2023).

2 *Ibid* 11.

3 *Ibid* 62.

International suggested that the second lowest number of executions had been conducted globally in over a decade (579 – the lowest being during the previous year, in which the Covid-19 pandemic occurred). This figure excludes China, which is the world's most prolific executioner;[4] with the vast majority being conducted in only a few countries (including Iran and Saudi Arabia).[5] Whilst a very small number of countries executed more people in 2021 than in the previous year, several countries either abolished the death penalty, imposed a moratorium on executions or took steps towards complete abolition (including in Sierra Leone, Kazakhstan, Papua New Guinea, Malaysia and the US state of Virginia – the first southern state to do so).[6]

15.2 The abolition of capital punishment in the UK

Whilst not the first country to do so, the UK was one of the earlier abolitionist states, last executing a convicted offender in 1964.[7] Nonetheless, the UK does have a long history of using the death penalty,[8] and the concept of capital punishment remains relevant despite its illegality in this jurisdiction in the modern era. The slow process of abolition began in the early 20th century with a series of incremental steps: for under 16s in 1908;[9] for pregnant women in 1931;[10] and for a range of types of murder deemed 'non-capital' (those considered less severe, and punishable by life imprisonment).[11] This effectively reduced the use of execution to the most serious murders.

This step resulted from work of the Royal Commission on Capital Punishment (1953), led by Sir Ernest Gowers. In the post-war period, the world reflected on the massive loss of life and large-scale abuse of individual rights recently perpetrated across the globe (most particularly by the Nazi regime). This new perspective led to Parliamentary pressure for abolition. Instead, the post-war Labour Government established the Royal Commission to consider a 'limited or modified' version of the death penalty – but not abolition.[12] The Commission's recommendations and the legislation resulting from it (the Homicide Act 1957) were described as 'an uncomfortable compromise' designed to defer complete abolition.[13] Yet this reprieve for the death penalty in England and Wales did not last long. By the mid-1960s, a majority in Parliament considered the legislation and the death penalty as 'unworkable'; lacking in any evident deterrent effect; and morally objectionable. A string of high-profile executions appeared to tip the balance in favour of abolition. Timothy Evans, executed in 1950 for the murder of his child, was a tragic example of an irreversible miscarriage of justice.[14] The case of Derek Bentley, executed in 1953, was

4 *Ibid* 7.

5 *Ibid.*

6 *Ibid* 8.

7 See Davies, C, 'Britain's last executions: hanging of two jobless criminals a "low key" affair' (*Guardian*, 13 August 2014): www.theguardian.com/world/2014/aug/13/britain-last-executions-hanging-criminals-low-key (accessed 22 April 2020).

8 See Knowles, J, 'The Abolition of the Death Penalty in the United Kingdom' (The Death Penalty Project, 2015): www.deathpenaltyproject.org/wp-content/uploads/2017/12/DPP-50-Years-on-pp1-68-1.pdf (accessed 22 April 2020).

9 Children Act 1908.

10 Sentence of Death (Expectant Mothers) Act 1931.

11 Homicide Act 1957.

12 See the Commission's Terms of Reference, quoted in Knowles (n 8), 20.

13 Homans, L, 'Swinging Sixties: The Abolition of Capital Punishment' (2008) 58 *History Today* (12), 46.

14 See **Chapter 16**.

'hugely controversial at the time, and has remained so'.[15] Bentley's trial for murder, having been an accomplice in a robbery which resulted in the shooting of a police officer, has been heavily criticised: particularly the summing of Lord Goddard (the trial judge) whose bias '[denied] the appellant that fair trial which is the birthright of every British citizen'.[16] Reginald Paget QC summarised the mood of Parliament and, arguably, the wider public, at the time:

> A three-quarter-witted boy of 19 is to be hanged for a murder he did not commit, and which was committed 15 minutes after he was arrested. Can we be made to keep silent when a thing as horrible and as shocking as this is to happen?[17]

Despite efforts to commute his sentence, Bentley was hanged. Ruth Ellis was lawfully convicted of murder in 1955 but the death sentence passed was met with opposition, primarily by a public who sympathised with her due to the abuse she had suffered at the deceased's hands prior to his death.[18] Despite a campaign for a reprieve, Ellis was hanged in 1955. These events, combined with the increasing criticism of the Homicide Act 1957, led to a landmark change in 1964.

Harold Wilson's Labour Government passed the Murder (Abolition of the Death Penalty) Act 1965, initially suspending the death penalty for capital murder for five years (made permanent at the end of 1969). Throughout the 1970s and 1980s, multiple attempts were made to repeal the legislation; in total, Parliament considered the issue 13 times between 1965 and 1994, with majorities against every time.[19] Four years after the last attempt, the death penalty was finally abolished for all remaining offences (including high treason).[20] The 1990s had seen multiple miscarriages of justice uncovered[21] and the election of New Labour, which quickly moved to enshrine international human rights obligations into domestic law as part of its social agenda. As such, the abolitionist movement secured its ultimate objective and became, legally and politically, the orthodox view on the death penalty in the UK.

Notwithstanding this, public opinion has appeared to – on balance – favour the death penalty. In 2009, Ipsos MORI found that 70% of respondents thought that the UK should have the death penalty as the maximum possible penalty for at least one of 12 different types of crime, with 73% believing that 'the views of the public are being ignored by politicians and the Government when setting maximum sentences and penalties for serious crimes'.[22] A significant majority (76%) thought that 'there should be more open debate in the UK about the penalties for serious crimes, including the death penalty'.[23] In 2014, YouGov found that 45% of people favoured reintroducing the death penalty, with 39% opposed, and 17% unsure;[24] very similar proportions

15 Knowles (n 8), 39.

16 *Bentley (Deceased)* [2001] 1 Cr App R 21, per Lord Bingham at [68].

17 Royal Prerogative (Disallowed Motion), HC Deb 27 January 1953, vol 510, cc 845-64, 851.

18 Knowles (n 8), 47.

19 Hansard, 21 February 1994, col 39.

20 Under the Crime and Disorder Act 1998 and the Human Rights Act 1998.

21 For example, the cases of the Birmingham Six (1991), Guildford Four (1989), Maguire Seven (1991), Cardiff Three (1992) and Judith Ward (1992).

22 Ipsos MORI, 'Survey for Channel 4 on attitudes towards the death penalty' (28 October 2009): www.ipsos.com/ipsos-mori/en-uk/survey-channel-4-attitudes-towards-death-penalty (accessed 23 April 2020).

23 *Ibid.*

24 YouGov, '50 years on, Capital Punishment still favoured' (13 August 2014): https://yougov.co.uk/topics/politics/articles-reports/2014/08/13/capital-punishment-50-years-favoured (accessed 23 April 2020).

believed it to be an effective deterrent.[25] More recently, the annual NatCen British Social Attitudes Report found that overall support for the death penalty had dropped below 50% for the first time in the three decades the survey had asked the question.[26] By early 2023, YouGov found that less than a third of Britons favoured death for all types of murder, with more than half opposed.[27]

15.3 For or against? Debates about capital punishment

Whilst debates about capital punishment are complex, nuanced, and often overlapping, some common themes can be identified in the narratives of the two opposing sides:

- those in favour of using the death penalty: retentionist (in countries which already use it) or proponent (in countries which do not);
- those against using the death penalty: abolitionist (in countries which already use it) or opponent (in countries which do not).

The following sections will summarise the major arguments for and against the death penalty.

15.4 Retribution and denunication

One of the primary moral debates about the death penalty is its use as a form of retribution and denunication for the most serious types of criminal behaviour. Whilst capital punishment has historically been used as the penalty for a wide variety of offences, most modern debates focus on its imposition for a small category of extremely serious crimes: primarily murder, terrorism and serious sex offences (particularly when related to children). This is justified by the need to exact retribution for the offence – that is, to inflict harm on the offender – and to mark its severity, which is so grave, damaging and offensive, that nothing less than death will be appropriate. As discussed in **Chapter 12**, retribution is backwards looking in that it is concerned with responding in a morally appropriate manner to wrongs previously committed, rather than considering how to avoid such wrongs occurring in the future. Similarly, 'the emphatic denunciation by the community for the crime' is therefore also backwards looking,[28] concerned with expressing the disapproval of society as regards the offence in question.[29] The question in this context is therefore: what type of action is appropriate to both punish and denounce the offence in question? This will depend on the offence. Like sentencing (discussed in **Chapter 13**), this requires some moral 'mathematics' in which the various factors which determine harm and culpability are used to calculate an appropriate sentence 'equal' to the crime. Since most debates focus on the use of the death penalty for murder, we will focus on this.

25 *Ibid.*

26 BBC News, 'Support for death penalty drops below 50% for the first time' (26 March 2015): www.bbc.co.uk/news/uk-32061822 (accessed 23 April 2020).

27 YouGov, 'Should the death penalty be reintroduced in all cases of murder?' (January 2023): https://yougov.co.uk/topics/politics/trackers/should-the-death-penalty-be-reintroduced-in-all-cases-of-murder (accessed 10 February 2023).

28 Gowers, E, 'The Royal Commission on Capital Punishment' (HMSO, Cmd No 8932, 1953), [53] *per* Lord Denning.

29 See **Chapter 12**.

Most arguments regarding the right level of retribution and denunciation for murder rely on theoretical concepts related to proportionality, such as 'just deserts',[30] and the biblical concept of *lex talionis*.[31] 'Just deserts' is, broadly, a form of revenge meted out by the state on behalf of a victim of crime. The type of revenge enacted is justified on the basis that:

- the offender deserves to receive it due to their own blameworthy actions (ie their culpability);
- it is proportionate to the results of these actions (ie the harm caused); and
- it will result in satisfaction, relief or closure for a victim (ie reparation – which is in itself a separate theory of punishment).[32]

A very traditional, and literal, method of determining what revenge is deserved is the Old Testament concept of *lex talionis*: that is, 'an eye for an eye, a tooth for a tooth'. Therefore, the punishment should resemble the offence that has been committed in both kind and degree. When applied to the crime of murder, concepts like these can be used to argue both against and (more commonly) for capital punishment. Interpreted literally, *lex talionis* would dictate that murder (the intentional taking of life) should be returned with murder (albeit, state-sanctioned). In short, a life for a life. This, it might be argued, satisfies the principle of 'just deserts' in a proportionate manner because the crime and the punishment are equal. Similarly, as a state sanctioned murder, the death penalty denounces (that is, disapproves of) the offence committed in the most extreme way possible. Finally, one might argue that the victims who can receive reparation (eg the family of the deceased) will receive satisfaction and closure from the death of the person who killed their loved one.

There are, of course, counter-arguments to the above. First, it could be argued that the 'exchange' theory of *lex talionis* reduces human life to a commercial bargain equivalent to 'paying' for the value of an object, like one would at a shop – an arguably dehumanising construct. The argument that the death penalty brings satisfaction to those victimised by the death of a loved one is also flawed, in that it is not guaranteed. In some cases, this will certainly (or at least superficially) be the case if the family of a victim express a desire for the death of the offender, receive this form of justice, and express satisfaction with this outcome; for others, it is clear this is not the case.[33] Many families have expressed that the death of their loved one's killer has provided no joy or closure.[34] In summary, this justification of the death penalty is simply too variable to apply broadly.

All of the above suggests that the moral debate – particularly around retribution and denunciation – is ultimately irresolvable, complex, and fraught with contradiction and counter-argument. Good examples of the latter might be the application of 'sanctity of life' type arguments to different areas of social life, such as euthanasia and abortion. If life is sacred in the context of the death penalty, is it also sacred in relation to these

30 *Ibid.*

31 *Ibid.*

32 *Ibid.*

33 For more on this, see Berns, N, 'Contesting the Victim Card: Closure Discourse and Emotion in Death Penalty Rhetoric' (2009) 50 *Sociological Quarterly* 3; and Barrile, L, 'I Forgive You, But You Must Die: Murder victim family members, the death penalty, and restorative justice' (2015) 10 *Victims & Offenders* 3.

34 See **Chapter 10;** Lifton, R and Mitchell, G, *Who owns death? Capital Punishment, the American Conscience and the end of executions* (Harper, 2002); and Bandes, S, 'Victims, "Closure," and the Sociology of Emotion' (2009) 72 *Law & Contemporary Problems* (2).

other areas of debate? These discussions rely on value judgements regarding the people and actions involved in such decisions, which will be variable depending on personal perspective, experience and beliefs. Indeed, moral debates about retribution and denunciation are highly subjective and personal. Any moral debate founded on retribution and denunciation is somewhat problematic as a means of robustly justifying or criticising the death penalty; nonetheless, it remains an important debate to explore. Retribution and denunciation are deeply emotive and personal concepts, inextricably connected to and influenced by each person's worldview. As such, each person will conceive of them differently depending on their value system and their relationship to the society in which they live. If we ignore these concepts and dismiss any discussion centred on them, we will fail to fully examine the nature of the death penalty as a punishment.

15.5 Incapacitation and public protection

One of the few undisputable arguments favouring the death penalty is that it incapacitates the person subject to it permanently. Unlike other punishments – particularly imprisonment – post-sentence reoffending by the individual executed is not a concern, because it is not possible: there is no 'post-sentence'. As such, rehabilitation is not necessary; the individual's contribution to crime is lowered to nothing; and the public is protected from any further harm by this individual, *ad infinitum*. In this sense, the death penalty is a reliable method of satisfying several of the sentencing objectives outlined in s 142 of the Criminal Justice Act 2003, and might therefore be described as effective. Of course, this is a literal interpretation and can only be applied to a single individual, whereas the sentencing objectives are aimed at impacting on more than just the individual offender in a particular case. Following these arguments, the crime rate is directly lowered in the smallest possible way (ie the contribution of one individual) and the public is protected from only one person – not the many others who might pose a threat of harm (though there is an argument to be made regarding the indirect impact of deterrence on wider crime rates – discussed below). Such arguments have slightly more credence when applied to offenders whose impact goes far beyond individual victims (for example, mass murders, terrorists or serial rapists),[35] since the crimes committed and the people affected by these individuals will be much more significant and numerous.

However, this line of argument makes one very important assumption – that the person executed is *in fact* guilty of the offence(s) in question. Permanent incapacitation and public protection are achieved only if the actual offender is punished in this way; otherwise, we face the twin nightmare (in criminal justice terms) of an innocent person being put to death, whilst the real perpetrator remains at liberty and able to commit further offences against an unknowing public. One need only refer to some of the major miscarriages of justice, discussed in other parts of this book, to illustrate this fundamental problem. Take, for example, the case of the Cardiff Three,[36] and place it in an alternate reality where the punishment for murder is death. Paris, Abdullahi and Miller – the three defendants wrongly convicted of the murder of Lynette White in

35 Examples might include Dr Harold Shipman (estimated to have murdered around 250 of his patients); Hashem Abedi (convicted of 22 counts of murder in relation to the 2017 Manchester Arena bombing); and Reynhard Sinaga (convicted of 136 rapes, and believed to have committed a further 200).

36 *Paris, Abdullahi and Miller* (1993) 97 Cr App R 99.

1989 – could have been executed shortly after conviction; the flaws in the investigation revealed by an appeal or by more extensive investigation might have remained hidden forever. The real killer, Jeffrey Gafoor, might have never been caught (as he was in 2003) because there would be no reason to believe that the real killer remained free.[37] Therefore, the death penalty would, in this alternative scenario, have entirely failed to either incapacitate or protect the public. For critics, this argument is an attractive one, though it also has problems. In the scenario above, incapacitation and public protection are not achieved because the convicted defendants were executed quickly. The likelihood of miscarriages of justice being discovered and corrected is partly contingent on the length of time between a death sentence and any eventual execution, because this period provides opportunities for appeal and other forms of investigation and scrutiny.[38] If the offender is killed within a matter of days, weeks or months, the likelihood is much lower; if years pass before the offender is put to death, the likelihood is much higher.

We might look to historic cases to demonstrate this. For example, Derek Bentley was convicted on the 11 December 1952 and executed on 28 January 1953 – an intervening period of 48 days (just under 7 weeks).[39] An even more pertinent example is the execution of Timothy Evans, 57 days after conviction (just over 8 weeks); the actual perpetrator, John Christie, not only testified against Evans at trial, but proceeded to murder his own wife two years later (for which he was executed).[40] That such cases were miscarriages of justice is now undisputed; but such arguments were completely rejected at the time, both at trial, on appeal, and by the Home Secretary in rejecting a pardon.[41] As such, it might be argued that the death penalty is a valid form of incapacitation and public protection if a sufficient period is allowed between sentence and execution, increasing the likelihood that any mistakes are uncovered and the right person is punished (or, at the very least, an innocent person spared). For an example of this, we might look to the use of 'Death Row' in the USA. This is best defined as 'the area in a prison which houses inmates awaiting execution',[42] and it is used for this purpose (collectively and for individuals) for long periods of time. Indeed, as of 2017, condemned prisoners spent an average period of 243 months (slightly over 20 years) on death row.[43] This would almost certainly satisfy the criteria of a 'sufficient period' for reviewing and correcting miscarriages of justice. Indeed, between 1973 and 2017, 161 prisoners on death row in the US were exonerated,[44] and research conducted by Gross et al suggested that if such prisoners remained on death row indefinitely, approximately 4.1% of them would be exonerated – described as a 'conservative' estimate.[45] However,

37 Whilst there is no evidence to suggest Gafoor killed or offended against others, he would have been free to do so (and, in reality, was so for more than two decades).

38 For example, by campaigners, the press, family, friends and lawyers.

39 See *Bentley* (n 16), [1].

40 *R (Westlake) v Criminal Cases Review Commission* [2004] EWHC 2779 (Admin), [4]. Also see Rubin, G, 'Posthumous pardons, the Home Office and the Timothy Evans case' (2007) *Crim LR* 41–59.

41 See Knowles (n 8), 41–44.

42 Hudson, P, 'Does the death row phenomenon violate a prisoner's human rights under international law?' (2000) 11 *Eur J of Int Law* (4), 835.

43 Death Penalty Information Centre, 'Time on Death Row': https://deathpenaltyinfo.org/death-row/death-row-time-on-death-row (accessed 23 April 2020).

44 Cornell Centre on the Death Penalty Worldwide, 'Justice Denied: A Global Study of Wrongful Death Row Convictions' (Cornell Law School, January 2018), 7: https://files.deathpenaltyinfo.org/legacy/files/pdf/innocence_clinic_report_2018_R4_final.pdf (last accessed: 24 April 2020).

45 Gross, S et al, 'Rate of false conviction of criminal defendants who are sentenced to death' (2014) 111 *PNAS* (20), 7234.

extending the length of time between sentence and execution raises another problem – the argument (discussed in more detail below) that to do so is inhumane, unjust, costly, and tantamount to life imprisonment for prisoners (some of whom will be innocent). Moreover, a lengthy period of time post-conviction provides no guarantee of the correction of a miscarriage.[46] This therefore presents an irresolvable problem in the context of the death penalty: wait too long to execute, and injustice is perpetrated against those on death row (and those, such as victims' families, wanting closure), with no guarantee of fixing mistakes. In contrast, fail to wait long enough, and the opportunity to question or challenge a conviction is lost, forever. Those who are wrongly executed receive no justice, and the only compensation will be posthumous vindication.[47]

Even if we accept that the death penalty is a valid and reliable form of permanent incapacitation and public protection, it might also be argued that to kill a person simply to achieve these ends will virtually never be proportionate in and of itself. This is because, logically, we could extend this argument to *any* criminal offence. A prolific thief could be permanently stopped if we chose to execute them; an individual could be permanently protected from harm if we opted to kill their domestically violent partner. Whilst true, such a response would be disproportionate. The punishment is excessive and inappropriate for this level of offending which, whilst obviously negative, is not serious enough to merit such a harsh outcome. As such, effective incapacitation and public protection cannot – on their own – justify the use of the death penalty. They must also be proportionate. It is at this point that we return to the debates about retribution and denunciation (which, as discussed above, are also problematic). Overall, this leaves this debate in the following position: whilst incapacitation and public protection are undoubtedly delivered (on a limited basis) by the death penalty, they are reliant on proportionality to be justifiable – and this has a range of problems too. This again leaves us with few certain and reliable answers, and room for continued discussion.

15.6 Impact on and relationship to individual rights

One of the most vociferous debates regarding capital punishment is the impact on individual rights, primarily those of the offender executed. In the modern era, the primary framework of laws governing the death penalty is human rights, as defined by various types of international law. In Europe, the key legal instrument in this context is the European Convention on Human Rights (ECHR). The ECHR, created by the Council of Europe (CoE), applies to signatory countries from across Europe – including all member states of the EU as well as a significant number of non-EU jurisdictions (which now include the UK). When it opened for signature in 1950, the ECHR allowed for the use of the death penalty as a form of punishment;[48] this has since

46 Many miscarriages of justice have taken decades to be corrected, and many will almost certainly remain undetected. Multiple cases involving detected miscarriages of justice – such as the Birmingham Six – have never been resolved, with no one convicted for the original offence. Even the Cardiff Three case (in which the actual perpetrator was eventually found) remained 'cold' for two decades after Paris, Abdullahi and Miller were freed.

47 For example, see *Mahmoud Mattan (Hanged)* [1998] EWCA Crim 676.

48 Organisation for Security and Cooperation in Europe, 'Exchange of views on the question of abolition of capital punishment' (Human Dimension Implementation Meeting, September 2014), 1: www.osce.org/odihr/124116?download=true (accessed 24 April 2020).

changed. In 1985, a binding protocol to the ECHR (No 6) was issued by the CoE, which abolished the use of the death penalty in peace time.[49] By 2003, this had been expanded to cover all circumstances (by Protocol 13), with no derogations allowable and an irreversible process imposed to prevent its reintroduction.[50] To date, 44 of the 47 CoE member states have ratified this protocol. As such, Europe has, legally, been a 'death penalty free zone' for nearly two decades.[51]

Globally, the most relevant international laws are the United Nations (UN) International Covenant on Civil and Political Rights (ICCPR) and the UN Economic and Social Council (ESC) Resolution 1984/50.[52] Unlike the ECHR, these do not specifically prohibit the use of the death penalty; however, Article 6 ICCPR and the ESC Resolution do place strict requirements on its use which, if breached, would constitute a violation of international law. Article 6(2) ICCPR states that the death penalty 'may be imposed only for the most serious crimes', which appear to be defined as 'intentional crimes with lethal or other extremely grave consequences'.[53] Additionally, the death penalty cannot be used 'contrary to the provisions of the present Covenant' under Article 6(2). As such, if other provisions of the ICCPR are breached in executing someone (such as Article 7, 'torture or cruel, inhuman or degrading treatment or punishment'), it will be unlawful. Importantly, the death penalty can only be carried out 'pursuant to a final judgement rendered by a competent court',[54] and 'after legal process which gives all possible safeguards to ensure a fair trial'.[55] As part of this, the standard of proof required before such a penalty can be imposed is high; that is 'when the guilt of the person charged is based upon clear and convincing evidence leaving no room for an alternative explanation of the facts'.[56] When the death penalty is carried out, it is required that it be done in a manner that 'inflict[s] the minimum possible suffering'.[57] Additionally, Article 6(5) ICCPR prohibits the use of the death penalty for those under 18 or for pregnant women, whilst the ESC Resolution extends this to include new mothers and the insane.[58]

A variety of rights are enshrined by these legal instruments which may be affected by the death penalty. The primary one is the right to life, guaranteed under Article 2 ECHR and Article 6 ICCPR. In relation to Article 2 ECHR, the modifications introduced by Protocol 13 absolutely prohibit the taking of life by the state as a punishment for crime. Thus, use of the death penalty would, legally, breach the right of any offender, regardless of the circumstances, the basis for this being the sanctity of life and the fundamental and irreversible loss suffered by any human being whose life is taken. Proponents of the death penalty might argue that those convicted of murder have clearly breached the Article 2 rights of the victim and that such a fundamental breach should be met with equivalent legal consequences. From a rights-oriented

49 Council of Europe, 'Protocol No 6 to the Convention for the Protection of Human Rights and Fundamental Freedoms concerning the abolition of the death penalty' (ETS No 114).

50 Council of Europe, 'Protocol No 13 to the Convention for the Protection of Human Rights and Fundamental Freedoms, concerning the abolition of the death penalty in all circumstances' (ETS No 187).

51 Organisation for Security and Cooperation in Europe (n 48), 1.

52 'Safeguards guaranteeing protection of the rights of those facing the death penalty'.

53 *Ibid*, para 1.

54 *Ibid*, para 5.

55 Article 6(2) ICCPR; and *ibid.*

56 *Ibid*, para 4.

57 *Ibid*, para 9.

58 *Ibid*, para 3.

perspective, this argument lacks validity. Ultimately, a death sentence (whatever its motivation) remains a breach of the right to life under the ECHR, though there are, of course, legal exceptions to the right to life (such as necessary, proportionate self-defence).[59] However, it is hard to see how such an exception can be extended to the death penalty as its use does not defend any specific person from unlawful violence (other than, possibly, future victims) and is clearly not necessary force. Unlike lethal self-defence, the death penalty is not a 'heat of the moment' reaction in a time of urgency; it is calculated and considered. As such, arguments that the death penalty can be likened to a form of 'self-defence' by the state are weak (particularly since the ECHR affords *individual* rights, not rights to the state as an entity).

Beyond Article 2, other rights under the ECHR – as well as the various rights and safeguards applicable under the ICCPR and ESC Resolution – are arguably affected by the use of the death penalty. These include:

- freedom from torture or cruel, inhuman or degrading treatment or punishment
- right to a fair trial
- minimisation of the suffering of those executed.

15.6.1 Torture or cruel, inhuman or degrading treatment or punishment (Article 3 ECHR and Article 7 ICCPR)

Both of these provisions are potentially engaged by capital punishment, not by the fact of an offender's death but by the process leading up to that moment. As discussed earlier, a substantial period of time post-conviction is arguably needed to ensure that appeals and proper scrutiny are afforded to those condemned to death, so as to lower the chances of a miscarriage of justice. However, if this period of 'limbo' (when the offender has been sentenced but not punished) continues for too long, then the state risks accusations of cruel and inhuman treatment, and possibly torture in the most extreme circumstances. As mentioned earlier, the average length of time on death row in the US is 20 years,[60] and between 2010 and 2019, 23 death row prisoners were exonerated after a wait of more than 25 years.[61] Such long periods are tantamount to life imprisonment; in some cases this may be imposed on innocent people, amounting to a serious breach of multiple individual rights and civil liberties. For those who are in fact guilty, the cloud of uncertainty hanging over their proposed execution may last decades, with an inevitable toll on their mental and physical health (as well as that of the family of a victim, whose rights are also threatened by long delays). When any execution eventually takes place after such a period, it may be interpreted as a 'double punishment' since a prisoner may already have spent many years in custody. In *Pratt and Morgan v Attorney General for Jamaica*,[62] the Privy Council ruled that executing a prisoner after five years on death row amounted to cruel and unusual punishment, stating:

> There is an instinctive revulsion against the prospect of hanging a man after he has been held under sentence of death for many years. What gives rise to this instinctive revulsion? The answer can only be our humanity; we regard it as an inhuman act to keep a man facing the agony of execution over a long extended period of time.[63]

---

59 Article 2(2).

60 Death Penalty Information Centre (n 43).

61 *Ibid.*

62 [1993] UKPC 1

63 *Ibid* [60].

These issues are even more acute when the offender is arguably a vulnerable person, such as someone with serious mental or physical health issues. In such situations, the offender's competence to be executed becomes a significant legal (as well as moral) issue. For example, in 2019, the US Supreme Court ruled that Vernon Madison – convicted of shooting a police officer in 1985 – was not fit to be executed in Alabama due to multiple health conditions, including advanced dementia that meant he was unable to remember his crime.[64] A stay was granted on the grounds that Madison could not comprehend the reasons for the execution, and that to carry it out would constitute a cruel and unusual punishment.[65]

Equally, the method of execution used might also breach Article 3 ECHR and Article 7 ICCPR (as well as ESC Resolution 1984/50, para 9, which requires minimal suffering – discussed below). Historically, a range of gruesome methods of execution have been used, including being hung, drawn and quartered, or burned at the stake. In the last few centuries of its use in the UK, the death penalty involved hanging by the neck, with very specific methods developed in the last years of its use (notably by Albert Pierrepoint) designed to achieve a swift, reliable and humane death.[66] In the modern day, the most common method used is lethal injection (the default in all US states that have the death penalty);[67] however, other methods continue to be available across the globe, including electrocution, gassing, beheading, hanging, shooting and even stoning.[68] All of the above pose human rights issues. Proponents argue that death by methods such as lethal injection are quick, painless and effective, ensuring that the individual rights under discussion are protected as much as is possible. However, evidence supporting this is mixed; no method of execution is guaranteed to be totally effective, in both achieving death and doing so humanely. The Royal Commission (discussed earlier in this chapter) considered methods of execution as part of its review of the death penalty, dismissing all but hanging as reliable (something which has subsequently been strongly disputed).[69] According to Sarat, just over 3% of executions conducted in the US between 1890 and 2010 were 'botched';[70] of these, lethal injection was the most problematic, with a rate of 7%.[71] This is troubling considering that lethal injection is regarded as the preferred option for execution. Others may be much less reliable and undignified, risking accusations of cruel and unusual punishment. For example, the Royal Commission concluded that shooting did not 'possess even the first requisite of an efficient method, the certainty of causing immediate death'.[72] In a renowned review of multiple methods of execution, Hillman concluded:

> [N]early all execution procedures are likely to be attended by pain to the condemned person. Nevertheless, despite the evidence presented above, it is

64 *Madison v Alabama*, 586 US __ (2019).

65 Prohibited under the 8th Amendment to the US Constitution.

66 See Knowles (n 8), 25.

67 National Conference of State Legislatures, 'States and Capital Punishment' (24 March 2020): www.ncsl.org/research/civil-and-criminal-justice/death-penalty.aspx (accessed 23 April 2020).

68 Both Iran and Brunei provide for stoning to death as a punishment, though it has not been used in a number of years. See Amnesty International, 'Death Sentences and Executions 2019' (April 2020): www.amnesty.org/download/Documents/ACT5018472020ENGLISH.PDF (accessed: 23 April 2020).

69 See Knowles (n 8), 25.

70 Sarat, A, 'Gruesome Spectacles: Botched Executions and America's Death Penalty' (Stanford University Press, 2014), 177.

71 *Ibid.*

72 Royal Commission on Capital Punishment (n 28), 710.

widely asserted that executions are humane and painless ... although no evidence to this effect appears to have been published.[73]

15.6.2 The right to a fair trial (Article 6 ECHR and Article 14 ICCPR)

The process underpinning the conviction and subsequent sentence of an accused person may be deeply flawed for reasons discussed elsewhere in this book. For example, suspects may be subject to oppression, violence or torture as part of an investigation, leading to convictions based on unreliable and false confessions.[74] Such actions may be driven by noble cause corruption,[75] and the belief that the suspect in question is guilty. The fact that a confession and conviction will likely result in the suspect's execution might even motivate such behaviour by investigators, rather than instilling a degree of caution. Indeed, the likelihood of a death sentence has potential repercussions for the entire pre-trial and trial process: including the charge selected, decisions about bail, and the eventual decision of a jury. Depending on the persons making such decisions, the fact that the death penalty may be the result could either persuade or dissuade decision-makers to lay more serious charges, deny bail, or convict a defendant. The impact of the availability of the death penalty on convictions and sentencing by both judges and juries is long recognised.[76] Clearly, the likely sentence should have no bearing on any of these decisions (except for bail, which will normally include consideration of likely sentence). Decisions about charges and conviction should be based entirely on the evidence in a case, in accordance with the law. Thus, the looming presence of the death penalty in such cases can in fact distort the fairness of a defendant's trial. Other important factors, such as inadequate legal representation (at both investigation and trial stages),[77] the inability of the defendant to comprehend proceedings and the sentence (discussed above), conviction and sentence *in absentia*, and the denial of an opportunity to appeal against a death sentence, all bear on the right to a fair trial. Indeed, it is arguable that, in some jurisdictions, these stringent standards are undermined or ignored in cases involving the death penalty, such is the desire to convict and execute the 'right person'.

15.6.3 Minimising suffering (ESC Resolution 1984/50, para 9)

Various 'safeguards' applicable to the use of the death penalty are identified by Resolution 1984/50 in light of the fact that the UN does not explicitly prohibit its use under the ICCPR. Nonetheless, there appear to be problems with compliance across the globe, suggesting that individual rights are routinely breached. In particular, the requirement to minimise suffering – whilst problematic in terms of the build up to an execution, discussed above – is most obviously threatened by the method of death utilised. In the modern era, the requirement to minimise suffering appears to be more commonly adhered to by those countries utilising the death penalty than in the past, with a comparatively narrow range of methods now used (discussed above). The most obviously problematic lawful method in the modern era is stoning. For example, the

---

73 Hillman, H, 'The possible pain experienced during execution by different methods' (1993) 22 *Perception* (6), 751.

74 See discussions in **Chapter 7**; and specifically in relation to the death penalty, see examples in multiple parts of Amnesty International (n 68).

75 See **Chapter 7**.

76 See, for example, Cowan, C, Thompson, W and Ellsworth, P, 'The effects of death qualification on jurors' predisposition to convict and on the quality of deliberation' (1984) 8 *Law & Human Behaviour*.

77 *Roderick Ricardo Went v The Queen (Criminal Appeal No 2 of 2014)* (2018) Court of Appeal of Barbados.

Iranian Penal Code provides for stones used for this purpose to be 'large enough to cause pain, but not so large as to kill the victim immediately', suggesting extended suffering is intended.[78] Both men and women are partially buried for this purpose (under Article 102 of the Penal Code), preventing flight and minimising defensive movement by the offender.[79] Notwithstanding this, stoning has not been lawfully used in Iran (or any other country) to execute an offender for over a decade.[80] However, it remains a lawful method of execution in a number of countries; most recently (in 2019) Brunei legalised stoning for homosexual intercourse and adultery, though quickly imposed a moratorium on its use amid an international outcry.[81]

15.6.4 Individual rights and the relationship with overall use of the death penalty

Finally, we might comment on the debate referenced above – that is, that rare use of the death penalty (conducted in a swift, reliable and painless manner) does not offend individual rights. Proponents of the death penalty might argue that, notwithstanding the arguments outlined in this section, if it is used sparingly, the infringement of individual rights is very limited. There is arguably some merit to this argument when applied to some jurisdictions; for example, of the 20 countries who were recorded as having executed offenders in 2019, just over 50% executed less than 20 (with the majority of these killing less than five people).[82] Superficially, this suggests rare use and therefore a limited impact on global human rights. However, attractive as this argument is, it is deeply problematic. For example, if we applied this logic to miscarriages of justice in the criminal justice system of England and Wales (which represents a comparatively small number of cases when juxtaposed with the overall number of convictions), this would represent a classic (and rather extreme) crime control approach; that is, miscarriages of justice are acceptable because they are rare. Yet, the individual impact is enormous and they indicate serious underlying problems in the criminal justice system, which threaten rights much more broadly. In the same way, rare use of the death penalty does not mean that its impact on individual rights is restricted only to the person executed. These arguments therefore recall Blackstone's formulation (discussed in **Chapter 8**), and the idea that small numbers do not equate to small impact. We might also point out that overall figures on the death penalty lack detailed context, such as how it is used and against whom. A good example might be heavy use of capital punishment during a specific period of time, such as the execution by Saudi Arabia of 37 people on one day for terrorism offences.[83] The overall number may appear small if measured over a long period; but it is hard to suggest that a single, mass execution has no implications for wider rights (particularly in light of the apparent fact that 14 of those executed had been involved in anti-government protests

---

78 Amnesty International, 'Iran: Death By Stoning, A Grotesque And Unacceptable Penalty' (15 January 2008): www.amnesty.org/en/press-releases/2008/01/iran-death-stoning-grotesque-and-unacceptable-penalty-20080115/ (accessed 28 April 2020).

79 *Ibid.*

80 A moratorium on executions (but not sentences) was introduced in Iran the early 2000s. See Amnesty International, 'Death Sentences and Executions 2009' (2010), 20: www.amnesty.org/download/

81 Documents/36000/act500012010en.pdf (accessed 28 April 2020).

82 Indeed, Brunei has not executed anyone since 1957. 104 Amnesty International (n 1), 9.

83 Amnesty International, 'Saudi Arabia: 37 put to death in shocking execution spree' (23 April 2019): www.amnesty.org/en/latest/news/2019/04/saudi-arabia-37-put-to-death-in-shocking-execution-spree/ (accessed 28 April 2020).

– another fundamental right).[84] Of course, the 'rare use' argument has little application as a rationale for countries such as China and North Korea, who are believed to execute thousands of people every year (though classify such information as state secrets which are not published).[85]

15.7 Deterrence

Of all the debates surrounding capital punishment, deterrence is arguably one of the oldest and most straightforward. In short, proponents of the death penalty argue that it is effective in reducing crime via the general deterrent effect, with a measurable impact on serious offences such as murder; whilst opponents would simply argue that no such conclusions can be drawn based on available evidence. In theory, the conceptualisation of the death penalty as a deterrent to serious crime has some basis in logic. Arguably, most (though perhaps not all) people would regard death as the ultimate loss.[86] If this is the legally and morally sanctioned consequence of certain kinds of behaviour – and, crucially, the populace believe that they are *likely* to be caught and this sanction *will* be enforced – then the impact should be to strongly deter that behaviour. The cost (death) can never be worth whatever might be gained (most likely, the death of another, but this will depend on the crime for which death is imposed). Economist Isaac Ehrlich characterised this, in his much discussed work on the death penalty, as a form of rational trade off:

> [I]f rational people fear death more than other punishment, the death penalty should have the greatest deterrent effect.[87]

This also neatly summarises a central contention of the pro-death penalty lobby: that death is a *more* effective deterrent than other punishments (primarily, life imprisonment without parole). This is referred to as the marginal deterrent effect.[88] As discussed in **Chapter 12**, the general deterrent effect on people beyond the offender punished does have theoretical difficulties, not least of which is its application to crimes of opportunity or impulsive 'crimes of passion'. The suggestion that the kind of rational thought process described by Ehrlich occurs during heated arguments or rushes of adrenaline is difficult to accept, and not supported by scientific evidence regarding

84 The right to protest is protected under Article 11 ECHR and Article 19 ICCPR.

85 See Amnesty International (n 1), 1. Amnesty has stopped publishing official estimates for China due to difficulty accessing reliable information. The last published figure (2008) was an estimate of 72% of global executions (just under 2,000 people), believed to be a gross underestimate. Amnesty International, 'Death Penalty: 2,390 Executions In 2008 Worldwide, 72 Per Cent In China' (24 March 2009): www.amnesty.org/en/press-releases/2009/03/death-penalty-2390-executions-2008-worldwide-72-cent-china-20090324/ (accessed 28 April 2020). The Dui Hua Foundation estimated that there were 12,000 executions in 2002; dropping (after significant reform) to 3,000 by 2012; and to around 2,000 in 2018 (Dui Hua Foundation, 'Death Penalty Reform: https://duihua.org/resources/death-penalty-reform/ (accessed 15 May 2020). For more on China's use of the death penalty, see Li, Y, Longmire, D and Lu, H, 'Death Penalty Disposition in China: What matters?' (2018) 62 *Int J of Offender Therapy & Comp Criminol* (1).

86 As famously suggested by Socrates at his trial, depicted in Plato's *Apology*.

87 Ehrlich, I, 'Capital Punishment and Deterrence: Some Further Thoughts and Additional Evidence' (1977) 85 *J of Political Economy* (4), 743.

88 See Weisberg, R, 'The Death Penalty Meets Social Science: Deterrence and Jury Behavior Under New Scrutiny' (2005) *Ann Rev of Law & Soc Science*, at 152 for a definition.

cognitive function.[89] Of course, the way in which criminal behaviour occurs varies widely, so it is difficult to dismiss a potential deterrent effect on this basis alone.

Unsurprisingly, many researchers – including criminologists, sociologists, psychologists and economists – have examined the deterrent effect of the death penalty in relation to homicide, in pursuit of some definitive answer to the question of whether, on balance, it works or not. At a rudimentary level, the death penalty could be deemed an effective deterrent if, for every execution, there was more than one homicide prevented. This rough calculation would therefore rely on utilitarian principles of the greatest happiness for the greatest number of people; one life is lost, but more than one is saved. Research in the US has focused on comparison of states with and without the death penalty. A multitude of methods have been used to determine whether US states with the death penalty have less serious crime (most specifically, murder), with a variety of conclusions drawn. The most basic approach is to directly compare homicide rates in states with and without the death penalty.

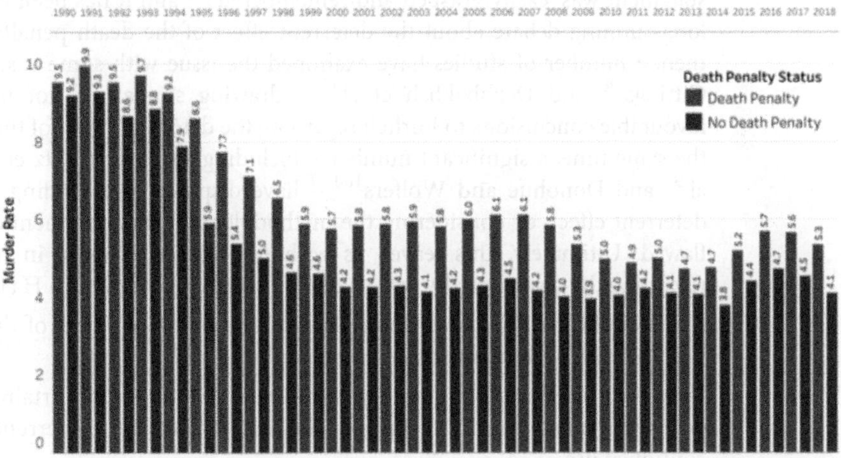

The above graph, produced by the Death Penalty Information Centre in the US, demonstrates a clear trend – states without the death penalty have lower murder rates than those which execute.[90] However, it would also be fair to say that this is a crude analysis. As Lamperti suggests:

> No deterrence can be seen here – but it might exist and yet be masked by other factors. Many things affect homicide rates; the problem is to separate the impact, if any, of capital punishment from that of all the other variables, known and unknown.[91]

89 See Roeder, O, Eisen, L and Bowling, J, 'What caused the crime decline?' (Brennan Center for Justice, New York University School of Law, 2015), 44.

90 Based on the FBI's 'Crime in the United States' statistical data. Death Penalty Information Center, 'Murder Rate of Death Penalty States Compared to Non-Death Penalty States': https://deathpenaltyinfo.org/facts-and-research/murder-rates/murder-rate-of-death-penalty-states-compared-to-non-death-penalty-states (accessed 28 April 2020).

91 Lamperti, J, 'Does Capital Punishment Deter Murder. A brief look at the evidence' (Dartmouth College, 2010): www.math.dartmouth.edu/~lamperti/my%20DP%20paper,%20current%20edit.htm (accessed 28 April 2020).

Factors such as varying demographics, overall crime rates, population densities and economic status might all influence murders in different states to varying degrees. Therefore, the above comparison can only take the debate so far.

In a landmark decision in 1972, the US Supreme Court concluded that there was 'no alternative but to conclude that capital punishment cannot be justified on the basis of its deterrent effect', deeming it unconstitutional.[92] This rationale reflected the academic consensus at the time regarding deterrence, based on research examining a wider range of factors and utilising more sophisticated techniques than the simple method above. Only a few years later, the Supreme Court reversed its decision and ruled the death penalty to be lawful, and its use resumed after a four-year suspension.[93] At this point, academic opinion began to markedly diverge as to the deterrent effect. In 1975, Ehrlich famously concluded that in the period between 1935 and 1969, 'an additional execution per year ... may have resulted, on average, in 7 or 8 fewer murders'.[94] Ehrlich did so based on relatively complex mathematical modelling, even if the headline was simple: the death penalty works. As Lamperti has suggested, this statement was 'easily grasped and remembered',[95] and it has been utilised as part of a long-running debate about the deterrent effect of the death penalty in the US. Since then, a number of studies have examined the issue with some – such as Mocan and Gittings,[96] and Dezhbakhsh et al[97] – drawing similar (if not more pronounced) favourable conclusions to Ehrlich regarding the deterrent effect of the death penalty. At the same time, a significant number – including studies by Katz et al,[98] Kovandzic et al,[99] and Donohue and Wolfers[100] – have disputed this, finding either little or no deterrent effect, or considering the methodology of the aforementioned studies to be flawed. Ultimately, this leaves us with no certain answers, in terms of research, regarding the death penalty and its deterrent effect. As Van Den Haag asserted:

> I doubt that the presence or absence of a deterrent effect of the death penalty is likely to be demonstrable by statistical means.[101]

However, he followed this by suggesting that '[i]t is on our uncertainty that the case for deterrence must rest'.[102] In short, the inability to rule out a deterrent effect justified its continued use.

In light of the debates above regarding individual rights and miscarriages of justice, this suggestion is questionable. There is considerable room for doubt about the deterrent effect in this context; thus a cautious approach to endorsing it would seem, arguably, wiser in light of the potential consequences. Indeed, one of these argued

---

92 *Furman v Georgia*, 408 US 238 (1972) *per* Justice Marshall.

93 *Gregg v Georgia, and others* 428 US 153 (1976).

94 Ehrlich, I, 'The Deterrent Effect of Capital Punishment: A Question of Life or Death' (1975) 65 *American Economic Rev.*

95 Lamperti (n 91).

96 'Getting off Death Row: Commuted Sentences and the Deterrent Effect of Capital Punishment' (2003) 46 *J of Law & Economics* (2).

97 'Does Capital Punishment Have a Deterrent Effect? New Evidence from Postmoratorium Panel Data' (2003) 5 *American Law & Economics Rev* (2).

98 'Prison Conditions, Capital Punishment, and Deterrence' (2003) 5 *American Law & Economics Rev* (2).

99 'Does the death penalty save lives? New evidence from state panel data, 1977 to 2006' (2009) 8 *Criminol & Public Policy* (4).

100 'Uses and Abuses of Empirical Evidence in the Death Penalty Debate' (2005) 58 *Stanford LR* (3).

101 Van den Haag, E, 'On deterrence and the death penalty' (1969) 60 *J of Crim L & Criminol, and Police Science* (2), 146.

102 *Ibid.*

consequences is the 'brutalisation effect', which suggests that '[e]xecutions create an atmosphere of brutality that spurs criminals to more violence'.[103] This generates a cycle of violence whereby individual citizens are more likely to have their right to be protected from violent crime breached,[104] resulting in more punishment of offenders for more serious crimes, and almost certainly more use of the death penalty; and thus amplifying the brutalisation effect in a continuing cycle. This was first theorised by Bowers and Pierce in 1980, who found that for every execution in the state of New York, there were two additional homicides in the following month.[105] More recently, Shepherd found evidence for both a deterrent and brutalisation effect in the use of the death penalty in different US states, depending on whether they passed what she termed a 'threshold' of executions.[106] In summary, if a state executed more than nine offenders (the threshold), 'executions, on average, deterred murder', whereas '[i]n states that conducted fewer executions than the threshold, the average execution increased the murder rate or had no effect'.[107] Her explanation for these 'two opposing effects' was as follows:

> First, the execution creates a brutalization effect: it contributes to creating a climate of brutal violence. The execution sets an example of killing to avenge grievances, an example that some private individuals then follow. Second, the execution creates some deterrence: potential criminals recognize that the state is willing to wield the ultimate penalty. For the first few executions, however, the deterrent effect is small. Only if a state executes many people does deterrence grow; only then do potential criminals become convinced that the state is serious about the punishment, so that the criminals start to reduce their criminal activity. When the number of executions exceeds the threshold, the deterrence effect begins to outweigh the brutalization effect.[108]

This novel analysis therefore implies, somewhat paradoxically, that for capital punishment to have any meaningful deterrent rather than an apparent brutalising effect on citizens, it must be used extensively and with limited restraint. This might explain why research is so mixed in finding a deterrent effect, since few US states use the death penalty extensively.[109]

However, this raises serious questions about the impact on individual rights and miscarriages of justice, and we must ask whether the inevitable sacrifices which would result from significantly increased use of the death penalty are worth the price of a

---

103 Shepherd, J, 'Deterrence versus Brutalization: Capital Punishment's Differing Impacts among States' (2005) 104 *Mich LR* 203, 229.

104 Protected under Article 3 ECHR – see, for example, *Commissioner of Police of the Metropolis v DSD and NBV* [2018] UKSC 11, in which the victims of 'Black Cab Rapist' Jon Worboys successfully sought damages against the Metropolitan Police for failing to effectively investigate his crimes and protect them from victimisation.

105 Bowers, W and Pierce, G, 'Deterrence or Brutalization: What Is the Effect of Executions?' (1980) 26 *Crime & Delinq.*

106 Shepherd (n 103), 205–06.

107 *Ibid*, 206.

108 *Ibid.*

109 Since 1977, approxmately 1,500 people have been executed in the US. Of the 27 states that currently use the death penalty, three have imposed a moratorium. Of the 24 remaining states, five (Texas, Oklahoma, Ohio, Florida and Virginia) account for nearly two-thirds of executions conducted in the last four decades. See Death Penalty Information Centre, 'Executions Overview': https://deathpenaltyinfo.org/executions/executions-overview (accessed 10 February 2023).

(certainly debatable) deterrent effect. The speculative nature of this effect is well demonstrated by Roeder et al:

> [T]he potential offender must consider the probability he would be caught, the probability he would be charged, the probability he would be convicted, the probability he would receive a death sentence, and the probability that he would be executed. After multiplying these probabilities together, the potential offender realizes a small probability of execution occurring, and therefore the possibility of being executed would essentially never affect a criminal decision.[110]

In this sense, increasing the number of executions to meet the 'threshold' for a deterrent effect would arguably not be enough. It would also need to be accompanied by better detection rates by the police (which would likely necessitate more police officers); higher charging rates (which would depend on more available evidence and, probably, more available criminal offences); increased conviction rates (dependent on many different factors); more death sentences (which depends on the offences for which it is available and the inclination of the decision-maker); before, finally, increasing the numbers of executions to pass the threshold for a deterrent effect. Achieving all of this would almost certainly have enormous implications for civil liberties and individual rights, and strongly resemble a pure crime control system. Overall, the deterrent effect of the death penalty is uncertain and difficult to establish. As Lamperti summarises:

> When we acknowledge that there must be instances when capital punishment helps deter a murder, we must also recognize that at other times it can encourage what it is meant to prevent. Since neither effect can be measured directly we are forced back to the statistical studies, which seek to determine the net effect. Their evidence does not prove that the death penalty is no added deterrent to murder, nor could it. It does show, I believe, that any 'deterrent' effect is very small in magnitude, *and it might go in either direction.*[111]

15.8 Practicality

Whilst the moral and legal arguments related to the death penalty tend to take centre-stage, another more pragmatic conversation – one with increased relevance in the era of economy and efficiency – always lingers in the background: the practical and logistical benefits and drawbacks of capital punishment. Supporters of the death penalty regard it as the most cost effective and, in penological terms, straightforward method of punishing the most serious offences (again, almost exclusively murder). Whether the death penalty is *cost* effective – that is, it achieves the same goals as other punishments at a lower financial cost – is contingent on various factors. If a death sentence is executed quickly using low cost methods, it might theoretically be argued that it is cost effective. This approach would ensure public protection, provide retribution, and reduce the chances of the individual reoffending to zero. It would achieve this for a one-off cost, as opposed to the long-term financial investment required to imprison someone for many years (with the potential for them to reoffend on release). Of course, this ignores all sorts of essential points: swift executions risk miscarriages of justice and may deny the chance for an offender to appeal. Low cost

110 Roeder (n 89), 44.
111 Lamperti (n 91).

methods tend to be crude, brutal and inhumane. A classic comparison would be stoning (a virtually zero cost method of execution, in terms of money and time) as opposed to lethal injection (which requires specific drugs and trained administrators). In short, promoting cost-effective use of the death penalty, measured purely in terms of money and time, ignores the *social costs* – the deleterious effect on individual rights and the moral legitimacy of state punishment.

The above debate is largely (though not entirely) theoretical; in reality, the use of the death penalty is less black and white, with limited examples of 'swift and simple' execution now being used. Instead, the tendency globally – and most notably in the US – is for a death sentence to be followed by a lengthy appeals process, whereby the legality of a conviction or sentence is challenged (possibly multiple times). This can take many years, as exemplified by the long-term imprisonment of offenders on death row in the US. Not only does this mean that the death penalty is not swift; the process preceding it can be extremely expensive. Additionally, lengthy delays in actually executing the death sentence have resulted in what has been termed the 'death row phenomenon':

> [T]hat execution after prolonged delay under the harsh conditions of death row constitutes cruel and unusual punishment. It is not the sentence of death that is being challenged, but the sentence of death after a torturous period of delay.[112]

As such, the process becomes self-perpetuating: delays lead to legal challenges, which generate cost and more delays, and so on. It has been noted that where 'the prisoner himself drives the delays by pursuing appeals', such an argument has limited validity.[113] However, outside of what might be termed 'frivolous' challenges (see **Chapter 11**), where delay is due to the natural pursuit of legitimate appeals – which are important for the reasons discussed earlier in this chapter – or are facilitated by the state rather than the prisoner, it would seem that a lengthy period between sentence and execution is reasonable and probably inevitable.

Prior to any eventual execution, the process can be broken down into a variety of stages, with associated costs.[114] First, there are initial legal costs, including for prosecution lawyers as well as legal representation for offenders who cannot afford them (likely to be the vast majority).[115] Second, there are pre-trial costs, such as the commission of experts like forensic and mental health professionals, as well as pre-trial detention of offenders.[116] Third, there is the trial itself, which has a variety of costs that differ depending on the jurisdiction. For example, in the US, jury selection is time-consuming and costly in capital cases.[117] The conduct of the trial is likely to be longer

112 Hudson (n 42), 833.

113 *Ibid*, 834.

114 For more on the costs of these various stages, see Alarcón, A and Mitchell, P, 'Executing the Will of the Voters?: A Roadmap to Mend or End the California Legislature's Multi-Billion-Dollar Death Penalty Debacle' (2011) 44 *Loy LA LR* S41; and Alarcón, A and Mitchell, P, 'Costs of Capital Punishment in California: Will Voters Choose Reform this November?' (2012) 46 *Loy LA LR* S1.

115 See US Department of Justice, 'Expert Working Group Report: International Perspectives on Indigent Defense' (September 2011): www.ncjrs.gov/pdffiles1/nij/236022.pdf (accessed 29 April 2020); and Primus, E, 'Defense Counsel and Public Defense' in Luna, E (ed), *Reforming Criminal Justice: Pretrial and Trial Processes* (Academy for Justice, 2017).

116 On the latter, it has been estimated that pre-trial detention generally costs the US approximately $13.6 billion a year (Wagner, P and Rabuy, B, 'Following the money of mass incarceration' (Prison Policy Initiative, January 2017): www.prisonpolicy.org/reports/money.html (accessed 29 April 2020).

117 Garey, M, 'The Cost of Taking a Life: Dollars and Sense of the Death Penalty' (1985) 18 *UC Davis LR* 257; Alarcón, 'Executing the Will of the Voters?' (n 114), S77.

(in line with other complex crime trials), with court running costs, legal and administrative personnel, and compensation for jurors.[118] Fourth, there is post-conviction imprisonment (death row), which is high security and often long term.[119] Fifth, there is the appeal process, which encompasses several of the costs above at a higher rate due to the enhanced complexity of proceedings and, in many cases, the need to gather further evidence. There can be multiple appeals (depending on the process in each jurisdiction), lasting several years.[120] The issue of high costs is particularly well documented in the US. A 2011 study of the death penalty in California found that the state had spent more than $4 billion on the punishment since 1978, resulting in only 13 executions.[121] These costs included most of those mentioned above: pre-trial and trial (42%, nearly $2 billion); appeals (37%, just over $1.5 billion); and imprisonment (22%, $1 billion).[122] Considering that life imprisonment would be the likely alternative to the death penalty, it is interesting to note that the lowest cost appears to be incarceration. Indeed, the authors of the study argued that by replacing the death penalty with life imprisonment, 'an immediate net savings of $170 million per year would be realized … and a savings of $5 billion over the next 20 years'.[123] Other studies over the last two decades have drawn similar conclusions about the costliness of the pre-execution process: in Maryland,[124] Pennsylvania,[125] Kansas,[126] Louisana,[127] Texas,[128] Oklahoma,[129] Oregon,[130] Nebraska[131] and Washington,[132] among others.

---

118 *Ibid*, S79.

119 *Ibid*, S102–08

120 See Cauthen, J and Latzer, B, 'Why So Long? Explaining Processing Time In Capital Appeals' (2008) 29 *Justice System J* (3).

121 Alarcón, 'Executing the Will' (n 114).

122 *Ibid.*

123 *Ibid*, S222.

124 Which found that death sentence cases cost three times as much as non-death sentence cases: Roman, J et al, 'The Cost of the Death Penalty in Maryland' (Urban Institute Justice Policy Centre, March 2008): www.urban.org/research/publication/cost-death-penalty-maryland (accessed 30 April 2020).

125 Brambila, N, Turner, F and Urban, M, 'Capital punishment in Pennsylvania: When death means life' (*Reading Eagle*, 14 December 2014): https://deathpenaltyinfo.org/news/pennsylvania-death-penalty-costs-estimated-at-350-million (last accessed: 30 April 2020).

126 Legislative Division of Post Audit State of Kansas, 'Costs incurred for death penalty cases: a K-GOAL audit of the Department of Corrections' (December 2003): https://cdm16884.contentdm.oclc.org/digital/collection/p16884coll58/id/266 (accessed 30 April 2020).

127 Johnson, C and Quigley, W, 'An Analysis of the Economic Cost of Maintaining a Capital Punishment System in the Pelican State' (Loyola University New Orleans, 2 May 2019): https://law.loyno.edu/sites/law.loyno.edu/files/images/Economic%20Cost%20Paper%20LA%205.1.2019.pdf (accessed 30 April 2020).

128 Lundberg, A, 'On the Public Finance of Capital Punishment' (5 April 2019): https://ssrn.com/abstract=3367170 or http://dx.doi.org/10.2139/ssrn.3367170 (accessed 30 April 2020).

129 Collins, P, Hickman, M and Boruchowitz, R, 'An Analysis of the Economic Costs of Capital Punishment in Oklahoma' (Oklahoma Death Penalty Review Commission, 2017): https://files.deathpenaltyinfo.org/legacy/files/pdf/Report-of-the-OK-Death-Penalty-Review-April-2017-a1b.pdf (accessed 30 April 2020).

130 Kaplan, A, Collins, P and Mayhew, V, 'Oregon's Death Penalty: A Cost Analysis' (Oregon Justice Resource Center, 2016): https://files.deathpenaltyinfo.org/legacy/files/pdf/OregonDeathPenaltyCostAnalysis.pdf (accessed 30 April 2020).

131 Goss, E, Strain, S and Blalock, J, 'The Economic Impact of the Death Penalty on the State of Nebraska: A Taxpayer Burden?' (Retain A Just Nebraska, 2016): https://files.deathpenaltyinfo.org/legacy/files/pdf/The-Economic-Impact-of-the-Death-Penalty-on-the-State-of-Nebraska.pdf (accessed 30 April 2020).

132 Collins, P et al, 'An Analysis of the Economic Costs of Seeking the Death Penalty In Washington State' (American Civil Liberties Union of Washington Foundation, 2015): https://files.deathpenaltyinfo.org/legacy/documents/WashingtonCosts.pdf (accessed 30 April 2020).

The actual execution also has associated (albeit lower) costs. This will vary depending on the nature of the execution. The most common method, lethal injection, generally comprises the administration of multiple drugs designed to sedate and paralyse the offender, before causing death by stopping the heart. However, protocols for administering a lethal injection vary depending on jurisdiction – and, indeed, from state to state in the US.[133] Some states use the 'standard' three drug protocol, whilst others use two or even one. In addition to debates regarding the effectiveness of varying protocols (both in terms of causing death and doing so swiftly and without suffering) is the cost of the drugs used. Such drugs are produced by pharmaceutical companies – but primarily for medical purposes, not for use in executions. As such, securing the appropriate drugs for this purpose is a delicate matter contingent on pharmaceutical companies being willing to sell them for executions. This has created problems (and increased costs) when pharmaceutical companies have refused to supply them to jurisdictions for this purpose. In 2011, Hospira ceased production of sodium thiopental, which had previously been used in executions,[134] on the grounds that it 'could not prevent the drug from being diverted to departments of corrections for use in capital punishment procedures'.[135] As the only US based supplier of the drug, this forced states to look abroad for supply; however, this became problematic for the same reason, with suppliers in Germany and Switzerland refusing to do so, and the UK and the EU later prohibiting export of sodium thiopental (or other drugs) for use in executions.[136] Like any product, the rarer it is, the more expensive it becomes. As such, in 2012, executing states paid 15 times more for lethal injection drugs than the previous year.[137] In summary, arguments that the death penalty is quicker and cheaper than, for example, life imprisonment without parole bear little weight in reality. To execute quickly would raise enormous risks of mistakes, unfairness and cruelty, a social cost which most agree is not worth paying. Of all the debates surrounding the death penalty, the discussion of practical benefits is arguably the simplest: there is little evidence to suggest that the death penalty is, in reality, more cost effective and straightforward than other methods of punishing serious crime.

15.9 Summary

- Debates regarding the death penalty are generally either moral or practical; overall global use has declined, but a number of jurisdictions still execute offenders for serious crime.
- The UK (including England and Wales) had a long history of using capital punishment, but it suspended its use as a punishment for murder in 1965 and finally abolished it for all offences in 1998.

133 See Death Penalty Information Centre, 'State by State Lethal Injection Protocols': https://deathpenaltyinfo.org/executions/lethal-injection/state-by-state-lethal-injection-protocols (last accessed: 30 April 2020)

134 McGreal, C, 'Lethal injection drug production ends in the US' (*Guardian*, 23 January 2011): www.theguardian.com/world/2011/jan/23/lethal-injection-sodium-thiopental-hospira (accessed 30 April 2020).

135 *Ibid.*

136 Lain, C, 'Death Penalty Drugs: A prescription that's getting harder to fill' (Richmond School of Law, 2013), 11: https://scholarship.richmond.edu/cgi/viewcontent.cgi?article=1279&context=law-faculty-publications (accessed 30 April 2020).

137 *Ibid*, 14.

- Debates about capital punishment include a range of arguments for and against its use:
  - *Retribution and denunciation*: death is appropriate and proportionate retribution for offenders who intentionally kill, marking the seriousness of the offence; but this arguably undermines the sanctity of life through state-sanctioned killing and brings no closure to victim's families.
  - *Incapacitation and public protection*: death permanently protects the public from an offender by stopping them killing again, making it the ultimate form of incapacitation; but if the wrong person is executed, not only is this untrue but a grave miscarriage of justice will occur – which cannot be fixed.
  - *Individual rights*: capital punishment respects individual rights if it used sparingly, swiftly and causes minimal suffering; however, it inevitably breaches the right to life and the reality of its use – including long delays and the methods used – means it arguably amounts to a form of torture.
  - *Deterrence*: death is the ultimate punishment, and if people fear this sanction, they will be deterred from committing serious crime; but evidence to demonstrate this is mixed, with no clear and compelling case that capital punishment leads to lower crime, particularly where offenders kill in the heat of the moment.
  - *Practicality*: the death penalty is cost effective if it is executed in a timely manner, saving time spent on imprisoning offenders for life; however, the reality of 'death row', costly methods of execution and various legal processes (necessary to avoid miscarriages of justice) mean that capital punishment is expensive and slow.

chapter 16

Miscarriages of Justice

16.1 Introduction

This chapter will cover a vital issue that has been referred to at various points throughout this book: the problem of miscarriages of justice. Miscarriages of justice can result from deliberate abuse of the criminal justice system; from unintended errors in procedures; or from plain incompetence. They can be caused by one of the many actors involved in the process, both internal and external to criminal justice institutions. Miscarriages can originate at all stages of the criminal justice process: from the treatment of a suspect at the police station, through to the conduct of a trial, and at various points in between. The impact of miscarriages of justice is both symbolic and real. They not only undermine the integrity of the criminal justice system and sap public confidence in it; they also severely damage the lives of those individual citizens affected. The long history of the English and Welsh legal system is littered with many examples of miscarriages of justice. They continue to occur in the 21st century and many will remain unproven or undiscovered.

To an extent, any realist must accept that, despite best intentions and notable efforts, miscarriages of justice will always occur. The criminal justice system is large and complex, and it is both designed and administered by human beings. It is therefore imperfect. Nobles and Schiff have suggested that miscarriages are part of a natural 'evolutionary' process; that is, they are 'an intrinsic side-effect of the system's operation' rather than a 'malfunction'.[1] From this broader, objective viewpoint, miscarriages of justice are perhaps akin to the mistakes we make as we learn in school or university. They are, however, arguably a natural result of the choices we make about the priorities of the criminal justice process – should we try to be certain about guilt or accept a margin of error? Should we maximise convictions or protect all innocents? This, of course, reminds us of the tensions between crime control and due process discussed in **Chapter 1**.

Notwithstanding these arguments, the damage done by miscarriages of justice can never be simply accepted on the basis that they are 'just part of the process'. Practitioners and observers (such as academics and students) should be alive to the risk of miscarriages occurring and work to minimise them. Much has been done (particularly in the last 40 years) to strengthen the systemic safeguards designed to prevent miscarriages of justice (and therefore reduce the likelihood of their occurrence), and to detect and correct those that slip through the net. This chapter aims to explore what miscarriages of justice are, why they are important, and how they occur. It will examine how responsive the criminal justice system has been when faced with miscarriages of justice and will examine some of their major causes.

1 Nobles, R and Schiff, D, 'Trials and Miscarriages: An Evolutionary Socio-Historical Analysis' (2018) 29 *Criminal Law Forum* (2), 225.

16.2 What is a miscarriage of justice?

It is important to start this chapter by exploring how a miscarriage of justice *could* be defined; there is no fixed way of describing this concept. It is a well-known term, often invoked by campaigners and the media to suggest that something fundamentally wrong has occurred within the legal machinery of the state. Clearly, it impacts those people directly involved (eg criminal defendants), but it resonates with a much wider audience in an indirect way. A miscarriage of justice implies that we cannot always rely on our legal system to reach the right result. Generally, the term is used to describe an outcome of the criminal justice process which is unfair, unjust, inaccurate or unreliable. This is but one potential definition and is quite broad. Leverick and Chalmers have suggested that, in the context of criminal procedure and punishment, the term 'miscarriage of justice' can 'be understood as having three overlapping meanings', namely:[2]

(1) Convictions which are quashed by the appeal court …
(2) The conviction of the factually innocent … where innocence had been positively established following conviction … [and] where guilt cannot be taken to be reliably established …
(3) The acquittal of the factually guilty: a use of the term popularised by Tony Blair.[3]

From this – and all potential definitions – we can determine that, at their core, miscarriages of justice suggest some wrongful or unfair result. The term is particularly associated with the conviction of a demonstrably innocent defendant ((2) above). When a defendant is subsequently shown to be factually innocent of the criminal offence in question, it is normally through the discovery of clear and irrefutable evidence that was not originally available (eg DNA evidence or a confession by the 'real' culprit).[4] In short, the person convicted can prove in a concrete way that they did not commit the offence for which they have been convicted. We will return to this particular situation shortly.

Beyond academic discussion, there are limited legal definitions of a miscarriage of justice in England and Wales. A miscarriage of justice is not, in itself, a ground of appeal and therefore does not have a legal definition in this sense.[5] Moreover, causing a miscarriage of justice is not, in itself, an offence; thus, the term does not fall within the substantive criminal law of England and Wales, although a range of specific offences may have occurred which caused a miscarriage of justice (eg perverting the course of justice, or the relatively new offence of corrupt or other improper exercise of police powers and privileges).[6] Neither is the term a formal aspect of the regulatory framework governing criminal procedure; rather, regulation is designed to avoid miscarriages happening by minimising certain risk factors (which will be discussed below). A miscarriage of justice is more akin to an umbrella term which can cover a range of mistakes or abuses that, as a whole, lead to a result that is objectively inaccurate or unreliable. Therefore, to paraphrase Balcombe LJ in *Lewis* in describing

---

2 Leverick, F and Chalmers, J, 'Causes of wrongful conviction' in J Chalmers, F Leverick and A Shaw (eds), *Post Corroboration Safeguards Review Report of the Academic Expert Group* (Scottish Government, 2014), 30.

3 *Ibid.*

4 See **11.4.4** on fresh evidence.

5 In Scotland, a 'miscarriage' is the sole ground of appeal; contrast this with 'unsafe conviction' in England and Wales (see **Chapter 11**).

6 Criminal Justice and Courts Act 2015, s 26.

arrest, a miscarriage of justice is a matter of fact, rather than a legal concept.[7] It is open to interpretation but, at the same time, is undoubtedly accepted as an issue of central importance in criminal justice.

The courts have provided some guidance on what the concept means, albeit in a very specific context. The only current statutory definition of a miscarriage of justice is provided by s 133(1ZA) of the Criminal Justice Act 1988 (as amended by s 175(1) of the Anti-social Behaviour, Policing and Crime Act 2014). This describes the concept for the purposes of awarding compensation to those wrongly convicted of an offence:

> [T]here has been a miscarriage of justice in relation to a person convicted of a criminal offence … if and only if the new or newly discovered fact shows beyond reasonable doubt that the person did not commit the offence.

This therefore implies that, for the purposes of this legislation, a miscarriage only includes demonstrably innocent persons (ie those who can prove it beyond reasonable doubt). This is a fairly narrow definition. For example, it would exclude cases where innocent defendants are convicted on the basis of coerced false confessions or unreliable witness evidence, but where the real offender has not been found or where there is no exculpatory forensic evidence. This is not fanciful; many miscarriages have involved this sort of scenario, a leading example being that of the Birmingham Six.[8]

The original provision contained no definition of a miscarriage at all and as a result generated a number of challenges in the courts, which sought to give meaning to the term. In *R (Mullen) v Secretary of State for the Home Department*,[9] Lord Bingham described a miscarriage of justice as being 'very familiar' but having 'no settled meaning'.[10] He went on to suggest that whilst the term usually described someone who was 'demonstrably innocent', it also included 'cases in which defendants, guilty or not, certainly should not have been convicted'.[11]

What exactly does this second category include? The more recent case of *Adams* provided some expansion, where Lord Phillips suggested four potential categories of miscarriage:[12]

(1) Where … fresh evidence shows clearly that the defendant is innocent of the crime of which he has been convicted.[13]

This clearly aligns with Lord Bingham's 'demonstrably innocent' category. Where a person can prove beyond reasonable doubt that they are innocent, then a miscarriage has occurred.

(2) Where … fresh evidence is such that, had it been available at the time of the trial, no reasonable jury could properly have convicted the defendant.[14]

This suggests that the jury were denied the opportunity to consider vital evidence which, whilst not conclusive of the defendant's innocence, would certainly have amounted to reasonable doubt about the defendant's guilt and therefore led to an acquittal. This appears to fall under Lord Bingham's second category ('cases in which defendants, guilty or not, certainly should not have been convicted').

---

7 [1990] EWCA Civ 5.
8 *McIlkenny, Hunter, Walker, Callaghan, Hill and Power* (1991) 93 Cr App R 287.
9 [2004] UKHL 18.
10 *Ibid* [9].
11 *Ibid.*
12 [2011] UKSC 18.
13 *Ibid* [9].
14 *Ibid.*

(3) Where ... fresh evidence renders the conviction unsafe in that, had it been available at the time of the trial, a reasonable jury might or might not have convicted the defendant.[15]

This is similar to category two, except that the evidence *may* have led to an acquittal – in short, the jury *might* have had reasonable doubt about the defendant's guilt. This does not appear to fall within Lord Bingham's second category.

(4) Where something has gone seriously wrong in the investigation of the offence or the conduct of the trial, resulting in the conviction of someone who should not have been convicted.[16]

This, arguably, covers a wide range of potential mistakes, abuses or flaws in the criminal justice process. It is a catch-all. It also certainly seems to fall within Lord Bingham's second category.

It is important to distinguish between two important concepts – demonstrable innocence and a wrongful conviction. Somebody who is demonstrably innocent will also have been wrongly convicted; someone who is wrongly convicted may not be demonstrably innocent. The wrongful conviction may involve a failure to meet the standard of proof or may be tainted by malpractice; but it does not follow that the defendant is necessarily factually innocent. For the purposes of compensation, *Mullen*, *Adams* and the relevant legislation have concluded that only the demonstrably innocent can be classified as having experienced a miscarriage of justice. Whether this is fair or accurate is a moot point (and continues to be challenged).[17]

However, in terms of this chapter, these sources assist in establishing a working definition – in the broadest sense – of a miscarriage of justice; this will enable us to examine examples, their causes, and how regulation of criminal justice attempts to minimise them.

We will primarily focus on conviction of the demonstrably innocent and the broader wrongful conviction of both the innocent and guilty, but we should briefly consider the acquittal of defendants who are factually guilty ((3) under Leverick and Chalmers' definition). It is legitimate to suggest that this is a miscarriage too; after all, when the outcome of the criminal justice process subverts its primary objectives (to both acquit the innocent and convict the guilty),[18] it can be reasonably stated, in a broad sense, that a miscarriage of justice has occurred. The system will have failed to deliver the 'right' result, as it is most commonly understood. For example, when a demonstrably guilty defendant is acquitted because of flaws in procedure or police abuse, a lay person might describe the defendant as having 'gotten away with it' or 'escaped on a technicality'. One might even expand this to include a failure to apprehend and prosecute people in time to prevent offending (an example being the 'Black Cab Rapist' John Worboys).[19]

15 *Ibid.*

16 *Ibid.*

17 See *R (Hallam) v Secretary of State for Justice; R (Nealon) v Secretary of State for Justice* [2019] UKSC 2, in which Victor Nealon and Sam Hallam (both wrongfully convicted of serious offences, which were later quashed on appeal) were denied compensation for miscarriages of justice. For commentary on this issue, see Hoyle, C and Tilt, L, 'Not Innocent Enough: State Compensation for Miscarriages of Justice in England and Wales' (2020) *Crim LR* (1).

18 See the 'Overriding Objective' of the Criminal Procedure Rules (CrimPR) 2020 (r 1.1(2)(a)).

19 Indeed, the police were recently found to have violated the human rights of two victims of Worboys by failing to properly investigate (*Commissioner of Police of the Metropolis v DSD and another* [2018] UKSC 11). The success of the victims implies that a miscarriage of justice had occurred – namely, that Worboys should have been apprehended and prosecuted earlier.

However, these arguments are fundamentally flawed. The concept of justice goes beyond simply convicting and acquitting the 'right' people, by whatever means necessary. Justice should arguably place equal value on fair and legitimate procedure. When procedure is frustrated to the point of impacting on the fairness of the verdict, a miscarriage of justice will have arguably occurred, regardless of guilt or innocence, because it becomes difficult to trust the ultimate decision made. It should also be remembered that establishing that someone is definitively, objectively guilty is not a simple matter – *and* in fact may be impossible in the purest sense, hence why the standard of proof demanded in criminal proceedings is 'beyond reasonable doubt' rather than certainty about guilt. As such, the criminal justice system requires high standards of proof, particularly because the consequences of conviction are potentially severe; moreover, until that threshold is reached, all defendants are presumed innocent until proven guilty. As such, the argument that the acquittal of the demonstrably guilty is a miscarriage of justice is fraught with difficulty and should probably be excluded from any conventional definition.[20]

16.3 A history of mistakes: how miscarriages have shaped criminal justice

Miscarriages of justice strike at the heart of the criminal justice system because they raise serious questions about its reliability and credibility. When the system gets it wrong, crucial ideals such as fairness, legality and justice are defeated. The conviction of innocent citizens is generally considered to be one of the most abhorrent distortions of justice. The rule of law is founded on the idea of punishing wrongdoers and protecting law-abiding citizens, as well as ensuring that no one is penalised without just cause (for more on the ideals behind punishment, see **Chapter 12**). The centrality of guarding against the conviction of innocent people is emphasised by Blackstone's formulation:

> It is better that ten guilty persons escape than that one innocent suffer.[21]

This statement, which has long guided the development of due process safeguards in criminal justice, places a strong emphasis on protecting innocence rather than securing convictions.[22] This idea is embodied in the presumption of innocence and the high standard of proof required to establish guilt in criminal proceedings. Why is this desirable? An explanation was offered by John Adams, the second US President and a Founding Father:

> We are to look upon it as more beneficial, that many guilty persons should escape unpunished, than one innocent person should suffer. The reason is, because it is of more importance to the community that innocence should be protected than it is that guilt should be punished

When considered, this is rational; the criminal justice system exists, primarily, for the benefit of innocent citizens. It protects and reinforces the rights of law abiders, and it is designed to serve this majority. Weighed against each other, the failure of the system to

---

20 It may be possible to argue that an exception is the case of a jury which ignores overwhelming evidence of guilt and acquits – that is, a perverse verdict. That being said, such cases may not in fact be miscarriages of justice. An example would be the case of Clive Ponting (see **Chapter 9** for more on this and the concept of jury equity).

21 Blackstone, W, *Commentaries on the Laws of England, Book IV* (1760), Ch 27.

22 A clear due process orientation – see **Chapter 1**.

protect the innocent is thus a greater problem for society as a whole than a failure to convict the guilty. As suggested above, failing to protect the innocent undermines the rule of law. It may also breach the human rights of innocent citizens, for example the right to a fair trial or their right to liberty.[23] Simultaneously, conviction of the innocent also fails to punish perpetrators; the real offender will remain at liberty (or, at least, free of formal responsibility for the crime) and thus the impact is doubled. When such miscarriages become apparent, they can seriously damage public confidence in the criminal justice system. Doubts are raised about how reliable, fair, honest and effective are the system and the people who operate it. People may wonder if they might become a victim of such gross unfairness for no justifiable reason.

Because miscarriages of justice highlight weaknesses or flaws in the criminal justice system, they have consistently been a catalyst for reform. Two major miscarriages in the early 20th century led directly to the creation of the Court of Criminal Appeal; prior to this, no formal system of appeal existed for criminal cases – only the prerogative of mercy, which could be exercised by the Home Secretary.[24] Between 1844 and 1906, 31 Bills were laid before Parliament on the issue of creating an appeal court for the criminal division, all of which failed.[25] Clearly, whilst there was some appetite for change, a significant number of parliamentarians did not believe a formal system for correcting errors was needed for criminal cases. This attitude eventually changed in the wake of the cases of George Edalji and Adolf Beck. In 1903, Edalji was convicted of mutilating animals and sending threatening letters. The police investigation was seriously flawed and the conviction based on dubious evidence (famously questioned by Sir Arthur Conan Doyle, the creator of Sherlock Holmes). Indeed, animals continued to be maimed when Edalji was in custody and even after his conviction. After a public outcry, Edalji was pardoned and released.[26] Adolf Beck was convicted of fraud in 1877, and then again in 1904, on the basis of handwriting and witness evidence. In both instances, Beck had been confused with the actual perpetrator – a man named John Smith. This case of mistaken identity twice led to the conviction of an innocent citizen.[27] In the wake of these serious miscarriages, Parliament finally passed legislation (the Criminal Appeal Act 1907), creating the Court of Criminal Appeal.

In the latter 20th century – particularly the 1970s – several miscarriages influenced the future shape of criminal justice in England and Wales. For example, in 1969, Laszlo Virag, a Hungarian immigrant, was convicted of theft and GBH after being wrongly identified by eight witnesses (five of them police officers).[28] In 1972, Luke Dougherty was wrongfully convicted of theft after being identified by two eye witnesses.[29] Another example, discussed in **Chapter 4**, is the 'Maxwell Confait' case.[30] These cases led to the creation of the Royal Commission on Criminal Procedure (the Philips Commission), whose recommendations both formed the basis of PACE 1984 and led to the creation of

23 See Articles 6 and 5 of the ECHR.

24 See **Chapter 11**, n 3.

25 Pattenden, R, *English Criminal Appeals 1844–1994: Appeals against Conviction and Sentence in England and Wales* (Clarendon Press, 1996), 6–16.

26 See *Ibid* 30.

27 See Naughton, M, *Re-thinking Miscarriages of Justice: Beyond the Tip of the Iceberg* (Palgrave, 2007), 80–82.

28 (1969, unreported). For a summary, see Davies, G and Griffiths, L, 'Eyewitness Identification and the English Courts: A Century of Trial and Error' (2008) 15 *Psychiatry, Psychology and Law* (3).

29 For a summary, see Robins, J, *The First Miscarriage of Justice: The 'Unreported and Amazing' case of Tony Stock* (Waterside Press, 2014), 126–27.

30 *Lattimore, Salih and Leighton* (1976) 62 Cr App R 53.

the CPS. The discovery of miscarriages in the 1980s and 1990s had a similar impact. In 1989, the Guildford Four were released after 14 years in prison for the bombing of two pubs in Guildford in 1974, whilst the Birmingham Six were released in 1991, having spent 16 years in prison for the bombing of two pubs in Birmingham in 1974. The conviction and lengthy imprisonment of 10 innocent people in these cases led to the creation of the Royal Commission on Criminal Justice (the Runciman Commission). Again, its recommendations resulted in significant changes to the criminal justice system, one being the creation of the Criminal Cases Review Commission (CCRC) – the extra-judicial body charged with considering potential miscarriages of justice not detected by the criminal courts system.[31]

A misconception is that miscarriages of justice are an 'old' issue – the subject of newspaper headlines from the 1980s, rather than an issue the modern criminal justice system needs to face today. They in fact remain a serious and significant problem, despite the substantial progress made over the last 40 years in particular. In 1999, solicitor Sally Clark was convicted of murdering her children and jailed; she was freed on appeal in 2003 after serious questions were raised about the expert evidence adduced at her trial.[32] In 2005, Suzanne Holdsworth was convicted of murdering a toddler. This conviction was ruled unsafe in 2008 after she had spent three years in prison; she was subsequently found not guilty at a retrial.[33] In 1997, Victor Nealon was convicted of attempted rape. He was freed on appeal in 2014, having spent 17 years in prison (see below).[34] In one of the most high-profile recent cases, 17-year-old Sam Hallam was convicted of murder in 2005; he was released in 2012 after serving seven years in prison for a crime he did not commit (although in both Nealon and Hallam's cases, the courts have not accepted that they were demonstrably innocent).[35] More recently, the conviction of Danny Kay was overturned after it emerged that the complainant had tampered with Facebook messages and the prosecution had failed to investigate when Kay challenged their accuracy.[36] In late 2017 and early 2018, a string of rape trials collapsed as a result of serious failures in police disclosure (the most high profile being that of Liam Allan).[37] Whilst the defendants were not convicted, they were variously bailed and detained for lengthy periods, and subjected to the stigma of such accusations. All of these cases have occurred since the last major investigation into the functioning of the criminal justice system (the Runciman Commission in 1993).[38] Miscarriages of justice have not retreated into the fog of history – they remain a modern problem. For example, during the Covid-19 crisis of Spring 2020, it emerged that several persons had been wrongly convicted using emergency police powers

31 See **Chapter 11**.
32 [2003] EWCA Crim 1020.
33 [2008] EWCA Crim 971.
34 [2014] EWCA Crim 574.
35 [2012] EWCA Crim 1158; see n 17.
36 [2017] EWCA Crim 2214.
37 As these cases collapsed before conviction, they are unreported. For an account of Liam Allan's case, see Metropolitan Police Service (MPS) and Crown Prosecution Service (CPS), 'A joint review of the disclosure process in the case of R v Allan: Findings and recommendations for the Metropolitan Police Service and CPS London' (January 2018): www.cps.gov.uk/sites/default/files/documents/publications/joint-review-disclosure-Allan.pdf (accessed 5 May 2020); and Smith, T, 'The "Near Miss" of Liam Allan: Critical Problems in Police Disclosure, Investigation Culture, and the Resourcing of Criminal Justice' (2018) *Crim LR* (9). See also **Chapter 17** for more on this issue.
38 Viscount Runciman, 'Report of the Royal Commission on Criminal Justice' (the Runciman Commission) (HMSO, 1993).

created under the new Coronavirus Act 2020,[39] including Marie Dinou – convicted *in absentia*, without a lawyer, for a non-existent offence.[40] This led the CPS to announce an unprecedented review of every charge, conviction and sentence under the legislation in May 2020 – 'the first time it has ever launched a review of every charge under a specific piece of legislation'.[41]

It should also be highlighted that miscarriages of justice have a severe personal impact on the innocent people imprisoned, most notably in the prevalence of early deaths. After serving 17 years in prison for a murder he did not commit, Stefan Kiszko died of a heart attack – only a year after release. Sally Clark, mentioned earlier, committed suicide in 2007. Yusef Abdullahi, one of the Cardiff Three (mentioned many times in this book), died in 2011 of a burst ulcer – aged only 49. Victims of miscarriages can also suffer physical, psychological and financial problems for significant portions of their lives after release. Paddy Hill, one of the Birmingham Six, has frequently discussed the serious emotional problems that have continued to dog him. Victor Nealon recently described his need for psychiatric care and an inability to work. Prior to his early death at the age of 60, Gerry Conlon (one of the Guildford Four) was frank about his institutionalisation and difficulty in living in the outside world. Families are affected as well. Conlon's father, Patrick 'Giuseppe' Conlon, was arrested after travelling from Northern Ireland to England to arrange legal assistance for his son. He was convicted of involvement in the bombings (one of the so-called Maguire Seven) and jailed for 12 years.[42] He died less than half way through his sentence – on the same day that Home Secretary William Whitelaw decided to grant him parole.[43] He was exonerated posthumously.[44] Sam Hallam's father took his own life whilst his son was still imprisoned. Outside of this jurisdiction, we might highlight those that use the death penalty – cases in which miscarriages of justice can never be corrected.[45]

All of these cases demonstrate powerfully the importance of reflecting upon miscarriages of justice – not only because they expose the reality of how our criminal justice system can go wrong but so that, hopefully, we can seek to improve it. Moreover, they underline the awful impact that a wrongful conviction has on innocent people as well as undermining our faith in the legal system.[46] Many of the cases mentioned here will be revisited during this chapter as we examine how miscarriages of justice occur.

---

39 Big Brother Watch, 'Emergency Powers and Civil Liberties Report' (28 April 2020), 66–69: https://bigbrotherwatch.org.uk/wp-content/uploads/2020/04/Emergency-Powers-and-Civil-Liberties-Report-april-2020.pdf (accessed 5 May 2020).

40 Dearden, L, 'Coronavirus: How woman "loitering" at train station was wrongfully convicted in shambolic case' (*Independent*, 2 April 2020): www.independent.co.uk/news/uk/crime/coronavirus-marie-dinou-lockdown-stay-at-home-loitering-arrest-fine-police-a9444311.html (accessed 5 May 2020).

41 Karim, F, 'CPS will review every charge under coronavirus law' (*The Times*, 2 May 2020): www.thetimes.co.uk/article/cps-will-review-every-charge-under-coronavirus-law-0l37rsg8f (accessed 5 May 2020).

42 (1991) 94 Crim App R 133.

43 Gupta, T, '"Secrets" over Patrick "Guiseppe" Conlon's pub bomb prison death' (*BBC News*, 13 March 2018): www.bbc.co.uk/news/uk-england-surrey-43357152 (accessed 5 May 2020).

44 *Ibid.*

45 See **Chapter 15**.

46 For a good summary of the impact of miscarriages of justice, see Hoyle, C, Speechley, N and Burnett, R, 'The Impact of Being Wrongly Accused of Abuse in Occupations of Trust: Victims' Voices' (University of Oxford Centre for Criminology, 2016), 4–5.

16.4 Causes of miscarriages of justice

16.4.1 External pressures on the justice process

External pressure – that is, publicity, opinion or commentary originating from outside of the formal court process – can lead to miscarriages of justice by influencing, distorting or disrupting the investigation of an offence or the trial of a defendant. It should be remembered that the police have a duty to investigate relevant evidence and facts in an objective manner, in order to decide on whether to charge a suspect with an offence. As such, extraneous opinion – such as public outrage at an alleged crime – should not form part of this decision. Equally, juries are expected to confine their consideration of a verdict to the evidence presented to them in court.[47] External pressure is therefore, by definition, anything falling outside of the relevant, legally sanctioned processes for determining whether to arrest, detain, charge and convict those accused of offences. External pressure usually takes the form of inappropriate media coverage, excessive public pressure, or influential outside commentators offering opinions about an ongoing investigation or trial. There are numerous examples. In 1994, the Sun newspaper published a photo of a man accused of murder, six weeks before a police identity parade was held in which he was picked out. Clearly, the report may have influenced this identification; the newspaper and editor were found to be in contempt of court and fined a total of £100,000.[48] In *Taylor (Michelle)*,[49] the conviction of two sisters for the alleged murder of a love rival was heavily influenced by news reporting. It was described as a 'media dream', with newspapers publishing headlines such as 'Love crazy mistress butchers wife'. On appeal, the media coverage was described as 'unremitting, extensive, sensational, inaccurate and misleading'.[50] The court stated:

> We are satisfied that the press coverage of this trial did create a real risk of prejudice against the defendants, and, for this second reason, as well as the first, the convictions are unsafe and unsatisfactory and must be quashed.[51]

More recently, the case of Tommy Robinson has generated headlines; he was convicted of contempt of court after broadcasting a video via Facebook in which he attempted to film defendants entering a court for trial and made prejudicial comments about the case.[52]

A major driver of external pressure is the concept of the 'outsider' suspect or defendant – that is, an unusual or stereotypical character, presenting opportunities for caricature or persecution which can unfairly influence the criminal justice process.[53] There are many examples, but this chapter will briefly cover two in order to

---

47 Ensuring this is a significant challenge in the age of social media and widespread internet access.

48 Crone, T, *Law and the Media* (Focal Press, 2013), 127. The *Sun* and the *Daily Mail* were also found guilty of contempt in 2011, after publishing pictures of a defendant accused of murder posing with a gun. Interestingly, this was only published online for a few hours, representing the strict approach taken to internet publication and its potential impact.

49 (1994) 98 Cr App Rep 361.

50 *Ibid* 386.

51 *Ibid* 369.

52 BBC News, 'Tommy Robinson jailed for contempt of court' (BBC News, 11 July 2019): https://www.bbc.co.uk/news/uk-48950672 (accessed 23 May 2023). Robinson successfully appealed against his original custodial sentence in August 2018; this was reheard in July 2019, and he was again convicted and sentenced to custody.

53 Although this is not necessarily limited to 'social outcasts' – for example, the *Sunday Mirror* was fined £75,000 for contempt of court after publishing an article which led to the collapse of the trial of Leeds United footballers Lee Bowyer and Jonathan Woodgate.

demonstrate the impact that external pressure can have on the investigation and trial of accused persons.

Chris Jefferies and the murder of Joanna Yeates

In mid-December 2010, landscape architect Joanna Yeates went missing after a night out with friends. On Christmas Day, her body was found in a rural lane just outside of Bristol. The case attracted widespread national media coverage – partly as a result of the extensive hunt for her, and the subsequent search for her killer. As part of the police investigation, her landlord Chris Jefferies was arrested and questioned. Jefferies was the subject of extensive negative media attention during the investigation. For example, the Sun newspaper nicknamed him 'Professor Strange', whilst the *Daily Mirror* suggested that he was a 'suspect peeping Tom'.[54] The media also contrived to link the Joanna Yeates case to an unsolved murder of a Bristol woman and highlighted a 'tenuous connection' between Jefferies and someone imprisoned for child sex offences.[55] As such, Jefferies was the subject, in essence, of witch hunts in more than 40 newspaper articles; he was presented as a 'dark, macabre, sinister villain' and appeared to be the victim of deliberate 'character assassination'.[56] The media coverage was so extreme that then Attorney General Dominic Grieve issued a rare warning to the press, saying:

> We need to avoid a situation where trials cannot take place or are prejudiced as a result of irrelevant or improper material being published, whether in print form or on the internet, in such a way that a trial becomes impossible.[57]

Despite this unusual caution from the Government's lawyer, press coverage continued unabated. As a result, both the Sun and Daily Mirror were prosecuted for contempt of court in *Attorney General v MGN Ltd and News Group Newspapers Ltd* and were fined £18,000 and £50,000 respectively.[58] In a separate legal action, Chris Jefferies successfully sued eight national newspapers for libel, resulting in a six-figure payout.

None of this occurred in a vacuum. The external pressure from the media, purporting to represent the views of the public, sought to portray Jefferies as a lurid character and therefore the likely killer (in spite of no actual evidence of this). Importantly, the media's coverage appeared to effect the criminal justice process. Chris Jefferies later commented:

> Because of the nature of the reporting, it merely served, I think, to encourage the police in their belief that they may have caught the actual murderer. Certainly, it was quite striking that during the interrogation of me the police were particularly interested in some of these fantastical stories that were being reported.[59]

---

54 Thomson, M, 'Yeates murder: There is no excuse for the wholly unbalanced media reporting' (*Guardian*, 5 January 2011): www.theguardian.com/law/2011/jan/05/chris-jefferies-media (accessed 5 May 2020). For a fuller review, see Lord Justice Leveson, 'An inquiry into the culture, practices and ethics of the press' (TSO, 2012), 558–64: http://webarchive.nationalarchives.gov.uk/20140122145023/; www.official-documents.gov.uk/document/hc1213/hc07/0780/0780_ii.pdf (accessed 5 May 2020).

55 For a full account, see *Attorney General v MGN Ltd and News Group Newspapers Ltd* [2011] EWHC 2074 (Admin).

56 Morris, S, 'Christopher Jefferies: tabloid frenzy hampered Joanna Yeates investigation' (*Guardian*, 16 March 2012): www.theguardian.com/uk/2012/mar/16/christopher-jeffries-tabloid-frenzy-joanna-yeates (accessed 5 May 2020).

57 Bentley, D, 'Newspapers warned over contempt law' (*Independent*, 31 December 2010): www.independent.co.uk/news/uk/home-news/newspapers-warned-over-contempt-law-2173008.html (accessed 5 May 2020).

58 [2011] EWHC 2074 (Admin).

59 *Guardian* (n 54).

After spending three months on bail, Jefferies noted that the police did little to correct the impression of him as a suspect. Yet during that period, Vincent Tabak (a neighbour of Joanna Yeates) was arrested and charged with her murder (and subsequently convicted). In an unprecedented move, Nick Gargan, Chief Constable of Avon and Somerset Constabulary, issued an apology to Jefferies in 2013, accepting that the police should have publicly clarified that he was no longer a suspect. Commenting on this failure, Jefferies stated:

> What happened was partly because the police were under such extreme media pressure themselves and they had to be seen to be acting.[60]

In short, the police felt pressure to do *something*, rather than exercise caution and restraint in their investigation. This is arguably a familiar problem in high-profile criminal investigations.[61] As Innes argues:

> [M]urder investigations are frequently performed under pressure where, particularly in the earlier stages of the investigative response, the [Senior Investigating Officer] is required to take consequential decisions on the basis of limited, flawed and/or unclear information.[62]

This context undoubtedly raises the risk of errors on the part of the police.

Barry George and the murder of Jill Dando

In 1999, TV presenter Jill Dando was shot on the doorstep of her home; an extensive manhunt began, resulting in the arrest, trial and conviction of Barry George in 2001. The case generated enormous media interest – particularly because Dando was a high-profile, well-loved media figure. In the time between the murder and George's arrest, the police appeared to be under substantial pressure, with the BBC commenting that the police 'must be aware that there will be deep anger if the man is not caught – and preferably soon'.[63] In an interview with the BBC about the Dando case, former Chief Superintendent Douglas Sharp commented:

> Any inquiry creates pressure. Obviously in this particular case, not only is the victim well known to the public, but she was associated with the media itself so there will be a great deal of interest. It will create interest in a way that the police are not used to dealing with.[64]

However, he also added, 'It was the case once that sensing public pressure for a result would affect the investigation – I don't think it's so much the case now.'[65] Yet, the investigation and conviction did seem to be influenced by such coverage. In 2007, the *New Statesman* argued that there were 'strong grounds for looking closely at the

60 'Christopher Jefferies told "sorry" by police over arrest distress' (*BBC News*, 16 September 2013): www.bbc.co.uk/news/uk-england-bristol-24104834 (accessed 5 May 2020).

61 For example, see the conviction of Colin Stagg for the murder of Rachel Nickell in 1993; the conviction and exoneration of the Darvell brothers in 1992; and the case of Barry George (below). Also see Home Affairs Committee, 'Police, the media, and high-profile criminal investigations' (October 2014).

62 Nicol, C, Innes, M, Gee, D and Feist, A, 'Reviewing murder investigations: an analysis of progress reviews from six police forces' (Home Office, 2004), 14, relying on Innes, M, *Investigating Murder: detective work and the police response to criminal homicide* (Clarendon Press, 2003).

63 'UK Murder hunt police face pressure' (*BBC News*, 30 April 1999): http://news.bbc.co.uk/1/hi/uk/331231.stm (accessed 5 May 2020).

64 *Ibid.*

65 *Ibid.*

contribution the media made to a notoriously dubious conviction'.[66] It observed, in the wake of Barry George's arrest, that

> papers were pumping out material about the weird loner and hypochondriac who lived in squalor, supposedly idolised Princess Diana and pretended alternately that he was an SAS veteran and Freddie Mercury's cousin. The vilification only stopped after he was charged.[67]

Coverage made frequent references to an historic conviction for attempted rape and an arrest for breaking into the grounds of Kensington Palace with a replica gun. After his conviction, the targeting of George's character was intensified, with the *Daily Mirror* declaring him to be 'Jill's mad assassin' and the Sun even declaring that he had tried to kill Princess Diana.[68] In 2007, after an unsuccessful appeal, the CCRC referred George's case back to the Court of Appeal (see **Chapter 11** for more on this process). The media reignited its interest in the case, with Nick Ross (co-presenter of 'Crimewatch' with Dando) writing an open letter to the court arguing that George was guilty. TV programmes were also broadcast, questioning the validity of George's conviction, including an interview with a juror at his trial. Lord Phillips – one of the appeal judges – stated that the judges had in fact been sent letters regarding the appeal; ignoring them, he said:

> Justice in this country is administered in public and it is important that the public should see or hear any submissions made to the court through the lawyers conducting the process.[69]

Lord Phillips also criticised the TV programmes, questioning the 'propriety of those broadcasts'.[70] In *George (Barry)*,[71] the original verdict was deemed unsafe; George was retried and found not guilty. Clearly, these examples demonstrate the potential impact of external pressure on the criminal justice process (at all stages). Where the results are lengthy prison sentences for innocent persons and continued freedom for the culpable, there has undoubtedly been a serious miscarriage of justice. Sadly, it continues be a source of concern. The recent investigations into public figures like Cliff Richard and Paul Gambaccini (see **Chapter 4**) ended with no action taken against them for criminal offences. In these cases and others, the external pressures exerted by the media (and the apparent police practice of 'advertising' a suspect to attract additional claims) had a severe impact on the lives of the suspects and could well have influenced a trial.[72] In the last decade alone, the Home Affairs Committee has twice inquired into and criticised the relationship between the media and the police at the earliest stages of investigations, arguing that:

66 Cathcart, B, 'Prejudice? What Prejudice?' (*New Statesman*, 28 June 2007): www.newstatesman.com/media/2007/06/barry-george-loner-conviction (accessed 5 May 2020).

67 *Ibid.*

68 *Ibid.*

69 Dowell, B, 'Media warned over Barry George retrial' (*Guardian*, 15 November 2007).

70 *Ibid.*

71 [2007] EWCA Crim 2722.

72 It should, however, be noted that publicising investigations has several benefits – particularly in cases involving sexual offences, where potential victims may be afraid to come forward. A primary example is the case of Jimmy Savile (see MPS and NSPCC, 'Giving Victims a Voice' (January 2013): www.nspcc.org.uk/globalassets/documents/research-reports/yewtree-report-giving-victims-voice-jimmy-savile.pdf (accessed 5 May 2020).

> we do not think it is ever acceptable for officers to identify individual suspects to the media before charge, as this has the potential to damage the investigation, any subsequent trial and the reputation of suspects released without charge.[73]

16.4.2 Prosecution misconduct

Prosecution misconduct can also cause miscarriages of justice. As the party primarily responsible for pursuing a case against the accused, the prosecution makes decisions that can affect the fairness of a case, including charging decisions (with the police), selection and disclosure of evidence, and advocacy and presentation of a case at trial.[74] In *Randall v R*,[75] the Privy Council heard an appeal from a defendant convicted of theft in the Cayman Islands. The defendant appealed on the basis that the conduct of the prosecuting counsel during the trial rendered it unfair; specifically, the prosecutor had made a number of prejudicial comments to witnesses, interrupted frequently during cross-examination and examination-in-chief, and interrupted the judge during his summing up. In considering the case, Lord Bingham summarised the duty of the prosecution:

> The duty of prosecuting counsel is not to obtain a conviction at all costs but to act as a minister of justice.[76]

He concluded that while 'not every departure from good practice … renders a trial unfair', in this particular case the prosecutor's misconduct had done so.[77] He stated that the prosecutor had 'conducted himself as no minister of justice should conduct himself' and concluded:[78]

> The right of a criminal defendant to a fair trial is absolute. There will come a point when the departure from good practice is so gross, or so persistent, or so prejudicial, or so irremediable that an appellate court will have no choice but to condemn a trial as unfair and quash a conviction as unsafe, however strong the grounds for believing the defendant to be guilty.[79]

As such, this demonstrates a strong due process approach – prosecution misconduct can lead to a miscarriage when the trial is rendered unfair, even if the defendant appears to be guilty.

---

73 Home Affairs Committee, 'Police and the Media' (December 2008), Conclusions and Recommendations [1].

74 On failures in prosecution disclosure, see n 38. This also includes the failure of the prosecution to challenge a lack of disclosure by the police, a key issue in the Liam Allan case (see also HM Inspectorate of the CPS (HMCPSI) and HM Inspectorate of Constabulary (HMIC), 'Making It Fair: A joint inspection of the disclosure of unused material in volume Crown Court cases' (July 2017)): www.justiceinspectorates.gov.uk/cjji/wp-content/uploads/sites/2/2017/07/CJJI_DSC_thm_July17_rpt.pdf (accessed 5 May 2020).

75 [2002] 2 Cr App R 17.

76 *Ibid* [10].

77 *Ibid* [28].

78 *Ibid* [29].

79 *Ibid* [28].

16.4.3 Police misconduct

Equally, police misconduct is a potent source of miscarriages of justice: arguably, it is the most common cause of wrongful convictions.[80] This can often be a result of what is known as 'noble cause corruption', defined by Crank and Caldero as

> [c]orruption committed in the name of good ends, corruption that happens when police officers care too much about their work. It is corruption committed in order to get the bad guys off the streets ... the corruption of police power, when officers do bad things because they believe that the outcomes will be good.[81]

In essence, this is a crime control imperative in that the ends justify the means. Convicting the guilty is more important than protecting individual rights. Of course, this logic fails when those whom the police pursue are not, in fact, guilty. Equally, it undermines the fairness and reliability of the process, creating scope for questions to be raised about all convictions, even of the guilty. Primary examples of police behaviour driven by 'noble cause corruption' are the fabrication of evidence, the fabrication of confessions, and police conduct which is oppressive, renders confessions unreliable or is otherwise unfair (see **Chapter** 7).

Fabrication of confessions has played a part in most of the major miscarriages in England and Wales, including the cases of the Birmingham Six, the Guildford Four and the Cardiff Three, amongst many more. A key problem, discussed in **Chapter** 7, is that such evidence will normally be put to a jury who must then decide whom to believe – the defendant or the police. It might be argued that this is not necessarily a fair match, as articulated by Deane J in the Australian case of *Carr v The Queen*:[82]

> An accused person who is confronted, on his trial, with fabricated evidence of an oral confession is placed in an extraordinarily unfair predicament. The police witnesses are likely to be practised in giving evidence. The accused is not. The police will enter the witness box with the respectability of officialdom. The accused will enter it from the dock.

In the case of the Guildford Four, the convictions of the defendants were primarily based on confessions – allegedly extracted from them by police brutality and during drug withdrawal. At their appeal,[83] Lord Lane described the confessions as being either 'a fabrication by the police from start to finish, invented by some fertile Constabulary mind' or 'amended to make them more effective'. Fabrication of evidence to convict 'the right person' is exemplified in *Mason*,[84] where the police fraudulently claimed to have found a bottle with the suspect's fingerprints on at the scene of the crime. The suspect confessed and was convicted – but the confession was later excluded under s 78 of PACE 1984 and the conviction overturned.[85]

80 The CCRC has stated that failure to disclose information to the defence is 'the single most frequent cause' of miscarriages (CCRC, 'Annual Report and Accounts 2015/16' (July 2016), 7: https://s3- eu-west-2.amazonaws.com/ccrc-prod-storage-1jdn5d1f6iq1l/uploads/2017/01/CCRC-Annual-Report- and-Accounts-2015-16-HC244-Web-Accessible-v0.2-2.pdf (accessed 5 May 2020). Whilst this will be dealt with below, this cause (amongst others) arguably falls under the umbrella of police and/or prosecution misconduct.

81 Crank, J and Caldero, M, *Police Ethics: The Corruption of Noble Cause* (Routledge, 2000), 2.

82 (1988) 165 CLR314.

83 *Richardson, Conlon, Armstrong and Hill* (1989).

84 [1988] 1 WLR 139.

85 This provision is not covered in detail in this book – see **Chapter 7** for a brief summary of s 78.

Additionally, the behaviours of police officers which are prohibited under s 76 of PACE 1984 (and can lead to the exclusion of confessions) are a cause of miscarriages. That is, behaviours which are oppressive or render any confession unreliable.[86] Again, these may result from 'noble cause corruption' – the desire to convict by whatever means necessary. As such, oppressive police behaviour can lead to unfair convictions. Oppression was described in *Fulling* as the

> exercise of authority or power in a burdensome, harsh, or wrongful manner; unjust or cruel treatment of subjects, inferiors, etc.; the imposition of unreasonable or unjust burdens.[87]

A good example of this is the Cardiff Three case,[88] in which Miller was 'bullied and hectored' in his police interview for 13 hours, over five days. The second limb for exclusion, unreliability, can vary since it can include 'anything said or done' in the circumstances which could render any confession unreliable. When the police lie or deceive, this can lead to unreliable confessions.[89]

Police misconduct might also be unfair, leading to exclusion under s 78 or the common law power of 'abuse of process'.[90] Again, there are various examples. In *Allan v United Kingdom*,[91] a defendant was induced to confess by a police 'stooge' in custody. The stooge's questions amounted to a disguised interrogation, undermining the right to silence; this was deemed a breach of the Article 6 right to a fair trial. In *ex parte Bennett* (No 1),[92] the defendant had been forcibly extradited by the police; the court ruled that this serious abuse of power meant that it could 'refuse to allow [the police] to take advantage'.[93] Thus, behaviours that amount to oppression, lead to unreliability or will affect the fairness of proceedings are examples of police misconduct that can cause miscarriages of justice – in some cases, where the defendant was likely guilty. This reinforces due process principles that underpin many of the safeguards designed to prevent miscarriages.

16.4.4 Unreliable witnesses

Witnesses have frequently been a cause of miscarriages; this can be as a result of mistake or deliberate deception. Mistaken identity is a particularly good example of the fallibility of witness evidence. An early example is the case of Adolf Beck, mentioned at the start of this chapter, who was convicted twice on the basis of mistaken identity. In the 1970s, both Virag and Dougherty (again, mentioned earlier) were wrongly convicted on the basis of eyewitness evidence. In 1976, the Devlin Report recommended that no defendant should be convicted solely on the basis of eyewitness evidence – something that has never been made into law.[94] The following year, in *Turnbull*,[95] Lord Widgery found that:

---

86 See **Chapter** 7.
87 [1987] QB 426, 432.
88 *Paris, Abdullahi and Miller* (1993) 97 Cr App R 99.
89 For examples, see **Chapter** 7.
90 See **Chapter** 7; see n 1 in that chapter for more on 'abuse ofprocess'.
91 (2003) 36 EHRR12.
92 [1994] 1 AC 42.
93 *Ibid* 62.
94 Lord Devlin, 'Report on Evidence of Identification in Criminal Cases' (1976).
95 [1977] QB224.

> Evidence of visual identification in criminal cases ... can bring about miscarriages of justice and has done so in a few cases in recent years.[96]

As a result, the Court of Appeal laid down the 'Turnbull Guidelines' for dealing with eyewitness evidence, compelling judges to direct juries to treat such evidence with caution and care.[97] Yet, three decades on, mistaken identity remains a problem. In 1997, Victor Nealon (again, mentioned earlier) was arrested for attempted rape, on the basis of a witness description of a 'man with a pock-marked face'. He was convicted on the basis of a disputed identification parade and imprisoned. After seven years, he became eligible for parole but was refused because he insisted upon his innocence and would not 'rehabilitate' himself. After another decade in prison, his conviction was quashed in late 2013 after DNA evidence suggested another perpetrator.[98] In 2008, William Mills was convicted of robbing a bank; four witnesses claimed to recognise Mills as the offender, including two policemen. After a year in custody, first on remand and then as part of his sentence, his conviction was quashed after DNA evidence implicated another man. At appeal, Lord Gill highlighted:

> This was a prosecution that stood or fell by eyewitness identification alone ... That is a form of proof that has been shown to be, in some cases, a dangerous basis for a prosecution.[99]

Reliance on eyewitness evidence and its place in the criminal justice system have been questioned more broadly. Pike asserted:

> Memory is not like a video of an event which can be replayed endlessly and is always perfect. Human memories alter over time, and are very suggestible.[100]

We might argue that the proliferation of CCTV and the use of video identity procedures should reduce the chances of mistaken identification, and thus miscarriages of justice.[101] However, Valentine has pointed out:

> There are currently up to 100,000 line-ups held per year, compared to around 2,000 at the time of the Devlin report ... Errors are going to be proportionate to the number of procedures that are run, so I wouldn't be surprised if there are more errors now than there used to be.[102]

To support this assertion, Davis and Valentine conducted research in which a third of participants identified the wrong person from close-up, high-quality video footage of the accused's face.[103] In a study conducted in 2017, it was suggested by Mojtahedi

---

96 *Ibid* 228.

97 *Ibid.*

98 See n 17.

99 Rowley, S, 'Wrongful conviction throws spotlight on unreliability of eyewitness evidence' (*Guardian*, 18 August 2009): www.theguardian.com/uk/2009/aug/18/eyewitness-evidence-wrongful-conviction (accessed 5 May 2020).

100 Cook, Y, 'Cutting down on cases of mistaken identity' (*Independent*, 6 April 2011): www.independent.co.uk/student/news/cutting-down-on-cases-of-mistaken-identity-2263950.html (accessed 5 May 2020).

101 See Webster, W, 'CCTV policy in the UK: reconsidering the evidence base' (2009) 6 *Surveillance & Society* (1) on CCTV; and Brace, N, Pike, G, Kemp, R and Turner, J, 'Eye-Witness Identification Procedures and Stress: A Comparison of Live and Video Identification Parades' (2009) 11 *International Journal of Police Science & Management* (2) on video ID parades.

102 Rowley (n 99).

103 Davis, J and Valentine, T, 'CCTV on trial: Matching video images with the defendant in the dock' (2009) 23 *Applied Cognitive Psychology* (4).

that approximately 100 people a year are wrongly convicted of sexual or violent crimes based on unreliable witness evidence.[104]

In addition to honest mistakes, witnesses can also lie. A primary example of this is the Cardiff Three case, in which the conviction rested not only on the confession of Miller but also on the evidence of two prostitutes (Leanne Vilday and Angela Psaila); the evidence of Mark Grommek, the victim's neighbour; the evidence of Jackie Harris, the common-law wife of one of the defendants; and the evidence of Ronnie Williams, the common-law brother-in-law of one of the defendants and a police informant. All of these witnesses either lied or provided unreliable or inconsistent evidence. Indeed, in 2008, Vilday, Psaila and Grommek were all convicted of perjury in relation to the Cardiff Three case.[105] Their evidence – alongside the confession of Miller – led directly to a miscarriage of justice.

16.4.5 Non-disclosure, faulty forensic evidence and inadequate investigation

Miscarriages of justice may also result from the way in which evidence is gathered and handled by the police, prosecution and others. This could cover a range of activities; but in this section we will focus on non-disclosure of evidence by the police and prosecution; problems with forensic evidence; and inadequate investigation by the police.

Disclosure is a particularly impactful and long-running problem. A classic example is the case of Judith Ward. In 1974, a coach exploded whilst travelling along the M62 motorway, killing several of its passengers (including British soldiers, thus linking the act to the IRA). Later in the year, Judith Ward, a woman with a history of mental illness, was arrested, confessed and was convicted; her conviction was quashed and she was released after spending 17 years in prison.[106] The prosecution had failed to disclose evidence to the defence that would have cast doubt on Ward's involvement; additionally, government forensic scientists withheld vital information. Summarising the seriousness of this misconduct, Glidewell J said:

> Non-disclosure is a potent source of injustice and even with the benefit of hindsight, it will often be difficult to say whether or not an undisclosed item of evidence might have shifted the balance or opened up a new line of defence.[107]

Emphasising the unacceptability of non-disclosure of evidence, he added, 'Our law does not tolerate a conviction to be secured by ambush.'[108]

This 'potency' of disclosure was demonstrated again in late 2017 and early 2018, when a series of rape and sexual assault trials collapsed after the police failed to disclose potentially exculpatory evidence to the defence.[109] Among the most high profile were

104 Mojtahedi, D, 'New research reveals how little we can trust eyewitnesses' (*The Conversation*, 13 July 2017): https://theconversation.com/new-research-reveals-how-little-we-can-trust-eyewitnesses-67663 (accessed 5 May 2020). For more on this issue, see Roberts, A, 'The Frailties of Human Memory and the Accused's Right to Accurate Procedures' (2019) *Crim LR* (11).

105 Horwell, R, 'Mouncher Investigation Report' (HMSO, 2017), 34–35: https://assets.publishing.service.gov.uk/government/uploads/system/uploads/attachment_data/file/629725/mouncher_report_web_accessible_july_2017.pdf (accessed 5 May 2020).

106 *Ward (Judith)* (1993) 96 Cr App Rep 1.

107 *Ibid* 22.

108 *Ibid* 52.

109 For a full examination, see Justice Committee, 'Disclosure of Evidence in Criminal Cases: Eleventh Report of Session 2017–19' (20 July 2018): https://publications.parliament.uk/pa/cm201719/cmselect/cmjust/859/859.pdf (accessed 5 May 2020).

the cases of Liam Allan, Samson Makele, Isaac Itiary and Oliver Mears. In all these cases, the police did not disclose the existence of crucial text and social media messages and pictures, suggesting that the sexual relationships in question had been consensual. This illustrates how disclosure in the 21st century is even more problematic – an age of vast quantities of digital information and evidence (such as social media and text messages). Indeed, in Allan's case, this amounted to approximately 60,000 lines of text messages.[110] Yet the information hidden in the large body of evidence cast significant doubt on the case against Allan, and it was revealed to no one (including the CPS) until the trial. Whilst Allan (and the others mentioned above) were not convicted, they suffered the stigma of suspicion for months (and in Allan's case, two years). Itiary spent several months in custody prior to the collapse of the case against him. In a human trafficking case in early 2018, a disclosure failure did not emerge until the defendants had been detained for several months, during which time one of them gave birth in prison.[111] As such, whilst these are not miscarriages in the traditional sense, they involve significant injustice (and could have easily been much worse had all the defendants been convicted). Clearly, there are likely to be a number of similar cases that will remain undiscovered, and the problem appears to go beyond cases involving sexual offences. The Justice Committee found that 'between 2013–14 and 2017–18 the number of cases stopped due to disclosure failures increased by 40%'.[112] Disclosure is therefore a serious problem, and unsurprisingly it has attracted widespread attention since 2018.[113]

Another important issue is weak or faulty forensic evidence. This is particularly problematic considering both the perceived reliance of the modern criminal justice system on DNA and other forensic evidence, as well as the assumption that such evidence (unlike human testimony) is 'infallible'. Less than 1% of crimes are detected using DNA;[114] moreover, in a US study by Peterson et al, it was suggested that DNA testing was rarely performed at crime scenes and was focused mainly on atypical offences like homicide and rape.[115] DNA detection is, in itself, complex and should not be regarded as a 'silver bullet' for securing correct identifications and appropriate convictions, but it undoubtedly represents a more reliable form of evidence than human witnesses. However, since it is rarely a key factor in most convictions, there may be over- reliance on other less robust forms of forensic evidence. The case against Barry George was heavily reliant on weak forensic evidence.[116] This included microscopic firearms residue found in one of George's pockets, allegedly lodged there from the gun

110 Smith (n 37).

111 Brown, D, Johnston, N and Gibb, F, 'Mother gives birth in jail as vital evidence is withheld' (*The Times*, 1 February 2018): https://www.thetimes.co.uk/article/mother-gives-birth-in-jail-as-vital-evidence-is-withheld-3fll0j9lk (accessed 5 May 2020).

112 Justice Committee (n 109), 12.

113 Alongside the Justice Committee's inquiry, the Attorney General conducted a review of disclosure. Various media outlets ran stories on the cases mentioned above (and others), including a 'Panorama' special on BBC One. As a result, the Attorney General Guidelines on disclosure were substantially revised and reissued in 2020 and again in 2022.

114 House of Commons Home Affairs Committee, 'The National DNA Database' (HC 222-I, HMSO, March 2010), 5: www.statewatch.org/media/documents/news/2010/mar/uk-hasc-dna-report.pdf (accessed 15 July 2020); Wallace, H, 'The UK National DNA Database: Balancing crime detection, human rights and privacy' (2006) 7 *EMBO Reports*, 29.

115 Peterson, J, Sommers, I, Baskin, D and Johnson, D, 'The Role and Impact of Forensic Evidence in the Criminal Justice Process' (US Department of Justice, September 2010), 122: www.ncjrs.gov/pdffiles1/nij/grants/231977.pdf (accessed 5 May 2020).

116 See above.

he used to kill Jill Dando. The significance of this evidence was questionable; the residue could, in the estimation of the forensic experts asked before George's trial, have equally come from another source, such as the armed police officers who arrested George. Yet the prosecution promoted the evidence as strong proof of his presence at the crime scene (as did the media). At George's appeal in 2007, the Court of Appeal ruled that the significance of this evidence had been overplayed and it was not included in his retrial. Additionally, a single fibre of polyester, allegedly from a pair of George's trousers, was found on Dando's coat; yet, the coat had been left lying on the ground for hours after the murder and the fibre could therefore have come from any number of sources.

In the case of *Maguire and others* (the Maguire Seven),[117] the forensic evidence used to convict the defendants was key. The seven were convicted in 1976 of supplying nitroglycerine to the IRA for making bombs, but they were eventually released on appeal in 1991. Forensic evidence showed traces of nitroglycerine in the home of the defendants; yet there was also evidence that the home could have been innocently contaminated. This possibility was not disclosed at trial; the selective interpretation of the forensic evidence and failure to disclose led to the convictions being overturned.

The case of Stefan Kiszko exemplifies the problems of both forensic evidence and non-disclosure. Kiszko, a 23-year-old who had a mental age of 12, was convicted of the sexual assault and murder of a child in 1976; he was freed on appeal in 1992 after 16 years in prison. Famously described as the 'worst miscarriage of justice of all time', Kiskzo confessed (without a lawyer) after being told by the police that he could go home if he did so; shortly afterwards, he retracted his admission. At trial, the prosecution produced forensic evidence linking Kiszko to the crime – specifically, semen on the underwear of the victim. However, the police forensic team failed to disclose evidence that Kiszko was unable to produce semen with a normal sperm count due to a rare medical condition. In contrast, the semen found on the victim had a normal sperm count and could therefore not have been Kiszko's. This major flaw in the presentation of the forensic evidence and the disclosure process substantially contributed to Kiszko's wrongful conviction.

More recently, the reliability of forensic evidence has been brought into question by the Randox Testing scandal. In January 2017, it emerged that manipulation of forensic tests had occurred at a private forensics firm (Randox Testing Services) – tests which had been used as evidence in criminal cases.[118] Two employees were arrested and questioned on suspicion of tampering with evidence. By the end of 2017, it was estimated that 10,000 cases (including murder and sex offences) may have been affected, with the potential for many miscarriages of justice as a result.[119] The aftermath has been significant. Several cases collapsed prior to trial, and the Court of Appeal heard four cases involving multiple persons, resulting in four convictions being quashed,[120] one sentence being reduced[121] and one conviction being upheld.[122]

117 (1991) 94 Crim App R 133.

118 Tully, G, 'Annual Report: November 2016 – November 2017' (Forensic Science Regulator, January 2018), 6: https://www.gov.uk/government/publications/forensic-science-regulator-annual-report-2017 (accessed 5 May 2020).

119 Swerling, G, 'Forensic testing scandal may ruin 10,000 crime cases' (*The Times*, 22 November 2017): www.thetimes.co.uk/article/forensic-testing-scandal-may-ruin-10-000-crime-cases-j72wnmsz0 (accessed 5 May 2020).

120 *Senior* [2018] EWCA Crim 837 and *Wilson (Jamie Lee)* [2019] EWCA Crim 2410.

121 *Bravender* [2018] EWCA Crim 723.

Moreover, mass retesting of samples was required. The Forensic Science Regulator estimated that this would take two to three years.[123] In addition, one of the private firms employed to do this became insolvent in 2018, leading to a government bail-out and further delays.[124]

The Randox scandal (and the collapse of the retesting firm) highlights a long-running concern about the role of private firms in forensic science for the purposes of criminal prosecutions. In 2012, the publicly owned Forensic Science Service closed and greater reliance has since been placed on the commercial sector. As with other areas of criminal justice practice discussed in this book, government and the courts have emphasised the need to increase efficiency and lower the cost of forensic evidence in the criminal justice system.[125] Richmond has suggested that such reforms 'carry the potential to contribute to miscarriages of justice at the pre-trial stage and may ultimately detract from the quality and content of expert scientific opinion'.[126] As a result, this could affect 'the court's ability to arrive at sound determinations on questions of fact'.[127] To compound the problem, the Forensic Science Regulator has issued a strong warning about the impact of cuts to funding for forensic science work.[128]

Finally, another evidential problem that can contribute to miscarriages of justice is the failure of the police and prosecution to investigate evidence which does not support a conviction. An example of this is the recent case of *Hallam (Sam)*.[129] The defendant was convicted of murder in 2005; his conviction was quashed in 2012. This was due, among other issues (such as mistaken eyewitness evidence), to the failure of the police to investigate evidence supporting an alibi contained on the defendant's phone. Indeed, similar points could be made about the cases of Liam Allan and Danny Kay, in which the suspects directed the police to specific exculpatory evidence – which they did not appear to fully investigate.[130] Such failures are arguably an issue particularly associated with adversarial criminal procedure, where parties engage in a battle to 'win', sometimes at the cost of the truth. This would suggest that the arguments of Baldwin regarding 'proof vs truth' (discussed in **Chapter 4**) continue to have credence.[131] Of course, we should also recognise that a failure to investigate can result in miscarriages of justice for victims of crime as well as defendants. This has been most recently demonstrated in *DSD and another*, in which two of the victims of the 'Black Cab

---

122 *Ward* [2018] EWCA Crim 872, in which the Court of Appeal emphasised that a mere connection to the Randox Testing scandal was not enough to render a conviction unsafe.

123 Tully (n 118), 6.

124 Burn, C, 'Firm's collapse into receivership sees forensic scandal retests delayed' (*Yorkshire Post*, 11 February 2018): www.yorkshirepost.co.uk/news/firm-s-collapse-into-receivership-sees-forensic-scandal-retests-delayed-1-9012046 (accessed 5 May 2020).

125 For example, see Streamlined Forensic Reporting (discussed in Richmond, K, 'Streamlined Forensic Reporting: "Swift and sure justice"?' (2018) 82 *J of Crim L* (2).

126 *Ibid* 157.

127 *Ibid.*

128 Forensic Science Regulator, 'Continuing cuts to forensic science threaten criminal justice' (19 January 2018): www.gov.uk/government/news/continuing-cuts-to-forensic-science-threaten-criminal-justice (accessed 5 May 2020).

129 [2012] EWCA Crim 1158, discussed earlier in this chapter.

130 MPS and CPS (n 37); and n 36.

131 For more on the influence of adversarial culture in this context, see Quirk, H, 'The significance of culture in criminal procedure reform: why the revised disclosure scheme cannot work' (2006) 10 *Int J of E & P* and Smith (n 37).

Rapist', John Worboys, successfully claimed damages from the Metropolitan Police Service.[132]

16.4.6 Ineffective representation

Finally, a consistent cause of miscarriages of justice relates to issues with legal representation; that is, when suspects and defendants either have no legal representation at crucial stages of the criminal justice process, or the representation they receive is inadequate. A very large number of miscarriages involve suspects who did not have a lawyer during the police investigation. The absence of legal representation often facilitates other causes of miscarriages, since protection against coercion or scrutiny of the investigation is non-existent or ineffective. Often, suspects confess to crimes or provide otherwise incriminating statements before consulting a lawyer. Suspects can confess for a variety of reasons aside from guilt, but, regardless of guilt or innocence, all suspects are entitled to legal advice at the police station under s 58 of PACE 1984 and according to the ECtHR case of *Salduz v Turkey*.[133] The Guildford Four and the Birmingham Six, alongside many other victims of miscarriages, were denied access to a lawyer at the police station. Both cases resulted in confessions which were later retracted and allegedly extracted through oppression and violence. In *Downing (Stephen)*,[134] the defendant was 17 years old when he was convicted of murder. This was in 1974, a decade before the passage of PACE 1984. After being arrested, Downing was neither cautioned nor offered legal advice, and he confessed after several hours in custody. On appeal, Pill J commented:

> [The defendant] had no friends or family and was not told of his right to legal advice. We regard such isolation of a 17 year old as being a very significant factor in this case.[135]

He concluded:

> That, in our judgment, is a serious breach of the treatment which should have been afforded to him.[136]

Downing was released after 27 years in prison. At present, this is the longest miscarriage of justice sentence in the history of the English and Welsh criminal justice system.[137]

The presence of a lawyer may, in some cases, be no better than the absence of one. A primary example is the Cardiff Three case, where the solicitor for the defendant Miller failed to intervene or provide any active representation during the oppressive police interview. As Lord Justice Taylor commented, 'the solicitor appears to have been gravely at fault for sitting passively through this travesty of an interview'.[138] The case of Stefan Kiszko also provides an example of inadequate legal representation. Kiszko was represented at trial by David Waddington QC (who later became Home Secretary). Despite Kiszko's insistence that he was innocent, Waddington persuaded him to

132 See n 19.

133 (2009) 49 EHRR 19.

134 [2002] EWCA Crim 263.

135 *Ibid* [40].

136 *Ibid*[38].

137 Jointly with Sean Hodgson, who also spent 27 years in prison for a murder he did not commit (*Hodgson (Robert Graham)* [2009] EWCA Crim 490). Hodgson died only three years after release from prison, aged 61.

138 *Paris* (n 88), 104.

present the partial defence of diminished responsibility as well as arguing that he had an alibi. Both of these arguments were rejected by the jury and Kiszko was convicted. Arguably, the first defence – in essentially admitting presence at the scene – substantially impaired the second, as it contradicted the argument that he was elsewhere and thus undermined Kiszko's claim of innocence. Moreover, the defence failed to call important, favourable witnesses at trial, such as Kiszko's endocrinologist (who would have been vital to explaining Kiszko's unusual medical condition) or people who could confirm his alibi. More recently, the importance of competent and informed representation was highlighted in *Zaredar*, in which the defendant's lawyers failed to advise him of a statutory defence available to him.[139] Moreover, this was only one of a string of similar failures; by the end of 2015, more than 30 similar cases had been referred back to the Court of Appeal by the CCRC.[140]

16.5 Summary

- A miscarriage of justice is generally understood to be an outcome of the criminal justice process which is unfair, unjust, inaccurate or unreliable.
- This arguably includes any wrongful conviction quashed on appeal; the conviction of the demonstrably innocent; the unfair conviction of the guilty; and the acquittal of the guilty.
- Miscarriages of justice have been highly significant in shaping the development of the criminal justice system, with reforms normally resulting from these critical mistakes.
- Miscarriages of justice are not an old problem; they continue to occur today and many will go undetected.
- They have a very serious impact on both the individuals affected and public confidence in criminal justice.
- Miscarriages of justice can have a range of causes, including:
  - external pressures (eg media coverage);
  - prosecution and police misconduct (eg inappropriate advocacy or the fabrication of confessions);
  - unreliable witnesses (eg being mistaken as to the identity of an offender);
  - non-disclosure of exculpatory evidence to the defence;
  - problems with forensic evidence (eg misinterpretation or tampering);
  - failure of the police to investigate fully (for both suspects and complainants);
  - ineffective representation (eg a lawyer who is passive during police interview).
- Miscarriages are primarily dealt with by the CCRC and the appellate courts (see **Chapter 11**).

139 [2016] EWCA Crim 877.

140 Aliverti, A, 'Prosecuting Refugees: Wrongful Convictions, Unlawful Practices' (*Border Criminologies*, 20 March 2017): www.law.ox.ac.uk/research-subject-groups/centre-criminology/centreborder-criminologies/blog/2017/03/prosecuting (accessed 5 May 2020).

chapter 17 Contemporary Issues in Criminal Procedure and Punishment

17.1 Introduction

This book has covered a number of important topics surrounding both criminal procedure and punishment. The process of detecting and investigating crime develops organically, constantly evolving and changing to adapt to new challenges. How we punish offenders is also changing, both in the actual punishment meted out and the justification behind its use. We might argue, perhaps due to the emotionally charged nature of punishing criminals, that the pace of change is slower as we cling to old ideas. With this context in mind, this chapter seeks to explore two contemporary issues that are the subject of significant debate and/or reform at the time of writing. Whilst we cannot cover everything that might be considered contemporary, we hope that this chapter will provide a more extensive insight into some of the most pressing current challenges in criminal justice that are not directly addressed elsewhere in this book.

17.2 New approaches to efficiency in criminal procedure

17.2.1 Disclosure and Pre-Charge Engagement

In **Chapter 8**, we discussed the evolution of the disclosure regime and its remit to make the criminal justice system, and in particular the pre-charge stage, more efficient. The rationale is simple and has two key elements. First, the inequality of resources between the two sides is somewhat balanced out by the prosecution disclosing to the defence information that might reasonably be considered as evidence that undermines the prosecution case or assists the case of the accused.[1] In return, and for trials in the Crown Court, the defence has to disclose the core facets of its case to the prosecution.[2] Whilst this is mandatory only for cases in the Crown Court, the Criminal Procedure and Investigations Act (CPIA) 1996 also provides for a voluntary system of disclosure for summary-only offences.[3]

As the chapter discussed, the goal of the disclosure regime was to make the process more efficient. By disclosing the core elements of each side's case, both parties ought to be better positioned not to waste time at the trial stage and to reach a conclusion in a swifter timeframe. The voluntary element of defence disclosure in summary-only trials was effectively circumvented by the creation of the Criminal Procedure Rules and its case management provisions. These provisions essentially mirror the defence disclosure obligations of the Defence Case Statement, but remove the voluntary element, so it is now mandatory for all summary-only cases to comply with a regime of defence disclosure.

---

1 Criminal Procedure and Investigations Act (CPIA) 1996, s 3.

2 *Ibid* s 5.

3 *Ibid* s 6.

As discussed in **Chapter 8**, the operation of the disclosure regime has been fraught with difficulty, and in the near 30 years of its operation, the statutory disclosure regime simply has not worked, so much so that it has been subject to numerous reviews and recommendations over its lifespan. As such, the latest version of the Attorney General's Guidelines on Disclosure introduced an extension to the disclosure regime, which is called Pre-Charge Engagement (PCE). Annex B of the Guidelines introduces and explains what PCE is; in a nutshell, it represents an opportunity for both the police and defence lawyer to engage, prior to charge, to discuss potential ways forward with the case, which might mean that the case is disposed of before trial – a clear efficiency and economic winner!

The advent of PCE further represents the changing culture of criminal procedure in England and Wales. Since the advent of the Criminal Procedure Rules in 2003, there has been a 'sea change'[4] in the way in which criminal cases are dealt with. The system no longer resembles an adversarial battle where both sides compete to either achieve a conviction (the prosecution and police) or the best result for their client (the defence) – eg an acquittal at a trial, a non-custodial sentence or the charges dropped completely. This adversarial culture was seen to be slow and cumbersome and, as a result of the piecemeal reforms, has been replaced (in theory at least) by a culture of mutual cooperation to achieve the goals of the justice system, namely 'to deal with cases justly'.[5]

How does PCE work?

The Guidelines describe PCE as 'voluntary engagement between the parties to an investigation after the first PACE interview, and before any suspect has been formally charged'.[6] To engage with the process, a defence solicitor (or an unrepresented suspect) and the police must agree that PCE is in the interests of progressing the case. If the police offer PCE to a suspect, the suspect has the right to reject the offer of engagement. If the request is rejected, and the suspect is eventually charged, the Guidelines explicitly provide that no inference can be drawn from the suspect's failure to participate in PCE.[7] The Guidelines provide a non-exhaustive list of what PCE might involve:

a. Giving the suspect the opportunity to comment on any proposed further lines of enquiry.
b. Ascertaining whether the suspect can identify any other lines of enquiry.
c. Asking whether the suspect is aware of, or can provide access to, digital material that has a bearing on the allegation.
d. Discussing ways to overcome evidential barriers to obtaining evidence, such as revealing encryption keys.
e. Agreeing any key word searches of digital material that the suspect would like carried out.
f. Obtaining a suspect's consent to access medical records.
g. The suspect identifying and providing contact details of any potential witnesses.
h. Clarifying whether any expert or forensic evidence is agreed and, if not, whether the suspect's representatives intend to instruct their own expert, including timescales for this.

4 *R (DPP) v Chorley Justices* [2006] EWHC 1795 (Admin) at [24].
5 Criminal Procedure Rules 2020, r 1.1.
6 *Attorney General's Guidelines on Disclosure*, effective from 25 July 2022, p 38.
7 *Ibid.*

At face value, this appears to be a lot of information coming from the suspect and very little being given in return. Furthermore, there is a potential danger in the midst, as the Guidelines further state that a 'no comment' interview by a suspect does not preclude them from being offered PCE.[8] This could mean, for example, where a suspect does not want to go 'on the record' (as anything gained from PCE cannot be used in evidence at trial) to say that his mate committed the offence and it was not him, he could propose a further line of enquiry (a. above) to the police. This could dispose of the charges against the first suspect and provide the police with lines of enquiry to discover exculpatory evidence against his mate. This theoretical danger holds ramifications for the right to silence in the police station, but it does suggest that Jackson was correct that the police interview is being 'transformed … into a formal part of the proceedings against an accused'.[9] By allowing 'no comment' suspects to engage with PCE, it means the scope of participation is wide, as no suspect will be precluded from being offered the chance to engage. Although the impact of this ought to be small – the official assumption is that between 1–3% of police station attendance cases will result in PCE being offered[10] – nevertheless, any success of PCE will impact on the use of the scheme and the understanding of all actors who use it.

Is PCE working?

Although little is known about the use of PCE, the short answer to this question is 'not yet.' Johnston conducted the first empirical study on the use of PCE and found disappointing results.[11] The understanding of PCE among respondents appeared to be very mixed in terms of those who knew what it entailed and what its purpose was. Whilst three (7.5%) respondents did not understand what PCE was, 11 respondents (27.5%) thought PCE existed to assist the police with their investigation. Two respondents (5%) stated that, by their understanding, PCE was effectively what they already did in the police station. The respondents said: 'I use it as an opportunity to raise reasonable lines of enquiry and have the police investigate them'; and 'I raise issues that help the police better understand the defence and/or direct them to evidence that undermines the allegations'.

Some lawyers claim that the police are using PCE as intended; however, there are some clear misunderstandings about its purpose and utility. It is not a mechanism to convince the police of the suspect's innocence or as a potential carrot to co-opt the suspect into talking, as if they remain silent, it is unlikely that PCE will hold much value and therefore will not be in the 1–3% of cases where it is offered. Whilst the Government suggests that PCE will only be used in a small number of cases, what PCE entails is likely to be more commonplace, as the majority of cases are likely to involve reasonable lines of enquiry (RLE) or seek details regarding encryption keys to electronic devices. As such, PCE ought to be trigged and a dialogue of engagement offered in more cases than the 1–3% estimate. However, as only 5% of respondents recognised this fact, it might point to a need for Continuing Professional Development (CPD) or other further training on how PCE can be utilised to advance the suspect's

8 *Ibid* p 36.

9 Jackson, J, 'Silence and proof: extending the boundaries of criminal proceedings in the United Kingdom' (2001) 5(3) *International Journal of Evidence and Proof* 145–73.

10 Ministry of Justice (2021) 'Government Response: Criminal Legal Aid Review: Remuneration for pre-charge engagement', para 41: https://assets.publishing.service.gov.uk/government/uploads/system/uploads/attachment_data/file/976301/pre-charge-engagement-consultation-response.pdf (accessed March 2023).

11 Johnston, E, 'Pre-charge (lack of) engagement: an empty gesture?' (2022) 9 Crim LR 737–54.

best interests. Such training might help lawyers recognise that when RLE are proffered, this should trigger a discussion concerning whether PCE is appropriate in this case. However, this would have a knock-on effect on both the volume of cases that use PCE and the budget allocated by the Government to fund the scheme. The Impact Assessment attached to the consultation suggests that the estimated cost of PCE is between £0.3m–£1.8m annually[12] and would need a vast increase if PCE were to be used in more than 1–3% of cases.

If PCE is not working, can it work?

In short, the answer appears to be yes. A follow-up survey was undertaken with a firm of solicitors offering a PCE version for private paying clients (ie non-legally aided clients). This version of PCE effectively mirrors the legal aid version but yields very different results. When dealing with private paying clients, it appears that PCE benefits both the client and the criminal justice system as a whole. One lawyer commented that with 'private paying clients, where we can spend an adequate amount of time on engagement, we can either compile a better case for mitigation (should the case go to trial) or divert the case from prosecution and receive an out-of-court disposal'. Of the sample of six lawyers, 40% claimed that early engagement had led to no further action being taken by police (ie the investigation ceased immediately and no sanction was placed upon the suspect). One lawyer claimed, 'Where I argue the case should not proceed, I estimate that 75% of [my] representations are successful.' This remarkable figure suggests that early engagement between the defence lawyer and the police can result in a diversion from prosecution. However, the lawyers surveyed indicated that they spent at least 14 hours on engagement (40%), and 60% claimed that this engagement takes over 20 hours. This highlights the problem with the scheme – there is not adequate funding for the legally aided client.

The rates of remuneration could further explain the low usage of legal aid PCE. The hourly rate for PCE work is £51.28 in London and £47.45 elsewhere and is subject to an extendable upper limit of £273.75.[13] This equates to a little over five hours of work in London and just under six hours elsewhere. However, using the private paying client as an example, to successfully engage and use PCE would take a minimum of 14 hours, which would cost £717.92 in London and £664.30 elsewhere, which means the spending set aside for PCE would have to increase greatly. One lawyer supported this increase, saying, 'It's not economically viable to undertake PCE on a legal aid basis.' Arguably, this places the legally aided client at a double disadvantage; first, their lawyer does not engage with PCE as it is not in their economic interests to do so. Perhaps this is because the rate of remuneration is too low, the volume of work involved will not be completed before the upper limit is reached or a combination of both factors. The second tier of justice is reserved for those without means. They are provided with an overworked and underfunded legal aid lawyer who does not have either the time or the inclination to engage with the police as it is not economically viable. Instead, their case progresses through the system and will be heard in court.

Although greater awareness about the use of PCE is needed, greater engagement is also required – legal aid lawyers are simply not using the scheme. The Impact Assessment of PCE estimated that the cost of the regime would be between £300,000

12 Ministry of Justice, 'Remuneration for pre-charge engagement, Impact Assessment', 11 March 2021: https://assets.publishing.service.gov.uk/government/uploads/system/uploads/attachment_data/file/976303/pre-charge-engagement-impact-assessment.pdf (accessed March 2023).

13 See Criminal Legal Aid (Remuneration) (Amendment) (No 2) Regulations 2020 (SI 2020/497).

and £1.8 million per annum. However, in 2021–22, only £9,000 was spent on PCE.[14] Using the higher London weighting as an example, this would account for 175 hours of PCE work. Again, using the upper limit would allow for only 5.3 hours per case. Using these estimates would show that there were approximately 33 claims for defence work under the PCE scheme. Clearly, the scheme is not being used to anywhere near capacity. Using the upper limit of £1.8 million in the Impact Assessment, the Government could fund 6,575 cases per year (using the London weighing), yet just 33 claims were made. This is a remarkable disparity which indicates that the scheme is not working as intended. If the system was working, the evidence suggests that a number of cases could be diverted from trial, thus helping to clear the backlog of cases that has been building over the last 10 years. By the end of June 2021, there were around 61,000 cases outstanding in the Crown Court and 364,000 in the magistrates' court.[15] PCE could be used to help clear this backlog for cases that do not warrant prosecution and could be diverted by other means.

The lack of engagement with PCE is concerning. If cases can be diverted from prosecution, defence lawyers should do all they can to advance that option for clients. However, they are under an inordinate amount of workload pressure and perhaps are missing the opportunity to engage actively with PCE. Ultimately, better engagement and a better understanding of the scheme could help achieve these goals, but the early findings are not encouraging.

17.2.2 The Single Justice Procedure Notice

The Single Justice Procedure Notice (SJPN) is another efficiency mechanism that is designed to make the process, from start to finish, much quicker for low-level offences. The offences that can be dealt with via a SJPN include, but are not limited to: a range of motoring offences, including both speeding and driving with a mobile phone, non-payment of TV licence fees, failing to ensure a dependent child's school attendance, and avoiding paying for a ticket on public transport. Ultimately, these criminal offences are at the lowest level, and can be dealt with in an extremely swift manner. If you are charged with an offence to be disposed of via an SJPN, you will receive a letter through the post providing brief details of the evidence the prosecutor has in their possession. You will have 21 days, from the date of posting, to respond, and as with a traditional hearing you have two options – you can plead guilty or not guilty. The Government claims that the SJPN is not a radical new innovation but merely a modification of existing procedures, which by virtue of the Magistrates' Courts Act 1980 means:

- the case may be heard by one magistrate, rather the normal two or three;
- the case need not be heard in open court;
- there is no fixed date for the hearing, and it can be heard any time from the 21 days after the notice was served on the defendant.

Furthermore, the Government claims that many of the features of the SJPN are not new. It states that 'trial in absence' has been standard for over 300 years. Trials based on written evidence were introduced in 1957; postal services summons to attend court

14 per Mike Freer, Assistant Whip, Parliamentary Under-Secretary of State for Justice: https://www.theyworkforyou.com/wrans/?id=2022-11-14.86596.h&s=afzal+khan#g86596.q0 (accessed March 2023).

15 House of Commons Committee of Public Accounts, 'Reducing the Backlog in Criminal Courts', 43rd Report of Session 2021–22: https://committees.parliament.uk/publications/9159/documents/159649/default/ (accessed March 2023).

were introduced under Queen Victoria; and the police previously prosecuted such offences in this manner, and therefore the CPS did not review all cases that led to a prosecution.[16]

If you enter a guilty plea, you will not have to be present in court. The court hearing will take place in your absence, and a single magistrate will consider both the prosecution evidence against you, as well as any mitigating factors you have offered. These mitigating factors might be reasons why you committed the offence and go some way to explaining your behaviour. If you enter a plea of not guilty, you will need to attend a trial to present your case. When you return the Notice, you must outline any witnesses you seek to rely on. You can elect to have a defence lawyer represent you or you can represent yourself. These decisions must be made within 21 days from the date the prosecution sent you the notice. Should you miss the deadline to return a plea, the court will accept this as a guilty plea and your case will be decided in your absence without any mitigation. Once the court has reached its decision, you will receive another letter with its decision and details of any financial penalty the court has imposed. The Government claim that the new case management system, the Common Platform, can automate the process and reduce administrative tasks, which will allow the process to run in a more efficient manner and for justice to be delivered swiftly. It suggests there are many benefits to the automation of the SJPN, which include: saving time for all participants, reserving court time for cases that need to be heard, and making the whole process clearer, less costly and more straightforward for defendants who have been accused of minor offences.[17]

Problems with the SJPN

Between January and October 2022, there were 530,000 cases disposed of using the SJPN.[18] This is a slight reduction from the 2020 figures, where some 535,000 cases were dealt with in this manner.[19] Nevertheless, it represents a large number of defendants who have their cases heard via the SJPN. There is very little evidence surrounding the use of the SJPN; it is for low-level offences and has seemingly not caught the eye of the criminal justice fraternity. However, the *Evening Standard* journalist, Tristan Kirk, has reported extensively on the use of the SJPN and how the courts deal with or, for a better word, process such cases. In September 2022, Kirk reported that, 'alarmingly', magistrates were handing out criminal convictions in as little as 90 seconds.[20] Kirk made a number of Freedom of Information requests to examine how the courts use these powers. He said that courts in South West London and Warwickshire were 'set a recommended base-line of 90 seconds' to analyse the prosecution evidence, consider the mitigating circumstances, decide whether to convict or acquit the defendant and then pass sentence on the offender. There are four stages the single magistrate has to consider in this process, which means they may spend approximately 22.5 seconds on each element. This is absolutely absurd; there is no other word for it. Criminal

16 Jones, S, 'Explaining the Single Justice Procedure in the magistrates' court', *Inside* HMCTS, 26 October 2021: https://insidehmcts.blog.gov.uk/2021/10/26/explaining-the-single-justice-procedure-in-the-magistrates-court/ (accessed March 2023).

17 HMCTS, Fact Sheet: Single Justice Service: www.gov.uk/government/publications/hmcts-reform-crime-fact-sheets/fact-sheet-single-justice-service#important-statistics (accessed March 2023).

18 *Ibid.*

19 Jones (n 16).

20 Kirk, T, 'Magistrates handing out criminal convictions in private hearings that last just 90 seconds', *Evening Standard*, 23 September 2023: www.standard.co.uk/news/crime/single-justice-procedure-magistrates-criminal-convictions-b1026894.html (accessed March 2023).

convictions are being meted out to defendants in a timeframe so quick that you would be unlikely to be able to decide what to have for dinner. Yet within 90 seconds, all the evidence is considered, a decision on guilt or innocence is made, and an appropriate sentence has been designed.

This picture is no better in other courts. Kirk reported that some London magistrates averaged around 2.5 minutes per case, but it would be expected that once magistrates became more familiar with the process, they would envisage 'higher levels of productivity'.[21] For breach of Covid-related restrictions, the picture was even bleaker. Kirk reported that a magistrates' court in Swindon handed out £54,000 in fines during a session that lasted 15 minutes – which meant that magistrate processed 40 cases at an average of 22.5 seconds each. For driving offences in Merseyside, a magistrate convicted 204 defendants in 55 minutes (an average of 16.1 seconds per case).[22] The point is clear – efficiency is king with low-level offences, but the decisions these courts make in a matter of seconds could hold stark ramifications in a person's life.

For example, you drive a vehicle for a living and receive an SJPN for a driving-related offence. Once the letter is posted, you have 21 days to respond and mitigate your case. Is it feasible that you will have the time to seek legal advice during this period? Some would say perhaps not. Furthermore, can you afford legal advice? If you were arrested, you would be offered a lawyer in the police station free of charge. But with the SJPN, there is no such recourse to legal advice. In the Impact Assessment Statement on the SJPN, the Government readily admitted that if a defendant sought legal advice regarding a plea, defence firms could experience additional 'resource pressures [although] this is expected to be of limited impact'.[23] Ultimately, the Government is not expecting many people to utilise defence advice and therefore will pass through the justice system alone.

Another problem with the SJPN is the digital nature of the plea. Whilst you receive your prosecution notice through the post, you cannot return your plea through the mail; you have to make your plea online. Ward rightly points out that no consideration appears to be given to those deemed vulnerable through a learning difficulty, with literacy problems or without access to or knowledge of how to use a computer.[24] With the quest for digitisation in the criminal justice system (and more will be coming with the passing of the Police, Crime, Sentencing and Courts Act 2022),[25] we appear to be ignoring those people who are vulnerable or 'digitally excluded' from society.[26]

Efficiency and conveyor belt justice

In **Chapter 1**, we discussed Packer's models of criminal justice, and in England and Wales nothing reflects the ideology of the Crime Control model (CCM) more than the use of the SJPN. As summarised there, the CCM holds the repression of criminal conduct as the most essential function of the criminal justice system. There is a great deal of trust placed in state actors; therefore, there is a presumption of guilt rather than

21 *Ibid.*

22 *Ibid.*

23 Ministry of Justice, 'Online convictions/statutory fixed fine, Impact Assessment', 15 September 2016: https://consult.justice.gov.uk/digital-communications/transforming-our-courts-and-tribunals/supporting_documents/Impactassessment.PDF (accessed March 2023).

24 See Ward, J, 'Contemporary Issues in Criminal Court Procedure' in Johnston, E, *Challenges in Criminal Justice* (Routledge, 2022), pp 65–83.

25 See the extension to the use of video and audio links in criminal proceedings under s 51 of the Criminal Justice Act 2003, as amended by s 200 of the PCSCA 2022.

26 *Ibid.*

innocence, ie that those accused of the crime have 'done it'. The model needs a high rate of both detection and conviction and a heavy emphasis on the speed of proceedings. The process ought to resemble a conveyor belt. This conveyor belt moves an endless stream of cases, and each stage of the conveyor belt moves toward finding the defendant guilty – acquittals are rare. The procedures used to convict a defendant ought to be uniform, and there should be little recourse to challenge a court finding. Finally, a full trial is deemed to be a waste of resources, the investigative work has been done pre-trial, and as we trust our state actors, we do not require a full trial.[27] In our opinion, the SJPN process follows each of the elements of Packer's CCM. There are few due process obstacles faced by the courts and prosecutors in these cases. Once you have been served an SJPN, you are highly likely to be convicted. And if you are vulnerable and 'digitally disadvantaged' – and therefore do not return your plea within 21 days because you do not understand it or you do not have the ability to log on to the platform – you will be convicted.

17.2.3 Concluding thoughts: why the push for efficiency?

Various governments have been pushing for a more efficient criminal justice system since the early 1990s. Earlier chapters have charted these changes to the right to silence, the advent of the disclosure regime and the creation of the Criminal Procedure Rules. However, there is a further crisis that requires attention. There is currently an enormous backlog in the criminal courts – and with cuts to almost every service involved in the criminal justice system, this is not surprising. In 2017/18 HM Courts & Tribunals Service had a reduction in spend (in real terms) of 23.2%; this decrease had 'improved' to a reduction of 8.1% by the end of 2020/21.[28]

The Institute for Government suggests that the failure of criminal courts to process more cases does not reflect a lack of spending or resources but an inefficient system.[29] Hence, the advent of the processes examined in this chapter. The Institute goes on to blame the recent barristers' strike[30] for producing more ineffective trials. Whilst undoubtedly the strike slowed down the process and caused further delays, the idea that resources or funding do not play a role in any inefficiencies is laughable. At the end of 2017, the backlog in the criminal courts stood at 336,846; at the end of the third quarter of 2022 it had risen to 410,586 – so a clear rise in cases, not helped by the global pandemic of 2020. It is clear there was an unsustainable backlog prior to both the pandemic and the barristers' strike. The Government hopes that the measures discussed in this chapter will go some way to alleviating the backlog in the courts, but the price of these measures are defendants' adversarial, fair trial rights.

There are particular concerns about the use of SJPNs. Whilst they appear to have satisfied the Government's desire for speed when dealing with low-level offences, we think they ought to remove the 'J' from the acronym – as it ought to be impossible to deliver 'justice' in under 30 seconds. In terms of the PCE, it further represents the one-way street to disclosure – it is another mechanism to extract more information from a

27 See Packer, H, *The Limits of the Criminal Sanction* (Stanford University Press, 1968), pp 163–70.

28 The Institute for Government, Performance Tracker 2022/2023: Spring Update – Criminal Courts: www.instituteforgovernment.org.uk/performance-tracker-2022-23/criminal-courts (accessed March 2023).

29 *Ibid.*

30 Siddique, H, 'Criminal Barristers in England and Wales Vote to End Strike Action', *Guardian*, 10 October 2022: www.theguardian.com/law/2022/oct/10/barristers-in-england-and-wales-vote-to-end-strike-action (accessed March 2023).

suspect at an early stage, with the carrot of a potential diversion from prosecution offered for compliance. Whilst the system has proven to work in the private sector, the legally aided client is unlikely to benefit from this carrot, as the scheme is simply not being engaged with.

17.3 Criminal justice responses to sex offending

The process of investigating sex offences can be physically and psychologically traumatic for complainants (affecting whether they report and if they remain engaged in the process). Indeed, a major issue in this area is that victims of sex offences may not report a crime at all; and when cases are reported to the police, they may not proceed through and beyond investigation (a concept known as attrition).

17.3.1 Impact on reporting of sexual offences

Various surveys conducted over the years have shown low reporting rates for sex offences, generally somewhere between 15 and 20%.[31] Non-reporting leads to a large 'invisible' population of victims (and perpetrators) – referred to as the 'dark figure' of sexual offending.[32] Many factors contribute to why people choose not to report, including problems with the case building, such as a lack of independent evidence, and the investigation process itself, which can be an invasive, traumatic, repetitive and lengthy experience. Many complainants fear being disbelieved by those they report to others (including family). Intimidation or coercion by an offender, especially an intimate partner or spouse, can discourage reporting. The emotional experience of being victimised – including feelings of anxiety, guilt, shame or embarrassment – can be key barriers.[33] A victim may also be uncertain about whether an offence has in fact occurred or, even if they believe it has, may attempt to 'normalise' the offence (that is, to accept it as simply a normal part of life). This may be done to protect others (including the offender),[34] to deal with the psychological intensity of the experience, or from a desire to forget about the incident and move on. Victims may also lack confidence in the criminal justice system, believing that reporting will achieve little of value. Finally, personal characteristics – such as age, ethnicity, gender, and disability or incapacity – may cause victims not to report (for example, being very young or fearing prejudice).

---

31 Most recently, HM Government's 2021 review of rape in the criminal justice system estimated that less than 20% of victims report (HM Government, 'The end-to-end rape review: report on findings and actions' (June 2021, CP 437), iii: https://assets.publishing.service.gov.uk/government/uploads/system/uploads/attachment_data/file/1001417/end-to-end-rape-review-report-with-correction-slip.pdf (accessed 15 March 2023).

32 Walker, S-J, Hester, M, McPhee, D, Patsios, D, Williams, A, Bates, L and Rumney, P, 'Rape, inequality and the criminal justice response in England: the importance of age and gender' (2021) *Criminology and Criminal Justice*, 21(3), 3.

33 See Angiolini, E, 'Report of the Independent Review of the Investigation and Prosecution of Rape in London' (2015), 16: www.cps.gov.uk/sites/default/files/documents/publications/dame_elish_angiolini_rape_review_2015.pdf (accessed 15 March 2023); Dos Reis, MJ, de Moraes Lopes, MH and Osis, MJD, '"It's much worse than dying": The experiences of female victims of sexual violence' (2017) *Journal of Clinical Nursing* 26 (15–16); and Rumney, P and McPhee, D, 'Vulnerability, resilience, and rape: Uncovering the hidden work of police officers during rape investigations' (2023) *International Review of Victimology*: https://doi.org/10.1177/02697580231151974 (accessed 15 March 2023).

34 Of relevance particularly because most sexual offences are perpetrated by 'known' persons, for example, within a relationship.

17.3.2 Investigation process

Sexual offences, particularly rape, are complicated and emotionally challenging for everyone involved. Victims can experience long-lasting impacts and aftermaths, while investigation and prosecution can be complex and difficult. Investigations can involve emotionally and physically challenging but (often though not always) necessary processes – for example, intimate, embarrassing, intrusive or traumatic lines of questioning; the need to recall or recount harrowing events; and physical examinations. Seeking corroborative evidence to establish whether an offence has occurred or not can be highly intrusive in a broader sense – for example, requiring access to the phones or social media of complainants:

> Imagine your most private thoughts and feelings from counselling held in your phone being seen by anyone, let alone your rapist. And imagine having no guarantee about how in the future this data may be used or stored. The decision to have my case dropped was a no-brainer for self-preservation, but I now feel that the requirement to surrender one's data is the same as being raped with impunity … The optimism I had at the beginning of this process of 'taking power back' has been replaced with a feeling of absolute helplessness.[35]

Even if conducted with great care and consideration, such processes will never be easy for a victim. In addition, investigation (if it progresses) may involve extensive waiting times for charging decisions and trial dates, and the possibility of attending at and being examined in court.

Historically, the investigation of sexual offences, especially rape, by the police was generally considered to be inadequate, characterised by being unpleasant, traumatic, invasive, discouraging, accusatory, and conducted by unskilled personnel.[36] However, since the 1980s, there has been a cultural shift in the approach to the investigation of sex offending, with many innovations introduced over the last four decades, including the introduction of a presumption of belief in the complaint,[37] sexual assault referral centres (SARCs),[38] specially trained officers (STOs)[39] and specific police strategies.[40] In 2010, the Stern Review made 23 recommendations to improve reporting of sexual

35 Anonymous, 'My sexual assault case was dropped when I refused to give police my phone' (*Guardian*, 26 April 2019): www.theguardian.com/commentisfree/2019/apr/29/sexual-assault-case-dropped-refused-police-phone-rape (accessed 15 March 2023).

36 See, for example, Hall, R, *Ask any woman* (Virago Press, 1985); BBC, *A Complaint of Rape* [TV Documentary] (1982); Blair, T, *Investigating Rape* (Oxford University Press, 1985).

37 In 2014, HM Inspectorate of Constabulary recommended that this presumption should be 'institutionalised' ('Crime-recording: making the victim count – The final report of an inspection of crime data integrity in police forces in England and Wales' (November 2014), 21): www.justiceinspectorates.gov.uk/hmicfrs/wp-content/uploads/crime-recording-making-the-victim-count.pdf (accessed 15 March 2023). However, this approach subsequently received criticism and has been to some extent reversed (see Angiolini (n 33), 57); Henriques, R, 'An Independent Review of the Metropolitan Police Service's handling of non-recent sexual offence investigations alleged against persons of public prominence' (October 2016), 19–28: www.met.police.uk/SysSiteAssets/foi-media/metropolitan-police/other_information/corporate/mps-publication-chapters-1---3-sir-richard-henriques-report.pdf (accessed 15 March 2023).

38 National Health Service, 'Help after rape and sexual assault' (October 2021): www.nhs.uk/live-well/sexual-health/help-after-rape-and-sexual-assault/ (accessed 16 March 2023).

39 McMillan, L, 'The role of the specially trained officer in rape and sexual offence cases' (2015) *Policing and Society*, 25(6).

40 See, for example, Stanko, B, 'Operation Soteria Bluestone Year One Report 2021-2022' (December 2022, CP 769): www.gov.uk/government/publications/operation-soteria-year-one-report (accessed 16 March 2023); see Rumney and McPhee (n 33).

offences, concluding that the area remained far from the ideal.[41] More than a decade on, this area remains highly problematic. In 2021, the Government published the 'End-to-End Rape Review', which was highly critical of the continued problems in managing sexual offences across the criminal justice system.[42] It highlighted that one in two victims withdrew, identifying an increased 'justice gap' despite a stable prevalence of offending.[43] Damningly, the report concluded that such findings were 'trends of which we are deeply ashamed'.[44]

17.3.3 Attrition

The latter point about withdrawal refers to a key issue in this area – that of attrition. This is the loss or drop-out of reported cases of sexual offences from the criminal justice system, most particularly during the investigation stage. This can occur when victims actively or passively withdraw or disengage from the investigation; or when the police close the investigation and opt to take no further action (NFA). The latter may be due to a perceived lack of evidence to charge; verifying that there was no crime; inability to identify or find the suspect; or it may be based on unique challenges such as demonstrating a lack of consent, the rarity of third-party witnesses, or inconclusive forensic evidence. There are several reasons why a complainant may withdraw from the allegation or not want a formal investigation, including their relationship with the perpetrator, or their own vulnerability. The phenomenon of attrition has a significant impact on meeting the standard of proof in court, as most prosecutions will be built around the complainant as the central component.

Studies on attrition have identified four key points of the criminal justice process at which this occurs: the reporting stage, the investigative stage, the charging stage and the trial stage.[45] Discounting those who never choose to report, the highest proportion of cases is lost during the investigative stage, with between half and two-thirds dropping out at this stage.[46] A significant proportion of cases do not proceed due to evidential issues, with major drivers of both NFA and victim withdrawal including mental health, learning disability, victim accounts, fear of disbelief and the trauma of the process.[47] Indeed, victim withdrawal has increased from 42% of cases in 2015/16 to 57% of cases in 2019.[48] Conviction rates for rape have slowly declined since 2012, with a faster decline in recent years, despite police recording nearly doubling between 2015/16 and 2019/20.[49] In contrast, charges/summons, prosecutions and convictions for adult rape

41 Stern, V, 'The Stern Review' (Home Office, 2010): https://evaw-global-database.unwomen.org/-/media/files/un%20women/vaw/full%20text/europe/stern%20review%202010/stern%20review%20-%202010.pdf?vs=4929 (accessed 16 March 2023).

42 HM Government (n 31).

43 *Ibid.*

44 *Ibid.*

45 Kelly, L, Lovett, J and Regan, L, 'A gap or a chasm? Attrition in reported rape cases' (Home Office, February 2005): https://webarchive.nationalarchives.gov.uk/ukgwa/20110218135832/rds.homeoffice.gov.uk/rds/pdfs05/hors293.pdf (accessed 16 March 2023).

46 *Ibid*, 27.

47 See *ibid*; Hohl, K and Stanko, B, 'Complaints of rape and the criminal justice system: Fresh evidence on the attrition problem in England and Wales' (2015) *European Journal of Criminology*, 12(3); Hester, M and Lilley, S-J, 'Rape investigation and attrition in acquaintance, domestic violence and historical rape cases' (2017) J *Investig Psychol Offender Profil*, 14; HM Government (n 31).

48 Rumney and McPhee (n 33),

49 HM Government (n 31).

have fallen by 13%, 59% and 47% respectively since 2015/16.[50] Considering that the vast majority of victims do not report at all, there is a clear, significant and increasing gap between the number of perpetrated, recorded, prosecuted and convicted sexual offence cases.

17.3.4 The role of myths and stereotypes

Myths and stereotypes play an important role in attrition, as they can shape prejudicial and inaccurate perceptions about sexual violence and the decisions made when investigating.[51] Examples of such myths and stereotypes include the following:

- Most sexual offending is committed by 'strangers' (people not previously known to victims).
- Victims will have injuries if they have been raped.
- Failing to resist or fight back indicates consent.
- Victims emotionally react to offences in a particular way (eg distressed).
- Sexual offences normally take place in remote public locations.
- Delayed reporting by a victim indicates that the allegation is false.
- The clothing and appearance of a victim can explain/justify offending.
- There is a high incidence of false allegations.

Some of these statements are occasionally relevant or accurate, but rarely – that is, they are stereotypes (for example, sexual offending can occasionally be perpetrated by strangers but is more commonly perpetrated by persons known to victims). Crucially, none of them are always true, and some are never true – that is, they are myths. Overestimation of and attaching disproportionate relevance to such myths and stereotypes contributes to attrition. For instance, if it is believed that violence is a requirement for rape, unmerited importance may be attached to a lack of injuries. This can lead to negative outcomes (such as NFA). They can also introduce a general sense of doubt about the honest and credibility of victims, which is not in fact justified. For example, it may be believed that false allegations are common when the evidence suggests that false allegations, whilst difficult to measure, are relatively rare.[52] Additionally, people may conflate both malicious and deliberate allegations (rightfully termed 'false') with mistaken or unproven allegations. This may be, to some extent, exacerbated by the tendency to publicise high profile false allegations (such as Carl Beech or Jemma Beale)[53] and the well documented issue of few reports progressing to the point of conviction (something affected by many factors, as we have discussed).

Myths and stereotypes play a crucial role at the investigation stage if police officers subscribe to such beliefs (a phenomenon termed Rape Myth Acceptance (RMA)).[54] If they do, a complainant's claim may be disbelieved or doubted, leading to disproving behaviour (eg trying to undermine the complainant); limiting the extent of the investigation; or assessing the allegation as too weak to charge or even false. In 2019,

50 Lovett, J, 'Review into the Criminal Justice System response to adult rape and serious sexual offences across England and Wales – Research Report' (Ministry of Justice and Home Office, 2021): https://assets.publishing.service.gov.uk/government/uploads/system/uploads/attachment_data/file/994165/rape-review-research-report-appendix-d.pdf (accessed 16 March 2023).

51 Ward, C, *Attitudes toward rape: Feminist and social psychological perspectives* (Sage, 1995).

52 See Kelly (n 45); Angiolini (n 33); and HM Government (n 31).

53 On Beech, see Henriques (n 37); on Beale, see *R v Beale* [2019] EWCA Crim 665.

54 Murphy, A and Hine, B, 'Investigating the demographic and attitudinal predictors of rape myth acceptance in U.K. Police officers: developing an evidence-base for training and professional development' (2019) *Psychology, Crime & Law*, 25(1).

Hine and Murphy found that officers with high RMA may consider victims to be more responsible, perpetrators less responsible, and cases less authentic than those with low RMA.[55] The influence of some rape myths and stereotypes on attrition is also evident from the findings of Hohl and Stanko, who note that police officers and prosecutors often rely on the ethnicity of the suspect and other factors to assess the truthfulness of the allegations.[56] Moreover, Hester et al highlight that various factors, such as the relationship to the accused, victim vulnerability and evidential issues, impact attrition differently, depending on whether the cases involve acquaintance, intimate domestic violence or historical child sexual abuse.[57] Overall, the concern is that RMA can unfairly lower belief in complainants, increase doubt and damage the victim's credibility, thereby affecting the outcome of the investigation.

17.3.5 Improving investigation

Improvements in addressing under-reporting and low conviction rates, combating harmful myths and stereotypes and enhancing support and care for victims have been a focus in recent years. Areas for improvement include the policies adopted by the police and CPS; specialisation in terms of training and knowledge; and engaging independent/non-police support services in processes. 'Victim-centered' investigations have been become a priority over the last decade; these place the care and support of victims at the heart of investigations, not only for promoting the wellbeing of complainants but to reduce attrition and encourage initial reporting. The police have attempted to improve communication and updates to complainants (a priority across the criminal justice system),[58] including informing them of major decision points in a case (such as charging or NFA). A major shift was the promotion of a presumption of belief, where the default position is that the complainant is telling the truth and that the allegation is genuine. Whilst this was pioneered and gained approval as a policy response in the 2000s, this approach has been criticised since 2015 on the basis of concerns about fair trials, failures to disclose evidence[59] and false accusations (see above). As such, this policy has since adapted, shifting towards a 'middle ground' where complaints are taken seriously, where officers focus on empathy, support, listening and being open, whilst not assuming that an offence has occurred.

Specialisation of investigators has long been considered crucial to successful investigations. Since the 1990s, it has become increasingly common for police to have STOs who take specific roles in sexual offence cases and have an appropriate set of skills, experience and mindset suited to sex offence investigation and victim care. Among the benefits are continuity of contact for complainants, appropriate signposting to support agencies, while partnering with other agencies, and understanding of the complexities of investigations in this area. An expansion of specialisation was the establishing of specialist teams within forces, which are specifically recruited and trained to provide enhanced victim care and support, better quality investigations, invested and dedicated support, and joined-up working with other agencies (such as the CPS and the NHS). However, whilst such officers and teams

---

55 *Ibid.*

56 Hohl and Stanko (n 47).

57 Hester et al (n 47).

58 M Government, 'Victims Strategy' (Cm 9700, September 2018): https://assets.publishing. service.gov.uk/government/uploads/system/uploads/attachment_data/file/746930/victim-strategy.pdf (accessed 16 March 2023).

59 Angiolini (n 31); and see **Chapter 8** on disclosure.

may be the ideal, specialisation has been restricted in its impact, with many forces disbanding such teams in recent years (primarily on resource grounds).[60] In 2015, the Angiolini Report recommended investing in such units,[61] yet there has been continuing disparity in the quality of investigations – generally good in specialist units, but often poor in non-specialist units.[62] It is concerning how few specialist units appear to exist across England and Wales, and for forces that have such units, there are concerns about over-stretched and under-resourced teams. Such problems have led to closures and disbandment of units in Greater Manchester, the Metropolitan Police (the single biggest force by some distance) and the British Transport Police. Indeed, high profile failures led to the reorganisation of the Metropolitan Police's flagship 'Sapphire' units.

Specialist support outside of the police includes Sexual Assault Referral Centres (SARCs) and Independent Sexual Violence Advocates (ISVAs). SARCs are independent facilities that provide specialist medical, forensic and counselling services to victims of sexual assault, free of charge and without the need to report the incident to the police. There are more than 40 SARCs across England and Wales, which are separate from the police and specially designed for rape victims. SARCs are designed to help improve support, engagement and reporting while lowering attrition rates. ISVAs are impartial advisers who provide tailored guidance and support to victims of sexual violence. They offer their services free of charge and are independent of the police. ISVAs provide continuity of contact and are often located in close proximity to SARCs. There are over 250 ISVAs across England and Wales. The benefits of ISVAs include being more able to manage and adapt to the complex and changing needs of victims and helping victims to have a better experience of the process.[63]

17.3.6 Beyond the investigation: prosecution

After the police investigation, the case is referred to the CPS to consider charging. The charging process is a critical step in the CJS;[64] however, concerns about charging practice in sex offence cases have existed for some time, with particular issues being low numbers of referrals by the police that are actually charged by the CPS; the time taken for charging decisions by the CPS; lack of specialism in charging decisions; inconsistent practice leading to a 'postcode lottery' for charging; and inadequate communication with victims during the process.

17.3.7 Explanations for prosecution issues

According to a 2016 review by HMCPSI, specialists were not used for charging/ prosecution in 40% of cases, there was a lack of continuity in contact for complainants, and there were high caseloads and pressure to increase prosecutions.[65] The review found that in over 10% of cases, the Code for Crown Prosecutors was not applied

---

60 Rumney, P, McPhee, D, Fenton, R and Williams, A, 'A police specialist rape investigation unit: a comparative analysis of performance and victim care' (2020) *Policing and Society*, 30(5).

61 Angiolini (n 31).

62 Rumney et al (n 60).

63 Hester, M and Lilley, SJ, 'More than support to court: Rape victims and specialist sexual violence services' (2018) *International Review of Victimology*, 24(3).

64 See **Chapter 4**.

65 HMCPSI, 'Thematic Review of the CPS Rape and Serious Sexual Offences Units' (February 2016): www.justiceinspectorates.gov.uk/hmcpsi/wp-content/uploads/sites/3/2016/02/RASSO_thm_Feb16_rpt.pdf (accessed 20 March 2023).

correctly at the charging stage, which was worse than the findings in relation to non-specialist cases.[66] Furthermore, it took too long for the CPS to provide charging advice, thereby increasing the anxiety for vulnerable victims.[67] More recently, HMCPSI/HMICFRS found that CPS/police relationships were strained, with both agencies blaming each other for failings.[68] Both had high and unmanageable workloads and an overly cautious approach; and decisions suffered from significant delays, over-investigation of victims and poor communication.[69] Furthermore, a third of police files sent to the CPS were considered inadequate.[70] According to the End-to-End Rape Review, the growth of digital evidence, reduced resources and an increase in workload have all put pressure on the police and CPS, creating greater strain in the workforce.[71] There are also increasingly strained relationships and difficulties in communication between the two agencies, which are impacting negatively on case progression and final outcomes. The lack of co-location, a shortage of detectives, workloads and inexperience were identified as issues that needed to be addressed. Perhaps most concerningly, questions have been raised about whether low charging rates may have been a result of the CPS informally raising the charging standard in order to weed out 'weak' cases (though a legal challenge on this matter was dismissed in 2021).[72]

There have been various responses to concerns about charging over the last decade. One has been a focus on better joint working between the police and CPS, and more specialisation for those making charging decisions. In 2015, the CPS and police jointly established a national protocol on best practice, including early consultation between the specialist prosecutor and the police.[73] The CPS now provides a specialist sexual violence prosecutor in each of the 42 CPS areas, with the responsibility to review every rape case referred by the police.[74] These prosecutors work in dedicated Rape and Serious Sexual Offences (RASSO) Units;[75] according to the CPS, they receive 'extensive, ongoing training in the complexities of these offences',[76] with efforts made to keep the same specialist prosecutor assigned to a case from start to finish ('cradle to grave'). However, significant concerns remain:

---

66 *Ibid.*

67 *Ibid.*

68 HMCPSI/HMICFRS, 'A joint thematic inspection of the police and Crown Prosecution Service's response to rape – Phase one: From report to police or CPS decision to take no further action' (July 2021): www.justiceinspectorates.gov.uk/hmicfrs/publication-html/a-joint-thematic-inspection-of-the-police-and-crown-prosecution-services-response-to-rape-phase-one/#communication-between-the-police-and-the-cps (accessed 20 March 2023).

69 *Ibid.*

70 *Ibid.*

71 HM Government (n 31).

72 *R (on the application of EVAWC) v DPP* [2021] EWCA Civ 350.

73 Association of Chief Police Officers/CPS, 'Protocol between the Police Service and Crown Prosecution Service in the Investigation and Prosecution of Rape' (2015): www.cps.gov.uk/sites/default/files/documents/publications/cps_acpo_rape_protocol_v2-1.pdf (accessed 20 March 2023).

74 CPS, 'CPS response to the HMCPSI 2019 Rape Inspection': www.cps.gov.uk/cps/cps-response-hmcpsi-2019-rape-inspection (accessed 20 March 2023).

75 CPS, 'Rape and Serious Sexual Offences (RASSO) 2025' (July 2020): www.cps.gov.uk/publication/rape-and-serious-sexual-offences-rasso-2025 (accessed 20 March 2023).

76 CPS (n 74).

> What we unfailingly found was the commitment and determination of individual RASSO lawyers to do the best they can for both complainant and accused in circumstances where their workload is often unreasonable.[77]

Initially, any NFA decision by the CPS needed to be confirmed by a second rape specialist, although this has not been mandatory since 2015 and its application has been found to be inconsistent.[78] Cases are reviewed post-charge to identify issues or stop cases when necessary. Additionally, the Victim's Code provides that victims are entitled to be notified of the decision to charge or NFA within five working days, or within one working day for the most serious crimes.[79]

17.3.8 Next steps

The End-to-End Rape Review resulted in a specific plan of actions, outlining further steps needed to improve the charging process. The initial goal is to return the number of charged rape cases back to 2016 levels (which, whilst better, remain markedly low).[80] The Government outlined the objective, by the end of the current Parliament, of ensuring that victims who report an offence to the police will not be without their mobile phone for more than 24 hours (a response to the concerns raised earlier about invasion of privacy).[81] The plan includes increased frequency of reviews and more data collection, the latter often being a problem in fully understanding criminal justice issues in practice. The Government also identified a £27 million national fund to expand the recruitment of ISVAs and Independent Domestic Violence Advisers (IDVAs) with statutory grounding and national standards, with the aim of, in essence, professionalising such services as an additional support alongside police responses to reports.[82] The plan of action also outlined that the ability of victims to challenge requests for information from them will be expanded, including provision of legal advice for victims on this matter.[83] As of 2022, the flagship police operations on responses to sexual offending – Operation Soteria and Project Bluestone – are oriented towards a focus on suspects while supporting victims (though, note, the 'presumption of belief' remains a sidelined policy). Additionally, the plan recognised an ongoing issue (discussed earlier) in requiring increased training on rape myths and stereotypes for both the CPS and police.[84] How successful these responses will be remains, at the time of writing, unknown; a cynical perspective might suggest that policy-driven, top-down responses to investigating sexual offences are nothing new – and have clearly not made significant progress in the last decade, hence the renewed focus in the early 2020s. Ultimately, time will tell; but undoubtedly this area of criminal justice remains a contemporary, controversial and challenging one.

---

77 HMCPSI, '2019 Rape Inspection: A thematic review of rape cases by HM Crown Prosecution Service Inspectorate' (December 2019): www.justiceinspectorates.gov.uk/hmcpsi/wp-content/uploads/sites/3/2019/12/Rape-inspection-2019-1.pdf (accessed 20 March 2023).

78 *Ibid.*

79 Ministry of Justice, 'The Code of Practice for Victims of Crime in England and Wales and supporting public information materials' (April 2021), Right 6: www.gov.uk/government/publications/the-code-of-practice-for-victims-of-crime (accessed 28 March 2023).

80 HM Government (n 31).

81 *Ibid.*

82 *Ibid.*

83 *Ibid.*

84 *Ibid.*

17.4 Conclusion

This chapter has attempted to tackle two core and contemporary issues at the heart of criminal procedure in England and Wales. First, we have examined the latest iteration of the ongoing quest for greater efficiency within the pre-trial stages, specifically the advent of Pre-Charge Engagement (PCE) and the Single Justice Procedure Notice. These developments are consistent with the approach policy makers have taken to the management of criminal justice over the last 30 years, but – as we argue above – both appear to conflict with traditional adversarial norms and values of England and Wales (discussed in **Chapter 1**). PCE is posited to have numerous benefits for promoting earlier resolution of cases, including potential diversion from prosecution and trial by enhancing the role of the suspect in developing further lines of inquiry the police should investigate. These lines of inquiry could provide exculpatory information – for example, they might illustrate to the police that the suspect has an account for their whereabouts at the time of an alleged offence, thereby pointing away from guilt. However, should the line of inquiry yield information that the police or prosecution wish to rely on at trial, the guidance makes clear that engagement needs to stop and the suspect should be re-interviewed under caution. This, of course, has implications for the way the interview is conducted. From an efficiency standpoint, if the scheme is actively engaged with and earlier revelation of information and cooperation between the parties occurs, the backlog in the criminal courts could be drastically reduced (primarily by stopping relevant cases as early as possible). However, the evidence so far suggests that defence lawyers, when representing legally aided clients, have very little appetite to engage with the scheme (in contrast to when working for privately funded clients). Clearly, this creates a danger of a two-tier system emerging. Equally, the police may see the scheme as simply another way to extract information from suspects, rather than as a method of developing co-working at the early stages of the investigation.

Secondly, we examined challenges in the way that the criminal justice system responds to cases involving sexual offences. We highlighted that, despite increases in recent years, there continues to be vast under-reporting of cases of this nature (called the 'dark figure') and suggested a number of reasons why such cases never reach the criminal justice system. For those cases that do, the investigative process poses a variety of challenges, which not only explain why complainants in rape and sexual assault cases do not wish to come forward, but also drop out (a concept known as attrition). Despite changes recommended by the Stern Review in 2010, there are continuing problems with how investigations are undertaken in England and Wales, most recently highlighted in the damning 'End-to-End Rape Review' of 2021. Problems include the traumatic nature of the process itself; the influence of rape myths and stereotypes; lack of specialised knowledge and experience; and attitudes towards complainants. We highlighted some of the key developments designed to improve the investigation of such cases and, ultimately, deliver justice, such as additional funding to expand the recruitment of ISVAs, increased specialisation and victim-centred approaches. We also explored challenges beyond the investigation – that is, when the CPS must determine whether or not to charge a suspect based on the evidence gathered. Similar challenges exist with concerns about the working relationship between the CPS and the police and problems with 'blame culture' – particularly when it comes to the undoubtedly low number of cases referred, charged, prosecuted and convicted. Whilst recent reviews have set out a variety of next steps to address trends in this area, it remains to be seen what difference they will make in the long term.

Both of the topics explored in this chapter have common ground. They focus on different aspects of the criminal process, yet they are focused on long-standing problems in criminal justice: for the first, cultures of adversarialism, the drive for efficiency, and the tension between these imperatives; and for the second, failures to detect, prosecute and convict sexual offences effectively and fairly. Despite being issues that are decades old, they continue to occupy policy makers and practitioners. New developments in these areas continue to emerge, with persistent uncertainty as to whether they will be effective or will represent more failed promises for improvement. As such, this chapter serves not only to explore (as the title states) contemporary issues in criminal procedure, but also to highlight that some of these tensions – in one guise or another – are always there in the background. In this way, this chapter is a look at the past, the present and the future of criminal justice.

INDEX

absolute discharge **251, 252**
active case management **149–50, 153, 154–5**
adversarialism **2–3, 5–6, 14, 18, 141, 152–5, 193, 338**
  defence lawyers 170–1
  impact of Criminal Procedure Rules 151, 152–5, 156, 164
  role of the judiciary 12–14, 163–4
  trial as centrepiece 159
advocacy **3, 7–8, 12, 91, 151, 154, 165, 170, 178, 194, 311**
alibi disclosure **142–3, 144–5**
allocation
  'either-way' offences 161–2
  indictable offences 160
  summary offences 159–60
'ambush defences' **5, 110, 170**
Amnesty International **32**
appeals **199, 216**
  from Crown Court 204–9
    'fit for appeal' 205
    fresh evidence 208–9
    prevalence 205–6
    result of appeals to Court of Appeal 209
    unsafe convictions 206–8
  from magistrates' court 200
    appeals against conviction or sentence 200–2
    appeals by way of case stated 203–4
    judicial review 204
    limitations 202
    prevalence 202–3
    to Crown Court 200–3
    to High Court 203–4
  'leapfrog appeals' 210
  need for appeals process 199–200
  post-appellate system 210
    Criminal Cases Review Commission (CCRC) 210–16
  to Supreme Court 209, 210
arrest **43, 60**
  ancillary powers and duties 55–6
  cautions 56
    see also **cautions**
  Code G 49, 53, 54
  context and intention 45–6
  definition 43–4
arrest – *continued*
  deprivation of liberty 46–8
  factual state of affairs 44
  impact on child witnessing 267
  lawfulness 43
  necessity 52–5
  organisational factors 58
  previous convictions and 58
  public order 57
  race and social class 59
  'reasonable force' 56
  'reasonable suspicion' 49–52
  relevant law 48–55
  research findings 57–60
  statistics 43
  status and rights of victims of crime 58
attrition **331–2**
Auld Review **78, 141, 145–6, 147, 150, 153, 156, 172, 182, 183**

bail **64–5**
  changes to the law 67–70
  conditions 65, 179–80, 188–9
  court bail 186–7
    grounds for withholding 187–8
    unconditional and conditional 188–9
  money bail 179
  without charge 65–7
'Best Use of Stop and Search' (BUSS) scheme **22, 27–8, 38–9**
Better Case Management (BCM) **153, 182–3**
bias **4, 12, 15, 173**
Bloody Code **10**
'brutalisation effect' **293**
burden of proof **99, 164–5, 193**

capital punishment **9–10, 222**
  abolition 278–80
  costs 294–7
  debates 277–8, 280, 297–8
  as denunciation 280–2, 298
  as deterrent 290–4, 298
  fair trial and 288
  incapacitation 282–4, 298
  individual rights and 284–6, 289–90, 298

capital punishment – *continued*
international law 284–6
methods of execution 287, 288–9
minimising suffering 288–9
miscarriages of justice and 278–9, 282–4
practicality 294–7, 298
public opinion 279–8
public protection 282–4, 298
as retribution 280–2, 298
statistics 277–8
torture or cruel, inhuman or degrading treatment 286–8
case management 149–50, 151–2, 153, 154, 165, 182
cautions 56
conditional caution 254–5
simple caution 253–4
use of 255
character evidence 10, 11–12
charging a suspect 76
decision to charge 78–9
Full Code Test 76–7, 169, 253
research on charging decisions 79–80
statutory charge 78
Threshold Test 77
children
impact of family member in prison 266–9
parentification 269
stigmatisation 273–4
witnessing arrest 267
civil law jurisdictions 2
civil liberties 14, 19, 20
coerced-compliant confessions 128
coerced-internalised confessions 127–8
coerced-passive confessions 128
common law jurisdictions 2
community relations 37–8
community sentences 240, 243–6
compensation orders 229
'competing truths' 4
conditional discharge 251, 252
confessions 62, 94, 95, 97, 123–4, 138–9
accuracy 123
'adverse' to the accused 124–5
'anything said or done' 136–7
'circumstances existing at the time' 137–8
definition 124
excluded evidence 138
false confessions 126–7
coerced-compliant confessions 128
coerced-internalised confessions 127–8
coerced-passive confessions 128
made by the accused 124
made to a person in authority or not 125
made in words or otherwise 125
partly or wholly adverse 125
police-invented confessions 129, 312–13
prevalence and significance 129–30
regulation 124, 125–6
confessions – *continued*
circumstances and environment 132
evidence used at trial 133–8
legal advice 131
oppression and inducements 97, 131–2, 133–5, 313
safeguards 132
unreliability 135–8
usefulness 123
contemporary issues 321, 337–8
efficiency
Pre-Charge Engagement 321–5
Single Justice Procedure Notice 325–8
responses to sex offending 329
attrition 331–2
improving investigation 333–4
investigation 330–1
myths and stereotypes 332–3
prosecution 334–6
reform 336
reporting 329
cost-effectiveness *see* efficiency
Court of Appeal 154, 204–9
post-appellate system 210–16
court bail 186–7
grounds for withholding 187–8
unconditional and conditional 188–9
court system *see* criminal courts; Crown court; magistrates' courts
Covid-19 pandemic
review of charges 312
social distancing 19
***Crime Control* model 16, 17, 56, 154**
criminal appeals *see* appeals
Criminal Cases Review Commission (CCRC) 210–11, 305
casework, applications and referrals 212–13
criticisms 215–16
independence 213
legal representation and funding 214–15
'real possibility' test 211–12
referral rates 213
relationship with the Court of Appeal 214
resources 213–14
criminal courts 159, 177–8, 179
see also **Crown Court; magistrates' courts**
before court: bail and detention 179–81
court bail 186–7
grounds for withholding 187–8
unconditional and conditional 188–9
defence lawyers 151–2, 169–71
first appearance at court 181–2, 196
equivocal guilty plea 201
guilty plea 181, 182–5
not guilty plea/no plea 181–2, 186
significance of early guilty plea 182–5
judges 164–5
see also **judiciary**
juries *see* **juries**

criminal courts – *continued*
- lay magistrates 165–6
- magistrates' and Crown Courts compared 162–3
- pre-trial detention (PTD) 179, 189–92
- pre-trial disclosure 184, 192–3
- prosecution 166–7
  - Crown Prosecution Service (CPS) 78–9, 166, 167–8
- sentencing 197–8
- special measures 194–7
- venue of trial and allocation of cases
  - 'either-way' offences 161–2
  - indictable offences 160
  - summary offences 159–60

Criminal Procedure Rules (CrimPR) 17, 147, 182
- 'acquitting the innocent and convicting the guilty' 147–8
- case management 149–50, 151–2, 153, 154, 165
- 'dealing with the case efficiently and expeditiously' 148
- 'dealing with the case in ways that take into account the gravity of the offence alleged, the complexity of what is in issue, the severity of the consequences for the defendant and others affected, and the needs of other cases' 149–51
- 'dealing with the prosecution and defence fairly' 148
- dilution of adversarialism 151, 152–5, 156
- 'ensuring that appropriate information is available when bail and sentence are considered' 149
- impact on defence lawyer's role 151–2
- overriding objective 147, 149, 155, 185
- 'recognising the rights of a defendant' 148
- 'respecting the interests of witnesses, victims and jurors' 148

criminal proceedings
- Auld Review 78, 141, 145–6, 147, 150, 153, 156, 172, 182, 183
- CPIA 1996 144–5
- *Crime Control* model 16, 17, 56, 154
- CrimPR *see* **Criminal Procedure Rules (CrimPR)**
- critical analysis 15–17
- disclosure *see* **disclosure**
- *Due Process* model 16–17, 154
- efficiency 144–5, 149, 154, 155
- importance of procedural models 1, 7
- trial *see* **criminal trial**
- truth vs proof 141, 152–5
  - *see also* **adversarialism**; **inquisitorialism**

criminal trial 193–5, 196–7
- degradation 8
- public nature 9
- purpose 7
  - adversarial and inquisitorial trials 10–12
  - argument 8–9
  - catharsis 9
  - finality 9–10, 199–200
  - truth 7–8
- special measures 194–7

cross-examination 8, 152, 193

Crown Court 159, 160, 182, 186
- appeals *see* **appeals**
- cost of hearings 161
- magistrates' courts compared 162–3
- responsibilities 163
- sentencing 197–8
- trial 193–7

Crown Prosecution Service (CPS) 78–9, 166, 167–8
- decision to charge 78–9

cruel, inhuman or degrading treatment 286–8

custodial sentences 198
- *see also* **imprisonment, impact of; prison**

custody centres 61
- *see also* **police stations**

custody officers 62–3
- *see also* **police custody**
- charging a suspect 76
  - decision to charge 78–9
  - Full Code Test 76–7, 169, 253
  - research on charging decisions 79–80
  - statutory charge 78
  - Threshold Test 77
- custody records 73
- decisions about detention 63–4
  - suspect can be charged 63–4
  - suspect cannot be charged 64
- effect 71–3
- release from police custody on bail 64–5
  - bail without charge 65–7
- reviews of detention 73–4

custody records 73

death penalty *see* **capital punishment**

'Death Row' 283, 286, 295

defence disclosure 144–5, 152, 153

defence lawyers 151–2, 169–71
- aggressive tactics 170
- ambush defences 5, 110, 170
- neutral partisanship 170

defence statements 144–5, 146, 150, 192–3

delay 155

denunciation theory 220, 226–8
- death penalty and 280–2, 298

deprivation of liberty 46–8, 61

detention
- *see also* **police custody**
- pre-trial 179, 189–92

deterrence 222–4
- 'brutalisation effect' 293
- capital punishment and 290–4, 298
- stop and search as 25

Devlin Report 142, 313

'Diplock Courts' 14

discharge 251–2

disclosure 155–7
- alibi disclosure 142–3, 144–5
- compulsory 144

disclosure – *continued*
continuing duty 193
defence disclosure 144–5, 152, 153
definition 142
evolution 142–4
Initial Details of Prosecution Case 184
key aspects 144
miscarriages of justice 192, 315–16
Pre-Charge Engagement 321–5
pre-trial 184, 192–3
sanctions for non-compliance 145
DNA evidence 314, 316
***Due Process* model 16–17, 154**
Dunpark Committee 229
duress 201
duty solicitor 86, 90

early disclosure cooperation 17
Early Guilty Plea regime 182–5
efficiency 144–5, 149, 154, 155, 161, 182
Pre-Charge Engagement 321–5
Single Justice Procedure Notice 325–8
'either-way' offences 160–2
equality of arms 3
equivocal guilty plea 201
ethnic minority communities *see* racial discrimination
European Court of Human Rights 6, 186, 191
Article 6 jurisprudence 82–3, 313
evidence
admissibility 14
character evidence 10, 11–12
confessions 133–8
eyewitness evidence 313–14
forensic evidence 316–18
fresh evidence 208–9
hearsay 194
oral 154
expert testimony 9
explanatory models 5, 6
eyewitness evidence 313–14

fact-finding 5, 11
fair trial right 10, 105, 148, 155, 204, 288, 313
false confessions 126–7
coerced-compliant 128
coerced-internalised 127–8
coerced-passive 128
families of prisoners
see also **children**
family ties 260–1, 271–2
impact of imprisonment on 260–6
financial impact 270–3, 274
maintaining relationships 261–3
letter writing 263–4
phone calls 265–6
stability of marriage 260–1
stigmatisation 273–4
as victims 274–5
Family Court 9
fatal stabbings 20–1
finality 9–10, 199–200
fines 247–9
impact 250
penalty notices for disorder 256–7
sanctions for non-payment 249
standard scale 247–9
Fisher Inquiry 81, 167
forensic evidence 316–18
Fraud Trials Committee 143
French criminal proceedings 10–11, 14–15
fresh evidence 208–9
Full Code Test 76–7, 169, 253

game theory 110–11
gangs 31–2
general deterrence 223
guilty plea 181, 182–5
equivocal guilty plea 201
guilty verdict 197

Halliday Report 232
hearsay evidence 194
Howard League for Penal Reform 190
human rights
see also **European Court of Human Rights**
civil liberties 14, 19, 20, 102–3
death penalty and 284–6, 289–90, 298
fair trial right *see* **fair trial right**
right of access to a lawyer 82–3
right to liberty 46
right to life 285
torture or cruel, inhuman or degrading treatment 286–8

identification parades 314
imprisonment, impact of 259–60
on children 266–9
families as victims 274–5
family ties 260–1, 271–2
financial impact 270–3, 274
loss of income 270
prisoners' costs 265, 266, 270, 271
social security benefits 270
visiting costs 272–3, 274
maintenance of relationships 261–3
letter writing 263–4
phone calls 265–6
stability of marriage 260–1
stigmatisation 273–4
incapacitation 225–6
death penalty and 282–4, 298
indictable offences 160
'individual fear calculus' 223
individual liberties 14, 19, 20, 44, 100–1
see also **human rights**
inducements 97, 131–2

Initial Details of Prosecution Case 184
inquisitorialism 2, 3–4, 5, 7, 8, 10–11, 18, 141
importance of pre-trial investigation 159
role of the judiciary 14–15, 164
'institutional racism' 35–6
interviews *see* police interviews
investigation
sex offences 330–1
improving 333–4

Judges' Rules 62, 81, 167
judicial intervention 154, 164–5
judicial review 204
judiciary
adversarial tradition 12–14, 164
inquisitorial tradition 14–15, 164–5
juries 14, 171
bias 173
comparison of lay vs professional justice 177
composition and selection 171–2
controversial cases 173–5
decline in use 172
equity and secrecy 172–3
external pressures on 307
reforms to jury service 171–2, 175–6
role 172
just deserts 221–2, 281
JUSTICE (legal reform charity) 146
Justices of the Peace 165
see also **magistrates' courts**
justification for punishment 219–20, 234
sentencing 231–4, 247

'kettling' 47–8
King's Bench Division (QBD) 203, 204
knife crime 20–1, 32, 58

Lammy Review 23, 39, 183
lay magistrates 165–6
see also **magistrates' courts**
'leapfrog appeals' 210
legal advice 81–2
adversarial defence of suspects' rights 92
agencies 89
confessions 131
duty to accused persons 91
effect on suspect behaviour 93–4
fixed fee 87–8
human rights 82–3
impact of PACE 1984, s 58 83–6
methods of provision 90–3
right to silence and 115–16, 120
solicitors and non-solicitors 86–7
telephone-only advice 90
legal aid 201–2
legal representation 3, 5
legal traditions 1–2
adversarialism 2–3, 5–6, 14, 18, 141, 152–5, 193

legal traditions – *continued*
defence lawyers 170–1
impact of CrimPR 151, 152–5, 156, 164
role of the judiciary 12–14, 163–4
trial as centrepiece 159
critique of ideological approaches 5–7
inquisitorialism 2, 3–4, 5, 7, 8, 10–11, 18, 141
pre-trial investigation 159
role of the judiciary 14–15, 164
***lex talionis* 221, 281**

Macpherson Inquiry 34, 35
magistrates 14, 165
community sentences and 245
training 165–6
magistrates' courts 159–60, 181
appeals *see* **appeals**
cost of hearings 161
Crown Court compared 162–3
proceedings 193–4
sentencing 160, 182
managerialism 142, 148, 149, 150, 151, 154, 157, 164, 182, 183
media coverage 307–11
medical experts 9
miscarriages of justice 97, 100, 199, 211–12, 215, 299, 320
abuse of process 313
causes
external pressures on the justice process 307–11
faulty forensic evidence 316–18
inadequate investigation 318
ineffective representation 319–20
non-disclosure 192, 315–16
police misconduct 312–13
prosecution misconduct 311
unreliable witnesses 313–15
death penalty and 278–9, 282–4
definitions 300–2
demonstrable innocence 300, 301, 302
history of mistakes 303–6
Jill Dando murder investigation 309–11, 316–17
Joanna Yeates murder investigation 308–9
media coverage 307–11
'outsider' suspects 307
personal impact 306
moral reasoning 222
myths and stereotypes 332–3

'name and shame' 227
natural justice 204
'noble cause corruption' 288, 312
non-custodial sentences 240–1
cautions
conditional caution 254–5
overall use 255
simple caution 253–4
community sentences 243–7

non-custodial sentences – *continued*
discharge 251–2
fines 247–9
impact 250
sanctions for non-payment 249
standard scale 247–9
out-of-court disposals 253–8
penalty notices for disorder 256–8
suspended sentences 241–3
normative models 5–6
not guilty plea/no plea 181–2, 186

open justice 179
oppression 97, 131–2, 133–5, 312, 313
oral evidence 154
out-of-court disposals 163, 253–8
'outsider' suspects 307

Packer's models 15–17, 18, 49, 154, 200, 327
penalty notices for disorder 256–8
Philips Commission 13, 62, 63, 83, 97, 167, 304
police custody 61, 80, 98
abuses 62
charging a suspect *see* **charging a suspect**
custody officers 62–3
custody records 73
decisions about detention 63–4
suspect can be charged 63–4
suspect cannot be charged 64
detention time limits 74–6
effect of the custody officer 71–3
history and development 61–2
impact on individuals 61
interviews *see* **police interviews**
Judges' Rules 62, 81, 167
'necessity' of detention prior to charge 70
presumption of release 179–80
release on bail 64–5, 179
bail without charge 65–7
changes to the law 67–70
release under investigation (RUI) 67–8, 70
remand in custody 179
reviews of detention 73–4
right of access to a lawyer 81–2
adversarial defence of suspects' rights 92
confessions 131
effect on suspect behaviour 93–4, 115–16
human rights 82–3
impact of PACE 1984, s 58 83–6
solicitors and non-solicitors 86–7
telephone-only advice 90
time limits 180–1
police interviews 94
confessions *see* **confessions**
definition 96
location 96
oppression and inducements 131–2, 133–5, 312, 313
purpose 94–5

police interviews – *continued*
right to silence *see* **right to silence**
safeguards 96–8
timing 96
police misconduct 214, 312–13
police powers
human rights implications 19, 20
investigating and controlling crime 19
power of arrest *see* **arrest**
social distancing 19
stop and search *see* **stop and search**
police stations 61
see also **police interviews**
'Popish Plot' 100n
poverty 36–7
power of arrest *see* **arrest**
Pre-Charge Engagement 321–5
pre-trial detention (PTD) 179, 189–92
pre-trial disclosure 184, 192–3
pre-trial investigation 4, 159
prerogative of mercy 199
presumption of innocence 99, 148, 180, 186, 193, 303
prevention theory 220, 222, 247, 251, 252, 258
deterrence 222–4, 243, 258
incapacitation and protection 225–6
reform and rehabilitation 224–5, 243, 258
previous convictions 58, 238–9
prison 235
see also **imprisonment, impact of**
aims and use 236
alternatives to custody *see* **non-custodial sentences**
categories 236
crisis in the prison system 239–41
immediate incarceration 236
overcrowding 237–8, 239, 246
population 237–8
rate of reoffending 238–9
visiting costs 272–3
privilege against self-incrimination 99, 103, 105
see also **right to silence**
procedural rules
CrimPR *see* **Criminal Procedure Rules (CrimPR)**
importance 1, 7
'proper inferences' 113–14
prosecution misconduct 311
prosecution witnesses 170
prosecutors 166–7
Crown Prosecution Service (CPS) 78–80, 166–7, 168–9
dependence on police 168–9
responses to sex offending 334–6
psychiatrists 9
public interest 3, 168, 174, 180
public order 57
public policy 58
public protection 225–6, 282–4, 298
punishment 235
custody *see* **prison**

punishment – *continued*
justification *see* **justification for punishment**
theories *see* **theories of punishment**
'punitive turn' 198

racial discrimination 23, 30, 31–2
arrest 58
composition of juries 175
direct discrimination 34–5
effect on decisions about plea 183
implicit and 'institutional' discrimination 35–6
poor relations between police and communities 37–8
poverty and marginalisation 36–7
Randox Testing scandal 317–18
'reasonable force' 56
'reasonable suspicion'
arrest 49–52
stop and search 26–7, 29–32, 38
reasonableness 114–16
recidivism *see* reoffending rates
reductivism *see* prevention theory
reform 224–5, 243, 258, 336
rehabilitation 10, 11, 224–5, 243, 258
previous convictions and rate of reoffending 238–9, 240
remand in custody 179, 189–92
reoffending rates 238–9, 240
reparation theory 220, 228–31
reporting
sex offences 329
restorative justice 229–31
retribution theory 220–2, 241, 251, 258
death penalty 280–2, 298
just deserts 221–2, 281
right to life 285
right to privacy 104–5
right to silence 99–100, 121
advantages 102
compensation for limitations of other procedures 105–6
protection against mistreatment and unfairness 103–4
protection of individual rights 104–5
cautions and 56
definition 99
disadvantages 102
'ambush defence' 110
counter-productive 109
encouraging mistreatment 109
exploitation by the guilty 106–7, 110–11
frustration of justice 106–7
unnecessary and excessive safeguard 107–8
'flushing out innocence at an early stage' 109
game theoretic analysis 110–11
impact of CJPOA 1994 reforms
convictions 119
delegitimisation of silence 120–1
silence, disclosure and legal advice 120

right to silence – *continued*
use of silence 118–19
origin of the right 100–1
scope of the right 101
'general' immunities 101–2
'specific' immunities 102
statistics on exercise of right 110
using silence against accused (CJPOA 1994) 111
'facts' and 'reliance' 112–13
failure to account for object, substance or mark 117–18
failure to give evidence 116–17
failure to mention fact later relied on 112–16
legal advice 115–16
proper inferences 113–14
reasonableness 114–15
rights of the accused 3
riots 37
Roskill Committee 153–4
rule of law 1, 9
Runciman Commission 110n, 111, 305

safeguards 5, 7
confessions 132
police custody 70, 73, 75
police interviews 96–8
stop and search 39–40
sentencing
determination 232–3
discretion 233–4
hierarchy 235
justifications for punishment 231–4, 236
procedure 197–8
Sentencing Council 232, 233, 234, 244, 249
Serious Fraud Office 143
sex offences 329
attrition 331–2
improving investigation 333–4
investigation 330–1
myths and stereotypes 332–3
prosecution 334–6
reform 336
reporting 329
sex offenders 227–8
shaming 227–8, 231
Single Justice Procedure Notice 325–8
social control 227, 230
'social fear calculus' 223
solicitors 86–90, 90
special measures 194–7
specific deterrence 223
stabbings 20–1
standard of proof 193, 303
state power 3, 4, 7
stigmatisation 273–4
stop and search 19–20, 41
BUSS scheme 22, 27–8, 38–9
case law and research 32–4

stop and search – *continued*
'consensual searches' 40
controversies 20–1, 23
as deterrent 25
effectiveness in combating crime 24–5
'fishing' 30–1
'hit rate' 24, 31
impact on individuals 23
importance 20–5
'information' requirement 40
prevalence 21–3
racial discrimination 23, 30, 31–2, 32
direct racial discrimination 34–5
implicit and 'institutional' discrimination 35–6
poor relationship between police and communities 37–8
poverty and marginalisation 36–7
'reasonable suspicion' 26–7, 29–32, 38
'recording' requirement 40
reform 38–9
relevant law 25–6
CJPOA 1994 and TA 2000 27–9
PACE 1984 26–7, 29
safeguards 39–40
subjectivity 4
summary offences 159–60, 161
Supreme Court 209, 210
suspended sentences 241–3

target-driven culture 58
telephone-only legal advice 90
theories of punishment 219
denunciation theory 220, 226–8, 280–2, 298
theories of punishment – *continued*
prevention theory 220, 222, 247, 251, 252, 258
deterrence 222–4, 243, 258
incapacitation and protection 225–6
reform and rehabilitation 224–5, 243, 258
punishment defined 219
reparation theory 220, 228–31
retribution theory 220–2, 241, 251, 258
death penalty 280–2, 298
just deserts 221–2, 281
torture 103, 104, 108–9, 286–8
treatment models 224–5
trial by jury *see* juries
trial process *see* criminal trial
trial venue
'either-way' offences 161–2
indictable offences 160
summary offences 159–60
truth-seeking 7–8, 10
Turnbull Guidelines 314

unsafe convictions 206–8

victims 58
vigilantism 228
***voir dire* 14**
vulnerable suspects 105
vulnerable witnesses 194–7

witnesses 170, 194–7
unreliable witnesses 313–15
wrongful convictions *see* miscarriages of justice